PROGRESS IN THE PSYCHOLOGY OF LANGUAGE
VOLUME THREE

Progress in the Psychology of Language

Volume Three

edited by

Andrew W. Ellis

University of Lancaster

LAWRENCE ERLBAUM ASSOCIATES, PUBLISHERS
London   Hillsdale, New Jersey

Lawrence Erlbaum Associates Ltd., Publishers
Chancery House
319 City Road
London EC1V 1LJ

British Library Cataloguing in Publication Data

Progress in the psychology of language.
  Vol. 3–
  1. Psycholinguistics—Periodicals
  401'.9   BF455
  ISBN 0-86377-044-4

Typeset by Acorn Bookwork, Salisbury, Wiltshire
Printed and bound by A. Wheaton & Co. Ltd., Exeter

Contents

Introduction   1
Andrew W. Ellis

1. **The Evolution and Dissolution of Language**   5
   Stephen Walker
   Introduction   5
   Phylogeny, Communication, and Vocalisation   7
   Language and Principles of Primate Brain Function   13
   Brain Mechanisms and Human Brain Damage: Evolution and
       Dissolution   23
   Training Chimpanzees in Symbolic Communication   28
   Nonverbal Systems of Communication Used with Aphasic Patients   38
   Conclusions and Summary   40
   References   42

2. **Nonpropositional Speech: Neurolinguistic Studies**   49
   Diana Van Lancker
   Introduction   49
   Heterogeneity in Language: An Hypothesis   53
   Hemispheric Specialisation for Language   57
   Cortical Control of Peripheral Speech Mechanisms   58
   Lateralisation of Other Cerebral Functions   64
   Lateralisation of Language: A Functional Interpretation   66
   Right Hemisphere Communicative Ability   67
   Subcortical Processing of Speech and Language   73
   Clinical Descriptions of Nonpropositional Speech   79
   Evidence from Normal Speech and Language   93

Summary and Conclusions   101
Appendix   104
References   108

3. **Rate-Dependent Processing in Speech Perception**   **119**
Joanne L. Miller
Introduction   119
Changes in Rate During Speech Production   121
Basic Phenomenon of Rate-Dependent Speech Processing   127
The Nature of Rate-Dependent Speech Processing   129
Concluding Remarks   153
Acknowledgements   153
References   153

4. **Computational Modes of Parsing**   **159**
Steven G. Pulman
Introduction   159
Parsing   165
What Should a Theory of Parsing Account For?   175
Parsing Strategies   183
Parsing and Grammatical Constraints   198
Interlude   208
Parsing and Understanding   211
Towards a Theory of Parsing and Interpretation   217
Centre Embedding   220
References   227

5. **Syntax, Semantics, and Garden Paths**   **233**
Dennis Norris
Introduction   233
The Case for Interaction   235
Serial Models of Comprehension   240
Garden Paths   244
Conclusions   250
References   251

6. **Understanding Anaphora**   **253**
Alan Garnham
Introduction   253
Sense, Reference, and Context   253
Anaphora   255
Linguistic Descriptions of Anaphora   257
Anaphor Interpretation in AI Programs   270
Psychological Questions About Anaphor Resolution   272
The Distance Between an Anaphor and Its Antecedent   275
Experiments on Structural Factors in Anaphor Resolution   276
What Do Deep Anaphors Reactivate?   285

The Use of Knowledge About the World in Anaphor Resolution   287
Experimental Studies of Knowledge-Based Anaphor Resolution   288
An Overview of the Process of Understanding Anaphors   293
Conclusion   295
Acknowledgements   296
References   296

7. **Understanding Verbs: Easy Extension, Hard Comprehension**   **301**
Valerie F. Reyna
References   314

8. **Change and Continuity in Early Language Learning**   **317**
Elena V. M. Lieven
Introduction   317
From Communication to Words   318
Learning the Words   320
Building Utterances   322
Discourse, Function, and Affect   329
Acknowledgements   332
References   332

9. **Co-ordinating Words and Syntax in Speech Plans**   **337**
J. Kathryn Bock
Introduction   337
What Does the Sentence Production System Have to Do?   339
Lashley's Analysis of the Co-ordination Problem   342
The Components of the Co-ordination Problem   344
Lexical-Syntactic Integration: Another Look   371
Conclusion   381
Acknowledgements   384
References   384

Introduction

Andrew W. Ellis
*Department of Psychology, University of Lancaster, Bailrigg,
Lancaster LA1 4YF, U.K.*

This volume is the third in the *Progress in the Psychology of Language* series which was inaugurated with the simultaneous publication in 1985 of Volumes 1 and 2. As stated in the Introduction to those two volumes, the series aims to provide those actively engaged in research on the psychology of language, as well as teachers and advanced students of the subject, with a means of keeping abreast of developments in its many areas.

The individual chapters may review an entire area, or may present an overview of an author's ideas and findings. Once again a high proportion of the contributors are younger researchers who might not normally take (or be offered) the opportunity to discuss their ideas in the relaxed and often frankly speculative style they have been encouraged to adopt here. Those who could present their thoughts concisely have done so, while others requested (and were usually granted) space enough to explore the various ramifications of their work. In the overcrowded world of scientific journals, authors are all too rarely afforded the luxury of space in which to expand and develop their ideas. I only hope that on perusing these contributions the reader considers the greater generosity shown here to have proved a worthwhile investment.

Another feature that I hope will distinguish this series from others is the range of topics covered under the broad heading of "psychology of language." In this and the previous volumes that umbrella term has been allowed to encompass subject matters as disparate as the psychology of morphemes, verbatim recall, reading, animal communication, syntax, language acquisition, speech perception, and aphasia. I am personally convinced that there is not an area of psychology which cannot be illuminated by insights from other areas, so I shall go on trying to produce volumes which are as eclectic and wide ranging as possible as a matter of very deliberate policy; I hope that readers who are attracted to a volume by one contribution will occasionally find themselves getting caught up in, and illuminated by, others which they might not normally have sought out.

Volume 3 contains 8 contributions. Stephen Walker opens with a discussion of language evolution and dissolution. Beginning with an account of John Hughlings Jackson's ideas on the hierarchical organisation of nervous activity, Walker goes on to consider the levels of organisation of communicative activity which might be held in common by humans and other animals, especially monkeys and apes. Their vocal communication, along with the neurological substrate which sustains it, is reviewed in detail. The later parts of the chapter extend the Jacksonian thinking to human communication and the human brain, taking in manual and artificial modes of communication as well as speech. Finally the role of language in reasoning and thinking is explored from a comparative perspective.

The second chapter, by Diana Van Lancker, neatly complements Walker's. The adage "to speak is to propositionalise" is one we associate with Hughlings Jackson: Van Lancker delves into those corners of human speech which are nonpropositional and arguably closer to the communicative systems of our evolutionary forebears. Again following a suggestion of Hughlings Jackson, Van Lancker proposes that while the left hemisphere of the brain may be specialised in most people for syntactically formulated propositional speech, the right hemisphere may possess a capability for nonpropositional or automatic speech such as expletives, stereotypic utterances, and recitation.

Chapter 3 is definitely concerned with a left hemisphere linguistic capability, though the author is not in fact concerned with issues of functional localisation. The capability in question is the identification of phonetic segments in the acoustic speech wave. This mapping is complex and subject to syntactic, semantic, and prosodic influences. Joanne Miller argues that "the listener uses multiple, context-dependent properties of the acoustic signal in deriving the phonetic structure of the utterances" and reviews her own work, focussing particularly on the effect of variations in speech rate on phonetic perception. Interestingly, Miller incorporates in her analysis the utilisation of visual cues from the speakers' lip and face movements.

The psychology of grammatical parsing is the concern of Chapters 4 and 5 by Steven Pulman and Dennis Norris respectively. Pulman reviews the successes and problems of attempts to induce computers to assign grammatical structures to sentences. The chapter is not limited to the artificial intelligence perspective, but also evaluates the evidence on whether or not the human "parser" is an independent functional component. Pulman shows that even if the parser is distinct it is nevertheless subject to influence from the listener's knowledge of the world. Such knowledge can affect whether or not listeners can be misled by so-called "garden path" sentences. Listeners' problems with garden path sentences (like *The florist sent the flowers was very pleased*) are expanded upon in Norris's chapter. Like Pulman, Norris maintains that the parser can be an independent functional component, even if it interacts with higher-level semantic processes.

High-level knowledge is indisputably involved in the topic of Alan Garnham's chapter, namely anaphor resolution. That is the term applied to such things as the process of deciding what the referents of pronouns like *it*, *him*, or *they* are. Garnham reviews both computational and psycholinguistic research on anaphor resolution, arguing in the process that work on the topic should be broadened to incorporate phenomena wider than the pronoun resolution which has dominated psycholinguistic research so far.

In Chapter 3 Miller includes work on infant speech perception in her review of acoustic-phonetic translation. Valerie Reyna (Chapter 7) also appeals to developmental as well as adult evidence in her discussion of the possible reasons for observed differences in comprehensibility and memorability between nouns and verbs. A problem with which many psycholinguists will sympathise arises from the fact that nouns and verbs typically differ not only on syntactic class but also on other dimensions such as imageability, age-of-acquisition, and number of meanings. In fact the last difference is favoured by Reyna as the ultimate cause of apparent noun-verb contrasts.

Chapter 8 by Elena Lieven is the first exclusively developmental chapter to appear in the series. Her theme is that language acquisition is not discontinuous with a quantal jump around the age of two years, but is rather "a process of constant reorganisation." This theme is developed through a survey of word learning, "babytalk," sentence formulation, and pragmatics. How children learn to use language to achieve goals is a neglected aspect of development which is now receiving greater attention. Lieven suggests that important aspects of more general individuation may be traced to these early steps in language mastery.

Finally, Kathryn Bock (Chapter 9) develops further a topic treated by Sternberger in Vol. 1 of this series and by Robinson & Moulton and Ellis in Vol. 2, namely speech production. She takes as a starting point the "linearization problem" of how a thought containing several elements are expressed sequentially. Speech is regarded as the product of several separate psychological processors which must be coordinated for fluent speech to occur. Dysfluences, including slips of the tongue, are traced either to errors in the subsystems or to failures of coordination between them.

My thanks to the contributors and also to those who read and offered comments upon draft chapters. I hope that readers feel that this latest volume has gone at least some way towards achieving its stated goals.

Andrew Ellis
Lancaster, August 1986

1 The Evolution and Dissolution of Language

Stephen Walker
Department of Psychology, Birkbeck College, University of London,
Malet Street, London WC1E 7HX, U.K.

INTRODUCTION

In this chapter I do not intend to violate the Paris Ban of 1866 on speculations about the evolutionary origin of human language, in the sense of discussing whether human linguistic skills were initially prompted by the necessities of co-operative hunting, the division of labour, or extra-terrestial intervention. Instead, my starting point is Hughlings Jackson's discussion of the evolution and dissolution of the nervous system, which makes connections between biological evolution, the brain, and language disorders.

Jackson was a fervent and uncritical admirer of Herbert Spencer, whose metaphysical speculations are rather out of place in the modern neo-Darwinian climate, and indeed Head (1926) suggests that Jackson's insistence on putting his observations in Spencerian terms led to obscurity and the neglect of Jackson's writings by his contemporaries. But Head's own championing of Jackson's clinical expertise and theoretical subtlety has meant that many of Jackson's Spencerian ideas, such as the concept of an evolutionary hierarchy of nervous centres, have not been forgotten.

Jackson, following Spencer, used the term "evolution" almost synonymously with "hierarchy": Evolution is a passage from the least to the most organised; from the simple to the complex; from the most automatic to the most voluntary—and in anatomical contexts, from the lowest to the highest centres. (See, especially, the Croonian Lectures; and other papers reprinted in the sections on "Evolution and Dissolution of the Nervous System" in Jackson, 1932). What interested Jackson most about evolution

5

was the peculiar concept of "dissolution;" this was Spencer's term for the reverse of evolution, and the Jacksonian generalisation was that all instances of brain dysfunction could be categorised as local or uniform reversals of evolution, including in particular of course epilectic seizures and aphasia, but also encompassing various forms of intoxication and insanity. This makes very little sense in the context of the Darwinian principle of natural selection. However, as an empirical generalisation it was helpful to stress the reduction from the voluntary to the automatic in many kinds of pathology, and to separate out syndromes according to a hierarchy of nervous centres supposedly affected.

The idea that psychological symptoms resulting from organic brain malfunction represent progressive loss in a hierarchy of centres of organisation, rather than an all-or-nothing loss of discrete psychological functions, may still be a useful one. However, I wish to use Jackson's complex and elaborate theories as an introduction to two other issues: (1) the relation of human language to cognition and communication in other species; and (2) the relation of language disorders following brain damage to principles of brain organisation shared with other species. In each case I shall narrow down the issue.

In the first case it is clear that on Darwinian grounds the capacities of our closest living relatives, the great apes, should be of most relevance, and I shall therefore review the evidence on the abilities of chimpanzees to utilise artificial systems of communication, such as gesture-sign language, which they are exposed to by human intervention. This work has added interest insofar as it involves attempts to establish linguistic skills in subjects who lack them as a matter of species constitution—training methods that prove successful in these instances might be expected to suggest techniques for the rehabilitation of human patients whose organic deficits are less profound. Jackson himself frequently discussed the use of "pantomimic actions" in aphasic patients, and made the connection with the symbolic use of homologues of these in lower animals (e.g. Jackson, 1883, 1932; p. 210).

In the second case, that of principles of brain organisation, I shall refer to the vexed issue of localisation of function. Jackson was a moderate on this, claiming to be neither a "localizer," nor a "universalizer" (1883/1932; p. 35), being most concerned initially with the implications of spread and sequence of epilectic spasms for the nature of motor representation in the cerebrum. But his emphasis on the separation of motor and sensory functions within each hemisphere, the separation of productive and voluntary speech in the left hemisphere with automatic and receptive processes in the right, in addition to his anatomical distinctions drawn within the hierarchy of centres, provides a framework for the discussion of the relation of speech disorders to brain function.

PHYLOGENY, COMMUNICATION, AND VOCALISATION

Insofar as language is unique to the human species, biological facts concerning other animals might be thought irrelevant. Jackson was very much aware of research such as that of Ferrier on the motor cortex of monkeys and dogs, but his interests in cross-species comparisons were confined to mammals. However, although human linguistic abilities may be unique, certain subsections of these skills may not be: Vocal production, hearing, vision, and perceptual and motor semantic organisation may be found in a wide range of species other than our own. I turn first, therefore, to the phylogenetic basis for cross-species comparisons. There should be no need to argue the point that the human species is phylogenetically closer to the apes than to any other group of animals—the only matter for debate is the precise assessment of the evolutionary distance between *Homo sapiens* and other primates in biological terms. This may be to some extent imponderable, but all physical measures indicate that, given the great psychological gulf separating people from other vertebrates, the purely biological differences between man and the great apes are remarkably minor. I shall discuss brain organisation in more detail later, but nothing has emerged in the last 100 years to invalidate Huxley's comment that the differences between the brain of a chimpanzee and that of a man are negligible by comparison with the differences between the brain of a chimpanzee and that of a small primate such as a marmoset.

   Detailed biochemical investigations into the structure of haemoglobin, the immunological response to proteins from another species, and the structure of DNA, confirm the view that, if anything, apes are more closely related to *Homo* than they are to other primates (Goodman, 1974; King & Wilson, 1975). However, according to most interpretations of the fossil evidence, hominid precursors diverged from the line leading to the anthropoid apes at least 15 million years before the present. By comparison, murid rodents (rats and mice) are estimated to have first split off from other rodent orders only 10 million years ago (Radinsky, 1976). The fact that rats and mice are a very recent type of rodent does not of course necessarily make them interesting as models for human behaviour, although it is possible that early rodents derived from early primates rather than (as do all other mammalian orders including primates) from early unspecialised insectivores (Radinsky, 1976). Next to the apes, the primates most closely related to ourselves are the Old World Monkeys, such as the rhesus macaque and the baboon, which separated from the Hominoid (apes and man) line about 40 million years ago, while the New World Monkeys (e.g. the squirrel, spider, and cebus) are somewhat more remote phylogenetically, and are guessed to have evolved from a line which diverged from human ancestry up to 50 million years ago (Simons, 1976).

If one defines communication as the transmission of information from one individual animal to another via sensory channels, then the whole range of vertebrate and invertebrate life could be surveyed, and the use of tactile, visual, and chemical signals in inter-individual exchange of information in the social insects would have pride of place. But for reasons of plausibility, as well as of space, I shall here concentrate in the first instance on the primates, within the background of communication in other airbreathing vertebrates. Although isolated species of fish produce noises (usually by teeth grinding), the evolution of human speech might be said to begin with the airbreathing of amphibians, about 350 million years ago. Early amphibians gave rise to reptiles, which have the phylogenetic distinction of being ancestral to both mammals and birds. One would have to go back over 300 million years to find a common ancestor of birds and primates, but it would be worth paying some attention to birds on the ad hoc grounds of their elaborate vocalisation. Twenty years ago birds might have been excluded from a survey of the relationship between brain function and vocalisation due to their lack of cerebral cortex, but it has become increasingly apparent that forebrain function in birds is not so radically different from that of mammals as this superficial anatomical distinction might suggest (Nauta & Karten, 1970; Karten, 1979).

Communication and Social Interaction

It is certainly part of the biological context of the evolution of human speech that many species in all vertebrate classes have well-developed forms of inter-individual exchange of information. There is a logical imperative for any vertebrate species to possess social signals sufficient at the very least to accomplish sexual reproduction, and the doctrines of inclusive fitness and sexual selection propose that the physical and psychological mechanisms involved in mate selection should have very high evolutionary priority. Systematic types of social organisation directly or indirectly related to courtship, including distinctions based on rank and territorial space, also occur in all vertebrate classes. These require more or less elaborate sets of instinctive social signals with some modifications according to experience, since both territory and rank are often aquired in animals by personal accomplishment rather than by birth. It was because of the very general connection between communication and sexual reproduction that Darwin developed his own theory of the origin of human speech: That it started as singing, used to charm potential sexual partners, or to impress rivals, and only later acquired its spoken and linguistic properties (the hypothesis that propositions began as propositions: Darwin, 1871/1901, pp. 133 & 872). The eventual complexity of grammatical constructions in human languages, even the "most barbarous" ones, Darwin suggested, should be explained by a process of linguistic evolution analogous to biological evolution.

A more widely applicable Darwinian thesis was that communication in animals could be viewed as the expression of the emotions. In the animal world the emotions expressed are usually various gradations of lust and hostility, but nevertheless there is perhaps more in common between "non-verbal" communication in man and other primates (for instance in facial expression; Van Hoof, 1972) than there is between human speech and primate cries and coos.

Auditory and Visual Channels of Communication

Of the five senses, taste could probably be excluded as a significant channel of inter-individual communication in most vertebrates. Touch is certainly a crucial proximal stimulus in sexual interactions, and hugging, stroking, grooming, biting, scratching, and so on form part of the communicative repertoire of many reptiles and mammals. Olfaction is a crude but effective method of transmitting social signals in some reptile species, and in many mammals, but is usually considered to be of relatively minor importance in primates; in general olfaction is even less important to birds than it is to primates. Clearly the vocal-auditory channel is the basis of human speech, but the visual cues of posture, gesture, and facial expression have interest as supplementary methods of human emotional exchange and social interaction. As a rule of thumb we may say that species in all the airbreathing vertebrate classes commonly make use of all four sensory channels of social communication, but the vocal-auditory channel is used for more elaborate signals in higher vertebrates (birds and mammals) than in amphibians or reptiles. There is something to be said for Spencer's (and Aristotle's) opinion that touch is the highest of all the senses, since mammalian fur and whiskers are more sensitive than the skin scales or feathers of other classes. It might also be claimed that the anatomical differentiation of the inner ear in birds and mammals, by which reptilian jawbones were converted to a mechanism for sound transmission, support the case the hearing is the most phylogenetically advanced modality.

The croaking of modern frogs and toads announces the origins of tetrapod vocalisation, and is involved in some fairly complicated rituals of male competition (one species of toad typically competes in trios, and there is chorusing in several species, but intensity and pitch are probably the main distinctive features detected). Reptiles as a class can be said to use the visual rather than the auditory channel for social communications (see below), but several species of geckos (a family of lizards) are highly vocal. Most of these are nocturnal, and either arboreal or burrow-dwelling (e.g. *Ptenopus garrulus garrulus*), which habits provide obvious reasons for developing the auditory modality, and some species go so far as to utilise "polysyllabic" chirps (Stamps, 1977). Others vocalise only when paired off during the breeding season, their vocalisation appearing to be primarily a male device for territorial assertion or courtship. Turtles and tortoises also produce sounds but little is known of their social function: Various of these chelonians have been reported to cluck like a hen, quack like a duck, meow like a cat, or whistle like a tea kettle, but no single species appears to make more than about half-a-dozen separate sounds (Carpenter & Ferguson, 1977). Although reptilian vocalisation is thus rather limited, neural organisation in both the peripheral and the central auditory pathways is roughly similar to that found in higher vertebrates (Foster & Hall, 1979; Mulroy & Oblak, 1985).

The vocal channel of social communication is of course more conspicuously developed in birds than it is in most mammals. The main lesson is simply that a large primate brain is not a biological necessity for the perception and reproduction of human phonology, as this can be achieved by parrots and mynah birds among others. But there is an enormous diversity of innate and experiental determinants of avian vocalisation (Marler, 1970). Social learning of vocal production and auditory discrimination presumably functions for the recognition of particular individuals, or of individuals sharing local dialects. Young terns respond selectively to the recorded vocalisations of their own parents when only four days old (Stevenson et al., 1970); there are undoubtedly "critical periods" of early vocal learning in some species, but in others vocal learning may be very protracted. Thorpe (1972) reports that individual pairs of an East African shrike develop idiosyncratic antiphonal duets, which he presumes serve to enable the members of a pair to keep in touch even in very dense foliage. The skills of acoustic pattern recognition and complex vocal production are thus not in themselves exceptional among higher vertebrates, the human species generally being differentiated more from other primates than from higher vertebrates in these respects. There are no doubt very profound differences in the mechanisms employed in the bird and human brain to produce control of vocalisation: For instance, it has been discovered that the annual learning of new songs in canaries is accompanied by annual cycles of neuronal growth and degeneration (Paton & Nottebohm, 1984; Burd & Nottebohm, 1985). This is a special case but may provide a model for other relationships between brain growth and complex vocal learning.

It is conceivable that rather more vocal learning occurs in monkeys and apes than is immediately obvious (Seyfarth & Cheney, 1984). Since the sounds produced by any single mammalian species are universal throughout the species and usually directly related to emotional states, it is reasonable to classify them as merely reflexive cries. In monkeys and apes (as also in domestic cats) a fairly wide range of emotional signals may be transmitted vocally—from 15 to approximately 30 sounds being categorised separately by human observers (Marler & Tenaza, 1977)—but it is not necessarily the case that primate cries never have any representation context, or external referents. Seyfarth, Cheney, and Marler (1980) suggest that vervet monkeys extend the meaning of warning cries on the basis of experience and, as adults, discriminate between warnings of "leopard," "snake," or "eagle" by adopting alternative defensive manoeuvres.

Be that as it may, such niceties do little to ameliorate the enormous disparity between primate vocalisations and human speech. In the context of primate communication, one of the most remarkable things about human spoken languages is their phonological diversity. If there was a plentiful supply of obvious linguistic universals, such as aspirated sounds at the end of vocal units always meaning a request, vowel alternations always indicating case—in other words if there were human species-specific sound-meaning universals—it would be possible to ask how these might have evolved from other primate species-specific vocalisations, rather as one can ask similar questions about facial expression (Jolly, 1972). Ignoring, for the moment, whether language expresses unique inner faculties or reason and thought, it is obvious from the diversity of human languages that vocalisation in the human species is serving radically different purposes from those accomplished by the use of the auditory-vocal channel in other primates. But it is worth noting that these unique functions of the vocal organs are accompanied by fairly minor changes in the vocal apparatus. It is possible to trace changes in the human supralaryngeal vocal tract that allow for more varied speech sounds (Lieberman, 1975) but by evolutionary standards this is a trivial anatomical change. Other primate species for which intensity rather than variety of vocalisation has become important, such as the New World howler monkey, or some of the lesser apes, have developed large vocal sacs on the throat. These provide a much clearer anatomical sign of a selection pressure than the anatomy of the human vocal organs. Similarly there are no obvious changes to the human ear, either internal or external, which are associated with the perception of speech.

The use of the visual channel for social communication may be said to be phylogenetically older than the vocal-auditory channel in the sense that visually detected social displays are common in fish, and in reptiles, as well as in birds and mammals. Perhaps the most primitive displays are colour changes in the skin—like elaborate forms of blushing. These point up the fact that although colour vision is a distinctively primate capacity among mammals, it is well developed in other vertebrate classes. Changes in the appearance of the head by extentions and colourings of dewlaps, crests, and frills are very common as social signals in lizards, and might be considered as specialised forms of facial expression. Lizards also have gestures such as submissive and aggressive circular forelimb waving, tail lashing, head bobbing, back arching, and so on (Carpenter & Ferguson, 1977). Therefore, lizards do not merely perceive simple colour cues but distinguish also form and movement as visual social signals. Most lizards, like most birds, have a well-developed cone-packed fovea in the retina of the eye—again a feature which humans share with primates, birds, and lower vertebrates, but not with other mammals. Many birds have two fovea in each retina: The standard one in the centre, which points to the side of the visual field, and an extra temporal fovea which, in both eyes, picks up the central region of the visual field in front of the head. I mention this to counter the impression sometimes given in discussions of human reading that the evolution of the fovea post-dated the invention of writing, or at least post-dated primate binocular vision.

Phylogeny and Pre-adaption

The general conclusion I wish to draw concerning the use of the vocal-auditory channel for social communication is simply that human speech has a general biological context, and did not evolve in a complete vacuum. Although conventionally one separates out courtship displays in reptiles or birds as merely "innate releasing mechanisms" of a reflexive stimulus-response kind, it is arguable that by these mechanisms a considerable variety of vocal or visual signals are obtained which possess a certain behavioural and emotional meaning for the animals involved. The task of the nervous system, even in these nonmammalian species, in detecting and reacting to the array of possible interspecies signals, is much more complicated than a series of lock-and-key releasing circuits. One may thus claim that both the auditory and the visual modalities have a long evolutionary history as channels of social communication.

The human species patently does something quite new and different with these channels, but at the same time makes use of many pre-existing anatomical and neural devices. At any rate, the eyes, ears, and throats of hominids did not have to change very radically to achieve radical results. I will discuss possible neurological changes later. However, the theme will remain that of achieving something new with pre-existing devices. One needs fingers and foveas to sight-read a piece of music on the piano or violin, but the fingers and foveas we use for this purpose have a phylo-genetic history even though sight-reading does not. One needs a larynx and a cochlea in order to speak and understand a human language, and these bits of anatomy are inherited from other primates, even though talking is not. Some of the brain circuits between the cochlea and the larynx must similarly have an evolutionary history, even if propositional speech does not.

LANGUAGE AND PRINCIPLES OF PRIMATE BRAIN
FUNCTION

As many and various cognitive disorders are caused by brain dysfunction, there ought to be at least a partial overlap between theories about cognition and theories about primate brain function. Given the mysteries and complexities of brain function, one may prefer to construct psychological theories and classifications of disorders of cognition and language without reference to the primate brain, or even to the human brain (Patterson, 1981). Moreover, the relationships between primate brain function and human language might be of the kind that human cognitive and linguistic disorders have absolutely nothing to do with primate brain function, as the uniqueness of human language means that the human brain works in a completely different way from all other primate brains (Geschwind, 1965). However, in our present state of ignorance about these matters it is surely a legitimate enterprise to continue to examine relationships between human and primate brain function (Weiskrantz, 1977).

On phylogenetic grounds we would look first and foremost at primate brain function, but in many cases the same theoretical issues apply to other mammals, and in some cases, even to rats. The most general theoretical issue, which has a particular history in connection with language, but bedevils all discussion of mammalian brain function, is the question of the anatomical localisation of psychological function. It is a very old and very strong tradition to distinguish separate psychological faculties, and identify them with different locations in the body. For more than a millenium before the 17th century it was a popular view that "common sense" (i.e. supramodal perception), reason, imagination, and memory could be located in the four brain ventricles. (A 15th-century illustration in Brazier, 1979, has "virtus imaginativa" in the left lateral ventricle and "virtus cognitiva" in the right, with "sensus communis" centrally in the third ventricle and "memoria" further down in the fourth.) Clearly this was a mistaken view, but it does not follow that all other attempts at localisation are equally mistaken (cf. Fodor, 1983). In the 17th century the ventricles lost their popularity and similar mental functions were assigned to more reasonable locations in the brain: The English anatomist Willis put common sense in the corpus striatum, imagination in the corpus callosum, memory in the cerebral cortex, and motor reflexes in the cerebellum—this is not too far from what one may find in current texts (Brazier, 1979). Creutzfeldt (1979) still puts consciousness in the corpus striatum (the basal ganglia) on the "sensus communis" grounds that multi-sensory inputs from the cortex converge there. In Spencer's *Principles of Psychology* (1855/ 1899; p. 105) it is asserted that "the seat of consciousness is that nervous centre to which, mediately or immediately, the most heterogenous impressions are brought." Jackson often quoted this passage, although he himself located the "substrata" of consciousness in the cerebral hemispheres fairly generally, with different kinds of consciousness in different places (Jackson, 1931; p. 152). Penfield, however, when requoting the same passage from Spencer, deduced that the seat of consciousness was in the thalamus—this is Penfield's "centrencephalic" theory (Penfield & Rasmussen, 1950; p. 235; also Penfield & Jasper, 1954; Penfield & Roberts, 1959; p. 247).

The first experimental basis for the anatomical localisation of functions was the discovery of the separation of sensory and motor pathways into the dorsal and ventral roots of the spinal cord, made independently by Sir Charles Bell and Francois Magendie. This holds for all living vertebrates with the exception of very primitive fishes such as the lamprey, whose spinal cord was the subject of Sigmund Freud's first publications, ten years prior to his work on aphasia (Sulloway, 1979). (Bell had clinical interests, and travelled to Spain in 1809 and Belgium in 1815 to study and treat the effects of gunshot wounds sustained in the battles of Coruna and Waterloo.) Extensive experimentation on laboratory animals took place in the 19th century in parallel with the localising claims of clinicians such as Broca and Wernicke: Ferrier's *The Localisation of Cerebral Disease* (1878), based largely on his experiments with monkeys and dogs, was accepted as conclusive by Jackson among many others, but controversies concerning cerebral localisation continued, as between Goltz and Munk over the visual functions of the occipital lobes (Weiskrantz, 1972). To a degree, these have continued to the present day, since there are some such as Barlow (1972, 1985) and Konorski (1967) who put forward theories in which individual neurons are supposed to have specific cognitive functions, while others (Anderson, Silverstein, Ritz, & Jones, 1977; Wood, 1978, 1982) would not only prefer to avoid giving individual neurons specific functions, but are prepared to support the extreme proposal (Lashley, 1950) that "all of the cells of the brain, are participating, by a sort of algebraic summation, in every activity. There are no special cells for special memories (p. 477)."

It certainly seems unlikely that a particular neuron should be responsible for a particular psychological property, since a single neuron can do hardly anything on its own. But the notion that all neurons participate in all brain activities, even if logically possible, is in conflct with much empirical evidence that particular neurons do indeed do particular things in mammalian brains (Sperry, 1958; Hubel & Weisel, 1977; Cowey, 1979; Zeki, 1978; Kaas, 1982; Perrett et al., 1985). I shall review in the next sections evidence of a conventional kind, that stimulating or lesioning specific locations in the primate brain has particular effects on vocalisation. The assumption behind this, of course, is that identifiable processes in the nervous system can be tied to these known anatomical locations. But this assumption is not necessarily incompatible with the notion that *psychologically* defined functions are achieved by serial and parallel and "distributed" sequences of brain circuits, and that it is therefore unwise to imagine that a psychological faculty resides at a particular geographical address in the brain.

Consider for a moment the metaphor of a pair of trousers held up by a pair of braces (suspenders) as well as a belt, each alone being just about sufficient to keep the trousers in place under normal conditions of physical exertion. Where is the function of "holding up the trousers" localised? If we remove both the belt and the braces, but the wearer is sitting or lying down, the trousers stay up anyway, and the supports may thus seem unnecessary (some vertebrates may survive, if hand fed, after the removal of the entire forebrain). On the other hand, if the wearer is standing, and we leave on the belt and braces, but cut all around the trousers below the belt, these garments, to all intents and purposes, fall: even the belt and braces together are not sufficient (optic nerve damage may blind). If we first remove the belt, and then simply snip off the buttons, to which the braces are attached, a dramatic failure of normal trouser stability may ensue—to what extent does the "holding up" function therefore reside in the buttons?

One could go on. The point is that the relationship between the presence and absence of structures, and their possible functions, may be logically complex, and the brain is at least as complicated as the belt and braces system. *But* this does not mean that it is foolish to say that trousers can be held up by belts or by braces, or that these localised items contribute in some way to the behaviourally defined function of holding up. To gather additional evidence for such assertions one might wish to perform more carefully controlled experiments involving the removal of the belt and/or braces under a variety of conditions of physical exertion, but the anatomical position of these physical structures, in relation to the trousers, by itself strongly suggests an anti-gravity effect. Similarly, in the vertebrate and mammalian brains, anatomical layouts alone virtually ensure some degree of functional specialisation: It might technically be possible to build a robot in which all inputs and outputs are randomly scrambled at a short distance from the sensory and motor peripherals, but brains are not like that. However, as the trousers metaphor indicates, and as discussed in some detail by Jackson (and also by Luria, 1974), it is *components* of functions rather than whole functions which are localised. While the holding up function is clearly distributed both within and between the belt and the braces, it is nevertheless the case that individual functional components of the system are discretely localised—for instance at the buckle and the buttons. Obviously there are limits to the applicability of this metaphor, but it is at least arguable that in the same way, although it would be misleading to claim that a behaviourally defined function in its entirety (e.g. vocalisation), resides at a single location in the primate brain, it is still possible that there are discretely localised brain structures which serve particular components of that function (e.g. premotor and motor cortex, the extrapyramidal motor pathway, and brainstem nuclei which feed the tongue, larynx and lips).

In Jackson's words, it is the "nervous arrangements," rather than psychological entities, that are anatomically discrete. Given this, there are three simplifying dimensions of brain localisation which, as used by Jackson, correspond roughly to the orthogonal axes of the primate brain. First is the up-down hierarchy, from medulla to cortex, but with some parts of the cortex being defined as higher than others. Second is the left/right lateral division of functions between the hemispheres, and third is the "front-to-back" dimension, often stressed by Jackson because it was then relatively novel, with movements and motor organisation in the frontal lobes, and sensory and perceptual functions generally in the rear of the hemispheres.

Hierarchical Control of Vocalisation in Monkeys and Apes

There is a large recent literature on several aspects of primate vocalisation (Steklis & Raleigh, 1979; Sebeok, 1977; Seyfarth & Cheney, 1984) but in many ways the most pertinent review for present purposes is that by Ploog (1979), in which a very Jacksonian scheme is put forward involving lower, middle, and higher levels of neural control of voicing in primates. Ploog's conclusion is that only in the human species is the highest neural level actively involved in the "vocal signalling process," this highest level being localised as the premotor cortex adjacent to the motor representations of the larynx, face, and throat. A corollary of this conclusion is that only human speech is voluntary, sub-human vocalisation being assumed to be emotional and automatic. Thus those aspects of human phonation which are primarily emotional and automatic—crying, shrieking, moaning, screaming, groaning, giggling, grunting, and so on—have more in common with subhuman vocalisation than does articulate speech. Ploog (1979) conjectures that: "the brain mechanisms of vocalisation which operate in the monkey are homologous to those in the human neonate (p. 95)."

In terms of the more peripheral aspects of human voice production, human speech differs from primate vocalisation mainly in the use of supralaryngeal cavities to produce a greater variety of vowel sounds, and in the correspondingly decreased importance of sound production during inhalation. An inhaled hiss may indicate a number of signalled emotions between people, from pain to wonder, but vocalisation during inhalation in

Homo sapiens could be completely ignored without serious loss of information. By contrast, three of the most frequent chimpanzee vocalisations, the pant-hoot, the pant-grunt and "laughing" are typically made both during inhalation and exhalation and, although data is scarce, it is probably that inhalation is used to produce phonation even more often in the orang-utan than it is in the chimpanzee or gorilla. One orang sound, the "kiss-squeek" is usually produced by sucking through pursed trumpet lips, but some (wild) animals have been observed making a similar noise by sucking on the backs of their hands (MacKinnon, 1974; Marler & Tenaza, 1977). Although observed phonation in the apes (and in other primates) thus has little in common phonetically with human speech, Lieberman (1977) suggests that the external apparatus in apes would be capable of producing a wide variety of phonetic features (voiced/unvoiced, glottal stops, and the consonants, b,p,d for instance). But any nonhuman primate would have to make do with one unspecified vowel. In practice, human observers usually distinguish only a couple of dozen distinct vocalisations at most, in a given primate species, and give them generic labels such as "bark" or "pant-hoot"—but this does not deal with the possibility that many gradations within the human categories may be distinguished by the animals concerned.

It should be remarked that practically all of the neuroanatomical work, and most of the behavioural observation, has been done with species other than the gibbons, which are in many ways the most interesting group as far as the evolution of language goes. For the half-dozen species of gibbon, and the Siamang (Tembrock, 1974): "The peculiar structure of the voice appartus, with an accessory vocal chord, the complete closure of the glottis, the formation of the aryepiglottic folds similar to *Homo*, the m. thyreoideus transversus impar and the extension of the m. cricoarytenoideus give rise to a voice unusually capable of modulation (p. 177)." This is apart from the large air sacs used by the black gibbon and the Siamang. All these lesser apes share with birds a highly arboreal habitat and a social structure based on the two-parent pair bond. Perhaps because of this, they all sing. The songs are made up from repetitions of elements in "stanzas," and repetitions of stanzas in songs, and are thus syntactically more complex than most other nonhuman primate vocalisations. Social co-operation in vocalisation is also complex. In all species of gibbon studied (except Kloss's gibbon) there is duetting, or antiphonal singing, between mated pairs. In the pileated gibbon, the Siamang, and the hoolock, the male and female songs overlap, but in the other species (the white-handed and dark-handed gibbons) the male and female strictly alternate. This "turn-taking" is facilitated by special signals—in the white-handed gibbon (Marler & Tenaza, 1977): "the female signals her readiness to sing by uttering a series of short monotonous notes. When she begins her full song the male normally stops singing until she has completed it, whereupon he adds a short coda, then pauses for several seconds before starting to sing again (p. 1007)."

In Bornean gibbons the male's role seems to be limited to adding the short coda at the end of female songs, and in the Siamang the male sings only stereotyped phrases which overlap with certain portions of the female song. In hoolocks both male and female produce more or less the same sounds, but the male sings in a lower pitch. There are thus large differences in singing style between these closely related species (which often inter-breed in captivity), but there is also a considerable degree of variation both within and between the performances of individuals. Apart from male-female duets, the other main occasion for singing is chorusing between neighbouring males, in which individual variations no doubt serve for inter-individual recognition (Marler & Tenaza, 1977). In Kloss's gibbon (the only species without male-female duets), the male pre-dawn chorusing is typically followed by *four hours* of all-female choruses, after the families have left their sleeping trees. Apart from all this, gibbons have a more typically primate selection of food-sighting cries, warning barks, play squeals, and copulatory grunts. One presumes that the central nervous system requirements for the control of vocalisation in these primates is somewhat greater than average.

Leaving aside the gibbons, on which virtually no neuroanatomical studies seem to have been performed, there is a fairly clear set of conclusions derived from experiments on the larger apes (usually chimpanzees or gorillas) and on laboratory monkeys such as the squirrel monkey (New World) and the rhesus macaque (Old World), which have been reviewed by Jurgens (1979) and Sutton and Jurgens (1985) as well as by Ploog (1979). The main points of these conclusions are that: (1) the basic neuroanatomical pathways for the control of vocalisation are roughly similar in man and other primates; (2) other primates apart from *Homo sapiens* do not make use of the highest levels of their available neuroanatomy in the course of species-specific vocalisations. Three kinds of evidence to support these points may be quoted: neuroanatomical structure; the elicitation of movements or vocalisations by electrical stimu-lation of the brain; and the effect on vocalisation of various brain lesions. A potentially valuable source of evidence would be electrical recording (or other intra-cranial forms of measurement) during vocalisation, but com-paratively little work of this kind has been reported.

Electrical Stimulation

"Artificially induced discharge of what in the monkey is homologous to Broca's region, produces movements of the tongue, palate, lips, etc. (Jackson, 1883/1932; p. 205)." This refers of course to the electrical stimulation of the regions of exitable motor cortex related to the face and throat, which are in the same relative position—at the bottom of the motor strip—in all mammals. Vocal fold movements can be elicited from points in this area (the inferior precentral gyrus) in the chimpanzee (Leyton & Sherrington, 1917), the rhesus monkey (Hast, Fisher, Wetzel, & Thompson, 1974), and the squirrel monkey (Jurgens, 1974). There is thus no doubt that the bottom of the motor strip in primates is associated with outputs which would be useful in vocalisation, but whether they are normally put to this use in nonhuman primates is another matter. Emphasis is usually given to the fact that, although motor strip stimulation may produce isolated lip and laryngeal movements in experimental animals, it seldom, if ever, prompts actual vocalisations. The contrast is then drawn with Penfield's finding that in human patients "occasional growls or grunts" and sometimes a vowel cry, are made involuntarily during stimulation at the bottom of the pre-central gyrus. (And with stimulation at the bottom of the post-central gyrus: In both cases the effect may occur in either hemisphere.) It would hardly be surprising if the human motor cortex was found to be more sensitive in this respect than that of other primates, but no such conclusion can properly be drawn from the stimulation studies just cited, since all the animal work was done under anaesthetic, while in Penfield's work the human patients were awake (Penfield & Rasmussen, 1950/57; e.g. pp. 88–89).

Electrical Stimulation—Supplementary Motor Area

Penfield obtained involuntary cries from awake human patients both by stimulation of the Rolandic facial region (bottom of the pre-central motor strip, as above) and by stimulation within the longitudinal fissure between the hemispheres, anterior to the central fissure, and just above the cingulate gyrus. (Again, even in human patients, this kind of phonation occurs equally often from stimulation of the right and left hemispheres.) Other motor effects were also observed in this region, and on the basis of experimental work with various mammalian species, the longitudinal fissure is expected to contain the "supplementary motor area"—a second map of the body surface, smaller than that on the main motor strip, and having more bilateral effects (Kruger & Stein, 1973). However, the cingulate gyrus, just below this secondary motor area, is classified as "limbic." For present purposes, the interesting thing about this limbic/ supplementary motor region is that stimulating it reliably produces vocalisations in monkeys (rhesus and squirrel: Jurgens & Ploog, 1970; Jurgens, 1979).

Electrical Stimulation—Subcortical Structures

The supplementary motor/cingulate regions of the frontal cortex are certainly not the only parts of the brain from which vocalisations in monkeys may be 'obtained by the technique of electrical stimulation. Stimulation of many parts of the limbic system, and of brainstem nuclei (in particular, the inferior olive, adjacent to the auditory nuclei of the superior olive) results in phonation, with certain types of vocal call "localised in certain sets of structures (for the squirrel monkey; Jurgens, 1979; 1982)." Shrieking and groaning seems most likely to come from a circuit based in the stria terminalis, and growling from a rather similar set of (limbic) locations, but cackling appears to follow a different path, starting in the cingulate region and continuing down through the thalamus; while chirping is evoked from five separate areas, including the nucleus accumbens, the rostral hippocampus, and the inferior olive. Broadly speaking vocalisation is most likely to be produced by the application of current to electrodes placed in the limbic system. Clearly this raises the question of whether the cries so produced are an indirect result of the induction of motivational states—the shrieks and growls resulting from current applied to the amydala might well be associated with pain or anger, since lesioning this area produces animals which, on more general behavioural grounds, are judged to be extremely placid, and relatively insensitive to pain. It would of course be expected that species-specific and innately determined emotional signals should be closely linked anatomically with other aspects of the emotions. In fact Jurgens (1976, 1979) found that the majority of his sites which were implicated in the elicitation of cries of any kind also gave rise to intracranial reinforcement effects (i.e. the animals would turn the stimulation on or off themselves, if given the opportunity to do so). The only sites from which vocalisation could be evoked without such obvious emotional connotations were in the cingulate gyrus, or thereabouts, or in the midbrain ("caudalmost periaqueductal grey"), as if emotionally neutral vocalisation circuits were emrging from the top and bottom of the limbic system (Jurgens, 1979; pp. 16–17, 22–25).

Anatomical Pathways for Vocalisation

Anatomical pathways are inferred from various kinds of evidence, all involving a margin of histological error. However, it seems probable that the output pathways utilised in human vocal production are not very different from those present in the chimpanzee, and many features of the human neural circuitry are characteristic also of monkeys. The limbic system and motor pathways through the basal ganglia are undoubtedly involved in both human and primate vocal output. (Fairly severe speech difficulties can occur in connection with disturbances of the extrapyramidal route through the basal ganglia in Parkinsonism: See Lamendella, 1977, for a review of the limbic system and language). In addition to the extrapyramidal pathway, it appears that both in man and in the chimpanzee there is a direct route from the larynx representation in the pre-central motor strip to the nucleus ambiguous in the medulla (from which branches of the vagal nerve supply the larynx, and branches of the hypoglossal nerve the tongue: Kuypers, 1958a, 1958b). But many of the fibres do not run in the main pyramidal tract output of the motor cortex. No direct route between the "cortical larynx area" and the cranial nerve nuclei is thought to exist in the squirrel monkey (or in the cat), and it is doubtful whether this direct route, observable both in the chimpanzee and the human brain, is shared by the rhesus monkey (Jurgens, 1979). However, many primate species may make use of peripheral feedback circuits with access to sensory input from the larynx (Jurgens & Kirzinger, 1985).

It would be unwise to consider vocal output pathways to be independent of auditory input, but there is no anatomical evidence at present to suggest that the human auditory pathways have become structurally specialised for speech perception. Other primates do not appear to have difficulty in discriminating the phonetic features of human speech: Indeed it has been shown that even chinchillas (rodents) are quite capable of the "categorical perception" of alveolar stops (Kuhl & Miller, 1975; Waters & Wilson, 1976). Ploog (1979) reports that the anatomical substrate for what must be a basic relationship between speech production and speech perception is present in the squirrel monkey: There are some cells in this species' auditory cortex which do not respond to self-produced calls (even those artificially elicited by brain stimulation) but which respond to tape recordings of the same sounds. Recent anatomical work suggests that there is a very high degree of organisation within auditory cortex at the neuronal level, probably comparable to that found by Hubel and Weisel (1977) in visual cortex (Mitani et al., 1985; Winer, 1985).

The Effects of Cortical Lesions on Primate Vocalisations

We should not take it for granted that lesioning any given block of human cerebral cortex would necessarily have a predictable effect on speech. However, it is a safe generalisation that lesions of frontal motor cortex are quite likely to produce speech output difficulties in human patients, especially if they are large, and surround the inferior precentral gyrus in the left hemisphere. Greater specificity of prediction may eventually become possible (Naesser, Hayward, Laughlin, Becker, Jernigan, & Zatz, 1981). A number of experiments have been performed to assess the effect on vocalisation in nonhuman primates of lesions in their frontal motor areas—"Broca area homologues" (Aitken, 1981; see also Sutton, Larson, & Lindeman, 1974; Franzen & Myers, 1973). Often included in the same experiments are "Wernicke homologues"—that is, lesions centred on the superior temporal and/or inferior parietal regions. The results of these experiments are often difficult to interpret, for a number of reasons, including uncertainties involved in selecting the "Broca and Wernicke homologues." However, four tentative generalisations have been made (Jurgens, 1979; Ploog, 1979; Sutton & Jurgens, 1985):

1. Very large bilateral lesions of the frontal lobes may severely impair both vocalisation and other social behaviours in monkeys (Franzen & Myers, 1973; Green & Walker, 1938).

2. Small bilateral lesions of the frontal or temporal lobes do *not* impair vocalisation in monkeys (Aitken, 1981; Sutton et al., 1974).

3. Small bilateral lesions of the cingulate/supplementary motor regions may very severely impair vocalisations in monkeys under some circumstances (Sutton et al., 1974; Sutton, Samson, & Larson, 1978; Sutton, Trachy, & Lindeman, 1981a, 1981b; Aitken, 1981) and this "limbic" area may therefore be needed for volitional control of vocalisation (Jurgens, 1985; Tanji, 1984).

4. Large bilateral lesions of the superior temporal lobes significantly impair the auditory discrimination of species-specific calls (Hupfer, Jurgens, & Ploog, 1977).

Brain Mechanisms and Primate Vocalisations—Conclusions

Ploog's hierarchical theory of the brain mechanisms involved in primate vocalisation, put forward on the basis of the kinds of evidence described earlier, can be paraphrased as follows. Instinctive and species-specific cries can be accomplished with the necessary co-ordination of the vocal organs occurring at the lowest levels (midbrain and medulla). The correlation of vocalisations with emotional states is developed in the limbic system. Of particular interest in primates is the cingulate/supplementary motor area within the longitudinal fissure, categorised as "limbic," which has to do with "readiness to vocalise" (Ploog, 1979) or is the "voluntary call initiation area" (Jurgens, 1979, 1985) in both monkeys and man. The highest level in this model is the neocortex surrounding and in front of the facial and laryngeal parts of the pre-central gyrus, which is used for "voluntary call *formation*" and is thus significantly involved in vocal signalling in only the human species. This is not unlike Jackson's (1883/ 1932) speculation:

> I suppose that the motor nervous arrangements of Broca's regions which are correlative with what are psychically words have arisen out of those for the "common place" movements of the tongue, palate and lips and have become greatly or completely detached from the latter and then serve, not for their own ends, but stand for operations. . . . If so Broca's region, in man, differs

from the homologous part of a dog in their being in it more specialised, new, nervous arrangements in addition to what we may call the ordinary or old ones (p. 209).

BRAIN MECHANISMS AND HUMAN BRAIN DAMAGE: EVOLUTION AND DISSOLUTION

In one sense, the way in which mammalian brain mechanisms are discussed by Jackson, and by modern comparative anatomists, simply reinforces the naive theories of the localisation of psychological functions put forward by Bastian and the other "diagram makers" (e.g. Bastian, 1898) who were so chastised by Head (1926). On the other hand, Head was able to use Jackson's writing as a stick to beat the diagram makers with, since Jackson's theories are anything but naive (and he refrained from drawing diagrams). Although Jackson (1882/1932) claimed "I am neither a universaliser nor a localiser (p. 35)" he noted that he was attacked as both, and he can be quoted in support of both. The reason for this paradox is that Jackson argued for the localisation of multiple and various physiological components of brain mechanisms which accomplish psychological functions, rather than simplifying the localisation to unitary "speech centres," "writing centres," and so on. He emphasised not only multiple localisation in his evolutionary up-down hierarchy but also, of course, multiple localisation across the hemispheres (the left being for voluntary expression of propositions, the right for automatic expression and propositional reception), and the anterior/posterior separation of motor and sensory centres.

Arguably, this means that Jackson was different from the diagram makers in being *more* of a localiser, rather than less. The Jacksonian theme is that *everything can be separated out*: The voluntary from the involuntary and automatic; the propositional from the nonpropositional; the receptive from the expressive; representations from re-representations; muscle co-ordinations from intentional movements. The more it is the case that the physiological components subserving cognitive functions are separated out in the brain, the more likely it is that brain-damaged patients will present with peculiar permutations and combinations of psychological symptoms. Very few, apart from Lashley, have been prepared to maintain that the particular permutation of psychological symptoms resulting from brain damage has nothing whatever to do with the site (almost always, of course, sites) of the damage. Brain (1965) points out that even Head (although Head was virulently opposed to anatomical centres for functions) becomes "involuntarily a psycho-anatomist" by clearly attributing each of his own four types of aphasia to four kinds of cerebral damage, in a way which is roughly comparable to the theories of the much-abused diagram makers.

According to Head (1926): "Verbal aphasia is more particularly associated with injury to the foot of the precentral and neighbouring gyri"; "syntactical aphasia is associated with lesions in and around the upper temporal gyri and the parts beneath them"; "A lesion situated in the left hemisphere between the post-central fissure and the occipital lobe (i.e. in the parietal lobe) tends to affect more particularly the meaning and categorical use of language"; and "When the lesion lies in the neighbourhood of the angular gyrus and the parts beneath it the defects of speech are liable to assume a nominal form (pp. 500–502)." Lord Brain himself gives a straightforward anatomical account for all the disorders of speech and writing which he discusses. Similarly, Luria (1974) accuses Head of preserving "the same principle of *direct* relation of language and brain (p. 4)" but Luria is willing to attribute "motor aphasia" to "disturbances of the lower part of the premotor zone of the major hemisphere" and to attribute the acquisition and use of "reversible grammatical structures" to "tertiary zones of the parieto-occipital parts of the cortex (p. 7)" (see Arbib, 1982, for a Jacksonian critique of Luria).

Head's (1926) own explanation of why "manifestations differ according to the site of the lesion" is that "Such topographical associations come about because particular parts of the brain were already required for some lower function, which played a part in the evolution of one of the many aspects of the use of language (pp. 431 & 502)." There is thus a considerable measure of agreement, even among those ostensibly opposed in principle to excessive claims for localisation, that the localisation of physiological components of the human brain, which is a result of evolutionary processes and can be predicted from the study of the brains of other primates, determines the way in which "manifestations differ according to the site of the lesion" in human brain damage. The largest measure of agreement is probably for the up-down dimension of the Jacksonian hierarchy: No-one doubts that bulbar paralysis of the face and throat results in a speech deficit that has different psychological connotations from those of a speech deficit resulting from an infarction around the left middle cerebral artery. Left/right localisations are nothing like so robust, but there is no doubt that the lateralisation of cognitive functions is clinically important, even though the biological basis for this remains obscure (Denenberg, 1981; Walker, 1980, 1981, 1985).

The most contentious of the Jacksonian dimensions, but one with many implications for cognitive neuropsychology, is localisation from front-to-back of a given hemisphere. The main evolutionary constraints on this have been known for approximately 100 years, but it is worth saying that the accumulation of evidence concerning mammalian brain function has continuously strengthened the original rough generalisations, even though we are still ignorant of many neuronal details. The first constraint is that the frontal lobes are predominantly motor whereas the temporal, parietal and occipital lobes are distinctly sensory, containing clearly separate auditory, tactile, and visual inputs, respectively. It is hard to imagine ever knowing quite why the occipital lobe receives a visual input, but the temporal lobe an auditory one, *but* we can say beyond a shadow of doubt that the reason why the human occipital lobe receives that optic radiation is that we are primates, and that this is what happens in primates. And the reason why the occipital lobe is visual in primates is that primates are mammals, and there is an optic radiation to the rear of the hemispheres in all mammals (Kaas, 1980).

Similarly, the reception of heard speech is initially in the temporal lobe, despite the uniqueness of human auditory requirements, because that was the immediate possibility offered by the primate brain. Although one might have supposed that the uniqueness of human linguistic demands on the modality of hearing, presumably over a long period, should have entailed the evolution of major departures from the typical primate plan, anatomically the departures are not very radical, either in the temporal lobe or anywhere else (Passingham, 1979, 1982; Walker, 1985). Where uniquely human elaborations of primate organisation can be guessed at, they appear to conform to the general principles of the mammalian system.

The most obvious instance is of course "Broca's area." Broca's original claims may have been excessive, but the clinical consensus surely remains that a large loss of tissue somewhere in the neighbourhood of the bottom rear quadrant of the left frontal lobe is likely to have a deleterious effect on speech output processes. It is clearly no accident that this region is adjacent to (and includes) the face and throat parts of exitable motor cortex (i.e. is close to cortical output to face and throat: Levine & Sweet, 1982). Hence Jackson's hypothesis that the serial co-ordination of the combinations of movements required for vocalisation are in some sense localised here. The argument is that other mammalian species do not possess nervous arrangements for the learned modifications of precise forms of vocal output (or for any grammatical structuring of this output) but that if they did, this is where they would have to start.

By and large, this sort of very coarse localisation of what Head (1926) called "lower functions" is relatively unproblematical, provided that the existence of multiple motor representations in the up-down hierarchy is not forgotten. In some way the striate cortex is involved with visual reception rather than vocal output, even though vision as a psychological function cannot reside in the striate cortex exclusively, and in some way the bottom of the frontal motor strip is involved with vocal output rather than visual reception, even though the frontal cortex is only one level of motor control—these are statements which apply to all primate species. And these constraints alone would be sufficient to account for profound deficits in speech (but not necessarily vision) in anyone deprived of the front half of both hemispheres, no matter how soon in life (and therefore how much time was allowed for brain plasticity to make itself felt) the deprivation began (e.g. Vargha-Khadem & Watters, 1985).

But what of the "higher functions"—the formation of propositions, syntactical organisation, and the understanding of the meaning of a sentence? As these apply only to human capacities, is there any point in even attempting to relate them to primate brain mechanisms? In many cases probably not, but consider the example of higher functions in vision, in particular in reading. First, whatever brain peculiarities may have arisen during human evolution, they most certainly do not include specialisations for reading as such, since the vast majority of all human generations, at least until the last one or two, have been illiterate. When we look at letters, we cannot use anything that has evolved for that purpose. Conceivably a million years or more of naming seen and unseen objects, and more generally applying vocalisation to the perceived and imagined world, has had anatomical consequences, but grapheme-morpheme and grapheme-phoneme correspondences can only make use of these much more general mechanisms for auditory/visual correlations. In evolutionary terms, therefore, there is something odd about Charcot's famous diagram of the 1880s, which includes a visual centre for reading words (and a graphic motor centre for writing them) as useful items built in to the human central nervous system. However, if we were to suppose that a general purpose primate brain had to undertake the task of decoding script, we should expect it to make use of fairly nontopographical combinatorial mappings in the extra-striate cortex for detecting graphemes and for detected graphemes to be put in correspondence with phonemic motor instructions somewhere in the frontal lobe. Morphemic matters would have to be dealt with much more diffusely, and even for this the brain would need a separate set of motor instructions for writing, near the arm rather than the mouth regions of the pre-central motor cortex. We should in fact end up with something not unlike Charcot's diagram, or Lord Brain's version of it with labels for auditory phoneme schemas and graphic letter schemas (and word-meaning schemas and sentence schemas). On the basis of primate cortical layout, it would not surprise us that many different aspects of visual analysis and synthesis necessary for reading had different locations in the extra-striate cortex (in the parietal and temporal as well as occipital lobes) and that some localised lesions therefore had highly specific and separable effects on reading and writing (Cowey, 1979; Barlow, 1985; Diamond, 1979; Mansfield, 1982; Merzenich & Kaas, 1980; Kaas, 1982).

As specific mechanisms for reading and writing cannot be "given by inheritance," general features of the primate brain can plausibly be put forward as alternative principles of organisation. But both in terms of the plasticity of any individual's output, and in terms of an innate human grammar, speech, as opposed to writing, may be thought to have acquired the evolution of specialised mechanisms in the human brain beyond the predictable primate pattern. As far as plasticity goes, the most remarkable thing about human spoken language (from the point of view of comparisons with other species) is the existence of comparative linguistics. In other species, things that, in Jackson's words, are "given by inheritance" are usually very stereotyped, and this applies to species-specific vocalisations as well as to other behaviours. The observer from Mars, anticipating the emergence of propositional speech from primate calls, would surely have expected that syntax should be species-specific—in other words that linguistic universals in human speech should be very much more obvious than they are in fact. Even if anticipating some hominid enterprise with the same consequences as the Tower of Babel, to cause speech in different human populations not to be mutually comprehensible, the Martian primatologist could be forgiven if he or she predicted frequent cross-language regularities—such as gender always having similar grammatical implications, or word endings or vowel alternations always having at least roughly the same kind of grammatical significance. But, by comparison with the instinctive behaviours of animals or human emotional expression, the symbolic and refential use of language appears to be almost completely free of such inherited constraints (Greenberg, 1966; Swadesh, 1972; Comrie, 1981; Waldron, 1985).

If it is the case that the "commonplace movements" of the tongue and lips have become widely symbolic, then it appears that almost any movement of these organs can stand for almost any symbolic operation. One inference that could be drawn from this is that although the complex set of rules required for motor output of a specific human language are likely to require the successful functioning of extremely powerful combinatorial motor mappings, whatever it is that is innate about meanings and propositions, linguistically expressed, cannot be tied up exclusively with motor speech output. If all human languages signified plurality by putting an "s" sound on the end of words, then one might suppose that the anatomical idea of plurality was localised in Broca's area, and in close association with the movements required to say "s's." As human spoken languages are prodigiously variable, even for such basics as the denotation of sex and plurality, it seems possible that within the vocal-auditory channel general purpose aspects of primate brain function and cognition influence the human use of language, in addition to any uniquely evolved mechanisms for speech.

TRAINING CHIMPANZEES IN SYMBOLIC COMMUNICATION

Much time and effort has been spent over the last two decades in attempts to demonstrate that the general purpose cognitive capacities of the chimpanzee brain are sufficient to achieve a significant degree of linguistic competence, if the chimpanzees' natural inclinations are diverted by human intervention in the form of extended training with artificial systems of signs or gestures. If human evolution was accompanied by very radical changes in brain function associated with the use of language, then one would not expect very much of chimpanzees, however much time was spent on their education. If, on the other hand, human language is a new way of utilising an already existing brain design, then it is conceivable that the chimpanzee brain might be coached well beyond its normal limits.

The results of coaching efforts of this kind have been described and discussed at length (Gardner & Gardner, 1969, 1971, 1985; Premack, 1970, 1976; Savage-Rumbaugh, Rumbaugh, & Boysen, 1978a; Passingham, 1982; Walker, 1985). The most familiar technique is the training of chimpanzees in gestures based on the American Sign Language system developed for use by the human deaf. It is appropriate here, therefore, to refer to Jackson's theories about "pantomimic actions." Jackson distinguished pantomime from gesticulation, since the latter is more automatic and emotional, and not necessarily voluntary, and is therefore lower in the hierarchy. He seems to mean "pantomime" partly in the sense of gestural acting out, but also as anything which is referential and symbolic: Pantomimic actions are propositional and are sometimes severely impaired in aphasia. In other cases, loss of speech is due to more limited damage to middle and lower centres, leaving words still available for internal use in mentation. There are also, Jackson supposed, "arbitrary images," unlike symbols derived from words or from pantomimic actions, which allow us to have mental processes corresponding to the proposition "gold is yellow," simply by "thinking that a gold thing is a yellow thing" (Jackson, 1883/1932; p. 210). Clearly, if one believes that chimpanzees have mental processes which correspond to the proposition "bananas are yellow," one would hope to be able to train them to make communicative gestures to the same effect. Jackson's discussion of the evolution of reasoning and of the importance of "visual and tactile ideas and words" is involved and Spencerian, but there is a fairly direct assertion about animal mentation (Jackson, 1883/1932): "Since lower animals think, it may be asked 'What are their symbols?' if symbols are necessary in mentation. They have no words but I submit that they have other symbols—inferior symbols, symbols but little symbolic—which serve in their lowly mentation (p. 205)." These symbols, he suggests, are very low homologues of what in people becomes pantomimic, and are like faint visual and tactile ideas, and faint ideas of actions, concommitant with cerebral activity which is disengaged from the lower centres. In any post-Darwinian context, the assumption is likely to be made that in the anthropoid apes "there is reasoning in its lowest form—or at least there is that out of which reasoning has been gradually evolved (p. 209)." But it is no easy matter to tie down what such a lower form of reasoning might consist of. Perhaps the simplest hypothesis is that the chimpanzee brain is equivalent to two small human right hemispheres, with the corollary that if a human being has lost entirely the special purpose language apparatus of the left hemisphere, there will be suffered a dissolution of cognitive capacities of very drastic proportions. Alternatively one could suppose that the larger overall size of the human brain, or a general superiority in its mode of operation, means that no amount of brain damage short of complete decerebration is likely to reduce human abilities to an ape-like level.

This is partly a matter of rhetoric, but there is now a considerable body of behavioural evidence to suggest that chimpanzees exhibit a substantial amount of cognition of a rudimentary kind, but remain firmly "aphasic" in the sense of resisting efforts to induce either vocalisation, or syntactic skills within alternative forms of communication. The evidence has been discussed extensively elsewhere, and I shall give only a brief survey of it here (Dingwall, 1979; Passingham, 1982; Terrace, 1985; Savage-Rumbaugh et al., 1985).

There are several accounts of young chimps, orangs and gorillas reared in human domestic environments, most of whom adopted civilised habits of dress and decorum, but none of whom showed any tendency to imitate human speech (Furness, 1916; Cunningham, 1921; Kellogg, 1968). The most systematic study of a "home reared" chimpanzee was that undertaken by Hayes and Hayes (1952, 1953; Hayes & Nissen, 1971). Their animal, Viki, demonstrated an extreme lack of ability at voluntary and learned vocalisation (though not a total lack) but a remarkable aptitude at many other kinds of imitation. The Hayes' were encouraged to attempt the training of vocalisation because Viki, when a few months old, appeared to go through a "babbling" stage, but their efforts to improve on babbling met with little success. Perhaps it is not surprising, in view of Lieberman's description of the acoustic limitations of the chimpanzee throat, that Viki could not master vowel sounds. But she seemed to have difficulty even in establishing voluntary control of lip position. The only approximations to spoken English words were forms of "mama" "papa," "up," and "cup." In learning the most recognisable of these, "mama" and "papa," Viki at first kept her lips in the appropriate position for the consonants *by holding her lips with her own hand*. This was after the experimenters had held her lips, but whether or not it was this she was imitating, her behaviour suggests that she had better voluntary control of arm and hand movements than of lip position. In Jacksonian terms, higher motor centres appeared to be readily available for arm movements and skeletal movements generally, but either lip movements simply lack adequate representation in pre-motor cortex, or they are so strongly wired in to innate vocalisation and facial expression that they are not easily learnable in the context of voluntary phonation.

On the other hand, in perceptual understanding and manual dexterity, the Hayes claimed that Viki, when three years old, closely approximated a three-year-old child. This was based on controlled comparisons with human children, when Viki was aged between three and six, on tasks such as number matching and picture sorting (e.g. pictures of children versus pictures of adults), and these support the contention that the absence of vocal learning by Viki was not due to lack of "higher mental abilities" generally (Hayes & Nissen, 1971). Domestic chimpanzees' intellectual strengths appear to be in: (1) visual perception; (2) manual skill; and (3) visual-motor imitation. Because apes (and children) are good at it, imitation is not usually given much weight as a cognitive skill. But if one imagines building a robot that could *watch* someone cleaning spectacles, or holding the telephone, and then, later, copy these seen actions, then visual-motor imitation seems just as difficult in principle, if not more so, that auditory-vocal imitation. For the latter, self-produced output can be matched against the memory of the original model with little transformation; but to know that one's own actions in cleaning spectacles are equivalent to someone else's actions as visually perceived is quite complicated. Head (1926) promoted the use of a particular kind of imitation test in the examination of aphasic patients (the tester touches one of his eyes or ears with a particular hand, and the patient has to copy this exactly).

Because chimpanzees are usually very good at visual comprehension and the imitation of actions, most "language training" methods since that of Hayes and Hayes (1952) have attempted to capitalise on these natural strengths. Three kinds of system involving the visual modality have been tried: the American Sign Language gesture vocabulary (Gardner & Gardner, 1969; Terrace et al., 1979), a manipulable set of plastic tokens (Premack, 1970, 1976), and a computer-controlled keyboard with back-projected visual symbols (Rumbaugh, Gill, Brown, & Glaser, 1973). I will first describe the methods, and then consider the implications of the results obtained by using them.

The American Sign Language (ASL) Gesture System

Gardner and Gardner (1969) first reported the use of this method with the female chimpanzee Washoe. Since then a virtually identical system has been used with several other chimpanzees by Fouts, Chown, and Goodin

(1976), Terrace et al. (1979), and Muncer and Ettlinger (1981), while Patterson (1978) has used the same method with gorillas. As far as its use with nonhumans goes, ASL can be considered as a set of between 100 and 200 separate actions, each independent of the others. Many of the individual gestures are iconic or pantomimic: *drink* is the thumb pointed to the mouth; *eat* the fingers placed on the lips; *toothbrush* is the side of the finger rubbed across the teeth; *up* is an arm extended skywards. Other signs appear to be more arbitrary: *dog* is slapping the thigh; *brown* is a flat palm pulled down the side of the face; *banana* is one index finger stroking the other; and there are arbitrary proper names for human and ape individuals. Training with these gestures is usually partly informal, by "total immersion" of the infant animal among signing human companions, but imitation may deliberately be encouraged, and moulding of correct responses, plus shaping by actively rewarding approximations to the correct response, can also be used (Fouts, 1973).

The Plastic Token System

The tokens used by Premack (1970, 1976) are entirely arbitrary. Colour names are various achromatic shapes and *apple* is a blue triangle. Initially the plastic tokens were metal-backed and "written" in a top-to-bottom sequence by placing them against a magnetised board in a vertical line. There were no problems, however, in switching to the procedure of laying out the same tokens on a shelf in a horizontal line in front of the animal. Step-by-step training with individual tokens is the training method, in the first instance with food rewards for correct responses, but later without this expedient.

The Keyboard System

Combinations of individual visual elements were described by Rumbaugh et al. (1973) but as used in practice the symbols on the keyboard can be considered to be arbitrary and unrelated, though formed from a standard set of crosses, circles and straight lines with in-line display units. Particular visual "lexigrams" of this kind were projected on the individual keys of a keyboard array of up to 56 (8 across by 7 down), but the location of each symbol was changed from day to day to ensure the animals inspected the keys they were pressing visually. When the chimpanzee pressed one of the keys, the lexigram on that key was written up in a horizontal display line above the keyboard. The initial training took the form of key pressing followed by reward—if the animal pressed the key designated *tickle*, the trainer came in and tickled it (the chimp), and various foods and drinks were automatically dispensed when appropriate keys were pressed. More elaborate training for naming has since been reported to be necessary to establish "representational symbolic ability" (Savage-Rumbaugh et al., 1980, 1983).

Satisfaction of Wants

In all the above cases young apes give every appearance of eagerly making use of the artificial methods presented to them in order to achieve certain tangible ends. After making a gesture for *tickle*, or pressing a key so designated, they appear to expect to be tickled, and to enjoy any tickling delivered as a consequence of their communicative activity. It has frequently been pointed out that this does not constitute a very complex linguistic milestone (Terrace et al., 1979; Seidenberg & Pettito, 1979). Sceptics may deny that there is even any intention to communicate—suggesting that the gesture for tickle is like a reflex response to an itch. This does not seem very plausible, but the use of signs simply to satisfy wants is rather similar to pantomimic gestures used by domestic cats and dogs (running to the food bowl, or scratching at doors) and therefore cannot be used as a measure of exceptional primate abilities.

Naming

Chimpanzees trained with the gesture-sign method appear to use the gestures to make comments as well as requests. When leafing through a picture book they may make spontaneous signs, such as rubbing their teeth when they see a picture of a toothbrush. Experimenters also elicit naming by a *what's this?* gesture. All those involved in performing such experiments believe that a large number of gestures are associated with object categories, and various "double-blind" methods have been employed to check the accuracy of these associations (Fouts et al., 1976; Gardner & Gardner, 1985). The most obvious control technique is for the chimpanzee to be shown objects on a screen or placed in a box, out of the view of the human observer, who translates any gestures made by the animal in response to seeing the objects. But even if objects are labelled reasonably reliably, as appears to be the case, many critics remain to be convinced that this is a preliminary to linguistic skill rather than a set of high-level conditioned reflexes. One would like to have some quantitative measure of how far the animals "understand the names" by comparison with human children (or adults). No such measure is directly available, but one can assess evidence for the labelling of absent objects, and for categorisation.

Labelling Absent Objects

Asking for a banana when none are visible could be taken as displaced reference, but would not be a very convincing example of disengagement from context (Bronowski & Bellugi, 1970). A marginally more interesting achievement is referring to a particular banana which was seen a few minutes ago. Two experiments reported by Savage-Rumbaugh et al. (1978a, 1978b), which are of this general type, are valuable both for their experimental controls and for the fact that two chimpanzees used the keyboard system to exchange information, and material objects, between themselves. In the first case (1978b), one animal communicated to the other the identity of a hidden food object. After several preliminary phases of training, the final performance included the following tests. The animals were in adjacent cubicles, separated by a window, each with his own keyboard. One of the apes was led out to another room, and shown one of 11 different foodstuffs being placed in a container, which was then sealed. (The comestibles included banana, beancake, bread, milk, and orange drink, whose names were already well trained. The animal led out alternated from trial to trial.) This informed animal was then led back to his keyboard and, observed by his partner, pressed one of the keys to produce a symbol recorded on the overhead display. The second chimpanzee then had to key in a request for the particular food in the container. The container was then opened, and both animals shown its contents; only if these corresponded to the final request were they allowed to consume them. The combined accuracy was between 90% and 100% in various phases of this sort of test.

One of the checks was to require the second animal to select a photograph of the appropriate food item just after he had keyed in the request for it—since the selections were accurate, it would appear that the identity of a distant object had been transmitted from one animal to the other. If the animal who had seen the hidden food item was denied the use of the keyboard, but allowed to interact socially with the other chimp, the second chimp did not succeed in correctly identifying the hidden food; this suggests that the transmission of object identity took place in the form of meanings attached to arbitrary visual signals.

A second experiment (Savage-Rumbaugh et al., 1978a), using the same two chimpanzees (Austin and Sherman), involved requests made by one animal to the other. They were in adjacent rooms, connected by a hatch which could be opened and closed only by the experimenter. In one room there were several problem devices, each requiring the use of a different tool: a padlocked box requiring a key; a bolted box requiring a wrench; a vending device requiring metal discs; and various tubes and containers needing a stick, a sponge on a string, or a straw, to obtain any food or drink placed in them. On a given trial, the chimpanzee in the problem room was shown just one of these apparatuses being baited with food, but not given any of the six possible tools. The hatch was then opened to provide access to the second chimpanzee in the next room, who had possession of all the tools, but did not know (and could not tell) which one was necessary. The task was for the animal in the problem room to key in the symbol corresponding to the correct tool on a keyboard available to him. The ape in the tool room needed to observe the symbol thus projected (sometimes the requesting animal pointed at this symbol), and hand the appropriate tool through the window. When this tool had been used to obtain the hidden food item, the two animals shared out their incentive (initially at the insistence of the experimenters). As the correct tool was both requested and provided on more than 90% of the trials, even when the experimenter was "blind", or absent altogether, it seems necessary to conclude that the identity of a tool could be communicated from one animal to the other. Pantomimic actions did not appear to be involved: When the keyboard was turned off no iconic gestures were observed, and the only success achieved under these conditions was when the tool room animal simply offered each tool in turn. In a later experiment (Savage-Rumbaugh et al., 1983) both Austin and Sherman were able to use the keyboard to indicate (to the computer) which of several objects on a distant table they intended to choose in the near future. On the basis of this evidence it is difficult to resist the conclusion that these chimpanzees formed mental associations between arbitrary visual symbols and object categories.

Category Names

In a further success for Austin and Sherman it has been demonstrated that the "lexigrams" which they used for tools and for the foodstuffs could come to take part in a certain minimal form of semantic organisation (Savage-Rumbaugh et al., 1980). Special lexigrams designated as category names for "foodstuff" and "tool" were taught by training the animals to press the appropriate lexigram on a keyboard when presented with real food objects or tools, or with photographs of objects and tools. After this, they were able to categorise lexigrams of individual foods and tools correctly by pressing the lexigram for *food* or *tool*. For instance, if shown the lexigram *wrench* they pressed the lexigram *tool*, but if shown the lexigram *sweet potato* they pressed the lexigram *food*. During this experiment the animals neither ate the foods, nor used the tools, which they were labelling. This should count as a degree of disengagement from context, but the view of the experimenters was that the categorising performance was only made possible by the previous experience of using the lexigrams actively, as a means to achieve desired ends in earlier experiments.

Reasoning

The evidence is quite strong that chimpanzees, lacking any assistance from innate linguistic universals or learned phonological codes, can nevertheless be trained to associate arbitrary visual labels with individual object types and class categories. There is very little indication that they are able to go on from this, and learn syntactical rules for the combination of labels that would amount to a functional grammar (see below). But, even when grammar is absent, apes may be not altogether without nous—there are several experimental procedures which allow one to infer the presence in them of intellectual processes that go beyond the mental associations required for symbolic labelling.

Transitive Inference

If one was told that the orange team always beats the white team; the white team always beats the reds; the reds always beat the blacks; and the blacks always beat the blues; then if one had to bet, one would probably bet on the white team beating the black team. It is to be hoped that chimpanzees are indifferent to the overtones of black and white—these stimuli were used in a test of their inferences in order to avoid preferences based on colour (Gillan, 1981) or generalisation from other hues. The testing was a simple choice between members of pairs of containers with coloured lids. After the following training: orange has food in orange/white; white has food in white/red; red has food in red/black; and black has food in black/blue; it was possible to give chimpanzees the test of a novel nonadjacent pair, black/white, in which preference could be attributed to a "mental representation of order information." The most telling control procedure was that, if the linearity of the sequence was disturbed by the result that the bottom team always beat the top team, all bets were off: If trials were given in which blue has the food in blue/orange, the preference in the black/white pairing disappeared. This result was obtained with only one chimpanzee, Sadie, but there was more variation in the colour sequences tested than I have described here. This particular animal had not had any language training and the result thus supports the hypothesis that linguistic processes are not an absolute necessity for the accomplishment of transitive inference.

Analogical Reasoning

The chimpanzee, Sadie, which appeared to have constructed a mental linear scale of colours in the transitive inference test, failed to demonstrate any comprehension of a matching-to-sample procedure designed as a simple version of analogical reasoning. The bases of the analogy were the concepts of sameness and difference: The sample was always of two objects, and if these were the same—two toothbrushes, say—an alternative of two matchboxes, rather than an array of an ashtray with a cotton reel, should have been chosen. One would have thought that chimpanzees should be capable of perceiving this sort of relationship, but Premack (1983) reports that four out of five of the apes which he attempted to train on this test failed it. Children below about four years of age also failed it.

Only one chimpanzee (and older children) succeeded, this being Sarah, who had more than a decade of training with the plastic token symbols for "same" and "different" behind her. This animal can apparently not only make choices based on sameness and difference, but also place the tokens designated *same* and *different* between pairs of related or unrelated objects. That ability has been utilised to demonstrate what would seem to be a more complicated kind of analogical reasoning (Gillan, Premack, & Woodruff, 1981). According to this report, when shown a peeled apple plus apple peel on the left, and a peeled orange plus orange peel on the right, Sarah places *same* in the centre, but if the orange peel is accompanied by a peeled banana, or orange seeds, she puts *different*. A can with a can opener elicits *same* when paired with a lock with its key, but *different* when paired with a padlock plus a paint brush. Although a very large number of tests of this kind were given, some using controlled variations of geometric figures, it is difficult to say just what cognitive processes might have been responsible for the animal's (usually correct) choices. Premack (1983) concludes that the long years of token training are responsible for the successful performance by Sarah, because they enhanced an "abstract code" only dimly present in other animals of the same species.

Reasoning About Number, Time, and Place

Although it would be valuable to establish whether or not, as Premack (1983) suggests, training with his token system produces greatly enhanced cognitive abilities in primates lacking spoken language, it is also useful to know what mental capacities can be relied on in relatively untutored animals. Sarah, the "language trained" chimpanzee (although not others) could match arbitrary numbers of objects from one to four. But even the younger animals seemed to comprehend the difference immediately between one and two pieces of fruit. Arguably the test used implies an intuition that two minus one leaves one. First a trainer shows a chimp that he has two pieces of fruit in his hand, then the trainer goes out into a field, unseen by the animal, and places the fruit in a large container. The animal is allowed to see just one piece of food being removed from the container. If then released on its own the chimpanzee rushes to the container to retrieve the remaining titbit. The necessary (and more surprising) control is that if the trainer starts off by showing that he has only one piece of fruit, and then this one piece is seen to be removed from the container (Premack, 1983): "after this demonstration the animal does not go out into the field at all, but sits behind the blind, grooming itself or gazing out into space (p. 131)." This result alone might not be convincing, but there is a sufficient amount of evidence to confirm that, in general, chimpanzees without special training have a rich mental mapping of the observed locations of pieces of fruit in external space (Kohler, 1925; Menzel, 1978).

At least after special training, and possibly without it, nonhuman primates may approach the Piagetian "concrete operations" stage, demonstrating, in Sarah's case, something very like conservation of volume (Pasnak, 1979; Woodruff, Premack, & Kennel, 1978; Muncer, 1982).

Syntax and Function Words

Memory for the location of pieces of fruit, and even the association of visual symbols with object categories, could be taken as semantic, visual-spatial, right-hemisphere abilities. There is relatively little indication that nonhuman primates, even those trained with signs or gestures, can develop the skills required for the use of grammar. All the anecdotal reports of the use of combinations of gestures in apes trained in American Sign Language should probably be discounted (Terrace et al., 1979). It is possible, however, that the use of correct gesture order in the context of prepositions such as "in," "on," "under," and "behind" is within the capabilities of chimpanzees.

After about one year of training with ASL gestures for a limited vocabulary, but including the prepositions "in" and "behind," Muncer and Ettlinger (1981) gave their single animal a series of "critical trials" (including regular double-blind trials) to assess both comprehension and production of novel phrases concerning a transparent plastic bag and a number of small opaque objects such as: bag in box; box in bag; box behind apple; apple behind box. Cases such as "carrot in bag" where the order cannot be reversed, were used in training, but not in the critical trials.) Test performance was significantly better than chance, though considerably less than perfect. Curiously, more errors were due to choosing the wrong preposition than to choosing the wrong order of gestures (or objects). There seemed to be absolutely no difficulty for the ape in always putting the prepositions second, in groups of three gestures. Semantically, "in" and "behind" could be confused on the grounds that "bag in box" and "bag behind box" both entail the occlusion of the bag by the box.

In a second experiment this chimpanzee was trained to produce and comprehend the signs for *and, or,* and *not,* in the context of the animal being instructed to *"take peanut and carrot"* from a display including a banana and an apple; or the chimpanzee signing *"Graham not take banana,"* when she herself would get what was not taken by Graham. Performance on critical trials was then measured, in which, for the first time, *not* was combined with *or* and *and.* Three objects not before used with conjunctions were involved in these trials: paper, bag, and box, with raisins placed on these for reward. The animal refused to produce the signs for *not* or *or* under these circumstances. However, comprehension was tested by giving gestural instructions in the form *"not paper and bag"* or *"not paper or bag."* In the first case, taking both or taking just the third choice was scored as incorrect. Under these rules the chimpanzee was significantly above chance (95%) for the NAND operation, but significantly below chance (10%) on the NOR. In both cases what the animal did on most trials was simply to refrain from taking the raisin from the object signed just after *not*, while collecting its reward from the two others. Muncer and Ettlinger rightly report this as a "failure to negate conjunctions," but the chimpanzee should surely be given credit for adopting its own syntactic rule, even if this violated Boolean algebra. When instructions were given in the form *"not paper and not bag"* it was capable of refraining from touching both forbidden objects. Taken together, these findings with prepositions and negations using the gesture-sign method lend credence to Premack's earlier claims, that his animals could follow simple instructions of the type *apple dish insert*, or *red card on green card*, transmitted by lines of plastic tokens. Although the skills of combining symbolic elements, either receptively or productively, may be said to be minimal in tests on chimpanzees so far conducted, the ability to modify the interpretation given to one symbol because of the presence of another is not necessarily completely absent in these animals.

NONVERBAL SYSTEMS OF COMMUNICATION USED WITH APHASIC PATIENTS

As the American Sign Language (ASL) system was developed for the use of disadvantaged people—the deaf—it is hardly a new idea to suggest that it could be used with categories of persons in whom the normal vocal-auditory channel is for some reason unavailable. Bouilland recommended the use of nonspeech signals with adult aphasic patients in 1825. Peterson and Kirschner (1981) have more recently reviewed reports of the training of aphasic persons with visual methods, including pantomime and American Indian signs as well as ASL. There is of course a general difficulty, in that patients with the severest loss of speech production skills may also be impaired in their ability to produce or understand messages in other symbolic systems (Feyereisen & Seron, 1982). However, Peterson & Kirschner's review suggests that there are many patients whose impairments are sufficiently specific to vocal production or heard speech to make training them in the visual modality worthwhile. The case history reported by Kirschner and Webb (1981) is of this type. The patient, having become mute and incomprehending of speech after a bitemporal infarction, was able to learn over 100 signs including both ASL and Amerind gestures, which she found useful in communicating with her family. Two other findings with this patient may have considerable generality: Some sparing of reading and writing skills is an indication that other ways of making use of the visual channel may be successful; but even so, gesturing in aphasic patients may lack fluency. More optimistically, there are suggestions that gestural and pantomimic training may improve thinking, and may even result in spontaneous verbalisation, in aphasic patients (e.g. Schlanger & Freiman, 1979).

The tangible plastic token developed by Premack (1970) for use with chimpanzees provides a very particular kind of visual channel for communication; it has the disadvantage, compared to gesture, that it requires special (though not expensive) equipment, but the advantages are first that this equipment serves as an external aid to short-term memory, and second that vision may if necessary be augmented by tactile information. A patient must be relatively quick to observe gestures, but a line of plastic chips may be inspected for as long as is necessary. The token system may therefore be useful for minimising the load placed on memory and visual attention. Hughes (1975) conducted what was virtually a replication of the Premack (1971) investigation of the chimpanzee Sarah with developmentally aphasic children. The 14 subjects, whose aphasia was either congenital or of very early origin, were between 8 and 13 years of age, but had vocal language abilities assessed at the 2-year-old level or less. None could use spoken prepositions. But during a twice-weekly half-hour session, over a period of months, they learned to produce and understand "sentences" and to communicate a knowledge of class concepts. They first learned "nouns" by associating arbitrary plastic symbols with particular toys, such as a car or doll. Then sentences of the kind *"Diane insert doll dish"* were correctly complied with, and accurate descriptions such as *"experimenter take-out car bucket"* were given of seen events. The preposition "on" was tested systematically by itself: The children either followed instructions like *"green on red,"* by placing a green card over a red card, or gave description of cards arranged by the experimenter, by placing tokens in correct order, from left to right on a magnified board.

Although it might be expected that, even with profoundly impaired linguistic competence, a natural intelligence should easily encompass a set of simple associations between symbols and perceptible objects, and also between symbols and clearly visible relations between objects such as "in," "on," and "under," it is something of a surprise that bits of plastic can just as easily come to represent concepts such as colour in general, or shape in general, which are not so tied to visual images. When certain tokens stood for "colour of" and "name of," the children were able to select *colour of* correctly when the colour word for red was presented along with an actual red circle; or to insert the token for "square," rather than that for "yellow" in the proposition "blank *shape of* actual yellow square." Perhaps this should only be surprising if one assumes the existence of an all-powerful and transmodal language acquisition device, which ought to be notable by its absence in developmentally aphasic children. But it is also possible that some higher-order concepts are not as difficult as we think they ought to be for primates who exhibit difficulties with spoken or heard syntax. In Premack's original studies the chimpanzee performed even more accurately than usual when she was required to fill in blanks with class concepts, given concrete instances. This was true not only for implying that the token *round* was the *shape of* a real apple rather than its colour, but also for indicating that the arbitrary token for a banana fell into the category *name of*, rather then the categories of colour or shape (Premack, 1976; pp. 162–164, 198).

The manipulable tokens have been taught to autistic children (DeVilliers & Naughton, 1974) and to adult global aphasics (Velettri-Glass, Gazzaniga, & Premack, 1973), and a small number of other forms of visual ideographic symbol have been shown to allow for increased communication with some very severely aphasic adults (e.g. Baker, Berry, Garner, Zurif, Davis, & Veroff, 1975; Gardner, Zurif, Berry, & Baker, 1976). Given the ready availability nowadays of computer controlled coloured graphic displays, an obvious direction for future research in both the testing and retraining of human brain-damaged patients with vocal/auditory difficulties will be ideographic and vivid visual communication systems which make use of a keyboard or joystick and a television screen.

CONCLUSIONS AND SUMMARY

My concern has been the biological backdrop of cross-species comparisons, against which the unimpaired human use of language stands out in brilliant contrast. When human abilities are dimmed, it is perhaps easier to catch a glimpse of shadowy scene-shifters, but it is certainly going too far to think of all human disabilities in the extreme Jacksonian fashion, as a set of localised reversal of evolution. Nevertheless, it is arguable that the specialities of human cognition, including those requiring the use of language, do not place human cognition for ever outside the reach of biological comparisons.

No new modalities of sense or new motor organs were thrown up by the evolution of language, and to this extent the apparatus used in speech has phylogenetic precedents. It is the mental content of speech, rather than its physical form, that is most important, and therefore it is the relation between the functioning of the brain in human language, and the principles of brain organisation which apply also to monkeys and apes, where we might expect biological comparisons to stand or fall. The broad outlines of Hughlings Jackson's views of human brain function usually command respect, and two aspects of the details of Jackson's speculations continue to be supported by both neuroanatomical and clinical evidence. Although the multiple representation of body parts and their movements in the Jacksonian hierarchy precludes the identification of unitary centres in the brain responsible for isolated psychological functions, all specifiable components of psychological activity are, in Jackson's scheme, assigned to physically separate "nervous arrangements." A simple corollary of this is that many of the localisations of the nervous arrangements in the human brain can be related directly to the similar organisation of the brains of closely related primates. Thus the special movements of the tongue and lips required for human speech are anatomically adjacent to where more commonplace motor representations of the lips and tongue would be found in a general-purpose primate brain. Physically separate neural specialisations appear to be the rule in primate brains, and a second corollary is that small-scale components of psychological skills may be anatomically localised in individual brains to a very high degree.

Primate species which lack those specialisations peculiar to human speech may have other abilities which enable them to master a range of manual gestures, or artificial visual symbols, which can certainly be employed for simple descriptions and requests. Although there is no evidence that grammatical rules of ordinary human complexity will emerge from these training experiments, one-to-one correspondence between distinct visual signals and distinct object categories appears to allow for production and comprehension of symbols that refer to such higher-order categories as prepositions and class descriptions (a food, a tool, a shape, a colour, a visual signal). Persons who lack or who have lost some of the cognitive specialisations peculiar to speech may similarly retain many other cognitive abilities, and in some cases recourse to gestural or ideographic alternatives to the vocal/auditory channel may be clinically helpful.

As a final word on the degree of specificity possible in cognitive and linguistic impairments which result from brain disorder, and in belated commemoration of the centenary of Darwin's death (Darwin, 1871/1901):

The intimate connection between the brain, as it is now developed in us, and the faculty of speech, is well shown by those cases of brain disease in which speech is specially affected, as when the power to remember substantives is lost, whilst other words can be correctly used, or where substantives of a certain class, or all except the initial letters of substantives and proper names are forgotten (p. 134).

REFERENCES

Aitken, P. G. (1981) Cortical control of conditioned and spontaneous vocal behaviour in rhesus monkeys. *Brain and Language, 13*, 171–184.

Anderson, J. A., Silverstein, J. W., Ritz, S. A., & Jones, R. S. (1977) Distinctive features, categorical perception, and probability learning: Some applications of a neuronal model. *Psychological Review, 84*, 413–451.

Arbib, M. A. (1982) Perceptual-motor processes and the neural basis of language. In M. A. Arbib, D. Caplan, & J. C. Marshall (Eds.), *Neural Models of Language Processing*. London: Academic Press.

Baker, E., Berry, T., Garner, A., Zurif, E., Davis, L., & Veroff, A. (1975) Can linguistic competence be dissociated from natural language functions? *Nature, 254*, 509–510.

Barlow, H. B. (1972) Single units and sensation: A neuron doctrine for perceptual psychology? *Perception, 1*, 371–394.

Barlow, H. B. (1985) The Twelfth Bartlett Memorial Lecture: The role of single neurons in the psychology of perception. *Quarterly Journal of Experimental Psychology, 37A*, 121–145.

Bastian, H. C. (1898) *A Treatise on Aphasia and Other Speech Defects*. London: H. K. Lewis.

Bouilland, J. B. (1825) Recherches clinique propres à démontrer que la perte de la parole correspond à la lésion des lobules antérieurs du cerveau. *Archives Générales de Médicine, 8*, 25–45.

Brain, Baron W. R. (1965) *Speech Disorders*. London: Butterworths.

Brazier, M. A. (1979) Challenges from the philosophers to the neuroscientists. In Ciba Foundation Symposium 69, *Brain and Mind*. Amsterdam: Excerpta Medica, 5–29.

Bronowski, J. & Bellugi, U. (1970) Language, name and concept. *Science, 168*, 669–673.

Burd, G. D. & Nottebohm, F. (1985) Ultrastructural characterisation of synaptic terminals formed on newly generated neurons in a song control nucleus of the adult canary forebrain. *Journal of Comparative Neurology, 240*, 143–152.

Carpenter, C. C. & Ferguson, G. W. (1977) Variation and evolution of stereotyped behaviour in reptiles. In C. Gans & D. W. Tinkle (Eds.), *Biology of the Reptilia, Vol. 7: Ecology and Behaviour A*. London: Academic Press, 335–403.

Comrie, B. (1981) *Language Universals and Linguistic Typology*. Oxford: Basil Blackwell.

Cowey, A. (1979) Cortical maps and visual perception. *Quarterly Journal of Experimental Psychology, 131*, 1–17.

Creutzfeldt, O. D. (1979) Neurophysiological mechanisms and consciousness. In Ciba Foundation Symposium 69, *Brain and Mind*. Amsterdam: Exerpta Medica, 217–233.

Cunningham, A. (1921) A gorilla's life in civilization. *Bulletin of the Zoological Society, New York, 24*, 118–124.

Darwin, C. (1871/1901) *The Descent of Man and Selection in Relation to Sex*. London: John Murray.

Denenberg, V. H. (1981) Hemispheric laterality in animals and the effect of early experience. *Behavioural and Brain Sciences, 4*, 1–49.

DeVilliers, J. & Naughton, J. M. (1974) Teaching a symbol language to autistic children. *Journal of Consulting and Clinical Psychology, 42*, 111–117.

Diamond, I. T. (1979) The subdivisions of neocortex: A proposal to revise the traditional view of sensory, motor and association areas. In J. M. Sprague & A. N. Epsteinm (Eds.), *Progress in Psychobiology and Physiological Psychology, Vol. 8*. New York: Academic Press, 2–44.

Dingwall, W. O. (1979) The evolution of human communication systems. In H. Whitaker & H. A. Whitaker (Eds.), *Studies in Neurolinguistics, Vol. 4*. New York: Academic Press, 1–95.

Ferrier, D. (1878) *The Localisation of Cerebral Disease*. London: Smith Elder.

Feyereisen, P. & Seron, X. (1982) Nonverbal communication and aphasia: A review. I. Comprehension. II. Expression. *Brain and Language, 16*, 191–236.

Fodor, J. (1983) *The Modularity of Mind*. London: MIT Press.

Foster, R. E. & Hall, W. C. (1978) The organisation of central auditory pathways in a reptile *Iguana iguana*. *Journal of Comparative Neurology, 178*, 783–832.

Fouts, R. (1973) Acquisition and testing of gestural signs in four young chimpanzees. *Science, 180*, 978–980.

Fouts, R. S., Chown, B., & Goodin, L. (1976) Transfer of signed responses in American Sign Language from vocal English to physical object stimuli by a chimpanzee (*pan*). *Learning and Motivation, 7*, 458–475.

Franzen, E. A. & Myers, R. E. (1973) Neural control of social behaviour: Prefrontal and anterior temporal cortex. *Neuropsychologia, 11*, 141–157.

Furness, W. H. (1916) Observations on the mentality of chimpanzees and orangutans. *Proceedings of the American Philosophical Society, 65*, 281–290.

Gardner, B. T. & Gardner, R. A. (1971) Two-way communication with an infant chimpanzee. In A. M. Schrier & F. Stollnitz (Eds.), *Behaviour of Nonhuman Primates, Vol. 4*. New York: Academic Press, 177–183.

Gardner, B. T. & Gardner, R. A. (1985) Signs of intelligence in cross-fostered chimpanzees. *Philosophical Transactions of the Royal Society B, 308*, 159–176.

Gardner, R. A. & Gardner, B. T. (1969) Teaching sign language to a chimpanzee. *Science, 187*, 752–753.

Gardner, H., Zurif, E., Berry, T., & Baker, E. (1976) Visual communication in aphasia. *Neuropsychologia, 14*, 275–292.

Geschwind, N. (1965) Disconnexion syndromes in animals and man. *Brain, 88*, 237–294.

Gillan, D. J. (1981) Reasoning in the chimpanzee: II. Transitive inference. *Journal of Experimental Psychology: Animal Behaviour Processes, 7*, 150–164.

Gillan, D., Premack, D., & Woodruff, G. (1981) Reasoning in the chimpanzee: I. Analogical reasoning. *Journal of Experimental Psychology: Animal Behaviour Processes, 7*, 1–17.

Goodman, M. (1974) Biochemical evidence on hominid phylogeny. *Annual Review of Anthropology, 3*, 203–228.

Green, H. D. & Walker, A. E. (1938) The effects of ablation of the cortical motor face area in monkeys. *Journal of Neurophysiology, 1*, 26–80.

Greenberg, J. H. (1966) Some universals of grammar, with particular reference to the order of meaningful elements. In J. H. Greenberg (Ed.), *Universals of Language*. Cambridge, Mass.: MIT Press, 73–113.

Hast, M. H., Fisher, J. M., Wetzel, A. B., & Thompson, V. E. (1974) Cortical motor representations of the laryngeal muscles in *Macaca mulatta*. *Brain Research, 73*, 229–240.

Hayes, K. J. & Hayes, C. H. (1952) Imitation in the home-raised chimpanzee. *Journal of Comparative and Psychological Psychology, 45*, 450–459.

Hayes, K. J. & Hayes, C. H. (1953) Picture perception in a home-raised chimpanzee. *Journal of Comparative and Physiological Psychology, 45*, 470–474.

Hayes, K. J. & Nissen, C. H. (1971) Higher mental functions of a home-raised chimpanzee. In A. M. Schrier & F. Stollnitz (Eds.), *Behaviour of Nonhuman Primates, Vol. 4*. New York: Academic Press, 59–115.

Head, H. (1926) *Aphasia and Kindred Disorders of Speech*. London: Cambridge University Press.

Hubel, D. H. & Weisel, T. N. (1977) Ferrier Lecture. Functional architecture of macaque monkey visual cortex. *Proceedings of the Royal Society of London, Series B., 198*, 1–59.

Hughes, J. (1975) Acquisition of a nonvocal language by aphasic children. *Cognition, 3*, 41–55.

Hupfer, K., Jurgens, U., & Ploog, D. (1977) The effect of superior temporal lesions on the recognition of species-specific calls in the squirrel monkey. *Experimental Brain Research*, *30*, 75–87.

Jackson, J. H. (1882) On some implications of dissolution of the nervous system. *Medical Press and Circular* (reprinted in Jackson, 1932).

Jackson, J. H. (1883) Words and other symbols in mentation. *Medical Press and Circular* (reprinted in Jackson, 1932).

Jackson, J. H. (1931) *Selected Writings of John Hughlings Jackson. Volume One. On Epilepsy and Epileptiform Convulsions*. J. Taylor (Ed.). London: Hodder & Stoughton.

Jackson, J. H. (1932) *Selected Writings of John Hughlings Jackson. Volume Two. Evolution and Dissolution of the Nervous System, Speech, Various Papers, Addresses and Lectures*. J. Taylor (Ed.). London: Hodder & Stoughton.

Jolly, A. (1972) *The Evolution of Primate Behaviour*. New York: Macmillan.

Jurgens, U. (1974) The exitability of vocalisation from the cortical larynx area. *Brain Research*, *81*, 564–566.

Jurgens, U. (1976) Reinforcing concommitants of electrically elicited vocalisations. *Experimental Brain Research*, *26*, 203–214.

Jurgens, U. (1979) Neural control of vocalisation in nonhuman primates. In H. D. Steklis & M. J. Raleigh (Eds.), *Neurobiology of Social Communication in Primates*. London: Academic Press, 11–44.

Jurgens, U. (1982) Amygdalar vocalisation pathways in the squirrel monkey. *Brain Research*, *241*, 189–196.

Jurgens, U. (1985) Implication of SMA in phonation. *Experimental Brain Research*, *58*, A12–14.

Jurgens, U. & Kirzinger, A. (1985) The laryngeal sensory pathway and its role in phonation. A brain lesion study in the squirrel monkey. *Experimental Brain Research*, *59*, 118–124.

Jurgens, U. & Ploog, D. (1970) Cerebral representation of speech in the squirrel monkey. *Experimental Brain Research*, *10*, 532–554.

Kaas, J. H. (1980) A comparative survey of visual cortex organisation in mammals. In S. O. E. Ebbesson (Ed.), *Comparative Neurology of the Telencephalon*. New York: Plenum Press, 483–502.

Kaas, J. H. (1982) The segregation of function in the nervous system: Why do sensory systems have so many subdivisions? In W. P. Neff (Ed.), *Contributions to Sensory Physiology*. New York: Academic Press.

Karten, H. J. (1979) Visual lemniscal pathways in birds. In A. M. Granda & J. H. Maxwell (Eds.), *Neural Mechanisms of Behaviour in the Pigeon*. New York: Plenum Press, 409–430.

Kellogg, W. N. (1968) Communication and language in the home-raised chimpanzee. *Science*, *162*, 423–427.

King, M. & Wilson, A. C. (1975) Evolution at two levels in humans and chimpanzees. *Science*, *188*, 107–116.

Kirschner, A. S. & Webb, W. G. (1981) Selective involvements of the auditory-verbal modality in an acquired communication disorder: Benefit from sign-language therapy. *Brain and Language*, *13*, 161–170.

Kohler, W. (1925) *The Mentality of Apes*. London: Kegan Paul, Trench, & Trubner.

Konorski, J. (1967) *Integrative Activity of the Brain*. Chicago: University of Chicago Press.

Kruger, L. & Stein, B. E. (1973) Primordial sense organs and the evolution of sensory systems. In E. C. Carterette & M. P. Friedman (Eds.), *Handbook of Perception, Vol. III*. London: Academic Press, 63–87.

Kuhl, P. K. & Miller, J. D. (1975) Speech perception by chinchilla: Voiced-voiceless distinction in alveolar plosive consonants. *Science*, *190*, 69–72.

Kuypers, H. G. J. M. (1958a) Some projections from the pericentral cortex to the pons and lower brainstem in monkey and chimpanzee. *Journal of Comparative Neurology, 110*, 221–255.

Kuypers, H. G. J. M. (1958b) Corticobulbar connexions to the pons and lower brainstem in man. *Brain, 81*, 364–388.

Lamendella, J. (1977) The limbic system in human communication. In H. Whitaker & H. A. Whitaker (Eds.), *Studies in Neurolinguistics, Vol. 3.* New York: Academic Press, 157–222.

Lashley, K. S. (1950) In search of the engram. In *Symposia of the Society of Experimental Biology (No. IV)*, Cambridge: Cambridge University Press, 454–482.

Levine, D. N. & Sweet, E. (1982) The neuropathological basis of Broca's aphasia and its implications for the cerebral control of speech. In M. A. Arbib, D. Caplan, & J. C. Marshall (Eds.), *Neural Models of Language Processes.* London: Academic Press, 299–326.

Leyton, A. S. F. & Sherrington, C. S. (1917) Observations on the excitable cortex of the chimpanzee, orang-utan and gorilla. *Quarterly Journal of Experimental Physiology, 11*, 135–222.

Lieberman, P. (1975) *On the Origins of Language.* New York: Macmillan.

Lieberman, P. (1977) The phylogeny of language. In T. A. Sebeok (Ed.), *How Animals Communicate.* London: University of Indiana Press, 3–23.

Luria, A. R. (1974) Language and brain. *Brain and Language, 1*, 1–14.

MacKinnon, J. (1974) The behaviour and ecology of wild orang-utans (*Pongo pygmaeus*). *Animal Behaviour, 22*, 3–74.

Mansfield, R. J. W. (1982) Role of striate cortex in pattern perception in primates. In D. J. Ingle, M. A. Goodale, & R. J. W. Mansfield (Eds.), *Analysis of Visual Behaviour.* London: MIT Press, 443–482.

Marler, P. (1970) A comparative approach to vocal learning: Song development in white-crowned sparrows. *Journal of Comparative and Physiological Psychology Monograph, 71* No. 2, Part 2, 1–25.

Marler, P. & Tenaza, R. (1977) Signalling behaviour of apes with special reference to vocalisation. In T. A. Sebeok (Ed.), *How Animals Communicate.* London: University of Indiana Press, 965–1033.

Menzel, E. W. (1978) Cognitive mapping in chimpanzees. In S. H. Hulse, H. Fowler, & W. K. Honig (Eds.), *Cognitive Processes in Animal Behaviour.* Hillsdale, N.J.: Lawrence Erlbaum Associates Inc., 375–422.

Merzenich, M. M. & Kaas, J. H. (1980) Principles of organisation of sensory-perceptual systems in mammals. In J. M. Sprague & A. N. Epstein (Eds.), *Progress in Psychobiology and Physiological Psychology, Vol. 9.* London: Academic Press, 1–42.

Mitani, A., Shimokouchi, H., Itoh, K., Nomura, S., Kudo, H., & Mizuno, N. (1985) Morphology and laminar organisation of electrophysiologically identified neurons in the primary auditory cortex in the cat. *Journal of Comparative Neurology, 235*, 430–447.

Mulroy, M. J. & Oblak, T. G. (1985) Cochlear nerve of the alligator lizard. *Journal of Comparative Neurology, 233*, 463–472.

Muncer, S. J. (1982) "Conservations" with a chimpanzee. *Developmental Psychobiology, 16*, 1–11.

Muncer, S. J. & Ettlinger, G. (1981) Communication by a chimpanzee: First trial mastery of word order that is critical for meaning, but failure to negate conjunctions. *Neuropsychologia, 19*, 73–78.

Myers, R. E. (1976) Comparative neurology of vocalisation and speech: Proof of a dichotomy. *Annals of the New York Academy of Sciences, 280*, 745–757.

Naesser, M. A., Hayward, R. W., Laughlin, S. A., Becker, J. M. T., Jernigan, T. L., & Zatz, L. M. (1981) Quantitative CT scan studies in aphasia. II Comparison of left and right hemispheres. *Brain and Language, 12*, 165–189.

46   WALKER

Nauta, W. J. H. & Karten, H. J. (1970) A general profile of the vertebrate brain with sidelights on the ancestry of cerebral cortex. In F. O. Schmidt (Ed.), *The Neurosciences: Second Study Program*. New York: Rockefeller Press, 7–26.

Pasnak, R. (1979) Acquisition of prerequisites to conservation by macaques. *Journal of Experimental Psychology: Animal Behaviour Processes*, 5, 194–210.

Passingham, R. E. (1979) Specialisation and the language areas. In H. D. Steklis & M. J. Raleigh (Eds.), *Neurobiology of Social Communication in Primates*. London: Academic Press, 221–256.

Passingham, R. E. (1982) *The Human Primate*. Oxford: W. H. Freeman.

Paton, J. A. & Nottebohm, F. N. (1984) Neurons generated in the adult brain are recruited into functional circuits. *Science*, 225, 1046–1048.

Patterson, F. G. (1978) The gestures of a gorilla: Language in another pongid. *Brain and Language*, 5, 72–99.

Patterson, K. E. (1981) Neuropsychological approaches to the study of reading. *British Journal of Psychology*, 72, 151–174.

Penfield, W. & Jasper, H. (1954) *Epilepsy and the Functional Anatomy of the Human Brain*. Boston: Little Brown.

Penfield, W. & Rasmussen, T. (1950/57) *The Cerebral Cortex of Man*. New York: Macmillan.

Penfield, W. & Roberts, L. (1959) *Speech and Brain Mechanisms*. Princeton: Princeton University Press.

Perrett, D., Smith, P. A J., Potter, D. D., Mistlin, A. J., Head, A. J., Milner, A. D., & Jeeves, M. A. (1985) Visual cells in the temporal cortex sensitive to face view and gaze direction. *Proceedings of the Royal Society of London. Series B.*, 223, 293–317.

Peterson, L. N. & Kirschner, H. S. (1981) Gestural impairment and gestural ability in aphasia: A review. *Brain and Language*, 14, 333–348.

Ploog, D. (1979) Phonation, emotion, cognition, with reference to the brain mechanisms involved. In Ciba Foundation Symposium 69, *Brain and Mind*, 79–98.

Premack, D. (1970) A functional analysis of language. *Journal of the Experimental Analysis of Behaviour*, 14, 107–125.

Premack, D. (1971) Language in chimpanzee? *Science*, 172, 808–822.

Premack, D. (1976) *Intelligence in Ape and Man*. Hillsdale, N.J.: Lawrence Erlbaum Associates Inc.

Premack, D. (1983) The codes of man and beasts. *Behavioural and Brain Sciences*, 6, 125–167.

Radinsky, L. B. (1976) Later mammalian radiations. In R. B. Masterton (Eds.), *Evolution of Brain and Behaviour in Vertebrates*. Hillsdale, N.J.: Lawrence Erlbaum Associates Inc., 227–244.

Rumbaugh, D. M., Gill, T. V., Brown, J. V., & Glaserfeld, E. C. (1973) A computer controlled language training system for investigating language skills of young apes. *Behaviour Research Methods and Instrumentation*, 5, 385–392.

Savage-Rumbaugh, E. S., Rumbaugh, D., & Boysen, S. (1978a) Linguistically mediated tool use and exchange by chimpanzees (*Pan troglodytes*). *Behavioural and Brain Sciences*, 1, 539–554.

Savage-Rumbaugh, E. S., Rumbaugh, D. M., & Boysen, S. (1978b) Symbolic communication between two chimpanzees. *Science*, 201, 641–644.

Savage-Rumbaugh, E. S. (1980) Reference: The linguistic essential. *Science*, 210, 922–924.

Savage-Rumbaugh, E. S. (1983) Can a chimpanzee make a statement? *Journal of Experimental Psychology: General*, 112, 457–492.

Savage-Rumbaugh, E. S., Sevcik, R. A., Rumbaugh, D. M., & Rubert, E. (1985) The capacity of animals to acquire language: Do species differences have anything to say to us? In L. Weiskrantz (Ed.), *Animal Intelligence*. Oxford: Clarendon Press, 177–185.

Schlanger, P. & Freiman, R. (1979) Pantomime therapy with aphasics. *Aphasia, Apraxia, and Agnosia, 1*, 34–39.

Sebeok, T. A. (1977) *How Animals Communicate*. London: University of Indiana Press.

Seidenberg, M. S. & Petitto, L. A. (1979) Signing behaviour in apes: A critical review, *Cognition, 7*, 177–215.

Seyfarth, R. M. & Cheney, D. L. (1984) The natural vocalisations of nonhuman primates. *Trends in Neurosciences, 7*, 66–73.

Seyfarth, R. M., Cheney, D. L., & Marler, P. (1980) Monkey responses to three different alarm calls: Evidence of predator classification and semantic communication. *Science, 210*, 801–803.

Simons, E. L. (1976) Primate radiations and the origin of Hominoids. In R. B. Masterson (Ed.), *Evolution of Brain and Behaviour in Vertebrates*. Hillsdale, N.J.: Lawrence Erlbaum Associates Inc., 383–392.

Spencer, H. (1855/1899) *The Principles of Psychology, Vol. 1*. London: Williams & Norgate.

Sperry, R. W. (1958) Physiological plasticity and brain circuit theory. In H. F. Harlow & C. N. Woolsey (Eds.), *Biological and Biochemical Bases of Behaviour*. Madison: University of Wisconsin Press, 401–424.

Stamps, J. A. (1977) Social behaviour and spacing patterns in lizards. In C. Gans & D. W. Tinkle (Eds.), *Biology of the Reptilia. Vol. 7, Ecology and Behaviour A*. London: Academic Press, 265–334.

Steklis, H. D. & Raleigh, M. J. (1979) *Neurobiology of Social Communication in Primates: An Evolutionary Perspective*. London: Academic Press.

Stevenson, J., Hutchinson, R. E., Hutchinson, J., Bertram, B. L. R., & Thorpe, W. H. (1970) Individual recognition by auditory cues in the common tern (*Sterna hirundo*). *Nature* London, *226*, 562–563.

Sulloway, F. J. (1979) *Freud, Biologist of the Mind*. London: Burnett Books.

Sutton, D. & Jurgens, U. (1985) Neural control of vocalisation. In H. Steklis (Ed.), *Comparative Primate Biology: III Neurosciences*, New York: A. R. Liss (in press).

Sutton, D., Larson, C., & Lindeman, R. C. (1974) Neocortical and limbic lesion effect on primate phonation. *Brain Research, 71*, 61–75.

Sutton, D., Samson, H. H., & Larson, C. R. (1978) Brain mechanisms in learned phonation of Macacca Mulata. In D. J. Chivers & J. Herbert (Eds.), *Recent Advances in Primatology*. London: Academic Press, 769–784.

Sutton, D., Trachy, R. E., & Lindeman, R. C. (1981a) Primate phonation: Unilateral and bilateral cingulate lesion effects. *Brain and Behaviour Research, 3*, 99–114.

Sutton, D., Trachy, R. E., & Lindeman, R. C. (1981b) Vocal and nonvocal discriminative performance in monkeys. *Brain and Language, 14*, 93–105.

Sutton, D., Trachy, R. E., & Lindeman, R. C. (1985) Discriminative phonation in macaques: Effects of anterior mesial cortex damage. *Experimental Brain Research, 59*, 410–413.

Swadesh, M. (1972) *The Origin and Diversification of Language*. London: Routledge & Kegan Paul.

Tanji, J. (1984) The neuronal activity of the supplementary motor area of primates. *Trends in Neurosciences, 7*, 282–285.

Tembrock, G. (1974) Sound production of *Hylobates* and *Symphalangus*. In D. M. Rumbaugh (Ed.), *Gibbon and Siamang, Vol. 3*. Basle: Karger, 176–205.

Terrace, H. S. (1979) Is problem solving language? *Journal of the Experimental Analysis of Behaviour, 31*, 161–175.

Terrace, H. S., Pettito, L. A., Sanders, R. J., & Bever, T. G. (1979) Can an ape create a sentence? *Science, 206*, 891–902.

Terrace, H. S. (1985) Animal cognition: Thinking without language. *Philosophical Transactions of the Royal Society, B, 308*, 113–128.

Thorpe, W. H. (1972) Duetting and antiphonal song in birds: Its extent and significance. *Behavior: Monograph Supplement*, No. 18, 1–197.

Van Hoof, J. A. R. A. M. (1972) A comparative approach to the phylogeny of laughter and smiling. In R. A. Hinde (Ed.), *Nonverbal Communication*. Cambridge: Cambridge University Press.

Vargha-Khadem, F. & Watters, G. V. (1985) Development of speech and language following bilateral frontal lesions. *Brain and Language, 25*, 167–183.

Velettri-Glass, A., Gazzaniga, M., & Premack, D. (1973) Artificial language training in global aphasics. *Neuropsychologia, 11*, 95–103.

Waldron, T. P. (1985) *Principles of Language and Mind*. London: Routledge & Kegan Paul.

Walker, S. F. (1980) Lateralisation of functions in the vertebrate brain: A review. *British Journal of Psychology, 71*, 329–367.

Walker, S. F. (1981) Necessary symmetries in bilaterally symmetrical brains. *Speculations in Science and Technology, 10*, 575–578.

Walker, S. F. (1985) *Animal Thought*. London: Routledge & Kegan Paul.

Waters, R. S. & Wilson, W. A. (1976) Speech perception in rhesus monkeys: The voicing distinction between synthesised labial and velar stop consonants. *Perception and Psychophysics, 19*, 285–289.

Weiskrantz, L. (1972) Behavioural analysis of the monkey's visual system. *Proceeding of the Royal Society of London, Series B, 182*, 427–455.

Weiskrantz, L. (1977) Trying to bridge some neuropsychological gaps between monkey and man. *British Journal of Psychology, 68*, 431–445.

Winer, J. A. (1985) Structure of layer II in cat primary auditory cortex (AI). *Journal of Comparative Neurology, 238*, 10–37.

Wood, C. C. (1978) Variations on a theme by Lashley: Lesion experiments on the neural model of Anderson, Silverstein, Ritz, and Jones. *Psychological Review, 85*, 582–591.

Wood, C. C. (1982) Implications of simulated lesion experiments for the interpretation of lesions in real nervous systems. In M. A. Arbib, D. Caplan, & J. C. Marshall (Eds.), *Neural Models of Language Processes*. London: Academic Press, 485–509.

Woodruff, G. & Premack, D. (1981) Primitive mathematical concepts in the chimpanzee: Proportionality and numerosity. *Nature, 293*, 568–570.

Woodruff, G., Premack, D., & Kennel, K. (1978) Conservation of liquid and solid quantity by the chimpanzee. *Science, 202*, 991–994.

Zeki, S. M. (1978) Functional specialisation in the visual cortex of the rhesus monkey. *Nature, 274*, 423–428.

2 Nonpropositional Speech: Neurolinguistic Studies

Diana Van Lancker, Ph.D.
Neuropsychiatric Institute, Center for the Health Sciences, University of California at Los Angeles, 760 Westwood Plaza, Los Angeles, California 90024, U.S.A.

"Jeeves," I said, "don't keep saying 'Indeed, sir?' No doubt nothing is further from your mind than to convey such a suggestion, but you have a way of stressing the 'in' and then coming down with a thud on the 'deed' which makes it virtually tantamount to 'Oh, yeah?' Correct this, Jeeves."

(P. G. Wodehouse, *Brinkley Manor*)

Hir othes been so grete and so dampnable
That it is grisly for to here hem swear.

(Chaucer, *The Pardoner's Tale*)

Caliban: You taught me language; and my profit on't
Is, I know how to curse.

(Shakespeare, *The Tempest* [I, ii, 362])

INTRODUCTION

Human language has been characterised by modern linguistic theory as a homogeneous class, composed of definable discrete elements which are combined according to specifiable grammatical rules. Speech and language abilities are lateralised to the left hemisphere of the brain. Together, these viewpoints (in harmony with other facts about brain and cognition) are compatible with a picture of the left hemisphere as a special analytic processor.

This chapter investigates aspects of language ability that are not necessarily specialised in the left hemisphere. A similar point has been made for

49

"levels" of prosodic information in speech, specifically that linguistic functions of prosodic contrasts in speech are lateralised to the left hemisphere (Van Lancker & Fromkin, 1973, 1978), whereas other functions of prosody also carried in the speech signal are *not* (Van Lancker, 1975; 1980).

This claim has recently been corroborated by several studies. Gandour and Dardarananda (1983) and Naeser and Chan (1980) have shown that aphasic speakers of a tone language with LBD were impaired in the perception and production of the tonal contrasts of their languages; conversely, emotional and attitudinal information is not lateralised to the left hemisphere in speakers of a nontonal language (Ross & Mesulum, 1979; Heilman, Scholes, & Watson, 1975; and Heilman, Watson, & Bowers, 1983) or in speakers of a tone language, Chinese (Hughes, Chan, & Su, 1983). Van Lancker and Canter (1981) showed that voice recognition (perception of the prosodic cues that signal voice identity in the speech signal) is not impaired in aphasics, but is often deficient in right-brain damaged (RBD) subjects. However, the evidence for domains of linguistic prosodic information larger than the tone, such as word-stress contrasts and sentence intonation contrasts, is not so unambiguous. Both hemispheres evidently participate in processing linguistic prosodic information (Blumstein & Cooper, 1974; Heilman, Bowers, Speedie, & Coslett, 1984).

How are these differences in hemispheric specialisation for pitch and other prosodic information to be explained? Emotional information is graded, and does not occur in discrete units, as the tones of a tone language do. Voice patterns are each unique, and do not form any kind of combinatorial system, as tones of a tone language do. The property of being made up of a complex pattern rather than discrete permutable units is correlated with right hemisphere specialisation in the prosodic component. In a model of functional strata of prosodic function in speech (Fig. 2.1), only the "most linguistically structured" levels give evidence of lateralisation to the left hemisphere, whereas the intermediate "levels" are bilaterally represented, and the "least linguistically structured" (prosodic information present as nonpermutable complex patterns) are specialised in the right hemisphere. Thus, roughly stated, the unit-and-rule kinds of phenomena described by generative grammars are lateralised to the left hemisphere whereas complex patterns, not reducible to component parts, are specialised in the right hemisphere.

A related observation about lateralisation of language abilities is that some "subsets" within language competence are different in essential ways from the others (Van Lancker, 1975). On the one hand novel expressions, the unit-and-rule phenomena familiar to generative grammars, are known to be lateralised to the left hemisphere. On the other hand there are certain phrasal types, often with specialised communicative function, which include expressions referred to in the aphasiological literature as "automatic speech" (and a lot more).

This distinction, most generally viewed, is of "propositional" versus "nonpropositional" or "formulaic" language. Propositional language is newly created according to grammatical rules. This is classical linguistic structure, or "ortholinguistic" structure.[1] Its components are phonology, syntax, and semantics, and the basic units are phonemes, morphemes, lexical units ("lexemes" or words), and the sentence. Nonpropositional speech includes conventional expressions, speech formulas, idioms, frozen metaphors, expletives, and others (to be discussed), all having in common a cohesive, unitary, unanalysed structure. The phrases are learned, used, and comprehended as a whole. Grammatical rules are largely irrelevant to production and comprehension of nonpropositional subsets in language.

The term "nonpropositional" is not strictly descriptive, because speech formulas can be used to express underlying propositions. For example, "it's a small world" expresses the complex proposition that "people who know each other can coincidentally meet in the same place often doing or saying the same thing, or wearing the same clothes, even though there are very many people in the world and it is statistically improbable that such a meeting should take place; and this can happen more than once." A speech formula can be, and often is, used to express an underlying proposition. But in this article, "propositional language" or "propositional speech" refers to the a novel sentence or a novel utterance, whereas "nonpropositional language" or "nonpropositional speech" refers to familiar, conventionalised, formulaic, more or less holistic and cohesive sentences and utterances.

Many of these nonpropositional subsets are referred to in the aphasiological literature as "automatic speech." This is an unfortunate misnomer, for reasons which I will discuss later. It has contributed to the attitude that these phenomena are peripheral to language behaviour and therefore undeserving of attention, an attitude that I will inveigh against.

This monograph is basically about these phenomena, their saliency in brain pathology, their nature and use in normal language behaviour, their properties, and their cerebral representation. It describes their ubiquity and importance in language behaviour and argues that nonpropositional subsets reflect a characteristic principle in human language which is manifest synchronically, developmentally, and diachronically. This principle is different from the one accounted for by the logicodeductive model of generative grammar, which is the principle of infinite creativity in human

---

[1]The term "ortholinguistics" to refer to basic linguistic structure, exclusive of pragmatics and nonlinguistic prosody, was suggested by Dr. Joseph E. Bogen.

language. Nonpropositional subsets are accounted for by the principle which Bolinger (1976) has termed "idiomatic stereotyping," i.e., the tendency for familiar phrases to form and be maintained. Hockett (1958) called this property "idiom formation"; and Jespersen (1965) described it as the "formation of formular units" occurring throughout a language (these and other linguistic commentaries will be reviewed later). Furthermore, these formulaic expressions exist alongside novel constructions. It is in this sense that language is structurally "heterogeneous."

The claims for heterogeneous structures, which posit the existence of structure types in language which cannot be described in a traditional generative model of grammar, arise from descriptive linguistic analysis and from psycholinguistic studies on normal subjects. Evidence for nonlateralised subsets within the domain of language behaviour comes from clinical case reports and from clinical research. These studies will be reviewed below.

Diversity of Evidence

There are many different forms of evidence for the claim of heterogeneity in speech and language. There is no algorithm that guarantees the relevance of data to a theory; but the theory of grammar is a theory of human ability, and therefore the study of language is appropriate in many contexts. We are consoled by the justification for this approach by the philosopher Hempel (1966), who argues that "diversity of evidence is a very important factor in the confirmation of a hypothesis," giving several examples to illustrate the "power of diversified evidence (p. 35)." A corollary adds that it is "highly desirable" for a scientific hypothesis to be confirmed also by "new" evidence—by facts that were not known or not taken into account when the hypothesis was formulated. Extending the general theory into new contexts is desirable (Hempel, 1966): "Many hypotheses and theories in natural science have indeed received support from such 'new' phenomena, with the result that their confirmation was considerably strengthened (p. 37)."

With a large universe of phenomena potentially available to the study of language, some notion of relevance of data is needed. The criterion of "testability" can serve as a guideline because data or evidence are relevant or not relevant only in terms of a hypothesis. Hypotheses are "invented" to account for observed facts but creative imagination is usually involved in their invention (Hempel, 1966; p. 15), and they must be tested in several ways. Hempel suggests that "A finding is relevant to a hypothesis if either its occurrence or its nonoccurrence can be inferred from the hypothesis." It is obvious that (Hempel, 1966): "tentative hypotheses are needed to give direction to a scientific investigation. Such hypotheses determine, among other things, what data should be collected at a given point in a scientific investigation."

HETEROGENEITY IN LANGUAGE: AN HYPOTHESIS

It is in this spirit that a tentative neurolinguistic hypothesis is proposed in this monograph: That certain phrase types which are functionally and structurally unique exist, contrasting with the rest of language structure (which conforms to the classic unit-and-rule system described in a generative grammar); and further, these subsets of language are represented differently in the brain from classic language structure.

An assumption here is that something may be learned about the structure of language by investigating how patterns in linguistic behaviour are associated with aspects of cerebral structure and function, and with subjects' performance on psycholinguistic tasks. Models of hemispheric specialisation for specific functions provide a primary basis for the investigations described here, in the form of three assumptions which are interrelated (and which many would call facts): (1) specific functions are lateralised to a cerebral hemisphere (in the majority of right-handed individuals); (2) classical linguistic ability is lateralised to the left hemisphere (in the same typical group); and (3) the left and right hemispheres operate in contrasting or different "modes."

Various characterisations of these hemispheric modes have appeared: propositional/appositional (Bogen, 1969a, 1969b), analytic/holistic (Bever, 1975; Bradshaw & Nettleton, 1981, 1983), sequential/parallel, featural analysis/pattern recognition (Segalowitz, 1983). Any of these serve to motivate the following procedure: Describe the properties and characteristics of speech and language behaviour (or "performance", or ability) that are lateralised to the left hemisphere and compare these with language behaviours that are not lateralised to the left hemisphere. If the hemispheric modes of processing differ (as they seem to), then something interesting must be different between the lateralised versus nonlateralised kinds of language behaviour. Such an investigation first establishes what language properties are uniquely specialised in the left hemisphere (determine nonlateralised abilities and "subtract" those features from a model of left-lateralised language). If it is assumed that differences in cerebral function are reflected in linguistic structure and process, then the finding that some aspects of human language are uniquely lateralised and some are not has implications for descriptions of language and for a model of cerebral processing of communication.

An illustration of this point comes from studies of voice recognition. Much information about the speaker is carried in the speech utterance: sex, age, geographical background, personality traits and mood, and sometimes personal identity. Although carried in the speech signal, research shows that much of this processing is accomplished by the right hemisphere. Familiar voice recognition can be achieved by global aphasics, persons with nearly total loss of "classical" language abilities (phonology, syntax, lexicon, and linguistic semantics—or "ortholinguistic" ability) as the result of brain damage, and, conversely, individuals with right-hemisphere damage are impaired in recognising familiar voices (Van Lancker & Canter, 1981; Van Lancker, Cummings, & Kreiman, 1985).

Another level of prosodic function, comprehension and production of emotional information in speech, is also preserved in severe aphasic disturbance and is disturbed in right-hemisphere damage (Ross, 1983; Heilman et al., 1983). These observations indicate that the prosodic material in the speech signal is not uniformly, "homogeneously" lateralised, but that different levels of information are lateralised differently: The left hemisphere knows *what* is being said while the right hemisphere knows *how* it is being said (with what kind of affect, mood, or attitude) and *who* is saying it (what sex, age, and in some cases, which person). This difference—whether left- or right-lateralised—as mentioned earlier, correlates with the amount of linguistic structure (Fig. 2.1).

Sociolinguistic Heterogeneity: An Analogy

The work of Labov (1970) and other sociolinguists has brought about a challenge to the theoretical orientation of generative grammar and mainstreams preceding it (Weinreich, Labov, & Herzog, 1968): The "identification of structuredness with homogeneity." Sociolinguistic research has demonstrated, instead, that variation in a speech community is expected and normal (Labov, 1970): "It is perfectly true that the language

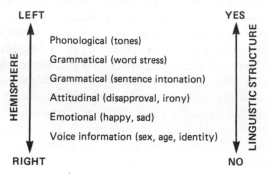

FIG. 2.1   Functional levels of prosodic information in speech. Hemispheric specialisation is correlated with presence or absence of linguistic structure.

of everyday life is certainly not homogeneous. Heterogeneity is the rule." There are ranges, varying with style appropriate to social context; there are strata, varying with socioeconomic context. There is ample evidence of those kinds of linguistic variability in that speakers can be observed to switch across styles and strata. Long ago, Weinreich et al. (1968) argued for a "model of language which accommodates the facts of variable usage and its social and stylistic determinants" to describe linguistic competence adequately. Of course, much work in sociolinguistic theory since then has filled out this picture. Those early claims that variations are not "errorlike vagaries of performance," but constitute a kind of "orderly heterogeneity" inherent in the competence of each speaker and common to the speech community have been borne out by work in many branches emanating from this original insight (Ervin-Tripp, 1972).

Yet it has also been observed that such quantitative data is not easily accommodated in generative models of grammar. An example of an observation not easily so accommodated is that speakers use different sets of linguistic variables depending on speech style. Some features are associated with casual speech, and these are distinct from a set of features used in more careful speech. The dimension which specifies this variation is the "amount of attention paid to speech." This fact was dramatically illustrated by a patient who inserted the syllable "sis" (or the variants -is, s) into his speech, usually at the ends of words and phrases, and did so more often during read and recited speech, and during more formal parts of the interview. The symptom decreased during free speech (Van Lancker, Bogen, & Canter, 1983). The speech problem clearly increased during periods of self-monitoring.

Propositional/Nonpropositional Dimension

I argue for another kind of heterogeneity, but not in speech, in language; I describe another dimension, like the "amount of attention paid" dimension mentioned above, that is needed to account correctly for language behaviour. This dimension might be called a "propositional/nonpropositional" dimension (Fig. 2.2). Phrase types at different points along this dimension have different properties. They comprise heterogeneous structure types in language. The main difference between these utterance types lies in the "degree of analyticity" versus the "degree of cohesion" in the configuration of the phrase. Propositional utterances have a full "analyticity"—the meaning follows from an analysis of the meaning of the component parts of the utterance. Familiar phrases of all kinds—idioms, greetings, speech formulas, proverbs—have a meaning that flows from the utterance *as a whole*. Analysis of the meanings of the component parts of the utterance results in the *wrong* interpretation.

PROPERTIES

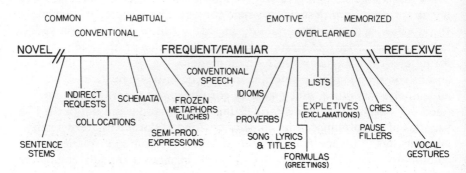

FIG. 2.2   Subsets of nonpropositional speech and their common properties, presented on a
hypothetical continuum from most novel to reflexive.

Propositional speech is made up of newly-created, original, novel utterances. Nonpropositional speech includes conventional and overlearned expressions of all kinds, including idioms, speech formulas, proverbs, expletives, serial lists, rhymes, song titles, sayings, quotations; in fact any expression which a group of native speakers would reliably rate as "familiar." The numbers of these expressions must reach several thousand, perhaps several hundred thousand; no upper limit has been seen in attempts to gather lists (Fillmore, 1977, personal communication). For an operational definition, give a list of any of these phrases, each with a portion missing, to a group of native speakers, and have them fill in the blank. They will do this flawlessly. There will be certain minor regional, age-related and socioeconomic variations, but overall subjects will accomplish this task and you will know they know the phrases you selected.

The differences between the various kinds of nonpropositional subsets will be discussed later. The reader must first consider the phenomena that are *not* novel sentences in the language, but are stored and processed as a very large set of phrasal entities *recognisable* by the native speaker as a familiar phrase. Evidence from aphasia, from psycholinguistic studies in normal subjects, and from linguistic analysis is presented to show that these are processed differently from propositional, newly generated language. In addition, the neurolinguistic hypothesis put forth here states that there is a neurophysiological basis to the propositional/nonpropositional dimension.

Nonpropositional Speech and Hemispheric Specialisation

It is well known that language processing is primarily lateralised to the left half of the human brain. Furthermore, the two cerebral hemispheres are specialised for different modes of processing. Propositional language is specialised in the left hemisphere, and nonpropositional language is a capacity either of both hemispheres or it is specialised in the right hemisphere. The role of subcortical structures must also be considered. The second part of my hypothesis is that human language is not homogeneous in structure. Nonpropositional subsets have a large place in human language function, and they cannot be described by a generative grammar.

HEMISPHERIC SPECIALISATION FOR LANGUAGE

Language function in the brain has been a topic of investigation since Biblical times, and modern thinking about hemispheric specialisation has progressed for well over a century. It was clinically observed in the 19th century that lesions in the left hemisphere cause disturbances of language, or aphasia, while lesions in the right hemisphere do not. Dax was said by his son (1865) to have read a paper with this discovery before a French medical society in 1836. The observation of left-hemisphere dominance for language was generally made known by Broca in 1861 by his article "Remarques sur le siege de la faculté du langage articulé, suivies d'une observation d'aphèmie ("Remarks on the seat of the faculty of articulate language, followed by an observation of aphemia," in Von Bonin, 1962).

The view well-attested since Broca's time is that the left hemisphere is dominant for language in most normal right-handed people. Figures suggest that about 90% to 95% of all right-handed people can be expected to be left-dominant for language; the case for dominance in left-handed individuals is unclear, however (Rasmussen & Milner, 1975), and the relationship between handedness and lateralisation for language remains unexplained (Kinsbourne, 1980).

There are reports that language is not lateralised to the left or to the right hemisphere in some people, particularly left-handers, but is to some degree bilaterally represented. In fact, Zangwill (1960) suggests that "cerebral dominance is in all probability itself a graded characteristic, varying in scope and completeness from individual to individual. Its precise relation to handedness and its vicissitudes still remain to be ascertained (p. 27)." Penfield and Roberts (1959) state from their extensive work in mapping language functions in the brain that "a definite possibility of bilateral representation of speech exists (p. 98)" especially in left-handers, and Luria (1970) reviews facts indicating that left-sided lateralisation for language is not always complete. He cites Jackson, Bastian, Goldstein, Nissl von Mayendorf, Zangwill, and Subirana as all having said that the right hemisphere may take part in the organisation of speech. In Luria's (1970) words:

... there is a whole series of intermediate stages from total and absolute dominance to the left hemisphere to partial or total transfer of the dominant role to the right hemisphere. Thus both the paradoxical appearance of aphasia following the injury of the subdominant right hemisphere in right handers and the absence of, or rapid recovery from, aphasia following the injury of the subdominant right hemisphere may be explained on the basis of variation among individuals in the degree of left hemisphere dominance which is reflected in variation in the relation of the right hemisphere to speech functions (pp. 56–57).

Thus some role of the right hemisphere in language production and comprehension can be assumed in many cases and individual differences must be considered in assessing the role of the right hemisphere in nonpropositional language abilities.

CORTICAL CONTROL OF PERIPHERAL SPEECH MECHANISMS

Phonation

The nature and source of central mechanisms in the brain for the initiation of movement in general, and speech in particular, are not entirely understood (Nauta, 1982). Motor sources for phonation and articulation are represented bilaterally in the primary and supplementary motor areas on the cortex. There are thus four cortical areas which, when stimulated by an electric current in surgery, cause the patient to emit a vowel-like phonation: the precentral Rolandic gyrus of both hemispheres, and the supplementary motor area of both hemispheres (Penfield & Roberts, 1959). Vocalisation can be initiated by electrode stimulation of either hemisphere, and specifically at points anterior to the speech centre. Words have never been elicited by cortical stimulation, although anomia and paraphasias have been observed (Ojemann, 1983).

Singing may be a capacity of the right hemisphere (Henschen, 1926; Luria, 1966) or it may be represented bilaterally (see review in Bogen, 1969a, p. 144). Observations in patients with left hemispherectomies have supported the early belief that the right hemisphere is capable of the motor control for singing words. Two adult left-hemispherectomy patients were able to recall and sing songs with lyrics, which suggested that the right hemisphere may play a significant role in "musical memory" and in the "neuromotor processes of singing," each of which involves many of the same mechanisms of vocalisation and articulation used in spoken language (Smith, 1966). Right-hemisphere singing was also observed in six patients using the Wada test to determine hemispheric dominance (Bogen &

Gorden, 1971). Subjects were asked to talk and to sing during sodium amytal injection of the left and right hemispheres respectively. During the left injection, subjects were able to sing the appropriate melody but the words were not intelligible. The authors conclude that the right hemisphere is more important for singing than speech and that it is specialised for tonal abilities.

There is evidence from several sources that abilities for phonation and articulation of speech are bilaterally represented. In Goldstein's (1948) view:

Even though there can be no doubt that, for the right-handed person, the left hemisphere is of paramount significance for language, it must be noted that for the *formation of sounds the corresponding area of the other hemisphere may play an important part, different in individual cases* . . . With regard to the bilateral speech movements, there is a *close relationship between the two motor speech areas* (p. 202).

Penfield and Roberts (1959) point out as further evidence that the motor sources for speech are bilaterally represented; that if the Rolandic motor strip of one hemisphere is destroyed, the other one takes over. They claim that "cortical control of the voice, including articulatory movements and vocalisation" can be served by either hemisphere alone. Excision of the lower Rolandic motor cortex (face, jaws, tongue, and throat) on either side only temporarily produces dysarthria or thickness of speech, which recovers fully to normal speech. Penfield and Roberts (1959) say: "It seems likely that such a patient is able to speak (after removal of the lower portion of the Rolandic strip) by employment of the cortical motor mechanisms of the other hemisphere (p. 16)."

Findings in adult right-hemispherectomised subjects support these statements. Hagen (1971) described three patients who underwent removel of the right hemisphere as a result of late-onset disease. Two sustained minimal dysarthria four weeks after surgery; the third retained a weakness of the left side of the tongue. That phonation and articulation remains a residual ability of left-hemispherectomised subjects has been demonstrated dramatically; the patient of Burkland and Smith, although deprived of normal abilities to speak and understand, nevertheless could produce expletives with normal articulation, and could sing "My country, 'tis of thee" (a rather complicated song) with clearly enunciated lyrics (Bogen, 1973).

Representation of most motor functions on the cortex is associated with movement on the opposite side of the body, or contralateral control of movement. However, the relationship between speech movements and lateralised function is more complex. Speech movements are mediated by cranial nerves V (sensory and motor portions serving face, mouth, and jaw); VII (with sensory and motor roots distributed into muscles of face and ears); VIII (the acoustic or auditory nerve); X (with sensory and motor fibres supplying pharynx, soft palate, base of the tongue, and supraglottal portion of the larynx); and XII (a motor nerve serving the tongue) (Van Riper & Erwin, 1958; Zemlin, 1968).

The motor pathway for articulation and phonation descends from Brodmann's area 4 on the cortex along the corticobulbar tract through the internal capsule to relay stations in the medulla, where the cranial nerves involved in articulation (IX, Glossopharyngeal) and XI (spinal accessary) and phonation (H, or Vagus) emerge. The upper motor neurons which descend via the corticobulbar tract to synapse at the cranial nerves are primarily crossed but are in portions also uncrossed.

In the case of the cranial nerves involved in speech, some of the motor fibres leave the brain stem above the level where the decussation occurs, so that the connections between hemispheric cortex and side of face and neck are in part ipsilateral. For example, the innervation of the muscles of the upper part of the face is actually bilateral, while the innervation of the lower part is primarily crossed (contralateral).

Anatomically there are bilateral connections between right and left cortical motor strips and the right and left cranial motor nuclei involved in speech. Eyelids, jaw, and trunk have the greatest degree of bilateral representation (Buchanan, 1951). For the larynx, the neuroanatomical findings are confirmed by clinical observations which suggest that the control of laryngeal muscles is to a large extent bilateral. Pitch control (as in singing, reciting memorised speech material, intonating contours in nonpropositional speech, and emotional vocalisations) often remains intact with left hemisphere damage or removal.

Pitch function in speech is often intact in left brain damage leading to aphasia, despite the usual teaching that "melody of speech" is disturbed in Broca's aphasia. Studies by Danly and Shapiro (1982) showed that the apparent impairment to speech melody is attributable to temporal, not pitch, errors. This apparent "amelodia" is actually an artifact of nonfluency; in patients who are able to produce utterances of two or more words, the intonation contours were not abnormal. What was notably lacking was prepausal lengthening, whereby the last word of a phrase is lengthened as compared to its duration in an embedded position. Prepausal lengthening is a subtle but robust phenomenon in normal speech (Gaitenby, 1965). It was intact in a Parkinsonian patient with accelerated speech, with other temporal features severely disturbed (Canter & Van Lancker, 1985). When this temporal feature is missing, speech melody appears strangely distorted.

Recent studies of control of pitch in speech production in left posterior brain damage have been somewhat ambiguous (Danly & Cooper, 1983). The observation that intonation contours are disturbed in Wernicke's aphasics, showing longer phrases with less steep declination lines, may actually reflect pragmatic deficits—the tendency for the fluent aphasic to "ramble" due to impairment of use of conversational turn-taking structure. Recent research on right-hemisphere damaged subjects has demonstrated an impairment in prosodic production, associated primarily with anterior damage (Ross, 1981).

The point here is that basic abilities for motor control of pitch in speech production are bilaterally represented. There are other neurophysiological bases for this bilaterality besides presence of both ipsilateral and contralateral innervation. One such basis lies in association and commissural neurons, which bring other areas in the cortex into relationship with the innervation of the cranial nerves of speech. Still another explanation has been advanced by Penfield and Roberts (1959), who emphasise the importance of subcortical mechanisms in speech processes, or the "centrencephalic centre," which is "bi-encephalic" in the sense of being a coordinating centre for both hemispheres. In this model, most of this centrencephalic mechanism is located in the higher brainstem, which includes the two thalami.

Penfield observes that babies organise vocalisation (which involves positioning the mouth, vocal cords, and controlling the breath) in a gesture similar to that observed during electrical stimulation of the four points on the cortex. Infants probably execute this gesture of phonation with little participation of the cortex. It is possible that initiation and execution of vocalisation, as well as some aspects of articulatory control, are in part subcortically controlled.

Penfield and Roberts (1959) take the position that although the motor sources of speech are bilaterally represented, "ideational" speech is organised in the left hemisphere. A similar conclusion emerges from studies on split-brain patients: The primary motor control of speech musculature is present in each half brain, but the neural organisation required for spoken language is lateralised (Gazzaniga, 1970; Bogen, 1969a). This reference is to propositional speech. Recent findings of impaired prosodic abilities in right-hemisphere damage have not been studied in the split-brain subject, nor have nonpropositional language abilities of the isolated right hemisphere been investigated.

Thus anatomical data reveal that the mechanisms for speech production, jaw, lips, tongue, and larynx, are bilaterally (i.e. redundantly) represented in the cortex. Therefore, for speech, only one side, (either side) is "needed." Various explanations have been proposed for the specialisation for speech and language abilities to one hemisphere in a potentially bilateral system (Semmes, 1968; Kinsbourne, 1980). Brain (1961) has written that the skilled integration necessary for speech requires that the motor cortices of each hemisphere should be under the control of a single co-ordinating area. Speech, in other words, because of its complexity, necessitates localisation. And indeed speech does require precision-timed integration of heterogeneous structures: Muscles of jaw, tongue, and larynx must not compete, but must work together in extraordinary orchestration within millisecond-long time windows.

Stuttering has been attributed to imperfect hemispheric specialisation for speech, or to abnormal bilateral representation of the "motor speech centre." One study reported a "cure" in three stutterers on whom surgery to the nondominant hemisphere was performed (Jones, 1966). Others, using the Wada test, showed bilateral representation in stutterers with organic brain lesions (Andrews, Quinn, & Sorby, 1972; Leussenhop, Boggs, Laborwit, & Walle, 1973). However, subsequent research has been unable to provide strong support for this theory in the general population of stutterers, using such techniques as evoked responses and dichotic listening (Andrews, Craig, Feyer, Hoddinott, Howie, & Neilson, 1983).

The "teleological" explanation (that speech is lateralised because it works better that way) does not accommodate certain observations. For example, as mentioned above, some individuals show "mixed" dominance in language comprehension. And in speech production, singing, emotional expressions, and the prosodic component of normal speech output (which involve the same complex articulations and integration of many of the motor skills as does propositional speech) are often preserved when classical language abilities are destroyed, as in global left-hemisphere damage or left hemispherectomy. These nonpropositional speech abilities may normally utilise bilateral pathways, the pathway from the nondominant hemisphere, or they may be subcortically mediated in part.

In summary, the two cerebral hemispheres are equipotential for motor control of speech. Specialisation is not at the level of motor organisation of speech gestures. Similarly, specialisation for speech perception is not to be explained at the level of peripheral processing.

Perception

The auditory pathways from the organ of Corti (in the cochlea of the ear) to the auditory cortex have been investigated in detail. Each ear projects to both auditory receiving areas in the cortex by ipsilateral and contralateral pathways. The asymmetry in projections from each ear to the auditory cortices has been observed in records of gross evoked responses to click stimulation recorded from the auditory areas of the right and left hemispheres (Thompson, 1967). In classic experiments, Tunturi (1946) and Rosenzweig (1951, 1954) demonstrated that, in animals, the amplitude of the evoked response is greater at the cortical area contralateral to the ear stimulated by the click. Experiments in animals have not revealed any differences in the auditory functions of right and left cerebral hemispheres (Neff, 1962). Instead, the only kind of auditory discrimination impaired by unilateral temporal lobe ablation in cats is sound localisation, a complex task requiring interaction between inputs at both ears.

The contralateral auditory pathways are stronger than the ipsilateral pathways, as measured by electrical activity. Clinically, the ear contralateral to a hemispheric lesion shows greater deficits than the ear on the side of the lesion (Milner, 1962). Anatomical and clinical studies in humans support the observations in animals. The majority of nerve pathways starting in one cochlear nucleus cross at the opposite side of the brain (Rosenzweig, 1951). However, there is considerable interaction between left and right ascending auditory pathways.

Much work has been done on processing of components of the acoustic signal: pitch, intensity, and duration (Rosenblith, 1961; Whitfield, 1967; Gulick, 1971). It is known that tone frequency has a spatial representation at all levels in the auditory pathway from the basilar membrane of the cochlea to the auditory receiving areas of the cerebral cortex. It is interesting to note that the auditory cortex is not required for pitch discriminations: Butler, Diamond, and Neff (1957) demonstrated that cats discriminate pitch even after extensive lesions of the cortex including all auditory areas. Studies on cats (Katsuki, 1961, 1962; Thompson, 1960 suggest that pitch discriminations are subcortically processed; bilateral transection of the auditory pathway below the level of the inferior colliculus does not impair pitch discrimination. Simple pitch discriminations can be made by patients with unilateral brain damage on either side (P. Milner, 1970). Right temporal lobectomy patients were observed to make more errors on pitch discrimination tasks than left temporal lobe patients, but the difference was not significant. A right-hemispherectomy patient performed better than normal subjects on both monotic and dichotic pitch discrimination tasks (Curry, 1967). In another study, three right-hemispherectomy patients performed normally in bilateral pure tones test and had a bilateral normal speech discrimination (Hagen, 1971).

Intensity discriminations can also be made by animals that lack auditory cortex (Dewson, 1964). Animal studies suggest that cortex and thalamus are not required for intensity discrimination (P. Milner, 1970). B. Milner (1962) found that right temporal lobectomy patients did only slightly worse on intensity discrimination tasks than left temporal lobectomy patients. Discrimination of different durations and timbres is impaired in cats (Neff, 1961) with lesions of the auditory cortex, and in humans with right temporal lobe damage (B. Milner, 1962).

Frequency, intensity, timbre and duration are all components of the speech signal. Frequency (pitch) and intensity (loudness) are subcortically and bilaterally processed in the brain, while normal timbre and duration discriminations require intact cortex in animals and intact right auditory areas in man. Independently, these components can be processed subcortically, bilaterally, or, in humans, better in the right cerebral cortex. Yet speech comprehension is a specialisation of the left hemisphere. Neff (1962) concludes that the differences in function of the two cerebral hemispheres in man "cannot be accounted for readily in terms of the manner in which sense organs project to, and motor organs receive innervation from contralateral and ipsilateral hemispheres (p. 196)." The hemispheric differences observed in man for processing of auditory stimuli are not based on the nature of the acoustic components.

Dichotic listening studies also suggest that perception of pitch contrasts is not lateralised, but that other, more abstract factors determine hemispheric specialisation of stimuli containing pitch contrasts. This is the functional hypothesis of hemispheric specialisation. It means that context and function of the stimulus determine laterality to a large extent (Spellacy & Blumstein, 1970a, 1970b). For example, Thai tones are lateralised to the left hemisphere in Thai speakers (Van Lancker & Fromkin, 1973) but not in native speakers of American English, whether or not musically trained (Van Lancker & Fromkin, 1978).

The right hemisphere is superior at processing complex auditory patterns, such as chords (Gordon, 1970) and complex tones (Sidtis, 1981), and is better at familiar melodies (McFarland & Fortin, 1982), whereas unfamiliar tonal sequences are processed better in the left hemispheres of trained musicians (Bever & Chiarello, 1974). Thus the mode of processing (whether analytic or holistic) interacts with the nature of the stimulus to determine hemispheric representation. This was also seen in PET-scan studies of perception of musical tonal sequences, in which hemispheric side of activation correlated with processing strategy, whether analytic or holistic, used to perform the task, as reported by subjects (Phelps & Mazziotta, 1985).

LATERALISATION OF OTHER CEREBRAL FUNCTIONS

It is now well recognised that speech/language is not the only lateralised function. The left hemisphere is thought to be superior for calculation (Sperry, 1964) and for temporal order processing (Efron, 1963a, 1963b; Carmon & Nachshon, 1971; Papcun, Krashen, Terbeek, Remington, & Harshman, 1974), and the right hemisphere for personal geography, visual pattern recognition including faces (Jung, 1962; Benton, 1980; Ellis, 1983), complex sound discrimination (Faglioni, Spinnler, & Vignolo,

1969), and familiar voices (Van Lancker & Canter, 1982; Van Lancker, Cummings, & Kreiman, 1985). Lateralised specialisation has been determined from clinical symptomology of brain injury to each hemisphere (Hecaen, 1962) and from studies on patients in whom the corpus callosum connecting the two hemispheres has been sectioned (Gazzaniga, 1970; Sperry, 1964; Springer & Deutsch, 1981).

Information about lateralised processing comes also from experimental testing of brain-damaged patients and normal subjects using special testing situations such as a tachistoscope, which projects an image to the hemispheres independently; and dichotic listening, in which two sounds are presented simultaneously. Another method involves recordings of electrical activity or evoked potentials over each hemisphere as visual or acoustic stimuli are presented to the subject. Greater or lesser activity associated with different stimuli implies greater or lesser functional involvement. Thus there is a large body of accumulating data describing details of specialised function, or preferred processing in the cerebral hemispheres (for review see Van Lancker, 1985; Bradshaw & Nettleton, 1983; Segalowitz, 1983).

In addition to demonstrating individual hemispheric preferences in detail, hypotheses about general differences between modes of processing have been proposed. Bogen (1969a, 1969b), for example, has assembled a list of dichotomies that describe mental activity, from which two different "modes" of processing can be distilled. These characterise the specific abilities of left or right hemisphere. Examples are: atomistic/gross; analytic or reductionist/synthetic or concrete; numerical/geometric; digital/ analogic; differential/existential; successive/simultaneous; rational/metaphoric; Buddhi/manas. Bogen hypothesised that the left hemisphere operates in a "propositional" mode while the right hemisphere has its own unique mode of function, an "appositional" mode. These differences correlate with folklore about right and left hands and right and left sides of the body, and with notions about two minds.

Many of these facts and myths are discussed by Ornstein (1972), interweaving findings from neuroscientific research with philosophy, mythology, and speculation. Ornstein presents his own list of dichotomies corresponding to two modes of consciousness. Some examples are: day/ night; intellectual/sensuous; analytic/Gestalt; focal/diffuse; verbal/spatial; intellectual/intuitive; argument/experience; masculine or Yang/feminine or Yin.

Although the terms used are often vague, "slippery," and subject to misinterpretation, neuropsychological research supports the view that the hemispheres operate according to different modes (Bever, 1975; Bradshaw & Nettleton, 1983). Analytic versus global processing of information corresponding to left and right hemisphere has been demonstrated for visual (Martin, 1979; Hellige, 1984; Bradshaw & Sherlock, 1982; Nebes,

1978) and auditory stimuli (Bever & Chiarello, 1974; Phelps & Mazziotta, 1985). Voluntary "control" over the two respective hemispheric modes was reported by Gott, Hughes, and Whipple (1984), describing a normal subject whose differential performances during the two conscious "states" were validated by behavioural and electrophysiological studies.

LATERALISATION OF LANGUAGE: A FUNCTIONAL INTERPRETATION

The bases for the specialisation of language function are not primarily to be found in the acoustic/physical system basic to speech. The peripheral processes of articulation and hearing are represented in both hemispheres, and there is evidence of subcortical involvement in speech and language. The specialisation must be viewed not as physical, but functional. Specialisation to one hemisphere involves properties of structure and organisation superimposed on the physical processes. It can therefore be inferred that speech and language are lateralised to the left hemisphere because of certain inherent properties. It is also possible that some aspects or components of overall language ability or performance may not have those properties. The point of this paper is, indeed, that some such components exist, and are so deftly interwoven in the fabric of language performance that it must be properly noted, in general, that they are stored, processed, used, learned, and lost differently from classical language ability. These are "formulaic" utterances; they make up the "nonpropositional" subsets of language, and they take many forms.

Thus the hypothesis that specialisation for language is functionally determined leads to interesting questions: What is unique to the structure and processing of language such that its functioning ("above" the motor and physiological levels) is specialised in the brain, and how are those language abilities not specialised in the left hemisphere different in principle from left hemisphere language?

What is the essential difference between the hemispheric "modes"? The left hemisphere operates on combinatorial units such as phonemes, morphemes, and lexical units, notes in a tonal sequence, or arithmetic entities, whereas the right hemisphere excels at whole complex patterns, nonanalysable and unitary, in visual, auditory, and tactile (Witelson, 1974) modalities. In general, the left hemisphere is best at managing permutable material, whereas the right is best at managing essentially nonpermutable material. The word "cat" for example, is eminently permutable: Exchanging the first and last sounds yields "tak". The sentence "The dog chased the cat" can easily be permuted to "The cat chased the dog." On the other hand, there is no meaningful way to talk about "permuting" portions of one face with another to yield a new face, except in a totally arbitrary way and one that intuitively engages other than recognition mechanisms. There is no reasonable way to discuss permuting details or "units" of one voice with those of another voice. The idiom "she has him eating out of her hand" does not have the same general structural properties as any novel utterance. It must be apperceived as a unitary, cohesive entity, unlike the novel utterance, which must be analysed in terms of its grammatical properties and lexical meanings. The idiom, in particular, must *not* be analysed in those terms; this is the kind of error made by nonnative speakers, demented persons, and persons with right hemisphere damage (Kempler, Van Lancker, & Hadler, 1984). Pattern recognition in all its manifestations is a different matter altogether from the kind of processing opportunities provided by language, mathematics, and musical tonal analysis.

Whereas propositional language or ortholinguistic structure is obviously the archetypical example of permutability, nonpropositional subsets of language are most appropriately processed as unitary patterns. Evidence has been presented that some of these subsets have a right hemisphere representation.

RIGHT HEMISPHERE COMMUNICATIVE ABILITY

Evidence for right hemisphere representation of nonpropositional language capacity comes from observations in aphasia (Jackson, 1958; Espir & Rose, 1970) and hemispherectomy studies. Two studies using the Wada procedure support the claim that residual aphasic speech is subserved by the right hemisphere (Kinsbourne, 1971; Czopf, 1981). In these studies, the Wada test was administered. In this test, one cerebral hemisphere is anaesthetised for a few minutes, leaving the other relatively operational. Patients tested were able to continue their aphasic production while the dominant hemisphere was anaesthetised. These observations are further supported by observations in adult left-hemispherectomised patients, in whom (in contrast to the aphasic) speech could not have been generated in any remaining, nondamaged portion of the left hemisphere.

It was over a century ago that John Hughlings Jackson (1878) proposed a right hemisphere role in language function. Damage to the left hemisphere interferes with the kind of speech he called *propositional*, whereas other types, or ways to use language, are typically spared. These other types have traditionally been referred to as *automatic speech*. Jackson proposed that these other types are retained by the healthy right non-language hemisphere. Jackson's suggestion was obscured by the more spectacular phenomenon of left-sided lateralisation of newly generated language, based in grammar and lexical units. Furthermore, there was no way of being sure that the residual speech (after damage to the left hemisphere) was not being processed in still healthy parts of that same dominant hemisphere. The role of the right hemisphere in speech, in normal use and in recovery from disease, remains unsettled. Individual differences in degree of lateralisation may be contributing to this unclear picture.

As reviewed earlier, the traditional view that language is processed in the left hemisphere has been modified by notions of "cerebral ambilaterality" and "cerebral dominance as a graded characteristic" pertaining to both left- and right-handed persons (Zangwill, 1960). Luria observes that "latent dominance" may play a role in performance after brain injury. He proposes (Luria, 1970) a "whole series of intermediate stages ranging from absolute dominance by the left hemisphere through equivalence of the two hemispheres, to dominance by the right hemisphere (p. 62)." Cases of "crossed aphasia," in which damage to the right hemisphere results in aphasia in a right-handed person, have supported these views (Ettlinger, 1967). Thus individual differences seen in residual aphasic speech may be attributed to variations in dominance.

The role of the right hemisphere in recovery from aphasia in strongly left-hemisphere-dominant individuals is not understood. Recovery of speech can be due to improved function of the injured left language area, takeover of a closely co-operating right area, or by a new activity slowly learned by either a right or a left area (Goldstein, 1948). The Wada tests cited above suggest that the right hemisphere is the site of aphasic speech. Another study, using dichotic listening, reported that task improvement over time was contributed by the left ear performance, suggesting that the right hemisphere was participating in recovery (Pettit & Noll, 1979). CT-analyses of 89 recovering aphasics suggested that increased capacity for right hemisphere contribution to language function might in part explain recovery patterns (Pieniadz, Naeser, Koff, & Levine, 1983).

Right-Brain Damage

In assessing the language abilities of patients who have right-hemisphere damage, Marcie (1965) demonstrated that 28 right-handed patients with right-hemisphere lesions were defective in written and spoken language, in both expression and reception. Repetition of nonsense words and syllables was defective. Perseveration was observed in the production of sentences. These authors conclude that in terms of linguistic symptoms and lesional topography, the right hemisphere seems to be (Marcie, 1965) a "weaker reflection of the dominant hemisphere and yet comporting its peculiar specificity and a qualitatively different role (p. 245)."

This prescient observation has been expanded amply in recent research in right-hemisphere communicative skills. Reviews of this material are available elsewhere (Heilman & Satz, 1983; Perecman, 1983; Young, 1983; Foldi, Ciconi, & Gardner, 1983). The role of the right hemisphere in communication, such as recognition of the emotional meanings carried in the prosody of speech (Ross, 1981; Borod, Koff, Lorch, & Nicholas, 1985), and of pragmatic features, such as conversational structure, has recently been supported (Gardner, Ling, Flamm, & Silverman, 1975; Gardner, Brownell, Wapner, & Michelow, 1983). In general, pragmatic and prosodic skills are impaired in right brain damage. These findings agree with clinical impressions so often given in aphasiological commentary, that even global aphasics can "converse," that is, they can utilise pragmatic information regarding conversational turn-taking, topic-maintenance, and openings and closings of conversational interaction, despite total loss of grammatical and lexical production or comprehension. Deficits in identifying idioms (Myers & Linebaugh, 1981; Kempler, Van Lancker, & Hadler, 1984) and metaphors (Winner & Gardner, 1977) have been reported in RBD patients. With regard to prosodic skills, patients with an impairment to lexical/grammatical ability can often produce and comprehend emotional and attitudinal meanings such as anger and surprise (Heilman et al., 1975; Ross, 1983; Ross & Mesulam, 1979).

Some time ago, Critchley (1962) submitted a number of "suggestive clinical data" on language deficits following right brain disease (pp. 211–212). These are:

1. Disordered articulation, often transient.
2. Severe effect on creative literary work.
3. Problems with word finding and resorting to circumlocution.
4. Delayed identification of language along visual or auditory channels.
5. Difficulties in learning novel linguistic material.
6. Difficulties in discussing patient's own illness.
7. Problems understanding pictures (symbolic formulation).

Similarly, Eisensen (1962) found right-hemisphere deficits on more abstract linguistic formulations; and Weinstein and Keller (1963) found right-hemisphere patients making naming errors relating to place and date and to illness-connected classes of objects.

Right Hemispherectomy

Hagen (1971) reported comparable results on three right hemispherectomy patients. Although all subjects' language abilities were normal with respect to vocabulary and syntax in conversational speech, some conceptual deficits were apparent. The Minnesota Test for Differential Diagnosis of Aphasia indicated a minimal language deficit in the definitions subset; deficits were also noted in tests for sentence building, picture interpretation, proverbs, absurd sentences, and absurd pictures. The deficits were: (1) difficulty in suppressing the whole concept when attempting to describe a part; and (2) difficulty in selecting the best possible response from a hierarchy of probable responses and suppressing the others. A tape-recorded interview with one of these patients (which I was permitted to analyse) revealed monotonic intonation and extreme conversational terseness. This may have been due to deficits in prosodic and pragmatic function as a result of the surgery, or may have been the patient's idiolect; premorbid speech information was not available. (See Appendix: Speech sample I.)

Left Hemispherectomy

In some cases of aphasia, autopsy indicated that the left hemisphere could have had little to contribute to the residual language performance of the patient. The speech of a patient, JS, who had suffered a stroke involving the left hemisphere, was limited to expletives and a few conventional utterances, such as "uh," "well," and "yeah." He had two years of speech therapy, during which time his performance did not improve beyond a competence of about 20 words, mostly nouns and a few verbs, which he could use singly and occasionally in strings of 2. (See Appendix: Speech sample II). The patient died and his brain was observed at autopsy. The entire left hemisphere was seen to be concave and atrophied in the region of the classical speech areas, involving the entire lateral portion of the frontal lobe, the temporal lobe, and the parietal lobe, including areas both superior and posterior to the angular gyrus.

The extreme test of nondominant hemisphere ability for language comes from left (dominant) hemispherectomy cases who undergo surgery as adults. The earliest reported case (Zollinger, 1935) lived only a few weeks after the operation. During that period, the patient could say "all right," "yes," "no," "goodbye," and "please." Another patient (Hillier, 1954) on the 16th postoperative day said "Mother," "Father," "nurse," "I don't know." Still another, who survived four months, could say "yes," "no," "I don't want any," and "put me back to bed" (Crocket & Estridge, 1951). Another patient (Smith, 1966), one year after surgery, showed some comprehension of commands and questions. He could clearly articulate swear words such as "goddamit" and "shit" (uttered as he attempted to respond to a question or command). He also had "pause fillers," such as "ah," "well," and "oh," all normally articulated and intoned. Repetition of other single words presented by the examiner was laborious and severely impaired, in sharp contrast to the fluent articulation of the swear words.

The patient could sing, correctly articulating lyrics for a familiar song and controlling the pitch for melody. He reportedly did not improve beyond this point (Bogen, 1973).

Another left-hemispherectomised patient, RS, is somewhat more difficult to evaluate because of the early removal of the hemisphere at age ten. She was observed to count, say her name, and sing "Jingle Bells" shortly after surgery; other language abilities were severely impaired. Articulation and pitch control were good for these abilities. Her singing ability was much better than her speech (Gordon, 1973); she could sing songs complete with lyrics while her speech was limited to single words and short phrases. She was able to produce the formulaic sequences in the Minnesota Test for Differential Diagnosis of Aphasia (Schuell, 1965) but could not respond to linguistically abstract tasks; and on the BDAE, she scored highest on automatic speech and music abilities (Goodglass & Kaplan, 1972). Examiners agreed that comprehension for language was reasonably good, in that when asked to point or move her hand, she would do so correctly.

RS recovered some use of language, showing mainly anomia and conceptual and memory losses as deficits. This recovery of speech might be ascribed to the early age at which hemispherectomy was performed, and thus to subsequent learning by the right hemisphere. In addition, RS had sustained some right hemisphere damage, and therefore her abilities are especially remarkable and difficult to assess.

These examples of speech ability after removal of the left (dominant) hemisphere have common features: (1) that some speech (production and comprehension) is possible without the "language" hemisphere; and (2) that some subsets of language ability are more in evidence than others. Although some shreds of what might be termed propositional speech have been observed in these cases, more common are the nonpropositional kinds, especially expletives, familiar song lyrics, and conventional speech formulas. What these have in common is that they are unitary expressions, not subject to grammatical or syntactic analysis in either production or comprehension, but are processed as a whole pattern.

As reviewed above, neurophysiological evidence shows that most muscles involved in speech have bilateral representation in the brain. Clinical evidence suggests that the nondominant (right) hemisphere can produce expletives, conventional phrases, speech formulas, and lyrics in familiar songs *with normal fluency and prosody*. Thus the unaided right hemisphere is capable of normal articulation and vocalisation of complex speech gestures in a certain category. Other forms of linguistic expression, propositional speech, are lacking in the adult left-hemispherectomised patient and in the globally aphasic patient. Repetition is impaired, especially of polysyllabic words. Levy (1974), having concluded that the right hemisphere can read words but not analyse them phonologically, has suggested that speech generated by the right hemisphere probably spills out in preformed motoric Gestalts.

RH Comprehension of Speech Formulas

Aphasic patients seem to comprehend more in conversational interaction than they do on formal testing of language comprehension; much of this may be attributable to RH comprehension of speech formulas. Espir and Rose (1970) suggest that recovery of receptive abilities in the aphasic depends on the function of the right hemisphere, and that additional injury to the right or to the corpus callosum will hinder recovery; this has been reported (Cummings, Benson, Walsh, & Levine, 1979). Similarly, Kreindler and Fradis (1968) have surveyed the clinical reports of cases of left and right hemisphere injury in aphasia, and note that bilateral lesions often cause irreversible receptive difficulties. Thus a lesion of the right hemisphere interferes with compensation of receptive disorders, whereas a right injury alone does not have such deleterious effects.

Studies on split-brain patients have occasionally indicated language comprehension in the RH, particularly of single words and short sentences (Zaidel, 1973). However, each patient presents a different clinical picture depending on history, extent of brain damage, and other factors, and therefore it is dangerous to generalise from a few well-tested individuals to right hemispheres in general. Of the 45 or so patients tested extensively so far, only 5 disconnected right hemispheres have shown clear evidence of language comprehension (Gazzaniga, Nass, Reeves, & Roberts, 1984). Although these studies are far from conclusive, they do not directly contradict the claim obtained from clinical studies that the right hemisphere is capable of some language comprehension. Tests of pragmatic and prosodic abilities have not been attempted on this population, nor have tests on their abilities to comprehend nonpropositional speech.

A study of the comprehension of formulaic expressions by LBD and RBD subjects was conducted (Kempler et al., 1984). Ten familiar phrases (formulas, such as "I'll get back to you later," or idioms, such as "That's enough to drive a man to drink") were presented with four line drawings depicting the correct meaning of each along with three other choices. In addition, ten novel sentences, matched for superficial sentence structure and number of words, were given. LBD subjects (all right-handed aphasic patients) were significantly better at recognising the familiar phrases than the novel phrases. Conversely, RBD subjects were significantly worse at recognising the familiar phrases than the novel sentences. This study indicated that comprehension of holistic expressions is available to the aphasic but impaired in right brain damage, and demonstrated for comprehension the difference that has been reported in production.

In another comprehension test, nonfluent aphasics were asked to decide as quickly and as accurately as possible if strings of words constituted possible English phrases (Dronkers, 1984). Some of the phrases were formulaic expressions (e.g. "heads or tails"), while others were common phrases matched overall for length and complexity (e.g. "making a profit"). In addition, aphasic subjects made similar judgments for single lexical items, both real and nonsense. A significant difference in subjects' reaction times and accuracy for fomulaic as compared with common phrases was found, suggesting that formulaic phrases are processed differently from novel phrases and, further, that they are processed like single lexical items, i.e. without involving syntactic analysis.

The findings in these two recent studies are similar to related observations that RBD subjects have impairments in recognising idioms (Myers & Linebaugh, 1981), metaphors (Winner & Gardner, 1977) and punchlines in jokes (Brownell, Michel, Powelson, & Gardner, 1983). Further work is obviously indicated here, for example, using split-brain subjects. It might be predicted that the RH's of split-brain subjects would show a pattern exactly opposite to the right-brain-damaged stroke patients: They would make significantly more accurate responses to familiar phrases than to novel expressions of matched length and complexity.

SUBCORTICAL PROCESSING OF SPEECH AND LANGUAGE

Residual speech production or comprehension in aphasia could be a function of the right hemisphere and/or of subcortical processes, when these structures remain undamaged.

The term *subcortical structures* in neuroanatomy refers to all parts of the brain between the spinal cord and the cerebral and cerebellar cortices (Thompson, 1967). It includes medulla, pons, midbrain, thalamus, and basal ganglia (caudate nucleus, putamen, and globus pallidus). Some neuranatomists use the term in a more restricted way, implying basal ganglia, thalamus, and rostral brainstem. Some evidence for subcortical involvement in language processing has been reported.

Penfield and Roberts (1959) claim that the subcortical areas of grey matter, particularly the pulvinar and other parts of the thalamus, play a large role in language processing. They propose (Penfield & Roberts,

1959), as a "speech hypothesis," that the "functions of all three cortical speech areas in man are co-ordinated by projections of each to parts of the thalamus, and by means of these circuits the elaboration of speech is somehow carried out (pp. 207–208)." The thalamic centre plays an "organising role," and constitutes "part of the centrencephalic system" in this functional view of the brain.

The centrencephalic hypothesis of brain function (referring to an integrating mechanism in subcortical structures) is based mainly on anatomical evidence, namely the connecting fibres from cortex to brain stem structures. Experiments in nonhuman primates show that the main functional connections of the cerebral cortex are to subcortical areas, and not from parts of the cortex to other cortical structures (Pribram, 1971). The corticothalamic projections are ipsilateral, but the thalamus receives sensory information from the opposite side of the body (Eyzaguirre, 1969). The role of this system relative to the secondary association area evolved for the parietal lobes, involving the ability to associate cross-modally (Geschwind, 1965), remains to be established.

The brain consists of the cerebrum, or two cerebral hemispheres, and the brain stem. Within the interior of the cerebrum are a group of structures forming the limbic system and a group of nuclei referred to as the basal ganglia. The limbic system is phylogenetically old and thought to be related to emotions and instincts. The basal ganglia include primarily the caudate nucleus, the putamen, and the globus pallidus.

The cerebral hemispheres are covered by the cortex and connected by the corpus callosum, a broad band of fibres. The cerebrum and the structures within it (limbic system and basal ganglia) form the telencephalon. The term *brain stem* refers to all structures between the cerebral and cerebellar cortices and the spinal cord. It consists of midbrain, pons, and medulla. Above the midbrain, the diencephalon is made up of the thalamus and other structures. The thalamus consists of many parts and connections (or projections) to surrounding parts. The cortical projections of the various thalamic parts have been studied extensively.

Speech/Language Disturbances in Subcortical Injury

Injury to or removal of the cortex has been considered a principle cause of aphasia. Of all brain structures, the cortex is the most recent in evolutionary history, and is most developed in the human (Sheer, 1961). Regions below the corpus callosum are phylogenetically more "primitive." Therefore, language faculties in the human have been assumed to be properties of cortical function. However, there is evidence that language processing may not be confined to the cerebral cortex only. Lenneberg (1967) cited "strong evidence" that language and speech-correlated functions involve subcortical and midbrain structures (p. 71); and Smith (1966) suggested the possibility that "some elements of language" may in part be processed by the higher brain stem.

In animals, parts up to midbrain can be demonstrated to exhibit complex behaviours such as walking, vocalising, eating, and sleeping, as well as emotional expression. Limited learning is also possible for animals in psychophysiological preparations in which brain tissue is destroyed above specified levels. For example, "striatal" cats (decortical animals with spared caudate nucleus, putamen, and globus pallidus) feed spontaneously, vocalise low intensity sounds, groom, and express fear and rage. In "thalamic" animals, all brain above the level of the thalamus is removed. These are also capable of supporting an extensive behavioural repertoire, including some learning (Buchwald & Brown, 1973).

Among subcortical structures in humans, the periaqueductal grey matter and the thalamus have been associated specifically with language function. The periaqueductal grey matter lies near the front of the aqueduct, between the third and fourth ventricles. Lesions in this area cause dysarthria or muteness. This area has also been associated with facio-vocal behaviour in emotional expression during electrical stimulation in cats (Kelly, Beaton, & Magoun, 1946) and in the squirrel monkey (Juergens & Ploog, 1970), while cortical involvement in vocalisation has never been observed (Juergens & Mueller-Preuss, 1977). These and related observations have led to the hypothesis that communication has evolved along two different tracks, with the cortical system developing uniquely to the human (Myers, 1968; Robinson, 1976).

There are two sources for facts about subcortical processing of speech: these are (1) observations from natural lesions in subcortical regions of the brain; and (2) explorations and surgery for disease, especially Parkinsonism and other movement disorders.

Several reports of aphasic disturbances following haemorrhage of thalamic nuclei, especially of the left thalamus, have appeared (Fisher, 1959; Ciemins, 1970); others have reported mild aphasia resulting from thalamic tumours (Smyth & Stern, 1938; Cheek & Taveras, 1966; Ojemann and Ward, 1971). Aphasia can result from other subcortical lesions (Brown, 1975). Recent PET-scan studies undertaken in conjunction with language testing noted that thalamic damage was not correlated with language measures other than verbal memory dysfunction (Metter, Riege, Hanson, Kuhl, Phelps, Wasterlein, Squire, & Benson, 1983). None of these have commented on an increase or a decrease in the comprehension or production of nonpropositional speech.

Electrical Stimulation of Subcortical Structures

Research into thalamic involvement in language and speech has been made possible by the development of surgical procedures for the treatment of Parkinson's disease. Several groups have published clinical observations of Parkinsonian patients before and after basal ganglia or thalamic surgery.

Parkinson's disease is a syndrome of unknown cause. Symptoms are tremor, difficulty with walking or balancing, failing memory, and eventual dementia. Some of the symptoms are due to disturbed functioning of subcortical systems in the basal ganglia, including the substantia nigra, corpus striatum, globus pallidus, and thalamus. Surgical intervention as treatment has given way to drug therapy.

In their review of subcortical correlates of speech and language, Riklan and Levita (1969) distinguish speech defects (dysarthrias) from language defects (dysphasia). Speech defects involve vocalisation and articulation, including rate, rhythm, volume, pitch, and phonation. The Parkinsonian syndrome includes defects of motor integration, and therefore disturbances in vocalisation and articulation may be expected. Because of the known participation of subcortical systems in motor and sensory processes, speech disturbances can also be expected to follow surgical lesions to these areas. For example, Guiot, Hertzog, Rondot, and Molina (1961) have reported changes in the rate of speech following electrical stimulation of the thalamus. These procedures involve deep stimulation before destruction of the afflicted region for the treatment of Parkinsonism. These authors have observed the effects on speech of the sectors passed through by the needle. Arrest or acceleration of speech (i.e. counting) occurs when the needle is in the ventrolateral nucleus of the thalamus. A Parkinsonian patient with accelerated speech resulting from such a surgical procedure is described in detail by Canter and Van Lancker (1985).

Anomia has also been observed during stimulation of the left thalamus, particularly in the pulvinar (Ojemann, Fedio, & Van Buren, 1968). Muttering, vocalisations, acceleration or interruption, and laughter have been elicited (Hassler et al., 1979).

Of special interest to this paper is a report by Schaltenbrand (1965). Stimulation of a specific area of the thalamus in a series of patients produced an arousal reaction, consisting of eyes turning, handgrasp, and a speech utterance. These acts were compulsory, in that the patient was unable to repress them even when so commanded beforehand. Each patient repeated the same utterance when stimulated; some of these utterances were speech formulas, such as "thank you," and "Let's go home." Schaltenbrand (1965) likened these responses to "the peculiarities of speech relics in aphasic patients which have been so well described by Hughlings Jackson (p. 839)." The vocalisations were more often evoked from the dominant portion of the thalamic nucleus. It is always difficult to interpret the implications of behaviour produced by brain stimulation for normal behaviour. However, it is interesting to note that *cortical* stimulation has never produced words (Penfield & Roberts, 1959; Ojemann, 1983).

Gilles de la Tourette's Syndrome

A provocative syndrome involving excessive production of a particular set of speech formulas—expletives—is Gilles de la Tourette's syndrome. This is a rare pathological condition which often includes among its complex of symptoms "coprolalia" (Greek for "foul speaking"), or compulsive swearing. The illness was first described by Gilles de la Tourette in 1885 (Goetz & Klawans, 1982). It is characterised by various motor symptoms which change and recur through life, including: facial tics; limb jerks; spitting; grimacing; blinking; shouting or barking; shaking; jumping; and fidgeting. The vocalised symptoms are: hisses; stuttering; odd emphasis of words or parts of words; unintelligible sounds or words; grunts and barks; coughs and throat-clearing; echolalia; and coprolalia. About half the patients with the disease develop coprolalia (Shapiro, Shapiro, Wayne, Clarkin, & Bruun, 1973; Shapiro, Shapiro, Bruun, & Sweet, 1978). Of 34 patients whose symptoms were described, 13 reported sounds (i.e. stammering, stuttering, throat-clearing), words, or coprolalia as the initial symptom. Coprolalia was a first symptom in three patients. The average age of onset of coprolalia was 14.5 and the range was 4–36 years. The symptom disappeared spontaneously in 6 patients after durations of from 1 to 17 years.

The vocalisations occur throughout normal speech, punctuating and interrupting fluent expression. However, the impulse to emit these expressions is sometimes controllable, often at the expense of increasing other symptoms (tics, coughing, grimaces, etc.). The vocalisation can be suppressed for minutes or hours in some cases (Cohen, Detlor, Shaywitz, & Leckman, 1982). Such patients find refuge in private places, such as a public toilet, to express their compulsive need to tic and vocalise. Patients describe the relief of being able to get off somewhere to "allow the words to come out" (Sweet, Soloman, Wayne, Shapiro, & Shapiro, 1973).

The words reported in the 18 patients with coprolalia were, in order of frequency, "fuck" (15 patients), "cocksucker" (5), "cunt" (3), "prick, dick" (3), "motherfucker" (3), "shit" (3), "bitch" (3), "bastard" (3), "cockey," "nigger," "whore," "blow me," "pussy," "wop," "pregnant," and "mother" (1). In addition, three patients had sentences or phrases, and three reported mental coprolalia. These expressions have one obvious feature in common: They are taboo expressions pertaining to sex or racial slurs, and as such take a sociolinguistic role of expletives. This is true cross-linguistically in Tourette's syndrome. Vocalisations fitting the criterion of taboo expressions have been reported in Spanish (Zuloaga, 1973; Briones, Aguiar, & Fernandes, 1974), Hindi (Perera, 1975 and 1981, personal communication), Italian (De Divitis, 1981, personal communication; Escalar, Majeron, Finavera, & Zamberletti, 1972), French (Yvonneau, 1972), Polish (Koprowska-Milewska, 1976), German (Hering, 1972; Beckers, 1973; Asam, 1978), New Zealand English (De Groot & Bardwell, 1970), and many other languages, including Hebrew and Dutch have appeared in the medical literature. The utterances are quite varied. They are complex, multisyllabic, and, with a very few exceptions, have in common only that they belong to the class of taboo expressions, constituting expletives, in the native language and culture.

The etiology of Tourette's disease is not known (Shapiro & Shapiro, 1982; Caine, 1985), although a genetic component is recognised (Kidd & Pauls, 1982). Previous psychiatric opinion that the symptoms are caused by psychological conflicts has been largely discredited in favour of an organic cause. Damage to subcortical systems, the basal ganglia or corpus striatum, has been implicated. Neurological impairments have been shown in a large number of the patients (Cohen et al., 1982). Frankel, Cummings, Robertson, Trimble, Hill, and Benson (1985) found a significantly higher incidence of obsessive-compulsive disorders in a group of Tourette's patients. Evidence for subcortical involvement is seen in the fact that the symptoms are alleviated by chemotherapy with haloperidol; the site of action of that drug is the corpus striatum. Of two postmortem examinations of the brains of Gilles de la Tourette's syndrome patients, one was normal and one showed some abnormal cells in the corpus striatum (Shapiro et al., 1973).

There are obviously differences between the swearing of the aphasic patient and the coprolalia of the Gilles de la Tourette patient. The Tourette patient has no difficulty expressing himself or herself, but continuously interrupts a normal sentence with coprolalic outbursts, while aphasic swearing is not compulsive, but happens as the patient tries to speak normally but instead substitutes an expletive (Bruun & Shapiro, 1972). The manner of use of these expressions may indeed differ substantially in the two patient groups. However, it is provocative to note that in the one group (Gilles de la Tourette's patients) speech production is normal but swearing is hyperstimulated, whereas in the other group (nonfluent aphasia), speech production is severely deficient, but swearing remains available. Seen this way, swearing can be said to have a "lower threshold" in speech production, and/or to be mediated by structures different from those that mediate normal speech production. Coprolalia, or excessive swearing, also occurs in a condition called *klasomania* following von Economo's encephalitis.

Thus the role of subcortical structures in some kinds of nonpropositional speech much be considered, either in hyperactivation or in representation of motor programs for expletives and other holistically produced phrases. Whether there is an interaction between subcortical structures and right-hemisphere abilities, or whether the right hemisphere produces some subsets but not others—these queries lurk at the moment in the dim shadows of speculation.

CLINICAL DESCRIPTIONS OF NONPROPOSITIONAL SPEECH

Evidence for differently processed subsets of language, those which may be processed by the right hemisphere or either hemisphere in the brain, is available in clinical cases of aphasia and other speech pathologies.

Several classification schemes for the aphasias have been advanced, and extensive testing procedures designed to demonstrate them. None of these is universally accepted, although many are convincing or useful for different purposes. The difficulties in establishing aphasic typology are due to individual variations, changes over time, involvement of extralinguistic factors such as cognition, memory, and attention, and nonagreement or misunderstanding of linguistic principles.

The traditional, most commonly used labels for aphasic phenomena are as follows:

1. Broca's aphasia, or a defect in production of language, also called motor aphasia, agrammatic, nonfluent, and telegraphic speech, classically described as the result of injury to the third frontal convolution of the left hemisphere.

2. Wernicke's aphasia, or deficit in comprehension, also called sensory or fluent aphasia, paraphasic or jargon aphasia, classically associated with posterior temporal lobe damage.

3. Mixed aphasia, or, when severe, global aphasia, in which language is defective in both production and comprehension.

4. Anomia, also called amnesic or nominal aphasia, or word-finding difficulties, usually associated with extensive or diffuse damage to the left hemisphere (although Geschwind [1967] has associated "a true anomia" with a well-defined angular gyrus lesion).

There are controversies with this traditional classification. It has been argued that all aphasias are mixed; that word-finding difficulties occur in all cases of aphasia; that comprehension is always impaired; even that the defects are intellectual or cognitive and that the emphasis on linguistic behaviour is misleading. These disputes need not be settled here. Clinical descriptions of aphasic speech are valid in any theoretical context, and these will be reviewed for their information about language abilities preserved in aphasia.

Most clinical observations of aphasic speech in the aphasiological literature are of aphasic *output*, mainly because comprehension is less "visible" and more difficult to assess and document. Furthermore, residual abilities refer to the nonfluent aphasic, who has extreme difficulty in speech production. The contrast between the deficit and the residual abilities is much clearer here than in the fluent aphasic, who produces a stream of more or less unintelligible speech. However, some clinicians have observed a similar dichotomous capacity in fluent aphasia, observing that the comprehension deficit in these patients often does not extend to some kinds of nonpropositional speech, such as greetings and other speech formulas, and in their impaired production, speech formulas and familiar expressions alone are recognisable interspersed in the jargon.

"Automatic/Propositional"

Perhaps the first mention of differential language abilities observable in aphasic speech was by Jackson (1958), writing in 1932, expressing his now well-known automatic/propositional speech dichotomy. It may well be that the unfortunate misnomer *automatic* universally used to refer to the residual speech output of the aphasic patient dates from these writings.

The term is meant to contrast with *voluntary*. It addresses the common observation in nonfluent aphasia that the patient can say a phrase, such as "son of a bitch," and does so quite fluently, but cannot say the word "son" to refer to his male offspring. But the dichotomy "automatic/voluntary" is inaccurate, because the nonfluent aphasic uses his/her recurrent utterance quite "voluntarily," with normal intonation, phrasing, and conversational structure. What cannot be accessed are the correct lexical items and the grammatical rules for combining them.

What does distinguish these two phenomena, then, are these very structural differences: The fact that one phrase is whole and unanalysable grammatically in its normal use, whereas the other is a lexical item that is combinable with others to make a novel phrase. The automatic/voluntary distinction is actually a difference between formulaic and novel speech, or between nonpropositional and propositional language. Nonpropositional language includes speech formulas, idioms, proverbs, greetings, frozen metaphors, pause-fillers, slang and jargon, and other overlearned utterances that, according to this view, are stored and processed in whole chunks, not in the units and combinatorial rules that characterise newly created language.

Jackson's astute observation was that patients with left-hemisphere damage could not speak propositions, but that they could produce some kinds of speech. He assumed these abilities for nonpropositional speech to be represented in the right hemisphere. Jackson (1958) argued that the left hemisphere is for the "voluntary revival of images," and the right for their "automatic revival (p. 141)." The speechless patient understands because "my words revive his words." That is, "the right half of the brain is for the automatic reproduction of movements of words, and the left the side for their voluntary reproduction."

The production of certain kinds of language, in Jackson's view, came because "the sensorimotor processes for words, even in the right cerebral hemisphere, may be so strong that these words are occasionally actually uttered." Evidence for this view is that "there is a loss of the most (special) voluntary form of language (speech) without loss of the more automatic (emotional manifestations). The patient smiles, laughs and varies the tone of his voice, and may be able to sing. We find that pantomime which stands half way suffers little, and gesticulation is not affected at all . . . there is loss of intellectual language with conservation of emotional language (p. 133 and *passim*)."

Jackson's observations are actually composed of several. The point that the patient "smiles, laughs and varies the tone of his voice, and may be able to sing" refers to preservation of the prosodic component in aphasia. The conservation of prosody despite loss of phonology, syntax, semantics, and lexicon has been discussed elsewhere (Van Lancker, 1975, 1980) and the role of the right hemisphere in producing and comprehending emotional meanings in speech has received considerable attention in the past few years (reviewed earlier). That the right hemisphere manages pragmatic features of communication, including maintenance of topic, turn-taking, and appreciation of humour is inferred from clinical and experimental work (Jaffe, 1978; Myers, 1979).

Jackson associates *propositional* with *voluntary*, and places *automatic* as the logical opposite. But the "voluntary/automatic" contrast does not describe the aphasic phenomena, even when viewed this casually and subjectively. As mentioned previously, the aphasic with nonpropositional residual utterances uses these quite voluntarily, varying intonation, facial expression, and gesticulation to communicate fairly effectively. What is not present is the intact grammar capable of generating propositional speech. That is, the aphasic cannot take individual linguistic units, such as phonemes, morphemes, and words, and arrange them according to the grammatical rules of his/her language. The typical instance of this state, and the most dramatic, is in the common observation of an aphasic who has a phrase, which is said fluently and with normal articulation, and with prosody appropriate to the sociolinguistic occasion; but that same speaker is totally unable to articulate a single isolated word in that phrase. This can easily be demonstrated in global or Broca's aphasia. For example, BW, a patient with damage to the entire temporal lobe extending into the temporoparietal junction, during a three-year period after the stroke, said only "to do." He repeated this phrase fluently and with normal prosody, communicating attitude and affect, and managing the pragmatic parameters of conversational structure. He was totally unable, however, to say the word "two," "to," or "too," given the written word or the number "2" which he could read with comprehension (but not aloud). Nor could he say "do."

The dramatic fact here is that the aphasic with this kind of deficit is able to produce the whole phrase but not any of its parts. Other holistic phrases are also available: greetings, recited material, serial lists, speech formulas of all kinds. Some of these can be thought of as "overlearned speech." But what they all have in common is a cohesive structure, which does not involve analysis or reorganisation into a newly formed string; the hallmark of generative grammar. Grammatical knowledge is irrelevant to production and comprehension of nonpropositional speech.

Testimonies from Aphasiology

In their survey of neurological aspects of speech, Espir and Rose (1970) provide a list of speech abilities typically retained in aphasics, possibly in the right hemisphere. Their term for these modes is "nonintellectual speech," and they include:

1. Emotional utterances
   a. ejaculations, expostulations;
   b. yes, no; i.e. "primitives" in the sense of first-learned;
   c. other words used inappropriately;
   d. jargon;
   e. recurrent utterances.
2. Automatic speech (songs, poems).
3. Serial speech (alphabet, days of the week).
4. Social gestures of speech (e.g. how do you do).

This observation, that some performances are less impaired than others, recurs throughout the aphasiological literature. Terminologies vary but the fact remains that some nonintellectual, or nonpropositional, kinds of speech are performed by many aphasics who are otherwise impaired in language abilities. Aphasiologists differ in their theories of aphasia, but agree in separating out nonpropositional speech abilities in the overall aphasic picture. For example, holding a currently unpopular view of aphasia, Bay (1964a) follows Marie (1925) in claiming that aphasia is a unitary disorder, the varieties observed being due to defects of input and output processing, or to underlying principles such as intentions of the speech activity. But the propositional/nonpropositional dimension also appears in this scheme. Aphasia affects the speech performances which convey "linguistically coded information" or contain a proposition. According to Bay, "mere emotional reactions (swearing) are unaffected," as are "stereotyped reactions to global situations (conventional phrases such as salutations, etc.), automatisms (serials) and, . . . undetermined word-finding in enumeration and association tests which mediated no sensible information." Next in line come reading and repetition; and most defective in their testing situation is naming and pointing to objects and story repetition.

Bay (1964b) has extended Jackson's notion (that the aphasic defect is an inability to use propositional speech) to most aphasias. That is, Broca's aphasia, anomia, and Wernicke's aphasia all have in common defective use of information-content-bearing language. This position is expressed in another way by Gloning, Gloning, and Hoff (1963), who discuss speech performances in terms of levels of complexity. The automatic greeting is a "very low-level symbol," as are the "semi-automatic sentences" of casual conversation. These authors observe that these processes are achieved faultlessly by the aphasic. It is the "complex speech processes" which are defective. The aphasic picture suggests that these different types of speech require "widely different brain processes."

Critchley (1970) endorses Jackson's automatic-propositional dimension in language behaviour. For Critchley, the functional roles proposed by Jackson explain observations in aphasic and normal speech, and serve to generate provocative hypotheses about human language in many other contexts. In his collection of papers on aphasiology, Critchley extends Jacksonian notions into more widely ranging areas of neurolinguistic thought, and to speculations about the definition, function, and evolution of human language and its relationship to animal language.

Pick (1973/1931) developed a production model to accommodate his observations in clinical aphasia. He also observed that certain kinds of speech behaviours are exempt in aphasic disturbances. His production model for normal speech production includes four stages, two preverbal and two verbal: (1) global awareness of the general import of the sentence; (2) activation of the specific mental content; (3) activation of the sentence schema; and (4) choice of words. Excepted are sentences which are "automatic," and do not go through all stages in production (cited in Goodglass & Mayer, 1958).

Head (1926) follows Jackson's views, adding that in recovery from severe aphasia, nonpropositional speech appears first: "The patient learns to utter those [words] in common use and can repeat them to order . . . Emotional expressions are uttered with greater ease and certainty." Similarly, in sensory aphasia, most spoken words are incomprehensible noises to the patient with receptive deficit, with the exception of "some isolated words and phrases, such as [patient's] name and 'How are you?' or similar expressions (Vol. 1, p. 90)." Head also described a hierarchy of disability in *receptive* aphasia parallel to that observed in expressive aphasia. As described earlier, this was supported by two recent studies of familiar phrase comprehension, in which fluent aphasics with comprehension deficits were significantly better at recognising familiar phrases than recognising novel sentences matched for length and structure (Kempler et al., 1984; Dronkers, 1984).

Luria (1970) reanalysed Jackson's original notions about "automatic" and propositional language within his own scheme of classification. In this scheme, aphasic syndromes are either acoustic-anmestic or expressive. Expressive aphasia takes four major forms (Luria, 1964; p. 150): (1) afferent-motor (errors in articulation); (2) efferent-motor (telegram speech); (3) semantic aphasia (alienation of meaning from word); and (4) dynamic (meaningless speech or jargon). Luria notes that generally, in expressive speech, some kinds of language are conspicuously facile while others are quite defective. In both "afferent" and "efferent" motor aphasia, habitual expressions and "well-established kinesthetic stereotypes" and other "lower levels of speech" remain intact.

Luria (1947) words it very much like other students of aphasia. He says that in a typical syndrome of expressive aphasia:

> . . . the patient is unable to formulate propositions, but he is sometimes able to name objects or repeat words; he may retain a few familiar speech expressions. He is able to utter spontaneous exclamations and to tell what his name is; he may even be able to run through certain speech sequences which have become automatic for him. Any speech pattern which might be used for the expression of a thought is impossible, but speech processes which are not a part of this system, i.e., those which involve simple verbo-motor habits or which express expressive states, may be retained.

Luria notes that the patient's remaining speech abilities are "based upon well-ingrained speech patterns (p. 281)." The patient often cannot select individual parts of his automatic sequence or expression, but produces it as a whole. Similarly, the "dynamic aphasic" usually retains verbal stereotypes, but is defective in "propositionising," or in the "predicative structure" of speech (Luria & Tsvetkova, 1968; p. 299).

Goodglass and Mayer (1958) refer to the Jacksonian distinction noting the commonly observed differences between propositional "as compared to exclamatory speech." They describe this as a "psychologically defined language phenomenon" which "presumably applies to aphasics of any nationality (p. 100)." It is a "fundamental psychological principle which reappears many times . . . that the aphasic is most apt to fail in communication which requires a volitional act of symbolic formulation but that he performs most readily in an automatized or otherwise highly structured speech situation (p. 101)." Here again, the emphasis in the distinction is on the "voluntary/automatic" dichotomy. But the notion "highly structured" must also refer to the kinds of speech observed: speech formulas, opening and closings in conversations (e.g., hello, goodbye), and other ritualised, routinised utterances. It is clear that several concepts have been intertwined in discussions of "automatic speech."

The range of such notions is seen in a similar view held by the aphasiologist Alajouanine (1956): "Situations leading to emotional, expletive, interjectional, automatic, habitual language are always more effective [in producing speech] than those requiring volitional or propositional speech (p. 28)." He has covered all the points usually mentioned to describe residual speech abilities in aphasia. All of these except "emotional": expletive, interjectional, automatic, and habitual; all fit the category of *formulaic speech*, meaning holistic phrases not subjected to or requiring grammatical analysis in either comprehension or production. (In fact, applying the usual grammatical rules to these utterances will cause a breakdown in communication.)

Myerson and Goodglass (1972) studied three agrammatic aphasics, who were described as having slow, halting and telegraphic spontaneous speech, with intonations and stress contours limited to word or phrase units.

In addition, however, each patient was found to have at his command a number of stereotyped familiar expressions which were not limited by the syntactic rules of his information-carrying utterances. Example; "I don't know," "Yes and no," "How are you today?" "Oh boy!". Basically these utterances, spoken in a holophrastic usage, serve the emotive or phatic functions of language as distinct from the referential function (pp. 41–42).

These authors wisely exclude any such expressions from their analysis of the generative grammars of the agrammatic patients.

Goldstein (1948) incorporates the Jacksonian distinction into his notions about "abstract and concrete attitudes" which he employs to describe human behaviour. He repeatedly observes that emotional language and "other speech automatisms" are less in impaired than novel speech production in aphasia; he calls the residual utterances "concrete," and explains that the brain-damaged patient is defective in his abilities to perform in the mode of "abstract attitude" (see R. Brown, 1968; pp. 288–292, for discussion). Concrete language (Goldstein, 1948): "consists of speech automatisms . . . one form of naming and of understanding of language in familiar situations for which it has been conditioned, and finally of emotional utterances." Abstract language, on the other hand, is: "volutional [sic], propositional voluntary speech (p. 25)."

Anomia

The propositional/nonpropositional dichotomy is observable in some cases of word-finding difficulty. Goldstein (1948) claims that "word-finding is different in emotional expression, in intentional speech, in speaking of motor series, of phrases in familiar connection of words." Thus for Goldstein (1948): "the problem of finding words is a very complex phenomenon. It depends on different underlying processes: on the readiness of speech automatisms, mental attitudes . . . emotional condition." The greater difficulty comes with "various forms of voluntary speech, as in conversation, description of facts, naming objects, etc. (pp. 59–60)."

Brain (1961) also reports that a patient with nominal aphasia can often produce words in an automatic or well-learned series which she cannot produce as independent symbols. For example, she can count, but cannot tell the number of days in a week; she can recite the days of the week in order, but cannot name the current day of the week.

Similarly, Bay (1963) concluded that word-finding difficulty varies with functional significance, and Wepman, Bock, Jones, & Van Pelt (1956) found that anomia affects not only nouns, but words of all categories, and that the typical anomic patient's speech is made up of "the conventional formulae of language." The defect, then, is "disruption of voluntary control of those relatively infrequent words" (with high information content), whereas the patient retains instead "more or less automatic use" of highly frequent expressions (pp. 476–477).

Palilalia

Palilalia is the involuntary repetition twice or more of terminal words or phrases. The patient is typically aware of the pathological behaviour and is unable to control it. Critchley's (1970) example is "Good morning, doctor, I'm not so well today, today, today, today. . . ." The repeated words become more and more clipped and are spoken more softly at a faster rate.

It has been reported that palilalia and types of mutism occur differentially according to "voluntary" (or propositional) and nonpropositional modes of speech. Marie (1925) observed that some kinds of nonpropositional speech were not affected: "as if the habitually fused modalities of voluntary activity and automatic activity have become dissociated (p. 274)." For example, a 33-year-old patient with palilalia of encephalic origin repeated her own words 2 to 21 times in a conversation, but did not repeat any words during recitation of a story, counting from 1 to 20, naming the letters of the alphabet, or singing. Marie observed that this phenomenon is difficult to explain "in a simple anatomic pathologic formula," being a question of a problem of "different modes of activity, voluntary and automatic, and of the very substratum of these two modes of activity." These observations were so striking, that "palilalia is worthy of being considered and deserves extensive research (p. 274)."

Similarly, according to Critchley (1970), the palilalic defect occurs during "voluntary" (or propositional) speech, *sometimes* in emotional speech (varying with individual patients), but *never* in read or recited speech:

> The palilalia occurs not only during spontaneous speech but also in reply to questions. But palilalia does not appear during the recital of an automatic speech-pattern, as for instance when the patient reads aloud, or recites a well-remembered verse or prayer, or when he declaims the days of the week, months of the year, letters of the alphabet, or when he counts. Palilalia occurs not only in the course of intellectual speech or 'propositionising,' but also—at times—during emotional cries, oaths, interjections and other forms of inferior speech. But this is not always the case, and in some palilalic patients, emotional speech may be free from such repetitions (p. 201).

Stereotypic Utterances: A Compendium

Jackson, in 1932, classified the residual speech of aphasics into *recurrent* and *occasional* utterances (Jackson, 1958a, 1958b). Recurrent utterances, which appear after the initial period of speechlessness (following the injury), can be nonsense words or phrases (e.g., watty, yabby); a single word (one, Jimmy, Battersea, yes, no); a phrase (come on, oh my God, yes but you know, to do, look inside and see, right on).

Occasional utterances occur in three "degrees," according to Jackson: First as swearing and ejaculations such as "oh dear," "bless my life," and interjections which are "deeply automatic" to the individual. Secondly, there are occasional utterances which are "inferior" speech. To Jackson, this means that the utterances are appropriately uttered, but are conventional phrases, such as "take care," "good-bye," "that's a lie." There are also "higher degrees of utterance" which come by surprise from the aphasic patient. But even these utterances show, for Jackson (1958b), that: "the speech possible by the right side of the brain is inferior speech. In nearly all cases it was well-organised, automatic, or 'old' (p. 183)."

These observations have in common (overlooking the value-judgments about degree of communicative excellence) that the expressions are unitary, not analysed into individual parts and recombined. These kinds of phrases occur in many communicative settings.

In the severe case of nonfluent aphasia, spontaneous speech is restricted to a single recurring utterance, termed a "hapax legomenon" by Alajouanine (1956), who studied patients with this condition. The term is well chosen, because it is often baffling that a single expression is the only one to remain in the stroke victim's productive speech. The solitary word or holophrastic word-cluster is reiterated, sometimes quite fluently, sometimes only very occasionally. The observation that nonpropositional speech occurs in emotional outbursts may well be attributable to the fact that only a strong impulse will motivate the person to speak using the only phrases still available.

The most frequently encountered residual utterance is "yes," "no," or both. In a study of 100 aphasic cases who retained only a single word, Henschen (1922) found that 63 patients retained yes and/or no, and the rest a diversity of expressions (cited in Critchley, 1970; p. 189).

The next most common recurrent utterances are undoubtedly expletives. Baudelaire retained only the phrase "cre nom" presumably from *Sacre nom de Dieu*. "Dammit," "shit," and "gerechter Gott" are often reported. (A survey of cross-linguistic expletives in aphasia has not been done.) The stereotype is often a familiar phrase: "Bon soir," "tout de meme," "the other day," "As de pique," "ace of spades," "Ai bien dit," "Voluntiers." Others are difficult to categorise: "les chose d'ici bas," "J'ai terriblement peur," "N'ya ypas de danger," "That's mine," "Boulevard de Grenelle 131."

The most difficult to explain are nonsense and apparently wholly idiosyncratic expressions. Idiosyncratic expressions are those that are not frequent, conventional, or formulaic in the language but which function as holistic, nonpropositional expressions in aphasic speech. These idiosyncratic expressions may be mistakenly taken to be propositional, because they do not fit into the usual classifications of "automatic" speech. However, in the context of the patient's performance, they are formulaic expressions and therefore nonpropositional, in that they occur as whole units, and are never decomposed or reanalysed into new phrases in the patient's speech.

Many nonsense and idiosyncratic expressions have been reported, such as: "pittimy," "monomentif" and "to do"; many expressions occur reduplicated, such as "watty-watty," "tan-tan," "tara-tara," "zu-zu," "cousisi-cousisi," "yes-yes," "come-come," "school-school," "dire-dire." Most other observations in preserved speech in aphasia fit the model that some familiar, holistic expressions, being not dependent on grammatical and lexical abilities, remain operative in aphasia. Idiosyncratic expressions might be produced as whole expressions, and therefore are somewhat accommodated by our model. But how would nonsense syllables be generated in this case? This remains to be explained. It is especially perplexing in view of the work of Levy (1974), who has given evidence that the right hemisphere is unable to perform a phonological analysis on words and thus cannot recognise phonological rhymes from words differently spelled (knows/rose). Thus, if stereotyped expressions are produced by right-hemisphere mechanisms, it is hard to understand how a nonsense phonological fragment, such as the famous "tan tan," constitutes nonpropositional output.

One study attempted to explain the origin of idiosyncratic recurrent utterances. The hypothesis was that these verbal stereotypies were *thought* or *said* at the time of injury, and therefore remained in the "foreground" of the patient's speech ability while the rest was lost. An investigation into what was happening at the moment of injury supported this theory for some of the utterances. One patient repeated "Farewell the things of this world"; the phrase "come on to me" was retained by a railway signalman; "gee gee" by a woman struck while riding a donkey; "list complete" by a clerk stricken compiling a catalogue; and "I want protection" and "on the booze" by two men injured in bar fights (Critchley, 1970).

The distinction between propositional and nonpropositional use of speech is demonstrated dramatically in patients with only one verbal stereotypy, in whom four stages of rehabilitation have been identified (Alajouanine, 1956):

1. Differentiation of the repeated phrase, with modification of expression and varying speech intonation. The phrase can be used to express needs and feelings, through prosodic variation alone.

2. The patient tries to check and control the recurring expression.

3. This is a fluctuating phase, during which other fixed expressions replace or are added to the original one. For example, a patient with one recurring phrase added to his own original stereotyped expression the phrases "after you, sir," and "pardon me."

4. In this last phase, the fixed phrases begin to disappear and "volitional" (propositional) speech appears, usually ungrammatical, developing into the usual picture of Broca's aphasia.

Agrammatism occurs in the newly developing speech, not in the old formulaic expressions. Speech formulas increase in number. Alajouanine (1956) observes the "very remarkable fact" that ready-made formulae of salutation, exclamations, and other speech formulas are grammatical, in contrast to the rest of the aphasic's speech; "the agrammatism does not extend to automatic language (p. 18)."

This fact is less "remarkable" given the explanation that unitary phrases, which are available to the aphasic whereas newly created utterances are not, are not "grammatical," in the sense of well formed according to the rules of the language; instead, they retain their overall "correct" form, to which grammatical rules are irrelevant. Speech formulas are notoriously exempt from grammatical analysis, and they often do not project the meanings normally implied by their constituent parts. The formula "she has him eating out of her hand" does not mean that he eats out of her hand. Furthermore, even if the meaning can be inferred from the parts, such as "I'm so glad you brought Harry (to the party tonight)," "that you brought Harry is pleasing to me" it is not acceptable (Pawley, 1980). These are "lexicalised sentence stems" which are "fixed" and, again, to which grammatical operations applicable to propositional expressions are irrelevant.

Therefore the course of the severely impaired aphasic who begins with one stereotypical utterance is actually quite predictable from our hypothesis about propositional and nonpropositional speech. The course parallels that in language learning: Formulas co-exist with grammatical utterances in first (Vihman, 1982) and second (Wong Fillmore, 1976) language learning.

At first, aphasics are unable to produce a constituent part of their residual utterance. This holds true equally for patients whose stereotyped utterance is a conventional speech formula ("right on!"), an idiosyncratic phrase ("to do"), or a nonsense expression: "da de da, do de da," "yabby," "me me," "committimy pittimy, sapon sapon." Later propositional utterances sometimes evolve alongside the stereotypies.

Goldstein (1948) describes a case that classically illustrates the evolution of aphasic speech from nonpropositional speech to some propositional speech. The patient was initially speechless except for "yes" and "no," which he could not repeat on demand. After some weeks, he said "I don't know," "please," "good night," "just so," and "to tell you the truth," all speech formulas; in addition, he was observed to say "dressing has moved," and "pineapple."

Unit Size in Residual Aphasic Speech

The question of unit size of the residual phrases arises here. The question of "chunk sizes" in cognitive storage, memory, retrieval, and other aspects of processing has been investigated extensively in normal subjects (see review by Simon, 1974). Studies have shown that lists of 4–5 familiar phrases, each consisting of 5–7 words, are equivalent in subjects' performance on various measures to 6–7 words. Thus we might not be surprised that long familiar phrases are occasionally observed as residual aphasic speech. For example, in a case described by Critchley a "cultured scientist" was speechless for three days after a left frontal topectomy. When he began talking again, he used only long technical and Shakespearean expressions

(Critchley, 1970) such as: "voluntary silence terminate," "methinks the lady doth protest too much," "scientific ineptitude," "vituperative old man," "there but for the grace of God go I (p. 260)."

Examples from Aphasic Interviews

An example of a fluent aphasic illustrates the use of nonpropositional speech including expletives ("God almighty," "goddamn it"), pause fillers ("I guess," "well," "huh"), conventional phrases ("I know," "and then"), and idiosyncratic recurrent expressions ("I gave him something," "over there").

First Interview
Patient: Over there, there, over there, . . . too, I guess, I gave him something too. God Almighty, and then I gave him something over there. I gave him cheese and everything else, I guess. I gave him something over there. I gave him something over there.
Doctor: What did you give him?
Patient: Yes, I know. And I gave him something.

Three months later, the patient had made some recovery. The second interview includes the original recurrent expressions along with new expressions, most of which are also highly frequent and conventional.

Second Interview
Patient: Yeah, yea. Things are great, I suppose, huh? And well . . . well understood, understood perhaps. I know, God Almighty! Thinkers. But when I go there, no no. I find that thinkers, good thinkers too, huh? Over there is, oh God, why? Perhaps later on I'll find that, and that, I don't know. I don't know because over there, over there okay, over here is all right . . .

Aphasic patients will often give an initial impression of fluency, because they rely on their set of formulaic expressions, and they utilise their intact prosodic and pragmatic abilities in communicative interaction. Further enquiry reveals that they have quickly exhausted their repertory. One patient, for example, got by on conversation openings, then continued with "I think . . .", she responded to queries with "I don't know and that's about all," "sure," "I guess so," and followed up with "I was . . . just . . . that was all . . . Well, I'm glad." On pursuing the dialogue, it could be ascertained that these expressions occurred over and over, with normal intonation, appropriate pragmatic gesturing and eye contact, and an air of sincerity each time. When pressed for propositional responses, the patient became halting and hesitant. In addition, her repetition ability was apparently restricted to her own set of phrases: She was able to repeat "how are you," "I'm fine," and "good morning," but not "thanks very much." Her speech production in attempts at novel expressions was laboured and anarthric, but the defects in speech production did not extend to her nonpropositional speech utterances.

Another patient answered "oh God," "godsakes," "okay," "I don't know," "no," and "I don't know what to do" to most questions directed to her. She tried to produce other answers, but after some attempts, said "wait," "God," "ah-shit-no," "goddammit," or "godsakes." She counted, on request, up to 28. She could not say the pledge of allegiance (often patients claim to have lost the ability to recite poems and passages learned at an earlier age). This patient could not say her own name. However, she often said "look inside and see . . . look inside . . . what to do . . . and wait." She said this with confidence and much expression. Later when asked whether she knew any songs, she began to sing a song with those lyrics ("Look inside and see, what to do, and wait"). Thus the lyrics of a familiar song functioned in this patient the same as her other residual nonpropositional speech. She also sang "Jingle Bells" with good pronunciation of the words and control of the melody. Singing with familiar lyrics existing side by side with production of formulaic speech is often observed in aphasics in whom other language abilities are quite impaired.

As reviewed previously, studies using the Wada procedure by Bogen and Gorden (1971) demonstrated that patients could sing when the left hemisphere was anaesthetised but not when the right hemisphere was inactivated, and an adult left-hemispherectomised patient could sing with lyrics.

Formulas in Production Tasks

In production, idiom completion in severely language-impaired patients has been described (Geschwind, Quadfasel, & Segarra, 1968; H. A. Whitaker, 1976). Canter, Coughlin, and Van Lancker (1978) presented repetition data from a conduction aphasic, who was able to repeat idioms with greater accuracy and fluency than comparable novel phrases.

Summary

Clinical evidence reveals that propositional and nonpropositional speech are differentially affected in language pathology. Descriptions of nonfluent and, although to a lesser extent, fluent aphasia, anomia, and conduction aphasia consistently mention that expletives, social formulas, stereotyped phrases and cliches, overlearned expressions, recitation, serial and memorised speech are selectively spared. Palilalia and Gilles de la Tourette's syndrome also feature some of these subsets. In addition, the clinical literature has suggested properties or attributes which distinguish the two modes in aphasia.

Kreindler and Fradis (1968) made this suggestion some time ago: "it is . . . in the nondominant hemisphere that especially stereotyped language, stereotyped formulas, of the most common and frequence use, polite expressions, typical and typified responses, slogan speech, etc., would be stored (p. 111)." The evidence is strong that some instances of residual speech abilities are subserved by the right hemisphere, but the relationship of these to subcortical systems remains to be investigated.

EVIDENCE FROM NORMAL SPEECH AND LANGUAGE

From the observation that some kinds of speech are differently affected from others in pathology, we turn to normal speech for evidence about "heterogeneity" in language, specifically about nonpropositional subsets and the properties associated with them. The sources of such evidence are diverse. They include descriptive comments about normal language, linguistic analyses, and psycholinguistic research. The Jacksonian notion of an "automatic/propositional" dimension underlying normal language use is considerably extended in this discussion.

It is often debated whether pathological states are qualitatively different from normal occurrences, or whether the differences are a matter of degree. For example, anomia, or difficulty in retrieving certain lexical items, is experienced by most normal speakers. The reduplication seen in the stereotypies of aphasic speech occurs as a regular grammatical process in some languages, and as baby talk and diminutives in others. Lenneberg (1967) remarks that a sort of "Broca's aphasia" occurs during emotional stress; and other aphasic patterns such as semantic and phonological paraphasias surface in the normal speaker with fatigue or under the influence of alcohol and other drugs.

An experience of mental caprolalia, a symptom of Gilles de la Tourette's syndrome, is described by a normal speaker in her autobiographical essays (Bengis, 1973):

> I am having a hard time concentrating, so I put the book down and stop to listen to my thoughts again. What I hear is a string of the crudest obscenities: "up your ass mother fucker cocksucker drip drip drip . . ." everything I've ever heard on the streets or seen scrawled on bathroom walls. They are words I would never use, invading some inner territory like armies of red ants preparing for a takeover. I listen more closely, but the unconscious voice seems to have exhausted itself from the effort of rising to that single outburst, or else perhaps it is retreating in the face of my shocked attention. All I can

hear are the same words, reverberating inside my mind, more softly now, less insistently (pp. 88–89).

Clinicians, observing the dissociation of language abilities in aphasia, have then "seen" the same phenomenon in normal speech. Jackson (1958), for example, claimed that:

there are in health all gradations from the most automatic use of words to their most voluntary use. Let us show the steps: (1) Receiving a proposition. (2) Simple and compound interjections, as "Uh" and "God bless my life!" and (3) Well-organized conventional phrases, as "goodbye," "not at all," "very well." (4) Statements requiring careful, and metaphorically speaking, personal supervision of the relation each word of a proposition bears to the rest (p. 133).

Similarly, Critchley (1970), having observed swearing in aphasic speech, speculates that swearing may be less vulnerable to injury because it is phylogenetically "more primitive." He further observes that analogies for stereotypical aphasia are found in "verbal mannerisms" such as "don't you know," "I say," "as a matter of fact," "do you know what I mean," "naturally," "actually," "of course," and even in folk music such items as "hey nonny nonny" and "fol-de-rol."

Speakers' Intuitions about Nonpropositional Speech

There is little linguistic work which systematically taps speakers' intuitions about differences in propositional and nonpropositional speech. Yet most speakers seem to have a casual awareness of idioms, greetings, and other speech formulas; they might be expected to notice instances of expletives, pause fillers, and unique recurrent expressions in the speech of others. Many might sense that these modes function differently. They might be aware, for example, of experiencing discomfort in trying to repress idiomatic phrases when speaking English to a non-native speaker of English; they might sense the importance of chosing the "right" formula in speech situations.

An example of such an awareness appeared in the comments of a New York secretary, telling her own life history, revealing clear intuitions about formulaic expressions (Olsen, 1972):

Most of my life had been spent completely alone, and I knew none of the code responses of young people. I didn't know what to *say*. Like when somebody comes up to you and says, "How you doing, kid?" you're supposed to say something back, you're supposed to know a code answer. But I didn't make the proper responses because I didn't know them. I would have given anything to know them! (p. 145)

The same insight was expressed by Robert Louis Stevenson in 1925 (in Bolinger, 1961): "the business of life is not carried on by words, but in set phrases, each with a special and almost a slang signification (p. 30)."

Awareness of differences between idiomatic and literal meanings was shown in a recent study (Van Lancker & Canter, 1981), in which subjects were asked to determine whether a literal or an idiomatic meaning was intended in a series of utterances which were ambiguous in just that way ("ditropically" ambiguous sentences). Subjects could reliably distinguish between idiomatic and literal productions of ambiguous sentences such as "I also had an axe to grind" when presented with a randomised tape-recorded list. A set of acoustic cues significantly distinguished the idiomatic from literal utterances (Van Lancker, Canter, & Terbeek, 1981). Acoustic analysis indicated the main cues to be pitch contour, pausing, durations, and pitch height.

Linguistic Descriptions

Jespersen (1965) described the "important distinction between formulas or formular units and free expression (p. 18)," a distinction that "pervades all parts of the grammar." Formulas, such as "how do you do," "good morning," and "thank you" are "felt and handled as a unit" and may often mean something quite different from the meaning of the component words taken separately (pp. 19–21). Jespersen claimed that formulas and free expressions involve different kinds of mental activity. Furthermore, for Jespersen, the distinction is important in a diachronic perspective of language. It correlates with the distinction between the role of regular formations as distinguished from irregular forms in morphology, therefore to productive versus unproductive affixes in word formation. Free expressions are associated with regular formations and productive rules for combining them. In contrast, irregular forms, which are unproductive, are preserved in the language as formular units.

A similar distinction was described by Lounsbury (1963):

Of two constructions made according to the same pattern, one may be an *ad hoc* construction of the moment and the other may be a repetition or reuse of one coined long ago, often heard, and much employed as a whole unit, e.g. as an idiom, a cliche, or a high frequency phrase of some sort. It is apparent that as behavioural events they are quite different and that in some sense their psychological statuses and in the actual speaking behaviour may be quite different (p. 561).

The existence of large-sized holistic units has been discussed by descriptive linguists, although these phenomena have not had much attention in transformation-generative grammatical description. De Saussure (1968) recognised a category of *"locutions toutes faites"* as part of *langue* in his langue/parole framework. Degrees of structural cohesion figure in his concept of *les rapports syntagmatique*. *"Locutions toutes faites"* are fixed and therefore belong to langue; but insofar as they have degrees of syntactic regularity, they interact with the productive processes of parole.

Lyons (1968) recommends separate analysis of "ready-made utterances," expressions which are learned as an unanalysable whole and employed in particular occasions by native speakers. Lyons' examples are "how do you do," not normally interpreted as a question, and "rest in peace," which is not to be regarded as an instruction, "but a situationally-bound expression which is unanalysable (and which does not require any analysis) with reference to the grammatical structure of contemporary English." Other instances of "ready-made utterances" are "the stock of proverbs passed on from one generation to the next." These are "not profitably regarded as sentences . . . Their internal structure . . . is not accounted for by means of rules which specify the permissible combinations of words." These must merely be listed in a dictionary along with an indication of the situations in which they are used and their meaning (Lyons, 1968; p. 177).

Lyons has noted that in addition to ready-made expressions "which permit no extension or variation," there are also what he calls "phrase-schemata" and "sentence-schemata," which are subject to certain kinds of productive rules, such as "what's the use of ___ing?" Lists will not accommodate schemata, because they are made up of different "ranks" (phrases and sentences) which can be combined and also because they are partly productive. Indefinitely large numbers of sentences can be generated from schemata (Lyons, 1968; p. 178). Lyons does not suggest a way to deal with these semi-productive processes, which are obviously ad hoc for each kind of phrase.

A thorough analysis of formulas and semi-productive phrases has been conducted by Pawley and Syder (1980), noting that mastery of a huge number of fixed expressions and sentence "stems" is part of native fluency in any language. "Memorised clauses" and "clause sequences" such as "think nothing of it"; "I'll believe it when I see it"; "I don't know and I don't care", are not strictly idiomatic (because the sentence meaning can roughly be predicted from the lexical meanings), but are "habitually spoken" in exactly that form. "Lexicalised sentence stems" are expressions such as "It's twenty to six"—stereotyped ways of saying things in a language, not subject to regular permutation or grammatical operations ("it's forty after five" is not acceptable). Similarly, Fillmore (1979) and

Bolinger (1976) have presented evidence from language structure for the natural status of speech formulas and other holistic phrases in normal speech behaviour amidst newly generated expressions. Holistic phrases resist grammatical rules and act totally differently with respect to semantic operations.

Similar observations were made by Weinreich (1969), who described idioms as "transformationally defective," requiring special treatment in a grammar. He recommended a "complex dictionary . . . for all compounds, complex words, idioms phrases, and sentences familiar to speakers of the language." He saw the differences between idiomatic (unproductive and semiproductive) constructions and free constructions as fundamental; and stated that (Weinreich, 1969) "the relation between idiomatic and literal meanings is so unsystematic as to deserve no place in the [generative-transformational] theory. Furthermore, these classes do not form dis-junctive sets; instead, differences fall along a spectrum from unanalysable, through semiproductive, to productivity in the strongest, Chomskyan sense (p. 23)."

In dealing with the problem of idioms in the generative model, Fraser (1970) also proposes a continuum or hierarchy. He classifies idioms by "degrees of frozenness" in terms of the transformational rules that may apply to them.

Weinreich's (1969) treatment adds a special dictionary to the generative model to account for idiomatic and other holistic phrases, although it does not specify how to deal with "semiproductive" constructions; Fraser's pro-posal includes special kinds of rules and a marking convention within the generative-transformational model. However, for Chafe (1968), idioms cannot be treated in the standard generative model of language. Chafe suggests that idioms constitute an anomaly of sufficient force as to require a Kuhnian "shift" out of the Chomskian paradigm. The properties attributed to idiomatic constructions are as follows: (1) although complex construc-tions, their meaning is like that of a single lexical item; (2) they show transformational deficiencies; (3) they are often not syntactically well formed; (4) the text frequency of the literal counterpart is much lower than the idiomatic construction. These facts about idiomaticity have not all been accounted for by any general model of language, although points (2) and (3) are easily observed in everyday idioms and speech formulas, and points (1) and (4) have been well substantiated by psycholinguistic studies; these will be reviewed below.

For Bolinger (1961), idioms are the extreme case along a continuum of the "bondage and freedom" of the parts of an utterance in relationship to the whole. There is a "gradient of idiomatic stereotyping" belonging to the "idiom grammar" of a language (p. 22).

Whereas Jespersen and Lyons included a few examples of idiom-like but particularly productive expressions, Hockett (1958) and Bolinger (1961) conceive of idiomatisation as a pervasive process in language.

Hockett (1958) places the "idiomatic composite form" alongside the morpheme as a basic element in language. These two kinds of basic units form the "raw materials" from which utterances are built. Phrases of all kinds, technical terms, verbal humour, abbreviations, figures of speech, and slang all qualify as idiomatic in Hockett's view. Furthermore, idiom formation is one of the grammatical processes to be accounted for in language. The "idiomatic value" of newly coined expressions is inversely related to the productivity of the pattern it is formed on. Derivation and idiom formation are different processes with different properties (p. 308).

Evidence for this point of view is present in English itself. Bolinger (1976) presented linguistic data demonstrating many kinds of idiom-like units. For example, the restricted occurrences of "ago" and "else" occupy a middle ground between what has traditionally been viewed as the bound forms of morphology and the free forms of syntax. Along the "vast continuum between morphology and syntax" are found fixed idioms, "loose" idioms, cliches, and the subtle but most pervasive of all, collocations. All these possess varying degrees of internal cohesion. It is this phenomenon, their relative cohesiveness, that distinguishes them. It is also this phenomenon—their cohesive structure—that makes them candidates for right-hemisphere processing. The property "degrees of cohesion" is developed in Firthian linguistics (Mitchell, 1971), but it is not a viable notion in descriptive or generative models.

Thus a number of linguists hold the view more or less explicitly that "idiomaticity" is a property or process in language. This property may be present in degrees: Expressions vary in their degree of cohesion. This property is present not only synchronically, but in diachronic processes as well. The distinction between frozen and free constructions is also present in language acquisition.

Language Acquisition

In child language, Moscowitz (1972) noted the co-existence of unanalysed or formulaic units alongside cognate expressions which have been analysed in accordance with phonological rules. Similarly, Clark (1972) claims that "imitated items, whether single words or longer stretches, are not fully analysed by the child for syntactic features or syntactic structure at the time they are imitated, but syntactic understanding proceeds in the course of production, usually after a lengthy period during which the utterances have been practiced as unanalysed wholes." Similarly, Peters (1983) observes that children learn language by first using whole phrases or "chunks," and later analysing these into their constituent parts as they learn the rules of language. Others have documented the distinctive role of formulas and other analysed expressions in first language acquisition (Vihman, 1982; Pollio & Pollio, 1974). This interaction between formulaic and rule-governed (propositional) was also observed in Spanish-speaking children learning English as a second language: All relied on the strategy of picking up and using a formula as much as possible, and then fitting new words into the formula (Wong Fillmore, 1979). And it seems obvious that the developmental process interacts with the diachronic: Across generations of speakers, irregular forms are transmitted as formular units, while regular and productive formations are acquired as the product of abstract rules.

Psycholinguistic Studies

To determine whether nonpropositional speech could be demonstrated to be nonlateralised in normal subjects, a dichotic listening study was designed in which appropriate words and short phrases were selected, such as "cut it out, don't, come on, get up, hurry, good morning, thank you, all right, damn you, and bastard, and shit" (Van Lancker, 1972). These were recorded by a male voice with natural intonation appropriate to each item.

The words were digitised, normalised for intensity, and aligned in pairs using a PDP-12 computer for the dichotic listening tape. The aligned pairs were recorded onto audio tape for the listening task. Twenty-three right-handed subjects responded by writing the two words they heard. Order of report was switched every ten items, and headphones were reversed for the second half of the set.

No difference in errors by left or right ear was found ($t = 107.0, P < .05$). Furthermore, substitution errors differed for stimuli presented in the two ears. There was a significant tendency for the left ear to have more nonpropositional-type substitution errors, and for the right ear to make more propositional-type errors, using a Chi-square analysis. (Chi-square is not strictly appropriate for pooled data; a Wilcoxon matched-pairs test performed on transformed scores was also significant.) The study was replicated on a second group of 20 subjects, yielding no significant ear difference and a significant difference between the error types by ear.

Although it is difficult to interpret negative results, this study suggests that comprehension (including both perception and interpretation) of nonpropositional words does not yield the usual right-ear advantage of linguistic stimuli. More dramatic were the errors generated by the subjects. The kind of error, whether propositional or nonpropositional, was significantly different, suggesting that perception of these items was influenced by the hemisphere contralateral to the ear stimulated.

Research by Goldman-Eisler (1968) on pauses in speech production supports the notion of differences in performance between propositional and nonpropositional speech. Pauses are more likely to occur in propositional or newly created speech than in formulaic constructions. Hesitation is correlated with originality of choice, novelty of language, and generative processes. In contrast, fluency is correlated with "high transitional probability, verbal sequences developed into habit, predictability, and associative linkage." These are all properties of nonpropositional speech. Goldman-Eisler claims that in planning and execution of the verbalisation insofar as they are revealed by pausing measures, differences are found between the production of formulaic and propositional speech.

Lieberman (1963) investigated differences between: (1) maxims and stereotyped phrases; and (2) novel sentences, each containing the same test word (a stitch in time saves *nine*; the number you'll hear is *nine*). The acoustically treated test word from the novel sentence was better recognised when excised and presented to listeners. This early study showed differences in how speakers produce these two kinds of sentences, formulaic and novel.

Since that early study, several different kinds of psycholinguistic studies point to essential differences between nonpropositional and propositional speech. Pickens and Pollio (1979), using questionnaires, revealed that novel and frozen usage represent two discriminably different aspects of figurative language. Horowitz and Manelis (1973) and Osgood and Hoosain (1974) showed that subjects are less able to remember the individual members of an idiomatic noun compound or an idiomatic phrase than members of other kinds of compounds; in addition, subjects were more likely to remember the entire idiomatic phrase, when given a cue, than the entire novel phrase. Both Gibbs (1980) and Ortony, Shallert, Reynolds, and Antos (1978), lending support to Chafe's farsighted comment that the idiomatic meaning is more common than the literal meaning of ditropically (having both an idiomatic and a literal interpretation) ambiguous sentences, demonstrated faster comprehension of the idiomatic than of the literal meanings of these kinds of sentences; and similarly, Van Lancker and Canter (1981) showed a bias toward their idiomatic interpretation. These studies provide evidence against the notion that on hearing a ditropically ambiguous sentence, the literal meaning is computed first, and then when that one does not fit the context, the second, idiomatic, meaning is selected.

When the task was to identify natural English phrases, Swinney and Cutler (1979) reported faster reaction times for visually presented idiomatic phrases than matched novel phrases, leading to a conclusion that idioms are processed like lexical items. This lends support to another of Chafe's observations about idioms, i.e. that although complex constructions, the meaning of idioms is like that of a single lexical item.

SUMMARY AND CONCLUSION

It has frequently been noted that aphasics with severe production deficits are able to produce certain utterances with normal fluency and articulation. This is true in nonfluent and fluent aphasias, and has been observed in anomia, conduction aphasia, and palilalia. In aphasia, it is particularly striking when the individual is able to say a whole phrase with intact phonetic/phonological structure and appropriate prosody, but is markedly impaired in producing constituent parts of the phrase, and in producing other propositional language. The nonfluent aphasic may produce only a few recurrent utterances and speech formulas while the rest of speech output is laboured and dysarthric; the fluent aphasic produces conventional expressions and speech formulas alongside empty and contentless speech, jargon, and paraphasias. This dissociation of abilities—with understanding of speech formulas superior to that of novel sentences—has also been observed in comprehension by aphasics. The Gilles de la Tourette's patient produces a compulsive stream of expletives. The varied nature of residual utterances in aphasia—ranging from nonsense syllables to speech formulas—has often been observed and described, but not explained; and the similarities between residual aphasic speech and speech phenomena observed in subcortical abnormalities have not been accounted for.

Evidence has been presented in this chapter that since both hemispheres are capable of the basic peripheral functions of production and perception of speech, it is probably the case that the right hemisphere is supporting residual speech production and comprehension in LBD and in left hemispherectomy. It was suggested that these formulaic expressions (often termed "automatic speech") are unitary in structure, comprising whole, unanalysable patterns, and that on that basis, it might be inferred that the right hemisphere, with its pattern-recognition abilities, would be able to store and process these kinds of speech entities, although it could not do so for propositional speech. However, involvement of subcortical structures has been inferred from studies of vocalisations in Gilles de la Tourette's syndrome and from stimulation during stereotaxic surgery for movement disorders. Our understanding of the relative roles of both these other-than-dominant-hemisphere sites in processing nonpropositional speech is at the earliest speculative stage.

The main property of nonpropositional speech is unitary structure. Evidence for this property co-existing with full generative productivity in normal language was reviewed, citing linguistic analysis as well as psycholinguistic studies. Intuitions about speech formulas and performance differences for idioms versus novel expressions strengthen the view that a propositional-nonpropositional distinction exists in normal language behaviour, which distinction could be represented on a continuum (Fig. 2.2, see p. 56).

I have been talking about what have been termed speech formulas, formulaic expressions, idioms, proverbs (Honeck & Hoffman, 1980), conventional phrases, habitually spoken clauses and clause-sequences (Pawley & Syder, 1980), lexicalised sentence stems, ready-made expressions (Lyons, 1968), schemata (Tyler, 1978), stable and familiar expressions with specialised subsenses, frozen metaphors (Pickens & Pollio, 1979; Lakoff & Johnson, 1980), cliches, and possibly also some indirect requests (Searle, 1975), collocations (Mitchell, 1971; Bolinger, 1961, 1976), and co-ordinate constructions (Malkiel, 1959; Cooper & Ross, 1975). These belong to native competence, and yet they do not fit the current key definition of human language, which involves potentially infinite creativity and productivity: In a word, *permutability*.

These have been classed, unfairly, I would insist, as the lowlife of language behaviours. Jackson (1958), in his discussions of "automatic language," referred repeatedly to these examples as "inferior speech," and Luria (1970) called them "lower levels of speech."

When extending his clinical observations into normal language analysis, Critchley (1970) commented on:

> ...the immoderate use of certain phrases, words, expressions, or even meaningless sounds which the speaker decorates his articulate utterance, such as "in fact," "you know," "actually," "of course," "naturally," "if you know what I mean" (p. 221)

and the

> ... irritating use of verbal mannerisms, where a person in conversation emits ad nauseum such trite little phrases as "don't you know," "I say," "as a matter of fact," "do you know what I mean." By gradual steps these verbal sillinesses graduate to sheer *verbal tics*, where a phrase is enunciated as an obsessional trait, without any pretense at meaning or congruity (p. 203).

Head (1926) referred to residual speech in aphasia as having the status of a "growl or a purr (p. 142)." Similarly, for Sapir (1921): "interjections are the least important of speech elements" and there is no record of "a noticeable tendency toward their elaboration into the primary warp and woof of language ... They are never more, at best, than a decorative edging to the ample, complex fabric (p. 7)."

I would argue quite the contrary: That familiar phrase formation *is* an integral part of language; if not the warp and woof, then definitely making up much of the vast woven pattern. I have tried to highlight the ubiquity of these phenomena and their deep involvement in everyday language use, in language learning, language history, and language evolution. Much more could be said about their role in literature, in poetry (e.g. the refrain), in humour, in establishing social group solidarity, and in transmitting cultural meanings across generations. Conventional, formulaic, and memorised expressions of all kinds play a large role in language play and linguistic creativity. The innumerable familiar phrases known to fellow native speakers are alluded to, toyed with, and varied just a little for emphasis and effect. Such phrases arise within families, organisations, and groups of all kinds. The world of advertising uses them extensively. Humorists and cartoonists draw on them constantly and journalists rely on them as "eye-catchers" in their story titles. Now, with instant, nationwide media, "familiar" phrases are born in an moment: Witness "one giant step for mankind"; "at this point in time." The multifaceted function of unitary phrases in social language use deserves an entire book of its own.

More could also be said, in a speculative way, about the relevance of holistic expressions to animal communication, recalling the hypothesis that communication has evolved along two tracks, cortical and subcortical (R. E. Myers, 1968; Robinson, 1976). Similar theories of phylogenetically earlier communication systems evolving in hierarchical strata have been elaborated by MacLean (1972), J. W. Brown (1975), and Yakovliev (1948). A bridge between nonpropositional speech phenomena and another controversial theory about the role of language in cultural evolution could easily be built: In that theory (Jaynes, 1976), holistic phrases as "auditory" directives were represented in the right hemispheres of "preconscious" humans and residues of this evolutionary feature are seen today in those who hear "voices" (see review by Van Lancker, 1979).

The message here, then, is that human language may be viewed as being made up of different subsets, which can be conceived as occurring along a continuum from fully propositional to nonpropositional, and which includes idioms, familiar and overlearned expressions, emotional phrases, memorised speech, pause fillers, swearwords, and other holistic and recurring phrases. Aphasics commonly lose propositional language abilities but not nonpropositional speech. Prosodic abilities are often also retained. In aphasia, then, holistic phrases, first uttered with stereotyped intonation, often develop a widely varying repertory of intonation contours. The aphasic regains facility of expression in control of intonation using his/her repertory of nonpropositional phrases.

Whatever their theoretical persuasion or model of brain function, most students of structure/function correlations of language and the brain agree that classical language abilities are represented in the left (dominant) hemisphere of right-handed adults. This, I maintain, is true of ortholinguistic structure: phonology, grammar or syntax, most of the lexicon (words), and linguistic semantics. This system makes propositional speech possible:

It provides for the generation of novel utterances. But the large component in language that does not rely on this system, that works differently, and is not lateralised to the left hemisphere, nonpropositional language, also deserves complete description in language analysis.

Jackson (1958; p. 132) hypothesised that "word processes are not of the same kind in each half of the brain." This was a farsighted remark, because much research on hemispheric function leads to the conclusion that the hemispheres operate according to different processing modes. Thus language function which is lateralised to the left hemisphere can be expected to proceed according to different principles, and have different properties, from language abilities not so lateralised. The evidence is strong that characteristics of general right-hemisphere function are compatible with observations about right-hemisphere production and comprehension of nonpropositional speech, and subcortical structures may play some as yet undefined role in their production.

These phenomena have been displayed, for heuristic purposes, on a continuum, extending from reflexive cries of pain through the opposite extreme, propositional language (Fig. 2.2, see p. 56). On such a continuum, features and properties of various kinds of nonpropositional speech can be seen. The properties and attributes indicated for nonpropositional speech are meant to be suggestive only; as more light is cast on this fascinating realm of language function, more will be revealed about their nature and use.

APPENDIX

Speech Samples from Two Patients Following Right (Sample I) or Left (Sample II) Hemispherectomy

Right Hemisphectomy Patient: Speech Sample I

1. Repetition (all items said by interviewer and repeated correctly by right-hemispherectomy patient)

   Baseball and bat
   Knife and fork
   My favourite vegetable
   Two times two
   Door and window
   Light the lamp
   Drive a car
   Sell the house
   Easy does it
   Thirty-three
   Father and mother
   All's shipshape
   A year yesterday

Bake a cake
Guess again
Sing a song
A kitchen chair
Orange juice

2. Interview

I. Would you say your voice sounds about the same now as it did before your operation?
P. No.
I. What's the difference?
P. It sounds a little weak.
I. Weak to you? Okay. Do you try and speak louder?
P. Yes.
I. And what happens?
P. Nothing.
I. How does it feel? When you try to speak louder.
P. I just can't express the feeling. I just can't get enough push behind it.

3. On request, patient counts from one to twenty, and names days of week.

4. Sentence completion

Interviewer	Patient
I want a cup of . . .	milk.
Do you think it looks like . . .	rain.
There's someone at the . . .	door.
I'd like a piece of . . .	pie.
The grass is . . .	green.
The sky is . . .	blue.
I like bread and . . .	jelly.
Please pass the salt and . . .	pepper.

5.

Interviewer	Patient
What do you use a hammer for?	drive a nail.
What do you use soap for?	wash with.
What do you use money for?	. . . (unintell) the things you need.
What do you use a razor for?	to shave.
What do you eat with?	a knife and fork.
What do you tell time with?	clock.
What do you write with?	a pen or a pencil.
What do you wear on your feet?	shoes or slippers.

6. Patient gives name and address on request.

I. Where were you born?
P. Denver, Colorado.
I. When is your birthday?
P. June 5, 1911.
I. And your age?

P. 57.
I. And what was the last school you went to?
P. Junior High School in Denver.
(Patient continues to answer questions about school and job)

7. I. Could you tell me three things you did today?
   P. Went to . . . ET.
      Those were the only places I went.
   I. Can you think of two other things you did?
   P. I went to breakfast.
   I. Okay. Could you tell me three things that a good citizen should do?
   P. Vote and obey the law.
   I. That's two.
   P. You wanted three.
   I. Three. Did you think of a third one? Okay.

8. I. Would you make up a sentence using the word "coat" in it?
      Would you make up a sentence using the word "coat"?
   P. I gotta leave now, would you please get me my coat?
   I. Would you make up a sentence using the word "new"?
   P. I have a new car.
   I. And a sentence using the word "want."
   P. (unintell) would you want.
   I. A sentence using the word "have."
   P. I have several of those.
   I. A sentence using the word "after."
   P. After I get back, I'll come over.
   I. And the last one, a sentence using the word "belongs."
   P. These items belongs to somebody else.

9. I. Look at this picture, and make up a story that has a beginning, a middle, and an
      end.
   P. The boy is with his kite, in Mr. Smith's yard. The kite flew over the house. He
      took his dog with him. There was a fire in the fireplace.

10. Naming task: Names concrete items pictured on cards.

11. *Interviewer*   *Patient*
    What is a robin?   a bird.
    What is an apple?   a fruit.
    What does the word "return" mean?   give back.
    What does the word "different" mean?   not alike.
    What does the word "bridge" mean?   (unintell).
    What does the word "continue" mean?   Go ahead.
    What does the word "history" mean?   past things.
    What does the word "material" mean?   solid substance.
    What does the word "decide" mean?   make a decision.
    What does the word "opinion" mean?   express yourself.

12. I. This is the comprehensive section of the WISK. I'll ask you some questions and you answer them, okay?

Interviewer	Patient
Why do we wash clothes?	For cleanliness.
Why does a train have an engine?	To pull the cars.
What is the thing to do if you find an envelope in the street that is sealed and addressed and has a new stamp?	Try to find out to who it belongs.
Why should we keep away from bad company?	To keep out of trouble.
Why should people pay taxes?	To help the country so you can have what you want.

Courtesy of Dr. Hagen

Patient with Severe Left-Hemisphere Damage: Speech Sample II

I. Would you give your name?
J. (Jack Smith)[2]
I. Jack Smith. Jack, what did you do yesterday?
J. Uh, ( ) (Unintell.)
I. What else?
J.   Oh! uh, sh- voice practice practice practice.
I. Anything else?
J.   uh, Well, practice ( )
I. What do you call this thing here?
J.   oh, table.
I. It has a back on it, a seat, and four legs. A Table? Are you sure that's a table?
J.   table. yeah!
I. What are you sitting in?
J.   um, huh?
I. What are you sitting in, right now?
J.   uh, well, um,
I. Yeah, that thing.
J.   sh-chairs.
I. Yeah, a chair, you're sitting in a . . . chair . . .
J.   uh huh. chairs.
I. What is this?
J.   chairs.
I. So this is a chair.
J.   yuh.
I. What is it used for?
J.   oh. well, uh, uh, table!
I. What is this thing here?
J.   um, um, (sigh) knife, no, uh,
I. Well you can put a knife on it.
J.   no no no no table? and uh uh well. Think. It's um
I. Put the food on the
J.   huh?

---

[2]Fictitious name given here.

I. Put the food on the
J.   table?
I. Table!
J.   No no
I. Yes it's a table.
J.   Table? Table?
I. Table. What's it used for.
J.   Oh. Table! huh. Oh, well, uh, do, um, uh. damn. Table! (Laughs)
I. All right, okay.

REFERENCES

Alajouanine, T. (1956) Verbal realisation in aphasia. *Brain*, *79*, 1–28.
Andrews, G., Craig, A., Feyer, A.-M., Hoddinott, K. S., Howie, P., & Neilson, M. (1983) Stuttering: A review of research findings and theories circa 1982. *Journal of Speech and Hearing Disorders*, *48*, 226–245.
Andrews, G., Quinn, P. T., & Sorby, W. A. (1972) Stuttering: An investigation into cerebral dominance for speech. *Journal of Neurology, Neurosurgery, and Psychiatry*, *35*, 415–418.
Asam, U. (1978) Das Gilles de la Tourette–Syndrome. *Acta Paedopsychiat.*, *43*, 267–276.
Bay, E. (1963) Aphasia and conceptual thinking. In L. Halpern (Ed.), *Problems of Dynamic Neurology*. Jerusalem: Hebrew University Hadassah Medical School.
Bay, E. (1964a) The history of aphasia and the principles of cerebral localisation. In G. Schaltenbrand & C. Woolsey (Eds.), *Cerebral Localisation and Organisation*. Madison, Wisconsin: University of Wisconsin Press.
Bay, E. (1964b) Principles of classification and their influence on our concepts of aphasia. In A. V. S. de Reuck & M. O'Conner (Eds.), *CIBA Foundation on the Disorders of Language*. London: J. & A. Churchill, Ltd.
Beckers, W. (1973) Zur Gilles de la Touretteschen Erkrankung anhand von fuenf eigenen Beobachtungen. *Arch Psychiat. Nervenkr.*, *218*, 169–189.
Bengis, I. (1973) *Combat in the Erogenous Zone*. New York: Bantam Books.
Benson, F. (1979) *Aphasia, Alexia, and Agraphia*. New York: Churchill Livingston.
Benton, A. (1980) The neuropsychology of facial recognition. *American Psychologist*, *35*, 176–186.
Bever, T. G. (1975) Cerebral asymmetries in humans are due to the differentiation of two incompatible processes: Holistic and analytic. *Annals of the New York Academy of Science*, *263*, 251–262.
Bever, T. G. & Chiarello, R. J. (1974) Cerebral dominance in musicians and nonmusicians. *Science*, *185*, 537–539.
Blumstein, S. & Cooper, W. E. (1974) Hemispheric processing of intonation contours. *Cortex*, *10*, 146–158.
Bogen, J. E. (1969a) The other side of the brain II: An appositional mind. *Bulletin of the Los Angeles Neurological Societies*, *34.4*, 135–162.
Bogen, J. E. (1969b) The other side of the brain III: An appositional mind. *Bulletin of the Los Angeles Neurological Societies*, *34.4*, 191–219.
Bogen, J. E. (1973) *Movie of a hemispherectomy patient and what it all means*. UCLA Conference on Cerebral Dominance, Los Angeles.
Bogen, J. E. (1979) The callosal syndrome. In K. M. Heilman & E. Valenstein (Eds.), *Clinical Neuropsychology*. New York: Academic Press.
Bogen, J. E. & Gorden, H. (1971) Musical tests for functional lateralisation with intracarotid amytal. *Nature*, *230*, 524–525.

Bolinger, D. (1961) *Generality, Gradience, and the All-or-none*. The Hague: Mouton.

Bolinger, D. (1976) Meaning and memory. *Forum Linguisticum, 1*, 1–14.

Borod, J., Koff, E., Lorch, M. P., & Nicholas, M. (1985) Channels of emotional expression in patients with unilateral brain disease. *Archives of Neurology, 42*, 345–348.

Bradshaw, J. L. & Nettleton, N. C. (1981) The nature of hemispheric specialisation in man. *The Behavioural and Brain Sciences, 4(1)*, 51–63.

Bradshaw, J. L. & Nettleton, N. D. (1983) *Human Cerebral Asymmetry*. Englewood Cliffs, New Jersey: Prentice Hall.

Bradshaw, J. L. & Sherlock (1982) Bugs and faces in the two visual fields: Task order, difficulty, practice and the analytic/holistic dichotomy. *Cortex, 1982, 18*.

Brain, Sir A. (1961) *Speech Disorders: Aphasia, Apraxia, and Agnosia*. London: Butterworths.

Briones, A. V., Aguiar, C. S., & Fernandes, A. C. (1974) El sindrome de Gilles de la Tourette. *Actas Luso-espanoles de Neurologia, Psiquiatria y ciencias afines, 2*, 15–20.

Broca, P. (1861) Remarques sûr le siège de la faculté du langage articulé, suivie d'une observation d'aphèmie. *Bull. Soc. Anatomie, 5*, 330–357.

Brown, J. W. (1975) On the neural organisation of language: Thalamic and cortical relationships. *Brain and Language, 2(1)*, 18–30.

Brown, R. (1968) *Words and Things: An Introduction to Language*. New York: Free Press.

Brownell, H. H., Michel, D., Powelson, J., & Gardner, H. (1983) Surprise but not coherence: Sensitivity to verbal human in right-hemisphere patients. *Brain and Language, 18*, 20–27.

Bruun, A. & Shapiro, A. (1972) Differential diagnosis of Gilles de la Tourette's syndrome. *Journal of Nervous and Mental Disease, 54*, 133–151.

Bryden, M. P. (1982) *Laterality: Functional Asymmetry in the Intact Brain*. New York: Academic Press.

Bryden, M. P., Hecaen, H., & DeAgostini, M. (1983) Patterns of cerebral organisation. *Brain and Language, 20*, 249–262.

Buchanan, A. (1951) *Functional Neuro-anatomy*. Philadelphia: Lea & Febiger.

Buchwald, J. & Brown, K. (1973) Subcortical mechanisms of behavioural plasticity. In J. Moser (Ed.), *Efferent Organisation and the Integration of Behaviour*. New York: Academic Press.

Butler, R., Diamond, I., & Neff, W. (1957) Role of auditory cortex in discrimination of changes in frequency. *Journal of Neurophysiology, 20*, 108–120.

Caine, E. D. (1985) Gilles de la Tourette's syndrome. *Archives of Neurology, 2*, 393–397.

Canter, G., Coughlin, J., & Van Lancker, D. (1978) *Observations on a conduction aphasic*. Paper presented at the American Speech and Hearing Association, November, 1978.

Canter, G. & Van Lancker, D. (1985) Disturbances of the temporal organisation of speech following bilateral thalamic surgery in a patient with Parkinson's disease. *Journal of Communication Disorders, 181*, 371–391.

Carmon, A. & Nachshon, I. (1971) Effect of unilateral brain damage on perception of temporal order. *Cortex, 7*, 410–418.

Chafe, W. (1968) Idiomaticity as an anomaly in the Chomskyan paradigm. *Foundations of Language, 4*, 109–127.

Cheek, W. & Taveras, J. (1966) Thalamic tumours. *Journal of Neurosurgery, 24*, 505–513.

Ciemins, V. (1970) Localised thalamic hemorrhage: A cause of aphasia. *Neurology, (Minneapolis), 20*, 776–782.

Clark, R. (1972) *Imitation, production, and comprehension and how they are related in children's performance*. University of Edinburgh, Department of Linguistics.

Cohen, D. J., Detlor, J., Shaywitz, B., & Leckman, J. (1982) Interaction of biological and psychological factors in the natural history of Tourette syndrome: A paradigm for childhood neuropsychiatric disorders. In A. J. Friedhoff & T. N. Chase (Eds.), *Advances in Neurology, Vol. 35, Gilles de la Tourette Syndrome*. New York: Raven Press.

Cooper, W. E. & Ross, J. R. (1975) World order. In R. E. Grossman (Ed.), *Parasession in Functionalism: Papers from the Parasession in Functionalism*, Chicago: Chicago Linguistic Society, 63–111.

Critchley, M. (1962) Speech and speech-loss in relation to the duality of the brain. In V. Mountcastle (Ed.), *Interhemispheric Relations and Cerebral Dominance*. Baltimore: Johns Hopkins University Press, 208–213.

Critchley, M. (1970) *Aphasiology and other Aspects of Language*. London; Edward Arnold, Ltd.

Crockett, H. G. & Estridge, N. M. (1951) Cerebral hemispherectomy. *Bulletin of the Los Angeles Neurological Societies*, *16*, 71–87.

Cummings, J. L., Benson, D. F., Walsh, M. J., & Levine, H. L. (1979) Left-to-right transfer of language dominance: A case study. *Neurology*, *29(1)*, 1547–1550.

Curry, F. (1967) A comparison of left-handed and right-handed subjects on verbal and nonverbal dichotic listening tasks. *Cortex*, *3*, 343–352.

Czopf, J. (1981) Über die Rolle der nicht dominanten Hemisphäre in der Restitution der Sprache der Aphasischen. *Archiven Psychiatrischer Nervenkrankheiten*, *216*, 162–171.

Danly, M. & Cooper, W. (1983) Fundamental frequency, language processing linguistic structure in Wernicke's aphasia. *Brain and Language*, *19(3)*, 1–24.

Danly, M. & Shapiro, B. (1982) Speech prosody in Broca's aphasia. *Brain and Language*, *16*, 171–190.

Dax, M. (1865) Lesions de la Moitie gauche de l'Encephale coincident avec l'oublie des signe de la Pensee. *Gaz. Hebdom.*, *2*, 259–260.

De Divitiis, H. (1981) Personal communication.

De Groot, M. H. & Bardwell, B. (1970) A case of Gilles de la Tourette's syndrome occurring in New Zealand. *Austrian and New Zealand Journal of Psychiatry*, *4*, 155–158.

De Saussure, F. (1968) *Cours de Linguistique General*. Paris: Payot.

Dewson, J. H. (1964) Speech sound discrimination by cats. *Science*, *144*, 555–556.

Dronkers, N. F. (1984) *The role of syntax in automatic speech processing*. Paper presented at the 22nd Meeting of the Academy of Aphasia, Los Angeles, California, 1984.

Efron, R (1963a) Temporal perception, aphasia, and déjà vu. *Brain*, *86*, 403–424.

Efron, R. (1963b) The effect of handedness on the perception of simultaneity and temporal order: Part II. *Brain*, *86*, 425–449.

Eisenson, J. (1962) Language and intellectual findings associated with right cerebral damage. *Language and Speech*, *5*, 49–53.

Ellis, H. D. (1983) The role of the right hemisphere in face perception. In A. W. Young (Ed.), *Functions of the Right Cerebral Hemisphere*. New York: Academic Press.

Ervin-Tripp, S. (1972) Language development. In L. Hoffman & M. Hoffman (Eds.), *Review of Child Development Research*. New York: Russell Sage Foundation.

Escalar, G., Majeron, M. A., Finavera, L., & Zamberletti, P. (1972) Contributo alla conoscenza della sindrome di Gilles de la Tourette. *Minerva Medica*, *15*, 3517–3522.

Espir, L. & Rose, F. (1970) *The Basic Neurology of Speech*. Oxford: Blackwell Scientific Publications.

Ettlinger, G. (1967) Analysis of cross-modal effects and their relationship to language. In C. H. Millikan & F. L. Darley (Eds.), *Brain Mechanisms Underlying Speech and Language*. New York: Grune & Stratton.

Eyzaguirre, C. (1969) *Physiology of the Nervous System*. Chicago: Year Book Medical Publishers.

Faglioni, P., Spinnler, H. & Vignolo, L. (1969) Contrasting behaviour of right and left hemisphere damaged patients on a discrimination and a semantic task of auditory recognition. *Cortex*, *5*, 366–389.

Fillmore, C. (1977) Personal communication.

Fillmore, C. (1979) On fluency. In C. J. Fillmore, D. Kempler, & S-Y. Wang (Eds.), *Individual Differences in Language Ability and Language Behaviour*. New York: Academic Press.

Fisher, C. M. (1959) The pathologic and clinical aspects of thalamic haemorrhage. *Transactions of the American Neurological Association*, *84*, 56–90.

Foldi, N. S., Cicone, M., & Gardner, H. (1983) Pragmatic aspects of communication in brain-damaged patients. In S. J. Segalowitz (Ed.), *Language Functions and Brain Organisation*. New York: Academic Press.

Frankel, M., Cummings, J., Robertson, M., Trimble, M. R., Hill, M. A., & Benson, D. F. (1985) Obsessions and compulsions in Gilles de la Tourette syndrome. *Neurology*, *34*, 16–22.

Fraser, B. (1970) Idioms within a transformational grammar. *Foundations of Language*, *6*, 22–42.

Gaitenby, J. (1965) The elastic word. *Haskins Laboratories Status Report on Speech Research*, *SR-2*, 3.1–3.12.

Gandour, J. & Dardarananda, R. (1983) Identification of tonal contrasts in Thai aphasic patients. *Brain and Language*, *18(1)*, 98–114.

Gardner, H., Ling, P. K., Flamm, L., & Silverman, J. (1975) Comprehension and appreciation of humorous material following brain damage. *Brain*, *98*, 399–412.

Gardner, H., Brownell, H. H., Wapner, W., & Michelow, D. (1983) Missing the point: The role of the right hemisphere in the processing of complex linguistic materials. In E. Perecman (Ed.), *Cognitive Processing in the Right Hemisphere*. New York: Academic Press.

Gazzaniga, M. S. (1970) *The Bisected Brain*. New York: Appleton-Century-Crofts.

Gazzaniga, M. S., Nass, R., Reeves, A., & Roberts, D. (1984) Neurologic perspectives on right hemisphere language following surgical section of the corpus callosum. *Seminars in Neurology*, *4(2)*, 126–135.

Geschwind, N. (1965) Disconnection syndromes in animals and man (Part 1). *Brain*, *88*, 237–294.

Geschwind, N. (1967) The varieties of naming errors. *Cortex*, *3*, 97–112.

Geschwind, N., Quadfasel, F. A., & Segarra, J. M. (1968) Isolation of the speech area. *Neuropsychologia*, *6*, 327–340.

Gibbs, R. (1980) Spilling the beans on understanding and memory for idioms in conversation. *Memory and Cognition*, *8*, 149–156.

Gloning, I., Gloning, K., & Hoff, H. (1963) Aphasia–A clinical syndrome. In L. Halpern (Ed.), *Problems of Dynamic Neurology*. Jerusalem: Hebrew University Hadassah Medical School.

Goetz, C. J. & Klawans, H. L. (1982) Gilles de la Tourette on Tourette Syndrome. In A. J. Friedhoff & T. N. Chase (Eds.), *Advances in Neurology, Vol. 35, Gilles de la Tourette Syndrome*. New York: Raven Press.

Goldman-Eisler, F. (1968) *Psycholinguistics: Experiments in Spontaneous Speech*. London: Academic Press.

Goldstein, K. (1948) *Language and Language Disturbances*. New York: Grune & Stratton.

Goodglass, H. & Kaplan, E. (1972) *The Assessment of Aphasia and Related Disorders*. Philadelphia: Lea & Febiger.

Goodglass, H. & Mayer, J. (1958) Agrammatism in aphasia. *Journal of Speech and Hearing Disorders*, *23*, 99–111.

Gordon, H. (1970) Hemispheric asymmetries in the perception of musical chords. *Cortex*, *6.4*, 387–398.

Gordon, H. (1973) *Verbal and nonverbal cerebral processing in man for audition*. Doctoral dissertation. California Institute of Technology.

Gott, P. S. (1973) Cognitive abilities following right and left hemispherectomy. *Cortex, 9*, 266-274.

Gott, P. S., Hughes, E. C., & Whipple, K. (1984) Voluntary control of two lateralised conscious states: Validation by electrical and behavioural studies. *Neuropsychologia, 22(1)*, 65-72.

Guiot, G., Hertzog, E., Rondot, P., & Molina, P. (1961) Arrest or acceleration of speech evoked by thalamic stimulation in the course of stereotaxic procedures for Parkinsonism. *Brain, 84*, 363-379.

Gulick, W. (1971) *Hearing: Physiology and Psychophysics*. Toronto: Oxford University Press.

Hagen, A. C. (1971) *Assessment of communication abilities in three right hemispherectomy patients*. Unpublished paper.

Hassler, R., Mundinger, F., & Riechert, T. *Stereotaxis in Parkinson Syndrome*. Berlin: Springer-Verlag.

Head, H. (1926) *Aphasia and Kindred Disorders of Speech*. Cambridge, England: The University Press.

Hecaen, H. (1962) Clinical symptomatology in right and left hemispheric lesions. In V. Mountcastle (Ed.), *Interhemispheric Relations and Cerebral Dominance*. Baltimore: The Johns Hopkins Press.

Heilman, K. M., Bowers, K., Speedie, D., & Coslett, H. (1984) Comprehension of affective and nonaffective prosody. *Neurology, 34*, 917-921.

Heilman, K. M., & Satz, P. (1983) *Neuropsychology of Human Emotions*. New York: Guilford Press.

Heilman, K. M., Scholes, R., & Watson, R. (1975) Auditory affective agnosia. *Journal of Neurology, Neurosurgery, and Psychiatry, 38*, 69-72.

Heilman, K. M., Watson, R. T., & Bowers, D. (1983) Affective disorders associated with hemispheric disease. In K. M. Heilman & P. Satz (Eds.), *Neuropsychology of Human Emotion*. New York: The Guilford Press.

Hellige, J. B. (1984) *Perceptual quality and cerebral laterality*. Symposium on Cognitive Models of Cerebral Laterality, International Neuropsychological Society, Aachen, West Germany, 1984.

Hempel, C. (1966) *Philosophy of Natural Science*. Englewood Cliffs, N.J.: Prentice Hall, Inc.

Henschen, S. E. (1922) *Klinische und Anatomische Beiträge zur Pathologie des Gehirns*. (5-7), Uppsala: Almqvist & Wiksell.

Henschen, S. E. (1926) On the functions of the right hemisphere of the brain in relation to the left in speech, music, and calculation. *Brain, 49*, 110-123.

Hering, A. (1972) Etiology and pathogenesis of Gilles de la Tourette's disease. *Annals of Psychosomatic Medicine and Psychoanalysis, 18*, 244-270.

Hillier, W. E. (1954) Total left hemispherectomy for malignant glioma. *Neurology (Minnea.), 4*, 718-721.

Hockett, C. (1958) *A Course in Modern Linguistics*. New York: Macmillan Co.

Honeck, R. P. & Hoffman, R. R. (1980) *Cognition and Figurative Language*. New York: Lea.

Horowitz, L. M. & Manelis, L. (1973) Recognition and cued recall of idioms and phrases. *Journal of Experimental Psychology, 100*, 291-296.

Hughes, C. P., Chan, J. L., & Su, M. S. (1983) Aprosodia in Chinese patients with right cerebral hemisphere lesions. *Archives of Neurology, 40*, 732-736.

Jackson, J. H. (1878) On affections of speech from disease of the brain. *Brain, 1*, 304-330.

Jackson, J. H. (1958a) On the nature of the duality of the brain. In J. Taylor (Ed.), *Selected Writings of John Hughlings Jackson, Vol. 2*. New York: Basic Books.

Jackson, J. H. (1958b) On affections of speech from disease of the brain. In J. Taylor (Ed.), *Selected Writings of John Hughlings Jackson, Vol. 2*. New York: Basic Books.

Jaffe, J. (1978) Parliamentary procedure and the brain. In A. W. Siegman & S. Feldstein

(Eds.), *Nonverbal Behaviour and Communication*. Hillsdale, New Jersey: Lawrence Erlbaum Associates Inc.

Jaynes, J. (1976) *The Origin of Consciousness in the Breakdown of Bicameral Mind*. Boston: Houghton Mifflin Co.

Jespersen, O. (1965) *The Philosophy of Grammar*. New York: Norton.

Jespersen, O. (1969) *Essentials of English Grammar*. London: George Allen & Unwin.

Jones, R. K. (1966) Observations on stammering after localised cerebral injury. *Journal of Neurology, Neurosurgery, and Psychiatry, 29*, 192–195.

Juergens, U. & Mueller-Preuss, P. (1977) Convergent projections of different limbic vocalisation areas in the squirrel monkey. *Experimental Brain Research, 29(1)*, 75–83.

Juergens, U. & Ploog, D. (1970) Cerebral representation of vocalisation in the squirrel monkey. *Experimental Brain Research, 10(5)*, 532–554.

Jung, R. (1962) Summary of the conference. In V. Mountcastle (Ed.), *Interhemispheric Relations and Cerebral Dominance*. Baltimore: The Johns Hopkins Press.

Katsuki, Y. (1961) Neurological mechanisms of sensations in cats. In W. A. Rosenblith (Ed.), *Sensory Communication*. Cambridge, Mass.: The MIT Press.

Katsuki, Y. (1962) Pitch discrimination in the higher level of the brain. *International Audiology, 1*, 53–61.

Kelly, A. H., Beaton, L. E., & Magoun, H. W. (1946) A midbrain mechanism for facio-vocal activity. *Journal of Neurophysiology, 9*, 185–189.

Kempler, D., Van Lancker, D., & Hadler, B. (1984) *Familiar phrase recognition in brain-damaged and demented adults*. Paper presented at the 22nd Meeting of the Academy of Aphasia, Los Angeles, California, 1984.

Kent, R. D. & Rosenbek, J. C (1982) Prosodic disturbance and neurologic lesion. *Brain and Language, 15(2)*, 259–291.

Kidd, K. K. & Pauls, D. L. (1982) Genetic hypotheses for Tourette syndrome. In A. J. Friedhoff & T. N. Chase (Eds.), *Advances in Neurology, Vol. 35, Gilles de la Tourette Syndrome*. New York: Raven Press.

Kinsbourne, M. (1971) The minor cerebral hemisphere as a source of aphasic speech. *Transactions of the American Neurological Association, 96*, 141–145.

Kinsbourne, M. (1980) A model for the ontogeny of cerebral organisation in non-right-handers. In J. Herron (Ed.), *Neuropsychology of Left-Handedness*. New York: Academic Press.

Koprowska-Milewska, E. (1976) Gilles de la Tourette's syndrome. In F. Abazzahab, Sr. & F. Anderson (Eds.), *Gilles de la Tourette Syndrome, Vol. 1: International Registry*. St. Paul: Mason Publishing Co., 117–122.

Kreindler, A. & Fradis, A. (1968) *Performances in Aphasia*. Paris: Gautier-Villars.

Labov, W. (1970) *The Study of Nonstandard English*. Champaign: National Council of Teachers.

Lakoff, G. & Johnson, M. (1980) *Metaphors We Live By*. Chicago: UC Press.

Lenneberg, E. (1967) *The Biological Foundations of Language*. New York: John Wiley.

Leussenhop, A. J., Boggs, J. S., Laborwit, L. J., & Walle, E. L. (1973) Cerebral dominance in stutterers determined by Wada testing. *Neurology, 23*, 1190–1192.

Levy, J. (1974) Psychobiological implications of bilateral asymmetry. In S. J. Dimond & J. G. Beaumont (Eds.), *Hemispheric Function in the Human Brain*. New York: John Wiley & Sons.

Lieberman, P. (1963) Some effects of semantic and grammatic context on the production and perception of speech. *Language and Speech, 6*, 172–187.

Lounsbury, F. G. (1963) Linguistics and psychology. In S. Koch (Ed.), *Psychology: Study of a Science*. New York: McGraw-Hill.

Luria, A. R. (1964) Factors and forms of aphasia. In A. V. S. DeReuck & M. O'Conner (Eds.), *Disorders of Language: CIBA Symposium*. London: J. & A. Churchill Ltd.

Luria, A. R. (1966) *Higher Cortical Functions in Man*. New York: Basic Books.

Luria, A. R. (1970) *Traumatic Aphasia*. Moscow: Academy of Sciences.
Luria, A. R. & Tsvetkova, L. S. (1968) The mechanism of "dynamic aphasia." *Foundations of Language*, *4*, 296–307.
Lyons, J. (1968) *Introduction to Theoretical Linguistics*. Cambridge, England: The University Press.
McFarland, H. R & Fortin, D. (1982) Amnesia due to right temporal-parietal infarct. *Archives of Neurology*, *39*, 725–727.
MacLean, P. D. (1972) The triune brain, emotion and scientific brain. In F. O. Schmidt (Ed.), *The Neurosciences Second Study Program*. New York: Rockefeller Press.
Malkiel, Y. (1959) Studies in irreversible binomials. *Lingua*, *8*, 113–160.
Marcie, P. (1965) Les realisations du langage chez les malades atteinte de lesions de l'hemisphere droit. *Neuropsychologia*, *3*, 217–245.
Marie, P. (1925) A singular trouble with speech: Palilalia (dissociation of voluntary speech and of automatic speech). *Le Monde Medical*, *664*, 329–344. Reprinted in M. Cole & M. Cole (Eds.), *Pierre Marie's Papers on Speech Disorders*. New York: Hafner Publishing Co., 1971.
Martin, M. (1979) Hemispheric specialisation for local and global processing. *Neuropsychologia*, *17*, 33–40.
Metter, E. J., Riege, W. H., Hanson, W. R., Kuhl, D. E., Phelps, M. E., Wasterlein, C., Squire, L., & Benson, D. F. (1983) Comparisons of metabolic rates, language, and memory in subcortical aphasias. *Brain and Language*, *19*, 33–47.
Milner, B. (1962) Laterality effects in audition. In V. Mountcastle (Ed.), *Interhemispheric Relations and Cerebral Dominance*. Baltimore: The Johns Hopkins Press.
Milner, B., Branch, C., & Rasmussen, T. (1964) Observations on cerebral dominance. In A. V. S. Reuck & M. O'Conner (Eds.), *CIBA Foundation Symposium on Disorders of Language*. London: Churchill, 200–214.
Milner, P. M. (1970) *Physiological Psychology*. New York: Holt, Rinehart, & Winston.
Mitchell, T. F. (1971) Linguistic "goings on": Collocations and other lexical matters arising on the syntagmatic record. *Archivum Linguisticum*, *11* (New Series), 35–70.
Moscowitz, A. B. (1972) *Phonological idioms and phonological change*. Unpublished paper, UCLA.
Myers, P. S. (1979) Profiles of communication deficits in patients with right cerebral hemisphere damage: Implication for diagnosis and treatment. In R. Brookshire (Ed.), *Clinical Aphasiology*. Minneapolis: BRK Publishers.
Myers, P. S. & Linebaugh, C. W. (1981) Comparison of idiomatic expressions in right-hemisphere-damaged adults. In R. H. Brookshire (Ed.), *Clinical Aphasiological Conference Proceedings*, 254–261.
Myers, R. E. (1968) Neurology of social communication in primates. *Proceedings of the 2nd International Congress of Primatology*, *3*, 1–9.
Myers, R. E. (1976) Comparative neurology of vocalisation and speech: Proof of a dichotomy. *Annals of the New York Academy of Science*, *280*, 745–760.
Myerson, R. & Goodglass, H. (1972) Transformational grammars of three agrammatic patients. *Language and Speech*, *15.1*, 40–50.
Naeser, M. R. & Chan, S. W.-C. (1980) Case study of a Chinese aphasic with the Boston Diagnostic Aphasic Exam. *Neuropsychologia*, *18*, 389–410.
Nauta, W. J. H. (1982) Limbic innervation of the striatum. In A. J. Friedhoff & T. N. Chase (Eds.), *Advances in Neurology, Vol. 35, Gilles de la Tourette Syndrome*. New York: Raven Press, 41–48.
Nebes, R. E. (1978) Direct examination of cognitive function in the right and left hemisphere. In M. Kinsbourne (Ed.), *Asymmetry of the Human Brain*. Cambridge, England: Cambridge University Press.
Neff, W. (1961) Neural mechanisms of auditory discrimination. In W. A. Rosenblith (Ed.), *Sensory Communication*. New York: Wiley.

Neff, W. (1962) Differences in the functions of the two cerebral hemispheres. In V. Mountcastle (Ed.), *Interhemispheric Relations and Cerebral Dominance*. Baltimore: The Johns Hopkins Press.

Ojemann, G. A. (1983) Brain organisation for language from the perspective of electrical stimulatory mapping. *The Behavioural and Brain Sciences, 6(2)*, 189–213.

Ojemann, G. A., Fedio, P., & Van Buren, J. M. (1968) Anomia from pulvinar and subcortical parietal stimulation. *Brain, 91*, 99–116.

Ojemann, G. A. & Ward, A. (1971) Speech representation in ventrolateral thalamus. *Brain, 94*, 669–680.

Olsen, J. (1972) *The Girls in the Office*. New York: Simon & Schuster.

Ornstein, R. (1972) *The Psychology of Consciousness*. New York: Freeman & Co.

Ortony, A., Shallert, D. L., Reynolds, R. E., & Antos, S. J. (1978) Interpreting metaphors and idoms: Some effects of context on comprehension. *Journal of Verbal Learning and Verbal Behaviour, 17*, 465–467.

Osgood, C. & Hoosain, R. (1974) Salience of the word as a unit in the perception of language. *Perception and Psychophysics, 15*, 168–192.

Papcun, G., Krashen, S., Terbeek, D., Remington, R., & Harshman, R. (1974) Is the left hemisphere specialised for speech, language, and/or something else? *Journal of the Acoustical Society of America, 55.2*, 319–327.

Pawley, A. & Syder, F. H. (1977) *Creativity versus memorisation in clause production: The role of lexicalised clauses in speech*. Unpublished manuscript.

Pawley, A. & Syder, F. H. (1980) Two puzzles for linguistic theory: Nativelike selection and nativelike fluency. In J. C. Richards & R. Schmidt (Eds.), *Communicative Competence*. London: Longmans.

Penfield, W. (1954) Mechanisms of voluntary movement. *Brain, 77*, 1–17.

Penfield, W. & Roberts, L. (1959) *Speech and Brain Mechanisms*. Princeton: Princeton University Press.

Perecman, E. (Ed.) (1983) *Cognitive Processing in the Right Hemisphere*. New York: Academic Press.

Perera, H. V. (1975) Two cases of Gilles de la Tourette's syndrome treated with haloperidol. *British Journal of Psychiatry, 127*, 324–326.

Perera, H. V. (1981) Personal communication.

Peters, A. M. (1977) Language learning strategies: Does the whole equal the sum of the parts? *Language, 55*, 560–573.

Peters, A. M. (1983) *The Units of Language*. Cambridge, England: Cambridge University Press.

Pettit, J. M., & Noll, J. D. (1979) Cerebral dominance in aphasia recovery. *Brain and Language, 7(2)*, 191–200.

Phelps, M. E. & Mazziotta, J. C. (1985) Position emission tomography: Brain function and biochemistry. *Science, 228*, 799–809.

Pick, A. (1913) *Die Agrammatische Sprachstoerungen*. Berlin: Springer-Verlag.

Pick, A. (1973) *Aphasia*. Springfield, Illinois: Charles C. Thomas. English translation by J. Brown, from *Handbuch der Normalen und Pathologischen Physiologie*. 1931, *15*, 1416–1524.

Pickens, J. D. & Pollio, H. R. (1979) Patterns of figurative language competence in adult speakers. *Psychological Research, 40*, 299–313.

Pieniadz, J. M., Naeser, M. R., Koff, E., & Levine, H. L. (1983) CT scan cerebral asymmetry measurements in stroke cases with global aphasia: Atypical asymmetries associated with improved recovery. *Cortex, 19*, 371–391.

Pollio, M. R. & Pollio, H. R. (1974) The development of figurative language in children. *Journal of Psychological Research, 3*, 195–201.

Pribram, K. H. (1971) *Languages of the Brain*. Englewood Cliffs, New Jersey: Prentice-Hall.

Rasmussen, T. & Milner, B. (1975) Clinical and surgical studies of the cerebral speech areas in man. In K. J. Zuelch, O. Creutzfeldt, & G. C. Galbraith (Eds.), *Cerebral Lateralisation*. New York: Springer.

Richardson, E. P. (1982) Neuropathological studies of Tourette syndrome. In A. J. Friedhoff & T. N. Chase (Eds.), *Advances in Neurology, Vol. 35, Gilles de la Tourette Syndrome*. New York: Raven Press, 83–88.

Riklan, M., & Levita, E. (1969) *Subcortical Correlates of Human Behaviour*. Baltimore: Williams & Wilkins & Co.

Robinson, B. W. (1967) Neurological aspects of evoked vocalisations. In S. A. Altmann (Ed.), *Social Communication among Primates*. Chicago: University of Chicago Press.

Robinson, B. W. (1976) Limbic influences in human speech. *Annals of the New York Academy of Science, 280*, 761–771.

Rosenblith, W. A. (Ed.) (1961) *Sensory Communication*. New York: Wiley.

Rosenzweig, M. R. (1951) Representation of the two ears at the auditory cortex. *American Journal of Physiology, 167*, 147–158.

Rosenzweig, M. R. (1954) Cortical correlates of auditory localisation and other related perceptual phenomena. *Journal of Comparative Physiology, 472*, 269–276.

Rosenzweig, M. (1972) Auditory localisation. In *Perception: Mechanisms and Models. Readings from the Scientific American*. San Francisco: W. H. Freeman & Co.

Ross, E. D. (1981) The aprosodias. Functional-anatomic organisation of the affective components of language in the right hemisphere. *Archives of Neurology, 38(9)*, 561–569.

Ross, E. D. (1983) Right-hemisphere lesions in disorders of affective language. In A. Kertesz (Ed.), *Localisation in Neuropsychology*. New York: Academic Press.

Ross, E. D. & Mesulam, M. M. (1979) Dominant language functions of the right hemisphere? Prosody and emotional gesturing. *Archives of Neurology, 36*, 144–148.

Sapir, E. (1921) *Language: An Introduction to the Study of Speech*. New York: Harcourt, Brace, & World.

Schaltenbrand, G. (1965) The effects of stereotactic electrical stimulation in the depth of the brain. *Brain, 88*, 835–840.

Schuell, H. (1965) *Minnesota Test for Differential Diagnosis of Aphasia*. Minneapolis: Minnesota Press.

Searle, J. R. (1975) Indirect speech acts. In P. Cole & J.L. Morgan (Eds.), *Syntax and Semantics 3: Speech Acts*. New York: Academic Press.

Segalowitz, S. J. (1983) *Two Sides of the Brain*. New Jersey: Prentice-Hall.

Semmes, J. (1968) Hemispheric specialisation: A possible clue to mechanism. *Neuropsychologia, 6*, 11–26.

Shapiro, A. & Shapiro, E. (1982) Tourette syndrome: History and present status. In A. J. Friedhoff & T. N. Chase (Eds.), *Advances in Neurology, Vol. 35, Gilles de la Tourette Syndrome*. New York: Raven Press, 17–24.

Shapiro, A., Shapiro, E., Bruun, R. D., & Sweet, K. D. (Eds.) (1978) *Gilles de la Tourette Syndrome*. New York: Raven Press.

Shapiro, A., Shapiro, E., & Wayne, H. (1973) The symptomatology and diagnosis of Gilles de la Tourette's syndrome. *Journal of the American Academy of Child Psychiatry, 12*, 702–723.

Shapiro, A., Shapiro, E., Wayne, H., & Clarkin, J. (1973) Organic factors in Gilles de la Tourette's syndrome. *British Journal of Psychiatry, 122*, 659–664.

Shapiro, A., Shapiro, E., Wayne, H., Clarkin, J., & Bruun, R. (1973) Tourette's syndrome: Summary of data on 34 patients. *Psychosomatic Medicine, 35.5*, 419–435.

Sheer, P. E. (Ed.) (1961) *Electrical Stimulation of the Brain*. Austin: University of Austin Press.

Sidtis, J. J. (1981) The complex tone test: Implications for the assessment of auditory laterality effects. *Neuropsychologia, 19*, 103–112.

Simon, H. A. (1974) How big is a chunk? *Science*, *183*, 482–488.

Smith, A. (1966) Speech and other functions after left (dominant) hemispherectomy. *Journal of Neurological and Neurosurgical Psychiatry*, *29*, 467–471.

Smith, A. R. & Burkland, C. W. (1967) Nondominant hemispherectomy: Neurophysiological implications for human brain function. *American Psychological Association Proceedings*. New York: American Psychological Association.

Smyth, G. E. & Stern, K. K. (1938) Tumours of the thalamus—a clinicopathological study. *Brain*, *61*, 339–374.

Spellacy, F. & Blumstein, S. (1970a) The influence of language set in ear preference in phoneme recognition. *Cortex*, *6*, 430–439.

Spellacy, F. & Blumstein, S. (1970b) Ear preferences for language and nonlanguage sounds: A unilateral brain function. *Journal of Auditory Research*, *10*, 349–355.

Sperry, R. W. (1964) The great cerebral commissure. *Scientific American*, *210*, 42–52.

Springer, S. & Deutsch, G. (1981) *Left Brain, Right Brain*. San Francisco: W. Freeman & Co.

Sweet, R., Soloman, G. E., Wayne, H., Shapiro, E., & Shapiro, A. K. (1973) Neurological features of Gilles de la Tourette's syndrome. *Journal of Neurological and Neurosurgical Psychiatry*, *36.1*, 1–9.

Swinney, D. A. & Cutler, A. (1979) The access of processing of idiomatic expressions. *Journal of Verbal Learning and Verbal Behaviour*, *18*, 523–534.

Thompson, R. (1960) Function of auditory cortex of cat in frequency discrimination. *Journal of Neurophysiology*, *23*, 321–334.

Thompson, R. (1967) *Foundations of Physiological Psychology*. New York: Harper & Row.

Tunturi, A. R. (1946) A study of the pathway from the medial geniculate body of the acoustic cortex of the dog. *American Journal of Psychology*, *147*, 311–319.

Tyler, S. A. (1978) *The Said and the Unsaid*. New York: Academic Press.

Van Lancker, D. (1972) *Language Processing in the Brain*. Paper presented at the American Speech and Hearing Association (November). San Francisco, California.

Van Lancker, D. (1973) Language lateralisation and grammars. In J. P. Kimball (Ed.), *Syntax and Semantics*. New York: Seminar Press.

Van Lancker, D. (1975) Heterogeneity in language and speech: Neurolinguistic studies. *Working Papers in Phonetics*, *29*. UCLA, Los Angeles.

Van Lancker, D. (1979) Review article: Review of J. Jaynes, *The Origin of Consciousness in the Breakdown of Bicameral Man*. *Forum Linguisticum. IV*, 72–91.

Van Lancker, D. (1980) Cerebral lateralisation of pitch cues in the linguistic signal. *Papers in Linguistics: International Journal of Human Communication*, *13*, 201–277.

Van Lancker, D. (1985) Hemispheric contributions to language and communication. In J. Darby (Ed.), *Speech Evaluation in Neurology*. New York: Grune & Stratton.

Van Lancker, D. & Canter, G. J. (1981) Idiomatic versus literal interpretations of ditropically ambiguous sentences. *Journal of Speech and Hearing Research*, *46*, 64–69.

Van Lancker, D. & Canter, G. J. (1982) Impairment of voice and face recognition in patients with hemispheric damage. *Brain and Cognition*, *1*, 185–195.

Van Lancker, D., Bogen, J. E., & Canter, G. J. (1983) A case report of pathological rule-governed syllable intrusion. *Brain and Language*, *20*, 12–20.

Van Lancker, D., Canter, G. J., & Terbeek, D. (1981) Disambiguation of ditropic sentences: Acoustic and phonetic cues. *Journal of Speech and Hearing Research*, *24*, 330–335.

Van Lancker, D., Cummings, J. L., & Kreiman, J. (1986) Voice perception: A dissociation between familiar and unfamiliar voices. *Journal of Clinical and Experimental Neuropsychology*, *7*, 6.

Van Lancker, D. & Fromkin, V. A. (1973) Hemispheric specialisation for pitch and "tone": Evidence from Thai. *Journal of Phonetics*, *1*, 101–109.

118　VAN LANCKER

Van Lancker, D. & Fromkin, V. A. (1978) Hemispheric specialisation for pitch and "tone": in musically trained and untrained speakers. *Journal of Phonetics, 3*, 19–23.

Van Riper, C. & Erwin, I. J. (1958) *Voice and Articulation*. Englewood Cliffs, New Jersey: Prentice-Hall Inc.

Vihman, M. M. (1982) Formulas in first and second language acquisition. In L. K. Obler & L. Menn (Eds.), *Exceptional Language and Linguistics*. New York: Academic Press.

Von Bonin, G. (1962) Anatomical asymmetry of the cerebral hemispheres. In V. Mountcastle (Ed.), *Interhemispheric Relations and Cerebral Dominance*. Baltimore: The Johns Hopkins Press.

Weinreich, V. (1969) Problems in the analysis of idioms. In J. Puhvel (Ed.), *Substance and Structure of Language*. Los Angeles, California: University of California Press.

Weinreich, V., Labov, W., & Herzog, M. (1968) Empirical foundations for a theory of language change. In W. P. Lehmann & Y. Malkiel (Eds.), *Directions for Historical Linguistics*. Austin: University of Texas Press.

Weinstein, E. A. & Keller, N. J. (1963) Linguistic patterns of misnaming in brain injury. *Journal of Neuropsychology, 1*, 79–90.

Wepman, J. M., Bock, R. D., Jones, L. V., & Van Pelt, D. (1956) Psycholinguistic study of aphasia: A revision of the concept of anomia. *Journal of Speech and Hearing Disorders, 21*, 466–477.

Whitaker, H. A. (1976) A case of isolation of the speech functions. In H. Whitaker & H. A. Whitaker (Eds.), *Studies in Neurolinguistics, Vol. 2*. London: Academic Press.

Whitfield, I. C. (1967) *The Auditory Pathway*. London: Arnold Publishers.

Winner, E. & Gardner, H. (1977) The comprehension of metaphor in brain-damaged patients. *Brain, 100*, 719–727.

Witelson, S. F. (1974) Hemispheric specialisation for linguistic and nonlinguistic tactual perception using a dichotomous stimulation technique. *Cortex, 10(1)*, 3–17.

Wong Fillmore, L. (1976) *The second time around: Cognitive and social strategies in second language learning*. PhD. dissertation, Stanford University.

Wong Fillmore, L. (1979) Individual differences in second language acquisition. In C. J. Fillmore, D. Kempler, & W. S-Y Wang (Eds.), *Individual Differences in Language Ability and Language Behaviour*. London: Academic Press.

Yakovliev, R. I. (1948) Brain, motility, and behaviour. *Journal of Nervous and Mental Disease, 107*, 313–335.

Young, A. W. (Ed.) (1983) *Functions of the Right Cerebral Hemisphere*. New York: Academic Press.

Yvonneau, M. (1972) Biological study of 2 cases of Gilles de la Tourette disease. *Revue Neurologique, 126*, 65–70.

Zaidel, E. (1973) *Linguistic competence and related functions in the right cerebral hemisphere following commisurotomy and hemispherectomy*. Doctoral dissertation, California Institute of Technology.

Zaidel, E. (1978) Lexical organisation in the right hemisphere. In P. A. Buser & A. Rougeul-Buser (Eds.), *Cerebral Correlates of Conscious Experience*. Amsterdam, North Holland: Elsevier.

Zangwill, O. L. (1960) *Cerebral Dominance and its Relation to Psychological Function*. Edinburgh: Oliver & Boyd.

Zangwill, O. L. (1967) Speech and the minor hemisphere. *Acta Neurologica Psychiatrica Belgica, 67*, 1013–1020.

Zemlin, W. (1968) *Speech and Hearing Science: Anatomy and Physiology*. Englewood Cliffs, New Jersey: Prentice-Hall Inc.

Zollinger, R. (1935) Removal of a left cerebral hemisphere: Report of a case. *Archives of Neurology and Psychiatry (Chicago), 34*, 1055–1064.

Zuloaga, R. L. (1973) La enfermedad de Gilles de la Tourette. *Revue Neuropsiquiatra, 36*, 222–232.

3 Rate-Dependent Processing in Speech Perception

Joanne L. Miller
Department of Psychology, Northeastern University, Boston, MA 02115, U.S.A.

INTRODUCTION

A fundamental problem of spoken language processing is the following: How does a listener, who possesses knowledge of a given language, process the continuously varying acoustic signal produced by a speaker of that language, so as to recover the speaker's intended message? Virtually every current theory of this process assumes that a number of analytic stages intervene between the initial presentation of the speech signal and the ultimate understanding of the message. During these stages information about the acoustic signal is combined with linguistic information about the lexical, syntactic, and semantic structures of the utterance, and with nonlinguistic information, which includes the immediate context and the world knowledge of the listener (e.g. Forster, 1979; Marslen-Wilson & Tyler, 1980; Morton, 1979; Swinney, 1981). Specific models differ widely in the precise levels at which the distinct sources of information are combined, and the manner in which they are combined. However, all assume an initial analysis of the speech signal in terms of those acoustic properties that specify the discrete linguistic units that define the individual items in the mental lexicon and thereby permit the recognition of spoken words.

The research discussed in this chapter focusses on the processes involved in these initial stages of language processing, during which the speech signal is converted into a set of discrete linguistic units—for the purposes of this chapter, I take these representational units to be the phonetic segments

119

of the language.[1] Within this framework, a primary goal of research on speech perception is to specify the mapping between the acoustic signal and the phonetic segments of the language and, moreover, to describe the perceptual mechanisms that take as input the segmentally relevant acoustic information and yield as output the intended sequence of segments. Research conducted over the past several decades has provided a rich source of information about the nature of the acoustic properties that specify segmental identity. Indeed, progress in understanding the acoustic-phonetic basis of language arguably constitutes one of the major accomplishments of the field of psycholinguistics.

A major finding of this research is that the mapping between acoustic signal and phonetic segment is highly complex. This complexity takes two major forms. First, the acoustic information underlying a given segment typically includes diverse properties of the speech signal that are distributed over a rather large stretch of speech and that overlap properties specifying other segments (Liberman, Cooper, Shankweiler, & Studdert-Kennedy, 1967; Repp, 1982). Second, the acoustic form of these properties typically varies substantially with a host of factors such as phonetic context, syntactic and semantic structure, stress pattern, speaker, and rate of speech (e.g. Klatt, 1976; Lehiste, 1972; Liberman et al., 1967; Peterson & Barney, 1952). I should note that there continue to be systematic attempts to find properties in the speech signal that remain invariant across the transformations introduced by these variables and, obviously, if such invariant properties existed, the mapping between acoustic signal and phonetic structure would be simplified (Stevens & Blumstein, 1981). However, from the existing literature it appears that if such properties do exist they are extremely elusive. Moreover, evidence is growing that listeners do not normally rely on a single property of the acoustic signal to identify a given segment, but make use of all the available relevant properties in the signal (cf. Whalen, 1984), even if putative "invariant" properties are available (e.g., Blumstein, Isaacs, & Mertus, 1982). Thus, it appears that the solution to the problem of speech perception will necessarily include an account of how the listener uses multiple, context-dependent properties of the acoustic signal in deriving the phonetic structure of the utterance.

Over the past few years, my colleagues and I have been engaged in a

---

[1]The nature of the representational units has been a matter of longstanding debate in the speech perception literature. Candidates have included, for example, phonetic segments, diphones, syllables, and words themselves (see Pisoni and Luce, in press). For purposes of explication I am assuming these units to be phonetic segments. It should be noted, however, that the findings discussed in the chapter are largely neutral with respect to the precise form of the units.

program of research on this issue. We have focussed on one of the primary factors that introduces variation in the speech signal, namely, the rate at which the utterance is produced. The essential problem is that alterations in speaking rate modify the temporal fine structure of the speech signal, thereby producing complex alterations in many of those temporal properties that convey segmental information. Thus the listener, in order to perceive the intended phonetic structure of an utterance across a range of speaking rates, must somehow process speech in a manner that takes into account the rate at which it was produced. That is to say, the processing of speech must be rate dependent. The goal of our research is to specify the nature of such rate-dependent processing, and our progress to date is described in the present chapter.

The discussion is divided into three main sections. In the first I describe evidence from studies of speech production that helps establish the extent of variation in speaking rate that typically occurs in normal conversation, and begins to specify the way in which changes in rate alter the fine structure of the acoustic signal. In the second section I describe research that establishes the basic phenomenon of rate-dependent processing; the means, in effect, by which listeners adjust for modifications in rate during speech perception. Finally, in the third and most extensive section, I describe a series of experiments that explored the characteristics of such rate-dependent processing. This research provides, or so I believe, at least initial answers to the question of how listeners might be able to comprehend spoken language despite the fact that it is not produced at a constant rate.

CHANGES IN RATE DURING SPEECH PRODUCTION

If one listens to everyday conversation with an attentive ear, it becomes apparent that people do not maintain a constant rate of speech while they talk; instead, speaking rate seems to change considerably throughout the course of conversation. Studies of spontaneous speech have confirmed these impressions, and have shown that overall speaking rate—typically measured in words or syllables per minute—varies substantially as a function of many factors, including the emotional state of the speaker, the speaking situation, and the familiarity of material being discussed (e.g. Goldman-Eisler, 1968).

Overall speaking rate is not a unitary variable, however, but is made up of two components: the rate at which the speech itself is produced (termed articulation rate), and the number and duration of pauses (termed pause rate). With respect to models of speech processing, the critical question is the extent to which the changes in overall rate are due to actual changes in the speech signal itself; that is, to changes in articulation rate, rather than to modifications in pausing.

For some time, the consensus among investigators has been that changes in overall rate are in fact due primarily to a modification in pause rate, with articulation rate remaining relatively stable across speaking situations (Goldman-Eisler, 1968; Grosjean & Deschamps, 1975). On this view, when a talker changes rate the actual speech signal itself is only minimally modified, with the consequence that the segmentally relevant acoustic information remains relatively constant. If this were indeed the case, there would be little need for rate-dependent speech processing. However, as we have argued recently (Miller, Grosjean, & Lomanto, 1984), a careful reconsideration of the data suggests that this conclusion is premature. For one thing, although the changes in articulation rate that have been observed are considerably less than the changes in pause rate, they are significant when considered in relation to the durational characteristics of phonetically relevant acoustic properties, which are typically in the order of tens to hundreds of milliseconds. Moreover, the available data underestimate the extent of rate variation, in that they are based on averages across relatively long stretches of speech and thus potentially obscure local variation in rate within a given utterance of a given speaker.

With respect to this last point, we have found that with appropriate measurement procedures the observed changes in articulation rate during conversational speech can be quite substantial (Miller, Grosjean, & Lomanto, 1984). Our analysis was based on the written protocols available from an earlier study by Grosjean and Deschamps (1975), which had examined various temporal aspects of the speech of 30 speakers being interviewed on a radio talk show. The protocols contained an orthographic representation of each speaker's responses to the questions posed by the interviewer, with various temporal variables marked. Specifically, each response was divided into successive runs of speech, with a run defined as the stretch of speech between 2 pauses and a pause defined as a silent interval of 250msec or longer. The total duration of each run and the number of syllables in the run were given on the protocol. For our analysis, we simply computed the articulation rate, in msec/syllable, for each run of speech. This gives a reading of the average syllable duration in the run (we should note that in the original Grosjean and Deschamps analysis, articulation rate was computed over considerably longer stretches of speech, thus averaging out potential variability). Of interest to us was the extent to which this measure—average syllable duration for a stretch of pause-free speech—changes across the interview for an individual speaker.

The data for a single speaker are graphically displayed in Fig. 3.1. For each of the two responses of the speaker, we have plotted the articulation rate, in msec/syllable, for successive runs of speech. (The mean number of

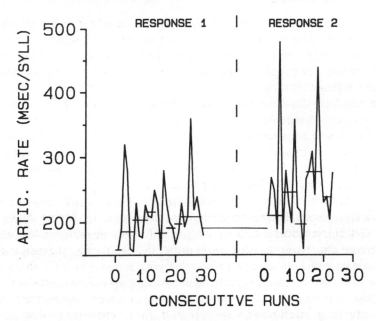

FIG. 3.1   The continuous lines represent mean articulation rate, in msec/syllable, for consecutive runs of speech in each of two responses of a single speaker. (The short horizontal lines represent an analysis conducted in the original Grosjean and Deschamps [1975] study, as described in Miller, Grosjean, and Lomanto [1984].) (Miller, Grosjean, & Lomanto, 1984.)

syllables per run was 8.97 and 7.00 for the first and second responses, respectively.) It is readily apparent that articulation rate varies during the course of the interview and that the change in rate is considerable. The actual rates for this speaker range from 156–480msec/syllable, thus yielding a difference of 324msec in average syllable duration across runs of speech. This magnitude of change was not unusual: For all but one speaker, the change from fastest to slowest rate during the interview was over 100msec, and for 20 of the 30 speakers it was 300msec or greater; across the 30 speakers, the average change in rate during the interview was 323msec/syllable. And it is important to keep in mind that since these data are based on average syllable durations, and not individual syllable durations, they are providing a conservative index of rate changes. The picture that emerges then is one of considerable variability in rate during spontaneous speech.

The important question that immediately arises is how these changes in articulation rate affect the acoustic fine structure of the speech waveform, in particular, those properties that convey segmental information. Ideally, one would want to assess this in the context of spontaneous speech, for example, by tracking the acoustic properties of a particular segmental contrast (in a given phonetic context) across changes in speaking rate.

Although such data have not been reported in the literature—and this is not surprising given the difficult methodological problems involved—there have been a number of studies investigating the issue in the context of elicited speech. The typical procedure in these studies is to ask a speaker to produce a given set of words or sentences at different rates of speech and then to measure the acoustic property of interest in each rate condition. On the basis of such studies, it is clear that for both vowels (e.g. Gay, 1978; Port, 1981) and consonants (e.g., Pickett & Decker, 1960; Summerfield, 1975) properties that are segmentally relevant are systematically altered in form as articulation rate goes from fast to slow (a review of this literature is provided in Miller, 1981a).

Let us consider two detailed cases from our own work, both of which involve consonantal contrasts in syllable-initial position. These will serve to exemplify the ways in which rate alters the fine structure of speech and to provide the basis for the perceptual studies to be discussed in the following sections.

The first case involves the contrast between stop consonant and semi-vowel, /b/ versus /w/ in this instance. The segments /b/ and /w/ differ from each other acoustically primarily in the abruptness of their onsets, with the onset for /b/ being more abrupt than that for /w/ (e.g., Dalston, 1975; Fant, 1960; Fischer-Jorgensen, 1954; Mack & Blumstein, 1983; O'Connor, Gerstman, Liberman, Delattre, & Cooper, 1957). This difference in abruptness manifests itself both in the amplitude contour at onset and the duration (and slope) of the initial formant transitions. Moreover, these properties are perceptually relevant: Tokens with abrupt amplitude onsets and short transitions are perceived as good exemplars of a stop consonant, whereas those with more gradual amplitude onsets and longer transitions are perceived as good exemplars of a semivowel (e.g., Cooper, Ebert, & Cole, 1976; Liberman, Delattre, Gerstman, & Cooper, 1956; Schwab, Sawusch, & Nusbaum, 1981; Shinn & Blumstein, 1984).

With respect to the issue of speaking rate, the important question is whether the onset characteristics of these consonants remain constant as speaking rate changes or, alternatively, whether changes in rate affect their form. To address this issue, we (Miller & Baer, 1983) investigated how the onset characteristics of the syllables /ba/ and /wa/ changed as a function of rate for four speakers. We asked each speaker to produce each of the two syllables across a wide range of rates. The task yielded approximately 200 syllables for each speaker, which spanned a range of syllable durations from roughly 100–700msec. For each syllable, the abruptness of the onset was estimated by measuring the duration of the first formant transition. The data, shown in Fig. 3.2, were very clear. For /ba/, as syllable duration increased there was little change in the duration of the first formant transition. However, quite a different pattern emerged for /wa/. As the

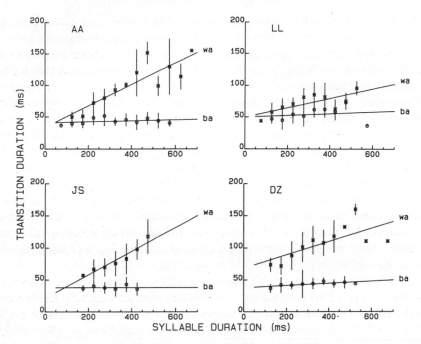

FIG. 3.2   Mean transition duration, in msec, of syllables within successive 50msec syllable duration intervals for each of 4 speakers. The data points are plotted at the midpoint of the 50msec interval, and the error bars indicate plus and minus one standard deviation from the mean. Linear regression lines are fit to each set of mean data. (Miller & Baer, 1983.)

syllable became longer, so too did the duration of the initial transition. And this was true for all four speakers.

These data have important implications for perception, if one conceives of the task of the perceptual system to be that of analysing the initial transition duration so as to identify the syllable correctly as beginning with /b/ verses /w/. The categorisation principle would at first appear to be simple: If the transition is short, the syllable begins with /b/; if it is long, it begins with /w/. But what is to be considered "short" and what is to be considered "long"? From the data in Fig. 3.2, it is clear that the criterion transition duration that optimally differentiates the /ba/ and /wa/ distributions is not constant. As syllable duration increases, the optimal criterion value also increases. The interesting question is whether the perceptual system operates accordingly, that is, whether when categorising tokens as /b/ or /w/, it treats transition duration in relation to syllable duration. As we shall see in the next section, there are data indicating that the answer is a clear yes.

Before turning to those perceptual data, however, consider our second investigation of how changes in rate alter the fine structure of speech

(Miller, Green, & Reeves, research in progress). The contrast of interest here was a distinction in voicing, namely, a distinction between the voiced consonant /b/ and the voiceless consonant /p/. The parameter we chose to study was voice-onset-time (VOT), defined as the interval between the release of the consonant and the onset of periodicity. It is well known that VOT values for voiced consonants are generally lower than those for voiceless consonants, and that listeners use this difference to categorise a consonant as being voiced or voiceless (Lisker & Abramson, 1964, 1970). We were interested in how this temporal property changed with a modification in rate. Essentially, our investigation was an extension of earlier work by Summerfield (1975), who had observed that VOT values of voiceless consonants (though not voiced consonants) increased as speakers slowed their rates of speech (cf. Diehl, Souther, & Convis, 1980). In contrast to Summerfield (1975), who measured speech at just three rates (fast, medium and slow), we wanted to assess change across a full range of rates, as we had done for the /b/-/w/ contrast.

In our study, we obtained tokens of /bi/ and /pi/ from 3 speakers across a range of rates; each speaker produced approximately 350 tokens that varied in syllable duration from roughly 100–800msec. Of interest is how VOT varied across this range. The general pattern of results was the same for all three speakers; the data from one speaker are graphically

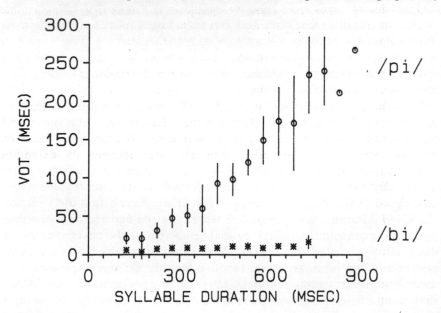

FIG. 3.3   Mean VOT values, in msec, of syllables within successive 50msec syllable duration intervals for a single speaker. The data points are plotted at the midpoint of the 50msec interval, and the error bars indicate plus and minus one standard deviation from the mean.

displayed in Fig. 3.3. For /b/, there was little change in VOT as syllable duration increased, but for /p/ there was a systematic increase in VOT. These data are in line with Summerfield's earlier findings and, like our /ba/-/wa/ data reported above, have clear implications for perception. Specifically, the criterion VOT value that optimally differentiates the /b/ and /p/ distributions is not constant, but increases with increasing syllable duration. The issue again is whether the perceptual system takes account of this, and treats VOT in a rate-dependent manner when categorising voiced and voiceless stop consonants. As we shall see in the next section, the answer again appears to be affirmative.

BASIC PHENOMENON OF RATE-DEPENDENT SPEECH PROCESSING

Let us begin our discussion by focussing on a single case, that of the /b/-/w/ distinction. Our acoustic measurements indicated that one important property distinguishing /b/ from /w/, duration of the initial formant transitions, was systematically influenced by a change in rate. We (Miller & Liberman, 1979) asked whether listeners take account of this modification during speech perception.

In order to investigate this, we synthesised a series of syllables that varied in transition duration and abruptness of amplitude onset so as to range from /ba/ to /wa/. Across this series, transition duration varied, in 4msec steps, from 16–64msec. (Since the amplitude reached its full value only by the end of the transition, this variation in transition duration was actually accompanied by a concomitant variation in the abruptness of the amplitude onset. For ease of explication, however, I refer to this complex change as one of transition duration alone.) The overall duration of each syllable in the series was 80msec. We then altered the rate (i.e., duration) of each stimulus in the series. This was accomplished by extending the steady-state portion of the syllable, which roughly corresponds to the vowel. By lengthening the syllable by various amounts we created 4 additional /ba/-/wa/ series, whose overall syllable durations were 116, 152, 224, and 296msec. For each of the five series, we expected that syllables with short transitions would be heard as /ba/ and those with longer transitions would be heard as /wa/. The critical question concerned the location of the /b/-/w/ crossover point. If, despite the effects of rate during production, listeners do not take account of changes in rate during perception, then the boundary will be located at the same transition duration for all five /ba/-/wa/ series. If, however, processing is done in a rate-dependent manner, then, as syllable duration becomes longer, the transition duration at the category boundary will also become longer.

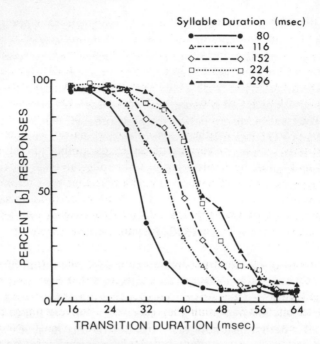

FIG. 3.4 Mean percentage of /b/ responses as a function of transition duration for five /ba/-/wa/ series that differ in syllable duration. (Miller & Liberman, 1979.)

In the experiment itself, many instances of each stimulus from each series were presented to listeners, who were asked to identify each syllable as /ba/ or /wa/. The group data are presented in Fig. 3.4. There was a highly reliable effect of syllable duration, indicating that listeners base their judgments of /b/-/w/ not on transition duration alone, but on transition duration in conjunction with syllable duration—clear evidence of rate-dependent perception.[2]

This basic phenomenon, a change in location of phonetic category boundary with a change in syllabic rate, is not limited to the /b/-/w/ contrast, but has been found for a number of acoustic properties that specify phonetic contrasts (for a review of this literature see Miller, 1981a). To take just one additional example, Summerfield (1981) has reported an analogous effect for a voicing contrast specified by VOT: As the syllables became longer, the criterion VOT value at the category boundary also became longer. Of course this is just what we would predict given the effect of rate on VOT values in production described earlier. The picture that begins to emerge, then, is one of a processing system that operates so as to

---

[2]For discussion of the precise fit of the perceptual data (Fig. 3.4) to the acoustic measurements (Fig. 3.2), see Miller and Baer, 1983.

adjust during perception for those changes in production that occur as a consequence of a change in speaking rate. This adjustment is reflected in a change in the criterion values of acoustic properties that differentiate phonetic segments. It should be noted, too, that the magnitude of these changes in category boundary location are often quite small. Nonetheless, they are highly reliable. For example, in the context of one of our subsequent studies on the /ba/-/wa/ contrast (Miller, Aibel, & Green, 1984) we have found highly reliable boundary shifts on the order of 1–2msec for successive 12msec increments in syllable duration. Data such as these have led us to view the adjustment for rate as a type of fine-tuning process that operates as the acoustic signal is analysed and mapped onto categorical phonetic representations.[3]

THE NATURE OF RATE-DEPENDENT SPEECH PROCESSING

In a series of investigations, we have begun to explore the nature of this fine-tuning process. Our research has been organised in terms of four primary questions, which are considered in turn.

Is the Adjustment for Changes in Rate Obligatory?

Consider the basic problem. During the course of normal conversation talkers change their rates of speech considerably and frequently. Thus, in order to engage effectively in conversation, the listener must make continual adjustments for speaking rate when processing the segmentally relevant properties of the speech signal. Given the need for such adjustments, it would be most efficient for the adjustment processes to be automatic in the sense of not requiring intent or conscious awareness (Posner & Snyder, 1975; Schneider & Shiffrin, 1977).

One way in which the adjustment for rate would be automatic is if it were

---

[3]An issue that has arisen in the literature is whether the mechanisms underlying this type of rate-dependent processing are part of a specialised system whose function is to derive the phonetic structure from the speech signal or, instead, are part of more general systems that are not specific to speech or language (cf. Liberman, 1982). It is interesting to note in this regard that effects analogous to some of those reviewed in this chapter have been demonstrated with nonspeech signals that have been patterned after speech signals (e.g., Pisoni, Carrell, and Gans, 1983). But it is not known whether the two sets of effects actually derive from the same underlying mechanism nor, if they do, whether this is a general processing mechanism that operates alike for speech and nonspeech or a speech-specific mechanism that has been mistakenly engaged by the nonspeech stimuli. For the present, then, the general issue remains unresolved.

built into the early perceptual processes themselves; that is to say, if those processes responsible for the initial analysis and/or interpretation of the speech signal functioned so as to take into account rate of speech. If adjustment for rate is a consequence of the operating characteristics of the early stages of speech processing, rather than a separate, auxilliary process, then not only would the adjustment for rate be automatic, but it would also be obligatory: In the course of deriving the phonetic structure of the utterance from the acoustic signal, the listener would necessarily take into account rate of speech. The strong prediction that follows from this line of reasoning is that there should be no set of circumstances under which the effect of rate would not be evidenced, and the effect of rate should not be under the strategic control of the subject (cf. Fodor, 1983; Pylyshyn, 1980).

Our first attempt to address the issue of obligatory processing (Miller, 1981b) grew directly out of our study of the /ba/-wa/ contrast described earlier. Recall that, in the original study (Miller & Liberman, 1979), subjects were asked to listen to each syllable and then indicate whether it was /ba/ or /wa/. Thus, due to the nature of the instructions, the listeners necessarily listened to the entire syllable before making an overt response; as the data clearly showed, they used information about syllable duration when making that response. But what if listeners were told *not* to wait until the entire syllable had been presented, but to indicate whether the syllable began with /b/ or /w/ as quickly as possible—would they be able to respond solely on the basis of the initial transitional information, ignoring the later-occurring syllable duration information?

In the new experiment, listeners were presented with randomised series of stimuli from 3 of the original /ba/-/wa/ series, those with overall syllable durations of 80, 152, and 224msec. They were told to indicate as quickly as possible whether each syllable began with /b/ or /w/ by pressing a response key; it was stressed that speed of responding was of utmost importance. Figure 3.5 presents the group identification data (top graph), as well as the group reaction time data (bottom graph). From the top graph it is clear that the requirement to respond quickly did not eliminate the effect. In fact, a comparison of these data with those from the original study revealed no diminution in the effect of rate.

The reaction time data shown in the bottom graph also reflect this use of later-occurring rate information. Each reaction-time curve has the form typical of speech experiments of this sort: Times are relatively fast for the stimuli closer to the endpoints of the series, and elevated for stimuli in the region of the category boundary. Thus, as the location of the category boundary changes, so too does the location of the elevated response times. However, the overall reaction times are also a function of syllable duration. On average, as the duration of the syllable increases, the time taken to

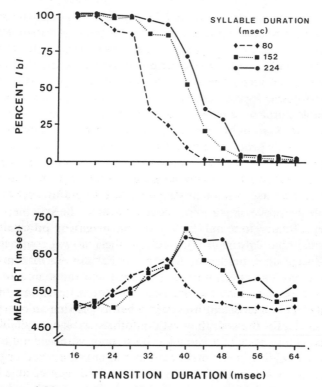

FIG. 3.5   Top panel: Mean percentage of /b/ responses as a function of transition duration for three /ba/-/wa/ series that differ in syllable duration. Bottom panel: Mean reaction times, in msec, for these identification responses. (Miller, 1981b.)

identify it also increases. Interestingly, this increase in reaction time is not limited to stimuli in the region of the boundary, that is, to stimuli whose identification depends on syllable duration. Even for those stimuli with long transition durations that are consistently identified as /w/, there is a reliable increase in reaction time with increasing syllable duration. This is not so for stimuli at the /b/ end of the series. Although the reason for this is not clear, it may be related to the fact that transition duration for /b/, unlike that for /w/, does not change with speaking rate during production. Whatever the reason for the asymmetry, however, the /w/ data suggest that in at least some cases rate plays a role in the identification process even when it does not affect the identification response itself.

There are two quite different ways in which the obligatory use of rate information within the syllable could come about. One possibility is that the processing unit of speech is the syllable per se (cf. Mehler, Segui, & Fraunfelder, 1981), and that the listener necessarily considers all information available in the syllable before making a response. In the /ba/-/wa/

case, the later-occurring durational information happens to be relevant, and thus is used when making the /b/-/w/ judgement. Another possibility is that the system does not treat speech in terms of set syllabic processing units as such, but instead considers precisely that stretch of speech that contains all the segmentally relevant information (cf. Eimas, Miller, & Jusczyk, in press). In the case of the /ba/-/wa/ contrast, the information about syllable duration is relevant and, consequently, the system takes that information into account. At least with respect to information about speaking rate, this process is obligatory.

One way of distinguishing these possibilities experimentally is to ask whether, for a contrast in which syllable duration is known not to play a role, it is still the case that, on average, it takes longer to respond to longer syllables. If the processing unit of speech is always the syllable, the answer will be yes; if the system only looks at later-occurring information in the syllable when the information is relevant, the answer will be no. We conducted such an experiment (Miller, 1981b) using a /ba/-/da/ contrast, for which the /b/-/d/ distinction was specified by a change in the form of the second- and third-formant transitions (Delattre, Liberman, & Cooper, 1955). For the experiment, we generated 2 /ba/-/da/ series that were identical except for the overall duration of the syllables, which was 80msec in one series and 260msec in the other. As expected, the change in syllable duration had no effect on identification responses. It was also the case, however, that the change in duration had no influence on response times. Thus, when the later-occurring information in the syllable was not relevant to the contrast being judged, listeners were able to respond solely on the basis of the relevant information at stimulus onset, without considering the entire syllable. These data strongly suggest that in the /ba/-/wa/ case, response times were affected by duration because the syllable contained relevant rate information and the processing system necessarily considers such information, and not because the system always considers all information within a syllabic unit.[4]

---

[4]The /ba/-/wa/ stimuli originally synthesised for Miller and Liberman (1979) and used in the subsequent reaction time experiment (Miller, 1981b) are patterned after natural speech, but they are schematised in certain ways. One of these involves the frequency values of the initial formant transitions: In natural speech these differ for /b/ and /w/, but in the original /ba/-/wa/ series they were kept constant. Recently, Blumstein (in press) reported that for /ba/-/wa/ series that varied not only in the duration of the initial transitions but also in their formant frequency values, syllable duration had little effect on identification responses. Taken together with the original findings, this result would appear to suggest that rate-dependent processing is employed only when listeners must base their /b/-/w/ decision on differences in transition duration.

But there is another possibility. Perhaps listeners always use all available relevant information in making the decision—for Blumstein's syllables, this would include both the transition

As indicated earlier, the /b/-/w/ distinction is but one of a family of contrasts whose perception is affected by a change in rate. If the adjustment for rate is truly an obligatory part of speech processing, it should be obligatory for all contrasts, regardless of the nature of the acoustic information underlying the phonetic distinction. An interesting case in point is the voicing contrast, specified by a change in VOT. As we saw earlier, a change in rate systematically alters the VOT values of (voiceless) consonants, and listeners adjust accordingly by treating VOT in relation to rate: As syllable duration increases, the VOT value at the voiced-voiceless category boundary also increases (Summerfield, 1981). But is this adjustment, like that for /ba/-/wa/, obligatory? Note that in the case of /ba/ and /wa/, the entire syllable is periodic, such that there is no simple change in acoustic form between the initial transitional segment and the later-occurring vocalic information. But this is not so for syllables varying in voicing as, for example, in the case of /bi/ versus /pi/. By their very nature, these syllables contain two quite distinct acoustic segments, the initial aperiodic segment and the periodic segment following the onset of voicing. The issue is whether, in this case, listeners are able to base their voicing judgments solely on the syllable-initial VOT information while ignoring the later-occurring information about syllable duration or whether here, too, the adjustment for speaking rate is obligatory.

To answer this question, we conducted a series of experiments focussing on the syllable-initial /b/-/p/ contrast, specified by a change in VOT (Miller, Dexter, & Pickard, 1984). Our primary interest was whether for this contrast, like the /b/-/w/ contrast, phonetic judgments would be influenced by syllable duration, even when the listener was under time pressure to respond as quickly as possible. But there was also a secondary purpose to the experiments. It is well known that phonetic perception can be influenced by many so-called "contextual" factors, not just speaking rate. One of these is the lexical status of the word to be identified, that is, whether the word constitutes an actual word of the language or a nonsense

---

duration and the formant frequency values of the transitions. But at least for stimuli near the category boundary, the formant frequency values carry the most weight, so that the effect of syllable duration—which operates through transition duration—is not seen in the identification responses. One test of this hypothesis would be to conduct a choice reaction time experiment with Blumstein's stimuli. We have seen that for the original /ba/-/wa/ stimuli, reaction time increases with increasing syllable duration and that in certain cases (the /wa/-end of the series), reaction time is affected by syllable duration, even though identification itself is not. Thus, reaction time is a particularly sensitive measure that can reflect the use of syllable duration in making the decision, even when the identification data do not do so. If the same reaction-time pattern were found for Blumstein's stimuli, we would have evidence that even for stimuli with variation in formant frequency values, listeners take account of the transition duration of the syllable during processing, and do so in a rate-dependent manner.

word. Ganong (1980) has shown that for words with acoustically ambiguous VOT values, the listener will tend to identify the initial consonant such that the word will form a real word, rather than a nonsense word. We were interested in comparing this lexical effect to the rate effect with respect to the obligatory issue.

The stimuli for the experiment were computer-edited tokens of natural speech. We created 4 series in all, each of which was composed of 13 consonant-vowel-consonant stimuli ranging in VOT value from 9–61msec. Stimuli with short VOT values were heard as beginning with /b/ and those with longer values were heard as beginning with /p/; the vowel was always /i/. The series differed from each other in two ways. First, 2 of the series had short syllables, 210msec in duration, and 2 had long syllables, 430msec in duration. Second, one 210 and one 430msec series ended with /f/, so as to create stimuli varying from the real word "beef" to the nonsense word "peef," whereas the other 210 and the other 430msec series ended with /s/, and created stimuli varying from the nonsense word "beace" to the real word "peace."

With this set of stimuli, it was possible to assess both the rate effect and the lexical effect as follows. With respect to the rate effect, we expected that for both the "beef"-"peef" and "beace"-"peace" sets, the /b/-/p/ category boundary would be located at a higher VOT value for the 430msec series than for the 210msec series. This would in effect be a replication of Summerfield's (1981) findings for the voicing contrast. As for the lexical effect, we expected that, for both the 210 and the 430msec sets, the /b/-/p/ category boundary would be located at a higher VOT value for the "beef"-"peef" series than the "beace"-"peace" series; that is to say, there would be a preponderance of responses yielding the real word "beef" on the "beef"-"peef" series, and the real word "peace" on the "beace"-"peace" series. This would in effect be a replication of Ganong's (1980) study. The critical question was whether these effects would be obtained not only in a standard identification task, but also in a speeded identification task.

In the first experiment of the series, the stimuli from all four series were randomised and presented to listeners. The listeners were fully informed as to the nature of the stimuli, that is, they were told they would be hearing one of four items, "beef" (a real word), "peef" (a nonsense word), "beace" (a nonsense word) or "peace" (a real word), and that there would be fast and slow versions of each. They were asked to listen to each word and then indicate whether it began with /b/ or /p/—a standard identification task, with no requirement to respond quickly. As the data in Fig. 3.6 indicate, we obtained both effects, as expected. For both the "beef"-"peef" and the "beace"-"peace" sets, the identification function is shifted toward longer VOT values for the longer stimuli (the rate effect), and for

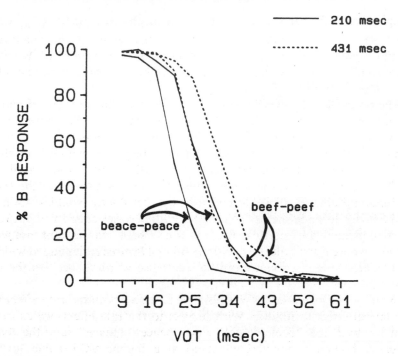

FIG. 3.6   Mean percentage of /b/ responses as a function of VOT value for a 210 and 430msec "beef"-"peef" series and a 210 and 430msec "beace"-"peace" series. (Based on Miller, Dexter, & Pickard, 1984.)

both the 210 and the 430msec sets, the identification function is shifted toward longer VOT values for the "beef"-"peef" series, compared to the "beace"-"peace" series (the lexical effect). Both effects were highly reliable.

Having established both effects successfully, we conducted a second experiment that was identical to the first, except that listeners were instructed to indicate whether each item began with /b/ or /p/ as quickly as possible. At issue, of course, was whether they were able to disregard the later-occurring information about rate and lexical status. The answer was a clear no—the data from this experiment were essentially identical to those of Fig. 3.6. Both the rate effect and the lexical effect were obtained under the speeded response task, and the magnitudes of the effects did not differ from those in the first experiment. Finally, in third and fourth experiments which employed a standard identification task and a speeded identification task, respectively, we found identical results when the listeners were told nothing about the nature of the stimuli, but simply were instructed that they would hear a sequence of speech items and that they were to indicate whether each began with /b/ or /p/. Even in this case, listeners apparently could not base their /b/-/p/ judgment solely on the basis of VOT information alone.

Taken together with our earlier studies of the /b/-/w/ contrast, the /b/-/p/ studies suggest that the use of rate information during phonetic perception may indeed be obligatory. For two very different kinds of contrasts, listeners apparently cannot make a phonetic judgment without taking account of rate, even when that rate information occurs later in the syllable. Interestingly, we also found in the /b/-/p/ studies that information regarding lexical status influenced phonetic judgments under all conditions. This at first suggests that lexical information, like rate information, might be obligatorily used in speech processing. But there is another possibility to consider, one which involves an interaction between these two factors. Perhaps the processing system always considers rate information when relevant to a phonetic contrast, as we have been arguing, but only considers lexical information when that information is already available. In the case of a contrast like /b/-/p/, the processing system obligatorily analyses the later-occurring information in the syllable with respect to rate and, at the same time, analyses that information with respect to the identity of the final consonant which, in conjunction with the initial consonant, defines lexical status. Since lexical status information is available, it is used in making the /b/-/p/ judgment. However, what if the contrast were not perceived in a rate-dependent manner, for example, a /b/-/d/ contrast? In that case, the listener does not need to analyse the later-occurring information in the syllable with respect to rate and (as we saw from the /ba/-/da/ reaction time experiment described earlier) there is evidence that the initial consonant can be identified on the basis of the onset information alone. It will be important to determine whether, for a contrast of this type, lexical status (as defined by the later-occurring information in the syllable) will still influence identification in a speeded response task.

Let us turn again to a consideration of the rate effect per se. Up to this point I have talked about this effect as if the critical information specifying rate were limited to the target word being identified. This is not so, however. It has been shown in a number of experiments that the rate of the surrounding sentence, especially the two or three syllables preceding the test word, systematically influences identification, although its influence is less than that of the rate of the target word itself (Port & Dalby, 1982; Summerfield, 1981; cf. Miller & Grosjean, 1981). Thus, word-external rate information, as well as word-internal rate information, plays a role in segmental processing. In my discussions of the obligatory issue so far, I have concentrated solely on rate information contained within the target word. But what about word-external rate information—is its influence also obligatory?

In an attempt to address this issue, we conducted a series of studies similar in form to those on word-internal rate information described earlier, again focussing on the voicing distinction (Miller, Green, & Schermer, 1984). Essentially, our strategy was to establish in a first experiment the word-external rate effect and then in subsequent experiments investigate whether this effect could be eliminated through a change in task requirements. That is, could we find conditions under which the identification of a target word was not influenced by the rate of its sentence context?

The stimuli for these experiments were computer-edited tokens of natural speech. The target words formed a 16-member series ranging from "bath" to "path"; the /b/-/p/ distinction was specified by a change in VOT, which ranged across the series from 7–73msec. Each target item was placed in a fast, medium, and slow version of the sentence frame "She is not thinking of the. . . ." On the basis of previous results, we expected that as the sentence frame became slower, the VOT value at the "bath"-"path" category boundary would become longer. In the first of three experiments, we randomised all test items and presented them to listeners, who were asked to perform two tasks on each trial. First, they were to indicate whether the target word was "bath" or "path" and second, they were to indicate whether the rate of the sentence frame was fast, medium, or slow. The latter task ensured that they would attend to the sentence context on each trial. The group identification functions, shown in Fig. 3.7, reveal the expected effect of sentence rate which, though small, was highly reliable.[5]

Having established the word-external rate effect, we proceeded to the second experiment, in which we asked whether the effect would also be obtained if on each trial the listener was required only to identify the word

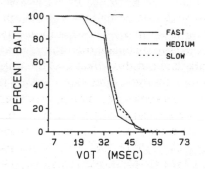

FIG. 3.7 Mean percentage of "bath" responses as a function of VOT value for a "bath"-"path" series in a fast, medium, and slow sentence context. (Miller, Green & Schermer, 1984.)

---

[5]That the effect was small was not unexpected, given the nature of the stimuli. Specifically, in constructing the stimuli we kept constant across sentence frames the rate of the "the" immediately preceding the "bath"-"path" target items, and it is known that the influence of word-external rate information decreases with distance from the target item (Summerfield, 1981). The reasons for constructing the stimuli in this manner are given in Miller, Green and Schermer, 1984.

as "bath" or "path," was not required to identify the rate of the sentence frame itself. Under these conditions, would the rate of the sentence frame still influence perception? The data from the second experiment mirrored those of the first, indicating that the answer was a clear yes. Thus, even when not explicitly required to attend to the sentential context of a word, its rate influenced the word's identification. Finally, in a third experiment, we attempted explicitly to focus the listener's attention on the target word at the expense of the sentence frame, by instructing the listener to identify the target word as "bath" or "path" as quickly as possible (of course, no identification of sentence rate was required). Again, the results of this study were as before; there was a highly reliable effect of the rate of the sentence frame on the location of the "bath"-"path" category boundary.

The three studies, considered together, indicate that listeners take account of the rate of the sentence context even when not explicitly required to do so, and even when attempting to identify the target word as quickly as possible. These results provide at least preliminary support for the hypothesis that word-external rate, like word-internal rate, plays an obligatory role in segmental perception. The results take on even more significance, however, when compared to those from a parallel series of studies conducted as part of the same investigation. In these studies, which employed the same "bath"-"path" target series as the rate studies, a different contextual effect was examined; that dealing with semantic congruity. Essentially, it had been shown previously that subjects tend to identify acoustically ambiguous target words such that they are semantically congruent with the sentence frame in which they occur, rather than incongruent (Garnes & Bond, 1976). We were interested in whether the semantic congruity effect, like the rate effect, would be obtained regardless of the requirement to attend to the sentential frame explicitly.

We investigated the semantic congruity effect by placing each of the "bath"-"path" target words in three sentence contexts (all produced at a moderate rate of speech): (1) She is not thinking of the . . . (neutral); (2) She needs hot water for the . . . (favours "bath"); and (3) She likes to jog along the . . . (favours "path"). We expected that, compared to the neutral "thinking" sentence, there would be more "bath" responses on the "hot water" sentence, leading to a higher VOT category boundary and, conversely, more "path" responses on the "likes to jog" sentence, leading to a lower VOT category boundary. Three experiments were conducted in all, analogous to the three rate experiments just described. In the first experiment, subjects were required on each trial to identify the target word as "bath" or "path" and to identify the sentence frame. Under these conditions, we obtained the expected semantic congruity effect. The second experiment was identical to the first, except that no identification of the sentence frame was required on each trial, only identification of the target word. Recall that under the analogous conditions, we still obtained the rate effect. In this case, however, the semantic congruity effect disappeared. And in the third experiment, in which speeded identification of the target word was required (and no sentence identification), we also failed to obtain the semantic congruity effect. These findings are important because of their marked contrast to the speaking rate data. Although it is easy to eliminate the influence of preceding semantic context on word identification, under precisely the same conditions the influence of preceding speaking rate prevails. This comparison lends force to the argument that the influence of speaking rate, whether word-internal or word-external, is not under strategic control of the subject, but is obligatory.

What is the Nature of the Critical Rate Information?

Up to this point, I have said little about the nature of the rate information to which the listener adjusts. A full account of the rate adjustment process will necessarily entail such a specification. There are many aspects to this issue; I will focus on three of them.

Characterisation of Acoustic Properties Conveying Rate Information

The first problem concerns how properly to characterise the properties of the speech signal that specify rate. Take as an example the case of /ba/ versus /wa/, which I have discussed at some length. When describing the /ba/-/wa/ perceptual rate effect (Miller & Liberman, 1979; Experiment 1), I talked of the influence of speaking rate, as specified by syllable duration, on the location of the /b/-/w/ category boundary. But we know that the nature of the critical rate information is more complex than simple syllable duration (cf. Summerfield, 1981). One such demonstration comes from a follow-up to the original /ba/-/wa/ study. In the follow-up study (Miller & Liberman, 1979; Experiment 3), we lengthened the syllables in one of the original /ba/-/wa/ series in two different ways: first, by extending the steady-state vocalic segment of each syllable and, second, by adding final transitions appropriate for the consonant /d/ to each syllable, thereby creating a series that ranged from /bad/ to /wad/. Although the overall syllable durations of the two resultant series were identical, the /b/-/w/ boundary locations were not. As before, extending the steady-state segment resulted in a shift of the boundary toward a longer transition duration, but adding the final transition segment had precisely the opposite effect. In other words, the acoustic-phonetic structure of the syllable, as well as its duration, contributes toward the specification of rate—although precisely how it does so is unknown (see Miller & Liberman, 1979, for further discussion).

The discussion so far has treated information for speaking rate as separate from the information proper for the phonetic contrast under test. In the /ba/-/wa/ case, for example, a distinction has been made between a critical property specifying the /b/-/w/ contrast, transition duration, and information specifying speaking rate; syllable duration. According to my characterisation of the basic phenomenon, when processing the transitional information listeners take into account the rate information. The important point is that on this type of account, rate information is extrinsic to the information about segmental identity, and is extracted separately during speech processing (cf. Fowler, 1977, 1980; Summerfield, 1981). A difficult, unresolved issue is how to characterise the critical rate information.

There is an alternative way of viewing the issue of rate-dependent processing, however, that solves the problem of specifying the rate information; it does so simply by eliminating it. On this view, the critical acoustic property specifying segmental identity—as properly characterised—actually remains invariant under transformations due to speaking rate. In a sense, timing information is intrinsic to the characterisation of the segment (Fowler, 1977, 1980; Summerfield, 1981). There is no need to extract rate information separately during perception because there is no need for a normalisation process as such. Phonetic perception is based solely on the (invariant) phonetically relevant acoustic properties.

Although such an intrinsic timing account eliminates the problem of how to specify the rate information, and does so in an elegant manner, it is not without its own problems. One of these is that it has been notoriously difficult to characterise the relevant acoustic properties specifying phonetic segments such that they in fact remain invariant under rate transformations. If there are such invariant properties, they remain to be discovered. But even if they do exist, there is yet another problem with an intrinsic timing account. This concerns the fact that, as noted earlier, the relevant rate information is not confined within the target syllable itself, but extends to both preceding and subsequent speech. Moreover, at least for preceding speech, relevant rate information extends to at least three syllables before the target—speech that is well removed from the acoustic consequences of the articulatory act that produced the segment in question (see Johnson & Strange, 1982; Miller, Green, & Schermer, 1984; Summerfield, 1981). It is very difficult to see how any specification of the critical segmental information could incorporate the properties of this distant speech. Thus, at least with respect to adjustments for word-external rate information, an extrinsic timing account appears to be required. Of course this raises the possibility that two processes are involved in what we have termed "rate adjustment"—one that accommodates for changes in word-internal rate and one that accommodates for changes in word-external rate. Our data on the obligatory issue, discussed earlier, suggest that if there are two distinct processes, the operation of each is obligatory.

Physical Versus Subjective Rate

Another aspect of the problem of how to characterise the critical rate information is whether it should be specified in terms of the physical rate of speech or the subjective rate of speech. To develop this issue, I consider again the case of /ba/-/wa/. Recall that in our original /ba/-/wa/ study (Miller & Liberman, 1979), we found that the location of the /b/-/w/ category boundary varied systematically as a function of syllable duration; as the syllable was lengthened, the boundary was shifted toward a longer transition duration. We interpreted this as an adjustment for a change in speaking rate, where speaking rate was specified by the change in syllable duration. But there are two distinct ways in which the change in syllable duration could have had its effect. The first is that the change in syllable duration produced a change in the subjective experience of the rate of the syllables—as they became longer, they were perceived to have been spoken at a slower rate of speech—and this change in subjective rate produced the change in boundary location. The second is that the change in subjective experience itself played no causal role but, instead, the change in boundary location was due directly to the change in the physical duration of the syllable, that is, to the physical rate of speech.

It is not possible to distinguish these alternatives on the basis of the original study, since the change in physical rate was confounded with a change in subjective rate. We (Miller, Aibel, & Green, 1984) thus designed an experiment in which physical and subjective rate could be dissociated. Specifically, we used a classic anchoring procedure (cf. Helson, 1964) to induce contrastive changes in subjective rate, while keeping physical rate constant. The target stimuli were syllables from a /ba/-/wa/ series with transition durations ranging from 16–60msec, and overall syllable duration of 116msec. These syllables were presented in three contextual conditions; neutral, fast, and slow. In the neutral condition, they were presented in the context of an equal number of fast (syllable duration of 80msec) and slow (syllable duration of 152msec) syllables. In the fast condition, they were presented with 3 times as many fast (80msec) as slow (152msec) syllables. Here we expected the 116msec target syllables to be perceived contrastively as relatively slow. In the slow condition, they were presented with 3 times as many slow (152msec) as fast (80msec) syllables. Here we expected the 116msec target syllables to be perceived contrastively as relatively fast. Given such induced shifts in subjective rate for the target syllables, the critical question was whether there would be a shift in the location of the

/b/-/w/ category boundary for these syllables. If subjective rate is the controlling factor, the answer will be yes; if instead physical rate is critical, the answer will be no.

In the experiment itself, we presented the stimuli in each of the three conditions to subjects, who were asked to perform two tasks on each trial. First, they were to identify each syllable as /ba/ or /wa/—a standard identification task—and second, they were to judge the speaking rate of each syllable—a rate judgment task. The latter was done by assigning a number from 1 to 10, with low numbers specifying a slow speaking rate and high numbers specifying a fast speaking rate. The top panel of Fig. 3.8 displays the results from the rate judgment task. Plotted are the rate judgments for the 116msec target syllables in each of the 3 conditions, along with the judgments for the fast (80msec) and slow (152msec)

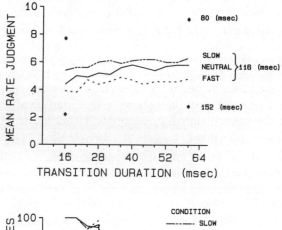

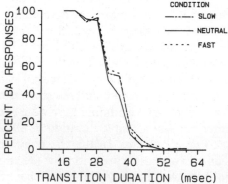

FIG. 3.8   Top panel: Mean rate judgment as a function of transition duration for syllables from a 116msec /ba/-/wa/ series in 3 anchoring conditions, as well as mean rate judgment for the fast (80msec) and slow (152msec) anchoring syllables. Bottom panel: Mean percentage of /ba/ responses as a function of transition duration for the 116msec /ba/-/wa/ series in the 3 anchoring conditions. (Miller, Aibel, & Green, 1984.)

anchoring syllables. Clearly, the anchoring procedure was successful in inducing contrastive shifts in subjective speaking rate for the 116msec target syllables, as expected. And these differences were highly reliable. However, the identification data, shown in the bottom panel of the figure, reveal no systematic influence of this change in subjective rate on /ba/-/wa/ judgments, and the functions do not differ reliably from one another. Moreover, in a control experiment we found that changes in subjective rate of the same magnitude as those induced by the anchoring procedure, when induced instead by a change in physical rate (syllable duration) itself, did lead to reliable shifts in the location of the identification function. It appears, then, that rate-dependent segmental processing is not mediated by changes in subjective speaking rate, but instead derives from changes in the physical characteristics of the speech signal that result from a change in rate.

Role of Visual Information for Speaking Rate

For some time, it has been known that visual information provided by the talker's face can play a role in the perception of speech. Typically this has been demonstrated by degrading speech in some fashion, for example, by presenting it in noise, and then showing that identification is enhanced if, along with the speech signal, appropriate visual information from the talker's face is also presented (e.g., Erber, 1969). More recently, however, it has been argued that visual information plays more than a compensatory role in speech perception. Essentially, McGurk and MacDonald (1976) discovered that, in specified cases, an undistorted auditory syllable presented in synchrony with a different visual syllable will lead to the percept of a single, coherent syllable that combines information from the auditory and visual syllables (see also Massaro & Cohen, 1983; Summerfield, 1979). For example, if the auditory syllables /ba/-/ba/ are presented in synchrony with the visual syllables /ga/-/ga/, many subjects report perceiving /da/-/da/. What is particularly interesting is that subjects are not always aware of the bimodal discrepancy; the phenomenal experience is often that of a single unified phonetic event. Data such as these are important in that they suggest that the processing system responsible for phonetic perception integrates relevant segmental information from the visual and auditory modalities and, moreover, that the output of the phonetic processor is an abstract, amodal phonetic representation (for further discussion, see Liberman, 1982; Summerfield, 1979).

In light of the current interest in the role of visual information in speech processing, we asked whether visual information about timing, as well as visual information about segmental identity per se, plays a role in speech perception. More specifically, some of the articulatory gestures that underlie a speaker's change in rate are visible on the face and, hence, provide potential visual information about speaking rate. Does this visual rate information influence phonetic perception?

Our experimental strategy (Green & Miller, 1985) was to pair acoustic tokens of the syllables /bi/ and /pi/, which were produced by a talker at a medium rate of speech, with a video display of the same talker producing these syllables at fast and slow rates of speech. The phenomenal experience that resulted from any particular audio-visual pairing was that of a unified single syllable, spoken at a single rate of speech. We asked the following two questions: First, would the visual information affect judgments of the speaking rate of the perceived syllable? Second, and more importantly, would the visual information about rate affect identification of the perceived syllable as /bi/ or /pi/?

The investigation involved three steps. The first step was concerned with the auditory stimuli that were to be paired with the visual stimuli. These were generated from a naturally produced /bi/ and /pi/. A computer-editing technique was used to modify these syllables so as to create a series of 13 syllables that varied in VOT from 7–57msec, and were perceived as ranging from /bi/ to /pi/. Overall syllable duration was 210msec. Before pairing these stimuli with the visual tokens, it was important to establish that an acoustic change in syllable duration would yield the expected rate effect. Thus we modified the vowel duration of each syllable in the 13-member series, thereby creating 2 new series with overall syllable durations of 161 and 302msec. Numerous randomisations of the syllables from all three series were presented to listeners, who were asked to perform two tasks. First, they were to judge the rate of each syllable using a scale from 1 to 10, with low numbers signifying a slow speaking rate and high numbers signifying a fast speaking rate. Second, the listeners were asked to identify each syllable as /bi/ or /pi/. The results of this first experiment were clear-cut: As syllable duration increased, the syllables were judged to be slower and, most importantly, the /b/-/p/ category boundary was located at a progressively longer VOT value. Both effects were highly reliable. Thus we demonstrated that, for the 210msec /bi/-/pi/ series, an acoustically based change in rate affected phonetic perception.

The second step of the investigation was to create the visual stimuli that were to be paired with the members of the 210msec /bi/-/pi/ series just described. This was done by asking the same speaker to say fast tokens of /bi/ and /pi/ and slow tokens of /bi/ and /pi/ while we videotaped his productions. The video display, without sound, provided the visual stimuli. The rationale of the investigation demanded that these visual stimuli provide information about speaking rate, but no direct information about segmental identity as /bi/ or /pi/ per se. To ensure that this was so, we presented numerous randomisations of the visual stimuli to observers, who were asked to perform two tasks: Judge the speaking rate of each syllable using a scale from 1 to 10, and identify each stimulus as /bi/ or /pi/. The results of this study were also clearcut. The observers readily judged the visual stimuli to differ in rate—a mean rating of 8.2 for the fast syllables and 2.4 for the slow syllables—but they were unable to identify them as /bi/ or /pi/ better than would be expected by chance. Thus, the visual stimuli did provide information about rate, but not about segmental identity.

In the third and final step of the investigation, we paired each member of the 210msec auditory /bi/-/pi/ series with an equal number of fast and slow visual /bi/'s and /pi/'s. As noted earlier, the phenomenal percept that resulted from any given audio-visual pairing was that of a unified single syllable, spoken at a single rate of speech.[6] Numerous randomisations of these audio-visual stimuli were presented to subjects who were asked first to judge the rate of each using a 1–10 scale and, second, to identify each as /bi/ or /pi/.

The top panel of Fig. 3.9 displays the results from the rating task, which revealed a highly reliable effect of visual information on judgments of speaking rate. When the syllables from the 210msec acoustic series were paired with the fast visual stimuli they received relatively high rate judgments, and when they were paired with the slow visual stimuli they received relatively low rate judgments. Did the visual information also influence the identification of the syllables as /bi/ or /pi/? As the bottom panel of Fig. 3.9 shows, the answer is yes. The identification function is located toward shorter VOT values when the visual information specifies a fast speaking rate and it is located toward longer VOT values when it specifies a slow speaking rate; this difference was highly reliable. This is, of course, precisely the pattern of results found in the first experiment, when we actually manipulated the rate of the auditory stimuli themselves. It appears, then, that visual as well as auditory timing information can influence segmental perception. This suggests that at least part of the effect of rate on segmental perception derives from operations beyond those provided by the auditory system itself (cf. Pisoni, 1983), perhaps operations at the level at which auditory and visual information combine to yield an amodal, phonetic representation.

Two comments are in order regarding the relation of this finding to our earlier results. First, although we have found that visual timing information influences both the judged rate of the audio-visual syllables and their identification as /bi/ or /pi/, we do not know whether there is a causal relation between the two effects. In the previous section of the chapter, I discussed

---

[6]For details of the way in which the auditory and visual syllables were paired, as well as further discussion of the failure to notice the asynchrony in the visual and auditory information, see Green and Miller, 1985.

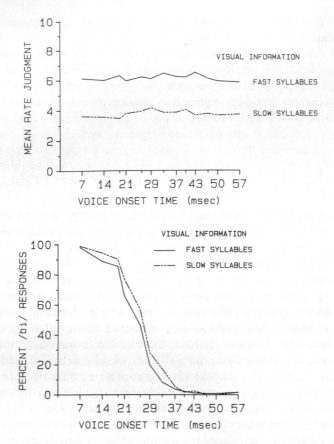

FIG. 3.9   Top panel: Mean rate judgment as a function of VOT value for syllables from a 210msec auditory /bi/-/pi/ series when paired with fast and slow visual syllables. Bottom panel: Mean percentage of /bi/ responses as a function of VOT value for these audio-visual syllables. (Green & Miller, 1985.)

evidence that, at least for auditory syllables, a change in segmental identity does not derive from a change in the subjective experience of the syllable's rate, but is based on a change in the physical rate of the syllable. An open issue is whether, for the audio-visual stimuli, identification also depends on a physically-based metric of rate—in this case a metric derived from both acoustic and optical information—or whether here a change in subjective rate is the causal factor. An experiment with audio-visual syllables that dissociates physical changes in rate from their subjective consequences should help resolve this issue.

Second, in this chapter I have raised the possibility that the listener's adjustment for rate is obligatory. The evidence presented in support of this hypothesis was based solely on experiments with auditory stimuli. A question raised by the present findings is whether the adjustment for visual timing information is obligatory as well. Although the answer to this is not yet known, we have replicated the visual rate effect when subjects were asked only to identify each syllable as /bi/ or /pi/, and not also to judge its rate. Thus it is at least the case that visual timing information influences segmental identity even when attention is not explicitly directed toward the changes in rate.

Do Adjustments for Rate Only Shift the Location of Phonetic Category Boundaries or Restructure the Mapping Between Acoustic Signal and Phonetic Categories?

Consider again the basic phenomenon. A change in speaking rate produces a systematic modification in the durations of temporal acoustic properties that specify segmental distinctions, and listeners adjust appropriately for these changes during speech processing.

The primary indicant of this adjustment for rate has been a shift in the criterion value of the critical property that perceptually distinguishes the two segments in question; that is to say, the value at the category boundary changes as speaking rate changes. Is it the case, however, that the change in category boundary location is, itself, the basic consequence of the adjustment process (whatever the underlying perceptual mechanism) or, alternatively, is this shift in boundary value part of a more comprehensive change in the mapping between acoustic signal and phonetic segment?

We have only begun to explore this issue systematically, but we have some data that are highly suggestive (Miller, Connine, Schermer, & Kluender, 1983). This study stemmed from a notion that phonetic categories may be structured in terms of prototypic, or "best" exemplars. Consider, as an example, a /ba/-/wa/ contrast and, in particular, a speech series that ranges from syllables with very short to very long transition durations. The category boundary on the series is located at some given transition duration value; stimuli with shorter transitions are perceived as /ba/ and those with longer transitions are perceived as /wa/. But all stimuli within a given category are not equally good representatives of the category. Informal listening reveals that, as the stimulus value begins to move away from the boundary, the syllable becomes a better exemplar of the category in question; that is, a better /ba/ as the transition becomes shorter and a better /wa/ as the transition becomes longer. However, if the transition value becomes too extreme in either direction, the syllable begins to be perceived as a less good exemplar of the category. In essence, then, phonetic categories would appear to have internal structure, with certain members serving as best exemplars, or prototypes (cf. Repp, 1977; Samuel, 1982).

In our investigation, we used a selective adaptation technique (cf. Eimas & Corbit, 1973) to assess the internal structure of phonetic categories. In the typical adaptation procedure, identification of members of a speech series (such as the /ba/-/wa/ series just described) is assessed before and after repeated exposure to a member of the series. A major consequence of this exposure is that identification of the stimuli, most notably in the boundary region, is altered such that fewer stimuli are identified as being members of the category of the adaptor after adaptation, compared to before adaptation. We were interested in whether members of a category would vary in effectiveness as adaptors, presumably reflecting differences in category goodness. For three series (/ba/-/pa/, /dae/-/gae/, /bae/-/wae/), we found that as the adaptor varied from a value near the boundary to one well within the category, the magnitude of adaptation progressively increased. However, beyond a certain value it progressively decreased. Thus we obtained nonmonotonic adaptation functions. We interpreted these as reflecting an underlying internal category structure, with certain category members being prototypic. (See Miller et al., 1983, for a discussion of the level of processing at which this structure may arise.)

As mentioned, one of the series we tested was /bae/-/wae/. As it happens,

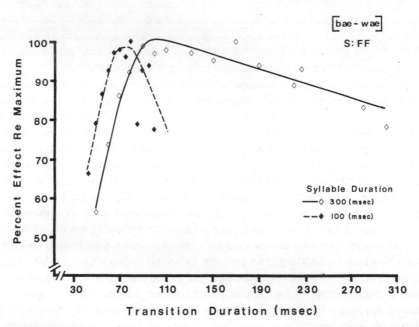

FIG. 3.10   Magnitude of adaptation effect as a function of the transition duration of the adapting stimulus for /bae/-/wae/ series with overall syllable durations of 100 and 300msec. The curves are fit by eye. (Based on figures and data in Miller, Connine, Schermer, & Kluender, 1983.)

the syllables had a duration of 300msec. From our previous work, we knew that if we reduced overall syllable duration to 100msec, the /b/-/w/ boundary would shift toward a shorter transition duration value—the standard rate effect. But would the mapping between internal category structure and transition duration, as revealed by the adaptation procedure, also shift? That is, if the entire adaptation experiment were carried out with 100msec syllables instead of 300msec syllables, would the adaptation function be shifted toward shorter transition durations, including that syllable that yielded maximal adaptation? We conducted this experiment and found the answer to be yes. This is shown in Fig. 3.10, which displays separately for the 100 and the 300msec /bae/-/wae/ syllables the magnitude of adaptation as a function of the transition duration of the adaptor. It is apparent that the adaptation function shifts with a change in syllable duration.

These data provide at least tentative evidence that the adjustment for a change in rate involves more than a shift in the criterion value that distinguishes phonetic categories. Instead, it may involve a comprehensive change in the mapping between acoustic value and phonetic category structure—a change which includes not only the location of the category boundary itself, but also the location of the prototypic category members.

What are the Ontogenetic Origins of Rate-Dependent Speech Processing?

The final issue to be considered concerns the ontogenetic origins of the type of rate-dependent processing that we have been discussing. Two major possibilities can be distinguished. On the one hand, it may be that the rate-dependent processing we have observed in adults arises in the course of language acquisition, perhaps as the young child begins to acquire the phonological and/or lexical system of a given language. Alternatively, more than a decade of research has shown that the young infant brings to the task of language acquisition highly sophisticated mechanisms for the processing of speech (for a review, see Jusczyk, 1984). Perhaps rate-dependency is an aspect of this presumably innate processing ability.

One way to address the issue experimentally is to assess whether young, pre-articulate infants show any evidence of processing speech in a rate-dependent fashion. We have undertaken such an investigation (Eimas & Miller, 1980; Miller & Eimas, 1983) with three–four-month-old infants. In designing our experiment, we took advantage of the fact that, for adults, a change in rate alters not only the identification of stimuli along a speech continuum, but their discriminability as well. Recall that in our original experiment (Miller & Liberman, 1979), we found that as syllable duration increased, the /b/-/w/ boundary was located at a progressively longer transition duration. It is typically the case that for any given speech series, stimuli drawn from one category (in this case, two /ba/'s or two /wa/'s) are considerably more difficult to discriminate than are stimuli drawn from different categories (one /ba/ and one /wa/). This results in a peak in the discrimination function in the vicinity of the category boundary. We might expect, then, that as syllables in a /ba/-/wa/ series are lengthened, there is not only a shift in the location of the identification function, but also a concomitant shift in the location of the discrimination function. That is to say, which syllables are discriminated best would depend jointly on transition duration and syllable duration. In a follow-up experiment (Miller, 1980) which focussed on the 80 and 296msec series, we found that this is indeed the case. As Fig. 3.11 shows, a change in syllable duration from 80 to 296msec produced a shift toward longer transition durations of both the identification function (top panel) and the discrimination function (bottom panel). Thus, when adult listeners are discriminating stimuli varying in transition duration, they take into account not only transition duration per se, but also the overall duration of the syllable.

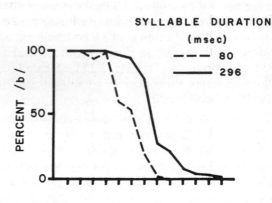

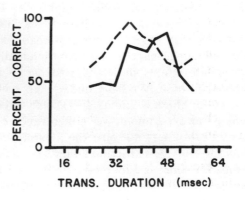

FIG. 3.11 Top panel: Mean percentage of /b/ responses as a function of transition duration for /ba/-/wa/ series with overall syllable durations of 80 and 296msec. Bottom panel: Percent correct discrimination of pairs of syllables that differ by 16msec of transition duration, from each series. The discrimination data points are plotted at the transition duration midway between the transition durations of the stimuli in the pair. (Miller, 1980.)

Given that sensitivity to rate (syllable duration) is reflected in discrimination performance, we were able to use an infant discrimination paradigm to assess the early existence of rate-dependent processing. Our experiment was based on the well-established finding that young infants process speech stimuli in a categorical-like fashion: If infants are tested on two exemplars from a given phonetic category, they typically show evidence of discrimination, whereas if they are tested on two exemplars from different phonetic categories, they typically do not. I should note that since languages differ in the precise location of phonetic category boundaries, and in the number of categories along any given continuum, the infants' categories do not necessarily match those of the parental language at the outset, and thus require modification in the course of acquiring the phonological system of the parental language (for a recent review of this literature, see Eimas et al., in press). The important point for our purposes, however, is simply that infants do categorise stimuli along speech continua. The issue at hand is whether they take account of speaking rate when doing so.

The design of the experiment was as follows. Discrimination was assessed on 4 pairs of stimuli, 2 from the 80msec /ba/-/wa/ series and 2 from the 296msec /ba/-/wa/ series. For each series, one pair consisted of the stimuli with transition durations of 16 and 40msec, and the other consisted of the stimuli with transition durations of 40 and 64msec. Note that the adult category boundary (see Fig. 3.11) is located between 16 and 40msec on the 80msec series, but between 40 and 64msec on the 296msec series. Thus, for the 80msec series, the 16msec stimulus (/ba/) and the 40msec stimulus (/wa/) are easily discriminated, but the 40msec stimulus and the 64msec stimulus (both /wa/) are not. Precisely the opposite is true of the stimuli from the 296msec series. In this case, the 16msec and the 40msec stimulus (both /ba/) are not easily discriminated, but the 40msec stimulus (/ba/) and the 64msec stimulus (/wa/) are readily differentiated. If the infant's categories, like the adult's, are determined by transition duration in conjunction with syllable duration, we should obtain the same pattern of results in the infant experiment: For the 80msec syllables, the infants should discriminate the 16–40 pair but not the 40–64 pair, whereas for the 296msec syllables, they should discriminate the 40–64 pair but not the 16–40 pair.

To assess infant discrimination, we used a variant of the high-amplitude-sucking procedure (see Miller & Eimas, 1983, for details). Infants were divided into five groups, one experimental group corresponding to each of the four pairs of stimuli to be tested, and one control group. Each infant was tested individually. The basic procedure is as follows. At the outset of the session, a baseline reading of the infant's high-amplitude sucking responses is obtained. Subsequently, the pretest phase of the experiment is initiated, in which one member of the pair of sounds to be tested is presented contingent upon the infant's sucking behaviour. This typically results in an increase in sucking responses, followed by a decrease in sucking. At a set point, the postshift phase of the session is introduced, in which the other member of the pair is now presented contingent upon sucking, rather than the original. A renewed increase in sucking responses, compared to the responses of control infants who receive the original sound throughout, is taken as evidence of discrimination. The specific dependent measure we used was the difference in sucking rate between the first two minutes of the postshift phase and the last two minutes of the preshift phase of the session. A positive difference score indicates an increase in sucking rate, whereas a negative difference score indicates a decrease in rate.

The data from the five groups of infants are shown in Fig. 3.12. It is plain that discrimination depended jointly on the transition duration and the syllable duration of the stimuli: The only groups to reliably differ from the control group were those that heard the 16–40 pair for the 80msec series and the 40–64 pair for the 296msec series. This pattern of results suggests that, in categorising stimuli along a /ba/-/wa/ series, infants, like adults, take into account changes in speaking rate, in this case specified by a change in

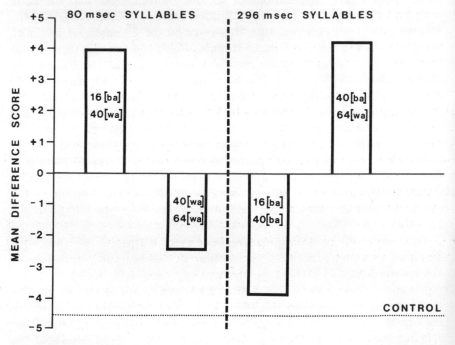

FIG. 3.12   Mean difference scores for four experimental groups and one control group of infants. (Miller & Eimas, 1983.)

syllable duration. Thus at least the rudiments of the ability to adjust for changes in rate during speech processing exist in early infancy.

CONCLUDING REMARKS

Our research has been concerned with the earliest stages of language processing, during which the listener derives the phonetic structure of the utterance. We have focussed on one very specific aspect of this process: How the listener is able to perceive speech despite the fact that its form varies considerably as a consequence of changes in speaking rate.

Taken together, and in conjunction with related work in the literature, our studies suggest that this is accomplished through a process of fine-tuning that operates during the course of speech perception. This process serves to alter the mapping between acoustic (and perhaps visual) signal and phonetic structure, taking into account the changes due to speaking rate that arise during production. This alteration in mapping entails a change in the location of the boundaries between categories and perhaps even the internal structure of the categories. Furthermore, it appears that this fine-tuning may be an integral, obligatory part of speech processing: Not only do listeners take account of changes in rate when perceiving speech, but they appear to be unable to perceive speech without doing so. Finally, our work with young infants suggests that at least certain aspects of this fine-tuning process are operative very early in life, before the onset of language.

The existence of rate-dependent speech processing thus appears to be firmly established, and we are even beginning to understand some of its dimensions. A major challenge for future research is to explicate the nature of the mechanisms that underlie this aspect of the earliest stages of spoken language understanding.

ACKNOWLEDGEMENTS

This research was supported in part by NIH Grant NS 14394 and NIH RCDA NS 00661 to the author, and by NIH BRSG RR 07143 to Northeastern University. Special thanks are due to Peter D. Eimas for valuable comments on an earlier version of the chapter.

REFERENCES

Blumstein, S. E. (in press) On acoustic invariance in speech. In J. S. Perkell & D. H. Klatt (Eds.), *Invariance and Variability of Speech Processes*. Hillsdale, New Jersey: Lawrence Erlbaum Associates Inc.

Blumstein, S. E., Isaacs, E., & Mertus, J. (1982) The role of the gross spectral shape as a perceptual cue to place of articulation in initial stop consonants. *Journal of the Acoustical Society of America, 72,* 43–50.

Cooper, W. E., Ebert, R. R., & Cole, R. A. (1976) Perceptual analysis of stop consonants and glides. *Journal of Experimental Psychology: Human Perception and Performance, 2,* 92–104.

Dalston, R. M. (1975) Acoustic characteristics of English /w,r,l/ spoken correctly by young children and adults. *Journal of the Acoustical Society of America, 57,* 462–469.

Delattre, P. C., Liberman, A. M., & Cooper, F. S. (1955) Acoustic loci and transitional cues for consonants. *Journal of the Acoustical Society of America, 27,* 769–773.

Diehl, R. L., Souther, A. F., & Convis, C. L. (1980) Conditions on rate normalisation in speech perception. *Perception and Psychophysics, 27,* 435–443.

Eimas, P. D. & Corbit, J. D. (1973) Selective adaptation of linguistic feature detectors. *Cognitive Psychology, 4,* 99–109.

Eimas, P. D. & Miller, J. L. (1980) Contextual effects in infant speech perception. *Science, 209,* 1140–1141.

Eimas, P. D., Miller, J. L., & Jusczyk, P. W. (in press) On infant speech perception and the acquisition of language. In S. Harnad (Ed.), *Categorical Perception*. New York: Cambridge University Press.

Erber, N. P. (1969) Interaction of audition and vision in the recognition of oral speech stimuli. *Journal of Speech and Hearing Research, 12,* 423–425.

Fant, G. (1960) *Acoustic Theory of Speech Production*. The Hague: Mouton.

Fischer-Jorgensen, E. (1954) Acoustic analysis of stop consonants. *Miscellanea Phonetica, II,* 42–59.

Fodor, J. A. (1983) *The Modularity of Mind*. Cambridge, Massachusetts: The MIT Press.

Forster, K. I. (1979) Levels of processing and the structure of the language processor. In W. E. Cooper & E. C. T. Walker (Eds.), *Sentence Processing: Psycholinguistic Studies Presented to Merrill Garrett*. Hillsdale, New Jersey: Lawrence Erlbaum Associates Inc.

Fowler, C. A. (1977) *Timing Control in Speech Production*. Bloomington: Indiana University Linguistics Club.

Fowler, C. A. (1980) Coarticulation and theories of extrinsic timing. *Journal of Phonetics, 8,* 113–133.

Ganong, W. F. III (1980) Phonetic categorisation in auditory word perception. *Journal of Experimental Psychology: Human Perception and Performance, 6,* 110–125.

Garnes, S. & Bond, Z. S. (1976) The relationship between semantic expectation and acoustic information. *Phonologica,* 285–293.

Gay, T. (1978) Effect of speaking rate on vowel formant transitions. *Journal of the Acoustical Society of America, 63,* 223–230.

Goldman-Eisler, F. (1968) *Psycholinguistics: Experiments in Spontaneous Speech*. New York: Academic Press.

Green, K. P. & Miller, J. L. (1985) On the role of visual rate information in phonetic perception. *Perception and Psychophysics, 38,* 269–276.

Grosjean, F. & Deschamps, A. (1975) Analyse contrastive des variables temporelles de l'anglais et due français: Vitesse de parole et variables composants, phénomènes d'hésitation. *Phonetica, 31,* 144–184.

Helson, H. (1964) *Adaptation Level Theory*. New York: Harper & Row.

Johnson, T. L. & Strange, W. (1982) Perceptual constancy of vowels in rapid speech. *Journal of the Acoustical Society of America, 72,* 1761–1770.

Jusczyk, P. W. (1984) On characterising the development of speech perception. In J. Mehler & R. Fox (Eds.), *Neonate Cognition: Beyond the Blooming, Buzzing Confusion*. Hillsdale, New Jersey: Lawrence Erlbaum Associates Inc.

Klatt, D. H. (1976) Linguistic uses of segmental duration in English: Acoustic and perceptual evidence. *Journal of the Acoustical Society of America, 59*, 1208–1221.

Lehiste, I. (1972) The timing of utterances and linguistic boundaries. *Journal of the Acoustical Society of America, 51*, 2018–2024.

Liberman, A. M. (1982) On finding that speech is special. *American Psychologist, 37*, 301–323.

Liberman, A. M., Cooper, F. S., Shankweiler, D. P., & Studdert-Kennedy, M. (1967) Perception of the speech code. *Psychological Review, 74*, 430–461.

Liberman, A. M., Delattre, P. C., Gerstman, L. J., & Cooper, F. S. (1956) Tempo of frequency change as a cue for distinguishing classes of speech sounds. *Journal of Experimental Psychology, 52*, 127–137.

Lisker, L. & Abramson, A. S. (1964) A cross language study of voicing of initial stops: Acoustical measurements. *Word, 20*, 384–422.

Lisker, L. & Abramson, A. S. (1970) The voicing dimension: Some experiments in comparative phonetics. In *Proceedings of the Sixth International Congress of Phonetic Sciences*. Prague: Academia.

Mack, M. & Blumstein, S. E. (1983) Further evidence of acoustic invariance in speech production: The stop-glide contrast. *Journal of the Acoustical Society of America, 73*, 1739–1750.

Marslen-Wilson, W. D. & Tyler, L. K. (1980) The temporal structure of language understanding. *Cognition, 8*, 1–71.

Massaro, D. W. & Cohen, M. M. (1983) Evaluation and integration of visual and auditory information in speech perception. *Journal of Experimental Psychology: Human Perception and Performance, 9*, 753–771.

McGurk, H. & MacDonald, J. (1976) Hearing lips and seeing voices. *Nature, 264*, 746–748.

Mehler, J., Segui, J., & Fraunfelder, U. (1981) The role of the syllable in language acquisition and perception. In T. Meyers, J. Laver, & J. Anderson (Eds.), *The Cognitive Representation of Speech*. Amsterdam: North-Holland.

Miller, J. L. (1980) Contextual effects in the discrimination of stop consonant and semivowel. *Perception and Psychophysics, 28*, 93–95.

Miller, J. L. (1981a) Effects of speaking rate on segmental distinctions. In P. D. Eimas & J. L. Miller (Eds.), *Perspectives on the Study of Speech*. Hillsdale, New Jersey: Lawrence Erlbaum Associates Inc.

Miller, J. L. (1981b) Some effects of speaking rate on phonetic perception. *Phonetica, 38*, 159–180.

Miller, J. L., Aibel, I. L., & Green, K. (1984) On the nature of rate-dependent processing during phonetic perception. *Perception and Psychophysics, 35*, 5–15.

Miller, J. L. & Baer, T. (1983) Some effects of speaking rate on the production of /b/ and /w/. *Journal of the Acoustical Society of America, 73*, 1751–1755.

Miller, J. L., Connine, C. M., Schermer, T. M., & Kluender, K. R. (1983) A possible auditory basis for internal structure of phonetic categories. *Journal of the Acoustical Society of America, 73*, 2124–2133.

Miller, J. L., Dexter, E. R., & Pickard, K. A. (1984) Influence of speaking rate and lexical status on word identification. *Journal of the Acoustical Society of America, 76*, S89.

Miller, J. L. & Eimas, P. D. (1983) Studies on the categorisation of speech by infants. *Cognition, 13*, 135–165.

Miller, J. L., Green, K., & Schermer, T. M. (1984) A distinction between the effects of sentential speaking rate and semantic congruity on word identification. *Perception and Psychophysics, 36*, 329–337.

Miller, J. L. & Grosjean, F. (1981) How the components of speaking rate influence perception of phonetic segments. *Journal of Experimental Psychology: Human Perception and Performance, 7*, 208–215.

Miller, J. L., Grosjean, F., & Lomanto, C. (1984) Articulation rate and its variability in spontaneous speech: A reanalysis and some implications. *Phonetica, 41*, 215–225.

Miller, J. L. & Liberman, A. M. (1979) Some effects of later-occurring information on the perception of stop consonant and semivowel. *Perception and Psychophysics, 25*, 457–465.

Morton, J. (1979) Word recognition. In J. Morton & J. C. Marshall (Eds.), *Psycholinguistics 2: Structures and Processes*. Cambridge, Massachusetts: The MIT Press.

O'Connor, J. D., Gerstman, L. J., Liberman, A. M., Delattre, P. C., & Cooper, F. S. (1957) Acoustic cues for the perception of initial /w,j,r,l/ in English. *Word, 13*, 25–43.

Peterson, G. E. & Barney, H. L. (1952) Control methods used in a study of the vowels. *Journal of the Acoustical Society of America, 24*, 175–184.

Pickett, J. M. & Decker, L. R. (1960) Time factors in perception of a double consonant. *Language and Speech, 3*, 11–17.

Pisoni, D. B. & Luce, P. A. (in press) Acoustic-phonetic representations in word recognition. *Cognition*.

Pisoni, D. B., Carrell, T. D., & Gans, S. J. (1983) Perception of the duration of rapid spectrum changes in speech and nonspeech signals. *Perception and Psychophysics, 34*, 314–322.

Port, R. F. (1981) Linguistic timing factors in combination. *Journal of the Acoustical Society of America, 69*, 262–274.

Port, R. F. & Dalby, J. (1982) Consonant/vowel ratio as a cue for voicing in English. *Perception and Psychophysics, 32*, 141–152.

Posner, M. I. & Snyder, C. F. (1975) Attention and cognitive control. In R. Solso (Ed.), *Information Processing and Cognition*. Hillsdale, New Jersey: Lawrence Erlbaum Associates Inc.

Pylyshyn, A. (1980) Computation and cognition: Issues in the foundations of cognitive science. *Behavioural and Brain Sciences, 3*, 111–132.

Repp, B. H. (1977) Dichotic competition of speech sounds: The role of acoustic stimulus structure. *Journal of Experimental Psychology: Human Perception and Performance, 3*, 37–50.

Repp, B. H. (1982) Phonetic trading relations and context effects: New experimental evidence for a speech mode of perception. *Psychological Bulletin, 92*, 81–110.

Samuel, A. G. (1982) Phonetic prototypes. *Perception and Psychophysics, 31*, 307–314.

Schneider, W. & Shiffrin, R. M. (1977) Controlled and automatic human information processing: I. Detection, search, and attention. *Psychological Review, 84*, 1–66.

Schwab, E. C., Sawusch, J. R., & Nusbaum, H. C. (1981) The role of second-formant transitions in the stop-semivowel distinction. *Perception and Psychophysics, 29*, 121–128.

Shinn, P. & Blumstein, S. E. (1984) On the role of the amplitude envelope for the perception of [b] and [w]. *Journal of the Acoustical Society of America, 75*, 1243–1252.

Stevens, K. N. & Blumstein, S. E. (1981) The search for invariant acoustic correlates of phonetic features. In P. D. Eimas & J. L. Miller (Eds.), *Perspectives on the Study of Speech*. Hillsdale, New Jersey: Lawrence Erlbaum Associates Inc.

Summerfield, A. Q. (1975) Aerodynamics versus mechanics in the control of voicing onset in consonant-vowel syllables. *Speech Perception* (No. 4), Department of Psychology, Queen's University of Belfast.

Summerfield, Q. (1979) Use of visual information for phonetic perception. *Phonetica, 36*, 314–331.

Summerfield, Q. (1981) On articulatory rate and perceptual constancy in phonetic perception. *Journal of Experimental Psychology: Human Perception and Performance, 7*, 1074–1095.

Swinney, D. A. (1981) Lexical processing during sentence comprehension: Effects of higher order constraints and implications for representation. In T. Myers, J. Laver, & J. Anderson (Eds.), *The Cognitive Representation of Speech*. Amsterdam: North-Holland.

Whalen, D. H. (1984) Subcategorical phonetic mismatches slow phonetic judgments. *Perception and Psychophysics, 35*, 49–64.

4 Computational Models of Parsing

Stephen G. Pulman
Computer Laboratory, University of Cambridge, Corn Exchange Street, Cambridge CB2 3QG, U.K.

INTRODUCTION

The notion of a computational model of something can be interpreted in at least three partially distinct ways. The first and most obvious of these interpretations is that under which some pre-existing theory or model is translated into a computer program which is then run to provide a simulation of whatever the original phenomenon was. Such programs will usually be capable of operating on different values of various parameters to reflect the behaviour of the theory under different conditions or assumptions. It is in this sense that we talk of a computer model of the economy, or of weather patterns over the Atlantic: Different parameter values enable different courses of events to be simulated and the resultant effects to be observed.

Computational models of this type are unrestricted in their subject matter, provided that it be well enough understood to be described formally in terms necessary for the construction of the programs. They provide two things: a consistency check on the theory, and a way of deriving predictions from a theory in cases where it may be too complex or cumbersome for these predictions to be easily apparent, or for them to be derived mechanically by hand.

Neither of these advantages should be underestimated: It is a salutary experience to take some apparently tight and complete theory of some domain and attempt to implement its principles in a computer program. Invariably there turn out to have been hidden assumptions that contain real problems; failures of logic in the interaction of components, or simply failure to specify in sufficient detail some element crucial to the operation of the overall system. Nevertheless, there is a good sense in which these advantages are not really dependent on the model being computational so much as formal. Any attempt at a complete formalisation of a theory might lead to similar results—the role of the computer is simply dictated by practical rather than other requirements.

A second way of being computational is via the employment of terms and concepts from computer science or artificial intelligence. Computers are a rich source of metaphors for the description of complex systems, using notions like subroutine or coroutine, data file, registers, concurrent processes, stacks, etc. In practice, psychological theories are probably those which draw most heavily upon ideas like these, but it is easy to imagine sociological, anthropological, or political models making fruitful use of them too.

Again, it could be argued that there is nothing essentially computational about this second type of computational model. The validity of the theories comes, after all, not from the terminology they use but from their accuracy or otherwise in capturing the properties of a system in functional terms; that is, describing the properties of each component in terms of its contribution to the whole. Even so, the benefits of the computational metaphor here too should not be underestimated: While we may eventually come to see theories using phrases like those above as being as quaint and inaccurate as those employing metaphors like Hume's "secret springs of the mind," at present there is no better or more fruitful set of metaphors for attempting to understand mental processes.

It is the third interpretation of "computational model" that we shall mostly be concerned with here, and it is to this interpretation that the computational element is indispensable. This interpretation (restricted to psychology and neighbouring disciplines) can best be summarised by saying that it combines the features of both of the preceding, with the extra twist that the computational vocabulary is not to be taken metaphorically but, within limits, literally. Mental processes (for the most part, but not exclusively) are seen as literally computational, in the sense that they are a species of information processing which takes place in a specifically computational way, involving operations on symbolic representations.

While this is not the place to go into great detail over the pros and cons of this approach (see Dennett, 1978; Fodor, 1981; Woodfield, 1982; Churchland, 1984 for further discussion), it is perhaps worthwhile to outline the major justification for, and the type of methodology associated with, what has come to be called the "computational theory of mind," the more so since, as an activity which professes to be part of psychology, it seems surprisingly remote from laboratory experiments and the usual methods of operation of the psychologist.

Two philosophical traditions have influenced psychological theorising about the nature of mental processes: dualism, which holds that there is some ineffably mental level independent of, and incapable of reduction to the physical; and materialism, which insists that there is nothing there over and above the physical. All forms of dualism respect our deep-seated intuitive feeling that our mental life is quite real, but have difficulty explaining how that mental life can affect our physical condition, and vice versa. Either the mental is not after all so ineffably mental as to be unable to interact causally with physical mechanisms (thus opening the door to materialism), or some thoroughly unsatisfactory not-quite-mental-or-physical intermediary must be postulated to effect this causal interaction. The strict materialist, on the other hand, has difficulty accounting for the apparent reality and partial autonomy of our mental life, since it can only be an inessential byproduct of physical events. Furthermore, any laws that there may be governing behaviour—laws of psychology—must either be stated in physical terms, or be reducible to statements which are couched in wholly physical terms. At present, however, it seems extremely unlikely that such a reduction is possible in any straightforward way: We have no single satisfactory instance of any such reduction in cognitive psychology, and many instances of generalisations which appear to hold across different species with differing physical makeups. Furthermore, it is easy to imagine encountering some alien life form having a different physical constitution but roughly similar cognitive capacities. By hypothesis, no physical account could capture the psychological similarities.

On the computational theory, all these problems are apparently solved. Mental processes are a species of computation, where this is understood in the literal sense, namely, of mechanical processes operating on symbolic representations. These mechanical processes may not even take account of what the representations represent—they may be purely syntactically governed—but this does not mean that they are merely shuffling symbols (pace Searle, 1984), for the symbols do have a meaning, whether or not that meaning is taken account of in the computation. What distinguishes computation from mere symbol-shuffling is precisely that the symbols have meaning, even if the meaning is, as it were, imposed on them from the outside.

The psychological theory describes the processes, and the representations operated on, but it leaves owing an account of exactly how the representations do get a content. On this approach, cognitive psychology would say exactly the same thing about a brain in a vat as about a brain in a person, and thus could be said to be solipsistic (cf. the chapter by Fodor on "methodological solipsism"; in Fodor, 1981). Obviously, though, we would expect some ecological account to supplement the cognitive one in giving us a complete picture of the organism.

On this view there is nothing mysterious about the interaction of the mental with the physical. In one sense, there is nothing going on in the brain over and above physical events, but of course the description of what is going on cannot be couched in purely physical terms. (Real) computer programs are a good analogy here (though a misleading one in other respects: The computational theorist is not necessarily claiming that all mental processes are programs, as this term is currently understood): Given a black computational box, we can give a full physical description of positive and negative electrical charges, signals going along data buses, gates open and closed, and so on. But as psychologists this does not help: We want to know what the box is doing—is it performing an arithmetical calculation, playing space invaders, composing a sonnet, or what? The answer to this question is at the program level—what type of instructions are being carried out—not at the hardware level.

While the program is dependent on the hardware for its execution, it need not be dependent on any particular type of hardware. The very same program can be run on a variety of different machines with quite different internal architectures and operating principles, still giving identical results. Conversely, it is by no means inconceivable that the very same sequence of physical events in some machine might at different times correspond to the running of two different programs, the symbols perhaps being identical in form but changed in interpretation. (As we said, the computational theory owes us an account of how the symbols do get an interpretation, otherwise it would not be capable of representing the facts of a case like this correctly.) Thus the description of the program and the hardware level must be logically independent: Particular instances of either will coincide, but there will be no general correspondence of types of one to types of the other, thus precluding any general, lawlike, reduction of the program level of description to the hardware level.

Thus both the autonomy of mental phenomena, and the fact of causal interaction between the mental and the physical, can be accommodated within the computational paradigm (with the provisos mentioned in the last paragraph). Mental phenomena can be described in terms which do not make essential reference to their physical instantiations; nevertheless, there is no mysterious entity over and above this physical instantiation as far as particular organisms are concerned. The logical coherence of this view of the relation between mental and physical is guaranteed by the existence of actual physical computers operating as described: The empirical accuracy of the research program based on it depends on how far those aspects of mental phenomena we are interested in turn out to be genuinely computational in the literal sense intended here.

So much for the philosophical underpinnings. The computational approach also has methodological consequences. Within this paradigm, the process of research into some cognitive ability will fall into logically, though not necessarily temporally, distinct stages. Firstly, taking account of whatever is available by way of evidence about the general cognitive capacities of the organism, or the exercise of the ability, we formulate a high level, abstract, logical theory of the ability. We will call this the "logical theory" (see Marr, 1977 for a clear statement of these distinctions, but note that his terminology is different). The logical theory characterises what the organism is doing as an information-processing task. It provides a description of what would be sufficient (and what may be necessary) for any organism to carry out that particular task given what we know about it. Examples of such theories might include Marr's (1982) theory of stereo vision, Morton's (1979) "logogen" theory of word recognition, Johnson-Laird's (1983) theory of syllogistic reasoning, the accounts of "deep dyslexia" given in Coltheart, Paterson, and Marshall (1980) as well as some of the theories of parsing we shall examine below. The logical theory should not, strictly speaking, be taken to make any claims about the precise nature of the computational processing, much less about physical instantiation, although it is usually suggestive of such claims. To see this, notice that if the logical level theory of an ability is a true one, it would be equally true of any artificial simulation of the original organism, provided that the simulation preserved the functional makeup of the original, even though it might employ different types of actual computation and be instantiated in a completely different physical medium.

The second stage concerns the computational interpretation of the logical theory. This is best illustrated with an artificial example: Consider the logical theory of the abilities of some black box whose sole forte appears to be the capacity to carry out multiplication when presented with two numbers. One logical theory might characterise this ability in the following way, taking the notion of addition of positive and negative numbers as a primitive:

multiply x by y:
if y = 1 then the answer is x
otherwise, add x to the result of:
multiply x by y − 1

(This definition takes multiplication by 1 as the basic case and reduces all other instances to sequences of additions to the basic case.)

The logical level theory, however, tells us almost nothing about what is happening inside the box—it only tells us that, whatever it is, it must produce the same results as the theory above. It is the second stage at which we begin to make claims about actual processes, or algorithms, involved in carrying out the computation. One algorithm might be a direct translation of the logical theory into statements of some programming language which we assume the box to have access to. Another possibility might be that the box uses the algorithm I was taught at school, which relies on the multiplications of all numbers less than ten being pre-stored. The algorithm is a bit tedious to describe in detail (and it gave me no understanding of what multiplication was), but you may recognise it from the following series of calculations:

$$
\begin{array}{ccccc}
25 & 25 & 25 & 25 & 25 \\
\underline{12\times} & \underline{12\times} & \underline{12\times} & \underline{12\times} & \underline{12\times} \\
0 & 50 & 50 & 50 & 50 \\
 & & 0 & 250 & \underline{250+} \\
 & & & & = 300
\end{array}
$$

A third alternative might be to add x to itself y − 1 times (not quite the same as the first), and a fourth might be to translate x and y into binary numbers and carry out various "bit rotation" operations on the resulting sequences of 0s and 1s—this is the way your electronic calculator does it.

This is the point at which experimental tests can be used to narrow down the possibilities. If we try to make the box perform under trying circumstances we may find it makes mistakes. If the pattern of mistakes corresponds to forgetting to "carry 1" in the second algorithm, that would be strong support for it. If we can somehow measure the amount of memory load needed to carry out a multiplication we might decide between algorithms one and three, for it can be shown that the first algorithm would need an amount of memory which increases quickly in proportion to the size of y, whereas the third alternative needs only a constant amount of memory, roughly speaking.

A third stage of inquiry, having found that one or the other of these algorithmic theories was supported over the others, would be to look for corroborative support from the physical composition of the box. (Of course if we knew enough about it, we might be able to verify our stage two hypotheses directly this way.) If we found evidence that the box was capable of the necessary bit manipulation operations, but not of storing precalculated numbers, then that would favour hypothesis four over two. If it had a small fixed amount of physical memory storage, that would favour three over one.

In practice we are almost never in the fortunate position of being able to proceed with the third stage, and there are very few areas where we have convincing second-stage algorithmic theories. To make matters worse, the distinction between first- and second-stage theories is often ignored: To some extent this is inevitable, as it is natural, when given a logical level theory, to translate it immediately into an algorithm (as we did with algorithm one). But if we are not careful, this can lead to much confusion over whether some aspect of a theory is intended as a claim about the logical properties of an ability or about the actual computational processes that are presumed to be involved in carrying out the ability.

Nevertheless, in principle, this is the logical sequence of events in the process of arriving at a satisfactory psychological theory of some cognitive ability within the computational paradigm, and it is in this light that we shall be discussing the various approaches towards the role of parsing in language comprehension in the next sections of this chapter.

PARSING

The term "parsing" is usually taken to mean the process of assigning grammatical structure to some string of words, although it has occasionally been used in a looser sense to mean also the process of extracting meaning from a sentence (e.g. Sparck Jones & Wilks, 1983; Introduction). Here we will be concerned with the original, stricter sense, and will try to demonstrate the roles of syntax and parsing within the overall process of language comprehension.

What exactly is grammatical structure? Linguists assume that sentences can be described, at one level, in terms of the sequence of word classes instantiated in the sentence, and in terms of groupings of these into higher-level constituents or phrases. This is usually represented by a diagram such as that in Fig. 4.1. Such structures can be generated by grammars like:

1 S → NP VP
 N → Det (Adj) N
 VP → V NP

The important thing to stress about labels like Det(erminer), N(oun), P(hrase), and suchlike is that they are assigned to words or sequences of

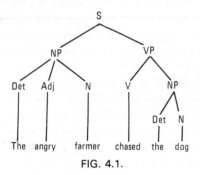

FIG. 4.1.

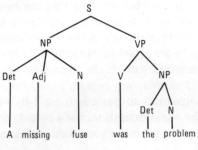

FIG. 4.2.

words purely in terms of their patterns of distribution in sentences: whether or not they can take certain affixes; what can follow or precede them; what type of item can replace them while still preserving grammaticality, and so on. (See e.g. Lyons, 1968, for more discussion and illustration.) Although there are some gross correlations between syntactic category and semantic value, they are only partial and not completely reliable. Thus a sentence with a completely unrelated type of meaning might receive exactly the same syntactic analysis, at this level of detail, as the example above (see Fig. 4.2).

There is no interesting semantic similarity between these two sentences: A syntactic representation of a sentence ignores most of its semantic properties.

Let us assume that we have available to us a grammar something like the one in Fig. 4.2, though obviously bigger, and a list, or dictionary, of all the words of the language and what syntactic categories they can belong to. Such a device gives us the information necessary to establish the following for any sequence of words: whether or not it is a sentence; how it is built up; whether or not it is syntactically ambiguous; how it is related to other sentences; and so on. Since it appears that these are all things that native speakers are able to do with a language, it is an irresistible move to attribute to them knowledge of the things expressed by the grammar, and to construe the latter as a description of that knowledge. Thus we would have taken the first step towards a logical theory of language comprehension. (See, for example, Smith and Wilson [1979] for a clear description of the notion "knowledge of language" which is presupposed here. My description of what a grammar makes possible begs certain technical and theoretical issues to do with the mathematical properties of such systems.)

This first step makes possible a theory of parsing, but it does not in itself provide such a theory. A grammar contains the information necessary for parsing (or generating) grammatical sentences but it is not itself a device which will do this.

At this point the question arises as to whether or not there is actually any evidence that parsing—the assignment of syntactic structure—plays any real part in sentence understanding, as was blithely assumed just now. In answering this question we must be careful to distinguish two separate claims about the involvement of syntax in sentence understanding:

1. We use the information contained in a grammar and a dictionary as part of the process of understanding a sentence.
2. We construct explicit syntactic representations as part of this process.

Clearly (2) is a much stronger claim and, as we shall see later, the evidence for and against is by no means conclusive. But (1) seems uncontroversial and obvious, although even this claim has been denied by some psychologists (Kintsch, 1974, cf. the discussion in Chomsky, 1980, pp. 202–205), several workers in artificial intelligence (e.g. Small, 1983, pp. 258–259; Schank, 1972; Rieger, 1976) and even, apparently, by some linguists (e.g. Moore & Carling, 1982; Sampson, 1980), insofar as all of these workers seem to deny that there is anything in reality corresponding to the type of grammar that linguists postulate.

The easiest way for one to become convinced of the truth of (1) is by considering the alternatives. Could we construct a device which "understood" sentences without making use of syntactic information? Such a device would be wholly reliant on semantic information stored with particular words, we must assume, for although one sometimes hears phrases like "semantic grammars" in this context, the idea of a "semantic grammar" is simply logically incoherent. If it is really semantic, then it must make reference only to the meanings of words. If to individual words, then it is not clear how a semantic grammar could be anything other than a list of meaningful combinations of them—but this is impossible as a basis for language understanding, for the list would have to be infinitely long. If, on the other hand, it groups words together in order to make more general statements, it will be inadequate semantically, for, unless operating entirely on groups of synonyms, it will have to ignore some aspects of their meaning to class them as similar. Indeed, to the extent that it ignores aspects of the meanings of words in order to group them together, such a grammar is already doing syntax by another name.

Another possibility which is sometimes raised is that we might somehow be able to understand sentences by working out the grammatical relations involved in them, which words function as the subject, object, predicate, etc. However, as these notions are properly understood, they are every bit as syntactic as those like NP or VP: In fact, in many theories the former are defined in terms of the latter (e.g. in Chomsky, 1965; see also Bresnan, 1982, for a more recent approach; one still strictly syntactic). No intrinsic semantic property of a word determines whether or not it can be a subject or an object, as examples like these show:

2 John opened the door with a key
The key opened the door
The door was opened
The surgeon performed the operation on the patient
The patient underwent the operation
The operation was successful

In each of these the first NP is the subject, according to traditional definitions ("what the verb agrees with", etc.).

In general, in a language like English, which does not mark grammatical relations by morphological affixes, determining what the relations are can only be done in conjunction with an analysis of the constituent structure of the sentence. And there are no languages, even morphologically rich ones, in which constituent structure is completely unnecessary for this purpose.

More plausible candidates as the basic elements for a semantically driven understander might be what are sometimes called "case" (misleadingly) or "thematic" relations (Fillmore, 1968; Jackendoff, 1972): notions like agent (of an action), patient (recipient of the action), beneficiary instrument, location, etc. To these we might also add the traditional categories of adverbial modification such as time and manner. They seem to fulfil our requirements, being apparently conceptually basic, and (for some at least) not necessarily restricted to language (see Braine & Hardy, 1982, and references therein). They seem to provide a level of description which is undeniably semantic, though not tied to the meanings of individual words. Furthermore, it seems likely that information about the thematic relations expressed by a sentence could be computed on the basis of information associated with particular words (for example that "kick" requires both an agent and a patient, and implies that the instrument was a foot) and some simple general principles which we can assume to be derived from our understanding of the nature of things in the world and how they interact with each other (for example that agents are typically animate, but patients do not have to be, and instruments seldom are).

Let us follow our own prescriptions and try to formulate a logical level theory of how sentence understanding might proceed on such a basis. We will assume a semantic dictionary in which some words have "slots" associated with them indicating what thematic roles they require or can have optionally:

AGENT eat   PATIENT
AGENT kick PATIENT (LOCATION)

AGENT ride PATIENT (LOCATION)
AGENT open PATIENT (INSTRUMENT)
AGENT give PATIENT BENEFICIARY (LOCATION)

and others have an indication of whether or not they are animate:

Animate: boy, girl, horse, bear . . .
Inanimate: apple, fence, door, car . . .

We will also assume some set of general principles about what things can fulfil what roles:

If animate then agent or patient, not instrument . . .
If inanimate then patient or instrument, not agent . . .

etc.—pretending for simplicity that these are absolute restrictions rather than preferences.

Roughly speaking, our semantically driven device attempts to assemble complete propositions by filling slots in the entries associated with the verbs. A proposition is complete if all obligatory slots are filled. Incoming words are labelled as to what slots they can fill or what empty slots they can introduce. These labelled words are held in a working memory while the device attempts to put words into slots, in accordance with the information in the dictionary and the general principles given.

1. No more words? then return any complete propositions, else:
2. Get dictionary information for next word.
3. Can it fill a vacant slot? If yes, fill the slot and go to 1.
4. Record any new unfilled slots introduced by the word. Go to 1.

Glossing over the role of determiners, the device as specified would produce the following sequence of events in "parsing" a sentence like:

3 The boy ate the apple
Memory:
1. boy = AGENT or PATIENT
2. boy = AGENT or PATIENT;
   [AGENT eat PATIENT]
3. [boy eat PATIENT]
4. [boy eat PATIENT];
   apple = PATIENT or INSTRUMENT
= [boy eat apple]

This is the only consistent assignment of words to slots in this sentence. Alternative versions of the same sentence like:

4 It was the apple that the boy ate
    The apple was eaten by the boy

will have the various slots filled in different orders, but the end result will be the same, as the reader might care to verify by working through the little procedure above. (Some orders do not result in a complete proposition, as for example if we had chosen to put "boy" in the PATIENT slot). Thus the device is able to recognise that the same proposition can be expressed in different forms merely by making use of the semantic information associated with individual words and a few general rules of interpretation. The ordering of the items is irrelevant, provided that all the slots are filled. The procedure is thus genuinely nonsyntactic in that this semantic information is allowed to override any syntactic arrangement or sequencing of items in the sentence.

If we now construe the procedure as not just an abstract characterisation, but a partial description of the actual algorithm used by people in understanding sentences, we can proceed to experimental testing, for we can derive some clear predictions from it:

1. Where semantic information conflicts with the syntactic sequencing of items in the sentence, it will be understood wrongly.
2. Where there is more than one consistent assignment of words to slots we might, in the absence of any further assumptions, expect the procedure to regard the sentence as ambiguous, or to be uncertain over the correct meaning.

Both of these predictions are clearly falsified by simple observations about normal natural language understanding. In the case of an example like:

5 The apple ate the boy

we have no difficulty interpreting the sentence as saying what it says, though we might have difficulty believing it, and there is no tendency to interpret it as synonymous with 3. Of course, on a particular occasion of utterance we might conclude that a speaker did not intend to convey the proposition expressed by 5, but rather that conveyed by 3: But that is a question about what the speaker meant rather than about what the sentence meant; the sentence has the meaning it has, whatever the speaker might have intended, and cannot change that meaning from occasion to occasion.

Nor do we find any particular difficulty or ambiguity in a sentence like

6 The tiger that the lion attacked was fierce

even though the order in which the participants are encountered is potentially misleading. It is possible that under some circumstances we might make a mistake more readily in cases like these than in cases where there is only one consistent assignment to slots, but that is a much weaker conclusion than would be predicted by our semantic theory.

It is fairly clear, pre-theoretically, I think, that there are at least two distinct factors involved in our processing of sentences like these: semantic plausibility—whether or not some collection of words and slots make up a coherent or plausible message given the background of our expectations and beliefs about the world; and syntactic information, which requires that a particular collection of words and slots must be assembled one way rather than another, and thus that sentence 5 is not synonymous with sentence 3. This latter type of information must of necessity be at least partly independent of semantic roles, of course, for otherwise it would be incapable of overriding them, and then sentence 5 would be synonymous with sentence 3.

Notice that it would not be sufficient to augment our procedure with additional information about word order, for example "if there is a choice, assume that the first word that can be an agent is an agent." This would in any case already count as a form of simple syntax, but is not sufficient to give the right results in the case of passives like "the boy was eaten by the apple" and in some relative clause cases, like those in 6. We need to recognise that these are indeed passives and relative clauses in order to assign the semantic relationships appropriately.

It would be tedious to demonstrate in further detail that this information must be grounded in the kind of syntactic properties discussed earlier. We need to categorise words as nouns or determiners in order to begin to break the sentence up into phrasal constituents, and we need to refer to syntactically stated generalisations to work out how these constituents are related to one another. It is quite possible that this process is aided by semantic generalisations of the type used by our procedure but it is not the case that it can be wholly replaced by them.

There is an important link to be made here with Chomsky's (1965) notion of "creativity." According to Chomsky, human linguistic ability is creative in that we have the capacity to create indefinitely many new sentences appropriate to any particular context, though not necessarily dependent on it. One component of this creativity is the ability to produce sentences different from any that have been produced before. This "infinite capacity," however, is only one component, and a relatively trivial one at that: Many computers count as creative language users in this sense, and even our semantically driven procedure could easily be equipped with the ability to "understand" an indefinite number of "new" messages obtained by combining sequences of old ones with "and" or "or." (Each such combination is a "new" message and immediately available for further recombination.) Real creativity is more than this: It is the ability to create truly new messages, not just new combinations of old ones.

It should now be clear that any device which allows semantic plausibility to be the driving force in comprehension is going to be incapable even in principle of accommodating this type of creativity. For the one thing that is required if we are to be sure of being able to create genuinely new messages is that we should be able to change our semantic expectations and notions of what is plausible. If what can be conveyed is limited to what is antecedently plausible, then on the occasion when the appropriate message is actually quite implausible, according to previous experience, then communication of it will not succeed. It is simply impossible to convey to our semantic procedure the message that the apple (from the kitchen garden of your local nuclear power station) really is eating the boy. More generally, for such a procedure, anything which can be construed in a way which does not contradict prior experience must be so construed, and anything which cannot will just be regarded as anomalous.

If, on the other hand, syntax is allowed to override semantic plausibility, then there is literally no limit to the number of new messages that can be conveyed. (Think of the number of things to which we can now attach literal truth but which would have been anomalous or metaphorical 100 years ago: "My Aunt Jan used to be my Uncle John," "We flew here over the North Pole." Carnivorous apples may be closer than you think.) It is in this sense that syntax is really the engine of linguistic creativity, paradoxical though it may seem that semantic freedom depends on nonsemantic resources.

Although the semantically driven device we have described is not a plausible model for normal natural language understanding, it is possible that some similar model might accurately characterise one type of pathological linguistic behaviour, namely, that observed in some Broca's aphasics. Adults suffering from cerebral lesions in Broca's area of the left hemisphere, usually as the result of strokes, display a reasonably uniform set of symptoms. While auditory comprehension appears to be fairly normal (though as we shall see, in fact it is not), the speech of Broca's aphasics is said to be typically hesitant and "agrammatic," consisting mainly of content words (nouns, verbs, etc.) with few function words or affixes to indicate any grammatical structuring. Clearly, this latter fact suggests that difficulty in producing syntactically structured speech may indicate a more fundamental syntactic disability reflected also in comprehension, for as we have argued, syntactic analysis is an essential part of sentence comprehension.

In a well-known experiment, Caramazza and Zurif (1976) tested some Broca's aphasics using a task which involved deciding which of several pictures a spoken sentence was true of. The sentences in question were carefully designed so that some were correctly interpretable on syntactic grounds alone, some required syntactic processing to choose between two semantically plausible readings, and some required syntactic processing to override semantic plausibility:

7a. The apple that the boy is eating is red
  b. The horse that the bear is kicking is brown
  c. The man that the horse is riding is fat

Compared to normal subjects, and to patients with different types of aphasia, the Broca's aphasics performed well on sentences of type (a), badly on sentences of type (c), and had only an at chance level of accuracy on sentences of type (b). (See Caramazza & Berndt, 1982; p. 506 for discussion.) It looks as if these patients are relying virtually exclusively on semantic plausibility to arrive at an interpretation of the sentence, and when this gives the wrong answer, or no determinate answer at all, they cannot instead use the syntactic structure of the sentence to guide them. Under most circumstances this disability would not be evident, for there is usually a great deal of redundancy in linguistic interchanges, and abundant semantic or contextual information is available to narrow down the range of plausible possibilities. It is only when these things have been factored out that it is revealed that this apparently normal comprehension is not normal at all.

Other studies have extended and repeated the findings, even for sentences much simpler than those in 7 (e.g. Schwartz, Marin, & Saffran, 1980). The obvious conclusion to draw is that in these patients the ability to carry out syntactic processing, or at least the ability to use the results of it, has been selectively damaged in some way, while apparently leaving other components of the comprehension mechanism more or less intact. This in turn supports the contention that syntactic processing is an isolatable subcomponent of the language processing system, as we have already argued.

Attractive though this explanation is, the picture it presents is vastly oversimplified. To begin with, there is some doubt as to whether the symptoms commonly regarded as constituting agrammatism reliably co-occur at all: At least some patients can have different types of production problem with apparently no corresponding problems in comprehension (Miceli, Mazzuchi, Menn, & Goodglass, 1983). Citing these findings, among others, Badecker and Caramazza (1985) argue further that there is sufficient disunity even among the different types of production deficit observed to cast doubt on the usefulness of agrammatism as a descriptive category. This makes any inference from problems of production to hypotheses about syntactic deficit in comprehension somewhat less compelling: Many other factors may be involved.

Even setting aside these methodological qualms, there are other explanations possible for the comprehension difficulties observed by Caramazza and his colleagues. Alternatives have been offered which locate the problem as a phonological one (Kean, 1978), or as one of lexical access difficulties for function words (Kean, 1980). Bradley, Garrett, and Zurif (1980) also offer a different version of this type of explanation. None of these alternatives threaten the claim about an isolatable syntactic subcomponent, in fact, although they do make its involvement somewhat more complicated.

However, a recent finding by Linebarger, Schwartz, and Saffran (1983) puts the support even for this claim into some doubt. They discovered that some Broca's aphasics, while unable to process sentences accurately in a task like that used by Caramazza and Zurif, were nevertheless able to provide correct yes/no judgements when asked about the grammaticality of sentences, even when the sentences were correctly structured nonsense. Linebarger et al. (1983) argue that this finding cannot be explained unless the subjects were in fact able to perform "complex syntactic analysis of sentences (p. 380)." Although there is some doubt over whether the patients were sensitive to every type of grammatical distinction they were presented with (Zurif & Grodzinsky, 1983), it is at first sight difficult to explain their behaviour without assuming some level of syntactic processing independently of semantic properties of the sentence.

Nevertheless, these patients are not able to bring whatever syntactic ability they have to the task of actually understanding sentences. This suggests that the correct interpretation of the nature of the syntactic deficit may be not that syntactic competence is no longer intact, but that full syntactic processing is no longer possible, perhaps for some relatively simple reason like lack of computational resources or working memory space.

Although at this stage such a suggestion is merely a speculation, it is one way of reconciling the various findings. Interestingly enough, results in formal linguistics provide a firm mathematical basis for the idea: It can be proved (Chomsky, 1963; Langendoen, 1975) that for grammars of certain types, including those demonstrably adequate for the description of

English (Gazdar, Klein, Pullum, & Sag, 1985), it is possible to construct a device which will recognise (i.e. simply say whether or not they are grammatical, as the patients were required to) the sentences generated by the grammar using only a constant, small amount of working memory that does not vary with the length of the sentence. But a full parsing procedure—a procedure constructing explicit trees describing the structure of the sentence—requires an amount of memory proportional to the length of the sentence and the depth of the tree being built, a proportion which may grow very rapidly indeed. If the amount of working memory available to these patients is limited in some way, then it may be that they are able to operate in the way described for the recognition procedure, but not in the manner required to assign full syntactic structures to the input, and thus to be able to interpret the sentences correctly.

It is not the case, then, as Linebarger et al. (1983) seem to be assuming, that full syntactic processing must be available in order to make grammaticality judgements of the type observed. This can be done without building any syntactic structures at all, in fact. However, to the extent that full syntactic processing is required for accurate comprehension, the same patients would then encounter difficulty with any task which demanded this higher level of processing, even while apparently retaining full syntactic competence.

WHAT SHOULD A THEORY OF PARSING ACCOUNT FOR?

Not surprisingly, there may be as many answers to this question as there are people working in the field. However, in practice, there are some general objectives which it is obvious should be addressed by any theory of parsing, and there have also emerged in recent years several sub-issues which have generated various proposals about parsing. In this section we shall survey the general objectives and present some of the phenomena of which theories of parsing have attempted to provide an explanation.

To begin with the most basic requirements, it is clear that a theory of parsing cannot proceed without making some assumptions about grammatical form. If we have no notion of what sort of grammatical information is used by people in comprehension, nor any theory of how that information may be organised or stored, we cannot design models of how that information may be used as part of the process of understanding a sentence. Assuming that we have a well-defined theory of grammar, however, we can say that one aim of a theory of parsing is to provide an equally well-defined procedure which, when presented with acceptable sentences of the language, will show how the information represented in the grammar is used during the process of comprehension. This will be part of the logical level theory of parsing. The procedure may take the form of showing how one or more explicit parse trees are built up for a sentence from the grammar, or may involve syntax in a less direct way: My neutral formulation is intended to avoid pre-judging the question.

A second general objective concerns the correspondence of syntactic processing, of whatever sort, with semantic interpretation. While some claims have been advanced that seem to suggest that a certain amount of syntactic processing must have taken place before semantic interpretation can begin (e.g. several of the theories discussed in Fodor, Bever, & Garrett, 1974; Carroll, 1981, and references therein), it seems intuitively obvious that we understand sentences, to some level at least, as fully as possible as soon as we begin processing them. Marslen-Wilson (1975) and Marslen-Wilson and Tyler (1980) describe experimental findings which support this claim: We shall not discuss any details but simply assume that an adequate theory of parsing should at least make available in principle the ability for instantaneous comprehension.

There are several more specific facts, the attempted explanation of which have motivated different approaches to parsing.

Centre Embedding

Any construction (X1) which contains another instance of itself (X2) is said to display "self-embedding." If there is no material in the containing constituent X1 to the left of the contained constituent X2, the latter is said to be "left embedded," or "left recursive"; if there is no material to the right of X2 in X1 then it is "right embedded" or "right recursive." If there is material to both left and right of the contained constituent then it is said to be "centre embedded."

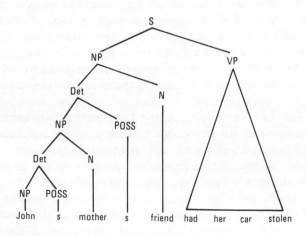

FIG. 4.3.

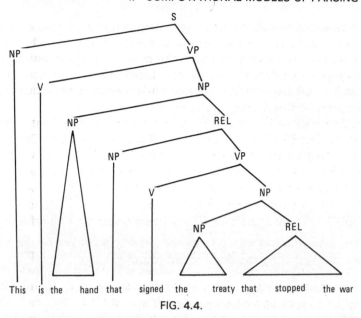

This is the hand that signed the treaty that stopped the war

FIG. 4.4.

On most assumptions about the structure of English a sentence like that shown in Fig. 4.3 would be an example of left embedding of NP and Det. Sentences like:

8a. This is the hand that signed the treaty that stopped the war
 b. John thought that Mary said she wanted to help

(see Fig. 4.4) display right embedding of S and VP (strictly, too, there is a limited degree of centre embedding of NP).

Clearly, left and right recursion are common properties of the grammars of natural languages, perhaps an inevitable consequence of the hierarchical nature of sentence structure. Cases of centre embedding are equally possible: In fact, given the rules necessary to generate the previous examples there is no way to prevent them from also generating structures like

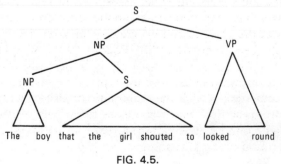

The boy that the girl shouted to looked round

FIG. 4.5.

9 The boy that the girl shouted to looked round

as shown in Fig. 4.5. With one layer of centre embedding such structures are perfectly acceptable. However, with more than one layer, they very rapidly become difficult or even impossible to process accurately:

10a. The man that the girl that the boy liked waved to looked round
  b. The man that the girl that the boy that the dog barked at liked waved to looked round

This cannot be due to any intrinsic semantic difficulty, for paraphrasing (a) and (b) by passivising their components results in a perfectly comprehensible, if somewhat stilted, sentence:

11 The man who was waved to by the girl who was liked by the boy who was barked at by the dog looked round

This paraphrasing removes all but one degree of centre embedding, as opposed to the several degrees in the original.

The difficulty associated with sentences of this sort has been amply documented and discussed (Chomsky & Miller, 1963; Miller & Isard, 1963; etc.). The conclusion reached by most people is that such sentences really are grammatical, even though difficult to process: The only way they could be declared ungrammatical is by imposing some arbitrary limit on the allowed degree of centre embedding. This would be unsatisfactory; with practice, people become more adept at understanding them, which suggests that the difficulty is not one of grammar. No amount of practice will make an ungrammatical sentence like "up the of isn't" acceptable.[1] In the

---

[1]The terms "grammatical" and "acceptable" are used here in the following way. The raw data of linguistic inquiry (of the type in question, at least) are judgements of "acceptability"—i.e. whether a sentence or a discourse, considered in isolation, sounds like ordinary, idiomatic English. Examples of unacceptable English will then include 10(a) and (b), "up the of isn't," "colourless green ideas sleep furiously," "daddy goed home," and "shall I compare thee to a summer's day." Judgements of acceptability can be collected and quantified in the same way as any other psychological data, if required.

To say that a sentence is grammatical or ungrammatical is not a judgement, but a statement of fact about the relationship between that sentence and a particular grammar, namely that the sentence is or is not characterised as grammatical by that grammar. Grammaticality is defined by the grammar. Thus not all unacceptable sentences might be characterised as ungrammatical by all grammars: The child's grammar, presumably, characterises "daddy goed home" as grammatical.

Many unacceptable sentences can be made to seem perfectly innocuous when embedded in a suitable context: It is precisely the fact that they need such contextualising which makes us characterise them as unacceptable, as different from run of the mill, banal English prose. Once it is remembered that there is no clear line of inference from unacceptability to ungrammaticality, nor from grammaticality to acceptability, this state of affairs should cause no confusion.

written medium, when presumably memory and processing difficulties can be, to some extent, artificially overcome, instances of centre embedding up to five or six deep can be found (de Roeck, Johnson, King, Rosner, Sampson, & Varile, 1982).

The fact that centre embeddings are difficult to process suggests, among other things, that the human parsing mechanism is not capable of parsing all the sentences that the grammar it has access to would declare to be grammatical. It may also, as we shall argue later, suggest something about the organisation of the memory available for parsing; at any rate, the rather striking and puzzling facts about centre embedding are something that a theory of parsing ought to have something to say about.

Parsing Preferences

Although we are not aware of the fact most of the time, many sentences are, logically speaking, ambiguous: In a particular context of utterance we do not generally notice that other construals of the sentence are possible. Some of these ambiguities are inherited from the ambiguity of particular words in the sentence, but some are a consequence of the fact that the sentence can be given two syntactically different analyses (some sentences display both properties).

For example, a sentence like:

12 They wanted to complete the cycle

taken in isolation could be about bicycles, or some repetitive circular process. With a different verb (ride, interrupt) the ambiguity would be invisible. But in a sentence like:

13 They saw the manager of the band's accounts

which can be understood as saying either that they saw the manager, or the accounts, there are no ambiguous words: The two possibilities are determined by the fact that on one syntactic analysis "the manager of the band" is a constituent, and on another it is not.

In isolation, the preference for one reading rather than another of the first example is determined entirely by the likelihood of one interpretation for "cycle" being preferred. In the second example, it seems to most people that in the absence of any contextual information to the contrary, the preferred reading is that on which it was the manager who was seen, not the accounts. The syntactic structures corresponding to the two readings are shown in Fig. 4.6. In fact, in some cases, this preference is so strong that people may not even notice that there is a second syntactically possible construal. For example, people do not generally notice that in (a) below, there ought to be a reading (b), analogous to that for (c) given in (d):

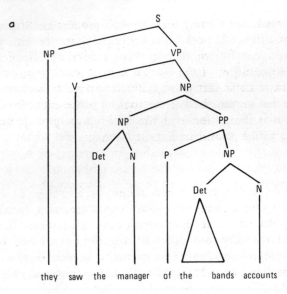

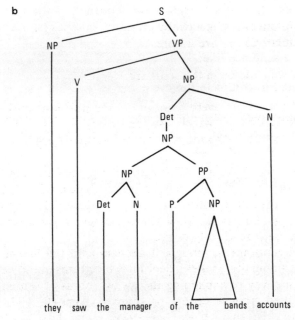

FIG. 4.6.

14a. The student took the job that was well paid
  b. The student that was well paid took the job
  c. The man arrived today that we were telling you about
  d. The man that we were telling you about arrived today

It has been claimed that there are systematic tendencies to prefer one over another of two logically possible readings in sentences like these. If this is so, then we clearly have an important source of evidence which might bear on the operation of the human parsing mechanism, for these preferences do not, on the fact of it, seem to derive from the intrinsic semantic properties of the words involved, but on preferences for one type of syntactic analysis over another, even though both are equally legitimate parsings according to the grammar of the language.

Garden Paths

Many sentences are ambiguous when taken as a whole in isolation ("global" ambiguity) but perhaps most sentences are, at a certain point when going through them left to right, temporarily ambiguous, in that the current portion of the sentence may be consistent with one or more possible parsings, all but one of which will actually be ruled out by material coming later in the sentence. This "local" ambiguity might be resolved almost immediately:

15a. Visiting relatives . . . is a chore
  b. Visiting relatives . . . are a bore

  or not until much later in the sentence:

16 Have the books which were damaged in the post last week
  a. . . . sent back to the warehouse (an order)
  b. . . . been sent back to the warehouse? (a question)

The ambiguity of "visiting relatives" is resolved by encountering the next word, but the ambiguity of "have" may not be resolved until several words later, and it is not difficult to construct examples which delay the point of resolution almost indefinitely. As with global ambiguity, for the most part local ambiguity is not consciously noticed.

Under some circumstances, though, it appears as if the listener, when faced with a local ambiguity, makes a decision which turns out to be wrong. At least, this is one way of explaining the awkwardness of sentences like the following, culled from a variety of sources (Kimball, 1973; 1975; Frazier, 1979; Ford, Bresnan, & Kaplan, 1982; Milne, 1982).

17a. John believes that Mary left is clear
  b. The man was angry was obvious
  c. The man pushed through the door fell
  d. Who did Mary give the present
  e. I told the girl the cat scratched Bill would help her

    f. While Mary was reading the book fell from her lap
    g. The granite rocks during earthquakes
    h. The old dog the footsteps of the young
    i. She wouldn't give the man who was reading the book
    j. Without her contributions would be inadequate
    k. The building blocks the sun shining on the house
    l. Before the king rides his horse is always groomed

This phenomenon is known for obvious reasons as the "garden path" effect. In sentences like these there is a conscious feeling of having been derailed suddenly in the course of understanding an apparently innocuous sentence—there are unexpectedly too many or too few components to fit together. Again, this phenomenon is assumed to give us some insight into the syntactic preferences of the parsing mechanism, the garden path effect then being explainable as cases where the purely syntactically driven expectations of the parser are not satisfied by that particular sentence. While the analogy is not exact, garden path phenomena have often been compared in significance to the study of visual illusions in perception.

    Of course, all three of the phenomena just described are subject to a greater or a lesser degree of semantic influence. Centre-embedded sentences with strong semantic cues are apparently less likely to present people with comprehension difficulties (Schlesinger, 1968), although they are still not models of elegance by any means:

    18 The snowball that the picture that the artist painted showed was pink.

Semantic bias can coincide with or alter the direction of preference in cases demonstrating preferences for one of two possible readings:

    19a. John said that he will phone your mother tomorrow
      b. John said that he will phone your mother yesterday

Sentences that, with one choice of words, exhibit the garden path effect, may become quite unproblematic with different lexical choices:

    20a. The man pushed through the door landed on the mat
      b. The letter pushed through the door landed on the mat

If any of the original observations are to be taken as evidence for or against particular models of the parsing mechanism, we must therefore be sure that the semantic effects are not actually the primary ones. If what we are taking to be a set of syntactically based preferences turn out to be explainable on nonsyntactic grounds, then we will learn little about the parser itself: Indeed, such a discovery might show that there was little to learn about it. This is a question that we will return to later, meanwhile taking for granted the assumption made by the vast majority of researchers in this field that these are indeed syntactic phenomena requiring a syntactic explanation.

PARSING STRATEGIES

Much recent work in natural language parsing was inspired by the model put forward by Kimball (1973, 1975) in which he attempted to show how all the phenomena we have discussed could be explained in terms of a particular set of strategies employed by the parsing mechanism.

Kimball assumed that grammatical knowledge was essentially as characterised in the "standard theory" of transformational grammar (Chomsky, 1965; Akmajian & Heny, 1975, is an approachable introduction). In this theory, the mechanisms that characterise sentences fall roughly into two components; a base component generating forms which are closest to the canonical simple sentence forms of the language, and a transformational component which maps these into surface structures, which may bear little overt relation to the forms which they derive from, having undergone various deletions, permutations, and so on.

Kimball assumed that parsing takes place in two stages. Firstly, the surface constituent structure analysis of a sentence is built up, and, piece by piece, shipped off to a second stage for a deeper level of processing. Kimball did not specify this second stage in any detail, beyond suggesting that the recovery of some kind of base structure could be assumed to be implicated, since this was generally assumed to be a necessary part of the semantic interpretation of a sentence.

Although this does not reduce the importance of Kimball's work, it turns out that the assumptions he was making were not consistent with the grammatical theory itself. In a standard transformational grammar, surface structures are not defined directly, but via a complex mapping from underlying ones. Since these are clearly not available to a parser prior to analysis of a sentence, the surface structures must be computed directly, but given an arbitrary transformational grammar, there is no guarantee that this is possible (see, e.g. Woods, 1970). Furthermore, even if we assumed the direct computation of surface structures to be possible, it also turns out that there is no guaranteed route back to the base structure from which they derived, in the general case at least. Thus it is by no means clear that any procedure could operate in the way that Kimball envisaged.

In practice, Kimball's work dealt solely with the recovery of surface structures themselves: In more recent grammatical theory, this level of structure has assumed many more of the properties earlier associated with deep structure, in particular being regarded as containing most of the information necessary for semantic interpretation. This means that we can ignore these technical problems and instead construe Kimball's account within a more surface-oriented grammatical theory (e.g. Gazdar, 1982; Bresnan, 1982; Chomsky, 1981; etc.) without thereby losing anything of importance.

Kimball made several other assumptions about the nature of parsing: (1) sentences are processed as rapidly as possible on a left to right basis; (2) trees are built "top down" rather than "bottom up"; and (3) some "lookahead" is possible. The first of these we have already discussed. The second assumption is that as much of the tree as is possible is built at a time. (Although Kimball calls this "top-down" parsing, this is not so in the strict sense of the term: See e.g. Aho and Ullman, 1972). Thus on encountering the beginning of a subject NP, for example, the parser will assume that this is to be dominated by S, as shown in Fig. 4.7, rather than waiting until the whole NP is complete.

The third assumption enables this process to be carried out with less fear of error: If the parser is allowed to look ahead one or two words then it will be able to verify that the tree it is currently hypothesising is compatible with what is coming later. This assumption is of course a modification of the first, for it is equivalent in its effects to a delay of one or two words in processing the input, this lag allowing the parser to check before building a portion of tree.

There is also an important consequence of the two-stage assumption which Kimball appeals to; that completed subconstituents are no longer easily available to immediate memory once they have been cleared to the secondary stage, and thus that it should be relatively difficult to modify parsing decisions which would involve alterations to structures already cleared.

The three most important of the specific parsing principles that Kimball postulates are:

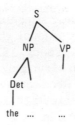

FIG. 4.7.

1. *Two Sentences*: Under normal conditions, no more than two sentences (i.e. one layer of self embedding) can be held in immediate memory at a time.
2. *Right Association*: Given a choice, incoming words should be attached to the lowest available part of the tree.
3. *Closure*: A phrase is closed (i.e. judged to be complete) as soon as possible; that is, unless the next node parsed can be regarded as an immediate constituent of the current phrase, the current phrase is closed.

Clearly, Two Sentences makes it a matter of stipulation that centre-embedded sentences beyond a depth of one are unparsable. In a sentence like:

21 The man the boy the girl saw waved to laughed

as shown in Fig. 4.8, parsing of the lower sentence violates the principle. Since left embeddings do not in general involve sentence-level constituents, they are parseable to any depth without violating the Two Sentences limitation. Right embeddings are rescued from the limitation by the assumption that completed subconstituents are cleared from immediate memory: Kimball assumes that a subconstituent can be regarded as complete if all its components have been recognised, even if the last one is not itself yet completed (see Fig. 4.9). So S1 can be regarded as complete when VP1 has been begun (since, we assume, we know from the grammar that

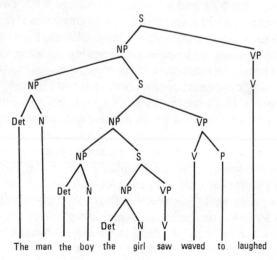

FIG. 4.8.

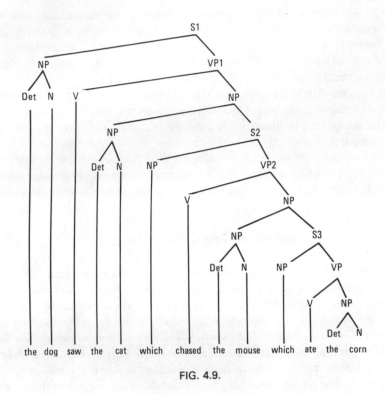

FIG. 4.9.

nothing can follow the VP), and likewise with S2 and VP2. Thus at no stage is there more than one uncompleted S in working memory, and the Two Sentences limitation does not come into play. Clearly this would always be so no matter how many right-embedded sentences were involved. This sequence of events is consistent with at least some of the experimental findings concerning the period of retention of surface syntactic structure in working memory (e.g. Jarvella, 1971; Caplan, 1972), and so Kimball cannot be accused of resorting to an ad-hoc mechanism to preserve the Two Sentences hypothesis in the face of apparent counter evidence.

The principle of Right Association explains many of the parsing prefer- ence examples and some of the garden path phenomena. The two possible readings of the sentences shown in Fig. 4.10 correspond to two different attachments of the adverb "yesterday." Right Association claims that the attachment to VP2 will be preferred, which does in fact coincide with the interpretation which most people find most natural for that sentence.

A similar preference is predicted for examples like our:

22 They saw the manager of the band's accounts

Although grammatically speaking the possessive markers could be associated with either "band" or the phrase "manager of the band," it is the latter which is preferred, as the NP "the band" is the lowest available. (Notice that strictly speaking we also need some mechanism to force the choice between construing "the manager . . ." as the direct object of "see" and as the determiner phrase belonging to "accounts." Kimball seems to have been assuming that the simplest tree compatible with the input would be constructed, but as we shall see later, this may not be sufficient to get the correct results. It is not clear that Right Association alone will suffice here.)

To account for many of the garden-path observations, Kimball suggests that both Right Association and Closure are involved, as well as the various effects consequent upon the two-stage assumption. Thus sentences like:

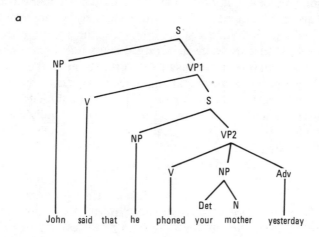

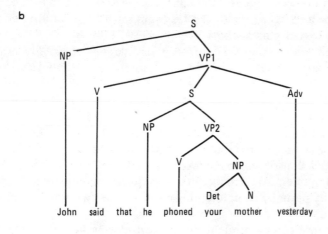

FIG. 4.10.

23a. [John believes [that Mary left]] is clear
  b. [The man was angry] is obvious
  c. [The man pushed through the door] fell

are parsed as indicated by the bracketings via Right Association: When the material outside the brackets is encountered Closure has decided that the current constituent is complete and, on one possible line of explanation, that constituent has been shuffled away out of working memory. Integrating the remainder of the sentence is then difficult because the original part has to be, in effect, reparsed, since the first parsing is no longer available.

As Kimball points out, his principles fit closely with the presumed mode of operation of the two-stage model, conspiring to reduce the load on working memory. Closure, in particular, is virtually redundant as a separate principle given the assumed preference to clear completed constituents as quickly as possible. But there is something rather unsatisfying about this: If the principles fit so closely, then surely we are missing something by regarding them as separate strategies at all? If the shape of the strategies is motivated by the operation of the parsing mechanism, then ought it not to be possible to explain the various linguistic phenomena directly in terms of that mechanism, rather than via some intervening separately stated principles that in effect just recapitulate features of the mechanism?

Frazier and Fodor (1978) offer a model which attempts to do this, and also to extend the range of data considered by Kimball. Theirs is also a two-stage parsing model, which distinguishes two components: the Preliminary Phrase Packager (PPP) and the Sentence Structure Supervisor (SSS). The idea is that the PPP is a relatively "shortsighted" analyser which inspects a portion of the input of no more than six or seven words at a time, chops it up into lower-level phrasal constituents like NP and PP and hands these over to the SSS, which assembles them into the structure needed to interpret the sentence as a whole.

Frazier and Fodor supply lamentably few details of exactly how this mechanism is supposed to operate beyond somewhat metaphorical descriptions of the type given above—theirs is a prime example of a theory which is too complex to assess by hand, and which cries out for a computational implementation to check on its consistency. The general principle, however, seems to be not dissimilar to that assumed by Kimball. The difference is that whereas Kimball's first-stage mechanism could, within limits, choose when to snip a constituent off, Frazier and Fodor's model requires the first-stage component to unburden itself as quickly as possible, even if the analysis is only partially complete, if the size of the "window" available to it is exceeded.

This difference can be brought out by considering how the Frazier and Fodor model would handle sentences like:

24 John said that your mother had phoned yesterday

On Kimball's account, as we saw, Right Association prefers to attach "yesterday" to the "had phoned" VP, although in principle both the lower and the higher attachments are possible at this point. On the Frazier and Fodor model, the PPP stage has moved its window over the earlier stage of the sentence and so by the time "yesterday" is reached the lower point of attachment is the only one visible. Thus the effects of Right Association follow automatically: The higher attachment reading is predicted to be more awkward, as it indeed (usually) is.

Notice that Right Association is now a misleading term to use: "Local Association" is a more accurate description, when the association can be either to the right or to the left. Frazier and Fodor suggest that this means that their model is better equipped to handle cases like the following (a somewhat clumsy sentence when encountered with no intonational groupings or punctuation—unfortunately such artificial examples are needed to ensure that the hypothesised "window" size is exceeded):

25 Though Martha claimed that she will be the first woman president yesterday she announced that she'd rather become an astronaut

Right Association would seem to predict that "yesterday" should prefer to be associated with the lowest verb phrase "will be . . . ," which is of course semantically impossible in this case. Instead, "yesterday" is fairly clearly interpreted as modifying the following sentence, "she announced. . . ." It is not obvious how Kimball's model deals with this, for that model would seem to suggest that the reading on which "yesterday" modifies "claimed" should be the next most favoured candidate. In Frazier and Fodor's model, however, this possibility is again no longer visible to the PPP at the point at which "yesterday" is encountered, and so the actual "left attachment" reading, on which "yesterday" modifies the sentence that follows it, is the only one feasible. (Notice that examples like these seem to show fairly conclusively that some nonsyntactic strategy for interpreting adverbs, like "attach to the nearest preceding semantically modifiable verb" is not sufficient, even though it may coincide with a syntactically based strategy in all but a few cases.)

Frazier and Fodor also claim that this explanation makes sense out of what would otherwise be a rather puzzling phenomenon: Examples which on Kimball's account are awkward because Right Association is not possible, mysteriously become much less so if the constituent involved is larger than the one or two words usually chosen for illustration:

26a. Red put the fire that had been burning for a long time out
  b. Red put the fire that had been burning for a long time out for good at last
  c. The man that the girl that the boy liked saw waved
  d. The man that the girl that the boy was waiting for in the garden had always liked returned her smile

The (b) and (d) examples seem a little less difficult than the others. Frazier and Fodor explain this in terms of the narrowness of the window of the PPP stage. They argue that in a case like (a), the PPP has lost sight of the constituent which the "out" should be associated with, and therefore runs into trouble, because it cannot make any coherent attachment to the items which are currently within its view. In an example like (b), however, the "out" can be grouped coherently with the words which follow it to make a constituent, and this constituent can then be handed up to the SSS second stage, which they assume to have a more global view of the structure of the sentence, and to be able to make the "long distance" attachment necessary to correctly interpret the sentence.

It is with "explanations" like this that the lack of clarity and precision in the description of the exact operation of the Frazier and Fodor model become crucial. While the above account seems superficially plausible, when examined more closely it does not stand up. Why, for example, when the PPP finds it cannot make an appropriate local attachment for "out" in sentence (a), does it not simply hand it up to the second stage? The necessary long-distance attachment then could proceed as for the (b) example. Frazier and Fodor are assuming that "out" cannot be a complete constituent, whereas "out for good at last" can be. Syntactically speaking, however, there is no warrant for this assumption: "Out" is a perfectly good, though short, constituent.

Another problem concerns what the difference is between the two stages. The intuitive difference between a phrasal level and sentence level analysis is clear enough; but does this mean that the phrasal level analyser is incapable of handling constituents of sentential level? Apparently not: We are told that that PPP is able to handle every type of constituent that the SSS can handle, provided that it is short enough to be encompassed within the narrow window available to it (Frazier & Fodor, 1978; p. 314). This is surely rather curious: We seem now to have two duplicated parsing mechanisms, differing only in that one of them is shortsighted and the other not. Furthermore, as several critics have pointed out (e.g. Wanner, 1980), this claim makes nonsense of the explanation Frazier and Fodor offer for the difficulty of centre embedding: According to them, the difficulty is caused by the fact that in these constructions the PPP is unable to package up its phrasal constituents correctly, and the SSS is handed a sequence of jumbled phrases that it is unable to make sense of. It is in any case unclear as to exactly how things are arranged so as to ensure that this does not happen in other circumstances, but seems to predict that cases where the window is wide enough to see all the sentence should be unproblematic. This is not so: The tentative measure of size given is "seven-plus-or-minus-one," which should comfortably encompass examples like this:

27 Committees politicians people elect form multiply

(The committees that are formed by the politicians that people elect multiply). This sentence is very difficult to parse without conscious effort.

We noted that Kimball's account of some of the Right-Association phenomena required a supplementary principle guaranteeing that the simplest tree compatible with the input will be built, under normal circumstances. Frazier and Fodor christen such a principle "Minimal Attachment": This is the only strategy they allow themselves, all other facts being supposed to follow from the architecture of their two-stage model. Thus in a sentence like:

28 John brought the book for Susan

which can be analysed in either of the ways shown in Fig. 4.11, Minimal Attachment would, on encountering the NP "the book," prefer the first

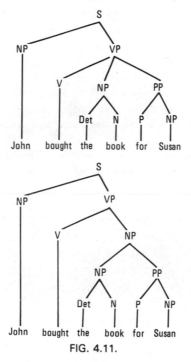

FIG. 4.11.

alternative, as this requires the smallest number of new nodes to be added to the tree.

Minimal Attachment is the basis of Frazier and Fodor's account of some of the garden path sentences: Of the two analyses shown in Fig. 4.12, the first is the only one that will lead to a complete parse, but it will be discarded by Minimal Attachment, other things being equal, in favour of the second, which attaches the NP directly to the S. This principle is an essential one for Frazier and Fodor's account of phenomena like this, for it is not plausible that the first-stage window is so narrow as to be unable to encompass the few words needed to provide the necessary information, and thus their normal pattern of explanation is unavailable.

Both of the approaches to parsing we have looked at so far assume that the phenomena are to be described in purely structural terms, in fact, in terms which make reference only to the syntactic categories of words and the labellings of the constituents to which they belong. It is assumed that semantic information can affect parsing decisions but it is not specified how, at what points, or to what extent this happens. The theory of parsing put forward by Ford et al. (1982) takes some small steps towards this, as the theory of grammar they presuppose incorporates more information of a type which might normally be considered semantic. Ford et al. also report experimental findings which show some measure of confirmation that the intuitive judgements taken for granted so far are indeed shared across

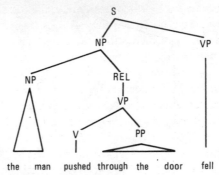

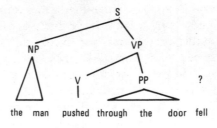

FIG. 4.12.

speakers to a significant extent—a step readers may feel somewhat over-due. They used a questionnaire-based survey, and found that while by no means all subjects agreed, there was enough agreement to convince them that a real phenomenon exists, and that (Ford et al., 1982) "one can observe syntactic biases operating in isolation from context (p. 744)," claiming that sentences like:

29a. They wanted everything there
  b. They positioned everything there

demonstrate this. The syntactic bias they mean here is actually something that is fairly clearly semantically grounded, namely the fact that the verb "want" is semantically complete with just an NP following it, whereas "position" usually requires not just an NP, but a locative of some kind (unless this can be easily inferred from context, as in "the captain positioned his fielders"). Thus, even in the absence of particular semantic information (there are as many semantically neutral pronouns used as possible), a particular preference for attachments shows: "There" in the first sentence is construed as belonging with "everything," not with the verb, whereas the reverse is true in the second. At the level of syntactic categories and constituents, however, the two sentences are actually identical, and in fact either parsing can be associated with either sentence in different contexts.

Ford et al. assume that each verb and adjective has associated with it information of this type about what other constituents are needed in its syntactic context. Thus a verb like "object" can take either a PP beginning with "to" or a sentential complement beginning with "that." All verbs require a subject, of course. In the case where there are several alternative possibilities for a particular verb Ford et al. assume they are ranked in terms of strength or likelihood of occurrence. Thus some important aspects of meaning (the constituents needed to assemble a complete proposition, and the most semantically likely possibility) are actually encoded syntactically and therefore available to the parser in the Ford et al. model. A parsing of a sentence which observes all these preferences is called the "lexically preferred" reading of it. Thus the lexically preferred parsings of the two example sentences in 29 are different, the difference being traceable to the rankings of contextual preferences or "subcategorisation restrictions" associated with the two verbs.

Ford et al. assume that parsing follows two strategies:

1. *Final Arguments*: On the lexically preferred reading of a sentence, when the final required item or argument is encountered, delay attaching it for as long as possible. (An "argument" is, roughly speaking, an NP or S

that bears some grammatical or thematic relationship to the main predicate of its clause.) Final Arguments has the effect of attaching as many constituents as possible to the final argument before attaching the argument itself. When processing nonfinal arguments the remaining default strategy, (2), applies.

2. *Invoked Attachment*: Attach a phrase within the partial constituent which caused it to be hypothesised. Invoked Attachment produces virtually the same effects as Frazier and Fodor's Minimal Attachment, though it is slightly more restricted in its application.

The strategies can be illustrated with the following examples:

30a. They objected to the guide that they couldn't hear
  b. They signalled to the guide that they couldn't hear

Assume that the lexically preferred reading of "object" is that on which it demands just a "to" PP following. Then "to the guide" is the final argument of "object" and the Final Argument strategy will delay doing anything with it. On encountering "that they couldn't hear," this will be attached as a relative clause to "the guide" (this may involve some reanalysis) and the whole thing is then attached to the original VP containing "object."

In (b), on the other hand, the preferred reading of "signalled" is that on which it takes the PP followed by an S, and so the S is the final argument. Since the default Invoked Attachment strategy is in operation until the final argument is encountered, "to the guide" will be attached immediately to the VP. Since nothing comes after the S, that too will be attached immediately to the VP as there is no reason to delay this particular final argument.

A theory which was not sensitive to these various lexical preferences would treat these sentences identically.

These two strategies account for by now familiar examples like:

31a. The man pushed through the door fell
  b. The letter pushed through the door fell

In (a), Invoked Attachment builds a simple [S [NP][VP]] structure, for at the point at which this decision has to be made no final arguments have been encountered. Then when "fell" is met, the parser flounders. For (b), the parser recognises that "the letter" is not a possible subject for "pushed" construed as a transitive verb (whereas "the man" could have been) and thus builds the more complex alternative on which "pushed" is in a reduced relative clause: [S [NP[NP REL]][VP]]. "Fell" is then attached correctly.

Ford et al. claim that their model is also capable of representing the influence of context on parsing preferences. We have up to now been dealing exclusively with sentences in isolation from context, on the assumption that removal of context will reveal those factors which we are interested in (we will return to the legitimacy of this assumption). It is of course clear that a particular contextual setting may bias us towards one reading of a sentence rather than another. The mechanism proposed by Ford et al. to allow for this possibility is in effect a reordering of the lexical preference rankings associated with particular verbs and adjectives. Thus whereas under normal circumstances the preferred reading of "buy" might expect both an NP and a PP, in a context like the following the reading on which it takes just an NP would be the preferred one:

32 We bought presents for each of the children. I bought the present for John, but Mary bought the present for Susan.

The first occurrence of "bought" displays the usual preference, but subsequent ones are more easily parsed as having just a single NP after them ("the present for Susan," etc.).

Ford et al. do not specify how this mechanism for recomputing preferences is to work (nor how the original preferences are determined). It is clearly going to be an extremely sophisticated mechanism, sensitive not just to the type of proposition expressed by certain verbs in particular contexts, but also able to take account of the referential properties of phrases: Notice that in the examples above we have moved from a plural NP to singular definite NPs. "Presents" introduces a set of items into the discourse that need not have been mentioned before, whereas "the present" assumes that we know which present is being talked about, that we are already familiar with the set of objects in question. In this sentence this is not the case, and so some further information needs to be added to tell us exactly which present "the present" is. Thus "the present for Susan" singles out a particular present by modifying it further with the PP, in exactly the way that we might also do with a relative clause.

At this point the suspicion begins to grow that this process of contextually influenced recomputation of preferences might be missing the point somewhat. If the mechanism is sufficiently powerful to recompute the syntactic information associated with a predicate during parsing so as to arrive only at the contextually appropriate parse, might it not also be powerful enough to arrive at the same result more directly, by intervening in the actual process of parsing to nip in the bud and discard syntactically possible but unpreferred readings? Furthermore, might this not mean that some of the effects that we have been assuming to be syntactic, in the strict sense of the word, might themselves be the result of a similar process?

These possibilities are investigated in Crain and Steedman (1985). Their suggestion is that when contextual influences are properly taken into account, many of the arguments for the existence of independent principles of parsing simply disappear. The argument is as follows: People have assumed that the garden path and parsing preference phenomena show the workings of a syntactic mechanism which operates in a kind of "default" way to prefer certain readings when no semantic or contextual information prejudices it to the contrary. The default preference is assumed to be that displayed when the sentence is presented in isolation to subjects: 'The "null" context. This is an assumption inherited from the practices of linguists, who assumed that judgements about the status of sentences can be made coherently in the absence of plausible contextualisation, as discussed earlier. Crain and Steedman argue that far from the null context being neutral, it is itself heavily loaded in favour of a certain type of interpretation of various phrases, by virtue of the mechanisms of reference mentioned in the examples above and other similar mechanisms. Thus the default preference itself turns out to be just another type of contextual resolution, and the null context just another type of context. There are no independent principles of parsing at all, at least as far as this range of phenomena is concerned.

Crain and Steedman back up this strong claim with some ingeniously obtained experimental evidence. Consider sentences like:

33a. The teachers taught by the Berlitz method passed the test
  b. The children taught by the Berlitz method passed the test

The first sentence is likely to induce the garden-path effect, whereas the second is not: Inherent plausibility of the situations described on the various syntactically available parsings decides which is correct. Now, however, consider sentences like:

34a. Teachers taught by the Berlitz method passed the test
  b. Children taught by the Berlitz method passed the test

These are structurally identical to the previous examples, in all but the very finest level of analysis, and thus a purely syntactically based strategy should give identical results. The inherent semantic plausibility factor cannot be significantly different, for the same content words are involved in both. But intuitively, and confirmed by their experiments, sentence (a) in this pair is not as difficult to parse correctly as its earlier counterpart.

The difference lies in the nature of the subject NP. "The teachers" presupposes some already identified set of teachers, and thus a modifying reduced relative clause is unlikely to be necessary. Such clauses function to narrow down the range of reference of the nouns that they modify, but if this is already uniquely identified then any further information as to the identity of the teachers will be redundant. But in the case of "teachers" this is not so: This noun phrase simply introduces the set of all teachers. Thus the following clause can be nonredundantly interpreted as a restricting relative clause serving to specify further exactly which teachers it is that we are talking about. The so called garden-path effect is produced by the "null" context biasing the listener or reader towards an inappropriate reading.

Crain and Steedman further support their case by creating garden paths in sentences placed in inappropriate contexts. The target sentences in question were like these:

35a. The psychologist told the wife that he was having trouble with her husband
  b. The psychologist told the wife that he was having trouble with to leave her husband

If the "to leave" is present the "that" clause is interpreted as a relative modifying "wife," otherwise it is interpreted as a sentential object complement to "told."

The sentences are ambiguous up to the point after "with." Two contexts were used which biased subjects to select one of the two possible interpretations:

1. *Complement*: A psychologist was counselling a married couple. One member of the pair was fighting with him but the other one was nice to him.

2. *Relative*: A psychologist was counselling two married couples. One of the couples was fighting with him but the other one was nice to him.

When the two target sentences were presented in appropriate contexts, no difficulty was found by the subjects in processing them correctly. When preceded by an inappropriate context, however, there was a significant tendency to "garden path" as predicted.

This seems like a fairly convincing demonstration in favour of a nonsyntactic account of parsing preferences and garden paths, undermining the rationale of the whole line of research that we have been describing in this section. For Crain and Steedman's work suggests that the original assumption, that the various phenomena demonstrated something about the syntactic mechanisms underlying language comprehension, was simply wrong: These are not syntactic facts at all, but illustrative instead of the profound level of integration between syntactic and semantic processing, the two being completely interleaved and guiding each other at every stage.

This is unlikely to be the end of the story, however. Notice that Crain and Steedman do not address themselves to many of the phenomena which are covered by principles like Right Association or some of the other principles. And they do not even suggest that the centre-embedding facts would yield to a semantic or contextual explanation. Many of these phenomena seem much more resistant to contextual manipulation than the garden-path examples they used, and it is thus quite possible that they do indeed demonstrate the workings of some syntactically conditioned mechanism.

What Crain and Steedman's work does show is that to arrive at a satisfactory overall explanation of parsing preferences and the like we need a much more sophisticated account than is presently available of the interaction between syntactic and nonsyntactic factors. Only by attempting to develop such a theory can we hope to unravel the various different influences which serve to reduce temporary and local ambiguities to a manageable level: A level which remains largely invisible to the conscious attention, moreover.

PARSING AND GRAMMATICAL CONSTRAINTS

A notion that will be important to us in this section is the notion of "determinism." As understood here, this weighty phrase has only a tenuous connection with philosophical issues concerning freedom of the will and the like, and can in fact usefully be given a dry and severely technical definition. The definition strictly applies to particular classes of "automata" (Aho & Ullman, 1972) but can be generalised informally to any kind of formal device whose operation can be thought of as a transition through several states, $S1 \rightarrow S2 \rightarrow \ldots Sn$. Such a device is said to be deterministic if the transition from one state, Si, to another, $Si + 1$, is entirely determined by the contents of the machine at state Si, and any relevant input available at Si. That is, what happens at the transition from Si to $Si + 1$ must not depend on what happened before Si (unless that information is somehow encoded into Si itself), nor on what may happen after Si.

Marcus (1980) presents a theory of parsing which is based on the claim that the parsing of English and other natural languages is deterministic in just this way, or at least very nearly so. This assumption is in turn used to try to explain certain properties of the grammars of these natural languages, and also to provide a slightly different explanation of the garden-path phenomena.

In effect, for Marcus, determinism amounts to the requirements: (1) that any structures once built cannot be changed; (2) that only one parsing path at a time can be pursued; and (3) that only a limited lookahead is possible.

All these things were implicit in the earlier models we have discussed: One difference is that Marcus actually did produce a computer implementation of his parsing theory. His parser makes use of two notions: an "active node" stack (a stack is a last-in-first-out store) of partially completed constituents and a buffer. A buffer is, in general computational terms, a device which allows for temporary storage of material which is input or output to some process, and where some preliminary processing can take place, or where the material can be held until the main routine decides what to do with it. Parsing in the Marcus model takes place by filling the buffer (within the limits of lookahead) with either words or phrases, and then applying grammatical rules to the contents in order to change or add to the stack. Occasionally, items can be taken off the stack and replaced in the buffer to allow further processing to take place; for example, in processing a question like:

36 Has John arrived?

the auxiliary verb "has" would be replaced in the buffer when "John" had been parsed, and the sequence "has arrived" would be treated as for a declarative sentence. In this way Marcus's model is able to provide mechanisms identical in their effects to the operation of transformational rules, and his model is explicitly tied to that particular theory of grammar.

Although their effects are similar to those of more familiar types, Marcus uses grammatical rules somewhat different in form from those we have been assuming for illustration so far. This is not important for his main thesis, however, and so in presenting his framework a more familiar grammatical background will be assumed.

Given the following sentence to parse, and assuming the necessary grammatical rules, the Marcus parser would begin in the following state:

37 John phoned your mother yesterday
Stack: [S . . .]
Buffer: [NP John] [V phoned] [Det your]

By examining the contents of the buffer the parser is able to attach "John" as the subject of S, the only active node on the stack so far. It is also able to anticipate a VP and to recognise "phoned" as the beginning of that VP:

Stack: [S [NP John][VP [V phoned] . . .]]
Buffer: [Det your] [   ] [   ]

After updating, the buffer becomes:

Buffer: [NP your mother] [Adv yesterday] [.   ]

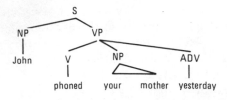

FIG. 4.13.

Notice that simple NPs can be recognised, as can other small constituents, and that when so packaged they occupy only one cell of the buffer. The full stop in the third cell simply indicates that we have reached the end of the input.

Now the NP and the Adv can be attached to the tree being built on the stack, giving the final parse tree as shown in Fig. 4.13.

Marcus's parser is deterministic in the sense that in any given state the operations of the parser are entirely determined by the contents of the stack and the three buffer cells (and the grammar). Of course, without some limitation on what access the parser has to the stack this reduces the notion to vacuity, for the stack could simply be used to encode everything that has been encountered so far: indeed, since the stack is building up the information to be represented in the final parse tree it must to some extent do this. Marcus assumes that access is, however, severely limited: The parser can only examine the stack as far back as, roughly speaking, the most recent S node.

There are clear similarities between Marcus's parser and the two-stage model of Frazier and Fodor (1978): In fact, the buffer mechanism would be one interpretation of their first-stage component (subject to the apparent problems with that claim). Like their model, Marcus's could be made to capture many of the Right Association phenomena through the limitation of the buffer length to three (under usual circumstances). The explanation for the difficulty of garden-path sentences that emerges from Marcus's theory is closer to that offered by Kimball, however. The reason why sentences like:

38 The boat floated down the river sank

are difficult is that the sequence "the boat floated down the river" will fit into the three-cell buffer naturally (given the particular rules and choices between them assumed by Marcus) with "sank" being invisible at the point at which the crucial decisions are made.

Stack: [S . . .]
Buffer: [NP the boat] [V floated] [P down]
Stack: [S [NP] . . .]
Buffer: [V floated] [P down] [NP the river]
Stack: [S [NP] [VP [V][PP]]
Buffer: [V sank] [.] [ ]

Because of the determinism requirement it is not possible to go back and alter the structure already built, and so the parser blocks.

In fact, as several commentators (Church, 1980; Briscoe, 1983) have pointed out, this is not a very satisfactory explanation, for there is no obvious reason why, if the buffer cells can contain small NP constituents, they should not also contain PP constituents and could therefore instead, at the second stage, have looked ahead to the end of the sentence:

Buffer: [V floated][PP down the river] [V sank]

The three-cell limit is not exceeded, and the parser should now be able to see that the only coherent parse is that on which the V and PP constituents modify the subject NP as a relative clause. Furthermore, it is not apparently possible, in Marcus's framework, to avoid the conclusion that a sentence like:

39 The letter pushed through the door fell (onto the mat)

should be equally difficult: If the first one violates the three-cell lookahead, this one will too. The obvious counter that the theory abstracts away from semantics or lexical interaction cannot be pushed too far, for it will run into the danger of acknowledging that determinism is not a strictly syntactic matter at all: There is no syntactic distinction between 38 and 39 in which to locate a difference in parsing behaviour.

However, it is not this aspect of Marcus's work which is of most interest to us. Rather, it is the type of explanation he attempts to derive from the operation of his parser for the existence and character of certain properties of grammars, within the framework he is assuming.

Within transformational grammar, it is assumed that there are, in addition to the type of grammatical rule that we have assumed so far, other types of grammatical operations which can move or displace phrases from their expected position, mark pairs of noun phrases as identical in reference, and so on. (Radford, 1981, is a good guide to the theory assumed by Marcus). For example, questions like:

40 Who did John see __?

are derived from a structure on which the Wh, or question word "who" occupies the place normally associated with the logical role it fulfils, namely, as object to "see." The same is true of Wh words in relative clauses:

    41 I know the man who John saw —

and the "gap" can be arbitrarily far away from the Wh word:

    42 I know the man who John thought he saw —
    I know the man who John thought Joe said that he saw —
    I know the man who John thought Joe said that Bill expected that he
    would see —

The position occupied by Wh words in cases like this is the one which can also be occupied by various complementisers, hence "Comp" position. The rule involved, Wh movement, is assumed to move a Wh phrase successively up through Comp positions sentence by sentence, leaving a "trace" or marker behind to show, ultimately, its origin:

    43 I know the man [who John thought [t Joe said [　t that Bill expected
    [t that he would see t　]]]]

While in general there seems to be no inherent semantic limitation on what constituents of a sentence can be questioned or relativised, there does seem to be a syntactic restriction. An unacceptable sentence like:

    44 I know the man who John worked for the firm which sacked —

is generally regarded by syntactic theorists as ungrammatical, though the proposition it is trying to express is a perfectly coherent one:

    45 I know the man such that the firm John worked for sacked the man

The restriction which disallows such constructions is the "Complex Noun Phrase Constraint" (CNPC) originating from Ross (1967): Essentially, it says that the process of Wh movement described above cannot take place if it would involve moving a Wh phrase out of a complex NP (an NP having the structure . . . [NP [S . . .]]. . .). Relative clauses are themselves a type of complex NP and so the difficulty with the example above is explained as due to the fact that the "who" referring to "the man" has had to be moved from a complex NP structure: [NP the firm [S which sacked who]]. Constraints like this play an extremely important role in recent theories of

grammar (see e.g. Chomsky, 1977; 1981), and their existence (and puta-
tively universal application) is regarded as important evidence for an
innately structured language-learning ability, given that they do not have
any obvious functional or semantic motivation. They seem to be just
logically arbitrary (though presumably not psychologically arbitrary) limitations on our ability to carry out certain types of symbolic operations.

The treatment of Wh phrases in Marcus's framework is more or less the
inverse of the "movement rule" analysis, and also depends upon the
grammatical fact that displaced Wh phrases appear in the sentence initial
Comp position. Thus when a Wh phrase is encountered it is either in the
correct position, in which case nothing needs to happen, or it is in Comp.
When a gap is encountered—a verb missing an object or subject, for
example—the parser creates a "trace" and inserts it in the gap, linking it to
the currently available Comp position. If when beginning a new sentence
the contents of Comp have not been identified with a gap, a trace is again
created, this time going in the Comp position of the new sentence.
However, this can only happen if this new Comp position does not itself
have a Wh phrase in it: Marcus assumes that only one such item at a time
can appear in Comp. Thus the linking of the Wh phrase with the gap, when
it is eventually encountered, is achieved via a sequence of traces, all but the
last of them in Comp, exactly as in the earlier transformational analysis.

This process can be illustrated as follows:

46 Who did John see?
Stack: [S . . .]
Buffer: [WH who] [Aux did] [NP John]
Stack: [S [Comp who][Aux did] [NP John]
Buffer: [V see][.   ][   ]
Stack: [S [Comp who][Aux did][Np John][VP [V see] . . .]
Buffer: [t   ][.   ][   ]

A trace is created and dropped into the buffer when the verb "see" is
discovered not to have an object. This is eventually put in the tree and
bound to "who": [S [Comp who(i)][Aux did][NP John][VP [V see] [NP
t(i)]]] (I am simplifying the grammatical facts in these examples).

In a case where the Wh phrase and the gap are not in the same sentence,
as in:

47 Who do you think that John saw?

then on encountering the beginning of the "that John saw" sentence, since
we have not yet found a gap to link the "who" to, a trace is created in the
Comp position: [S [Comp who(i)][do you think][S [Comp t(i) that] . . . .]]].

When the gap after "saw" is encountered it can be associated with this trace and hence indirectly with "who," as before. Identifying the trace with the currently available Comp position will get the right results: Recall that in order to make determinism a strong claim, access to the stack is limited to the most recent S, roughly speaking, and so the current Comp position is the only one available.

The interesting thing is that this treatment will not work in all cases. If the most recent Comp has already been "used up" for the purpose of interpreting a trace created to fill a gap, then any further gaps or traces will not be able to be handled correctly. This is exactly the case for the CNPC example we looked at. The structure that the grammar would assign to it would be something like:

48 [I know [NP the man [S [Comp who(i)] John worked for [NP the firm
   [S [Comp which(j)]][[NP t(j)] sacked [NP t(i)]]]]

(ignoring the application of the constraint itself). However, the parser is not able to assign this structure: When processing the second relative clause "the firm which sacked . . . ," the first "who" has not yet been linked to a gap, but the parser is not able to create a trace in order to carry this fact down, for Comp already has its own Wh phrase in it. When the subject gap is encountered ("which" must be in Comp, so cannot simultaneously be in subject position) a trace is created and put into it, and bound to the contents of the current Comp position, i.e. "which." When the second object gap is encountered there is now nothing for it to be bound to: The current Comp position has been used up, and no other higher Comp position is available, by the determinism hypothesis. Thus the parser will automatically fail to parse such structures: Its mode of operation reflects the restrictions expressed by the CNPC, although that constraint does not have to be stated separately as a special principle.

The details of Marcus's explanation of this and other constraints can be criticised, and the real picture is by no means as straightforward as has been suggested here. What is really of interest, however, is not the particular mechanism which does or does not suffice to bring about the desired effects so much as the type of explanation being offered. Grammatical theory typically tries to assume a simple set of syntactic rules, which might include a rule like Wh movement "move any Wh-phrase to Comp," rules which, if left to their own devices, will cheerfully generate impossible sentences like those above. To encode the restrictions necessary to exclude them as constraints on individual rules would be intolerably complex and probably unworkable: The alternative is to postulate a set of constraints on possible rule applications, like the one we have seen prohibiting movement out of a complex noun phrase. Seen from one perspective, such constraints are arbitrary—we could equally well have had a constraint, for example, which instead of prohibiting movement from inside such positions, *required* movement from them. As stated earlier, there is no obvious semantic motivation for the form assumed by these constraints—they are not constraints on what is sayable, but constraints on the way sayable things can and cannot be said.

What Marcus is offering us can be construed in two ways. On the strongest construal he is able to explain away the constraints themselves and to dispense with them as an independent part of grammatical description. This line of explanation can be somewhat baldly summarised in the following terms. Take some optimally simple set of grammatical rules, of such a kind that, if left to themselves, they will overgenerate in exactly the ways we have seen. Now assume the simplest parsing mechanism capable of correctly parsing the grammatical sentences generated by our rules, and which also obeys various other a priori computationally plausible restrictions on its operation, in particular determinism, and the other consequences of that, such as the passing of traces down from Comp to Comp. Now the claim is that the conjunction of these two, with no further work whatsoever, will quite naturally fail to parse exactly the set of overgenerated sentences, sentences which are ungrammatical but which require constraints to rule them out as ungrammatical if the grammar is taken in isolation. Thus the constraints themselves are misplaced: They are only a rather clumsy way of encoding into the grammar phenomena which are strictly speaking not to do with grammar per se so much as side effects of the parser's normal mode of operation. If this explanation could be carried through successfully it would eliminate the need for a statement of grammatical constraints as an independent subsystem of grammar.

For various reasons, this strong construal is probably not feasible (see e.g. Fodor, 1981; Pulman, 1983). It does not seem possible to explain all constraints that seem to be necessary in terms of the operations of the parsing mechanism. A weaker version can still be maintained, however; one which sees the operation of the parser not as replacing the independent statement of constraints, but rather providing a *raison d'etre* for their existence in that particular form: They have, in other words, a functional explanation in terms of the interaction between the demands of the linguistic system to maintain as much freedom as possible in the way it can express the messages a language user may need to convey, and the demands of the parser to the effect that the messages should be structured in such a way as to be able to parse them without undue difficulty or ambiguity within the limits of determinism. (See J. D. Fodor, 1981, 1983a, 1983b, for an extended exploration of this approach to syntactic constraints.)

Berwick and Weinberg (1984) attempt to extend this type of explanation to a wider range of phenomena, again using a model of parsing related to that proposed by Marcus. Their discussion centres around the notion of "subjacency," a principle of the theory of transformational grammar which says, roughly speaking, that the domain of application of grammatical rules can only extend to adjacent "cyclic nodes" (cyclic nodes, for our purposes, are just NP and S). Thus a rule may refer to elements X and Y in a configuration like: ... X ... [S ... Y ... but not in: ... X ... [NP ... [S ... Y .. or: ... X ... [S ... [S ... Y ... The first of these prohibited configurations is equivalent in its effects to the CNPC constraint which we discussed earlier: This can be seen as a special case of the more general principle of subjacency.

Subjacency applies to a wide variety of grammatical rules of different types, and appears to be a truly central grammatical principle, manifesting itself, sometimes in slightly different ways, in the grammars of all languages. (See e.g. Chomsky, 1981, and references therein for discussion.) Berwick and Weinberg see subjacency as motivated directly by the determinism requirement, by the following line of argument. Determinism requires that the state of the parser at any particular time determines its actions on a given input. As we have seen, this could be trivially guaranteed by allowing the parser to encode on the stack as much information about the preceding context as might be necessary. Of course, since there is no theoretical limit on the length of sentences, this could mean that the stack could grow indefinitely, a clear violation of the spirit of the determinism requirement, and also, presumably, involving considerable memory overheads if we were to interpret the parsing model as an algorithmic-level description of what is going on in parsing. The imposition of subjacency means that the encoding—if any is allowed—will be limited to the immediately preceding NP or S domain, for anything earlier can safely be forgotten: Subjacency states that no grammatical rule could ever refer to an item in the context that far back and so the information need no longer be retained. Thus the constraint ensures that at most one sentence or NP's-worth of left context at a time need be encoded, enabling the parser to operate effectively and safely while still observing the requirements of determinism. This was exactly the way in which Marcus treated Wh phrases, of course: Moving from Comp to Comp only one sentence at a time enables the effects of subjacency to be circumvented.

To illustrate the type of argument that Berwick and Weinberg are advancing, consider the phenomenon of "verb gapping" displayed in:

49 John ran after Sue, and Bill __ after Mary

In a conjoined sentence, a repeated verb can be omitted, although it is understood to be there. An apparently similar construction is "VP ellipsis," where this time a whole verb phrase rather than a single verb can be omitted, only a tense-carrying auxiliary being retained:

50 John ran after Mary, and Bill did __ too.

It is immaterial at present whether these grammatical processes are thought of as literally deleting repeated words and phrases or as filling in gaps with reference to earlier parts of the sentence. The interesting point is that although apparently so similar, gapping observes subjacency, while VP ellipsis does not:

51 *John ran after Mary, and [S I think [S that Bill __ after Sue]]
52 John ran after Mary, and [S I think [S that Bill did __ too]]

What decides whether some construction obeys subjacency or not? Berwick and Weinberg suggest that the difference between these two is that gapping creates a situation in which a particular syntactic decision cannot be made without reference to the preceding context, whereas VP ellipsis does not. This is not the decision as to what material is missing in the second conjunct of the sentence, for there is no clear evidence that this is a syntactic rather than a semantic decision at all. The decision in question is how the VP itself is to be structured. For example, in the two sentences:

53 John arrived after Sue, and Bill __ after Mary
54 John looked after Sue, and Bill __ after Mary

there is a decision to be made in the second conjunct as to how the sequence "after Mary" is to be attached to the VP. The preposition "after" may be associated with the missing verb, as in the second, or the NP "Mary," as in the first. These syntactic differences can be inferred from examples like:

55 It was after Mary that Bill arrived
56 *It was after Mary that Bill looked

Clearly the decision hinges on the subcategorisation properties of the missing verb: "Looked," in this sense, requires "after," whereas "arrived" does not. Subjacency guarantees that this information will be available in the preceding sentence, and so the decision can be made deterministically.

In contrast, for VP ellipsis, this question does not arise. The whole VP is missing, and so no properties of the verb in the earlier conjunct are relevant to the parsing of the remainder. (They may be semantically relevant, of course.) Thus the parser can simply record the fact that a VP is missing, and proceed with its analysis: No further syntactic decision needs to be made.

INTERLUDE

Let us review the story so far. We have illustrated a range of observations—limitations on centre embedding, parsing preferences, and garden paths—that seem prima facie to demonstrate something about the internal workings of the human parsing mechanism. We have examined several attempts to describe parsers operating along certain guiding principles which would account for some of these observations. We have also seen that, in fact, some of the observations themselves may not reveal anything about syntactic processing, but may instead be artefacts of a failure to take into account the role of context in resolving local ambiguities. (This does not apply to centre embeddings: Their difficulty is one of the most enduring observations to be found in the linguistics literature, and the difficulty remains unexplained by the mechanisms appealed to by Crain and Steedman (1985).)

We have also discussed deterministic parsing and attempts to ground a functional explanation for the existence and nature of syntactic constraints on this feature of the operation of a parser, itself perhaps motivated on functional grounds of robustness and economy of temporary memory storage. Now, however, given that at least part of Marcus's (1980) original motivation for the determinism hypothesis was the allegedly syntactic nature of the garden-path phenomena, it is perhaps worth asking whether the other consequences derived from determinism are equally spurious in the explanation of the real facts of the case. Does the human parsing mechanism operate deterministically, or is it guided by such powerful mechanisms of contextual resolution that it appears to do so? If the latter, do the findings of Crain and Steedman threaten the other explanatory functions of determinism?

Somewhat surprisingly, perhaps, the answer turns out to be no. The grounding of constraints like subjacency in functional properties of the language understanding mechanism can still be carried through, albeit in a slightly different form. On the Marcus/Berwick and Weinberg (1984) approach, the parser is seen as developing only one syntactic analysis at a time: This, coupled with the limited lookahead available, and the limitations on the storage of left context, is what makes the parser fully deterministic. On the model which fits most naturally with the Crain and Steedman findings, the parser also only develops one analysis at a time, though not because of any internal constraints: Rather, at any point at which local ambiguity becomes evident, the parser searches for some nonsyntactic resolution of the ambiguity. Once the ambiguity is resolved, one of the possibilities is discarded and only the remaining one pursued. Thus, strictly speaking, it is not the parsing mechanism which is deterministic in this sense but the overall comprehension process—the determinism of the parser is merely inherited from this: There is no need to assume that the parser is in itself unable to carry along more than one analysis at once, and thus may not be deterministic at all.

The motivation for subjacency need not be abandoned, however. The aspect of determinism essential to Berwick and Weinberg's explanation is not the pursuance of a single parse at a time, but the restriction to a limited left context (contrary to what they seem to be claiming on, e.g. Berwick & Weinberg, 1984; pp. 168–169). This latter requirement is actually the one doing the work, and although there is likewise no overwhelming reason so far to consider that this is a feature of the parser rather than of the overall comprehension process, the explanation for subjacency will survive. The assumption that comprehension proceeds as quickly as possible as words are encountered leads to pressure to resolve local ambiguities by reference to local context as soon as they are encountered. Thus the parser is able to abandon one possible line of analysis, even though, we may assume, it is in principle capable of carrying on pursuing different possibilities in parallel. It may even be that decisions like that in the gapping case are made partially by reference to the local context, including of course the meaning of the most recently processed conjunct, rather than by purely syntactic means. Nevertheless there would still be clear advantages in making sure that such grammatical processes observed subjacency, as the amount of semantic context which had to be searched would be likewise constrained. Thus although the causal connections between the parser and other components of the comprehension mechanism might be a little different, the overall pattern of explanation can be preserved: The determinism arguments simply apply to a different level.

It might be thought that the model we are moving towards, on which it is the overall process of comprehension that is deterministic (as far as possible), is somewhat vacuous, amounting only to the claim that humans manage to understand sentences somehow without making too many mistakes. But this is not completely true: In fact, the model makes some straightforwardly testable predictions, for example that at any point at which the parser is faced with more than one possible syntactic analysis path, then there should be some nonsyntactic information available in the input to provide the necessary disambiguation. This information might be semantic, contextual, or prosodic. Only under the circumstance where there is no such information would we expect to find anything like the garden-path effect.

This prediction has been investigated for the case of prosodic information by Briscoe (1982, 1984). He argues that the evidence for the garden-path and parsing-preference phenomena obtained in studies like those of Frazier (1979) and Ford et al. (1982) is misleading, as the subjects were forced to operate under conditions where a source of information normally present was not available to them: The subjects in the latter experiment, recall, were faced with written, unpunctuated sentences with no contextual settings. You may have felt intuitively when we discussed garden-path sentences earlier that many of the problems should disappear if the sentences were pronounced in a realistic way. Briscoe (1982) found that when garden-path sentences are read aloud with an appropriate intonation contour they provide little difficulty for comprehension. Acoustic analysis reveals that at crucial points in sentences like:

57 While Mary was mending the sock fell off her lap

namely, between "mending" and "the," there is a small but measurable prosodic break (Warren, 1985). In the written form, of course, it would be natural to insert a comma at just this point.

If, on the other hand, it turns out that the garden-path effects can be found to persist in sentences even when there is no unnatural lack of necessary information, then it seems likely that some of the original claims about the internal structure and preferences of the parser can be sustained. Briscoe's (1984) preliminary results indicate that in most cases, this is not so, and thus that Crain and Steedman's conclusions are for the most part borne out.

There remains still, though, the tendency for Local Attachment to be explained, in by now familiar examples like:

58 John said that he phoned your mother yesterday
59 We saw the manager of the band's accounts

It seems likely that this can best be explained in something like the way suggested by Frazier and Fodor (1978): If the comprehension mechanism is trying to integrate incoming input into a meaning representation of some kind as quickly as possible, then there is no reason for it to retain syntactic structure any longer than it has to. Thus if it is possible to parse incoming constituents in a way which does not require reference to prior structure, it will do so, and proceed to "forget" that prior structure, since it can now be absorbed into the nonsyntactic representation being built up. This is always assuming that no contextual conflicts are generated: Clearly, the following two settings will produce different preferences for sentence 59:

60 Who did you see?
61 What financial checking did you carry out?

Alternatively, it might be possible to develop an explanation (in the spirit of Crain and Steedman) in terms of notions like "topic." The low attachment reading of 58 seems to presuppose that what is being talked about is "John phoning your mother" and says that "yesterday" is when he did it. The high attachment reading, however, requires that what is being talked about is "John saying X" and says that "yesterday" is when he did that. Thus neither reading would be appropriate as an answer to a question about the other topic:

62. When did John phone her?
63. When did John tell you this?

Unfortunately, notions like "topic" are, in any nontrivial sense, vagueness incarnate at the present stage of linguistic theory, and the task of formulating a computationally precise and testable explanation in these terms is one for the future.

PARSING AND UNDERSTANDING[2]

We are assuming that parsing proceeds hand-in-hand with understanding. We have a fairly clear idea of the type of grammatical information that the parser must have access to: We now turn to the question of how that information is related to semantic information, and what type of parsing model we must contemplate in order to allow for the continuous integration of these two. It is striking that none of the models we have looked at so far makes any claims about this in any detail.

---

[2]I have had to assume some knowledge of formal logic in this section. For a quick introduction to some of the concepts presupposed here see Johnson-Laird (1983) and, for more detail, Dowty, Wall, and Peters (1981). Formulas like "(for-all (x) (P (x) → Q (x)))" are read as "for all x, if x is P then x is Q." The lambda notation is just a way of making new predicates or functions from old ones: A formula like "[lambda (x)(rich (x)] (John)" can be informally paraphrased as saying something like "the property of those x that are rich applies to John," and something like "[lambda (P)(P (John)](rich)" says something like "the property of those properties that apply to John applies to 'rich'." Both are logically equivalent to the formula to which they will reduce by making an appropriate substitution of the lambda variable: "rich (John)." This process is called "reduction" ("beta-reduction," strictly). In what follows, x and y are individual variables, and P and Q are predicate variables.

In most current theories of grammar the relation between syntax and semantics is a close one. One particular view of this relationship is that it is to be expressed on a "rule-to-rule" basis: For each grammatical rule stating how some items are to be grouped to form a constituent, there is to be a semantic rule saying how the meanings of the components are to be combined to form the meaning of the whole. All current theories of grammar also assume that some important aspects of the meaning of a sentence can be captured via a translation into some kind of logical form. Under the rule-to-rule assumption this is most naturally thought of as happening in the following way. Firstly, the sentence is syntactically analysed and a parse tree built for it in the familiar way. Secondly, the semantic rule associated with each syntactic rule involved in building the parse tree is executed, resulting in a complete logical form for the sentence being built up from the meanings of all the words and constituents in it.

As an example of such a procedure, let us assume the following grammar and semantic rules:

$$S \rightarrow NP\ VP : NP'\ (VP'\ )$$
$$NP \rightarrow Det\ N : Det'\ (N'\ )$$
$$VP \rightarrow V : V'$$

The portion after the colon is the semantic rule: $NP'(VP'\ )$ can be paraphrased as saying that the meaning of S is what you get by applying the meaning of NP to the meaning of VP as function to argument. We assume that the meaning of "every" can be represented as [lambda (P)(lambda (Q)(for-all (x)(P (x) $\rightarrow$ Q (x))))], and that other words just translate directly to constants of the logic being used.

Now given a tree like that in Fig. 4.14, applying the NP and VP rules gives us:

[lambda (P)(lambda (Q)(for-all (x)(P (x) $\rightarrow$ Q (x))))](man)

for NP, which reduces to

(lambda (Q) (for-all (x)(man (x) $\rightarrow$ Q (x)))).

The VP meaning is just that of the verb, and the S meaning is obtained by applying the first to the second:

[lambda (Q)(for-all (x)(man (x) $\rightarrow$ Q (x)))] (sleeps)

which in turn reduces to:

(for-all (x)(man (x) $\rightarrow$ sleeps (x))),

i.e. for any x, if x is a man then x sleeps.

The details of this process can rapidly become overwhelming, but for the moment the important points to note are that such a procedure for

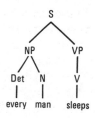

FIG. 4.14.

translation into logical form (which we are of course regarding as a highly abstract description of a process corresponding to the interpretation of a sentence) seems to presuppose two things: (1) that a complete syntactic analysis of the sentence is available; and (2) that it has to be available before the process of interpretation can begin, at least on a constituent by constituent basis.

This "classical" view of the relation between syntax and semantics seems straightforwardly at odds with what we have been assuming about the nature of parsing, namely, that it is at every stage interleaved with nonsyntactic decisions. At the very minimum we require partially completed constituents to be semantically interpretable in some fashion, so that logically possible but contextually implausible lines of analysis can be discontinued as quickly as possible. If meanings only become available once syntactic constituents have been completed this process is likely to be somewhat inefficient, at least where local ambiguities extend over more than a couple of words, as several analyses may have to be carried along in parallel. (Some researchers have, of course argued that this is indeed the case: E.g. Lackner and Garrett, 1973. Theirs was, however a highly artificial task conducted with isolated sentences, and thus subject to similar objections as with the garden-path phenomena, namely that a usual source of information is not available. Other evidence points to the virtually immediate resolution of ambiguity, as we have been assuming: See Tyler and Marslen-Wilson, 1977, and Pynte, 1978.)

Motivated in part by these considerations, Ades and Steedman (1982) and Steedman (1983) have advanced a model of grammar and an associated theory of parsing which is capable of allowing, in principle, for the word-by-word semantic integration that we seem to require. This model uses an extended "categorial" grammar (see Lyons, 1968, for an introduction); a grammar which assumes that information associated with syntactic rules in other theories is instead associated with individual words. For example, the treatment of the example earlier might posit a grammar/lexicon like:

every: NP/N (something which combines with an N to its right to form an NP) man: N

sleeps: S\NP (something which combines with an NP to its left to form an S)

(Their model is "extended" categorial grammar because it allows for more than these usual modes of combination: We will not illustrate or need these extensions here.) A parsing of the example sentence will illustrate this:

[NP/N every].

On encountering "every" its category is noted and an N is expected. When it is found the two are integrated into an NP by the rule of "Forward Combination" (given X/Y followed by Y, combine them to form an X).

[NP [NP/N every][N man]].

When "sleeps" is encountered:

[NP [NP/N every][N man]][S\NP sleeps];

this is combined with the NP by "Backward Combination" (given Y followed by X/Y combine them to form an X).

[S[NP[NP/N every][N man]][S\NP sleeps]],

which represents a derivation tree as shown in Fig. 4.15.

How does this theory allow for continuous semantic interpretation? The answer lies in the intended interpretation of the combination rules and the categorial symbols associated with words and constituents. For although we have regarded them as syntactic labels, it is equally appropriate to regard them as semantic formulas, in particular as a variety of logical formulas akin to those used earlier. Under this interpretation a label like NP/N means "a function which requires the meaning of an N to make the meaning of an NP," i.e. something which requires a noun to form a complete semantic unit. Likewise the meaning of an intransitive verb like "sleeps" requires the meaning of an NP to make the meaning of a complete sentence. Although these notions of partial meanings have a clear intuitive basis, they can also be given a rigorous formal interpretation via the lambda notation used above.

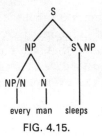

FIG. 4.15.

Once the labels are construed as semantic, then of course there is actually no difference whatsoever between the process of parsing a sentence and the process of assigning a semantic interpretation to it. Each time a new constituent is encountered, it is either used to complete the meaning of one already being built, ·or is itself a partial meaning waiting for other items to complete it. Thus there is no difficulty at all in the assumption that the process of semantic interpretation takes place incrementally word-by-word through the sentence.

Let us see how this might work in the case of the garden-path examples. In the case of:

64 The horse raced past the barn fell

let us assume that at some stage in the interpretation of this sentence we have the constituent "the horse" with two possible labellings (as we do within the categorial framework). Ades and Steedman (1982) assume that determiners are lexically ambiguous according to whether they introduce a simple or a complex NP, and thus we have two parsings of the first constituent:

[NP/S [NP\S/N the][N horse]]

and

[NP [NP/N the][N horse]].

(The complex NP type of determiner is "something which combines with an N to give something which combines with an S to give an NP.")

Contextual resolution is called into play at this point, as we have two possible parsings: In a setting where more than one horse had already been introduced, and no particular one was in focus, then a unique referent for "the horse" cannot yet be located. On the basis of this information the parser could throw away the simple NP analysis, for on this, NP is complete and should therefore be interpretable. It can continue, expecting to find a relative clause which will identify which horse is being talked about. If, on the other hand, a unique reference can be found (or postulated: If no horse has been mentioned at all, the NP could plausibly be taken to be introducing a new discourse referent) then the parser can reasonably confidently throw away the NP/S analysis. This will of course result in the garden-path phenomenon in this instance.

In contrast, on the classical view, it would not be until the end of the "raced past the barn" constituent that the information necessary to make this choice would become available, for it is not until then that the parse trees have been built and the semantic information associated with the syntactic rules used can be retrieved. This is not a very plausible description of what is happening here.

The model proposed by Steedman and his colleagues is the first, to my knowledge, to be compatible formally with these simple well-known facts about the comprehension process, and to be explicit enough to avoid charges of handwaving. (At least one computer implementation of the theory exists, described in Briscoe, 1984.) Neither of these achievements should be underestimated. Nevertheless, there are several grounds on which the theory can be criticised, mainly to do with the nature of the categorial framework on which it rests.

As will have been evident from the examples we have discussed, the constituent structures implicit in the categorial analysis of sentences are distinctly odd. Further illustration would have revealed more oddities: For example, on Steedman's analysis, in a sentence like:

65 I will eat the cakes

the sequence "I will" has to be regarded as a constituent. But there is virtually no evidence from the usual tests for constituent structure that this is correct, and several compelling reasons why it cannot be. This is not just a matter of aesthetics or preference: A grammatical theory, whatever its connection with semantic interpretation, should assign constituent structure in a way consistent with distributional evidence, intonational contours, and so on. It is by no means clear that categorial grammar is capable of doing this satisfactorily, and it is for this reason that linguists have not usually been attracted to the framework. (Those who have used it, like Montague, 1973, have been motivated by semantic, not syntactic concerns.)

A possible response might be that the structures which emerge from an analysis are merely an artefact of that process, and should not be taken to be making syntactic claims of the usual sort at all. Rather, the syntactic information about the language is encoded in the complex categorial entries associated with words in the lexicon. At first sight, this seems like a plausible response, for presumably the assignment of such entries to words depends on a prior classical analysis of the language in terms of ordinary phrasal constituents like NP, VP, PP, and S. In fact this reply raises more problems than it solves: Are we to assume, then, that people have access to two grammars; one which encodes the distributional facts about the language, and a further one, parasitic upon the first, which represents this information in a different form in the lexicon (in a highly redundant fashion, moreover)? We would surely need a very great deal of persuasion before accepting such a bizarre conclusion.

What we need at this point, I suggest, is some way of reconciling the classical picture with the demands of word-by-word semantic integration. This would allow us to avoid the problem of the categorial grammar-based approach, while preserving the attractive features of the categorial parsing model. In the final section we attempt to develop the beginnings of a theory of parsing and semantic interpretation with the necessary properties.

TOWARDS A THEORY OF PARSING AND INTERPRETATION

Our parsing model, like that of Steedman and his colleagues, and indeed those of Berwick and Weinberg and (to a lesser extent), Marcus, is a variant on a basic "shift-reduce" algorithm. The mechanism assumes a stack, or last-in-first-out store, on which incoming constituents are placed. In the categorial model, the basic operations of the parser are "shift"—i.e. put the next word, appropriately labelled, on top of the stack—and "reduce," if possible, the top two items on the stack by combining them using one of the combination rules, placing the result in turn on top of the stack. When the only item on the stack is labelled S, or whatever the distinguished symbol of the grammar is, and all the input has been consumed, the parse is successful.

To illustrate, the successive states of the stack in parsing "the man slept" in the categorial framework would be:

shift:
1. ⟨ NP/N the⟩ → shift

2. ⟨N man⟩
   ⟨ NP/N the⟩ → forward combination:

3. ⟨NP the man⟩ → shift

4. ⟨S\NP slept⟩
   ⟨NP the man⟩ → backward combination:

5. ⟨S the man slept⟩

In our model, parsing proceeds differently, but the same stack mechanism is presupposed. The parser assumes something like the phrase structure grammars of the type used earlier, repeated here:

$$S \rightarrow NP\ VP : NP'(VP')$$
$$NP \rightarrow N : N'$$
$$NP \rightarrow Det\ N : Det'(N')$$
$$VP \rightarrow V : V'$$
$$VP \rightarrow V\ NP : V'(NP')$$

although the central idea should transfer to most other contemporary models of syntax, in essence.

As well as the basic shift operation, which puts an entry of the form

⟨syntactic category, meaning⟩ on the stack for a word, the following operations are assumed to be available:

Invoke (a Rule). If there is an entry on top of the stack of the form ⟨X, Y⟩, and a rule in the grammar of the form "A → x B:⟨interpretation⟩," where B is a (possibly null) sequence, then create from that entry and the rule a new entry by the following process. The syntactic category is A, followed by (B), if B is not null. Interpret this as meaning "an A which needs a B to be complete." The interpretation is the result of first substituting Y in the appropriate place in the interpretation part of the rule and then lambda abstracting over all the symbols in B which appear in that interpretation, if any.

This sounds very complicated, but the idea is quite simple. If we have, say, a determiner on top of the stack: ⟨ Det every⟩ and a rule in the grammar like the one above, then we can create a new entry of the form:

⟨ NP(N), (lambda (x) (every' (x)))⟩.

The first part of the entry can be interpreted as meaning "an NP looking for an N." The second part is what we get by putting in the interpretation of the Det in the appropriate place, giving "every' (N)." Then we lambda abstract over the N, since it appears in the syntactic part of the entry, giving the final result. Thus (lambda (x) (every'(x))) is more or less the semantic counterpart of the syntactic part of the entry, except that it is more specific. What we are doing here, of course, is computing the meanings of partial constituents as does the categorial model: The difference is that we are doing it as the parse proceeds, and we are not using anything other than the standard types of syntactic and semantic rules.

Combine. Unlike the categorial and more standard shift-reduce parsers, we do not require both constituents to be complete before they can be combined. If the top item on the stack is of the type expected by the next item down they can be combined. Thus, given a stack like:

⟨N boy⟩
⟨NP(N) (lambda (x) (every'(x)))⟩

the two can be combined to give:

⟨NP [lambda (x)(every'(x))] (boy')⟩.

The interpretation is of course logically equivalent to "every'(boy')," and we will assume that all such necessary simplifications are carried out.

Clear. Under certain circumstances—roughly, when the size of the items grows beyond a certain threshold—an incomplete constituent can be "cleared" to some longer-term semantic storage, for reasons familiar from our earlier discussions. We are not much concerned with the precise mechanism for this until the next section: Suffice it to say that this can be achieved in such a way as not to throw away any necessary information, and to continue to build up an appropriate semantic interpretation. (A precise definition of a version of clear, and a description of a computer implementation of a parser operating in a similar way to the one outlined here, can be found in Pulman, 1985.)

As an illustration, here is a "trace" of the parser on the sentence:

66 The man sleeps
shift:
⟨Det the'⟩ → Invoke:

⟨NP(N) (lambda (x) (the'(x)))⟩ → shift:

⟨N man'⟩
⟨NP(N) (lambda (x) (the'(x)))⟩ → Combine:

⟨NP the'(man')⟩ → Invoke:

⟨S(VP) (lambda (y)[the'(man')](y))⟩ → shift:

⟨V sleeps⟩
⟨S(VP) (lambda (y)[the'(man')](y))⟩ → Invoke:

⟨VP sleeps'⟩
⟨S(VP) (lambda (y)[the'(man')](y))⟩ → Combine:

⟨S [the'(man')](sleeps)⟩

On the assumption that the meaning of "the" is something like:

(lambda (P)(lambda (Q)(exists (x) (contextually-unique (x) & P(x)
& Q(x))))),

this is equivalent to a form such as:

(exists(x) (contextually-unique(x) & man(x) & sleeps(x)));

("there is some contexually identifiable x such that x is a man and x sleeps").

There are two features of this model of parsing which are important. Firstly, as with the categorial model, at any stage whatever has been parsed can be interpreted immediately. The partial meanings constructed via lambda abstraction are objects which are just as semantically viable as complete formulas, within the logic assumed here: Indeed, they can be regarded as a formal reconstruction of the notion "meaningful fragment of a sentence." Secondly, although syntax is used to guide the operations of the parser, it does not explicitly build a parse tree en route to the logical forms it produces and thus has none of the counterintuitive (and counter-factual) properties of the classical view. In some sense, though, such a parse tree is implicit in the series of actions taken by the parser. The same is true of the categorial parser: The difference is that the parse tree implicit here is an uncontroversial labelling of the syntactic categories and constituents encountered by the parser. It nevertheless embodies the view of the relationship between syntactic and semantic rules expressed by the classical view; but syntactic rules here are used as a kind of key, rather than as something to produce structure. They tell the parser what kind of constituent to expect next and they provide the semantic information necessary to begin the interpretation of the constituent. Both of these types of information are available as soon as the first element of the constituent is recognised.

We can think of the parser as behaving like the categorial parser in contextual resolution: The invoke procedure will at times produce two or more candidate new entries to place on the stack. We assume that the one which is most coherent semantically and contextually will be the one chosen, and so the parser will not under normal circumstances have to pursue more than one analysis at a time. It will thus satisfy our requirements that it be capable of accounting for the possibility of word-by-word semantic integration of a sentence. It also provides a straightforward answer to the question of how semantic and syntactic knowledge is used in parsing: We merely assume that the parser has access to this knowledge in some neutral form between comprehension and production. We do not have to assume any special form of organisation of it for parsing.

CENTRE EMBEDDING

Let us now return to the topic of the difficulty of centre embedding, one of the few phenomena which seem to survive the findings of Crain and Steedman (1985) as being fairly uncontroversially syntactic.

We saw earlier that the proposals of Frazier and Fodor (1978), that the difficulty of centre embedding is caused by the narrowness of their parser's first stage "window," is not successful, for there are examples which should fall within the window but which are still difficult. The proposal that we began with, Kimball's (1973) "two sentences" limitation, is not a satisfactory solution either: While it achieves the right effects in the centre-embedding cases, it does so somewhat by brute force, and in other cases does not describe what is going on accurately. For example, while centre embeddings are one instance where more than two sentences need to be processed simultaneously, so are instances of nesting of nonidentical sentential constituents, as in:

67 [1 If [2 John sent the shop [3 that the girl bought the book from] a rude letter][then . . .]]

While such sentences can be clumsy, they do not seem to be anywhere near as difficult as centre embeddings of identical constituents of the type we have illustrated earlier. This extra element of difficulty is left unaccounted for by a simple "two sentences" limitation.

Alternative explanations for the centre-embedding difficulties have been offered. One influential proposal, in the context of a theory of syntactic processing influenced by transformational grammar, was made by Fodor et al. (1974). Their explanation is in terms of their "canonical sentoid" processing strategy, according to which incoming material on a left-to-right parse is assembled into constituents which roughly correspond to deep-structure sentences. Once assembled they can be cleared from immediate memory for full semantic processing. (This can be regarded as a version of the "classical" view sketched earlier.) The difficulty of centre embedding is explained (Fodor et al., 1974): ". . . if we assume, first, that there is only a limited amount of short-term memory available for the perceptual processing of sentences, and second, that no constituent of a sentence can be dismissed from short-term memory until it has been assigned to a sentoid (p. 342)." Since the head NP of a multiply-centre-embedded relative clause cannot be associated with its VP until the last embedded VP is processed, this represents the worst possible case for a procedure like theirs in terms of short-term-memory demands, for all intermediate results must be stored in memory until the earliest constituent is complete.

However, there are several objections which can be raised to this account (there are also objections that can be raised to the canonical sentoid strategy itself: e.g. Marslen-Wilson and Tyler, 1980). Firstly, as with the Two Sentences theory, it seems to be the case that this account predicts that all nested constructions should be just as difficult to process as centre embeddings. If memory for all incomplete constituents is limited, as it must be, then the beginnings of nested constituents, which are just as incomplete as the beginnings of centre-embedded constructions, should impose an equally severe burden on short-term memory. As we have seen, however, nonrecursive nestings are not as difficult as genuine centre embeddings.

Secondly, as intuition suggests, and as Miller and Isard (1964) confirmed in their experiment, the difficulty with centre embedding seems to set in immediately after the most deeply embedded sentence:

68 The man the boy the girl knew *liked was ill

If we take Fodor et al.'s account at face value, things should instead be getting better at this point, for by the time "liked" is encountered, the sentoid "the girl knew the boy" can be assembled and immediately dismissed from short-term memory, thus reducing the load. In other words, things should be no more difficult at this point than after "the boy." The time of maximal difficulty should be after "girl," where three NPs are awaiting assembly into sentoids.

The correct account of centre embedding seems to require two factors: a memory limitation for incomplete constituents of the type often proposed, accounting for the difficulty of all types of repeated nestings of constituents; and a specific limitation on recursive nesting—nesting of the same type of constituent within itself. (In theories which regard constituent labels as complexes of features, rather than unitary items, the two may be collapsed: Nesting would become more difficult in proportion to how similar the two constituents were.) The specific prohibition on recursive nesting is actually that made in one of the earliest discussions of this phenomenon (Miller & Isard, 1964), though later discussions seem to have ignored it.

Miller and Isard's proposal assumed that every grammatical rule or construction had associated with it a parsing routine. In particular, there would be an identifiable relative clause subroutine. Centre embedding corresponds to a situation where, in parsing, a particular routine is called on encountering the topmost instance of the construction, and then needs to be called again during the course of the original call. Their suggestion was that the human parsing mechanism is organised in such a way that this recursive calling is difficult or impossible (Miller & Isard, 1964): "if this recursive feature were not available, confusion would result; the temporary memory for the point of re-entry into the main routine might be erased, for example, so that when it resumed, the main routine would have to treat subsequent words as if they began a new constituent of the sentence (p. 300)."

This claim pinpoints exactly the nature of the difficulty, it seems to me, and, moreover, it locates the point of the onset of confusion accurately (this is of course on the assumption that relative clauses are not just S constituents, for otherwise even one level of centre embedding should be difficult).

Unfortunately the "no recursion" claim, in its straightforward form, makes some further predictions that seem to be wrong. To place a limit on recursion does not in itself distinguish centre embedding from either right or left embedding: All are equally instances of recursion. So the "no recursion" claim would seem to suggest that both left and right embeddings should be just as difficult to parse or interpret as centre embeddings and this is, as we have seen, simply not true.

An explanation for this emerges when we consider how the no recursion limitation might be imposed on a parser operating as the one we have described. The natural way of interpreting the restriction is to take Miller and Isard's proposal fairly literally, within the framework of the parsing procedure, as imposing a limitation on the "invoke" operation: A new (incomplete) constituent of a particular type can be begun only if there are some limited number of entries on the stack already of the same type. Exactly what the limit is will depend, we assume, on many factors: length of constituents; semantic and contextual properties; whether the written or the spoken medium is involved; and so on. If "invoke" is faced with a situation in which the limit would be exceeded we will assume that the earliest instance of the incomplete constituent is overwritten or forgotten in some way, thus losing the information necessary to complete it later on.

Let us see how this might work out in detail. We will add to the simple grammar we have been assuming some equally simple rules for relatives:

$$NP \rightarrow NP\ REL : REL'(NP')$$
$$REL \rightarrow NP\ VP : NP'(VP')$$

and we will ignore the question of how Wh words are linked appropriately with gaps. Notice that we are assuming that relative clauses are a constituent distinct from S. We assume, to make things simpler, that no recursion at all is allowed: This is not a realistic assumption, of course (nor is any other assumption of a permanently fixed limit). Also, for clarity, rather than build the incremental semantic interpretations yielded by the parser we will display the partial tree that a more conventional parser might build. These are considerably easier on the eye than complex lambda expressions.

For a sentence like:

69 The man the girl the boy knew waved to laughed

we ought to build a tree like that shown in Fig. 4.16. Things proceed as follows:

1. ⟨ NP   [NP the man]⟩
2. ⟨ NP (REL) [NP [NP the man][REL . . .]]⟩
3. ⟨NP [NP the girl]⟩
   ⟨ NP (REL) [NP [NP the man][REL . . .]]⟩

At this point, if we are to find the correct interpretation or build the appropriate parse tree, Invoke must recognise the NP "the girl" as the beginning of another relative clause, and place on the stack an entry like: ⟨NP(REL) [NP[NP the girl][REL . . .]]⟩. This, of course, will violate the recursion restriction, for there is already an NP(REL) on the stack. Let us assume that this earlier one is "forgotten," or at least inaccessible. Things

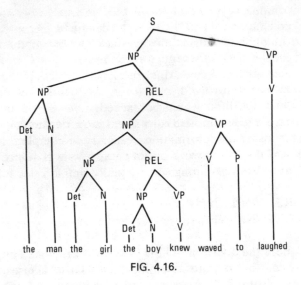

FIG. 4.16.

now proceed—I omit the details—until we have recognised the sentence as far as the word "knew":

4. ⟨NP   [NP [NP the girl][REL [NP the boy][VP knew]]]⟩

At this point we run into trouble. If the parser merely continues with "waved to" it will be stuck: "Waved to" on its own is not a complete VP, for it is missing an object. So a possible parse in which what is on the stack is the subject of "waved to" will fail. There is no other option available for it, however. In order to treat "waved to" correctly, the parser needs to know that it is part of a relative clause and thus can legitimately have a missing object; but this, of course, is precisely the information that is no longer available to it. Thus our model predicts exactly the point of onset of difficulty in the centre-embedding cases.

So far, we can show that imposing the no-recursion limitation on the way our parser operates produces the right effects for the centre-embedding cases, but we still have to show how this limitation can be overcome for the left and right recursive examples which apparently present no difficulty.

The case of left recursion is easy. Our parser shares with other shift-reduce algorithms the fact that left recursion can be successfully parsed to any depth without ever having to have more than one instance of the same incomplete construction at the same time. Thus the limit is automatically observed and we would not expect to find any difficulty in parsing such constructions. For example, if we have a pair of rules A → Aa; A → a, producing left embeddings of A, it is clear that any invocation of the recursive rule can only be made when an A constituent has already been recognised. So only one entry at a time of the form: ⟨A(a) . . . ⟩ will be present.

Right recursion is a different matter. It is easy to see that we will have the same thing happening as in the centre-embedding cases, in that, in order to be able to continue with a parse, we will have to "forget" earlier instances of the recursive constituents. Why, then, does this not lead to the same kind of difficulty?

There are two answers that it is possible to give here. The one that would be most satisfactory would be to maintain that we do indeed "forget" the syntactic information recorded in earlier entries for recursively occurring constituents, but that this is harmless because, being right embedding, we never encounter any further material which needs to be integrated with a forgotten constituent: This is not so for centre embedding, of course, and therein lies the difference. So in parsing a sentence like:

70 [S John [VP said [S that Mary [VP expected [S that he [VP would help her . . .

where there is right embedding of S and VP, we can confidently "forget" the earlier instances of entries which record S(VP), VP(S), etc., in moving to the later ones. Once "John" has been recognised as the subject of the sentence and "said" as the beginning of a VP, we know that we have all the ingredients of the S and so the parser can continue to parse the VP. (This is essentially the same rationale that Kimball (1973) appealed to for his forgetting procedure.)

There is a problem with this approach, although it would provide a very neat and parsimonious explanation of the various facts we have been discussing. The problem is that if these earlier instances of S and VP are forgotten, then in cases where reference to them at a later stage does need to be made, we should find ourselves in as much trouble as we do with the multiple centre-embedding cases.

It is not difficult to construct examples of the type required to test this prediction:

71 The man that John said that Mary expected that the police would arrest is still on the run

If the structure associated with ". . .[S that John [VP said . . ." is forgotten, as we might assume, then it is difficult to believe that the structure associated with "the man" is retained (although it is interesting that the parser as we have described would only actually remove the recursive constituents, leaving the earlier ones untouched, parsing and interpreting the sentence correctly). We should thus have exactly the same difficulty in integrating the sequence "is still on the run" as we did with the sequence "waved to" in the centre-embedded case. To my ear at least, this is not confirmed: The later example is unproblematic.

The second answer we can give to the right recursion question overcomes this objection and is the one implicit in the earlier description of the "Clear" operation of the parser. If we assume that a separate mechanism is able to "forget" information about already-begun constituents so as to be able to continue, then the recursion limitation could be overcome in all these cases. We must assume that the "Clear" procedure knows exactly which parts of the structure can be safely thrown away: In cases like the first right-recursive ones we looked at it is safe to throw away everything that precedes a new S or VP node when that is encountered; in the second type of example the higher NP node must be retained if the VP at the sentence is to be integrated satisfactorily. Of course, even some things retained by "Clear" could be overwritten if the recursion limit is exceeded.

The mode of operation of Clear required to produce this behaviour is as follows: if at some point on the stack there are two incomplete items such that the topmost, if completed, would in turn complete the first, then combine them to form a new single item. For example, if at some point we have entries like:

$$\ldots$$
$$\langle VP(X) \ldots \rangle$$
$$\langle S(VP) \ldots \rangle$$
$$\ldots$$

i.e. we have a VP looking for a constituent of type X, on top of an S looking for a VP, then we know that the S will be completed if the VP is. Clear produces a combined single entry, in this case of the form: $\langle S(X) \ldots \rangle$ (with appropriate adjustments to the semantics, amounting to composition of functions). Anything below the S on the stack will still be satisfied if an S is found, and anything of type X above it will satisfy the new entry. Obviously, such a procedure will allow any number of right recursions involving S and VP without violating the recursion limitation.

In the case of multiple centre-embeddings, however, Clear cannot operate to rescue the structure. The relevant portion of the stack for the earlier example will look like:

$$\langle NP(REL) \ldots \rangle$$
$$\langle NP(REL) \ldots \rangle$$
$$\langle S(VP) \ldots \rangle$$

Clear cannot combine any of these constituents, and so the recursion limitation will be triggered, the lower constituent being overwritten by the higher (if this is how the limitation is to be modelled).

This explanation is less parsimonious that the preceding one, as we have to postulate an extra mechanism. Nevertheless it seems quite plausible: We are claiming that there is one type of forgetting which is simply a throwing away of syntactic information when it has already been used to produce an appropriate partial interpretation and is serving no further purpose, the remainder of the sentence being sufficiently predictable for the parser to continue without it. This is the sort of procedure that most people have assumed to operate on general grounds of economy of effort. The second, and fatal, type of forgetting is when a particular piece of syntactic information is overwritten and lost by the postulation of another of a similar kind, this situation corresponding to a violation of the recursion limitation. This in turn is a consequence of the presumed organisation of the human parsing mechanism: The way that the computational resources available to the parser are organised is such that the necessary recursive mode of operation is just not a possibility without great conscious effort.

What explains this remains a mystery. It is a fact well known to computer scientists that recursive processing is more profligate of memory resources than nonrecursive processing. However, the nonrecursive nesting examples would take just as much memory, we argued, and so memory limitations cannot be the only factor. It is even possible that this type of processing is in general a cognitively difficult operation, not just in the syntactic domain: "Self-reference" seems to demand a similar kind of recursion and concepts like that in Russell's paradox "the set of all sets that are not members of themselves" are notoriously difficult to comprehend on first encounter. Perhaps the syntactic facts are just a reflex of a more general phenomenon.

REFERENCES

Ades, A. E. & Steedman, M. J. (1982) On the order of words. *Linguistics and Philosophy*, 4, 517–558.

Aho, A. V. & Ullman, J. D. (1972) *The Theory of Parsing, Translation, and Compiling, Vol I*. Englewood Cliffs, New Jersey: Prentice Hall International Inc.

Akmajian, A. & Heny, F. (1975) *Introduction to the Principles of Transformational Syntax*. Cambridge, Mass.: MIT Press.

Badecker, W. & Caramazza, A. (1985) On considerations of method and theory governing the use of clinical categories in neurolinguistics and cognitive neuropsychology: The case against agrammatism. *Cognition*, 20, 97–125.

Berwick, R. C. & Weinberg, A. S. (1984) *The Grammatical Basis of Linguistic Performance: Language Use and Acquisition*. Cambridge, Mass.: MIT Press.

Bradley, D., Garrett, M. F. & Zurif, E. B. (1980) Syntactic deficits in Broca's aphasia. In D. Caplan (Ed.), *Biological Studies of Mental Processes*. Cambridge, Mass.: MIT Press, 269–286.

Braine, M. D. S. & Hardy, J. A. (1982) On what case categories there are, why they are, and how they develop. In E. Wanner & L. Gleitman (Eds.), *Language Acquisition: The State of the Art*. Cambridge, England: Cambridge University Press.

Bresnan, J. (Ed.) (1982) *The Mental Representation of Grammatical Relations*. Cambridge, Mass.: MIT Press.

Briscoe, E. J. (1982) Garden path sentences or garden path utterances? In F. Nolan, J. Harrington, P. Warren, & E. J. Briscoe (Eds.), *Cambridge Papers in Phonetics and Experimental Linguistics, Vol I*. Dept. of Linguistics, University of Cambridge.

Briscoe, E. J. (1983) Determinism and its implementation in PARSIFAL. In K. Sparck Jones & Y. Wilks (Eds.), *Automatic Natural Language Parsing*. Chichester: Ellis Horwood Ltd., 61–68.

Briscoe, E. J. (1984) *Towards an understanding of spoken speech comprehension: The interactive determinism hypothesis*. PhD Dissertation, Dept. of Linguistics, University of Cambridge.

Caplan, D. (1972) Clause boundaries and recognition latencies for words in sentences. *Perception and Psychophysics*, 12, 73–76.

Caramazza, A. & Berndt, R. S. (1982) A psycholinguistic assessment of adult aphasia. In S. Rosenberg (Ed.), *Handbook of Applied Psycholinguistics*, Hillsdale, New Jersey: Lawrence Erlbaum Associates Inc., 477–535.

Caramazza, A., & Zurif, E. (1976) Dissociation of algorithmic and heuristic processes in language comphrehension: Evidence from aphasia. *Brain and Language*, 3, 572–582.

Carroll, J. M. (1981) On fallen horses racing past barns. In Chicago Linguistic Society, *Papers from the Parasession on Language and Behaviour*. Illinois: Chicago University.

Chomsky, N. (1963) Formal properties of grammars. In R. Luce, R. Bush, & E. Galanter (Eds.), *Handbook of Mathematical Psychology, Vol II*. New York: John Wiley.

Chomsky, N. (1965) *Aspects of the Theory of Syntax*. Cambridge, Mass.: MIT Press.

Chomsky, N. (1977) On Wh movement. In P. W. Culicover, T. Wasow, & A. Akmajian (Eds.), *Formal Syntax*. New York: Academic Press, 71–132.

Chomsky, N. (1980) *Rules and Representations*. Oxford: Basil Blackwell.

Chomsky, N. (1981) *Lectures on Government and Binding*. Dordrecht: Foris Publications.

Chomsky, N. & Miller, G. (1963) Finitary models of language users. In R. Luce, R. Bush, & E. Galanter (Eds.), *Handbook of Mathematical Psychology, Vol II*. New York: John Wiley.

Church, K. W. (1980) *On Memory Limitations in Natural Language Processing*. Report MIT/LCS/TR-245 Laboratory of Computer Science, MIT.

Churchland, P. M. (1984) *Matter and Consciousness: A Contemporary Introduction to the Philosophy of Mind*. Cambridge, Mass.: Bradford Books, MIT Press.

Coltheart, M., Patterson, K. E., & Marshall, J. C. (Eds.) (1980) *Deep Dyslexia*. London: Routledge & Kegan Paul.

Crain, S. & Steedman, M. J. (1985) On not being led up the garden path: The use of context by the psychological parser. In A. Zwicky, L. Kartunnen, & D. Dowty (Eds.), *Natural Language Parsing: Psycholinguistic, Theoretical, and Computational Perspectives*. Cambridge, England: Cambridge University Press.

De Roeck, A., Johnson, R., King, M., Rosner, M., Sampson, G., & Varile, N. (1982) A myth about centre-embedding. *Lingua*, 58, 327–340.

Dennett, D. C. (1979) *Brainstorms: Philosophical Essays on Mind and Psychology*. Hassocks, Sussex: Harvester Press.

Dowty, D., Wall, R., & Peters, S. (1981) *Introduction to Montague Semantics*. Dordrecht: D. Reidel Publishing.

Fillmore, C. J. (1968) The case for case. In E. Bach & R. Harms (Eds.), *Universals in Linguistic Theory*. New York: Holt, Rinehart, & Winston.

Fodor, J. A. (1981) *RePresentations: Philosophical Essays on the Foundations of Cognitive Science*. Brighton, Sussex: Harvester Press.

Fodor, J. A., Bever, T. G., & Garret, M. F. (1974) *The Psychology of Language*. New York: McGraw-Hill Book Company.

Fodor, J. D. (1981) Does performance shape competence? In *The Psychological Mechanisms of Language*. London: The Royal Society and the British Academy, 71–81. (Proceedings of a joint symposium: Also in *Philosophical Transactions of the Royal Society, London, series B, 295*, (no. 1077), 213–423.)

Fodor, J. D. (1983a) Constraints on gaps: Is the parser a significant influence? *Linguistics, 21–1*, 9–34.

Fodor, J. D. (1983b) Phrase structure parsing and the island constraints. *Linguistics and Philosophy, 6*, 163–223.

Ford, M., Bresnan, J., & Kaplan, R. M. (1982) A competence-based theory of syntactic closure. In J. Bresnan (Ed.), *The Mental Representation of Grammatical Relations*. Cambridge, Mass.: MIT Press.

Frazier, L. (1979) *On Comprehending Sentences: Syntactic Parsing Strategies*. Bloomington, Indiana: Indiana University Linguistics Club.

Frazier, L. & Fodor, J. D. (1978) The sausage machine: A new two stage parsing model. *Cognition, 6*, 291–325.

Gazdar, G. (1982) Phrase structure grammar. In P. Jacobson & G. Pullum (Eds.), *The Nature of Syntactic Representation*. Dordrecht: D. Reidel Publishing Co., 131–186.

Gazdar, G., Klein, E., Pullurn, G., & Sag, I. (1985) *Generalized Phrase Structure Grammar*, Oxford: Basil Blackwell.

Jackendoff, R. (1972) *Semantic Interpretation in Generative Grammar*. Cambridge, Mass.: MIT Press.

Jarvella, R. (1971) Syntactic processing of connected speech. *Journal of Verbal Learning and Verbal Behaviour, 10*, 409–416.

Johnson-Laird, P. N. (1983) *Mental Models*. Cambridge, England: Cambridge University Press.

Kean, M. L. (1978) The linguistic interpretation of aphasic syndromes. In E. Walker (Ed.), *Explorations in the Biology of Language*. Hassocks, Sussex: Harvester Press, 67–138.

Kean, M. L. (1980) Grammatical representations and the description of language processing. In D. Caplan (Ed.), *Biological Studies of Mental Processes*. Cambridge, Mass.: MIT Press, 239–268.

Kimball, J. (1973) Seven principles of surface structure parsing in natural language. *Cognition, 2*, 15–47.

Kimball, J. (1975) Predictive analysis and over-the-top parsing. In J. Kimball (Ed.), *Syntax and Semantics, Volume 4*. New York: Academic Press.

Kintsch, W. (1974) *The Representation of Meaning in Memory*. New York: John Wiley.

Lackner, J. R. & Garrett, M. (1973) Resolving ambiguity: Effects of biasing context in the unattended ear. *Cognition, 1*, 359–372.

Langendoen, D. T. (1975) Finite state parsing of phrase structure languages and the status of readjustment rules in grammar. *Linguistic Inquiry, 6*, 533–554.

Linebarger, M., Schwartz, M., & Saffran, E. (1983) Sensitivity to grammatical structure in so-called agrammatic aphasics. *Cognition, 13*, 361–392.

Lyons, J. (1968) *Introduction to Theoretical Linguistics*. Cambridge, England: Cambridge University Press.

Marcus, M. (1980) *A Theory of Syntactic Recognition for Natural Language*. Cambridge, Mass.: MIT Press.

Marr, D. (1977) Artificial intelligence: A personal view. Reprinted in J. Haugeland (Ed.), *Mind Design*. Cambridge, Mass: Bradford Books, MIT Press, 129–142.

Marr, D. (1982) *Vision*. San Francisco: W. H. Freeman & Co.

Marslen-Wilson, W. D. (1975) Sentence perception as an interactive parallel process. *Science, 189*, 226–228.

Marslen-Wilson, W., D. & Tyler, L. K. (1980) The temporal structure of spoken language understanding. *Cognition, 8*, 1–71.

Miceli, G., Mazzucchi, A., Menn, L., & Goodglass, H. (1983) Contrasting cases of Italian agrammatic aphasia without comprehension disorder. *Brain and Language, 19*, 65–97.

Miller, G. & Isard, S. D. (1964) Free recall of self-embedded English sentences. *Information and Control, 7*, 292–303.

Milne, R. W. (1982) Predicting garden path sentences. *Cognitive Science, 6*, 349–373.

Montague, R. (1973) The proper treatment of quantification in ordinary English. In K. J. J. Hintikka, J. M. E. Moravcsik, & P. Suppes (Eds.) *Approaches to Natural Language*. Dordrecht: D. Reidel Publishing.

Moore, T. & Carling, C. (1982) *Understanding Language: Towards a Post-Chomskyan Linguistics*. London: The Macmillan Press Ltd.

Morton, J. (1979) Word recognition. In J. Morton & J. C. Marshall (Eds.), *Psycholinguistics Series 2: Structures and Processes*. London: Paul Elek, 109–156.

Pulman, S. G. (1983) Trace theory, parsing, and constraints. In M. King (Ed.), *Parsing Natural Language*. London: Academic Press, 171–196.

Pulman, S. G. (1985) A parser that doesn't. In *Proceedings of the Second Conference of the European Chapter of the Association for Computational Linguistics*, Geneva, ACL, 128–135.

Pynte, J. (1978) The intra-clausal syntactic processing of ambiguous sentences. In W. Levelt & G. Flores d'Arcais (Eds.), *Studies in the Perception of Language*. New York: John Wiley.

Radford, A. (1981) *Transformational Syntax*. Cambridge, England: Cambridge University Press.

Rieger, C. (1976) Viewing parsing as word sense discrimination. In W. O. Dingwall (Ed.), *A Survey of Linguistic Science*, Stamford, Conneticut: Greylock Publishing.

Ross, J. R. (1967) *Constraints on variables in syntax*. MIT Phd dissertation.

Sampson, G. (1980) *Making Sense*. Oxford: Oxford University Press.

Schank, R. C. (1972) Conceptual dependency: A theory of natural language understanding. *Cognitive Psychology, 3*, 552–630.

Schlesinger, I. M. (1968) *Sentence Structure and the Reading Process*. The Hague: Mouton.

Schwartz, M. F., Marin, O. S. M., & Saffran, E. M. (1980) The word order problem in agrammatism. *Brain and Language, 10*, 249–262.

Searle, J. (1984) *Brain and Behaviour: The Reith Lectures*. London: BBC Publications.

Small, S. (1983) Parsing as co-operative distributed inference. In M. King (Ed.), *Parsing Natural Language*. London & New York: Academic Press.

Smith, N. & Wilson, D. (1979) *Modern Linguistics*. Harmondsworth: Penguin Books.

Sparck Jones, K. & Wilks, Y. (Eds.) (1983) *Automatic Natural Language Parsing*. Chichester: Ellis Horwood Ltd.

Steedman, M. J. (1983) On the generality of the nested dependency constraint and the reason for an exception in Dutch. *Linguistics, 21-1*, 35–66.

Tyler, L. K. & Marslen-Wilson, W. D. (1977) The on-line effects of semantic context on syntactic processing. *Journal of Verbal Learning and Verbal Behaviour, 16*, 683–692.

Wanner, E. (1980) The ATN and the sausage machine: Which one is baloney? *Cognition, 8*, 209–225.

Warren, P. (1985) *The temporal organisation and perception of speech*. PhD Dissertation, University of Cambridge.

Woodfield, A. (Ed.) (1982) *Thought and Object: Essays on Intentionality*. Oxford: Clarendon Press.

Woods, W. A. (1970) Transition network grammars for natural language analysis. *Communications of the ACM*, *13:10*, 591–606.

Zurif, E. & Grodzinsky, Y. (1983) Sensitivity to grammatical structure in agrammatic aphasics: A reply to Linebarger, Schwartz, and Saffran. *Cognition*, *15*, 207–213.

5 Syntax, Semantics, and Garden Paths

Dennis Norris
MRC Applied Psychology Unit, 15 Chaucer Road, Cambridge CB2 2EF, U.K.

INTRODUCTION

In recent years psycholinguists have become increasingly interested in determining the relation between the processes involved in syntactic and semantic analysis during comprehension. The question which has been of greatest concern to most researchers is whether syntactic analysis can be considered to be a completely autonomous stage of processing. Does syntactic analysis proceed independently of semantic processing, or do these processes interact? The answer to this question is seen to be central to our understanding of language comprehension. If we knew whether the processes involved in comprehension were highly interactive then this knowledge would place some very general constraints on the kind of processing models which would be viable. An answer to this very broad question would provide a framework within which much more specific theories of comprehension could be couched.

Proponents of the autonomy view argue that whether or not their theories turn out to be correct in the long run, they are adopting a far better research strategy than those who start from the premise that syntactic and semantic processes are interactive. A theory which proposes that comprehension consists of a series of autonomous processes has two major advantages over interactive theories. First, serial theories are more readily refutable. Whereas any demonstration that processes did interact would clearly refute a serial theory, it is impossible to refute a general claim that some interaction does take place. Experiments failing to demonstrate interaction might undermine the plausibility of an interactive theory, but they could never provide conclusive evidence against it. The second advantage of serial models is that they are more parsimonious than their interactive counterparts; they do not require any of the mechanisms for interaction. The best research strategy is therefore to start with the simplest and most refutable theory, and to see how far it will take you. Only when the simple theory fails should you concede the need for a more complicated one.

However, despite these arguments in favour of adopting the autonomy view as a research strategy, the dominant opinion in the psychological literature is that syntactic and semantic processes interact. While a large number of authors have argued in favour of interaction (Crain & Steedman, in press; Herriot, 1969; Slobin, 1966; Steedman & Johnson-Laird, 1978; Tyler & Marslen-Wilson, 1977; Marslen-Wilson, Tyler, & Seidenberg 1978), only Forster (Forster, 1979; Forster & Olbrei, 1973; Forster & Ryder, 1970) and Garrett (1978) have made strong claims for the independence of syntactic and semantic processing.

In order to make the argument that there is an autonomous stage of syntactic analysis, one would like to begin with some evidence that there is a clear psychological as well as a linguistic distinction between the processes of syntactic and semantic analysis. The best evidence for the existence of psychologically distinct syntactic and semantic processing systems comes from work with aphasics. Caramazza and Zurif (1976) studied patients with either posterior or anterior lesions of the dominant hemisphere. Patients were presented with centre-embedded sentences which were either reversible, such as "the lion that the tiger is chasing is fat," or nonreversible, such as "the bicycle that the boy is holding is broken." The patients' task was to decide which of two pictures corresponded to the meaning of the sentence. The interesting results in this experiment are those for the patients with anterior lesions (agrammatic aphasics). Caramazza and Zurif found that although these patients responded correctly about 90% of the time when the choice could be facilitated by semantic information (nonreversible sentences), performance dropped to chance level when the choice could only be made on the basis of syntactic information (reversible sentences). It seems that these patients are unable to make full use of syntactic information, but that they can comprehend reasonably well when there are semantic cues to the logical relationships. Indeed, it had previously been thought that these patients had near-normal comprehension ability and a syntactic deficit only in production.

The behaviour of these patients strongly suggests that there is a clear distinction between those psychological processes responsible for syntactic analysis and those responsible for semantic analysis. Syntactic processing can be impaired without any comparable impairment of the ability to utilise semantic information. However, this does not imply that syntactic and semantic processes are autonomous, merely that they are functionally distinct. In normal subjects who are in possession of a fully functional syntactic processing system, the operation of that system may well be influenced and guided by the results of semantic analysis.

The present paper begins by defending the autonomy hypothesis. It argues that all of the experimental data which is presented as evidence against the autonomy of syntax is actually quite consistent with the notion that syntactic analysis takes place completely independently of any semantic analysis which might be going on elsewhere in the system. In fact, models with an autonomous stage of syntactic analysis are actually far more powerful than is usually assumed. However, even these models run into difficulties in accounting for the comprehension, or rather the failure to comprehend, garden-path sentences. To explain how we can recover from parsing errors in garden-path sentences there must be some minimal provision for interaction which is incompatible with the strong form of autonomy model proposed by Forster.

THE CASE FOR INTERACTION

The most vigorous proponents of the view that comprehension must be characterised as a set of highly interactive processes have been Marslen-Wilson and his colleagues (Marslen-Wilson & Tyler, 1980; Marslen-Wilson, Tyler, & Seidenberg, 1978; Tyler & Marslen-Wilson, 1977). However, although Marslen-Wilson has claimed that syntax and semantics are interactive, he has not provided any clear specification of what form the interaction might take. The only well-formulated proposals for an interactive model of semantic and syntactic processing have been provided by Steedman and Johnson-Laird (1978) and by Crain and Steedman (in press). Steedman and Johnson-Laird have suggested that semantic information can facilitate syntactic analysis by eliminating semantically unacceptable parses. If semantic information can save the parser from pursuing parses which are known to be semantically unacceptable, then syntactic analysis will proceed more rapidly. In support of their theory, Steedman and Johnson-Laird present the results of an experiment by Quin, which demonstrates that semantic information is of greater value in comprehending syntactically complex than syntactically simple sentences. In Quin's experiment subjects were required to press a button when they had understood a sentence presented to them visually. The syntactic difficulty of the sentences was varied by preposing the indirect object in sentences such as 1 and 3, to produce sentences such as 2 and 4. Previous work by Dewart (1975) had indicated that sentences such as 2 and 4 are harder to understand than sentences such as 1 and 3. The sentences also varied as to whether or not there was a semantic cue to their logical structure (1 and 2 versus 3 and 4).

1   The man took the boy to the girl. (3.13sec)
2   The man took the girl the boy. (3.40sec)
3   The man took the coat to the girl. (2.87sec)
4   The man took the girl the coat. (2.96sec)

Quin predicted that the effect of the syntactic manipulation should be less in the semantic-cue condition than the no-semantic-cue condition, as the semantic cue should facilitate the syntactic analysis of the sentence. As can be seen from the mean response latencies shown after each sentence, this experiment did produce the predicted statistical interaction. The effect of the syntactic manipulation is only .09sec in the semantic-cue condition, as compared with .27sec in the no-cue conditions. However, even the results of such a simple experiment have a number of possible explanations, not all of which involve the assumption that syntactic processing is under any degree of control by semantic processes.

The simplest account of these data does involve some control of the syntactic processor by higher-level processes. In Quin's experiment the "no-cue" sentences tend to be less plausible than the sentences with a semantic cue. All that one needs to do to account for the statistical interaction in this experiment is to assume that subjects sometimes do a double-take when presented with an implausible sentence, so that they can check that the implausibility did not arise from an error in processing. If subjects do perform a double check on implausible sentences, then the time taken to process the syntax will be doubled, as the syntax will have been processed twice. There will therefore be a statistical interaction between syntactic complexity and the presence of a semantic cue (plausibility). This explanation of Quin's data does assume that higher-level processes exert some control over syntactic processing operations, but this control is of the simplest form imaginable. The high-level processes control *what* the syntax does, but not *how* it does it.

A second explanation of Quin's data involves the assumption that where there is any syntactic ambiguity, the syntactic processor computes all possible parses and continuously feeds all of its output to the semantic processor. According to this explanation, the statistical interaction arises because semantic cues facilitate processing by enabling the semantic processor to avoid unnecessary processing of partial syntactic analyses. If the semantic processor attempts to construct a semantic representation of all of its input as it arrives, any local syntactic ambiguity will result in more possible semantic analyses and will therefore lead to increased processing time. This increase in time will be less when semantic cues enable some of the potential semantic analyses to be abandoned at an early stage in processing. Such a model would predict a statistical interaction between semantic and syntactic factors which would arise entirely as a result of operations within the semantic processor and which would involve no interaction between processing stages or top-down flow of information within the system.

Crain and Steedman's proposals for interaction between syntactic and semantic processing deserve special attention. They have made the interesting suggestion that parsing preferences, such as minimal attachment (Frazier, 1978), which appear to be purely syntactic, are in fact due to semantic or pragmatic biases. It follows, therefore, that all purely structural garden paths can be eliminated by suitable semantics and context.

In Crain and Steedman's model semantics carries out an immediate word by word interpretation of the syntactic analysis. All syntactic alternatives are generated in parallel, or "proposed" in parallel to use Crain and Steedman's terminology. Semantics then "disposes" or chooses between parallel analyses on the basis of plausibility. An important feature of the model is that it contains a more elaborate notion of plausibility than other theories. Other things being equal, the more plausible of two readings will be the one carrying fewer unsatisfied presuppositions or entailments. For example, in the absence of context, the classic garden-path sentence 5 should be harder to understand than 6 because it presupposes that there is more than one horse, only one of which was raced past the barn, whereas 6 need only presuppose the existence of a single horse. The complex noun-phrase analysis appropriate for 5 is therefore less plausible than the simple noun-phrase analysis required for 6. Sentence 5 is therefore initially given a simple noun-phrase analysis which causes a garden path; this is discovered when the parser reaches "fell."

5 The horse raced past the barn fell.
6 The horse raced past the barn quickly.

In order to examine their claim that context can eliminate structural garden paths, Crain and Steedman obtained grammaticallity judgements to sentential complement (minimal attachment) sentences or relative clause (nonminimal attachment) sentences such as 7 and 8. In the absence of any context subjects show a preference for a minimal attachment analysis of 8. Crain and Steedman would explain this preference in terms of relative plausibility rather than in terms of any purely structural bias. The relative-clause analysis presupposes that there are at least two wives whereas the complement analysis requires only a single couple.

7 The psychologist told the wife that he was having trouble with her husband.
8 The psychologist told the wife that he was having trouble with to leave her husband.

Sentences such as 7 and 8 were presented to subjects preceded by a context biased towards either a complement or a relative analysis. In this example, a sentence describing a psychologist counselling a single married couple was designed to induce a complement analysis and a sentence describing a psychologist counselling two couples was designed to induce a relative-clause analysis. Although sentences were judged as ungrammatical over a third of the time when preceded by a context intended to induce an inappropriate reading, sentences were hardly ever judged ungrammatical when preceded by the appropriate biasing context. The contextual manipulation was clearly successful in inducing and eliminating garden paths. However, while this study helps us to understand the contextual variables controlling which reading of a sentence subjects finally arrive at, it really tells us little about how the syntactic and contextual information is actually combined on-line.

Crain and Steedman are insistent that competing syntactic analyses must be examined in parallel in order to compare their relative plausibility. They argue that to base decisions simply on the basis of the plausibility of a single analysis would too often lead to backtracking where, although the chosen analysis was plausible, it turned out not to be the most plausible in the context. However, it is really not clear that this would be a serious problem unless it is frequently the case that two alternative analyses are both fairly plausible and that the ambiguity cannot quickly be resolved on the basis of following structural information. For example, it could be the case that only a single structurally preferred analysis is initially computed, and that this analysis is abandoned as soon as it turns out to be either syntactically anomalous or it falls below a certain plausibility criterion. However, in order to distinguish between these accounts we need to resort to a more sensitive experimental measure of on-line processing.

On-Line Evidence for Interaction

Earlier we saw how a statistical interaction between semantic and syntactic factors in the experiment by Quin can be accounted for by a very simple model which requires only that there is a double-take of the less plausible sentences more frequently than of the more plausible ones. Such an explanation cannot, however, account for the interaction between semantic and syntactic factors found in an ingenious experiment by Tyler and Marslen-Wilson (1977). Subjects in this experiment heard sentence fragments such as 9 and 10 followed by a visual presentation of either "is" or "are."

9   If you are a pilot, landing planes
10 If you walk near runways, landing planes

The subjects' task was to pronounce the visually presented word as quickly as possible. Where the semantic context and probe word were consistent with the same syntactic analysis of "landing planes," response latencies were shorter than when the context suggested, say, an adjectival analysis and the probe word corresponded to a gerundive analysis. Tyler and Marslen-Wilson point out that until the probe word is seen there is no syntactic basis for preferring one parsing to the other. Therefore, they argue, the semantic context must be biasing the subject towards one particular parsing, or else there would be no difference between the conditions. This is considered to be evidence of an interaction between semantic and syntactic processors.

However, a problem arises when we attempt to specify the exact mechanism of the interaction. What must the semantic processor do in order to determine which parsing of "landing planes" is more appropriate? If we assume that "planes" can be interpreted unambiguously in this context, what is the semantic processor to make of "landing"? Is it an adjective or a gerund? How should it be integrated with the previous clause? Possibly the semantic processor can attempt both the adjective-noun and gerund-noun combinations and decide which fits best with the context. The results of this operation could then guide the syntactic processor to expect input consistent with either an adjectival or gerundive parse as appropriate. The problem with such a model is that, in differentiating between the two analyses, the semantic processor has performed what is effectively a syntactic operation. The same result would have been achieved by having the syntactic stage pass both alternative parsings to the semantic stage where they could then be evaluated on semantic grounds alone. There is even no need for the semantic processor to make the result of this evaluation available to syntax. If the probe word is inconsistent with the preferred semantic interpretation, this incongruity alone may be sufficient to interfere with the naming process. This is the only study demonstrating an interaction between semantic and syntactic factors using a response measure which might be expected to reflect the duration of processes occurring during comprehension. However, it should now be clear that statistical interactions provide no evidence of interactions between processes.

In a more recent paper, Marslen-Wilson, Tyler, and Seidenberg (1978) have used rhyme- and category-monitoring tasks to investigate the interaction between semantic and syntactic processes. In this study the subjects' task was to listen to a sentence and press a button as soon as they heard a word which rhymed with (or was a member of a semantic category specified by) a target specification presented before each sentence. Subjects were required to monitor for targets located either immediately before or immediately after clause boundaries. Response latencies were found not to be determined solely by the position of the target relative to the clause boundary, as would have been expected by a purely syntactic account of clausal structuring, but were also determined by the "completeness" of the semantic representation of the clause. Latencies were significantly faster before the boundary than after when the "completeness" was high, but not when the clause was less complete. Marslen-Wilson et al. interpreted this finding as evidence of interaction between the syntactic effect of the clause boundary and the semantic effect of completeness. However, the assumption that the clause boundry effect is entirely syntactic may not be fully justified. As Johnson-Laird (1974) has pointed out, syntactic boundaries tend to coincide with the points at which semantic interpretation would be expected to occur. Therefore, it is possible that the clause boundary effect is a consequence of operations at the semantic rather than the syntactic level, and that the apparent interaction is entirely due to effects within the semantic level alone. It should also be noted that even if it were correct to attribute the clause boundary effect to syntactic processes, these results would only refute a model of sentence processing such as that of Fodor, Bever, and Garrett (1974), in which all syntactic processing takes place at clause boundaries.

Despite the ingenuity which has gone into devising experiments designed to reject the idea of an autonomous syntactic processor, it is quite clear that none of these experiments provide clear evidence of interaction. Even the superficially impressive results from the Tyler and Marslen-Wilson study can be explained by assuming that the parser produces all analyses of syntactically ambiguous sentences in parallel. But what of the experimental work which is claimed to provide support for the autonomy of syntax? Is this work any more conclusive?

SERIAL MODELS OF COMPREHENSION

The experiments described so far have attempted to demonstrate an interaction between syntax and semantics. However, a number of experiments by Forster and his colleagues have been designed to show that syntactic and semantic processes are completely serial and independent. Forster and Olbrei (1973) have argued that the comprehension system is best viewed as consisting of three autonomous processing stages corresponding to lexical, syntactic and semantic levels of analysis. Each stage in the model receives input only from the immediately preceding stage and the system operates in a completely serial manner. In support of this view of the comprehension process Forster and Olbrei performed a number of experiments which, they claim, demonstrate that syntactic processing is uninfluenced by semantic constraints. Forster and Ryder (1971) had used the RSVP task to demonstrate that the relative difficulty of different syntactic constructions remained approximately constant while the plausibility of the sentences was varied. Forster and Olbrei (1973) replicated this finding in a sentence classification task and claimed that the positive correlation between difficulty of syntactic processing under varying conditions of plausibility indicated that syntactic processing was performed independently of semantic processing.

To test Slobin's (1966) claim that reversibility influences performance on a sentence-picture verification task, Forster and Olbrei investigated the effect of reversibility as a cue to syntactic structure. Slobin had demonstrated that reversible sentences such as 11, where subject and object can be reversed to produce an acceptable sentence, are harder to comprehend than irreversible sentences such as 12, where only one ordering of subject and object is possible.

11   The girl obscured the flowers.
12   The girl watered the flowers.

More significantly, Slobin found that the difference between reversible and irreversible sentences was greater for passive than active sentences. In a later experiment Herriot (1969) obtained similar results using sentences in which reversibility was determined by pragmatic rather than semantic information. These experiments were interpreted as providing evidence for an interaction between semantic and pragmatic information, and parsing. Forster and Olbrei noted that Slobin's experiment confounded reversibility with plausibility, nonreversible sentences tending to be more plausible than three studies using a sentence classification task, and one using the rapid serial visual presentation (RSVP) task, Forster and Olbrei found no effect of reversibility when the materials were controlled for plausibility, and no interaction between reversibility and syntactic structure. Again they considered these results to indicate that syntactic processing was not influenced by semantic cues to syntactic structure.

However, the reasoning leading to Forster and Olbrei's conclusions from these experiments contains a number of flaws. In their first experiment, in which they replicate the Forster and Ryder study, Forster and Olbrei claim that the positive correlation between processing difficulty and syntactic complexity indicates that syntax and semantics are processed independently. However, this result is not in the least incompatible with an interactive model. In order for an interactive model to predict anything other than a positive correlation between processing difficulty and complexity it would have to predict that plausibility could reorder the relative difficulty of the various syntactic structures. That is, it would have to predict that where one syntactic structure would be easier than another at one level of plausibility, the relative difficulty of the two structures would be reversed at some other level of plausibility. The most likely prediction of an interactive model is that increased plausibility would facilitate the processing of complex sentences more than it would simple ones. Such a prediction is quite compatible with a positive correlation between complexity and difficulty across a wide range of variations in plausibility.

Forster and Olbrei's experiments on reversibility also lead them to the conclusion that syntax and semantics are independent. But this conclusion is arrived at by default in the light of a null result; a result which is specific to reversibility as a semantic cue. Reversibility may not influence syntactic processing, but other cues may well do.

Forster's 1979 Model

In a later paper Forster (1979) has elaborated on his earlier model of the comprehension system. At the core of the model remain the three autonomous processes responsible for lexical, syntactic, and semantic processing, although the semantic processor has now been renamed the "message" processor. Each of these processes is now described as having access to information in the lexicon.

Forster describes the output of the syntactic processor as being the surface structure of the sentence in the sense of Chomsky (1975). The products of syntactic processing can be passed on to the next processor as soon as "viable syntactic constituents" are identified. In this way the message processor may commence analysis before the syntactic structure has been completely determined. The message processor is intended (Forster, 1979) to "convert a purely linguistic representation into a conceptual structure representing the intended message (p. 35)."

The major difference between the new model and the previous one is that each processor now delivers its output not only to the immediately following stage, but also to the "General Problem Solver" (GPS). It is the GPS which is responsible for delivering a decision on which responses in psycholinguistic experiments are based. The GPS has no direct access to the lexicon, but does have access to a source of information not available to the other processors; "general conceptual knowledge." General conceptual knowledge refers to a person's general knowledge and beliefs about the real world. Forster takes care to make it clear that the GPS is not itself part of the language processor, and it has no information about the operation of the language processor other than that obtained by observing the output of the lexical, syntactic, and message processors. The exact nature of the GPS, however, is not clear. The GPS (Forster, 1979): "consists simply of a device for collecting information from the various subsystems of the language processor and acting on that information (p. 33)."

The role of the GPS is best illustrated by Forster's account of a sentence classification experiment by Ratcliff. Ratcliff presented subjects with ungrammatical sentences such as 13 and 14 along with a number of syntactically acceptable sentences.

13   The musicians their played new songs.
14   The musicians shook the new rifle.

The subjects' task was simply to decide as quickly as possible whether the sentences were grammatical. It was found that there was a greater number of errors in classifying sentences such as 13, where reversal of the order of two adjacent words results in a plausible sentence, than in classifying sentences such as 14 where this is not the case. Forster's explanation of these results is that the error responses are due to the operation of the GPS. Correct responses in this experiment are assumed to be due to the syntactic processor being able to determine the grammaticality of the sentence before the GPS has produced an output. However, on some trials the GPS will derive a plausible interpretation of the sentence before the syntactic processor has detected the ungrammaticallity, and this will cause subjects to make the wrong response. Forster assumes that the subjects' final response is determined by the outcome of a race between the syntactic processor and the GPS. When the GPS wins, sentences such as 13 will be misclassified.

Although Forster has added more detail to his model, the underlying principles of organisation remain unchanged. Each stage of the language processor operates independently and receives input only from the immediately preceding stage. Much of Forster's justification for such a model lies in his belief that the model makes strong claims about the performance of the language processor. In principle at least, a model consisting of a series of autonomous processors is testable. If the processors can be shown to interact the model can be refuted. Unfortunately, the properties of Forster's model which give rise to its claim to testability also give rise to problems in obtaining empirical support for it. Although Forster considers the theory to be descriptively adequate, its adequacy can only derive from a failure to demonstrate interaction. Forster is therefore under a very strong obligation to ensure that, in those experiments cited in support of his theory where no interaction is found, there is some interactive theory which would actually predict interaction under those circumstances.

Forster's case for the refutability of his own model is to some extent undermined by the role played by the GPS. Although the GPS is an important component in the overall model, it is not itself part of the "language processor." So if behaviour which seems to be interactive is argued to be the responsibility of the GPS, it can still be maintained that the language processor is serial. In accounting for the results of Ratcliff's experiment Forster has already claimed that the use of semantic and pragmatic cues to interpret a sentence in the absence of a syntactic analysis is performed by the GPS. Why not endow it with other linguistic capacities?

The GPS has access to the output of each stage in the language processor other than the lexicon. Therefore the only real constraints on comprehension are the constraints on the operation of the GPS. So unless the GPS and its relation to the language processor are specified more clearly, there is a loophole in Forster's model which would allow the autonomy hypothesis to be maintained in the face of all possible evidence to the contrary. Any evidence for interactive processes can be deemed to arise from the operation of the GPS, not the language processor.

GARDEN PATHS

Are syntax and semantics autonomous or are they interactive? To say the least, the experimental work reviewed so far is inconclusive. There is certainly no strong evidence for interaction, but then there is none which would suggest that interaction does not take place. A major problem appears to be that it is not clear what kind of experiment one could perform to get evidence against the multiple-parse version of the autonomy.

The conventional view is that serial models are to be preferred to interactive models as they lay themselves open to the possibility of being refuted. However, this is really only true of the less powerful serial single-parse model, and it is probably fair to say that the mere fact that we can deal with syntactic ambiguity is sufficient grounds for rejecting such models. However, this doesn't apply to the far more powerful serial multiple-parse models. What can't such a model do? It's serial, it's autonomous; but it's very difficult to refute. Models of this general form would seem to be able to account for any finding which appeared to indicate that semantic information influenced syntactic analysis by means of the device outlined earlier: Semantic information can always be said to influence choices between alternative *semantic* analyses.

However, this form of model actually runs into a problem through being too powerful to be considered as a serious theory of human comprehension. If the syntactic processor always computed all possible parses of a sentence there should be no such thing as a syntactic garden path. That is, although there could be garden paths where semantic information led to semantic analysis of a parse being abandoned prematurely, a parse should never be abandoned on the grounds of being syntactically improbable. If it is at all possible for a parse to be computed then that parse should always be computed. Otherwise, if the parse which is dropped turns out to be the parse which is required for the correct semantic interpretation of the sentence, then the semantic processor would have to instruct the syntactic processor to compute another parse and that would constitute interaction between processes. Consider sentence 11 (taken from Frazier & Fodor 1978).

11 Tom said that Bill will take the cleaning out yesterday.

Most people are garden-pathed by sentence 11. They come to a point where they realise that if the sentence makes sense, then they have parsed it incorrectly. Yet there is no semantic information which should lead them to abandon the semantic interpretation of the correct parse. If the garden path isn't due to the semantic interpretation of the parse being abandoned prematurely, then it must be the case that the correct parse was never produced in the first place. How, then, do we ever get the correct parse? The syntactic stage has produced a perfectly good parse: Perfect apart from the fact that it isn't semantically acceptable. There is nothing an autonomous parser could know about which would make it realise the error of its ways. Only the semantic processor knows that something has gone awry.

The fact that we are garden-pathed at all is clearly evidence against a multiple-output model in which all parses are semantically interpreted, and the fact that we can understand this sentence second (or third) time round would seem to be evidence of an interaction between processes. It would appear that the semantic processor must instruct the syntactic processor to compute another parse for the sentence.

In fact, there is a way to avoid even this concession to interaction. We know from the work of Swinney (1979) that we do not continue with parallel semantic analyses of a sentence corresponding to all the possible interpretations of ambiguous words. Within a few hundred milliseconds of a lexically ambiguous item, all but one interpretation of the word has been abandoned. Such a strategy makes sense. Ambiguity is so ubiquitous that to attempt to analyse all possible readings of a sentence we would have to construct an enormous number of unwanted interpretations along with the desired one. It would greatly reduce the overall processing load if all but the most promising semantic analysis were to be abandoned as soon as possible. Something similar might happen with syntactic ambiguity. As already mentioned, there will often be good semantic grounds for selecting one parse rather than its competitors, but sometimes there won't be. To reduce semantic processing load in these cases it would be wise to select the parse which is most probable on syntactic grounds (or the simplest computationally). Many syntactic constructions, though possible, are rarely encountered. If the syntactic processor tagged its output with a measure of the frequency of constructions of this kind then the semantic processor could use this information to decide which parse to pursue.

This sort of behaviour would account for our observations with the garden-path sentences. The infrequent parse wouldn't be used as the basis of the semantic interpretation because the semantic processor would choose the parse which the syntactic processor had tagged as being more probable. When it transpires that the wrong choice has been made, the semantic processor can go back and work on the remaining correct parse. So, according to this modified version of the multiple-output model there is no longer any need for interaction, even when processing garden-path sentences. Once again it has been possible to push all of the processes which look interactive into the semantic processor.

However, these modifications have created a very strange and highly implausible model. The semantic processor is operating in such a way as to minimise the number of parallel analyses it has to deal with. However, the parser produces all possible outputs all of the time, no matter how improbable they might be and regardless of whether or not they are known to be semantically anomalous. If we consider the model in computational terms it would seem far less parsimonious than an interactive account. It would surely be more efficient to permit interaction than always to compute every parse. In terms of the demands which this model would make on memory capacity it is clearly contrary to all we know about human memory to assume that all possible parses of a sentence are stored throughout the whole sentence. What evidence we have about memory for linguistic information suggests that knowledge of the surface form of a sentence is lost within a very short space of time. It would be rather surprising if there were a special store to hold multiple parses which was found to be accessible only to the semantic processor and which had evolved simply to save the semantic processor from telling the parser when it had backed a loser. In fact, as with the previous model, this version of the multiple-parse model also runs into problems through being too powerful. As the semantic processor should have access to all parses there should never be any reason to reread a garden-path sentence. If the system makes the wrong choice to begin with, then it can go back and work on another parse held in memory. There should be no need to have a second look at the sentence. However, recent work by Frazier and Rayner (1982) has shown that people do make more regressive eye movements when reading sentences in which they are likely to be garden-pathed. It seems that the strongest forms of the multiple-parse models are untenable. It is not only implausible to suggest that all possible parses are computed and stored throughout the sentence, but it is also quite inconsistent with what we know about performance on garden-path sentences. Rather ironically, the first class of model we have been able to reject is a strictly serial model: Not because of its simplicity, but rather because in order to handle some situations we have had to make the model so powerful that it over-predicts in others. In order to defend the most extreme version of serial autonomy theory we have been forced to consider a model that performs better than people do.

So far we have established that models which are purely serial can be rejected, but how much of a concession to interaction must we make? In a later eye-movement study, Rayner, Carlson, and Frazier (1983) attempted to test the predictions of interactive theories by examining whether the initial syntactic analysis of a sentence with a local structural ambiguity could be influenced by the relative plausibility of the alternative analyses. Rayner et al. had subjects read sentences such as 15, 16, 17, and 18.

15 The florist sent the flowers was very pleased. (reduced implausible)
16 The performer sent the flowers was very pleased. (reduced plausible)
17 The performer who was sent the flowers was very pleased. (unreduced plausible)
18 The performer sent the flowers and was very pleased with herself. (active implausible)

The sentence fragment "The florist sent the flowers" is syntactically ambiguous. The preferred syntactic analysis is the simple active reading in which the florist sends the flowers, rather than the reduced relative analysis in which the florist is the recipient of the flowers. Frazier (1978) explains this preference in terms of the minimal attachment strategy according to which the structure is parsed using the fewest syntactic nodes possible. However, in sentences 15, 16, and 17 the minimal attachment strategy will temporarily lead subjects up the garden path. These sentences require the relative clause analysis rather than the simple active analysis favoured by minimal attachment. In 15 there is a further problem caused by the implausibility of the florist receiving rather than sending the flowers. However, 16 and 17 more plausibly have the flowers being received by a performer rather than a florist.

Rayner et al. (1983) argue that if subjects initially select the parse corresponding to the most plausible analysis of the ambiguity they should be garden-pathed in the implausible sentences 15 and 18, but not in 16 and 17. However, if the parser simply follows the minimal attachment strategy regardless of plausibility, then subjects should be garden-pathed in 15 and 16 but not in 17 and 18. The pattern of eye movements observed in the experiment strongly suggested that subjects' comprehension was being driven by an autonomous parser whose first pass parse of the sentence was not influenced by the relative plausibility of the competing analyses. Not only were fixation durations in the disambiguating region of both of the reduced relatives (15 and 16) significantly longer than in the controls (17 and 18) but there were also more regressive eye movements in the reduced relatives.

One might wish to argue that this experiment isn't really a fair test of interactive models like Crain and Steedman's (in press). The manipulation of pragmatic plausibility might not be sufficient to exert a strong enough biasing effect to influence the decision between alternative parses. However, Ferreira and Clifton (1986) have carried out a similar eye-movement study in which the biasing context was provided by a complete paragraph designed to alter the plausibility of alternative readings according to the principles outlined by Crain and Steedman. Their results, like those of Rayner et al., show no sign of any pragmatic or contextual influence over first-pass parsing. The evidence that the parser is operating in a completely autonomous fashion during its *initial* analysis of a sentence begins to look overwhelming.

Rayner et al. point out that their result raises an interesting question. Since we now know that not all syntactic analyses of a sentence are initially computed, then, in fully ambiguous sentences, we cannot simply make use of the plausibility of the alternative analyses to select the most plausible reading. If the parser initially selects a plausible reading, how will it ever know there is a more plausible one? One possibility would be for the language processor to evaluate the plausibility of all logically possible relationships between the major phrases of the sentence to see if there is a more plausible set of relations than that suggested by the parser. However, such a process would greatly increase the overheads involved in understanding unambiguous sentences and, if it were totally unconstrained by the syntactic analysis, it would involve consideration of potential relations which would not correspond to any possible grammatical analysis of the sentence.

Rayner et al. suggest instead that the language processor might take advantage of information about the possible thematic structures associated with verbs and heads of phrases. They give as an example the verb "see," which may occur with at least two thematic structures. "See" may occur with an *experiencer* and a *theme* as in sentence 19:

19   The spy saw the cop.

or with an *experiencer*, a *theme*, and an *instrument* as in sentence 20:

20   The spy saw the cop with the binoculars.

According to what Rayner et al. call the *thematic selection hypothesis*, the initial syntactic analysis identifies the major phrases. The language processor then makes use of knowledge of the world and the current discourse to compare the plausibility of the sets of relations between phrases listed in the thematic structure associated with the head of a phrase. If the thematic selection process discovers a more plausible set of relations than the ones consistent with the current syntactic analysis then an attempt will be made to revise the analysis. The main prediction of the thematic selection hypothesis is that the parser should always arrive at the most plausible analysis of a structurally ambiguous sentence.

21   The spy saw the cop with binoculars but the cop didn't see him
22   The spy saw the cop with a revolver but the cop didn't see him

Rayner et al. examined this by presenting subjects with sentences such as 21 and 22. They found that sentences like 21, where the minimal attachment reading is more plausible, were read faster than sentences such as 22 where the nonminimal attachment reading is the more plausible. Furthermore, in the biasing regions of the sentences (binoculars, revolver) subjects took longer than in the preceding section in the nonminimal attachment sentences, but not in the minimal attachment sentences.

As well as providing further evidence for the autonomy of the first-pass syntactic analysis, Rayner et al. claim that this result provides support for the thematic selection hypothesis. However, this pattern of results is also compatible with a far simpler hypothesis which was described earlier in conjunction with Crain and Steedman's (in press) claim that the language processor must compare the relative plausibility of alternative parses. Perhaps all that the language processor really needs to do is to monitor the plausibility of a single analysis at a time and to ask for a further parse to be attempted if the plausibility falls below a preset criterion. The crucial aspect of the thematic selection hypothesis is that it will always ensure that the most plausible reading is selected. However, in almost all of the sentences used by Rayner et al. the less plausible analysis is either anomalous or highly implausible. For example, the reading of 21 corresponding to "The spy used the revolver to see the cop" is so implausible that a system which simply monitored the plausibility of the current parse would produce the same pattern of results as the thematic selection hypothesis. Note that the thematic selection hypothesis and the simple plausibility monitoring hypothesis will only make different predictions where there are two parses with plausible interpretations but where the structurally less-preferred parse is much more plausible than the other. In this case the plausibility monitoring hypothesis has to predict that the structurally preferred parse will be selected regardless of whether or not a more plausible parse also exists. As long as the structurally preferred parse is plausible the plausibility monitoring system will be happy. However, the thematic selection hypothesis predicts that the most plausible hypothesis will always win out.

Both Rayner et al. and Crain and Steedman seem to believe that we need to have some means of comparing the relative plausibility of alternative syntactic analyses. One of Crain and Steedman's reasons for making such a claim was that they thought that the parser would otherwise have to back up to perform a reanalysis if it did not select the most plausible analysis. However, Rayner et al.'s data show that the parser does have to back up and reanalyse parts of sentences even when there is disambiguating semantic or pragmatic information. Whether some other mechanism such as the thematic selection process is required to help the language processor find the most plausible interpretation of a sentence really depends on how often we encounter syntactically ambiguous sentences where the structurally preferred reading is plausible, but not the most plausible reading possible. Perhaps such sentences do occur occasionally, but when one does it seems more than likely that disambiguating information will be provided by the next sentence. The occasional misunderstanding may be a small price to pay to save the computational cost of computing alternative thematic structures.

CONCLUSIONS

Concern with whether comprehension is serial or interactive has been seen as part of a search for some general principals of operation which can guide us in our construction of models of language understanding. I have argued that, so far, that enterprise has not born fruit. However, general principles do seem to be emerging from elsewhere. Swinney's (1979) work tells us that the system tries to minimise the number of semantic interpretations of lexical items being attempted at any one time. The work of Caplan (1972) tells us that surface information is purged from memory at points corresponding roughly to the clause boundary. Both of these findings indicate that the system attempts to minimise the demands on short-term memory. These results, in conjunction with the more direct evidence from studies of garden-path sentences, argue against the most powerful version of the autonomy model in which all possible parses are sustained throughout the sentence. The implication is that there must be at least some minimal interaction between syntactic processing and higher-level processes. However, this interaction need only be of a very simple form. All that is required is that the semantic processor can instruct the syntax to abandon implausible parses before being led too far down the garden path. Marslen-Wilson and Tyler (1980) have described language comprehension as an interactive processes in which: "knowledge sources communicate and interact during processing in an optimally efficient and accurate manner (p. 1)." However, the arguments against the multiple-parse model also apply to claims that comprehension is optimally efficient: If comprehension were optimally efficient we should never be troubled by ambiguity or garden paths. It is precisely because the system is not optimally efficient, and must process language with a limited memory capacity, that some degree of interaction between semantic and syntactic processing is necessary.

REFERENCES

Caplan, D. (1972) Clause boundaries and recognition latencies for words in sentences. *Perception and Psychophysics*, *12*, 73–76.

Caramazza, A. & Zurif, E. B. (1976) Dissociation of algorithmic and heuristic processes in language comprehension: Evidence from aphasia. *Brain and Language*, *3*, 572–582.

Chomsky, N. (1975) *Reflections on Language*. New York: Pantheon.

Crain, S. & Steedman, M. (in press) On not being led up the garden path: The use of context by the psychological parser. In D. Dowty, L. Karttunen, & A. Zwicky (Eds.), *Natural Language Parsing*. Cambridge: Cambridge University Press.

Dewart, M. H. (1975) A psychological investigation of sentence comprehension by children. Unpublished PhD thesis, University College London.

Ferreira, F. & Clifton, C. (1986) The independence of syntactic processing. *Journal of Memory and Language*, *25*, 348–368.

Fodor, J. A., Bever, T. G., & Garrett, M. F. (1974) *The Psychology of Language*. New York: McGraw-Hill.

Forster, K. I. (1979) Levels of processing and the structure of the language processor. In W. E. Cooper & E. C. T. Walker (Eds.), *Sentence Processing*. Hillsdale, New Jersey: Lawrence Erlbaum Associates Inc.

Forster, K. I. & Olbrei, I. (1973) Semantic heuristics and syntactic analysis. *Cognition*, *2*, 319–347.

Forster, K. I. & Ryder, L. A. (1971) Perceiving the structure and meaning of sentences. *Journal of Verbal Learning and Verbal Behaviour*, *9*, 285–296.

Frazier, L. (1978) On comprehending sentences: Syntactic parsing strategies. Doctoral dissertation, University of Connecticut.

Frazier, L. & Fodor, J. (1978) The sausage machine: A new two-stage parsing model. *Cognition*, *6*, 291, 325.

Frazier, L. & Rayner, K. (1982) Making and correcting errors during sentence comprehension: Eye movements in the analysis of structurally ambiguous sentences. *Cognitive Psychology*, *14*, 178–210.

Garrett, M. F. (1978) Word and sentence perception. In R. Held, H. L. Teuber, & H. Liebowitz (Eds.), *Handbook of Sensory Physiology, Vol. 8, Perception*. New York: Academic Press.

Herriot, P. (1969) The comprehension of active and passive sentences as a function of pragmatic expectations. *Journal of Verbal Learning and Verbal Behaviour*, *8*, 166–169.

Johnson-Laird, P. N. (1974) Experimental psycholinguistics. *Annual Review of Psychology*, *25*, 135–160.

Marslen-Wilson, W. D. & Tyler, L. (1980) The temporal structure of spoken language understanding. *Cognition*, *8*, 1–71.

Marslen-Wilson, W. D., Tyler, L. K., & Seidenberg, M. (1978) Sentence processing and the clause boundary. In W. J. M. Levelt & G. B. Flores d'Arcais (Eds.), *Studies in Sentence Perception*. New York: Wiley.

Rayner, K., Carlson, M., & Frazier, L. (1983) The interaction of syntax and semantics during sentence processing: Eye movements in the analysis of semantically biased sentences. *Journal of Verbal Learning and Verbal Behaviour*, *22*, 358–374.

Slobin, D. I. (1966) Grammatical transformations and sentence comprehension in adulthood and childhood. *Journal of Verbal Learning and Verbal Behaviour*, *5*, 219–227.

Steedman, M. J. & Johnson-Laird, P. N. (1978) A programmatic theory of linguistic performance. In R. W. Campbell & P. T. Smith (Eds.), *Advance in the Psychology of Language—Formal and Experimental Approaches*. New York: Plenum Press.

Swinney, D. A. (1979) Lexical access during sentence comprehension: (Re)Consideration of context effects. *Journal of Verbal Learning and Verbal Behaviour, 18*, 545–569.

Tyler, L. K. & Marslen-Wilson, W. D. (1977) The on-line effects of semantic context on syntactic processing. *Journal of Verbal Learning and Verbal Behaviour, 16*, 683–692.

6 Understanding Anaphora

Alan Garnham
Laboratory of Experimental Psychology, University of Sussex,
Brighton, BN1 9QG, U.K.

INTRODUCTION

An ubiquitous feature of expressions in natural languages is that their interpretation depends on the context in which they occur. This context dependence is particularly apparent with expressions such as pronouns and simple definite noun phrases. It is not possible, for example, to know what *it* or *the stone* refers to, unless a context, either linguistic or nonlinguistic, is provided. This chapter discusses how people understand one common class of expressions that have context-dependent interpretations—anaphoric expressions. Some preliminary remarks on anaphora and the problems that anaphoric expressions pose for the language understanding system are followed by a survey of linguistic descriptions of anaphora, from which some conclusions are drawn about psychological theories of anaphor comprehension. The survey is also intended as a reminder of some of the complexities of anaphora that have yet to be incorporated into processing theories. It is followed by a discussion of how the problem of anaphora has been tackled in artificial intelligence (AI) programs for understanding natural language. Again, the relation of this work to human language processing is considered. The remainder of the chapter describes psychological work on adults' comprehension of anaphors. Finally, a theory of anaphor interpretation is outlined.

SENSE, REFERENCE, AND CONTEXT

One way in which natural languages manage their resources economically is by having the same expression refer to different things on different

253

occasions. Even a semantically complex noun phrase (NP), such as *the brightest star in the Galaxy*, may have different referents in a discussion of the real world and in a science-fiction novel. Of course, some aspects of the meaning of such expressions remain constant whenever they are used. A theory of language understanding explains our grasp of this fixed semantic content by postulating stored knowledge of the meanings of words, and of how the meanings of complex expressions depend on the meanings of their parts. However, such a theory must also explain how we interpret expressions in discourse or text on the basis of the context in which they are encountered. More particularly, it must explain how people compute and remember the situation that a text is about—which they are good at—whilst forgetting the detailed way in which the facts were presented (see e.g. Sachs, 1967; Johnson-Laird & Stevenson, 1970; Anderson & Bower, 1973; ch. 9; Anderson & Hastie, 1974; Garnham, 1981a). Syntax and fixed semantic content are used only to determine reference, and then they are forgotten.

Frege (1892/1952) contrasted the *sense* (*Sinn*) of an expression with its *reference* or *denotation* (*Bedeutung*). Its reference is the thing in the world that it stands for—a definite pronoun, for example, typically refers to an object of some kind. The sense of an expression provides a method of picking out the referent. Frege illustrated the difference between sense and reference by considering the expressions *the morning star* and *the evening star*. The sense of *the morning star* indicates that its referent can be picked out by looking for a star-like object in the morning sky. The evening star appears in the evening. It was an astronomical discovery that the two are one and the same heavenly body—the planet Venus. More generally, any object (a referent) can be described in indefinitely many different ways (using expressions with different senses). The goal of language understanding is (usually) to identify referents via senses—to find out what is under discussion rather than how it is being described. Grasping senses is only a means to an end.

Frege assigned senses (and references) to *expressions*. He made no allowance for the fact that expressions of ordinary language change their meaning from context to context. In fact Frege regarded context-dependence as a *defect* of natural languages, and invented (Frege, 1879/1972) his own language, *conceptual notation* (predicate calculus), in which it was eliminated. The sense of an expression in conceptual notation always picks out the same reference.

The psycholinguist, however, must explain how people understand natural languages, in which the same expression typically has different denotations on different occasions of its use. For example, in direct speech *I* refers to whoever happens to be speaking.

Workers in the Fregean tradition who, unlike Frege, consider that their ideas should be applied to natural languages, have developed accounts of context dependence. The most detailed proposal is that of Kaplan (1978), who divides the sense of an expression into two parts, its *character* and its *content*. The character of an expression determines its content in any context (it is "a function from contexts to contents"). In particular, sentences express different *propositions* on different occasions of their use. The character of *I* states that it denotes the speaker in any context. The content of an expression fixes its denotation in any set of *circumstances of evaluation*. In the case of *I*, its content determines which person it refers to, given the state of the world in which it was uttered. Many expressions have context-independent characters. For example the meaning of common nouns, such as *dog* (though not that of definite NPs, such as *the dog*), is the same in all contexts.

From the psycholinguists' point of view, Kaplan has done little more than label a problem. A theory of text understanding must explain *how* people determine the content (in Kaplan's sense) of the expressions that they hear, taking account, where necessary, of context, and how they determine what things in the real or an imaginary world the text is about.

ANAPHORA

Kaplan's concern was with indexical expressions such as *I, you, here, there, now*, and *then*. This chapter is concerned with a wider class of expressions whose interpretation depends upon the context in which they occur. The term *anaphora* has been used in several different ways (see Bosch, 1983; ch. 1, for a historical survey); here the term will be used in a broad sense. Anaphoric expressions are those that take their meaning in certain ways (to be detailed later) from some preceding or following part of the text, or from nonlinguistic context. Thus, under the head of anaphora are included what Halliday and Hasan (1976) call cataphora, where the so-called *antecedent* follows the anaphor:

As he entered the room, John tripped over the mat

and what they call exophora, in which reference is made directly to something outside of the text:

(indicating someone the hearer can see)
He is a fool.

The reason for adopting this broad definition of *anaphora* is that all three cases pose parallel problems for the language understanding system. In particular, they all require a similar search of a representation for a referent, since, according to the theory of mental models (Garnham, 1981a; Johnson-Laird, 1980, 1983), text representations and representations of the world are, in crucial respects, similar, despite being constructed from different inputs. On this account an anaphor with a textual antecedent may not be interpreted via a representation of its antecedent, but may access directly the element in the mental model introduced by the antecedent.

Natural languages contain a wide variety of anaphoric expressions. Table 1 shows the main types in English.

TABLE 6.1
Examples of Anaphoric Expressions

Full Noun Phrases
(a) Definite noun phrases:
    The murder was committed at midnight. The crime had wide press coverage.
(b) Epithets:
    John slammed the door on leaving the room. The inconsiderate fool needs a talking to.

Pronouns
(c) Reflexive pronouns:
    John hurt himself
(d) Definite pronouns:
    The building was admired by many people. It was in the town centre.
(e) Indefinite pronouns:
    My brother has a new shirt and I want one, too.
(f) Sentential *it* anaphora:
    Bill said that Martha eats insects, but I don't believe it.

Elliptical Verbal Constructions
(g) Null-complement anaphora:
    Nobody else would take the rubbish to the dustbin, so Bill volunteered.
(h) *Do it* anaphora:
    Bill wants to go to university, and I think he'll do it.
(i) *So* anaphora (one of several types):
    Maisie feels that she should have a new coat, and so she should.
(j) *Do so* anaphora:
    Suzie went swimming yesterday, and Teresa did so today.
(k) Sluicing:
    Someone's coming to dinner but I don't know who.
(l) Verb-phrase ellipsis:
    Margie wanted the recipes. Tom did, too.
(m) Gapping:
    Stuart likes sparrows, Phil rooks, and Dennis magpies.
(n) Stripping:
    Sally likes watching rugby matches, but not hockey matches.

Interpreting Anaphoric Expressions

The fact that expressions in discourse have context-dependent interpretations poses three problems for language understanding:

1. The expressions in a discourse that have such interpretations must be identified.
2. For each such expression the linguistic or nonlinguistic context relevant to its interpretation must be determined.
3. The meaning of the expression must then be derived.

Anaphoric expressions take their meaning from context in a particular way. Such expressions have *the same meaning*, either same sense or same reference, as some other part of the text. However, not all expressions with context-dependent interpretations are anaphoric. For example, as Garnham (1979) showed, the interpretation of *cooked* differs in the sentences:

The housewife cooked the chips.
The housewife cooked the peas.

though *cooked* is not anaphoric in either.

Anaphoric expressions have meanings of different kinds, which depend on those of their antecedents. Definite pronouns, for example, usually refer to people or things and elliptical verb-phrases (VPs) to actions (e.g. hit the ball) or states (e.g. was lying on the bed). This fact restricts the set of appropriate antecedents for any particular anaphor—only actions and states need be considered as possible antecedents of elliptical VPs, for example—but it raises the further question of how context, including the preceding text, makes antecedents available.

Although most psychological studies have focussed on a restricted set of anaphors—chiefly definite pronouns and definite noun phrases—a theory of text processing should account for our ability to understand all types. The development of such a theory requires a detailed knowledge of anaphors such as that provided by linguists. The following section summarises a range of facts that must eventually be considered by psycholinguists attempting to develop a comprehensive theory of discourse understanding.

LINGUISTIC DESCRIPTIONS OF ANAPHORA

Wasow (1979) identifies three kinds of question that linguists can ask about pronouns. More generally, these questions can be asked about any kind of anaphor. They correspond loosely to the three questions that the reader or listener is faced with in interpreting anaphoric expressions:

1. First, there are strictly syntactic questions. What syntactic categories do anaphors belong to? What are their distributions? What sort of inflections do they take? These questions relate to the recognition of anaphoric expressions before they have been interpreted.

2. Second, there are questions about how anaphors are associated with their antecedents. Are there any sentence-level restrictions on what expressions can be antecedent and anaphor? What pragmatic factors affect the interpretation of anaphors? These questions relate to the search for the antecedent.

3. Third, there are questions about the meaning of anaphors. How does an anaphor take its meaning from its antecedent? Under what conditions would a sentence containing an anaphor be true?

Wasow argues that the failure to distinguish between these three kinds of question hindered the study of pronominalisation in generative grammar. Before looking in more detail at how the questions might be answered, an outline of early treatments of anaphora will be given to provide a background against which subsequent work can be assessed.

The Transformational Approach to Anaphora

In the 1960s syntacticians attempted to solve all three problems by treating anaphors as transformationally derived from copies of their antecedents in underlying structure—pronouns, for example, replaced full noun phrases. Since transformations apply to *phrase markers*, such accounts were restricted to those aspects of anaphora that can be explained at the level of single sentences. They put to one side facts about anaphora that might have to be explained at the level of discourse.

On these accounts the distribution of an anaphor was determined by that of the corresponding full form in underlying structure. The association between the anaphor and its antecedent was established by the transformation, with constraints on transformations prohibiting certain antecedent-anaphor pairings. In the Standard Theory of *Aspects* (Chomsky, 1965), the meaning of the anaphor was identical to that of the full form, since transformations did not change meaning.

This early approach can be illustrated using verb-phrase ellipsis as an example. Ross (1967) proposed that elliptical verb phrases were produced by a transformation called verb phrase deletion, which eliminates one of two identical VPs. A sentence such as:

John has eaten some ham, and Mary has, too.

was derived from the same underlying form as:

John has eaten some ham, and Mary has eaten some ham, too.

The transformational account was initially appealing but, at least in the case of pronominalisation, it is now universally rejected. Two of the main reasons for its rejection were, first, that it encountered problems in sentences with quantifiers, just as many other early transformational analyses did:

John likes his dog.

might plausibly be derived from the same underlying structure as:

John likes John's dog.

However, if transformations preserve meaning:

Everyone likes his dog.

cannot be related in the same way to:

Everyone likes everyone's dog.

because the two sentences mean different things.

Second, the transformational account is highly implausible for Bach-Peters, or crossing coreference, sentences:

The pilot who shot at it hit the MIG that chased him.
The boy who deserved it won the prize that he longed for.

In these sentences the antecedent of each pronoun contains the other pronoun. *Him* in the first sentence refers to *the pilot who shot at it*. On the transformational hypothesis this antecedent must be explicit in underlying structure. However, it contains a pronoun, *it*, which must also be expanded in underlying structure. That pronoun expands to *the MIG that chased him*, and so on *ad infinitum*. If every pronoun in surface structure derives from a full NP in underlying structure, then the underlying structures of Bach-Peters sentences must be infinitely large. In fact, the two pronouns in a Bach-Peters sentence are of different types (Bosch, 1983; 146–147). The first is referential, and the second is a bound variable (see later).

These arguments against a transformational account of pronominalisation led to a theory in which pronouns were inserted directly into underlying structure and assigned meanings by interpretive semantic rules. Interpretive theories for other kinds of anaphor were also developed.

Syntactic Form and Distribution of Anaphoric Expressions

Wasow's first kind of question is about the syntactic properties of anaphors. It will receive little discussion here. Many anaphors are specific lexical items: *he, she, it, they, do so*; and others are null elements—bits missing from what would otherwise be full sentences. These null elements must be distinguished from syntactic gaps in constructions such as relative clauses and topicalisations. For example, the "missing" verb phrase after *likes* in:

Eating grapes, Tom likes

is not elliptical. However, distributional facts distinguish syntactic gaps and null anaphors.

Wasow (1979) showed that the transformational approach failed to give an accurate account of the syntactic properties of anaphors. For example, if pronouns are derived from full NPs in underlying structure, the distribution of pronouns should be *more restricted* than that of full NPs, because there are constraints on where pronouns can appear in surface structure. In fact, it is the distribution of full NPs that is more constrained (Wasow's 13 [a] and [b]):

John left, didn't he
*John left, didn't the man

Mary lost her temper.
*Mary lost Sue's temper.

Wasow's observations on pronouns and full NPs show that description of the syntactic distribution of anaphors requires some care, but there is no reason to think that linguistic accounts of their distribution are different from the ones required in a psycholinguistic theory.

The Relation between Antecedent and Anaphor

The Backwards Anaphora Constraint

A transformation such as a verb phrase deletion cannot simply delete either one of two identical verb phrases, since in the following sentence the missing VP cannot take its meaning from the VP in the second clause:

John has, too, and Mary has eaten some ham.

Neither can there be a blanket restriction on deleting the first of two identical VPs. In some cases such deletions are permitted.

Because John has, Mary has eaten some ham.

Such examples led to the observation that *backwards anaphora* (Halliday and Hasan's cataphora)—where the antecedent *follows* the anaphor—is more restricted than "forwards" anaphora. They provoked a search for the *backwards anaphora constraint*, envisaged initially as a constraint on transformations.

The Precede and Command Condition

A formulation of this constraint—the *precede and command* condition—emerged in the mid-1960s (Langacker, 1969; Ross, 1967). It stated that an anaphor must not both precede and command its antecedent. The relation of commanding is defined for a phrase structure tree, and is, therefore, only applicable within a single sentence. If X and Y are two nodes in a tree, X commands Y if every clausal (S) node dominating X also dominates Y. For example, in the tree below, NP1 commands NP2, but NP2 does not command NP1, because S2 dominates NP2, but not NP1.

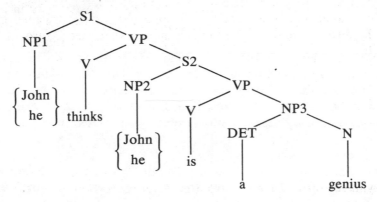

Therefore, *he* and *John* can be coreferential in:

John thinks he is a genius.

but not in:

He thinks John is a genius.

In the latter the pronoun both precedes and commands *John*. The effect of the precede and command condition is that if an anaphor precedes its antecedent it must be in a subordinate construction, so that a clausal node—the one corresponding to the subordinate clause—dominates the anaphor, but not its antecedent. In such a construction, by definition, the pronoun does *not* command any constituent in the main clause.

The precede and command condition was discussed in most detail in relation to definite pronouns, which are usually coreferential with their antecedents. Chomsky (1965) and others proposed that coreferentiality should be represented by indices in syntactic structure—indices that would later be interpreted by the semantic component of the grammar. The pronominalisation transformation applied to phrase markers with two identical co-indexed NPs, but was prohibited if its output would contain co-indexed NPs that violated the precede and command condition.

The transformational approach confined itself to intrasentential relations between anaphors and their antecedents. An anaphor could only be generated if it had an antecedent in the same sentence, and the precede and command condition disallowed certain outputs of these transformations. Nothing was said about anaphors such as *he* in:

John opened the door. Then he entered the room with great caution.

Such pronouns were labelled as *discourse anaphors* and deemed to fall outside the scope of sentential syntax. However, it has since been recognised that many pronouns with antecedents in the same sentence behave in the same way as discourse anaphors. This idea is compatible with later accounts of indexing and the precede and command condition. Indexed pronouns are inserted directly into underlying syntactic structure and may be co-indexed with NPs either in the same sentence or in other sentences. The precede and command condition disallows some co-indexings. For example, it forbids coreferentiality between *he* and *John* in:

He thinks John is a genius.

but it leaves open the possibility that *he* is coreferential with *Bill* in a preceding sentence.

In parallel with the rejection of a transformational account of pronominalisation, further investigation of the possible syntactic relations between anaphors and their antecedents led to a revision of the precede and command condition itself. Reinhart (see 1981) proposed the *C-command* condition—an anaphor must not C-command its antecedent. In this version of the constraint the left-to-right ordering of the antecedent and anaphor is irrelevant—there is no mention of precedence. The right-branching structure of English phrase markers ensures that backwards anaphora is more restricted than forwards anaphora. The relation of C-commanding, like that of commanding, holds between nodes in a phrase marker. X C-commands Y if every branching node dominating X also dominates Y. A node commands every node that it C-commands, but the reverse is not true, because there may be branching nodes between it and the next highest S node. For example, in the previous diagram NP3 commands NP2, but does not C-command it. The C-command condition, therefore, allows a greater range of antecedent-anaphor relations than the precede and command condition. The predictions of the precede and command condition and the C-command condition depend to some extent on other decisions about syntactic strucutre. However, the predictions of the C-command condition are more accurate. For example, it rightly predicts possible coreference between *John* and *his* or *him* in:

His mother loves John.
Near him, John saw a snake.

whereas the precede and command condition forbids it. A recent development (Chomsky, 1981) is the introduction of the notion of *government*, which is related to that of C-command, to explain intrasentential restrictions on antecedent-anaphor relations.

Nonsyntactic Approaches to Constraints on Anaphora

Not all linguists believe that the constraints on anaphora are syntactic. On the one hand there have been attempts to explain them in terms of discourse structure (e.g. Bolinger, 1979), and on the other there have been arguments that they should be explained semantically. People who favour the first approach start from the question: Why is an anaphor rather than a full form (or vice versa) appropriate at this point in a text? Their answers to this question appeal to notions such as topic and theme, and, to the extent that these notions are ill-defined, so are such explanations.

The semantic approach to constraints on anaphora is taken by some proponents of formal semantics (e.g. Keenan & Faltz, 1978; Bach & Partee, 1980). According to these theorists the meaning of a complex expression is built up from the meaning of its parts in such a way that some parts are treated as functions (in the mathematical sense), and others as arguments of those functions. On this approach the "backwards anaphora constraint" states that an anaphor cannot occur in an argument of the function containing its antecedent, and vice versa. Reinhart (1983) argues that this approach is equivalent, except in a few cases that are problematic for both theories, to the C-command condition.

Bosch (1983) combines these two nonsyntactic approaches. His definition of the "backwards anaphora constraint" makes use of the notions of function and argument. Indeed, he argues that the constraint follows from the definitions of those terms, and that a semantic formulation is better motivated than a syntactic one. However Bosch, unlike most formal semanticists, holds that expressions do not have fixed function-argument structures, but structures that are *focus-sensitive*. New information is treated as function and old as argument. If the answer *Fred walks* is given to the question:

How does Fred get home?

then *walks* is the function, and Fred its argument. However, if the same answer is given to the question:

Does anyone walk home?

then the roles are reversed. Bosch argues that by appealing to focus, he is able to account for antecedent-anaphor relations which remain problematic for the C-command analysis, in particular some that were first pointed out by Lakoff (1968/1976). Lakoff noted that there are pairs of sentences with two NPs in the same syntactic relations, in one of which an antecedent-anaphor relation cannot hold (first sentence below) and in the other of which it can (second sentence below):

Julia hit him before Max left.
Julia hit him before Max left in his Rolls-Royce for a dinner engagement at the Ritz.

By considering to what questions they are appropriate answers, Bosch shows that the focus of the two sentences is different. The sentences, therefore, have different function-argument structures and different antecedent-anaphor possibilities.

A related proposal is that of Reinhart (1983). She challenges the idea, which emerged in the mid-1970s (e.g. Lasnik, 1976), that the "backwards anaphora" constraint states the conditions under which two NP *must* be noncoreferential. She claims that the apparently negative constraint arises from a positive constraint on bound anaphora (see later) together with pragmatic principles that favour unambiguous modes of expression as opposed to potentially ambiguous ones—most violations of the constraint are potentially ambiguous between a bound and a referential reading of the anaphoric expression. In support of this view Reinhart shows that, unlike the constraint on bound anaphora, that on coreference is often violated. This pattern of data is exactly what would be expected if coreference options are determined by pragmatic principles that: (1) recognise the (nonpragmatic) constraints on bound anaphors; and (2) may be overridden by further pragmatic considerations. Since focus is a pragmatic notion, Reinhart's attempt to account for cases in which the C-command principle is violated has parallels with Bosch's.

Are There Syntactic Constraints on Antecedent-Anaphor Relations?

One question that remains to be resolved, and which is raised again by discourse structure approaches to constraints on anaphora, is whether there are *any* genuinely sentential constraints, as opposed to ones that sometimes happen to apply within a single sentence. The answer to this question is undoubtedly yes, at least in the case of pronouns. It has long been recognised (e.g. Langacker, 1969) that reflexive (e.g. *herself*) and reciprocal (e.g. *each other*) pronouns (R-pronouns) behave differently from other pronouns. For example, *Mary* and *her* cannot be coreferential in the first of the following sentences, but *Mary* and *herself* must be, in the second:

Mary likes her.
Mary likes herself.

R-pronouns must be related to certain NPs that C-command them (NPs in functions/arguments of which they are arguments/functions). They can only be interpreted if they have an appropriate antecedent NP in the *same* sentence. Although there is some dispute about whether:

John hurt herself.

is ungrammatical as well as uninterpretable, its ill-formedness is explained at the sentence level. In recent versions of transformational grammar (Chomsky, 1981), reciprocals and reflexives (Chomsky's overt anaphors) obey a different *binding principle* from other pronouns (Chomsky's pronominals).

On Bosch's (1983) analysis R-pronouns do occur in functions (arguments) of which their antecedents are arguments (functions). He argues that this fact is compatible with the definitions of function and argument, because R-pronouns are not coreferential with their antecedents, but are simply syntactic agreement markers.

Another class of pronouns that are subject to sentence-level restrictions are *bound anaphors*—those that are interpreted as if they were variables bound by quantifiers in a logical calculus. In ordinary language the relation between pronouns and quantificational NPs is different from that between pronouns and other NPs. Compare, for example, the following sentences (from Reinhart, 1983). In the first, *him* can refer to Siegfried. In the second it cannot be bound by *each of the managers*. (In both cases *him* can be exophoric.)

The secretary who works for him despises Siegfried.
The secretary who works for him despises each of the managers.

Reinhart (1983) proposes the following (intrasentential) constraint on bound anaphora. An NP can (*can* because the pronoun could be exophoric) bind a pronoun if and only if it C-commands the pronoun. This condition is the same as that on the relation between an R-pronoun and its antecedent, except that R-pronouns can never be exophoric, and contrasts with the condition for coreference, which states that coreference is *impossible* between an NP (full or pronoun) and a nonpronoun that it C-commands. On this view proper names sometimes act as quantifiers and sometimes they do not. On the one hand *his* in:

John loves his mother.

is bound (on the nonexophoric reading), since this sentence parallels:

Nobody loves his mother.

On the other hand *him* and *Siegfried*, in the sentence earlier, stand in a coreference relation. Bosch proposes a "nobody" test for deciding which pronouns are bound (syntactic in his terminology).

The Meaning of Anaphoric Expressions

There are at least two types of pronoun; those subject to intrasentential syntactic constraints (R-pronouns and bound variables); and what Bosch calls *referential pronouns*. This second type typically have the same meaning as their antecedents, whereas *syntactic pronouns* do not. Bosch argues that syntactic pronouns are syntactic agreement markers that contribute to the meaning of "compound verbs" or "complex predicates." For example, there is a compound verb *to love one's mother*, which declines *I love my mother, you love your mother, he loves his mother, she loves her mother*, etc. Such pronouns are not referential, since their antecedents need not be referring expressions:

Nobody loves his mother.

Reinhart and Bosch are concerned primarily with full NP anaphora and pronouns. Other kinds of anaphor cannot be interpreted as bound variables, and must always be discourse anaphors. Syntactic theory need concern itself only with the form and distribution of the anaphors themselves.

It might be thought that these other kinds of anaphor would all be similar, and contrast with pronouns and anaphoric full NPs. However, they are not. There are two distinctions that are relevant to the question of how anaphoric expressions are assigned meanings, neither of which corresponds to that between pronouns and NPs and other kinds of anaphor. The first is that between *identity of reference* anaphora and *identity of sense* anaphora. Nonsyntactic (definite) pronouns are usually coreferential with their antecedents. Consider, however, the elliptical VP in:

Susan has bought a flat, and Kerry has, too.

This anaphor does not refer to the same event as its antecedent—there are two different flat-buyings. Rather it has the same sense. Another example of an identity of sense anaphor is the indefinite pronoun *one*. In:

Joan has a yellow T-shirt and Paul has a red one.

there are two T-shirts, so *one* and *T-shirt* do not corefer. Nevertheless, the meaning of *one* is *T-shirt*. Some definite pronouns are identity of sense anaphors, notoriously the *it* in Karttunen's (1969) "paycheck" sentence:

The man who gave his paycheck to his wife was wiser than the man who gave it to his mistress.

However, such cases are less straightforward than "ordinary" identity of reference definite pronouns. Bosch (1983) argues that such uses of definite pronouns are strongly constrained by social facts—in this case the fact that almost everyone (in the USA) gets a paycheck. Because not everyone has a Ford dealer, the following sentence does not work in the same way:

John ordered a Fiesta from his Ford dealer, and Peter ordered an Escort from him.

Him cannot be Peter's Ford dealer.

The distinction between identity of reference and identity of sense anaphora is one that has implications for psychological theories of text comprehension. Occurrences of the two kinds of anaphor call for different modifications to the model of the discourse so far.

The second distinction—that drawn by Hankamer and Sag (1976) between *deep* and *surface* anaphora—is likewise important. As discussed above, pronominalisation is not a transformational process. In current transformational grammars, pronouns are inserted directly into underlying syntactic structure. For this reason Hankamer and Sag refer to pronouns as deep anaphors. In common with other deep anaphors—indefinite pronouns, full NPs, epithets, sentential *it*, *do it*, and null complements—pronouns can be distinguished from surface anaphors in two principal ways:

1. Deep anaphors can take their antecedents from real world context—they can be *pragmatically controlled* (they can refer *exophorically*). Both of the following are acceptable:
    Don't throw your orange peel onto the floor,
    put it into the bin!
    (A throws some orange peel on to the floor)
    B: Put it into the bin!
Surface anaphors cannot be pragmatically controlled:
    John threw some orange peel on the floor,
    and Bill did, too.
    (John throws some orange peel on the floor)
    A: *Bill did, too.
2. The antecedent of a surface anaphor must have an identical, or almost identical, surface form to that of the antecedent. Compare:
    Ted tidied the kitchen, because Barbara wouldn't.
    * The kitchen was tidied by Ted, because Barbara wouldn't.
The second of these two examples is not acceptable, though the corresponding sentence with the deep anaphor *do it* is.
    The kitchen was tidied by Ted, because Barbara wouldn't do it.
The qualification that the surface form must be "almost" identical is required to cover cases such as:
    A: Please scratch my back.
    B: OK, I will (scratch your back).

Hankamer and Sag proposed that surface anaphors were derived transformationally. More recently (Sag & Hankamer, 1984) they have suggested that the correct account of the distinction is in terms of processing—deep anaphors are interpreted with reference to a mental model, surface anaphors with reference to a representation of surface form. Murphy (1985a) proposes an alternative functional explanation—surface anaphors are potentially more ambiguous than deep anaphors, and therefore require additional constraints on their occurrence to make them interpretable. He claims that his own empirical data (1985b) show that, in comprehension at least, the two types of anaphor are not processed differently.

It follows from the second property of surface anaphors that, *in general*, their correct interpretation depends on an accurate memory for the surface form of the antecedent, though this interpretation may be difficult to compute. However, it is possible to guess the meaning of some surface anaphors without remembering surface form, just as it is possible to interpret some passive sentences (nonreversible passives) without producing a full parse of those sentences. Two suggestions have been made about how such guesses might be made. The first is the use of "selectional restrictions" or plausibility. For example, if a text contains the sentence:

An Apache had scalped a sheriff.

And a later elliptical clause that says *a Sioux had, too*, then, since a Sioux scalping a sheriff is a plausible event, it is reasonable (and in this case correct) to guess that the Sioux had also scalped a sheriff. However, if the surface form of the antecedent has been forgotten, there is no guarantee that it was not the passive:

A sheriff had been scalped by an Apache.

In that case the elliptical clause describes a comparatively implausible event (a Sioux had been scalped by an Apache), and a plausible guess will produce the wrong interpretation. Memory for (surface) syntax is necessary to derive the correct meaning. Guesses based on plausibility should not be allowed to override the interpretation of a sentence indicated by its full syntactic analysis, because one function of syntax is to allow unlikely events to be described (cf. Forster, 1979). However, our comparative inability to remember surface form may lead to errors in interpreting surface anaphors (see Murphy, 1985b, for some evidence that surface anaphors are often interpreted from memory for content).

The second suggestion is less plausible. It is that a representation of topic or focus might somehow be used to interpret an elliptical VP. There are two possibilities. One is that the overall topic can be used to guess an elliptical predicate. Such guesses will usually be incorrect, since topics rarely suggest a single predicate, and missing VPs may be only very indirectly related to overall topics. The other is that an elliptical VP predicates of the current (local) topic the same thing as was predicated of a previous topic. In the sense that this claim is true, remembering a topic can only mean remembering the surface subject of a previous clause, and remembering what was predicated of that topic is remembering a VP. So this version of the claim is equivalent to the statement that we interpret surface anaphors by remembering certain aspects of surface form.

Summary

Linguists have shown that anaphora is a complex phenomenon, and have described many aspects of it that are relevant to a psychological theory of language understanding. For example, the parser must have access to information about the syntactic categories of anaphoric expressions, and the message processor must be aware of restrictions on the position of anaphors in relation to their antecedents, and of the kinds of meaning that anaphors can have. When considering the psychological literature on anaphora, which is comparatively restricted in scope, it is important to remember the range of facts that psychological theories must eventually cover.

ANAPHOR INTERPRETATION IN AI PROGRAMS

A number of natural language-understanding programs in artificial intelligence (AI) perform impressively with texts that contain anaphoric expressions, primarily definite noun phrases and pronouns. It might, therefore, be asked if these programs help to explain how people understand anaphors.

In evaluating such programs it is easy to be overimpressed with outputs chosen to show the program at its best. However, a program whose output appears natural need not incorporate any very profound insights into the processes of language understanding, as Weizenbaum's (1966) ELIZA demonstrated. ELIZA can be made to look very foolish, even to someone who insists on evaluating it by its output, but the real lesson is that programs should not be evaluated by their output, but by the principles that they embody.

The AI program that comes most readily to mind in the context of anaphor understanding is Winograd's (1972) SHRDLU. SHRDLU can cope with a wide range of pronouns, both definite and indefinite, anaphoric definite noun phrases, and elliptical constructions. However, SHRDLU's procedure for resolving definite pronouns uses complex structural criteria that probably have no direct relation to the way people understand pronouns. For example, SHRDLU would misinterpret sentences such as:

I put the pencil in my pocket but because it had a hole it fell out.

because it assumes that two occurrences of the same pronoun in one sentence have the same referent. Frederiksen (1981) showed that people do not make this assumption. More generally, any purely structural strategy for pronoun resolution is bound to fail, because different assignments are possible in sentences with the same structure, for example:

John sold his car to Bill because he hated it.
John sold his car to Bill because he wanted it.

Other aspects of SHRDLU's procedure are psychologically more plausible. They include a preference for subject antecedents over object antecedents, and a preference for antecedents in main clauses over antecedents in subordinate clauses.

Although it is easy to construct sentences on which simple structural strategies for pronoun resolution fail, such strategies do give the right answer for a high proportion of sentences from actual texts. Rumelhart and Levin (1975) formulated the following simple structural strategy, which accepts the first antecedent it finds that agrees in number and gender with the pronoun:

1. If the pronoun is reflexive search the current clause.
2. If not, search the previous clause.
3. Check other pronouns first.
4. Then check, in order, subject NPs, object NPs, other NPs.

This strategy correctly interpreted 90% of pronouns in a random sample of sentences from the World Book Encyclopedia. These observations show that although structural strategies should not be relied on to *resolve* pronominal references, structural *preferences* in the search for antecedents may be useful.

An example of a linguistically more sophisticated approach to anaphora within AI is that of Webber (1978, 1981). Webber addresses the problem of what entities a discourse makes available for anaphoric reference, and introduces the concept of a *discourse model* (cf. Stenning, 1978; Johnson-Laird & Garnham, 1980; Kamp, 1981), in which those entities are represented. Webber shows that the relations between expressions in a text and the entities they introduce into a discourse model are complex. For example, in:

No intelligent woman likes Nixon.
She would be crazy to.

she refers to something like the prototypical intelligent woman (Webber, 1978; p. 49).

Another topic that has received attention in AI is the role of focussing in the interpretation of pronouns and definite noun phrases (Grosz, 1981; Sidner, 1978, 1981). Focussing is one method of restricting the set of possible referents for an anaphoric expression. Grosz (1981) studied the effect of task structure on reference in dialogues between instructors and apprentices performing tasks such as the disassembly of an air compressor. She found that people use their knowledge of what they are trying to achieve in order to focus on particular items, and to provide unambiguous interpretations for definite noun phrases such as *the screw*, which have a number of potential referents in the scene that they are looking at.

However, differences in knowledge between instructors and apprentices sometimes led to misunderstandings.

PSYCHOLOGICAL QUESTIONS ABOUT ANAPHOR RESOLUTION

Psychological studies have almost invariably been addressed to the second of the three kinds of question about anaphora—questions about how anaphoric expressions are associated with their antecedents. More specifically, the experiments tackle two related questions: (1) when there is a choice between antecedents for an anaphoric expression, which antecedents are easy to make connections with and which hard? and (2) what aspects of a given anaphor and antecedent affect the ease with which a link can be made between them?

Questions about the identification of anaphors and about the assignment of meanings to them have largely been ignored by psychologists. The main reason is that almost all of the studies have investigated two kinds of anaphor: pronouns (excluding R-pronouns and bound variables); and definite descriptions. Both are readily identified syntactically and both are identity-of-reference anaphors that take their meanings from their antecedents in a straightforward way, at least in the kinds of text that have been used in psychological experiments.

It was argued earlier that anaphors can be identified from their syntactic properties and environments. Since this chapter is not about parsing, their identification will not be described in detail. Once an anaphoric expression has been identified, its antecedent must be sought. Each type of anaphoric expression has a specific type (or types) of antecedent. In the general case, preceding text and, for deep anaphors, context will have made available several antecedents of the kind required by a particular anaphor (see Webber, 1978, for a discussion of the antecedents that may be available for definite pronouns, indefinite pronouns, and elliptical VPs), and the anaphor resolution system must choose between them.

There are two ways in which this choice could be made. Either the set of possible antecedents could be accessed or constructed, and a search made through that set, or context could restrict access to the actual antecedent. This distinction parallels that between multiple access and context-guided access models of the interpretation of ambiguous words. However, even in the case of ambiguous words, it is difficult to imagine a general mechanism by which context could guide access. One possibility is that context could ensure that the entries accessed from semantic memory had certain "semantic features." For example, the context:

The tennis player stretched out his racket and just hit the . . .

might limit the meaning of the following word to one with the feature ⟨+PHYSICAL OBJECT⟩, and exclude those with the feature ⟨+SOCIAL OCCASION⟩.

In the case of "referentially ambiguous" pronouns, methods that could restrict access to one member of the set of possible referents are harder to conceive. The reason is that it would be necessary to restrict access not to words with certain semantic features, but to people or things with certain properties. Since the properties that make a person or thing a plausible or implausible antecedent for a pronoun may be indefinitely complex, it is hard to see how context could be used on-line (or even off-line) to compute those properties and use them to exclude potential antecedents from consideration (see Lockman & Klappholz, 1980, for a similar argument). It is simpler to consider the properties of all potential antecedents, and determine which is the most plausible.

This idea is supported by several experimental findings. First, Corbett and Chang (1983) found that after reading:

Karen poured a drink for Emily and then she put the bottle down.

a decision about whether the word *Emily* (the non-antecedent) was in the sentence was faster than when the referring expression in the second clause was a proper name:

Karen poured a drink for Emily and then Karen put the bottle down.

This finding suggests that when the pronoun is encountered, both potential antecedents are accessed, even though context strongly favours one antecedent.

Second, Frederiksen (1981) found that the referent of a pronoun was harder to name if it had two syntactically possible antecedents than if it had one. Third, in an unpublished self-paced reading experiment, I found that subjects spent longer reading the second sentence of:

The knife and the rope were found beside the corpse.
The knife had been effective.

than the second sentence of:

The knife was found beside the corpse.
The knife had been effective.

The mean reading times were 2167 and 2012msec respectively.

Finally, Tyler and Marslen-Wilson (1982a) applied Swinney's (1979) cross-modal priming technique to the study of pronouns. They presented subjects with sentences such as:

The sailor | tried to save the cat | but | it/he | fell | *overboard* | instead.

The "|"'s indicate points at which words were presented for visual lexical decision. They found speeded decision for both *boat* (related to *sailor*) and *cat* (related to *dog*) at all points in both versions of the sentence. There was no differential facilitation, even after the pronoun. This finding suggests that both antecedents are active when the pronoun is encountered.

However, this result is qualified by that of Shillcock (1982). Shillcock presented subjects with sentences such as:

The teacher | did not board the train for the | simple reason that he/it | was not going to the South Coast of England.

The decision word for this sentence was either *school* or *street*. Lexical decision for *school* was speeded at all three points, and it was speeded after both pronouns. However, the amount of facilitation was not significant after the pronoun with a referent unrelated to the decision word (*it*) though it was significant after *he*. Unfortunately, however, the crucial interaction between decision word (related or unrelated) and pronoun was not significant. A further problem in interpreting these studies is that in neither was facilitation abolished before the pronoun, perhaps not surprisingly, since both potential antecedents might be relevant to the interpretation of subsequent parts of the passage. At least some of the effect detected after the pronoun is attributable to priming from the original occurrence of the antecedent.

The ease of finding potential antecedents for anaphors depends on the organisation of text representations. For example, if lists of antecedents of various kinds were explicitly maintained—and the ubiquity of anaphora might justify this—then the search for the set of possible antecedents for a given anaphor would be trivial. However, if, as seems likely, such lists are not kept, then a more complex search is required. In this second case anaphors might be resolved by a two-stage process in which a list of potential antecedents was first constructed, and then checks made to see which was the actual antecedent. Alternatively, each candidate might be checked when found, and accepted if suitable. A further dimension on which models of anaphor resolution could vary is whether the search is a serial or a parallel process. There are many possible processing models of anaphor resolution, and the data to hand resolve only a subset of the questions that can be asked about the search for antecedents.

One possibility that the data do eliminate is a model in which all possible antecedents are checked in parallel. In such a model the time taken to resolve an anaphor would not depend on such variables as the position of the antecedent in the text. To the extent that structural factors do influence the time taken to resolve a pronoun, this kind of model is implausible.

THE DISTANCE BETWEEN AN ANAPHOR AND ITS ANTECEDENT

The simplest structural factor that might influence anaphor resolution is the distance between an anaphor and its antecedent. This idea prompts the question: What is the significance for a theory of text comprehension of the fact that an anaphoric expression is usually separated in a text from its antecedent by only a short distance?

The first relevant observation is that distance effects might be expected for surface anaphors, but not for deep anaphors. A distance effect means that the greater the distance, as defined by some metric—say, number of words, number of clause boundaries, or number of sentence boundaries—between an anaphor and its antecedent, the more difficult the anaphor will be to interpret. As was argued earlier, surface anaphors must usually be interpreted with reference to a representation of the surface form of the preceding text. Memory for surface form is short-lived (e.g. Sachs, 1967; Jarvella, 1971; Johnson-Laird & Stevenson, 1970; Dooling & Christiaansen, 1977) except in two circumstances. First, subjects who are warned that they will be tested on surface form are better at remembering it (e.g. Johnson-Laird & Stevenson, 1970). Second, if some aspect of surface form conveys pragmatically important information, then it is more likely to be remembered (Kintsch & Bates, 1977; Keenan, MacWhinney, & Mayhew, 1977; Bates, Masling, & Kintsch, 1978; Bates, Kintsch, Fletcher, & Guiliani, 1980). Therefore, under normal circumstances, a surface anaphor should be difficult to interpret if it occurs too far from its antecedent, simply because the antecedent is difficult or impossible to recover. For deep anaphors the case is different, since no representation of surface form is necessary to interpret them. However, since all anaphors can match many possible antecedents—*she*, for example, could refer back to any female—the mechanism for ruling out possible antecedents may have the effect that, even for deep anaphors, antecedents will tend to be near. Furthermore, because of the kind of antecedents that they have and because of the different ways in which those antecedents are ruled out, some deep anaphors may give rise to purer distance effects than others.

It might be thought that deep anaphors with distant antecedents should be hard to interpret simply because the search for antecedents that are further back takes longer. However, this explanation is the same as one in terms of surface form. It is only in a representation that preserves surface features that "distant" antecedents are far away. A representation of content need have no linear structure.

EXPERIMENTS ON STRUCTURAL FACTORS IN ANAPHOR RESOLUTION

Surface Anaphors

A number of experimental studies suggest that structural factors influence anaphor resolution. Although the most straightforward prediction is of a distance effect for surface anaphors, there have been few psychological studies of such anaphors. In two unpublished experiments I found that clauses containing elliptical verb phrases were read more quickly if the antecedents were in the immediately preceding clause. For example, the elliptical clause in the second passage below was read more quickly than that in the first.

Margie wanted the recipes,
because the main dish was mouthwatering,
and the dessert was delicious.
Tom did too.

Because the main dish was mouthwatering,
and the dessert was delicious,
Margie wanted the recipes.
Tom did too.

A distance effect for elliptical VPs has also been obtained by Murphy (1985b), though he found parallel effects for the deep anaphor *do it*.

Malt (1985) reports some findings that suggest that, even for surface anaphors, simple distances may not be the crucial variable. She found that an elliptical VP was easier to interpret when it was an answer to a question than when it reaffirmed a factual statement, and easier to interpret when there was no topic shift between it and its antecedent.

Deep Anaphors and Distance

There are many more studies of deep anaphors, at least of definite pronouns and definite noun phrases, than of surface anaphors. Some of these suggest a distance effect, but their interpretation is complicated by a number of considerations.

Daneman and Carpenter (1980) asked subjects to answer questions about passages that they had just read. Some of the questions were about the referent of a definite pronoun in the last sentence of the passage. The number of errors tended to increase with increasing distance between the pronoun and its antecedent, and the effect was particularly marked for poorer readers. However, this result is not directly relevant to the interpretation of pronouns during reading.

Clark and Sengul (1979) showed that both definite pronouns and definite noun phrase anaphors are resolved more quickly if their antecedents are in the preceding sentence than if they are further back in the passage. They also showed that the effect was confined to antecedents in the final clause of the sentence before the pronoun, and concluded that clause boundaries rather than sentence boundaries were important in producing the effect. However, they did not include a condition in which the antecedent was in a previous clause of the sentence containing the pronoun, and in which there was, therefore, no sentence boundary between antecedent and anaphor. In an unpublished study, I compared such a condition, in a systematic way, with those used by Clark and Sengul, to see if a single clause boundary behaved in the same way as a sentence boundary. It is reasonable to suppose that it might not, since two clauses of the same sentence are more likely to depend on each other for their interpretation than are separate sentences. I measured the reading times for the C clauses of passages constructed from clauses of the following kinds:

A. (While) Mark supported the plank.
B. (While) Dora hammered the nails
C. She felt very cold.
D. (As) a wind blew from the north

The passages had the six structures in Table 2, and a pronoun in C had its antecedent in either A or B. The inclusion or exclusion of the subordinating conjunctions is indicated by s in the table. The figures indicate the mean time in milliseconds that subjects spent reading the C clauses in the passages. There were no significant differences among the times. Although it was no easier to resolve a pronoun in the preceding clause than in the preceding sentence, with distance controlled, the Clark and Sengul effect was not replicated either.

Two eye-movement studies also suggest distance effects in the interpretation of pronouns. Ehrlich (1983) measured the duration of the three closest fixations to a pronoun in a short text. She found an increase in the

TABLE 6.2
Structure of Passages and Reading Times
for "C" Clauses in an Experiment Following-up
the Findings of Clark and Sengul (1979)

	Antecedent	
	In B	*In A*
1. A, sB. C, sD.	1880	1907
2. A, sB. sC, D.	1907	2030
3. sA, B. C, sD.	1927	1881
4. sA, B. sC, D.	1860	2105
5. A. sB, C. D.	2146	1739
6. A. B, sC. D.	2030	2104

s indicates that the clause is subordinate.

duration of fixations around the point at which the pronoun occurred. However, the exact location of the increase depended on the distance back of the antecedent—the further back the antecedent, the later the effect arose, suggesting that more distant antecedents took longer to locate. Ehrlich also found that regressive eye movements were more likely following a pronoun for which there was no antecedent that agreed in number and gender in the preceding text, but which should have had such an antecedent. She concluded that in normal circumstances pronoun resolution does not require regressive eye movements.

The possible importance of regressive eye movements in pronoun resolution had been suggested by Carpenter and Just (1977). They found that, about 50% of the time, people looked back to the antecedent of a pronoun either as they read the pronoun, or at the end of the line in which it occurred. The frequency of such regressions did not depend on whether there was one or more than one potential referent for the pronoun in the preceding text. When there was more than one possible antecedent, the regressive eye movement was almost always to the correct antecedent. Such movements cannot, therefore, select the referent, and their exact function remains unclear. Furthermore, as Ehrlich and Rayner (1983) point out, Carpenter and Just's findings may have been an artefact of their experimental task—subjects had to decide at the end of each line of the display whether what they had just read was consistent with what had gone before.

In two further experiments Ehrlich and Rayner (1983) showed that lines of text containing pronouns were read more slowly when there were two sentences between the antecedent and the pronoun than when the antecedent was in the preceding sentence. They also replicated Ehrlich's finding that the location of the increase was delayed for distant antecedents. However, there were no significant differences for antecedents at different positions in the preceding clause, suggesting that all candidates in a single clause are checked together.

Although the distance between an anaphor and its antecedent is easy to measure, it is not necessarily a linguistically or psychologically important variable. Most obviously, the nature of the material between the two may affect how easy the anaphor is to understand. In particular, if that material is related to the antecedent, then resolution is likely to be easier than if it is not. This prediction was tested by Lesgold, Roth, and Curtis (1979).

Lesgold et al. varied the distance between a definite NP anaphor, for example *the forest*, and its antecedent, which was the same definite NP. In some passages the intervening material kept the antecedent foregrounded, and in others it did not. For example, in the following passage the two intervening sentences maintain the antecedent in the foreground:

A thick cloud of smoke hung over the forest.
The smoke was thick and black, and began to fill the clear sky.
Up ahead Carol could see a ranger directing the traffic to slow down.
The forest was on fire.

If the middle two sentences are replaced by:

Glancing to the side, Carol could see a bee flying around the back seat.
Both of the kids were jumping around, but made no attempt to free the insect.

then the forest becomes backgrounded. Lesgold et al. found that subjects spent longer reading *the forest was on fire* when the forest had become backgrounded than when it had not. They found no main effect of distance, though only three distances were used, zero (foreground only), two, and four intervening sentences.

Whitehead (1982) obtained similar results for definite pronouns with up to eight sentences between the pronoun and its antecedent. When there were two or more sentences that did not maintain the antecedent in focus, the pronoun was more difficult to understand. However, if the antecedent remained in focus, there was no effect of the distance between antecedent and anaphor.

Examination of passages for which distance effects have been found show that antecedents of pronouns that were difficult to resolve had become, at least to some extent, backgrounded by intervening sentences. This point is illustrated by the following passage from Ehrlich and Rayner

(1983), who concede that their findings on distance could be explained as a topic effect (something that has become backgrounded is no longer a topic):

> A group of people who shared an interest in photography had recently started writing a newsletter of their activities. Mark wrote most of the copy but the other members did a lot of work as well. In fact, in one room Cathy was mailing a copy of the paper to Susan. He was very involved in photography and spent every weekend taking pictures (p. 80).

For definite pronouns, only references back to foregrounded items are appropriate (cf. Sanford & Garrod, 1981). This fact is reflected in the awkwardness of the above passage, and in that of the following, much simpler, one from Tyler and Marslen-Wilson (1982a):

> The little puppy trod on a wasp.
> The puppy was very upset.
> It started to buzz furiously.

This restriction on possible referents for pronouns is necessary because pronouns have little semantic content of their own. It allows them to be resolved in a reasonable time, which is particularly important for spoken language with its transient signal. Sanford and Garrod (1981) suggest that the antecedent of a pronoun is sought only in a division of memory called *explicit focus*. The concept of explicit focus formalises the idea that pronouns have a *reference maintaining*, rather than a *reference establishing*, function. Another way of expressing this idea is to say that pronouns can refer only to the current topic of the discourse. However, the notion of topic is a problematic one that has been described (Brown & Yule, 1983) as "the most frequently used, unexplained, term in the analysis of discourse (p. 70)." It would be unfortunate if the notion of topic had to play a central role in a theory of text comprehension, unless it could be more satisfactorily formulated.

Garrod and Sanford (1982) report a finding that suggests a further complication. In passages such as:

> It was a fine Saturday morning.
> John and Mary went into town.
> She/they/Mary wanted some new clothes.

> The library was quite full.
> Linda and Jim could not sit down anywhere.
> The librarian told him/them/Jim to wait.

the plural pronouns were easy to understand in both subject and object position, but the singular pronouns were only easy in subject position. Garrod and Sanford argue that these results show that subject and object pronouns trigger different kinds of search for antecedents. However, their particular proposal, which assumes that plural antecedents such as *Linda and Jim* are represented as two individuals in explicit focus and as a group in *implicit focus* is not consistent with their general position. Implicit focus is the repository of information made available indirectly by a text—which may or may not be about groups of individuals—and pronouns cannot refer to implicit entities. If Linda and Jim were represented as a group only in implicit focus, it should not be possible to refer back to them using a plural pronoun.

Anderson, Garrod, and Sanford (1983) provided a further demonstration that the availability of an antecedent is not a simple function of how far back it was mentioned. They showed that the set of focussed items is updated when there is a time change that indicates the end of the current episode. Episode-bound characters move out of focus at the end of an episode, and subsequent anaphoric references back to them are difficult to resolve. For example, the waiter is an episode-bound character in a text about a visit to a restaurant, such as:

The Browns were eating a meal in a restaurant.
The waiter was hovering round the table.
The restaurant was well known for its food.
Forty minutes/Five hours later the resturant was empty.

Forty minutes after hovering round a table a waiter is still likely to be in the restaurant. After five hours he has most probably gone home. The passages continued in one of two ways. In the first kind of continuation there was a reference back to the main characters, the Browns in this case:

They had enjoyed eating all the good food.

This sentence was read equally quickly in the two conditions. It did not matter whether forty minutes or five hours had elapsed. In the second kind of continuation there was a pronominal reference to the episode-bound character:

He had enjoyed serving all the good food.

Subjects read this sentence more quickly when the time change did not take the action beyond the bounds of the episode. This result suggests that when episodes finish, episode-bound characters move out of focus. Main characters, however, remain focussed throughout several episodes.

Anderson et al.'s (1983) experiment shows that the passage of time can signal changes in focus, and that those changes may depend on knowledge about the world. However, no complete account has yet been given of how items mentioned in a text are maintained in focus or of how they go out of focus. Nevertheless, focus plays an important role in the interpretation of anaphoric expressions. Indeed, the natural use of a definite pronoun can serve as a diagnostic of whether something is still in focus. To refer back to things that are not in focus, and bring them back into the foreground, requires the use of other types of anaphor, typically definite descriptions—often complex ones, perhaps with restrictive relative clauses.

Another factor affecting the ease of resolution of anaphoric expressions, which might be mistaken for distance between antecedent and anaphor, was investigated in experiments by Ehrlich and Johnson-Laird (1982). They showed that the first of the following passages is easier to understand than the second.

> The knife is in front of the pot.
> The pot is to the left of the glass.
> The glass is behind the dish.

> The knife is in front of the pot.
> The glass is behind the dish.
> The pot is to the left of the glass.

In the second passage, anaphors are further from their antecedents than in the first. However, antecedents and anaphors are just as widely separated in:

> The pot is to the left of the glass.
> The knife is in front of the pot.
> The glass is behind the dish.

but this passage is not so hard to understand. Ehrlich and Johnson-Laird identify the crucial difference between the first and second passages as that of *referential continuity*. In the first passage the anaphoric noun phrases in the second and third sentences each refer back to something in the preceding sentence. In the second passage the first two sentences are disjoint in reference, and require two separate spatial layouts to be held in memory. In the third passage, although the last two sentences have no objects in common, they each refer back to something previously mentioned.

Finally, it should be pointed out that a more distant antecedent may be strongly favoured over a closer one. For example, Morrow (1985) showed that when people had to choose a referent for an ambiguous pronoun, they preferred a more distant foregrounded antecedent to a closer backgrounded one.

The conclusion suggested by all of these studies taken together is that distance per se is probably not a factor in determining how easy a deep anaphor is to understand.

Other Structural Strategies for Interpreting Deep Anaphors

Grober, Beardsley, and Caramazza (1978) claim to have demonstrated the use of parallel function in pronoun comprehension. Two expressions have parallel functions if each plays the same role (e.g. subject or object) in the clause in which it occurs. The importance of parallel function in language comprehension was demonstrated in a developmental study by Sheldon (1974). Sheldon showed that children found relative clauses easier to understand if the head noun of the relative clause played the same role in the matrix clause and the relative clause. For example:

The boy hit the man that the girl saw.

is comparatively easy for children to understand because *the man* is the object of both *hit* and *saw*. However:

The boy hit the man that saw the girl.

is harder because the functions of *the man* in the two clauses are not parallel. Sheldon speculated that adults might use a parallel function strategy to choose between two possible antecedents for a pronoun. If this hypothesis is true, sentences in which a pronoun plays the same role as its antecedent should be comparatively easy to understand. An example of such a sentence is:

John sold Bill his car because he hated it.

Both *John* and *he* are subjects, but if *hated* is replaced by *needed*:

John sold his car to Bill because he needed it.

a parallel function assignment is incorrect, and the sentence should, therefore, be more difficult to understand. Grober et al. asked subjects to complete sentence fragments such as:

John may scold Bill because he . . .

They found that in most of the completions the pronoun referred back to the subject of the first clause, as predicted by parallel function. However, in this study it is not possible to distinguish a parallel function strategy and a strategy of choosing the subject of the preceding clause as the antecedent. No examples in which the pronoun was the object of its clause could be used, for obvious reasons. Preference for antecedents in subject position, which will often also be current discourse topics, has often been noted. It is part of SHRDLU's pronoun resolution procedure, and has been demonstrated experimentally, for example by Frederiksen (1981), and by Caramazza and Gupta (1979), who showed that with a passivised first clause, which more strongly suggests the role of the surface subject as topic, the preference for "parallel function" in sentence completion increased.

Grober et al. (1978) found that their results depended to some extent on the verb in the first clause of the sentence fragments that they presented. This finding reflects that of Caramazza, Grober, Garvey, and Yates (1977), who showed that people used the semantics of the verb in one clause to "predict" whether its subject or object is likely to be pronominalised in a subsequent clause. For some verbs (e.g. *sell, question*) the referent of a pronoun in a following clause was named more quickly if its antecedent was in subject position, and for others verbs (e.g. *punish, envy*) naming was quicker if the antecedent was in object position. However, these findings are qualified by those of Ehrlich (1980), who obtained different results when the clauses were linked by *but* or *and* from when they were linked by *because*, as they were in Caramazza et al.'s experiments. It is also worth mentioning that the explicit computation of pronominal reference that is required for the naming task is not necessarily related to the "implicit" resolution of anaphors that occurs in ordinary reading. However, Garnham and Oakhill (1985) obtained results similar to those of Caramazza et al. in a self-paced reading study.

For nonpronominal anaphors, parallel function is not necessarily expected. For example, a passage such as:

The girl walked down the street.
The girl waved to a friend.

sounds stilted. Yekovich, Walker, and Blackman (1979) found that a definite NP anaphor was easiest to understand when it was in the given portion of a sentence, and its antecedent was in the new part of the previous sentence. With simple active declarative sentences, the NPs satisfy these conditions if the anaphor is a sentential subject, and the antecedent an object.

The lifeguard spotted the shark from a tower on the shore.
The shark attacked the diver near the reef.

This passage contrasts with:

In a cage beneath the boat, the diver photographed the eel.
The shark attacked the diver near the reef.

in which the antecedent is the subject and the anaphor the direct object, and which was the hardest type in the experiment. The prepositional phrases were included to control for distance effects.

Finally, Cirilo (1981) showed that the importance of the sentence containing the antecedent of a definite NP anaphor may affect how easy that anaphor is to resolve, regardless of its distance from the pronoun. This effect disappeared when only fragments of the passages were presented, from which the overall structure could not be deduced. This finding may reflect yet another "topic" effect, since important sentences usually introduce global topics.

WHAT DO DEEP ANAPHORS REACTIVATE?

When a pronoun contacts its antecedent, or the representation of that antecedent in a mental model, is it just the antecedent that is reactivated, or does other, related, information also become easier to access? A number of studies have used priming techniques to investigate this question. Chang (1980; Experiment 2) demonstrated the possibility of using such techniques to investigate pronoun comprehension. He showed that a definite pronoun in the final clause of a sentence facilitated a decision about whether its antecedent (a proper name in the penultimate clause) had been in the sentence. For example, subjects were faster to judge that *John* was in the sentence:

John and Mary went to the grocery store and he bought a quart of milk.

than they were to make a similar judgement when *she* was substituted for *he*. However, they were not as quick as when *John* was repeated in the second clause.

McKoon and Ratcliff (1980) used a similar technique, in which subjects read whole paragraphs, and then had to decide if a probe word had been in the paragraph. They found that a superordinate NP anaphor in the final sentence (e.g. *the criminal* referring back to *the burglar*) speeded decisions about whether *burglar* had been in the passage. However, they failed, in this experiment, to rule out the possibility that priming was mediated by category-instance associations. In a second experiment McKoon and Ratcliff showed that after a passage whose last sentence was:

The burglar/criminal slipped away from the streetlamp.

recognition of the probe word *garage*, which had occurred in the first sentence:

A burglar surveyed the garage set back from the street.

was also facilitated. They argue that an anaphoric NP reactivates not only its antecedent, but also other concepts from the same *proposition* as the antecedent. However, this result does not demonstrate the importance of a propositional representation, as opposed to any other structured representation of content (e.g. a mental model). In their final two experiments McKoon and Ratcliff showed that, when subjects were asked to make a series of decisions about whether words had been in passages of this kind, a decision on *streetlamp* was facilitated when it followed one on *burglar* when either *burglar* or *criminal* was in the final sentence of the passage above. However, when the sentence:

A criminal slipped away from a streetlamp.

was presented, effectively out of context, and *a criminal* was not anaphoric, there was no priming of *streetlamp* by *burglar*. This finding suggests that the priming does not result from pre-existing associations. McKoon and Ratcliff argue that these experiments show that information about the same person from the two sentences has been combined in a long-term memory. However, it is difficult to imagine a theory of comprehension that would deny this fact.

Dell, McKoon and Ratcliff, (1983) extended the priming technique by presenting subjects with paragraphs word by word—every 250msec an additional word appeared on a computer screen. Occasionally a word appeared in upper case for lexical decision. Dell et al. found that subordinate antecedents and other concepts from the same proposition were activated 250msec after an anaphor had been presented. However, only the referent produced priming for a longer period. These results were interpreted to mean that antecedents are not activated alone, but in the form of complete propositions. However, it is possible that the priming of words in the same proposition as the antecedent is mediated, and not direct.

THE USE OF KNOWLEDGE ABOUT THE WORLD IN
ANAPHOR RESOLUTION

Many anaphoric expressions can only be interpreted correctly with the help of knowledge about the world. The antecedent for an anaphoric definite description may have to be determined by a bridging inference (Clark, 1977). For example, to understand:

John was late for work.
The bus had been caught in a traffic jam.

it is necessary to assume that the bus mentioned in the second sentence was John's means of transport to work. For pronouns, world knowledge may be needed to decide between two or more potential antecedents; for example in the sentence:

Sue sold her car to Pam because she had decided to take up cycling.

she refers to Sue. This assignment depends upon knowledge about alternative means of transport, and the consequences of buying and selling.

A further aspect of knowledge about the world that is crucial for the interpretation of anaphors is knowledge about the other participants in the current discourse (Johnson-Laird & Garnham, 1980; Clark & Marshall, 1981). What a person knows will determine how they interpret phrases such as *the film John saw last night*, for example whether they take it to be coreferential with *The Sound of Music*. Although the onus is on speakers and writers to produce anaphoric references that can be interpreted correctly, it can be assumed that discourses are meant to be understood, and that assumption can be used in attempting to understand them.

These observations about the use of knowledge in understanding anaphoric expressions raise two questions, neither of which is specific to the interpretation of anaphors. The first is, how is knowledge in long-term memory organised and, in particular, how does that organisation aid language understanding? The second is, what cues in text and context are used to access knowledge from long-term memory? Neither of these questions has received a satisfactory answer. Both have been more intensively studied in AI than in psychology, partly because, in a language understanding program that makes use of knowledge about the world, decisions have to be made about how that knowledge is stored and accessed.

AI's approach to the structure of knowledge in long-term memory has been to provide very general methods of describing structured information. The best-known example is Minsky's (1975) frame-system theory. Related ideas that have been developed more specifically to explain language understanding are Schank and Abelson's (1977) theory of plans, goals, and scripts, Rumelhart and Ortony's (1977) schemata theory, and Sanford and Garrod's (1981) scenario theory. To a greater or lesser extent all these ideas have their roots in Bartlett's (1932) work.

The main shortcoming of this approach is that a method of representation does not necessarily provide constraints on what can be represented, or on how it should be represented. It merely provides a framework in which theories about long-term memory can be constructed. However, psychologists have often mistaken these frameworks for the more specific theories that they require—theories that specify what information is made explicit and what remains implicit in memory representations.

AI approaches to the use of textual and contextual cues for accessing information from memory are less well developed. One proposal is that the occurrence of a word in a text makes available the corresponding frame (or script or whatever). The implications of this proposal depend on what information is represented in a frame, and what the consequences of accessing a frame are. Are related frames accessed with it? Do they become easier to access? And what is meant by "related"? Another proposal is that frames can be accessed by *keywords*. This idea has been most clearly formulated for scripts, which are frame-like structures representing stereotypical sequences of events. For example, the visit-to-the-doctor script might be accessed by words such as *surgery* or *prescription*.

Although these ideas are a step towards a theory of how information in text accesses long-term memory, they must eventually be supplemented, for two reasons. First, scripts can be accessed not only by keywords, but also by phrases that do not contain such words. For example, *the one hour journey from London to Amsterdam* suggests the plane-flight script. However, none of the words in that phrase should on their own, otherwise the script would be accessed inappropriately on many occasions. Second, a keyword should not always access a script. The description *the off-duty waiter* signals explicitly that the restaurant script is not appropriate. Keywords do not function in a contextual vacuum.

EXPERIMENTAL STUDIES OF KNOWLEDGE-BASED ANAPHOR RESOLUTION

A number of experimental studies address the question of how knowledge about the world is used to interpret anaphoric expressions. One basic finding is that use of such knowledge to tie an anaphor in written text to its antecedent takes time (Haviland & Clark, 1974; but see Tyler & Marslen-Wilson, 1982a, 1982b for the suggestion that inference-making does not necessarily slow down the interpretation of pronouns in spoken language). Haviland and Clark showed that, if the sentence:

The beer was warm.

is presented in the context:

We got some beer out of the trunk.

it is easy to understand, because *the beer* has an explicit antecedent. However, in the context:

We checked the picnic supplies.

the sentence takes longer to understand, because the antecedent has to be established by a bridging inference. The effect cannot be explained by lexical repetition, because *The beer was warm* is comparatively difficult to understand after:

Andrew was especially fond of beer.

which contains the lexical item *beer*, but in which it has a nonspecific reference, so that it cannot provide an antecedent for *the beer* in the second sentence.

This last finding is similar to one from a study by Yekovich and Walker (1978). They found that:

The puppy had eaten a piece of poisoned meat.

was difficult to understand after:

The forlorn child longed for a puppy and cried.

since the verb *longed for* does not establish the existence of its direct object. Changing *a* to *the*, which by itself establishes a referent, facilitated integration. This difference between the definite and indefinite article was not found for contexts such as:

The angry boy threw a/the rock and ran away.

because the action of throwing establishes the existence of the object thrown.

Some non-explicit antecedents do not cause difficulties in comprehension. Garrod and Sanford (1981) found that:

The clothes were made of pink wool.

was no more difficult to understand after:

Mary dressed the baby.

than after:

Mary put the clothes on the baby.

However, there is an important difference between Garrod and Sanford's materials and those of Haviland and Clark (1974). The definition of the verb *to dress* makes reference to clothes—to dress means to put clothes on (cf. Cotter, 1984). Therefore, simply by constructing the meaning of the sentence—*Mary dressed the baby*—from the meanings of its parts, a representation that contains "clothes" will be produced. No knowledge about the world, other than that in the lexicon, has been used to make an inference in this case.

Garrod and Sanford (1977) provided further evidence that knowledge about the world can influence anaphor resolution. Passages such as:

A robin would sometimes wander into the house.
The bird was attracted by the larder.

were easier to understand than passages such as:

A bird would sometimes wander into the house.
The robin was attracted by the larder.

In the second passage the anaphoric definite noun phrase contains extra information about its referent (a bird need not necessarily be a robin), whereas in the first passage it does not (a robin must be a bird). Garrod and Sanford also found that high-frequency exemplars, such as robin, were easier to connect with their antecedents than low-frequency exemplars such as goose.

The interpretation of these results is far from straightforward. One explanation is that the extra time that subjects take to read the second sentence in the second passage is used to add the additional information carried by the anaphor into the text representation. Alternatively, the results may reflect knowledge of the typical structure of passages. In accordance with Grice's maxims of quantity, anaphors are usually not more specific than their antecedents. Subjects may consider the possibility that a more specific anaphor has a disjoint reference from its antecedent—a hypothesis that later sentential context forces them to reject.

Sanford and Garrod (1980) were forced to propose yet another explanation of their 1977 results in the light of further experimental findings. In this experiment, passages of the two kinds given earlier were included, along with two other types in which either the category noun or the instance noun was repeated (*bird-bird* and *robin-robin*). In neither of these cases does the anaphoric noun phrase contain extra information; the new passages ought, therefore, to produce results similar to the robin-bird passage. In fact, Sanford and Garrod found that the difficulty of integrating the information in the second sentence depended only on the specificity of the noun in the *first*.

Sanford and Garrod's explanation of this result is based on their theory of how information from long-term memory is used in understanding text. They assume that cues in a text make scenarios available for understanding subsequent sentences, and that more specific nouns access more specific scenarios. Furthermore, more specific scenarios facilitate the integration of subsequent information.

Garnham (1981b, 1984) failed to support Sanford and Garrod's proposal, and produced results compatible with the "extra information in the anaphor" theory. For example, Garnham (1984) found that, after taking account of the lengths of the subject NPs, *The small dog barked at a shadow* was difficult to understand after *The dog was sitting by the fire*, but the other three kinds of passage with *the dog* or *the small dog* as sentential subjects were comparatively easy. It is, perhaps, unclear whether *dog* and *small dog* should evoke different scenarios, but this failure to make a prediction is a weakness of scenario theory.

In some unpublished experiments I have attempted to resolve the question of how the relation between antecedent and anaphor affects resolution. In particular I hypothesised, on the basis of Sanford and Garrod's (1980) example:

The vehicle/lorry could not get up the hill.
The vehicle/lorry was overloaded.

that the second sentences in their passages were more coherently linked to the first sentences that those in Garnham's (1981b, 1984) experiments, in which the two sentences merely stated two facts about a person or thing. Perhaps in coherent passages coreference is established as a by-product of coherence, as suggested by Hobbs (1979), and therefore depends on the knowledge made available for establishing coherence. In the above example, if it is assumed that the text is coherent, then the fact that a lorry could not get up a hill can be integrated with the fact that a vehicle was overloaded by identifying the lorry and the vehicle, since being overloaded can explain not being able to get up a hill. In less coherent passages the nature of the anaphor and antecedent themselves might be more important. To test this hypothesis the reading times for second sentences in passages of the following kinds were compared:

The ship/liner turned back to its home port.
The ship/liner had one hundred passengers on board.

The ship/liner turned back to its home port.
The ship/liner needed one of its engines repaired.

However, in two experiments, there was a cross-over interaction between the kind of noun phrase (category versus instance) in the two sentences, with the repetition conditions (ship-ship and liner-liner) being easier. There was also a tendency for the category followed by instance condition to be the most difficult. Furthermore, there was no interaction of these factors with coherence, and a main effect of coherence in one experiment disappeared in a covariance analysis with the length in characters of the second sentence as the covariate.

A further question concerns the temporal relation between the integration of information from different parts of a passage, which typically requires use of knowledge about the world, and the assignment of antecedents to anaphors. Are anaphors resolved before, during, or after more global integration takes place?

Hirst and Brill (1980) showed that subjects were quick to name the referent of a pronoun when there were strong contextual constraints on its interpretation, for example in:

Henry spoke at a meeting while John drove to the beach.
He lectured on administration.

When the constraints were weaker or absent, the naming task was harder.

Henry spoke at a meeting while John drove to the beach.
He looked toward a friend.

Furthermore, these findings were replicated when the pronoun could only have one possible antecedent—when the sentences were "transformed" as follows:

Henry spoke at a meeting.

He $\left\{ \begin{array}{l} \text{lectured on administration} \\ \text{looked toward a friend} \end{array} \right\}$ while John drove to the beach.

Hirst and Brill argued that pronoun assignment and information integration are concurrent processes, otherwise pragmatic constraints could not influence referent naming time when there was only one syntactically possible antecedent. However, their arguments are not convincing. First, even if the two processes are concurrent, the referent can be named as soon as the antecedent has been found. Since syntactic matching is a simple process, it should be completed more quickly than information integration using knowledge about the world. Second, the texts vary in plausibility, and it is more difficult to make judgements about implausible texts. Perhaps an antecedent is assigned first, at least in the syntactically constrained case, but the response is not made until pragmatic checks have been made. These checks will be easier for more coherent passages.

In Hirst and Brill's first experiment, it is more likely that assignment and integration overlap. When there are two syntactically possible antecedents for a pronoun, an inference based on knowledge about the world and about the structure of texts must decide between them. Since such inferences also help to integrate the information in the pronoun-containing and antecedent-containing clauses, integration and assignment will be concurrent processes. This point restates Hobbs' claim that problems about coreference are often solved as a by-product of establishing the coherence of a text. Coherence is established by knowledge-based inferences, and therefore integration aids assignment.

AN OVERVIEW OF THE PROCESS OF UNDERSTANDING ANAPHORS

In understanding language, expressions whose interpretation depends on context are frequently encountered. Anaphoric expressions are a subset of those expressions. Although there is, as yet, no complete processing theory of how they are interpreted, the general form of such a theory is clear, as are some of its details.

There are three main aspects of the interpretation of anaphoric expressions:

1. Determining that an expression in a text is an anaphor.
2. Determining which aspects of linguistic and nonlinguistic context are relevant to its interpretation.

3. Assigning it a meaning on the basis of those aspects of context, and its relation to them.

Throughout this chapter it has been assumed that there is no special difficulty in recognising anaphoric expressions or expressions that might turn out to be anaphoric. Some, such as pronouns, are members of fixed lexical classes. Others, such as definite noun phrases, are members of structural classes that must be processed on the assumption that they might be anaphoric. However, elliptical constructions, such as verb-phrase ellipsis, null complement anaphora, gapping, sluicing, and stripping, may be more difficult for the parser to identify. Research is urgently needed on this topic.

Once an anaphoric, or potentially anaphoric, expression has been recognised, its antecedent must be sought. For deep anaphors an antecedent can be provided by either linguistic or nonlinguistic context. Within those contexts, there are further restrictions on where the antecedent should be found, particularly in the case of pronouns. For surface anaphors the antecedent must occur in linguistic context. The rare cases in which a surface anaphor has no linguistic antecedent are deviant, though they are usually interpretable.

In this overview the processing of anaphoric singular definite noun phrases will be used to illustrate the process of anaphor resolution. Semantic rules specify that a singular definite description denotes one thing of the kind denoted by its content (e.g. a man in the case of the description *the man*). The referent of *the man* is some particular man. There are many men in the world, so the referent of the noun phrase on any occasion of its use must depend on the context in which it occurs, and on knowledge shared by the speaker/writer and hearer/reader. *The man* should only be used in a context in which the relevant set of men can be reduced to one. If the phrase is used in a discourse in which only one man has been previously mentioned, or in which only one man is foregrounded, then its interpretation is straightforward. The focussed part of the representation of the preceding discourse and/or the context is searched, by hypothesis it contains just one man, so that man is the referent of the expression. Slightly more problematic are the cases in which the representation contains more than one man or no men. In the first case the discourse will be referentially indeterminate and, strictly speaking, uninterpretable, though it may be possible to guess which man was intended. In a conversation, clarification can be requested; written text is less redeemable. If there is no man in focus, a bridging inference must be made in an attempt to put one there. If no such inference is feasible, than the definite description introduces a new referent, as though it were indefinite. Some authors use definite descriptions at the beginning of a text as a literary device to suggest familiarity with the characters or places in the story.

In general, the interpretation of an anaphoric expression requires a search for its antecedent within some space of possibilities. The nature of the search varies for different kinds of anaphoric expression. For definite noun phrases the search must ensure that there is only one antecedent of the appropriate type. The antecedent of a definite noun phrase need not have the same linguistic form, though some divergences, particularly those in which the anaphor is more specific than its antecedent, can make identifying the antecedent difficult. In other cases, for example that of definite pronouns, the search involves the identification of several possible antecedents, and a decision among them on the basis of plausibility. For pronouns this search is comparatively well understood, but for other anaphors there have been few psychological investigations, often none.

Once the antecedent has been identified, a meaning can be assigned to the anaphor on the basis of the meaning of the antecedent. For definite noun phrases and definite pronouns, the two types of anaphor most widely studied in psychology, the anaphor typically has the same referent as its antecedent, though there are other possibilities (see e.g. Webber, 1978, for details). For these identity-of-reference anaphors, information in the sentence or clause containing the anaphor is attached to the token in memory representing its antecedent. Other types of anaphor do not refer to the same object as their antecedents, but, rather, have the same sense. For example, in the sentence:

Mary popped a red balloon, and John popped a yellow one.

the function of *one* is to introduce a new referent of the same *type* as one that was previously mentioned, in this case a balloon. Such identity-of-sense anaphors require a different kind of modification to a representation of the text so far than do identity-of-reference anaphors, such as definite pronouns.

Once the anaphoric expressions in the current sentence or clause have been resolved, and other connections to the preceding text established, the revised representation of the text so far serves as part of the context for the interpretation of the next sentence or clause. It provides some of the possible antecedents for anaphors in that clause.

CONCLUSION

Three main questions that a psychological theory of anaphor understanding must answer have been identified, and a sketch of a processing theory of anaphor resolution has been given. The major problems for a psychological theory are to specify what potential antecedents are made available by a text and its context, and how anaphoric expressions can be mapped onto members of that set of potential antecedents. Particularly in the case of pronouns, a major problem is to explain how the set of possible antecedents is restricted as narrowly as it is. Most psychological experiments have concentrated on a small number of anaphors, but even with these the results are not always clear-cut or easy to interpret. In a comprehensive theory of anaphor understanding, psychologists must take account of linguists' descriptions of the whole range of anaphoric processes, and decide how their distinctions are relevant to a processing account. They also need to determine whether their experimental results can be generalised to other kinds of anaphors.

ACKNOWLEDGEMENTS

The unpublished studies cited in this chapter were carried out while the author was a Science Research Council (now Science and Engineering Research Council) Research Fellow at the Experimental Psychology Laboratory, University of Sussex. I would like to thank Jane Oakhill for discussing and commenting on previous versions of this chapter. Phil Johnson-Laird, Greg Murphy, and two anonymous reviewers also provided many useful comments.

REFERENCES

Anderson, A., Garrod, S. C., & Sanford, A. J. (1983) The accessibility of pronominal antecedents as a function of episode shifts in narrative text. *Quarterly Journal of Experimental Psychology, 35A*, 427–440.

Anderson, J. R. & Bower, G. H. (1973) *Human Associative Memory.* Washington, D.C.: Winston.

Anderson, J. R., & Hastie, R. (1974) Individuation and reference in memory: Proper names and definite descriptions. *Cognitive Psychology, 6*, 495–514.

Bach, E. & Partee, B. H. (1980) Anaphora and semantic structures. In J. Kreiman & A. Ojeda (Eds.), *Papers from the Parasession on Pronouns and Anaphora.* Chicago: Chicago Linguistics Society.

Bartlett, F. C. (1932) *Remembering: A Study in Experimental and Social Psychology.* Cambridge, England: Cambridge University Press.

Bates, E., Kintsch, W., Fletcher, C., & Giuliani, V. (1980) On the role of pronominalisation and ellipsis in texts: Some memory experiments. *Journal of Experimental Psychology: Human Learning and Memory, 6*, 676–691.

Bates, E., Masling, M., & Kintsch, W. (1978) Recognition memory for aspects of dialogue. *Journal of Experimental Psychology: Human Learning and Memory, 4*, 187–197.

Bolinger, D. (1979) Pronouns in discourse. In T. Givon (Ed.), *Syntax and Semantics 12: Discourse and Syntax.* New York: Academic Press.

Bosch, P. (1983) *Agreement and Anaphora: A Study of the Role of Pronouns in Syntax and Discourse*. London: Academic Press.

Brown, G. & Yule, G. (1983) *Discourse Analysis*. Cambridge, England: Cambridge University Press.

Caramazza, A., Grober, E. H., Garvey, C., & Yates, J. (1977) Comprehension of anaphoric pronouns. *Journal of Verbal Learning and Verbal Behaviour, 16*, 601–609.

Caramazza, A. & Gupta, S. (1979) The roles of topicalisation, parallel function, and verb semantics in the interpretation of pronouns. *Linguistics, 17*, 497–518.

Carpenter, P. A. & Just, M. A. (1977) Reading comprehension as the eyes see it. In M. A. Just & P. A. Carpenter (Eds.), *Cognitive Processes in Comprehension*. Hillsdale, New Jersey: Lawrence Erlbaum Associates Inc.

Chang, F. (1980) Active memory processes in visual sentence comprehension: Clause effects and pronominal reference. *Memory and Cognition, 8*, 58–64.

Chomsky, N. (1965) *Aspects of the Theory of Syntax*. Cambridge, Mass.: MIT Press.

Chomsky, N. (1981) *Lectures on Government and Binding*. Dordrecht: Foris.

Cirilo, R. K. (1981) Referential coherence and text structure in story comprehension. *Journal of Verbal Learning and Verbal Behaviour, 20*, 358–367.

Clark, H. H. (1977) Bridging. In P. N. Johnson-Laird & P. C. Wason (Eds.), *Thinking: Readings in Cognitive Science*. Cambridge, England: Cambridge University Press.

Clark, H. H. & Marshall, C. R. (1981) Definite reference and mutual knowledge. In A. K. Joshi, B. L. Webber, & I. A. Sag (Eds.), *Elements of Discourse Understanding*. Cambridge, England: Cambridge University Press.

Clark, H. H. & Sengul, C. J. (1979) In search of referents for noun phrases and pronouns. *Memory and Cognition, 7*, 35–41.

Corbett, A. T. & Chang, F. R. (1983) Pronoun disambiguation: Accessing potential antecedents. *Memory and Cognition, 11*, 283–294.

Cotter, C. A. (1984) Inferring indirect objects in sentences: Some implications for the semantics of verbs. *Language and Speech, 27*, 25–45.

Daneman, M. & Carpenter, P. (1980) Individual differences in working memory and reading. *Journal of Verbal Learning and Verbal Behaviour, 19*, 450–466.

Dell, G. S., McKoon, G., & Ratcliff, R. (1983) The activation of antecedent information during the processing of anaphoric reference in reading. *Journal of Verbal Learning and Verbal Behaviour, 22*, 121–132.

Dooling, D. J. & Christiaansen, R. E. (1977) Levels of encoding and retention of prose. In G. H. Bower (Ed.), *The Psychology of Learning and Motivation, 11*. New York: Academic Press.

Ehrlich, K. (1980) Comprehension of pronouns. *Quarterly Journal of Experimental Psychology, 32*, 247–255.

Ehrlich, K. (1983) Eye movements in pronoun assignment: A study of sentence integration. In K. Rayner (Ed.), *Eye Movements in Reading: Perceptual and Language Processes*. New York: Academic Press.

Ehrlich, K. & Johnson-Laird, P. N. (1982) Spatial descriptions and referential continuity. *Journal of Verbal Learning and Verbal Behaviour, 21*, 296–306.

Ehrlich, K. & Rayner, K. (1983) Pronoun assignment and semantic integration during reading: Eye movements and immediacy of processing. *Journal of Verbal Learning and Verbal Behaviour, 22*, 75–87.

Forster, K. I. (1979) Levels of processing and the structure of the language processor. In W. E. Cooper & E. C. T. Walker (Eds.), *Sentence Processing: Psycholinguistic Studies Presented to Merrill Garrett*. Hillsdale, New Jersey: Lawrence Erlbaum Associates Inc.

Frederiksen, J. R. (1981) Understanding anaphora: Rules used by readers in assigning pronominal referents. *Discourse Processes, 4*, 323–347.

Frege, G. (1879/1972) Conceptual notation: A formula language of pure thought modelled upon the formula language of arithmetic. In T. W. Bynum (Ed. & trans.), *Conceptual Notation and Related Articles*. Oxford: Oxford University Press. (First published in German in 1879, Halle: L. Nerbert.)

Frege, G. (1892/1952) On sense and meaning. In P. Geach & M. Black (Eds.), *Translations from the Philosophical Writings of Gottlob Frege*. Oxford: Blackwell. (Originally published in German in *Zeitschrift für Philosophie and Philosophische Kritik*, *100*, 25–50.)

Garnham, A. (1979) Instantiation of verbs. *Quarterly Journal of Experimental Psychology*, *31*, 207–214.

Garnham, A. (1981a) Mental models as representations of text. *Memory and Cognition*, *9*, 560–565.

Garnham, A. (1981b) Anaphoric reference to instances, instantiated and noninstantiated categories: A reading-time study. *British Journal of Psychology*, *72*, 377–384.

Garnham, A. (1984) Effects of specificity on the interpretation of anaphoric noun phrases. *Quarterly Journal of Experimental Psychology*, *36A*, 1–12.

Garnham, A. & Oakhill, J. V. (1985) On-line resolution of anaphoric pronouns: Effects of inference making and verb semantics. *British Journal of Psychology*, *76*, 385–393.

Garrod, S. C. & Sanford, A. J. (1977) Interpreting anaphoric relations: The integration of semantic information while reading. *Journal of Verbal Learning and Verbal Behaviour*, *16*, 77–90.

Garrod, S. C. & Sanford, A. J. (1981) Bridging inferences and the extended domain of reference. In J. Long & A. Baddeley (Eds.), *Attention and Performance IX*. Hillsdale, New Jersey: Lawrence Erlbaum Associates Inc.

Garrod, S. C. & Sanford, A. J. (1982) The mental representation of discourse in a focussed memory system: Implications for the interpretation of anaphoric noun phrases. *Journal of Semantics*, *1*, 21–41.

Garvey, C., Caramazza, A., & Yates, J. (1975) Factors influencing assignment of pronoun antecedents. *Cognition*, *3*, 227–243.

Grober, E. H., Beardsley, W., & Caramazza, A. (1978) Parallel function in pronoun assignment. *Cognition*, *6*, 117–133.

Grosz, B. (1981) Focussing and description in natural language dialogues. In A. K. Joshi, B. L. Webber, & I. A. Sag (Eds.), *Elements of Discourse Understanding*. Cambridge, England: Cambridge University Press.

Halliday, M. A. K. & Hasan, R. (1976) *Cohesion in English*. London: Longman.

Hankamer, J. & Sag, I. A. (1976) Deep and surface anaphora. *Linguistic Inquiry*, *7*, 391–428.

Haviland, S. E. & Clark, H. H. (1974) What's new? Acquiring new information as a process in comprehension. *Journal of Verbal Learning and Verbal Behaviour*, *13*, 512–521.

Hirst, W. & Brill, G. A. (1980) Contextual aspects of pronoun assignment. *Journal of Verbal Learning and Verbal Behaviour*, *19*, 168–175.

Hobbs, J. R. (1979) Coherence and coreference. *Cognitive Science*, *3*, 67–90.

Jarvella, R. J. (1971) Syntactic processing of connected speech. *Journal of Verbal Learning and Verbal Behaviour*, *10*, 409–416.

Johnson-Laird, P. N. (1980) Mental models in cognitive science. *Cognitive Science*, *4*, 75–115.

Johnson-Laird, P. N. (1983) *Mental Models*. Cambridge, England: Cambridge University Press.

Johnson-Laird, P. N. & Garnham, A. (1980) Descriptions and discourse models. *Linguistics and Philosophy*, *3*, 371–393.

Johnson-Laird, P. N. & Stevenson, R. (1970) Memory for syntax. *Nature*, *227*, 412.

Kamp, J. A. W. (1981) A theory of truth and semantic representation. In J. Groenendijk, T. Janssen, & M. Stokhof (Eds.), *Formal Methods in the Study of Language*. Amsterdam: Mathematical Centre Tracts.

Kaplan, D. (1978) On the logic of demonstratives. *Journal of Philosophical Logic, 8,* 81–98.

Karttunen, L. (1969) Pronouns and variables. *Chicago Linguistics Society, 5,* 108–116.

Karttunen, L. (1976) Discourse referents. In J. D. McCawley (Ed.), *Syntax and Semantics 7: Notes from the Linguistic Underground.* New York: Academic Press.

Keenan, E. L. & Faltz, L. M. (1978) Logical types for natural languages. *UCLA Occasional Papers in Linguistics, 3.*

Keenan, J. N., MacWhinney, B., & Mayhew, D. (1977) Pragmatics in memory: A study of natural conversation. *Journal of Verbal Learning and Verbal Behaviour, 16,* 549–560.

Kintsch, W. & Bates, E. (1977) Recognition memory for statements from a classroom lecture. *Journal of Experimental Psychology: Human Learning and Memory, 3,* 150–159.

Lakoff, G. (1968/1976) Pronouns and reference. Distributed by Indiana University Linguistics Club. Reprinted in J. D. McCawley (1976 Ed.), *Syntax and Semantics 7: Notes from the Linguistic Underground.* New York: Academic Press.

Langacker, R. (1969) On pronominalisation and the chain of command. In D. A. Reibel & S. A. Schane (eds.), *Modern Studies in English.* Englewood Cliffs, New Jersey: Prentice-Hall.

Lasnik, H. (1976) Remarks on coreference. *Linguistic Analysis, 2,* 1–22.

Lesgold, A., Roth, S., & Curtis, M. (1979) Foregrounding effects in discourse comprehension. *Journal of Verbal Learning and Verbal Behaviour, 18,* 291–308.

Lockman, A. & Klappholz, A. D. (1980) Toward a procedural model of contextual reference resolution. *Discourse Processes, 3,* 25–71.

McKoon, G. & Ratcliff, R. (1980) The comprehension processes and memory structures involved in anaphoric reference. *Journal of Verbal Learning and Verbal Behaviour, 19,* 668–682.

Malt, B. C. (1985) The role of discourse structure in understanding anaphora. *Journal of Memory and Language, 24,* 271–289.

Minsky, M. (1975) A framework for representing knowledge. In P. H. Winston (Ed.), *The Psychology of Computer Vision.* New York: McGraw-Hill.

Morrow, D. G. (1985) Prominent characters and events organise narrative understanding. *Journal of Memory and Language, 24,* 304–319.

Murphy, G. L. (1985a) Psychological explanations of deep and surface anaphora. *Journal of Pragmatics, 9,* 785–813.

Murphy, G. L. (1985b) Processes of understanding anaphora. *Journal of Memory and Language, 24,* 290–303.

Reinhart, T. (1981) Definite NP-anaphora and C-command domains. *Linguistic Inquiry, 12,* 605–635.

Reinhart, T. (1983) *Anaphora and Semantic Interpretation.* London: Croom Helm.

Ross, J. R. (1967) Constraints on variables on syntax. Unpublished PhD dissertation, MIT.

Rumelhart, D. E. & Levin, J. A. (1975) A language comprehension system. In D. A. Norman, D. E. Rumelhart, & the LNR Research Group, *Explorations in Cognition.* San Francisco: Freeman.

Rumelhart, D. E. & Ortony, A. (1977) The representation of knowledge in memory. In R. C. Anderson, R. J. Spiro, & W. E. Montague (Eds.), *Schooling and the Acquisition of Knowledge.* Hillsdale, New Jersey: Lawrence Erlbaum Associates Inc.

Sachs, J. S. (1967) Recognition memory for syntactic and semantic aspects of connected discourse. *Perception and Psychophysics, 2,* 437–442.

Sag, I. A. & Hankamer, J. (1984) Toward a theory of anaphoric processing. *Linguistics and Philosophy, 7,* 325–345.

Sanford, A. J. & Garrod, S. C. (1980) Memory and attention in text comprehension: The problem of reference. In R. S. Nickerson (Ed.), *Attention and Performance VIII.* Hillsdale, New Jersey: Lawrence Erlbaum Associates Inc.

Sanford, A. J. & Garrod, S. C. (1981) *Understanding Written Language: Explorations in Comprehension Beyond the Sentence*. Chichester: Wiley.

Schank, R. C. & Abelson, R. P. (1977) *Scripts, Goals, Plans, and Understanding*. Hillsdale, New Jersey: Lawrence Erlbaum Associates Inc.

Sheldon, A. (1974) The role of parallel function in the acquisition of relative clauses in English. *Journal of Verbal Learning and Verbal Behaviour, 13*, 272–281.

Shillcock, R. C. (1982) The on-line resolution of pronominal anaphora. *Language and Speech, 25*, 385–401.

Sidner, C. L. (1978) The use of focus as a tool for disambiguation of definite noun-phrases. In D. Waltz (Ed.), *Theoretical Issues in Natural Language Processing 2*. New York: Association for Computing Machinery.

Sidner, C. L. (1981) Focussing for interpretation of pronouns. *American Journal of Computational Linguistics, 7*, 217–231.

Stenning, K. (1978) Anaphora as an approach to pragmatics. In M. Halle, J. W. Bresnan, & G. A. Miller (Eds.), *Linguistic Theory and Psychological Reality*. Cambridge, Mass.: MIT Press.

Swinney, D. A. (1979) Lexical access during sentence comprehension: (Re)consideration of context effects. *Journal of Verbal Learning and Verbal Behaviour, 18*, 545–569.

Tyler, L. K. & Marslen-Wilson, W. D. (1982a) The resolution of discourse anaphora: Some on-line studies. *Text, 2*, 263–291.

Tyler, L. K. & Marslen-Wilson, W. D. (1982b) Processing strategies in discourse contexts: On-line resolution of anaphors. *Journal of Semantics, 1*, 297–314.

Wasow, T. (1979) Problems with pronouns in transformational grammar. In F. Heny & H. S. Schnelle (Eds.), *Syntax and Semantics 10: Selections from the Third Groningen Round Table*. New York: Academic Press.

Webber, B. L. (1978) *A Formal Approach to Discourse Anaphora*. BBN Technical Report No. 3761.

Webber, B. L. (1981) Discourse model synthesis: Preliminaries to reference. In A. K. Joshi, B. L. Webber, & I. A. Sag (Eds.), *Elements of Discourse Understanding*. Cambridge, England: Cambridge University Press.

Weizenbaum, J. (1966) ELIZA—a computer program for the study of natural language communication between man and machine. *Communications of the Association for Computing Machinery, 10*, 474–480.

Whitehead, E. L. (1982) *Distance and foregrounding effects on pronoun interpretation*. Paper presented to the Experimental Psychology Society, Cambridge, March 1982.

Winograd, T. (1972) Understanding natural language. *Cognitive Psychology, 3*, 1–191.

Yekovich, F. R. & Walker, C. H. (1978) Identifying and using referents in sentence comprehension. *Journal of Verbal Learning and Verbal Behaviour, 17*, 265–277.

Yekovich, F. R., Walker, C. H., & Blackman, H. (1979) The role of presupposed and focal information in integrating sentences. *Journal of Verbal Learning and Verbal Behaviour, 18*, 535–548.

7 Understanding Verbs: Easy Extension, Hard Comprehension

Valerie F. Reyna
University of Texas at Dallas

Until recently, theories of meaning and comprehension treated verbs and nouns alike. Representational formats were developed and applied similarly to both classes of word (e.g., Katz, 1972). Analyses focussed on the comprehension of nouns, leaving the impression that the extension to verbs was straightforward (e.g., Cohen, 1979). Evidence is beginning to emerge, however, that there are psychological differences in the processing and representation of nominal and verbal meaning. Differences have been observed in both children (e.g., Reyna, 1985) and adults (e.g., Gentner, 1981a; Reyna, 1981). This chapter concerns observations of difficulty in processing verbal meaning on the one hand, and its pliancy and extendability on the other hand.

The terms "noun" and "verb" refer to syntactic classes, not semantic ones. The claim here, however, is that meaning differences attend this syntactic distinction. In general, nouns more often refer to objects, whereas verbs more often refer to relations. Because such systematic differences in meaning attend the syntactic distinction of noun and verb, the effects discussed in this chapter are probably semantic rather than syntactic. This is *not* to say that linguistic constituents should be defined semantically rather than syntactically. The independence of syntactic and semantic information in linguistic rules is not of concern here. Instead, the concern is with what we call "nominal meaning" and "verbal meaning," referring to the usual or typical meanings that nouns or verbs carry, respectively, in ordinary speech.

As stated above, verbs typically refer to relations (Gentner, 1978), whether these relations are implicated in actions (e.g. "kick"), states (e.g. "terrify"), or events (e.g. "marry"). For example, in "kick" an agent is related to the recipient of an action, and in "terrify" a cause of an emotional state is related to an experiencer of that state. Usual referents for nouns are objects, including people, animals, plants, and nonliving objects. Again, that is not to say that some nouns do not refer to relations (e.g. "employee") or to concepts other than objects (e.g. "party"). Neither is it claimed that verbs never refer to objects (e.g. "hammer"), nor are they always relational (e.g. "sleep"). Nevertheless, in the main, verbs are relational (and sometimes refer to objects as participants in relations) and nouns name the objects that verbs implicitly relate. An analogous distinction is made in mathematics between functions and arguments.

Whereas the prototypical concept is a relation for verbs and an object for nouns, for adjectives, it is a property. A property can be expressed as a one-place predicate (in the logical sense), whereas a relation is a two-or-more-place predicate. Thus, verbs and adjectives are both represented as predicates in formal logic. In addition, verbs and adjectives are closely linked in that many verbs express properties and are also one-place predicates, for example such intransitive verbs as "sleep." One might argue that the major distinction between nouns and verbs is not between object and relational meanings but between subject and predicative meanings (again in the logical sense). The latter distinction casts meaning into two moulds: characterisations (mostly verbs and adjectives) and what is characterised (mostly nouns). In this view, a characterisation can either ascribe a property or describe a relation.

For most of the noun-verb comparisons to be considered here, whether they involve differing empirical observations or theoretical descriptions, conclusions will not be affected by choosing a subject-predicate distinction over an object-relation distinction, or vice versa. Empirical results cannot decide the issue since comparisons including adjectives, or explicit comparisons of one-place versus two-place verbs, are virtually nonexistent. Thus, noun-verb empirical differences cannot be attributed specifically to verb meaning being essentially relational as opposed to predicative. As for theories of verbal and nominal differences, adding property predication to prototypical verbal meaning would not substantially change conclusions about nouns and verbs. For example, nominal concepts are described as less abstract than verbal concepts, in terms of having a more concrete, perceptible manifestation in the world. Relations can be more (e.g. "move") or less (e.g. "push") abstract and properties can be more (e.g. "good") or less (e.g. "red") abstract, but the typical level of abstraction of both properties and relations exceeds that of such typical nominal concepts as people, plants, other natural kinds, and artifacts. Thus, the inclusion of properties in verbal meaning does not alter the conclusion that verbal meaning is generally more abstract than nominal meaning.

The foregoing claim about relative abstractness of verbs and nouns has been made in order to explain certain empirical findings. Those findings include one which shows that children acquire noun meanings before verb meanings, and this advantage is maintained across diverse languages and cultures (e.g. Clark, 1978; Gentner, 1978, 1982; Goldin-Meadow, Seligman, & Gelman, 1976; Huttenlocher, 1974; Nelson, 1973). As late as middle childhood (around 9 years of age), differences between nouns and verbs can be detected using such sensitive tasks as metaphorical interpretation (Reyna, 1985); the difficulty of processing verbal meaning is apparent in such tasks although the interpreted vocabulary items are highly familiar.

For adults, verbs have been found to differ from nouns in being less memorable (e.g. Kintsch, 1974; Reynolds & Flagg, 1976; Wearing, 1970). This difference occurs in both recall and recognition tests. Adults are also less able to reproduce original verbs as opposed to nouns in a double translation task (Gentner, 1981a). In double translation, a bilingual translates a text and a second bilingual translates the translation back to the original language. In comparing the doubly translated text and the original, now in the same language, more nouns than verbs from the original survive.

A possible explanation for the translatability results is that verbs seem to vary across languages more than nouns in terms of the concepts they cover. In other words, one is more likely to find a close equivalent for a noun in another language, and less likely to be similarly fortunate with a verb (Gentner, 1981a). The latter observation more directly concerns language itself than language users.

Another linguistic, rather than psychological, observation that has been made is that verbs have more extended meanings than nouns do. Gentner (1981a) sampled nouns and verbs at each of four levels of word frequency in the Kucera and Francis (1967) corpus: a frequency of roughly 1000, and narrower ranges of frequency around 100 per million, 10 per million, and 1 per million. For a subset of nouns and verbs at each frequency level, the mean number of senses listed in a dictionary for each word was computed. At each frequency level, the verbs had a greater mean number of senses than the nouns.

Unfortunately, verbs occur more often in the higher-frequency levels than in the lower levels, and nouns show an even stronger but opposite trend by occurring increasingly often in lower-frequency levels. This resulted in small numbers of observations in some cells in Gentner's sample; only six nouns at the highest frequency and eleven verbs at the lowest frequency. Compounding this uneven distribution of nouns and verbs across frequency levels, frequency and number of senses covaried such that more frequent words had more senses. Given that the Kucera and Francis norms are an imperfect estimate of actual frequency, it is possible that the verbs at supposedly equal frequency levels had more senses than nouns because they were actually more frequent than nouns. Thus, inadequate sample sizes and confounding of frequency with number of senses in Gentner's data make it difficult to attribute a greater number of senses to some intrinsic property of verbs (as opposed to being explained by covarying differences in word frequency). As Jastrzembski (1981) has shown, word frequency, number of meanings, and number of related senses are easily confounded, and though these factors are independent, they exert similar effects.

Gentner (1981a) notes the covariation of form class and frequency, but explains this as a: "pattern of wide usage of a small number of verbs (p. 163)." It is certainly plausible that if verb tokens had a greater number of meanings they would be used more often than if they had fewer meanings. More importantly, experimental results using large samples of nouns and verbs demonstrate that, across a wide range of matched frequencies, people far more readily extend verbal meanings than nominal meanings (Reyna, 1981). This propensity to extend verbal meanings is bound to produce a greater base rate of spontaneous extensions for verbs compared to nouns, supporting Gentner's claim that verbs have more senses. Since verbs would supply more opportunities for adding to the stock of conventionalised meanings, the conclusion that verbs in fact have a greater number of conventionalised meanings, that they have greater breadth of meaning, is highly plausible.

In sum, verbs differ psychologically from nouns in being less memorable, later learned, and more difficult to interpret, and as linguistic entities they have a greater range of meanings and are more variable in meaning across languages, with their attrition in double translation probably another incarnation of their cross-linguistic variability.

These differences between nouns and verbs have been accounted for by an abundance of nonindependent explanations. Verbs have been characterised: as more abstract than nouns (in the sense of being less perceptually concrete); as having more variable reference to the world; as being less constrained by the nature of the physical world; as being more sensitive to context; as invoking less mental imagery; as being less salient in the ongoing stream of perceptual-cognitive information; as being more decomposable into meaning elements; as having meaning components that are more separable or independent; and so on (Gentner, 1978, 1981a, 1981b, 1982). Gentner (1981a) boils down these alternatives to two: verbs are more reactive to context and verbs have less "compositional latitude". That is, a noun is more "constrained to fit with our natural perceptual choice of objects (p. 170)." The latter idea reappears in Gentner (1982) as the natural partitions hypothesis. Thus Gentner claims that such assumptions "explain . . . phenomenological differences (p. 170)" between nouns and verbs. Those differences included differential acquisition, memory, breadth of meaning, cross-linguistic variability, and translatability (which she treats as a phenomenon distinct from cross-linguistic variability). The natural partitions hypothesis, for example, attributes the later acquisition of verbs to an assumption that nominal categories are more *natural* than verbal ones. The naturalness of nouns as conceptual packages simplifies the mapping problem for children between referent and word.

The natural partitions hypothesis may be true, but it seems at some remove from the data it is supposed to explain, and more importantly, it seems resistant to empirical test. Any obvious test of such a claim in the linguistic realm seems doomed to circularity in that the evidence in favour of the hypothesis is also the evidence that the hypothesis is supposed to explain (for example, that nominal meanings are acquired earlier than verbal meanings).

One strategy for testing a hypothesis of naturalness is to look for linguistic universals. The assumption is that what is universal is also natural, and sometimes innate, as Chomsky has claimed (e.g. Chomsky, 1968). Gentner (1982) utilised the strategy of looking for linguistic universals, comparing the order of acquisition of nouns and verbs simultaneously across different languages and cultures. She found that nouns were acquired before verbs in the six languages she studied. Such support for the hypothesis of greater naturalness for nominal concepts is indirect, and again the effect (acquisition order) that naturalness explains is also the evidence for the hypothesis itself. Hypotheses about quintessential naturalness, although often intriguing and perhaps true, are prone to the problem of confounding effect and explanation.

The tack taken here is more conservative. Sticking more closely to the data, two types of empirical effects are discernible: those that have to do with difficulty in understanding and those that have to do with flexibility of meaning (the latter both within and between languages). Difficulty in understanding would seem to subsume later acquisition, interpretation difficulty persisting into middle childhood, and lower memorability to the extent that memory is positively related to comprehensibility, as it has indeed been shown to be in many instances (e.g. Bransford, 1979).

Later acquisition of verbs is classified under difficulty in understanding since the effect cannot be accounted for without appeal to meaning differences, as opposed to other differences between nouns and verbs (Gentner, 1982). Indeed, analyses typically point to profound differences in conceptual complexity between nouns and verbs. Miller and Johnson-Laird (1976), for example, state that: "The kind of organisation we have found in verbal [semantic] fields is more complex than in the nominal fields (p. 666)." The nature and direction of difficulty between nominal and verbal meanings in acquisition seems directly derivative of differences in conceptual complexity. In addition, such differences in conceptual complexity can be established independently. For example, sufficient nonlinguistic evidence exists to support the idea that the concept of causal relation is more difficult to understand than the concept of object (e.g. Gardner, 1982). Thus, other factors being equal, one can predict that verbs will be acquired later than nouns because they involve more difficult concepts such as causal relations, whereas nouns more often refer to easier concepts such as objects. (Undoubtedly language acquisition involves other cognitive and linguistic factors, but the strategy here is to make the minimum number of assumptions in order to account for a set of relatively global differences between nouns and verbs.)

Including difficulties in interpretation of metaphors in middle childhood under the heading of "difficulty in understanding" does not require strenuous argument since interpretation is an instance of understanding. In other words, verbal metaphors are more difficult for children than nominal metaphors because verbs are harder to understand than nouns. Again, the postulated differences between nouns and verbs are semantic rather than syntactic. More complex subclasses of nouns, for example abstract nouns, might be learned by children before most verbs are learned (although direct summary evidence of such observations is lacking).

In sum, differential ease of acquisition, of memory, and of metaphorical interpretation seem classifiable under the rubric of difficulty in understanding primarily on the basis of logical and well-established empirical links, rather than additional theoretical assumptions. Similarly, breadth of meaning and cross-linguistic variability (or alternatively weak translatability) appear to be *prima facie* instances of flexibility of meaning.

Flexibility of meaning as it is used here is not identical with Gentner's (1981a) notion of differential adjustability. She treats differential adjustability as an "explanation" and as an "assumption (p. 168)" as opposed to a description of empirical results. More importantly, she attributes comprehensibility differences to differential adjustability, for example explaining poorer memory for verbs in terms of greater adjustment of meaning during comprehension. The position here is that differential flexibility and comprehensibility are distinct empirical patterns. Thus, in contrast to Gentner, empirical results concerning noun-verb differences are organised as examples of two dichotomous types of findings, differences in understanding or in flexibility.

Few researchers have studied the psychological phenomenon of flexibility of meaning in nouns versus verbs. Gentner (1981a) briefly alludes to an experiment she conducted in which subjects paraphrased sentences whose nouns and verbs were "semantically mismatched (p. 165)." Independent groups of subjects were better able to identify original nouns in sentence paraphrases as compared to original verbs. Gentner interpreted this result to mean that verbal meanings in the original sentence were adjusted more than nominal meanings during paraphrase.

Coincidentally, also in 1981 but conceived independently, a series of experiments was reported using stimuli similar to Gentner's and addressed in part to similar concerns. In Reyna (1981), semantically inconsistent sentences were presented in order to examine the psychology of meaning modification (or flexibility) of nouns compared to verbs. Since data bearing on this point are sparse, I will report the findings in some detail.

The sort of semantically inconsistent sentences used in the experiments are what Chomsky (1965) once called selectionally deviant; they are grammatical sentences in which word meanings are improperly combined, of which the now famous "colourless green ideas sleep furiously" is an example. Unlike Chomsky's example, sentences in the experiments usually involved only one conflict of meaning between a noun and a verb as in "the thunderstorm spanked the boy" in which the meanings of "thunderstorm" and "spanked" conflict. Half of such sentences contained conflicts between the subject noun and the verb, and half had conflicting verbs and object nouns. Another subset of sentences contained two meaning conflicts involving both subject and object noun, as in "the boulder berated the pebble."

A wide range of semantic content was sampled for both verbs and nouns. Nouns were sampled from the categories of: humans, animals, plants, inanimate objects, and abstractions. Verbs were sampled from the domains of: emotion, speech, crime, commerce, religion, physical action, and social interaction.

Usually working with a set of 36 sentences, independent groups of subjects performed tasks such as: paraphrasing the sentences; rating the difficulty of understanding the sentences; evaluating the aptness of or verifying the correctness of suggested interpretations; and so on. The results of the paraphrase task showed that subjects are generally quite adept at wresting meaning from such sentences, usually interpreting them metaphorically. Although children's books seem to have more instances of sentences such as "the thunderstorm spanked the boy" than do adults' books, children have greater difficulty with these sentences than adults do (see Reyna, 1985 for a detailed discussion).

When semantic conflict involves just one noun and verb, there are three ways to interpret the sentence so that it makes sense: to modify the meaning of the noun; to modify the verb; or to modify both. Usually context signals which word or words should be modified. For example, in a conversation in which the topic is weather, "the thunderstorm spanked the boy" would probably provoke verb modification to produce an interpretation such as "the thunderstorm pelted the boy with rain." If the topic instead were the misdeeds of a boy confronted by his father, the noun "thunderstorm" would probably be modified to yield an interpretation such as "raging father." The simultaneous modification of both words in that conflict is awkward and rare.

In the task most comparable to Gentner's, subjects were not given any instructions as to the context of sentences, nor as to which word they should modify; they were simply asked to paraphrase the sentences. Subjects never modified the meaning of a word not involved in conflict of meaning, and very rarely modified both noun and verb when both conflicted with one another. Rather, subjects typically chose to preserve one word in the conflict verbatim and metaphorically modify the meaning of the other word. Most germane to the discussion of relative flexibility of meaning, verbs were modified far more often than nouns. For one-conflict sentences, 77% of modifications involved only verbs, whereas 22% involved only nouns. The preference for modifying verbs was even more striking for two-conflict sentences in which 92% of modifications involved verbs.

Flexibility of meaning as descriptive of the willingness to extend conventional meaning seems far more characteristic of verbs than of nouns. One might argue, however, that subjects merely employed a given-new strategy such that the subject noun was construed as the topic, and therefore inviolable, and the verb was seen as part of the comment, and therefore a candidate for change. The given-new explanation can be ruled out for at least two reasons. First, in one-conflict sentences, half of the time a conflicting noun was in what would be topic position, the grammatical subject mentioned first, and the other half of the time the offending noun was the grammatical object in what would be comment position. If a given-new strategy were influencing which word were modified, one might expect that conflicting nouns in object position (comment) would be modified more often than nouns in subject position (topic). The percentages of noun modifications, however, were not statistically different: 23% for the object position sentences and 19% for the subject position sentences. Especially compared to the enormous difference between percentages of noun versus verb modifications, it appears that a given-new hypothesis would be hard-pressed to account for the noun-verb differences.

Additional evidence against a given-new strategic explanation was obtained by Gentner (1981a) who explored such a possibility by varying the verb's position in the sentence. Even when the verb occurred first, clearly marked as topic, it was modified significantly more often than the noun.

In Reyna (1981), changing some aspect of the conflicting nouns did alter the probability of verb modification significantly. When the category of the conflicting noun became incrementally closer to the category of noun conventionally required by the verb, the probability of noun modification increased (and that of verb modification correspondingly decreased). That is, as the incompatibility of the noun decreased, the probability of its being modified in accordance with the verb's meaning increased. For example, given a (prototypically) human-requiring verb such as "sobbed," nouns drawn from such nonliving categories as events or inanimate objects were generally less likely to be modified than nouns from the categories of animals or plants. Nevertheless, the preference for modifying verbs is sufficiently robust that fully 65% of modifications for one-conflict sentences consisting of a human-requiring verb and an animal noun eventuated in modifying the verb rather than the animal noun. This is despite the prevalence of such animal personification in literature, advertising, cartoons, and so on.

The foregoing results join the linguistic observations of breadth of meaning and cross-linguistic variability in supporting the conclusion that verb meanings are more flexible than noun meanings. In addition to data relevant to flexibility of meaning, observations were made in Reyna (1981) concerning relative difficulty in understanding verbs and nouns. Consistent with what one might expect given the results above when subjects were instructed to paraphrase interpretations of nouns, difficulty with interpretation as measured by the frequency of literal (that is failed) interpretations increased as nouns became less and less compatible with conflicting verbs. More direct evidence of difficulty with understanding was obtained in the task in which subjects rated ease of interpretation. Again, for subjects directed to interpret nouns, the rated ease of interpretation decreased as the noun became increasingly incompatible with the verb. (All differences reported in this chapter based on my work are statistically significant.)

The consistent pattern of results reported above regarding noun incompatibility cross-validates the different measures of difficulty in understanding. Given such a consistent and replicable pattern, one would conclude that the rating task, for example, validly tapped differences in difficulty of interpretation. Thus, the rating task was used for an additional comparison. One group of subjects was instructed to interpret (modify) the nouns in a set of 36 sentences while the same sentences were given to another group who were told to interpret the verbs. Both groups of subjects rated the difficulty of interpretation. When difficulty ratings of the two groups were compared, recalling that the physical stimuli were identical and that the only difference was the word interpreted, verb interpretation was rated as significantly more difficult than noun interpretation ($P < .001$). The differential was found for 27 of the 36 sentences, and was found irrespective of the position—topic or comment—of the conflicting noun.

That verb interpretation is harder than noun interpretation is consistent with the empirical generalisation discussed earlier concerning the greater difficulty in understanding verbs. As do children in middle childhood, adults appear to have increased difficulty in metaphorically interpreting verbs compared to nouns. Thus, the results for adults are consistent with the findings discussed earlier (e.g. later acquisition, poorer memory) under the rubric of greater difficulty in understanding verbal meaning.

The results for noun and verb interpretation in Reyna (1981), however, are not superficially consistent in terms of their overall pattern. Previously, findings of flexibility and difficulty in understanding were segregated. When investigation of both is done using comparable tasks and stimuli, the apparently intrinsic contradiction between the two claims emerges. The paradox is that people freely choose to interpret verbs rather than nouns even though they are significantly harder to interpret. Why would subjects plod through 36 sentences, uniformly modifying verbal meanings, if modifying those meanings was indeed harder than modifying noun meanings? Recall that modifying either the noun's meaning or the verb's meaning resolves the problem of semantic conflict equally well.

Lest we attribute this conundrum to some peculiarity of metaphorical sentences, it is important to note that the paradox also applies to conventional language. Verbal meaning is both hard to process, difficult to understand, and easy to process in the sense of being easy to extend. These two apparently contradictory empirical properties of verbs are reflected in more specific paradoxes involving conventional meaning. For example, given that verbal meanings are so easily extended or modified, and so frequently used since they perform double-or-more duty, why is their greater frequency not linked with ease of understanding (as it is for nouns)? Similarly, age of acquisition for a term and frequency of usage are generally correlated; since verbs are more flexible and therefore more frequent than nouns, why are they acquired after rather than before nouns? Also, since ordinary language comprehension is characterised by pragmatic, contextually dependent meaning, why is the contextual sensitivity and flexibility of verbs not a distinct advantage in understanding ordinary language in context? Each of these inconsistencies involving conventional language can be quibbled with. Even if these specific paradoxes of conventional language can be dismissed, however, the striking contradiction for the nonconventional sentences between the results for the paraphrase and rating tasks cannot be so easily dismissed. The finding is essentially that subjects choose the harder task of modifying verbs, as opposed to nouns. The fundamental question, in any case, is: Which theoretical assumptions about meaning could straightforwardly predict for verbs both greater difficulty in processing meaning, harder rated comprehension, and greater ease in processing meaning, easier metaphorical extension? (Ease of extension here refers to ease of meaning modification.)

One claim regarding verbs that was discussed earlier is that verbs are more abstract than nouns in the sense of referring to less conceptually concrete concepts. Verbs appear to be more abstract than nouns in another way as well, namely in being more *general*. The theoretical argument corresponding to this claim is that verbs have fewer aspects or components of meaning. The argument that verbs in general have fewer components of meaning than nouns is not the same as the argument that words having fewer meaning components should be processed more efficiently than words with more components (cf. Gentner, 1981b). What is being claimed here is that, since verbal meaning contains less detail, there are fewer constraints on its use.

The empirical results organised under the heading of flexibility of meaning seem easily accounted for with this argument. Since verbal meanings are more general than nominal meanings, it is nouns which contribute the greater proportion of detail in sentences. In sentences, verbal meanings become instantiated by virtue of nominal meanings. This division of linguistic labour suggests that habits of thought probably develop such that nominal meanings are ordinarily assumed to be relatively fixed, and verbs are looked to for adjustments in meaning. The under-specification of verbal meaning would allow such a strategy to be successful since fewer constraints would be placed on the final product of interpreta-tion. In this view, the differential modification of meaning observed in Reyna (1981), then, is a habitual mode of thought only made more apparent by extreme conflict in meaning between noun and verb.

Greater breadth of meaning for verbs in terms of a greater number of conventionalised meanings is explained by the idea that verbs' generality gives them an entrée to a greater range of situations; fewer constraints on meaning are available to prevent the use of verbs in a broader range of situations. As was argued earlier, the propensity for extending verbal meanings creates a larger pool of extensions, and therefore there are simply more opportunities for conventionalisation. Cross-linguistic varia-bility probably has to do with an interaction between greater propensity for extension and cultural biases in deciding what is important enough to be conventionalised.

The argument for greater generality of meaning in verbs has as corol-laries many of the descriptions of verbal meaning mentioned earlier, including greater variability in reference, less association with mental imagery, and less conceptual concreteness, as already indicated. Again, these effects are derivable from the claim that the intension, the sense, of verbs is more skeletal for verbs than for nouns. (The word "intension" is always used in this chapter to refer to that aspect of meaning which is a word's sense, as opposed to its reference.)

On the face of it, the claim for greater generality of meaning does not theoretically explain why verbs should be more difficult to understand than nouns. Indeed, in having fewer elements of meaning to work with, verbs might be expected to be easier to process than nouns. However, these fewer elements of meaning are more complex in verbs. Relational or predicative meaning makes the structure of verbal meaning relatively complex. Verbs are also harder to understand because the generality of their meanings makes mapping them onto specific referents more difficult. Therefore, under ordinary conditions, difficulty in understanding verbs is explained by their generality (and resultant vagueness in reference), as well as their complex connections among components.

The crucial distinction in simultaneously being able to account for difficulty in understanding and flexibility of meaning may have to do with whether a task is approached as entailing an intensional (as in Frege's notion of sense) judgment or both an intensional and extensional (as in *referential*) judgment. The initial distinction to draw is between two types of understanding. Everyday verbal comprehension typically involves concrete specification of reference. A reader or listener may "understand" the words, their intensions, but does not feel as though true understanding has occurred until the situation of the utterance is understood (e.g. Bransford & Johnson, 1973). Understanding in ordinary life involves putting the communication into a frame of reference both cultural and individual, and making reference to knowledge about the world; that is, discovering the extension (referents) of words (e.g. Bartlett, 1932).

Acontextual judgments based only on intension can, however, be performed. For example, students learning to solve abstract logical problems with premises such as "all A are B" can be trained to ignore interfering inferences based on instantiating the premises (e.g. Copi, 1972), although such training in logic is often accomplished with difficulty (Falmagne, 1975). In solving a problem in formal logic, a student is called on to process the intensions of terms, especially the senses of the logical terms (e.g. "all" and "if"). However, the solver must ignore possible references to the real world, for example knowledge about the actual truth of premises. As an exercise in maintaining such a barrier between the real world and the formal argument, students are often required to reason with premises they know to be false or absurd (e.g. "all bees carry raincoats"). Thus, a distinction between formal logical reasoning and plausible deduction about the real world is analogous to the distinction between intensional understanding and everyday verbal comprehension (which is based both on the sense of what is said and also on what is being referred to).

The claim is that the paraphrase or meaning modification task in Reyna (1981) was approached as an intensional judgment, and is influenced by intensional complexity, but language acquisition in the world, for example, is affected by both intensional and referential complexity. The paraphrase task in which subjects usually elected to modify verbal meanings involved a lengthy list of disconnected sentences. It is likely that subjects did not necessarily relate their understanding of each sentence to a situation in the world. Especially when such interpretation would be difficult, as when complex verbal meanings were involved, it is plausible that subjects opted for a minimal intensional processing of that sentence. Consistent with this notion of minimal processing that does not result in concrete instantiation of sentences, most paraphrases of verbs were what was called "disjunctive," that is, very general. The verbal interpretations were general enough to subsume both literal and metaphorical readings of the verb disjunctively. Subjects solved the immediate intensional problem of semantic conflict, but did not proceed to respecify the verb's meaning as one would have to in everyday life if one wanted to know which situation was being referred to.

The central claim of verbal generality of meaning indicates why intensional processing should be relatively easy for verbs while extensional (as in *referential*) processing is difficult. In intensional processing, the advantage of manipulating fewer components of meaning can be exploited. Verbs, having fewer components of meaning, could be intensionally processed more efficiently. Also, linguistic habits would encourage adjustment in the verb's meaning (those habits having been acquired because verbal meaning is relatively general. Although the complexity of verbal components would attenuate the effect somewhat, overall verbs should be processed more quickly than nouns in tasks calling for strictly intensional judgments; for example, acontextual laboratory tasks performed under time pressure involving single words or phrases, such as judgments of semantic absurdity or semantic equivalence. In such tasks, the fewer components of meaning a word has, the faster a response could be computed. (Of course, frequency of usage and other nonsemantic factors must be held constant, and the stimulus-response pairs should not be overlearned so that semantic processing is required.) Similarly, if class inclusion statements were verified intensionally as was once thought, "a robin is an animal" would be verified more quickly than "a robin is a bird" because presumably fewer components would need to be matched up in the former than in the latter. Of course, such verification judgments were found to depend on real-world knowledge and experience, including exposure to referents. Such acontextual tasks as meaningful word association—being given "hot" and responding "cold"—are probably based on intensional processing since they occur under some time pressure, encouraging minimal processing: When subjects are given more time, they produce associations to the real world of their own lives (e.g. Clark & Clark, 1977).

Referential processing is difficult for verbs for the same reason that intensional processing is easy, namely generality of meaning. The lack of detail or constraints on meaning makes the search for possible referents less guided. Also, given the lack of constraints, the ultimate interpretation might often remain fairly abstract for verbs. It is not difficult to see how such lack of specificity at the comprehension stage could deleteriously affect memory, which is augmented by manipulations that increase specificity at encoding (e.g. Tulving, 1983). Since ordinary understanding is usually taken to be both understanding the words and determining their referents, people are liable to experience the search for verbal meaning as less satisfying than the search for nominal meaning: The road to the referent is well marked for nouns, but on reaching a destination for verbs one cannot be sure one has "gotten to the right place." Subjects would have less confidence in interpretations of verbs according to their everyday standards for interpreting sentences because they could not be sure a specifically appropriate interpretation had been derived. It is consistent with this characterisation that, when asked for a judgment of their difficulty in interpreting words, subjects rated the search for verbal meanings as more difficult than the search for nominal meanings.

In summary, observations regarding nominal and verbal meaning can be organised under two general headings; difficulty in understanding and flexibility of meaning. When directly compared, these two kinds of findings can produce apparent paradoxes, for example people electing to process verbal stimuli in a manner that they rate as more difficult, as opposed to choosing an acknowledgedly easier route. Such paradoxes can be resolved by introducing the theoretical premise that verbal meanings have fewer components than nominal meanings. Intensional judgments, those based solely on sense, will be easier for verbs because fewer components are involved. However, for extensional judgments, where some referential correspondence to the world must be achieved, underspecified verbal meaning is a poor guide.

REFERENCES

Bartlett, F. C. (1932) *Remembering: An Experimental and Social Study*. Cambridge, England: Cambridge University Press.

Bransford, J. (1979) *Human Cognition: Learning, Understanding and Remembering*. Belmont, California: Wadsworth Publishing Co.

Bransford, J. & Johnson, M. K. (1973) Considerations of some problems of comprehension. In W. G. Chase (Ed.), *Visual Information Processing*. New York: Academic Press.

Chomsky, N. (1965) *Aspects of the Theory of Syntax*. Cambridge, Mass.: MIT Press.

Chomsky, N. (1968) *Language and Mind*. New York: Harcourt Brace Jovanovich,

Clark, E. (1978) Discovering what words can do. *Papers from the Parasession on the Lexicon*. Chicago: Chicago Linguistic Society.

Clark, H. & Clark, E. (1977) *Psychology and Language: An Introduction to Psycholinguistics*. New York: Harcourt Brace Jovanovich.

Cohen, J. (1979) The semantics of metaphor. In A. Ortony (Ed.), *Metaphor and Thought*. London: Cambridge University Press.

Copi, I. (1972) *Introduction to Logic*. New York: Macmillan.

Falmagne, R. (Ed.) (1975) *Reasoning: Representation and Process.* Hillsdale, New Jersey: Lawrence Erlbaum Associates Inc.

Gardner, H. (1982) *Developmental Psychology.* Boston: Little, Brown, & Company.

Gentner, D. (1978) On relational meaning: On the acquisition of verb meaning. *Child Development, 49,* 988–998.

Gentner, D. (1981a) Some interesting differences between verbs and nouns. *Cognition and Brain Theory, 4,* 161–178.

Gentner, D. (1981b) Verb semantic structures in memory for sentences: Evidence for componential representation. *Cognitive Psychology, 13,* 56–83.

Gentner, D. (1982) Why nouns are learned before verbs: Linguistic relativity versus natural partitioning. In S. Kuczaj (Ed.), *Language Development: Language, Cognition, and Culture.* Hillsdale, New Jersey: Lawrence Erlbaum Associates Inc.

Goldin-Meadow, S., Seligman, M., & Gelman, R. (1976) Language in the two-year-old. *Cognition, 4,* 189–202.

Huttenlocher, J. (1974) The origins of language comprehension. In R. L. Solso (Ed.), *Theories in Cognitive Psychology: The Loyola Symposium.* Hillsdale, New Jersey: Lawrence Erlbaum Associates Inc.

Jastrzembski, J. (1981) Multiple meanings, number of related meanings, frequency of occurrence, and the lexicon. *Cognitive Psychology, 13,* 278–305.

Katz, J. J. (1972) *Semantic Theory.* New York: Harper & Row.

Kintsch, W. (1974) *The Representation of Meaning in Memory.* Hillsdale, New Jersey: Lawrence Erlbaum Associates Inc.

Kucera, H. & Francis, W. N. (1967) *Computational Analysis of Present-Day American English.* Providence: Brown University Press.

Miller, G. A. & Johnson-Laird, P. N. (1976) *Language and Perception.* Cambridge, Mass.: Harvard University Press.

Nelson, K. (1973) Structure and strategy in learning to talk. *Monographs of the Society for Research in Child Development, 38,* 149.

Reyna, V. F. (1981) The animated word: Modification of meaning by context. Doctoral dissertation, Ann Arbor, Michigan: *University Microfilms International,* reference number 82-03153.

Reyna, V. F. (1985) Figure and fantasy in children's language. In M. Pressley & C. Brainerd (Eds.), *Cognitive Learning and Memory in Children: Progress in Cognitive Development Research.* New York: Springer-Verlag.

Reynolds, A. G. & Flagg, P. W. (1976) Recognition memory for elements of sentences. *Memory and Cognition, 4,* 422–432.

Tulving, E. (1983) *Elements of Episodic Memory.* New York: Oxford University Press.

Wearing, A. J. (1970) The storage of complex sentences. *Journal of Verbal Learning and Verbal Behaviour, 9,* 21–29.

8 Change and Continuity in Early Language Learning

Elena V. M. Lieven
Department of Psychology, University of Manchester, Manchester M13 9PL, U.K.

INTRODUCTION

Unlike other aspects of development, the information relevant to the study of language learning is relatively accessible. This accessibility may account for the range and depth of the research which has been undertaken in the last decade. Children talk without being asked to and, as a result, experimental studies, with all their problems of ecological validity, have played only a minor part in the study of early language learning. In all this research the questions implicitly or explicitly posed are: How do we describe the changes in a child's ways of talking? What new skills have been added and on what continuity are they based? How do we explain these new skills? In this chapter I explore the various answers to these questions in terms of what they have to say about continuity and change in development. I hope to show that language learning is a process—not a once-and-for-all leap into "language" around the age of two years. It is rather a process of constant reorganisation. Children increase the sophistication of their language skills by working on their current representation of language to produce a less context- and content-dependent representation. In other words there is both continuity and change.

These questions of continuity and change have often been seen as inextricable from the question of the biological basis of language. Much of the force and polemic of the old argument between Chomsky and Skinner as to the innateness of language has died down for two reasons. First, there is a better understanding of the process of language development and, secondly, there is more general acceptance of the part that the evolution of

317

the brain has played in language. However, there is also more general acceptance that knowing that language has a biological basis tells us nothing about what that basis is, how it manifests itself in children's language learning, or what its relation to more general cognitive skills is.

FROM COMMUNICATION TO WORDS

In her chapter in *The Integration of a Child into a Social World* (Ryan, 1974), Joanna Ryan outlined the theory of speech acts and argued that its application to child language was likely to prove very illuminating. The use of speech act theory in child language research is part of a general approach which analyses the pragmatics of children's communicative behaviour and argues that there is a continuity between children's preverbal and verbal behaviour. The strong claim of this approach would be that there is continuity not just in communicative behaviour but that preverbal communicative behaviour is a basis for the structure of children's early speech. As we shall see, there appears to be partial, but not complete, truth in this idea.

It seems that at least some children achieve a certain amount of regularity and primitive signification in their communications prior to learning words. Both Piaget (1952) and Bruner (1975a), from very different theoretical frameworks, argue that children come to be able to make part of a situation stand for the whole (i.e. to re-present it to themselves). For Piaget, the interest lies in the cognitive developments that underlie the child's capacity to recall absent objects and events—hence his detailed study of the development of delayed imitation and his attempt to specify the stages through which the child passes; from something that is close to a stimulus-response connection between the whole event and its representation (e.g. the tinkling of the bottle generating anticipatory behaviour) to a situation where the baby can use a word to represent an event or object. Bruner is more interested in the ways in which the child comes to be able to use some part of an interactional routine to communicate the desire that the whole routine be restarted. Thus he draws attention to the ways in which games start off as very highly structured by the caretaker, with the child playing a fairly passive role. The child then starts to be able to reverse roles and, finally, is able to use some small part of the game to signal a desire that the game be played again. This idea—that children gradually develop the capacity to use the part to signify the whole—is generally regarded as being a critical starting point for the development of a conventional sign system.

A related line of research suggests that children come to differentiate certain communicative functions and to transmit these functions using idiosyncratic but systematic signs to represent them. Halliday (1975), Carter (1978), Dore, Franklin, Miller, and Ramer (1976), and McShane (1980) provide evidence of this. The children in all these studies did appear to use sounds systematically to realise communicative functions such as requesting and rejecting, although what the sound actually was varied from child to child. Again, the ability to use a more or less arbitrary sound systematically to convey communicative function seems to be an important stepping stone both to the use of words and to the capacity to distinguish between various kinds of functions for utterances.

Thus far it seems incontrovertible that at least one way into language is through these sorts of developments in preverbal communication, though since the total number of children studied probably does not exceed 20, caution is in order. However stronger claims than these are made about the preverbal period. For instance, Bates, Camaioni, and Volterra (1975) describe the first distinctions that children make communicatively as "proto-imperatives" and "proto-declaratives"; the first when the child is making a demand on an adult for some action, the second when the child seems to be pointing out objects to gain the adult's attention. By using the terms "imperative" and "declarative," there is the implication that these early communicative distinctions are related to later syntactic methods of forming the declarative and the imperative. Another example is the attempt by Bruner to find the precursors of case grammer (Fillmore, 1968) in the interactions of caretaker and child (Bruner 1975a).[1] The potential benefit of these approaches is that they suggest functional continuity between preverbal and verbal communication. There are two problems that require careful attention, however. First, there is the possibility that linguistic categories (e.g., "imperative," "agent," "instrument") are imposed on the child's preverbal communications in order to show continuity but that these preverbal communications do not, in fact, fall naturally into these distinctions. The way to deal with this is through a detailed and careful longitudinal study which searches for real functional continuity between preverbal communicative distinctions and their eventual linguistic encodings. Such a study has not yet been undertaken. The second potential problem with these approaches is that they may be taken to be saying that all linguistic distinctions are present in some form preverbally, i.e. that structure is merely grafted onto categories already

---

[1]Case grammar works on the semantic roles created by different groups of verbs, e.g. agent, instrument, beneficiary. It was regarded as a very hopeful candidate in the search to find a linguistic theory which would allow the child's preverbal cognitive development to form the basis for its linguistic development. Its promise has not been upheld either in linguistics or in developmental psycholinguistics but it formed an important approach ten years ago and generated some crucial research.

present. As we shall see, this hugely underestimates what is involved in starting to talk and to put words together in utterances.

LEARNING THE WORDS

How do children learn words and what do words mean to them? Segmenting words and inflections out of the speech stream is no easy task. There is no one-to-one relation between a word and an acoustic signal, since the latter varies according to the context in which the word is spoken (Lieberman, 1972). Peters (1980), in a comprehensive approach to answering the question of how children segment words out of the speech stream, argues that aspects of "babytalk" will help. First, many adults explicitly teach words to children. Once some words are learnt, it will be possible for the child, in a kind of "bootstrapping" operation, to work out some of the context in which the word is spoken. Second, many features of "babytalk", which appear to be universal (Ferguson, 1977), will help a child to identify important content words, their inflectional contexts, and to distinguish between different types of functional utterance (e.g. "requesting" as opposed to "ordering" or "describing"). Thus stress and intonation patterns tend to highlight the content words in an utterance and the repetition of utterances with the words slightly changed around will also serve to emphasise certain words. All of this depends, of course, on rapid, temporal order, auditory processing which may well be part of the biological underpinning to language which has evolved in the brain.

An interesting consequence of these ideas about the importance of "babytalk" for children's segmentation of the speech stream is that those children who are not hearing much "babytalk" may have difficulties breaking into language. I have suggested (Lieven, 1982) that they may also depend more on rote-learned phrases and on a very functionally based use of a small number of words when they first start using words to communicate. Nelson (1973) makes a related distinction between "referential" and "social-expressive" children, and argues that the former are more object-word based while the latter concentrate more on the social use of language. While agreeing with Nelson that children can differ considerably in their early use of words and that this is, in part, due to their environment, I have argued that this is not because the "social-expressive" children have a greater interest in social interaction per se (Lieven, 1980). Rather, children's different approaches to early word learning and use is due to a complex of factors, not all of which necessarily hold for each child. Thus the child's own temperament, the richness of speech addressed to her/him and the relationship between the child and those around will all be involved in determining how s/he approaches language learning. This then calls into question the practice of dividing up language learning into stages based on the average number of words that children use in their utterances. It is more important, in terms of understanding how a child is doing in learning to talk, to look in depth at what words the child is using in what circumstances. One will then find that children who seem, superficially, to be at a similar stage are, in fact, doing very different things in terms of the sophistication of their speech. And what they are doing has consequences for how they move on.

This can be demonstrated by considering McShane's (1980) suggestion that at least some children make a decisive cognitive change in their learning of words a considerable time after the first words have been spoken. McShane argues that initially children learn words as part of ongoing actions (as claimed by Piaget, see earlier) or in scripts, as suggested by Nelson and Gruendal (1979) or Barratt (1978). However, in the end, words have to be detached from these contexts and seen as entities in themselves. When children "realise" this, McShane argues, they will start rapidly to increase vocabulary and may start requesting the names of things. Not until words have this status is a child going to be able to start working out the beginnings of structure—i.e. what goes with what. There is evidence that some children do go through a "naming boom" but some children do not (McShane, 1980). One suggestion about those that do not is that they have not yet understood the status of words. I have argued that children can move into the "two-word stage" without yet having made this cognitive advance (Lieven, 1980) and that their multiple-word utterances reveal this. Since, of course, all children have to work out "what goes with what" in order to start structuring utterances, the claim is that these children do this after they have started to produce some multiple-word utterances which are either rote-learned or generated by simple word associations. A second prediction is that children who do not go through a "naming boom" might be children defined as "social-expressive" by Nelson's or my criteria.

Here, then, is an example of both continuity and change: Continuity in the sense that the child's learning of words is clearly based on preverbal interactions and cognition. There is also real change: The child has to make a cognitive leap forward. Whether this cognitive development is specific to language or whether it is more general and has parallels in other spheres of development is, of course, a different question. It is also the case that the understanding of what a word is that the child achieves at this point in development is not a once-and-for-all adult understanding (see, for instance, the problems that children have with nominal realism at a much later age, Piaget, 1973). But that such a development, or something like it, occurs during the early stages of language development seems not to be in doubt.

BUILDING UTTERANCES

When children start to put words together in one utterance, these words will not be randomly ordered. From almost the first multiple-word utterance that a child produces there will be structure and regularity. Despite the fact that children do learn some phrases as a whole, e.g. phrases like *what's that* and *here you are*, and that children undoubtedly do sometimes put words together in the ad hoc way described by Clark (1977), it is clear that the internal composition of many of the utterances of young children show evidence of being governed by structural regularities. The question is: How should these regularities be described and where do they come from? Are they part of some innate language acquisition device, do they reflect more general cognitive development, or are they constructed from the pragmatics of the communicative interchanges in which the child takes part? For instance, when an English-speaking child systematically places the agent of an action before the action itself in all utterances, a number of explanations are possible. The child could be operating with a large number of specific associations which order every word in his or her vocabulary with every other word. This would not work for very long in the development of language and I shall not consider it further.[2] Or the child could have learnt that, for a particular action word, words for the performers of the action go in front of the word for the action itself (a lexically based strategy). Or the child could be ordering topics before comments (a pragmatic or functional strategy). Or the child could be placing agents before the actions that they perform (a semantically based categorical approach). Or, finally, the child could be operating in terms of the categories of noun phrase and verb phrase and their relation. Thus, other things being equal, the noun phrase dominating the main verb phrase is the subject of the sentence and, in English, goes in first position. These alternative explanations for the structure of children's two-word utterances suggest different precursors in the child's cognitive and communicative development and have implications for what is considered innate. They therefore make different claims about continuity and change and pose different theoretical difficulties.

Before considering some of these alternative approaches to analysing children's early language skills, a brief note about what the language-learning child is aiming for might help the discussion. I think that the average adult speaker of a language does require the capacity to manipu-

---

[2]Chomsky (1959) showed that (1) the number of associations involved would be beyond the scope even of human memory; and (2) that it is precisely the capacity of language to form an infinite number of novel utterances which disproves a purely associationist theory of language development and adult language skills.

late a formal, relatively meaning-free, syntax. There is no doubt, for instance, that in adult speech the linguistic role of subject is played by words which cannot be united into one semantic category, and that this is true for other linguistic roles and categories.[3] On the other hand this does not necessarily mean that children start out with such linguistic categories; they may build them out of simpler and more accessible distinctions.

The approaches to language learning which are most directly based in linguistics are those which come under the heading of learnability theory (Wexler & Cullicover, 1980, see Atkinson, 1980.) They are linguistically based in the sense that they follow Chomsky's thinking very closely, both at the philosophical level and at the level of the specific kinds of linguistics that they use in their studies. More specifically, they attempt to work out formally (i.e. mathematically and logically) what the requirements are on the child's language learning capacities (language acquisition device) given: (1) the properties of natural language; and (2) the fact that the child does not receive negative syntactic information (correction of grammatical errors or information about what cannot be said in the language). This interesting and reasonable approach is hampered, to my mind, by a number of difficulties. The first is that there is no necessary connection between the formal analysis of language and the psycholinguistics of how people learn, speak, and understand speech. Until we have a convincing and psychologi-cally realistic theory of language there will be an unchartable gap between linguistics and psychology. Following on from this there is the problem that learnability theorists seem not to be interested in what small children actually do. Thus it is well known by now that young children appear to be working either with low-scope semantic categories or with a set of associa-tions between different words (Braine, 1976). The obvious question then, is: How do they get from this to a more formal and linguistic set of rules and categories? Learnability theorists seem to take one of two approaches. The first is to acknowledge the existence of lexically based rules and to try to work out how the child gets from these to transformational rules (e.g.

---

[3]To use Schlesinger's (1981) examples with some of my own:

1. The bells are ringing.
2. People are good.
3. The wine glass is empty.
4. Sincerity is best.
5. Mary hit John.
6. The key opened the door.

The nouns in the role of subject do not cohere into one semantic role; there are agents, abstract entities, etc. Children have to learn to unite all these under the linguistic role of subject.

from the active to the passive; Randall 1985). Where this works it seems to me to be no different to various phrase structure approaches to these problems. The researcher, however, will often try to account for this learning in terms of Chomsky's most recent theories. This causes real problems for the psychologist since the debates over Chomsky's theories rage so hard within linguistics (e.g. Keenan, 1980; Gazdar, 1982), that it is hard to find the confidence in his specific formulations which would be required before the details of learnability theory could be accepted.[4]

The most extreme approach adopted by some of these theorists is to argue that although children start off with semantically based speech, their development into more complex syntax is governed by innate rules over which the "primitive language" has no effect or influence (Gleitman, 1981). These innate "rules" add an order of complexity (in terms of the movement of constituents in sentences, e.g. embedding, the passive transformation), and the researchers argue that it is the increasing neurological complexity of the brain which allows for and underpins the child's developing capacity for complex linguistic skills (Wexler & Cullicover, 1980). Borer and Wexler (1984), in a more reasonable approach to this idea, argue that neurological maturation allows the child new processing complexity in relation to the organisation of linguistic constituents, rather than that there is a complete break between earlier and more advanced development. The idea that neurological maturation may be involved in the development of certain skills—either specifically linguistic or more general cognitive skills—may be true. Mounoud (1982) also argues that brain maturation is responsible for the different kinds of representational skill that are roughly indicated by Piaget's three stages of cognitive development. These are very general statements, however. The burden of proof lies in pinning down, as Mounoud has attempted to do for cognition, how exactly such maturation is reflected in the child's behaviour, in showing that there is indeed real discontinuity as the child learns to talk, and in explaining the individual differences that occur in language development.

Few researchers reject the idea of biological underpinnings to language learning completely, though they may differ as to what precisely is being underpinned and as to how specific to language such capacities are. Thus

---

[4]Borer & Wexler (1984) argue that A-chaining, a rule that underpins both agent passives and "tough movement," results from biological maturation in the brain. They explain the fact that agentless passives develop before agent passives by arguing that the brain has not yet reached sufficient maturity for A-chaining, and agree with other linguists that agentless passives can be formed using a lexical rule. The problems with this are: first, that one would have to show that, indeed, all the skills underpinned by A-chaining developed together in children; and, secondly, the existence of A-chaining as a linguistic entity is challenged by many linguists (Keenan, 1980; Gazdar, 1982).

Slobin (in press) suggests that the capacity to look for meaningful segments in the speech stream (words and morphemes) may be innate in the sense that the processes involved may have evolved as part of the biological apparatus of the human. This would seem to be specific to language since it is difficult to think of a parallel in the domain of cognition. Gentner (1983) makes an interesting suggestion which relates a linguistic category, not to innate biological underpinnings for language, but to perception. She argues that the category of noun or "object-like thing" is derivable from perception—that is, our perceptual system is organised in such a way that objects tend to be perceived easily and to behave in similar ways. She suggests that once this category has been derived, children will be able to start identifying the morphological contexts in which such words occur and thus to start identifying other parts of the language. If this turns out to be correct it is interesting, because it shows how it might be possible for aspects of language learning to depend on human biology without necessarily being specific to language. Thus the universality of the category of noun may depend not on innate linguistic universals but on innate perceptual universals. This may well be reinforced by the fact that stress and intonation in babytalk seem universally to pick out content words, most especially nouns. However, it is not just the categories of words that children must learn but also rules for placing these words in particular grammatical roles in the utterance, whether these roles be syntactic (e.g. subject and predicate), semantic (e.g. agent and action), or pragmatic (e.g. new and given information).

At the opposite end of the continuum to innatist theories of language development are those theories that look to pragmatic factors to explain the early ordering of children's multiple-word utterances. Thus it has been argued that children order their utterances in terms of: comment and topic (Bates & MacWhinney, 1979); new and given information (Bates & MacWhinney, 1979); or rheme and theme (Sinha & Paprotté, in press).[5] Such claims are interesting because they explicitly or implicitly draw a connection between preverbal interaction and the internal ordering of children's utterances. The claim is that the child is already able to distinguish between given and new information or between topic and comment prior to being able to use words to do it. Thus there is a continuity between preverbal and verbal development which provides the possibility of the child using order in speech with categories which are already present. Bruner (1975b) argues that the interactional exchanges of adult and child show a topic-comment structure, and work by Greenfield and Smith (1976) suggests the same for new and given information. Greenfield and Smith's work attempts to demonstrate that children are observing given-new

---

[5]"Theme" refers to the "psychological subject" of a clause; "rheme" to the body of the clause which carries the message about the theme (Halliday, 1967).

distinctions in their one-word speech in that their utterances always present new information. This, of course, gives even more support to the idea of continuity from preverbal communication, through the one-word stage to multiple-word utterances. One difficulty with these approaches has been the problem of defining what is given and what is new for the child. The method used is that of rich interpretation, which can yield a number of different solutions to what exactly the child intended to say with any particular utterance. This is particularly the case, I think, when the method is being used to provide the underlying pragmatic structure of the inter-change (Howe, 1976). A second difficulty, which most of these researchers admit, is that however children start off ordering their utterances, they rapidly come to do so using various semantic or lexical strategies and thus there is the question of how and why the pragmatic strategies give way. This is a particular problem since the evidence for some kind of internal utterance structure in children's speech seems strong even if there is considerable argument about what form it takes. Although pragmatic factors seem to be of great significance when discussing why a child produces a particular utterance at a particular point in a conversation, the case for pragmatic factors being involved in the internal construction of the utterances of children of this age remains weak. If we had a grammatical theory that related syntax to pragmatics (as for instance Givón, 1979, attempts) it might be possible to move beyond this statement.

Most of the evidence suggests that children build their early utterances in one of two ways. They either have a formula based on combining a particular word, in a fixed position, with a group or groups of other words (e.g. *more* + X where X can refer to objects, actions, or events), or they have rules for combining semantic categories of words (e.g. agent + action). Both methods are used by most children, although there is a wide range of individual differences in the extent to which a child uses one or the other method (Lieven, 1980). As Maratsos and Chalkley (1980) point out, both strategies represent knowledge that a child has to have about lan-guage. Categorical information and information about "what goes with what" are equally essential in putting words together in sentences. What is interesting is where such approaches might derive from and how they develop into later language skills.

The last ten years have shown a gradual shift from analysing children's utterances using broad semantic categories such as "agent" and "action" to hypothesising much narrower categories based on the child's experience and cognitive understanding. Thus Braine (1976) demonstrates that chil-dren can be working with what he calls "low-scope formulae" in order to generate utterances with systematic word order (e.g. *article of clothing* + *on/off*). These formulae can be productive in the sense that the child can generate utterances that s/he has never heard or said before. It is easy, in general terms at least, to see where such formulae might come from. The child has learnt the individual words, can start to work out the linguistic environment in which they occur (e.g. words for articles of clothing occur often with *on* or *off*), and is cognitively capable of identifying the similarity of situations in which articles of clothing come on or off. For Braine the word order itself comes from the ordering of adult speech (e.g. *take your coat off* giving *coat off* vs. *take off your coat* giving *off coat*). This has not been looked into in great detail, however, and it might be necessary to postulate a strong instinct for ordering in the child which will lead to the attempt to order words and morphemes even when there is no clear order in the adult speech.

It is important and interesting to note that what children do with their early utterances can tell us something about how they think about and categorise the world around them. Thus Deutsch's (1984) example of the expression of possession in the speech of Adam (Brown, 1973) shows that Adam does not treat possession as the unitary category that it is, linguistically speaking, in English. Instead he distinguishes between alienable and inalienable possession, using his own name in utterances of the first type and *me* in utterances of the second. Of course it is not necessary to suppose that Adam thinks of it in these terms. It would almost certainly be more accurate to describe him as distinguishing between "laying claim" and "describing parts of," which are functional and interactional categories rather than pure semantic ones.

Another example of this is provided by Slobin (1981). He demonstrates that children find "highly transitive events" very salient in terms of what they try to express in language. Highly transitive events are those in which an actor performs a dynamic action upon some object (e.g. chopping, hitting, tearing). Languages all have an unmarked way of describing such an event—in English it is the simple, active, declarative sentence. Often this sentence structure will also be used to describe nontransitive events (e.g. in the sentences "*John is sleeping*" and "*Mary is reading*," *Mary* and *John* are still in first position subject despite the fact that these are nontransitive events). Slobin uses the pattern of children's over-extensions and under-extensions to show that children are sensitive to transitivity and use it to identify the canonical form of a transitive sentence (the unmarked form). Thus he reports a Russian-speaking child who only uses the accusative form with these transitive events rather than with all object words requiring an accusative in that language. An example that demonstrates the same thing comes from Schieffelin's (1981) study of children learning Kaluli (a language from Papua New Guinea). Kaluli is an ergative language, i.e. the agents of highly transitive events are marked. Thus in Kaluli *John is chopping wood* would have *John* marked with an ergative while in *John is sleeping on the bench*, *John* would not be marked. Children learning Kaluli never over-extend the ergative marker to sentences like this last one, despite the fact that in both cases *John* is the agent of the action. So, argues Slobin, children are not only *not* using the role of subject, they are *not* using the semantic category of agent either. He suggests that they are working with an event structure which they try to put into words. It seems clear from such work that children do not, initially, use syntactic categories nor, in many cases, pure semantic ones, but work with functional and/or event structure categories which have then to develop into more formal ones. In general terms it is possible to argue that these sorts of cognitions are available to the child prior to learning to talk; there is, however, a great deal of work to do to clarify this and to identify other frameworks that the child has available as s/he moves towards attempting to structure utterances. But although the child may, and indeed must, use preverbal cognition to break into language, there is no simple question of just grafting language onto preordained cognitive categories. It seems clear that the child comes to language with interests and predispositions as to what is salient, but there must be an interaction between this and whatever is already known or being learnt about language. I would expect the developing linguistic skills to be interacting with the child's cognitive categorisations of the world to change them, equally as much as preverbal cognitions are structuring the way that the child learns to talk.

Children continue to develop and reorganise language for many years. In doing so they make "errors" which allow us to see what their representation of language is (Bowerman, 1982; Karmiloff-Smith, 1981). Language learning consists of a movement away from a one-to-one mapping between form and meaning (Slobin, in press) and of an integration of initially separate systems. Schlesinger (1981) has shown one way in which categories, at first fully based in the child's cognitive and semantic system, can lose their meaning base and become fully syntactic. An example is the way that agents and topics become subsumed under the role of subject, which explains why the subject always retains some remnants of agenthood (see footnote 3 earlier). Slobin describes this process as the "bleaching out" of semantics into syntax.

This section has raised more questions than it has answered. It is clearly the case that language development does consist of quite radical reorganisations of the child's capacity to use language to represent; that is, in the child's rules and categories for producing and understanding language. Thus there is real, discontinuous change. And yet there are a number of suggestions about how such change could be based on prior cognitive development and on the functional aspects of interaction. In the last section of this chapter we look at the function of language for the child in a little more detail.

DISCOURSE, FUNCTION, AND AFFECT

The work that I have been discussing is concerned with individual utterances and how they are constructed. There are a good many criticisms of this kind of approach and, indeed, Ryan's (1974) article started from such criticisms. She argued that since utterances occur in conversation it is impossible to understand an utterance unless its context is analysed. Following on from this, the major criticism of all the approaches that have been discussed in the previous section, with the exception of the functional theories, is that they tend to suggest that language develops *sui generis* and thus to ignore the role of the social world in the development of language (Adlam, Henriques, Rose, Salfield, Venn, & Walkerdine, 1977; Urwin, 1984). They take the individual and her or his cognition as given, and then study language as if it had no connection with the social framework in which the child is developing or with the child's emotional world. This results in an inability to deal theoretically with the way in which the development of language affects the child's emotions and ways of thinking and in an inability to understand individual difference in any depth.

Taking the smaller problem first, let us look at where, specifically, pragmatics come into the story. First, children distinguish communicative functions before they distinguish semantic functions. Second, what an utterance is for, communicationally, must determine why children say what they do when they do. In other words, pragmatic considerations are crucial in accounting for the placing of particular utterances at particular points in the conversation. Pragmatic considerations may also be responsible for the very early ordering of words in some utterances according to the dimensions of "given" and "new" information, although we have seen that the evidence is weak on this. However, I do not think that pragmatic factors, in the sense of the child's communicative needs and intentions, can alone account for all aspects of the ways in which children's language develops. Children seem to be sensitive to structure and to semantics in ways that are relatively independent of communicative function, though this does not necessarily mean that language springs out of the mind fully formed. Previous sections of this chapter have shown, I hope, that children's language skills are built in part on prior skills, though it is also true that new skills do seem to come in, whether these be specific to language or more general cognitive skills. Children's language play, experimenting as it does with order, seems to indicate an interest in this for its own sake (Weir, 1962). Also, evidence from Karmiloff-Smith (1981) shows that children take a long time before they can manipulate sentence structure to achieve pragmatic ends such as topicalising, moving the focus of an utterance, and co-ordinating thematic structure across utterances.

The more comprehensive criticism of current studies of language learning, that they pay no attention to social and emotional factors, has, I think, more weight. My own work (Lieven, 1978, 1980, 1982) and that of Nelson (1973) suggests that aspects of the relationship between children and the adults who look after them may affect the ways in which children first start to work out language. I have argued that this is not only because the nature of the relationship may actually affect the kind of speech that a child hears and the ways in which adults respond, but also may be to do with the emotional relationships in which the child is involved. For instance a child who "needs" attention may use language in a very different way to a child whose parents are very "child-centred." Initially such differences may produce children who differ in their language learning strategies such as, for instance, the differences between "social-expressive" children and "referential" children or between "lexical" children and "categorical" children. I have suggested that these differences may have consequences for later development both in terms of what the child uses language for and how s/he copes with school (Lieven, 1984), but I also think that the range of differences in how children put together their early utterances will be constrained by the options that languages make available. However in the long term we would not expect, I believe, to see any great difference in the basic grammar that children use to manipulate speech. Differences which initially show up in what children say and how they say it will manifest themselves in other ways later in development. As well as telling us about how the child is learning language, they are symptoms of the ways in which the child's subjectivity is being formed—that is of the ways in which the child's sense of itself is created out of the social world in which s/he lives. This idea of language being the medium through which the child's subjectivity is being formed has been explored using two paradigms: discourse theory and psychoanalytic theory. The question that I am concerned with here is whether these approaches can be reconciled with the sort of psycholinguistic approaches discussed in the previous sections of this paper.

In learning to talk the child's subjectivity is created. Urwin (1984) traces this process from the ritualised and regularised actions of routines in which the child's communicative intentions are first formed. She argues that, as a result, these communicative intentions are socially created. Thus the child's understanding of its own self and others, of relationships and how to control them, is gained by being positioned in interaction with others. This approach derives from the idea that subjectivity consists of the positioning of the subject within discourse (Foucault, 1972) and it can provide an important and interesting approach to how the child's subjectivity might develop (Walkerdine, 1982). But, as Urwin argues, in the attempt to relate such ideas to the situations in which children learn to talk, a too-literal equation is made between the word "discourse," as used in studies of child language development, and the word as it is used by Foucault in the historical study of written documents. There is a great deal of both theoretical and empirical work to do before it is going to be possible to know how to relate these ideas. Of course this approach also suffers from the other criticism made of psycholinguistic studies, which is that they completely ignore the emotional significance of language learning. It is in relation to this that attempts have been made to use psychoanalytic theory to study language development.

Psychoanalytic theories of infancy emphasise the role of fantasy in helping the child to cope with pain and fear while also, during the second half of the first year, allowing the child to represent pleasurable feelings as well. Thus, in psychoanalytic theory, the child already has the capacity for internal representation before language is learnt but language learning is the fixing of these representations and their conventionalisation, and this involves loss as well as gain (Lacan, 1977). The loss consists of feelings and emotions becoming channelled in language while certain feelings (e.g. of omnipotence or destructive rage) become repressed. In Urwin's hands this approach illuminates a number of aspects of language development ignored by psycholinguists.

Urwin emphasises that language can be pleasurable to children, which we know from the amount that children play with and practice language (Weir, 1962; Kuczaj, 1983), but which is an idea rarely raised or considered. Language gives children a kind of control that they have not had before—the capacity to name objects also means, in psychoanalytic theory, the capacity to control them even when they are not present. Language also provides a means whereby children can control others more effectively. The idea that language gives pleasure to children might help to explain why children learn to talk. Some accounts of language development seem to suggest that effective communication is all that is needed to learn to talk—if this were the case one wonders why the child should bother. Urwin emphasises that the learning of language constitutes a radical break for the child but she does this in terms of the child's emotional world rather than in terms of linguistic or cognitive capacities. For instance, she points out that children's earliest utterances are often about rejection (*no*) and about reappearance and disappearance (*more, allgone*); both, according to psychoanalytic theories of infancy, are highly emotionally loaded. These are obviously interesting and important points, but it is not clear to me that they invalidate the study of language development as it has been presented in this chapter. There are two reasons for this. First, to quote Urwin (1984): ". . . as far as the entry into language and development in infancy is concerned, it is important to recognise that a psychoanalytic account cannot be immediately translated into empirical predictions, and possibly not even into directly observable phenomena (p. 279)." There is no one-to-one correspondence between observable behaviour and a psychic process. The same behaviour may have quite different psychic origins which can only be understood by detailed study of the particular individual. It seems to me, however, that the process of language learning is more universal than this, and that there are remarkable consistencies which have been discovered. This is not to deny individual difference nor the importance of social and emotional factors, but rather to argue for some separation between these various aspects of language learning.

These ideas of discourse theory and of psychoanalysis may help us to refine our understanding of how children learn to talk and how they develop their language skills; or, possibly, we will discover that we are talking about two different levels of analysis and that the one does not preclude the other. The approaches are concerned with slightly different issues—the one with how a child builds up a language and the other with what that language is used for. This will be an unpopular solution in some quarters, since it allows for partial independence in the study of social, cognitive, and linguistic aspects of development. And, despite the fact that language development is built on previous developments at every stage and is intertwined with cognitive, social, and emotional development in each child, it may be that, for the child as well as the researcher, language can come to be partially separated out from these other aspects of development and enjoyed for its own sake.

ACKNOWLEDGEMENTS

I would like to thank the editors of this book and the following people for their helpful comments on the first draft of this paper: Karen Clarke, John Churcher, Pat Devine, Alison Frankenberg, Margaret Johnston, Ivan Leudar, Peter Lloyd, and Cathy Urwin. All opinions and mistakes remain my own.

REFERENCES

Adlam, D., Henriques, J., Rose, N., Salfield, A., Venn, C., & Walkerdine, V. (1977) Psychology, ideology, and the human subject. *Ideology and Consciousness*, *1*, 5–56.

Atkinson, M. (1980) *Explanations in the Study of Child Language Development*. London: Cambridge University Press.

Barratt, M. (1978) Lexical development and over-extensions in child language. *Journal of Child Language*, *5*, 205–219.

Bates, E., Camaioni, L., & Volterra, V. (1975) The acquisition of performatives prior to speech. *Merrill Palmer Quarterly*, *21*, 205–224.

Bates, E. & MacWhinney, B. (1979) A functionalist approach to the acquisition of grammar. In E. Ochs & B. Schieffelin (Eds.), *Developmental Pragmatics*. New York: Academic Press.

Borer, H. & Wexler, K. (1984) *The maturation of syntax*. Paper presented at Conference on Parameter-Setting, University of Massachusetts, Amhurst.

Bowerman, M. (1982) Reorganisational processes in lexical and syntactic development. In E. Wanner & L. Gleitman (Eds.), *Language Acquisition: The State of the Art*. London: Cambridge University Press.

Bresnan, J. (1978) A realistic transformational grammar. In J. Bresnan & G. A. Miller (Eds.), *Linguistic Theory and Psychological Reality*. Cambridge, Mass.: MIT Press.

Braine, M. (1976) Children's first word combinations. *Monographs of the Society for Research in Child Development*, *41*, Serial No. 164.

Brown, R. (1973) *A First Language: The Early Stages*. Cambridge; Mass.: Harvard University Press.

Bruner, J. S. (1975a) From communication to language. *Cognition*, *3*, 255–287.

Bruner, J. S. (1975b) The ontogenesis of speech acts. *Journal of Child Language*, *2*, 1–19.

Carter, A. (1978) The development of systematic vocalisations prior to words: A case study. In N. Waterson & C. Snow (Eds.), *The Development of Communication*. New York: Wiley.

Chomsky, N. (1959) A review of B. F. Skinner's "Verbal Behaviour." *Language*, *35*, 26–58.

Clark, R. (1977) What's the use of imitation? *Journal of Child Language*, *4*, 341–358.

Deutsch, W. (1984) Language control processes in development. In H. Bauma & D. G. Bouwhuis, *Attention and Performance X*. Hillsdale, New Jersey: Lawrence Erlbaum Associates Inc.

De Villiers, J. G. & De Villiers, P. A. (in press) The acquisition of English. In D. I. Slobin (Ed.), *The Crosslinguistic Study of Language Acquisition*. Hillsdale, New Jersey: Lawrence Erlbaum Associates Inc.

Dore, J., Franklin, M., Miller, R., & Ramer, A. (1976) Transitional phenomena in early language acquisition. *Journal of Child Language*, *3*, 13–28.

Ferguson, C. (1977) Baby talk as a simplified register. In C. Snow & C. Ferguson (Eds.), *Talking to Children*. London: Cambridge University Press.

Fillmore, C. (1968) The case for case. In E. Bach & R. J. Harms (Eds.), *Universals in Linguistic Theory*. New York: Holt, Rinehart & Winston.

Foucault, M. (1972) *The Archaeology of Knowledge*. London: Tavistock.

Gazdar, G. (1982) Phrase structure grammar. In G. K. Pullum & R. Jacobson, (Eds.), *The Nature of Syntactic Representation*. Dordrecht: Reidel.

Gentner, D. (1983) Why nouns are learned before words: Linguistic relativity vs. natural partitioning. In S. Kuczaj (Ed.), *Language Development: Language, Thought, and Culture*. Hillsdale, New Jersey: Lawrence Erlbaum Associates Inc.

Givón, T. (1979) *On Understanding Grammar*. New York: Academic Press.

Gleitman, L. (1981) Maturational determinants of language growth. *Cognition*, *10*, 103–114.

Greenfield, P. M. & Smith, J. H. (1976) *The Structure of Communication in Early Language Development*. New York: Academic Press.

Halliday, M. (1967) Notes on transitivity and theme in English, part 2. *Journal of Linguistics*, *3*, 177–274.

Halliday, M. (1975) *Learning How to Mean*. London: Edward Arnold.

Hickman, M. (Ed.) (in press) *Social and Functional Approaches to Language and Thought*. New York: Academic Press.

Howe, C. (1976) The meaning of two-word utterances in the speech of young children. *Journal of Child Language*, *3*, 29–47.

Karmiloff-Smith, A. (1981) The grammatical marking of thematic structure in the development of language production. In W. Deutsch (Ed.), *The Child's Construction of Language*. New York: Academic Press.

Keenan, E. L. (1980) Passive is phrasal (not sentential or lexical). In T. Hoekstra, H. v. d. Hulst & M. Moorgat (Eds.), *Lexical Grammar*. Dordrecht: Foris.

Kuczaj, S. (1983) *Crib Speech and Language Play*. New York: Springer-Verlag.

Lacan, J. (1977) *Ecrits: A Selection*. London: Tavistock.

Lieberman, P. (1972) *Speech Acoustics and Perception*. New York: Bobbs Merril.

Lieven, E. V. M. (1978) Turn-taking and pragmatics. In N. Waterson & C. Snow (Eds.), *The Development of Communication*. London: Wiley.

Lieven, E. V. M. (1980) Different routes to multiple-word combinations. *Papers and Reports on Child Language Development*, *19*, 34–44.

Lieven, E. V. M. (1982) Context, process, and progress in young children's speech. In M. Beveridge (Ed.), *Children Thinking Through Language*. London: Edward Arnold.

Lieven, E. V. M. (1984) Interactional style and children's language learning. *Topics in Language Disorders*, *4*, 15–23.

McShane, J. (1980) *Learning to Talk*. London: Cambridge University Press.

Maratsos, M. & Chalkley, M. (1980) The internal language of children's syntax: The ontogenesis and representation of syntactic categories. In K. Nelson (Ed.), *Children's Language, Vol. 2*. New York: Gardner.

Mounoud, P. (1982) Revolutionary periods in early development. In T. Bower (Ed.), *Regressions in Mental Development*. Hillsdale, New Jersey: Lawrence Erlbaum Associates Inc.

Nelson, K. (1973) Structure and strategy in learning to talk. *Monographs of the Society for Research in Child Development*, *38*, *Serial 149*.

Nelson, K. & Gruendal, J. (1979) At morning, it's lunchtime: A scriptal view of children's dialogues. *Discourse Processes*, *2*, 73–94.

Peters, A. (1980) The units of language acquisition. *Working Papers in Linguistics*, *12*. Dept. of Linguistics, University of Hawaii at Manoa.

Piaget, J. (1952) *The Origin of Intelligence in the Child*. London: Routledge & Kegan Paul.

Piaget, J. (1973) *The Child's Construction of Reality*. London: Paladin.

Randall, J. (1985) *Negative evidence from positive*. Paper presented at 1984 Child Language Seminar, Reading, England.

Ryan, J. (1974) Early language development. In M. P. M. Richards (Ed.), *The Integration of a Child into a Social World*. London: Cambridge University Press.

Schieffelin, B. (1981) A developmental study of pragmatic appropriateness of word order and case marking in Kaluli. In W. Deutsch (Ed.), *The Child's Construction of Language*. New York: Academic Press.

Schlesinger, I. (1981) Semantic assimilation in the development of relational categories. In W. Deutsch (Ed.), *The Child's Construction of Language*. London: Academic Press.

Sinha, C. & Paprotté, W. (in press) Functionalism, semiotics, and language acquisition. In M. Hickman (Ed.), *Social and Functional Approaches to Language and Thought*. New York: Academic Press.

Slobin, D. I. (1973) Cognitive prerequisites for the development of grammar. In C. A. Ferguson & D. I. Slobin (Eds.), *Studies of Child Language Development*. New York: Holt, Rinehart, & Winston.

Slobin, D. I. (1981) The origin of grammatical coding of events. In W. Deutsch (Ed.), *The Child's Construction of Language*. London: Academic Press.

Slobin, D. I. (in press) Crosslinguistic evidence for the language-making capacity. In D. I. Slobin (Ed.), *The Crosslinguistic Study of Language Acquisition*. Hillsdale, New Jersey: Lawrence Erlbaum Associates Inc.

Urwin, C. (1984) Power relations and the emergence of the subject. In J. Henriques, W. Holloway, C. Urwin, C. Venn, & V. Walkerdine (Eds.), *Changing the Subject*. London: Methuen.

Walkerdine, V. (1982) From context to text: A psychosemiotic approach to abstract thought. In M. Beveridge (Ed.), *Children Thinking Through Language*. London: Edward Arnold.

Weir, R. (1962) *Language in the Crib*. The Hague: Mouton.

Wexler, K. (1982) A principle theory for language acquisition. In E. Wanner & L. Gleitman (Eds.), *Language Acquisition: The State of the Art*. London: Cambridge University Press.

Wexler, K. & Cullicover, P. (1980) *Formal Principles of Language Acquisition*. Cambridge, Mass.: MIT Press.

9 Co-ordinating Words and Syntax in Speech Plans

J. Kathryn Bock
Michigan State University, East Lansing, Michigan, U.S.A.

INTRODUCTION

What we say and how we say it depends in some important way on what and how we think, as well as on how, where, and why we communicate. But because language use cannot wholly be explained by features of thought and the communicative environment, there are other issues to be addressed by a linguistic performance theory. In particular, language requires the recruiting of special elements and structures, including the retrieval of words, the generation of syntactic frameworks, and the integration of the two into complete utterances. The processes that enter into this have their own special demands, over and above the exigencies of thought and communication. The goal of this chapter is to consider what these demands might be, and what kind of theory provides the best account of them.

The premise of the argument is that there are variations in the way language is used that may better be explained in terms of the specific computational problems that have to be solved by the sentence production system than in terms of general communication factors. It is clear that these information-handling problems are solved with a great deal of reliability: The speech that people produce, even spontaneously, is by and large remarkably well formed (Deese, 1984). Within this uniformity, however, there is nonetheless variability; variability revealed in errors, in dysfluencies, and in utterances that occur in one form when they might easily have occurred in another.

Variations such as these, particularly the errors and dysfluencies that occur in everyday speech, have provided a rich observational base for the

337

development of models of the language processing system (Boomer, 1965; Boomer & Laver, 1968; Dell & Reich, 1981; Fay & Cutler, 1977; Fromkin, 1971, 1973b; Garrett, 1975, 1980; Goldman-Eisler, 1968; MacKay, 1970; Maclay & Osgood, 1959; Meringer & Meyer, 1895; Nooteboom, 1973; Stemberger, 1985). Recently, methods have been developed for the controlled, systematic exploration of the cognitive or information-processing correlates of errors and other types of language variation (Baars, Motley, & MacKay, 1975; Bock, 1986, in press; Dell, 1986; Meyer & Gordon, 1985). Together, these observational and experimental studies suggest that variations in linguistic form, deviant or otherwise, can often be traced to perturbations in the flow of information within the language production system itself. These in turn seem to arise from the way the system retrieves, represents, and operates on linguistic information, and not exclusively from features of the speaker's thoughts or communicative goals.

This position is in many respects similar to one taken by Meringer and Meyer (1895) and disputed by Freud (1920). Whereas Meringer and Meyer explained speech errors in terms of a view that emphasised differences in valence, transient levels of activation, and competition among linguistic elements, Freud (1920) argued in opposition "that the result of the slip may perhaps have a right to be regarded in itself as a valid mental process following out its own purpose, and as an expression having content and meaning (p. 39)." Although there is evidence for ideational and motivational effects in some speech errors (Harley, 1984; Motley, 1980), a great many appear to be governed by intrinsic linguistic relationships (including most of the errors adduced by Freud; Ellis, 1980). Even errors that can be traced directly to momentary aberrations in the speaker's thought or attention exhibit strong linguistic conditioning. For example, Harley (1984) has shown that when an unintended word intrudes in an utterance from the speaker's "cognitive environment," there is very commonly a phonological relationship between the intended and the intruding word (as when someone who was packing books in boxes said "at least they'll be good for boxes," when "books" was intended).

To understand language production fully, then, we must be able to relate it not only to the speaker's communicative intentions, but to the endogenous states and operations of a system that manipulates and organises the elements of language. These states and operations may adjust in systematic ways to changes in the ease of retrieving and organising linguistic elements, to lingering effects of prior processing, and to random noise. As a result, the production system may make a contribution to the formulation of speech that is independent of the propositional content or structure of speakers' intended messages.

This chapter will explore the kinds of information processing problems that the language production system confronts and how it seems to cope with or adapt to them. It follows other work which suggests that variations in the forms of utterances commonly reflect variations in the processing of linguistic information (Bock, 1982; Dell, 1986; Garrett, 1975, 1980; MacKay, 1982; Stemberger, 1985). A major purpose of this exploration is to bring together studies of errors with studies of normal structural variation to provide a firmer rationale for a computational approach to sentence production.

The first section of the chapter lays out the central information processing problem, the need to transform a multidimensional conceptual structure into a structure that is fundamentally constrained by the single dimension of time. Following Lashley (1951), this central problem is analysed in terms of three basic issues: (1) the retrieval or preparation of lexical elements; (2) the formulation of a syntactic plan; and (3) the co-ordination of the lexical elements with the syntactic plan. These three components of the production problem serve as the framework for reviewing evidence, both observational and experimental, about the lexical and syntactic components of speech planning. Several alternative proposals about sentence production are then contrasted in light of this evidence. The available evidence appears to favour a syntactic formulation system with two interacting processing levels, each of which is influenced by probabilistic variations in the accessibility of information. A model incorporating these features is sketched along with some of its predictions about errors and normal, error-free production. The final section considers the role of such a system in human communication.

WHAT DOES THE SENTENCE PRODUCTION SYSTEM HAVE TO DO?

The basic problem of language production is to transform the many dimensions of a thought into a code that is fundamentally constrained by the single dimension of time. An idea that is present to the mind may seem *simultaneously* to embody actions, role relations, modalities, locations, and myriad other features. For example, people commonly have the experience of apprehending all the steps of an argument without verbally proceeding through them, or visualising a rich mental image of an event to be recounted. However, the features of these thoughts cannot be communicated all at once. Instead, the speaker must *sequentially* produce elements whose identity and arrangement will evoke an idea with the same critical features in the mind of the hearer.

To achieve this, the production system must do two interrelated things. First, for a unitary conceptual structure to be instantiated in a linear string, there must be a code that relates or links each element in the string to the representations of other elements. Second, there must be a systematic way of accessing or retrieving the stored representations of the linguistic elements that will comprise the utterance. Without such a retrieval plan, access would be haphazard and unreliable; with one, the process can be regulated and, if used repeatedly, routinised or automatised. These two demands need not be fulfilled independently, since the relational code can spell out a scheme that is used to guide retrieval.

Considerations such as these lead to the general view of syntax that underlies the processing arguments to be presented. The syntax of a language can be regarded as the system that enables the recoding of a multidimensional conceptual structure into a linear array by providing relational principles that define permissible links among morphemes or lexical elements, independent of their identities, and a scheme for retrieving the appropriate linguistic components from memory to form a temporal sequence.

A reflection of these fundamental demands on syntax can be found in the connection between language typology and mnemonic systems. Languages appear to rely on either of two basic types of relational linking systems, inflectional or configurational. Those languages that employ rich inflectional systems to convey relationships among constituents generally do so by marking lexical elements. The relative order in which the elements occur is not critical: What matters is their inflection. For example, most Slavic languages inflect nouns in sentences to indicate their relationship to the verb, so that the subject, direct object, and various oblique objects (genitive, dative) of the verb are indicated by special affixes. Their location with respect to the verb is largely irrelevant to conveying these relationships, so their order is relatively free.

An alternative to such inflectional systems is the use of hierarchical organisation, as found in configurational languages. In such systems, constituents are related to one another through clustering, embedding, and co-ordinating principles. These hierarchical arrangements serve at least two functions: (1) they group items into larger chunks of material; and (2) they specify superordinate, subordinate, and co-ordinate links that relate the items to one another. Thus, if the lexical elements in a sequence fall into hierarchically organised groups, their relationships to one another can be recovered from their location in the hierarchy. English provides a familiar example of such a language.

Inflectional and configurational systems are not mutually exclusive, of course. Features of both appear to some degree in most languages, so inflectional languages have hierarchical organisation (though their structures tend to be flatter than those of configurational languages) and configurational languages occasionally use inflection to mark grammatical roles (as in the marking of pronouns in English). In general, however, one or the other predominates.

These syntactic systems bear interesting similarities to the kinds of mnemonic systems that serve as effective aids in the recall of sequential material. One class of mnemonic systems involves the use of distinctive markers that relate the to-be-remembered material to a known coding scheme. For example, to use the peg-word system, one first learns the coding scheme (e.g., a rhyme such as "one is a bun, two is a shoe, three is a tree," etc.). To memorise a random list of words, each successive word in the list is "pegged" to the corresponding element in the code (for example, by forming an image which symbolises the first word interacting with a bun). A similar principle is involved in the use of the number-consonant alphabet (Lindsay & Norman, 1977, pp. 363–364) and the method of loci (Yates, 1966).

A second type of effective system involves the creation of hierarchical relationships among items that must be remembered sequentially. For example, Ericsson, Chase, and Faloon (1980) report the case of an undergraduate who successfully increased his digit recall span from fewer than 10 digits to 80 digits by recoding the numbers into a hierarchy. He first chunked the numbers into meaningful units (foot race times, ages, or dates), and eventually developed a scheme for organising these chunks into a hierarchy which he could then retrace or reconstruct during retrieval. Other examples of the effectiveness of hierarchical retrieval structures are reported by Bower, Clark, Lesgold, and Winzenz (1969) and Seamon and Chumbley (1977).

The similarity to language typology is intriguing, suggesting a link between mnemonic systems and syntactic systems that may be traced to their retrieval functions. However, the analogy is limited in its ability to illuminate the detailed intricacies of language structure. Nor can it be taken as comfort for the view that syntactic systems are built from more general cognitive competences (since mnemonic systems might well work as they do because of their resemblance to syntactic principles that are somehow accessible to language users). Still, the analogy does lend credence to the argument that syntactic systems are designed to help speakers and hearers cope with the difficult problems of retrieving linguistic material from memory and relating rapidly-presented sequences of transient items to more stable knowledge structures.

This view of syntax yields three basic representation and processing problems. The first has to do with the nature and role of the lexical elements. Languages are compositional, meaning that utterances are constructed from a large but finite set of basic elements, used in different arrangements to convey different underlying propositions. These elements have both characteristic meanings and characteristic sounds, either of which might have a critical effect on the way an utterance is assembled. The first question, then, has to do with the nature of lexical representations as they enter into the production process.

The second problem arises from the fact that these elements must be strung out in time, but their relationships to one another have to be recoverable for the underlying thought to be reconstructed by a listener. This requires a relational ordering scheme. We need to know the nature of the scheme, and how it is created.

The final and, perhaps, most fundamental problem is a consequence of the logical independence of the relational scheme from the elements it contains. Because the same elements appear in an unlimited number of different orders, often with very different meanings, the elements cannot be an integral part of the relational ordering scheme itself. The production system must therefore include a co-ordination process in which lexical elements are assigned to positions in the structure responsible for serial order. At bottom, the central issue addressed by theories of sentence production concerns the nature of this process. This is the co-ordination problem.

LASHLEY'S ANALYSIS OF THE CO-ORDINATION PROBLEM

Viewed very broadly, the requirement that items be ordered in some way is a common feature of many tasks, not only one of speech production. The similarities among these ordering problems led Lashley (1951) to an insightful analysis of the co-ordination problem, under the heading of "the problem of temporal integration (p. 114)." Lashley pointed out that the order of elements within virtually all skilled movements must be determined by something other than direct associative connections. He inferred the necessity of such independent ordering mechanisms from a number of observations. For example, he argued that the orders of sounds in words cannot wholly be determined by direct associative relations among the sounds themselves, since the same sounds can occur in different orders creating different words. He applied a similar argument to words within sentences, noting the possibility of such utterances as "The millwright on my right thinks it right that some conventional rite should symbolize the right of every man to write as he pleases (p. 116)." The arrangement of words cannot be explained by direct associations between the word *right* (or the sound sequence /rayt/) and other words, since the various positions that /rayt/ assumes has to do with the "meanings" of the positions themselves (e.g., noun, adjective, verb) as given by a structure that is independent of the specific words used.

Not all of Lashley's arguments drew on language. He also claimed that the different gaits of horses involve basically the same patterns of muscle movements in individual legs; the gait itself arises as a result of a mechanism over and above direct physiological connections among the centres responsible for the movements of the legs. Likewise for finger movements in piano-playing: The order in which they occur is determined by the composition, not associations between individual movements.

It is clear that Lashley did not think that serial order arose from relations among the movements themselves, as the dominant associative theories of the era implied. It is less often noted that he was equally opposed to the theory that the order arose directly from the thoughts that underlie speech. He subscribed to the views of Pick (1913) and the Würzburgers (see Humphrey, 1963), according to which the elements of thought are unordered and largely cotemporal. As evidence, he cited (Lashley, 1951) "the readiness with which the form of expression of an idea can be changed, [and] the facility with which different word orders may be utilized to express the same thought (p. 118)."

As an alternative to direct associations among movements or an inherent order of thought, Lashley proposed that there is an independent ordering mechanism that determines relationships among the elements of a sequence. He found evidence for such independent organisational structures in typing errors. Errors such as *iil* or *lokk* (where *ill* and *look* were intended) suggested to him the existence of an abstract "doubling schema" operating on the wrong elements. In addition, he cited the importation of syntactic forms from one's native language into a new language and the facility with which children acquire pig Latin as evidence that syntax arises from a separate, abstract pattern imposed upon individual acts.

These kinds of considerations led Lashley to define the temporal integration problem as originating from "the existence of generalized schemata of action which determine the sequence of specific acts, acts which in themselves or their associations seem to have no temporal valence (p. 122)." To solve the problem requires an account of the determining tendency or idea that motivates and constrains the act. But beyond this, Lashley argued, there must be an explanation of two other things: (1) the activation of the expressive elements; and (2) the ordering schema or abstract pattern that is imposed on those elements. These are, of course, the components of the co-ordination problem identified in the preceding section. The next section takes up both of them in the context of research on sentence production.

THE COMPONENTS OF THE CO-ORDINATION
PROBLEM

Because the co-ordination problem can arise at many points in the production process, including the ordering of sounds in words or morphemes, words in phrases, phrases in clauses, clauses in sentences, sentences in paragraphs, and so on, it is important to be clear about the level that is at issue. If there are representations of lexical and syntactic information that are to some degree independent, as Lashley argued, there must be some point in the creation of an utterance at which they are integrated. The discussion will assume that there is at least one level of processing at which lexical representations—semantic or phonological representations of words or morphemes—are co-ordinated with syntactic units such as phrases or clauses. What has to be determined is the nature of the lexical representations that are co-ordinated with syntactic structures, the nature of the syntactic units with which they are co-ordinated, and the processes responsible for their co-ordination. We will take up the issue of lexical representation and retrieval first.

Preparing the Units of Expression: Lexical
Representation and Retrieval

There is ample evidence that lexical information is in some way prepared for use before it appears in fully-fledged form in spoken sentences. Three rich sources of information about the nature of these preparatory processes and the representations they work on have received attention. The first type of evidence comes from speakers' sometimes imperfect awareness of the words that they intend to employ in an utterance, as found in tip-of-the-tongue states. The second involves the contaminations of overt speech that suggest activation or excitation of words other than those intended. These contaminations include word substitutions and blends. The last source of information encompasses experimental studies that have attempted to study the nature of lexical retrieval and its time course under more controlled conditions. Each of these will be considered in turn.

Tip-of-the-Tongue States

The frustrating inability to bring a word to mind was vividly described by William James in 1890:

> Suppose we try to recall a forgotten name. The state of our consciousness is
> peculiar. There is a gap therein; but no mere gap. It is a gap that is intensely
> active. A sort of wraith of the name is in it, beckoning us in a given direction,
> making us at moments tingle with the sense of our closeness, and then letting

us sink back without the longed-for term. If wrong names are proposed to us, this singularly definite gap acts immediately so as to negate them. They do not fit into its mould. And the gap of one word does not feel like the gap of another, all empty of content as both might seem necessarily to be when described as gaps . . . The rhythm of a lost word may be there without a sound to clothe it; or the evanescent sense of something which is the initial vowel or consonant may mock us fitfully, without growing more distinct (pp. 251–252).

James' intuitions about the nature of such gaps have been confirmed repeatedly. People in tip-of-the-tongue states give surprisingly accurate estimates of the number of syllables, the stress patterns, and the initial and final sounds of the words they are seeking (Brown & McNeill, 1966; Rubin, 1975; Woodworth, 1938; Yarmey, 1973). These characteristics are often apparent in the incorrect recalls made when seeking a particular word. For example, Woodworth (1938, p. 37) lists the names Rogers, Walliston, Stevens, Picquard, Casenaugh, and Hirschberg as the first ones recalled when seeking the names Richards, Warburton, Stowell, Lapicque, Ranelagh, and Fishberg, respectively.

We will see below that these features of words—numbers of syllables, stress patterns, and initial and final sounds—also play a prominent role in word substitutions, blends, and misorderings. The pervasiveness of their influence strongly suggests that the speech planning process includes the readying of a set of abstract lexical items that specify the word's rhythmic pattern (stress and number of syllables) and, minimally, the initiations and terminations of words. These could help in guiding the construction of phrases, providing the basic information needed to create a rhythmic plan for larger units and to program word-to-word transitions (Rubin, 1975). They may also serve to control the phonetic elaboration of the items in the sentence.

Errors of Lexical Selection

The errors of lexical selection that have received the most detailed analysis are substitution and blending. Substitutions involve the use of a word other than the one intended, and include both semantically related substitutions (e.g. "he rode his bike to school tomorrow" where *yesterday* was intended; Garrett, 1980) and phonologically related substitutions (e.g. "He's the kind of soldier a man looks up to and wants to emanate" where *emulate* was intended). Both types of substitutions occur much more often for open- than for closed-class words (Fay & Cutler, 1977; Stemberger, 1984). One way to interpret this difference is that the lexical selection processes responsible for substitutions operate only on open-class words, although the same pattern would appear if the very high frequency of closed-class words made them invulnerable to substitution errors (Stemberger, 1984).

Semantic substitutions have one obvious feature: The substituted word tends to be similar in meaning to the intended word. There is, however, some evidence for phonological contamination. Dell and Reich (1981) noted a better-than-chance occurrence of phonological relationships between the substituted and target words in semantically related substitutions. At the same time, it appears from Dell and Reich's graph of these data that the effects of phonological similarity are not the same for semantic substitutions as for nonsemantic substitutions. Specifically, the effects of sound similarity at word-initial positions seem to be substantially smaller for semantic substitutions, suggesting that the phonological effects arise somewhat differently.

Phonologically related substitutions, often called malapropisms, reveal very strong similarities between the target word and the word actually used: In general they have the same number of syllables, the same stress patterns, the same initial sounds, and the same form-class categorisation (Fay & Cutler, 1977). There is such a striking convergence between malapropisms and the erroneous words retrieved during tip-of-the-tongue states that they almost certainly arise in the same way—the phonological form of a known word eludes the speaker, and what comes to mind instead—if anything does—is a word from the same form class with the same basic phonological structure.

In the same way that subtle phonological relations appear in semantic substitutions, subtle semantic effects appear in phonological substitutions. Kelly (1986) has found that the substitutions in the Fay and Cutler corpus are significantly more imageable or concrete than the intended words. Stemberger (1983) suggests that substitutions may be more likely to occur when there is both a *semantic* relationship between the substituted word and a word elsewhere in an utterance and a *phonological* relationship between the substituted word and the intended word (as in "mandatory requirement policy," where *retirement* was intended). There is rarely a clear phonological relationship between the substituted word and the other words in the same sentence (Stemberger, personal communication). It appears that when the words for an utterance are retrieved, it is primarily their semantic characteristics that promote lexical selection errors, though such errors can be helped along by phonological similarity. Phonological specification takes place too late to bias the lexical selection process.

Blends involve the merging or blending of two words to produce examples such as "momentaneous" (instantaneous/momentary), "splisters" (splinters/blisters), and "slickery" (slick/slippery) (Fromkin, 1973b). There is often a strong semantic relationship (Garrett, 1980) as well as a phonological relationship (Dell & Reich, 1981). Like phonological substitutions, the phonological similarities in blends seem to be greater in the earlier parts of words (Dell & Reich, 1981). Blends appear to originate in the simultaneous retrieval of two words that are equally appropriate to the occasion, aided by phonological similarity, although the reasons for blending are unclear. MacKay (1973) and Stemberger (1985) have offered the interesting suggestion that *both* words are inserted into the single available syntactic slot, leaving the phonological system to come up with an appropriate form.

All types of selection errors are constrained by certain syntactic factors. Thus, substitutions and blends obey a strict grammatical category constraint, with the errors observing the form class specifications on the words for the intended utterances. The syntactic constraints could arise in either or both of two ways: the priming processes may be under the control of syntactic representations, or selections from the activated set may be carried out under the control of processes that observe syntactic form class and structural constraints. We will return to this question later.

To summarise, there seem to be at least two separable but not fully independent sets of processes involved in word-level errors. There are semantic selection processes that sometimes go awry, in which case an unintended but semantically related word or word blend may appear in speech. There are also phonological retrieval or elaboration processes that occasionally yield phonological substitutions, or nothing at all, as in tip-of-the-tongue states. Phonological relationships pervade all categories of errors, including semantic substitutions and blends, although the relationships are clearest for phonological substitutions. In the same way, there may be subtle semantic effects on phonologically-related errors. Finally, there is a nearly inviolable identity of syntactic form class between the erroneous and intended words.

Experimental Studies of Lexical Retrieval in Sentence Production

Relatively few experimental or quasi-experimental studies have been done on the retrieval of words during the production of complete utterances. Those investigators who have taken this approach have often been concerned with the predictability of words in their context of occurrence, motivated by theories of language use that emphasised the role of sequential associations in determining the serial order of words (e.g., Lounsbury, 1954) and interest in the determinants of hesitations in spontaneous speech (e.g., Boomer, 1965; Goldman-Eisler, 1968; Maclay & Osgood, 1959). The general finding has been that the words following hesitation points in speech tend to be less predictable than words in fluent speech (Goldman-Eisler, 1958a, 1958b; Maclay & Osgood, 1959; Tannenbaum, Williams, &

Hillier, 1965). Predictable words also tend to be produced more rapidly (Daneman & Green, 1986).

Unfortunately for the understanding of lexical retrieval processes, such predictability measures by themselves reveal little about the role of basic semantic or phonological factors. What they suggest is that Marbe's law (Thumb & Marbe, 1901) describes the production of words in sentences as well as in free association tasks: The more frequent a particular response (across subjects), the faster that response will be given (by an individual). An unpredictable word will thus be produced more slowly or more hesitantly than a predictable word. This descriptive relationship is interesting, but cannot substitute for an explanation of the cognitive processes responsible for the selection of words during speech.

Other experiments have looked at lexicalisation processes in the context of object naming. Although it is conceivable that the processes of lexical retrieval used in naming are completely different from those used in producing words in a syntactic context, they may well have interesting similarities. One conclusion from experiments that have considered the role of semantic and phonological processes is that naming involves at least an object identification or categorisation stage, and a stage at which the phonological form of the word is retrieved (Balota & Chumbley, 1985; Clark & Clark, 1977; Huttenlocher & Kubicek, 1983; McCauley, Parmelee, Sperber, & Carr, 1980; Oldfield & Wingfield, 1964, 1965; Wingfield, 1968). Semantic variables such as category relationships between pictures appear to influence the identification/categorisation process, while variables such as word frequency, age of acquisition, and name agreement seem to influence phonological retrieval.

These two hypothesised stages of the naming process correspond in a general way to the semantic and phonological processes hypothesised to underlie lexical errors in spontaneous speech. The same variables might therefore be expected to influence phonological substitution errors and phonological retrieval in naming tasks, while a different set of variables should influence semantic substitution errors and categorisation in naming tasks. Although there is very little research that has examined effects of similar variables across the two different areas, a preliminary and suggestive convergence has been found for frequency. Frequency has reliable effects on naming (Lachman, 1973; Lachman, Shaffer, & Hennrikus, 1974; Oldfield & Wingfield, 1965), and a greater impact on phonological substitutions than on semantic substitutions (Kelly, 1986). It remains to be shown whether the influence of variables such as concreteness is greater for semantic than for phonological substitutions, as it should be if these errors do indeed arise at different levels of the lexical preparation process, levels responsible for semantic categorisation and phonological retrieval.

Some Major Features of Lexical Preparation:
A Summary

The regular constellations of results appearing across these observational and experimental investigations suggest a number of fundamental characteristics of lexical retrieval and preparation. First, there appear to be semantic processes that prime words to convey meanings consistent with the speaker's intended message. These processes prepare sets of content words from appropriate semantic and syntactic form class categories. Occasionally an unintended word from the same category will replace the intended word, or two words from the same category will be selected in tandem and blended. Second, there are phonological retrieval or elaboration processes that prime the phonological forms of the semantically specified words. Just as semantic priming sometimes results in the selection of an unintended word from the same semantic category, phonological priming sometimes results in the selection of an unintended word from the same phonological "category." Phonological retrieval processes seem to be more heavily influenced by word frequency than are semantic retrieval processes, both when they operate correctly (Huttenlocher & Kubicek, 1983) and when they produce errors (Kelly, 1986).

The evidence from speech errors suggests that semantic and phonological preparation cannot be completely independent stages, since there are subtle but reliable phonological effects on "semantic" errors, and subtle but reliable semantic effects on "phonological" errors. However, the fact that semantic effects on phonological errors are weak in comparison to the relationships found in semantic errors, and that the phonological effects on semantic errors are weak in comparison to the relationships found in phonological errors, suggests that the phonological and semantic processes are at least in part dissociable. The picture that begins to emerge is one in which lexical retrieval proceeds through successive semantic and phonological priming processes that interact with one another.

There are, of course, many difficult issues in lexical preparation that are untouched by the research just reviewed. A particularly important question has to do with whether there are linguistic representations of the meanings of words that are different or separable from nonlinguistic conceptual representations (e.g. a specification of the meaning of the word *book* isolated from representations of our general knowledge about those objects in the world that we call books, including their usual size, shape, function, composition, authors, those read recently, those that made bad movies, and so on). Along these lines, Clark and Clark (1977) and Katz (1977) make a distinction between a mental "encyclopaedia" and a mental "dictionary," with the former representing general and particular knowledge, and the latter representing knowledge of word meanings. If the organisational principles of the encyclopaedia are different from those of the dictionary, a mapping from nonlinguistic to linguistic concepts may be a necessary part of language production (see Kempen & Huijbers, 1983, for an attempt to separate nonlinguistic and linguistic representations in a production experiment).

At a minimum, however, there appear to be two different levels at which words are prepared or activated in the course of formulating sentences: a semantic level and a phonological level. At some point, these lexical representations must be integrated with "the schema for order." We turn now to a consideration of that schema.

The Schema For Order

The two basic questions that have to be addressed about relational structures for word and constituent order in language production have to do with the nature of the structures themselves and the nature of the processes that create them.

The Structures

Most of the proposals about syntactic structure in natural language have originated in linguistics. There is relatively little consensus within theoretical linguistics about the nature of abstract syntactic levels, or in theoretical psycholinguistics about the role of such levels in processing, but there is considerable evidence and agreement in both areas that phrase- or constituent-structure representations provide a good account of the internal organisation of utterances as they are actually produced. The psycholinguistic evidence comes from experiments on and observations of pausing and intonation, from recall studies, from research on the learning of artificial languages, and once again from observations of errors.

Studies of Pausing and Intonation. The rhythms and intonation of speech created by pauses, vowel or word lengthening, and changes in fundamental frequency seem to reflect closely the phrase structure of utterances. In an examination of pause durations in slow speech, Grosjean, Grosjean, and Lane (1979) found a mean correlation of .76 between pause durations and an index of branching complexity reflecting the sentence's phrase structure. Klatt (1975) found that words at the ends of phrases tend to be lengthened, and Sorenson, Cooper, and Paccia (1978) showed that words in phrase-final positions were spoken with longer durations than the same words (or their homophones) in non-phase-final locations (compare *dyes* and *dies* in *If the tailor dyes the cloth we'll refuse to buy the suit* and *If the tailor dies the cloth in his shop will all be sold*). Cooper, Paccia, and Lapointe (1978) observed the conjunction of these effects—both phrase-final lengthening and increased pause durations at phrase boundaries—in oral readings conveying the alternative interpretations of ambiguous sentences (e.g. *Pam asked the cop who Jake confronted*). Lengthening and pausing increased at boundaries separating constituents with nodes higher in the phrase structure tree (i.e. stronger or more major syntactic boundaries, comparable to Grosjean et al.'s [1979] measure of branching complexity). Finally, Cooper and Sorenson (1981) replicated the results of Cooper et al. (1978) using measurements of fundamental frequency, and found a greater fall in pitch before stronger syntactic boundaries. Clearly, the timing and intonation of speech are conditioned by representational or procedural correlates of phrase structure descriptions.

Recall Studies. Some early investigations of the role of phrase structure in language production used immediate or delayed sentence recall as a method for tapping structural organisation. It might be objected that such recall could be accomplished without any reliance on sentence generation procedures, but this does not seem to be the case: Even when sentences are recalled immediately, people appear to draw on normal sentence production processes (M. C. Potter, 1985). Longer-term, reconstructive recall is also very likely to reveal such effects (see Bock, 1982, for discussion). Using recall tasks, Johnson (1965, 1966a) showed that the points at which errors in recalling the next word were most likely to be made corresponded to transitions between phrases, as defined by phrase structure descriptions of the sentences. Thus, the probability of recalling the next word in a sentence was significantly greater if it was in the same phrase as the word just recalled. Such a pattern indicates that subjects tended to organise the sentences at a level higher than that of individual words, a level that is well described in terms of hierarchical constituent structure.

Artificial Language Learning. Research on the learning of artificial languages tends to support this conclusion. For example, Braine (1963) found that it was easier to learn to construct sentences in an artificial language in which the units were presented as phrases (whose positions could be defined in terms of a hierarchy) than in a language in which the units were presented as single words (whose positions were determined relative to the positions of other words). Although Braine's tests were not adequate for deciding whether his subjects had in fact learned phrase structure rules (Bever, Fodor, & Weksel, 1965; Braine, 1965; Morgan &

Newport, 1981), Morgan and Newport (1981; see also Green, 1979) showed that subjects were significantly more likely to induce phrase structure and word-class dependencies in an artificial language when cues to the constituent membership of items were provided. Only with such cues were subjects able to go beyond simple linear connections to a hierarchical phrase organisation. Taken together, these results suggest that it may be easier to produce "utterances" in an artificial language if one has learned hierarchical phrase structure rules that characterise its sentences, instead of simple left-to-right or finite-state relationships between the elements of the language.

Evidence from Speech Errors.   Some of the most interesting evidence for phrasal organisation in production comes from sound exchanges, or spoonerisms. "Genuine" spoonerisms, those attributed to the Reverend Dr. Spooner himself (Fromkin, 1973a), include dubbing a group of farmers "noble tons of soil," and chiding an undergraduate who had "hissed all my mystery lectures." Though they are often used to illustrate the phenomenon, they are poorly attested (the Oxford undergraduates of the time may have improved on nature in their recounting of Spooner's errors; J. M. Potter, 1980). More reliable evidence about such errors has been assembled by the collectors and analysts of large corpora of mistakes in spontaneous speech (Bawden, 1900; Boomer & Laver, 1968; Dell & Reich, 1981; Fay & Cutler, 1977; Fromkin, 1971, 1973b; Garrett, 1975, 1980; MacKay, 1970; Meringer & Mayer, 1895; Nooteboom, 1973, 1980; and Stemberger, 1982, 1983, 1984, 1985).

Analyses of sound exchange errors have revealed several striking regularities. These can roughly be divided into similarity constraints and distance constraints. The similarity constraints are of several well known types. The articulatory features of exchanging sounds tend to be similar to one another, particularly in voicing or manner of articulation (MacKay, 1970; Nooteboom, 1973); exchanging sounds appear overwhelmingly in the same position in the syllable, with syllable-initial origins predominating (Boomer & Laver, 1968; Fromkin, 1971; MacKay, 1970); exchanges are more likely to occur when sounds precede, follow, or are in the general vicinity of repeated phonemes (MacKay, 1970; Dell, 1984); and finally, the syllables in which exchanging sounds originate tend to have the same stress, usually primary word stress (Boomer & Laver, 1968; Garrett, 1975). These similarity constraints are illustrated by such errors as "caught tourses," "Fats and Kodor," "heft lemisphere," and "poppy of my caper," (when "taught courses," "Katz and Fodor," "left hemisphere," and "copy of my paper" were intended; Fromkin, 1973b).

The distance constraints are more revealing of syntactic planning processes. The major ones have to do with the amount and type of material separating the exchanging elements. Sound exchanges typically occur between adjacent syllables and words (Garrett, 1975; MacKay, 1970; Nooteboom, 1973), and these are very often in the same phrase (Boomer & Laver, 1968; Garrett, 1980). According to Garrett (1980), 87% of the sound exchanges in his corpus originated in the same phrase. These patterns strongly suggest that the retrieval, elaboration, or programming of the sound structure for the words in an utterance occurs in a phrase-by-phrase fashion.

Sound exchanges may in fact be very infrequent events, though variations in recording practices make it difficult to determine the relative incidence of different error types with any certainty. In Nooteboom's (1973) tabulation of errors in Dutch, exchanges constituted about 5% of the corpus. In comparison, roughly 75% were anticipations and 20% perseverations (anticipations and perseverations are, respectively, errors such as "noman numeral" and "phonological fool", where "roman numeral" and "phonological rule" were intended; Fromkin, 1973b). Nooteboom's (1980) tabulation of phonological errors in the Meringer corpus (1908, cited by Nooteboom) revealed similar percentages—11% exchanges, 61% anticipations, and 28% perseverations.

These more common types of sound errors have received considerably less scrutiny than sound exchanges, because there is more ambiguity about the nature of the mistake. It is therefore unclear whether they obey the same constraints. Nooteboom (1973) did not separate anticipations and exchanges in his analysis of distance constraints, but Garrett (1980) noted that, unlike sound exchanges, anticipations and perseverations were about as likely to originate in different phrases as within the same phrase, and were more likely than exchanges to occur between open- and closed-class words. Such differences between exchanges and anticipations suggest possible differences between the point in processing at which sound errors are made versus the point at which they are detected. For example, anticipations may represent the first halves of exchanges, with the error being detected before the second half is produced. The full exchanges that actually appear in speech may tend to be phrase internal because the probability of detecting errors within phrases is lower.

This speculation gains credence from evidence that self-interruptions and other manifestations of speech monitoring are sensitive to certain constituent structure constraints. Levelt (1983) found that errors in colour naming that occurred at the ends of constituents were more likely to result in interruptions and corrections than errors earlier in constituents, perhaps because the likelihood of detecting an error increases at constituent boundaries. It is conceivable, then, that some of the restrictions on sound exchanges arise from monitoring rather than planning processes.

There is clearly a need for more investigation of errors other than exchanges, including comparisons of dysfluent and fluent anticipations (i.e. anticipations that are or are not followed by a hesitation). These might help to reveal the role of error detection in exchanges, and provide converging evidence for hypotheses about the scope of phonological or phonetic elaboration in speech.

Conclusions about Phrase Structure.   The evidence for phrase structure organisation in speech is very strong, though other factors are also at work. A powerful one is related to the length of constituents. For example, Grosjean et al. (1979) reported a tendency for speakers to "bisect" constituents, pausing at the halfway point of longer constituents. Along with phrase structure, this factor accounted for 72% of the variance in pause durations, compared to 56% with phrase structure alone (see also Dommergues & Grosjean, 1981; Grosjean, Lane, Barrison, & Teuber, 1981). Nonetheless, an impressive range of phenomena in speech can be explained with the assumption that the linguistic representations that guide speech output are hierarchically structured.

Evidence for More Abstract Levels of Syntactic Structure in Production.   In contrast to the case that can be made for phrase structure organisation, the empirical evidence for other levels of structure in language performance is relatively weak. Considerable controversy has centred on the need for an abstract level to capture the basic grammatical relations represented in sentences. This level would be the processing correlate of deep structure in transformational generative grammar (Chomsky, 1965, 1981) or the functional structure of lexical-functional grammar (Bresnan, 1982).

Some evidence that a representation of this sort may play a role comes from research by Ford (Ford, 1982; Ford & Holmes, 1978). Ford and Holmes found that subjects' latency to detect random auditory signals while they were speaking extemporaneously was more regularly related to deep-structure than to surface-structure clause boundaries. Thus, latencies were elevated at the ends of deep clauses, even when they did not correspond to surface clauses. Analyses of pause times (Ford, 1982) tended to produce similar results, though somewhat more equivocally.

These findings are provocative, but the difficulty of controlling for extraneous sources of variation in such research leaves open the possibility that the effects are attributable to something else. One possibility is the lexical complexity of the kinds of verbs that enter into constructions that create deep structure boundaries without corresponding surface boundaries, and another is the conceptual complexity of such constructions, which are often complements. In this connection, it is interesting that Rochester and Gill (1973) found that noun phrase complements were much more often responsible for speech disruptions than superficially similar relative clauses. Since both of these constructions involve a deep clause, it may be that there is something special about complements that complicates their formation in speech.

More detailed arguments for the underlying structure hypothesis come from analyses of speech errors, particularly word exchanges. Examples of such errors (with the exchanged words italicised) include "Is there a cigarette *building* in this *machine?*," "I left the *briefcase* in my *cigar*" (Garrett, 1980), "a *wife* for his *job*," and "*dinner* is being served at *wine*" (Fromkin, 1973b). Garrett (1975, 1980, 1982) has argued that these errors arise at a level at which words are specified in terms of their syntactic features rather than their phonological characteristics. The evidence for this claim is the very strong constraint on form class that is exhibited by word exchanges: The exchanging words regularly come from the same grammatical class (nouns, verbs, prepositions, and so on; Fromkin, 1971; Garrett, 1975, 1980; Nooteboom, 1973). In Garrett's corpus (1980), 85% of the word exchanges observed the form-class constraint.

Garrett's argument for attributing word exchange errors to an abstract syntactic processing level comes primarily from the ways in which they differ from sound exchanges. Recall that sound exchanges reveal strong adjacency effects, suggesting that they occur at a point at which the order of words has been specified. In word exchanges, however, the errors tend to span larger distances, generally crossing phrase boundaries. For example, Garrett (1980) observed that 81% of the word exchanges in his corpus occurred between words in different phrases. Word exchanges are thus much less affected by contiguity in the surface string than are sound exchanges.

Two further contrasts between sound and word exchanges point to possible differences in the representational levels at which they originate. First, sound exchanges do not seem predisposed to occur between words of the same form class, as they might if form class were specified when they happen. Second, sound exchanges rarely involve the closed-class vocabulary, but closed-class *word* exchanges are reasonably common (Garrett, 1975). All of these differences lead Garrett to argue that word and sound exchanges occur at different points in the formulation of an utterance. Though he does not explicitly identify the more abstract of these levels with deep structure, he acknowledges its similarity.

At least one important implication of this framework has not been supported. If word exchanges occur at a different level of processing than sound exchanges, one at which phonological form is unspecified, word exchanges should not exhibit phonological similarities. This prediction has been disconfirmed by Dell and Reich (1981), who showed that such similarities occur more often than would be predicted by chance (also see

Harley, 1984; Stemberger, 1985). Another troublesome feature of word exchanges is the number that occur between noun phrases in prepositional phrases. Garrett (1980) noted that 60% of the word exchanges in his corpus were of this type (e.g. "on the *room* to my *door*"). This led Butterworth (1980) to cast some doubt on the generalisations drawn about the form-class constraint, suggesting that there may be some (unspecified) peculiarity of paired prepositional phrases that predisposes them to exchanges, rather than a special level of processing at which exchanges occur. Stemberger (1985) proposed that the form-class constraint could emerge from the way that words are attached to phrase structure slots, with the label on the slot serving to limit selection to only words of the right form class. If so, such errors could be a consequence of surface phrase-structure elaboration, rather than a more abstract compositional process.

Despite such concerns, several interesting features of word exchanges remain. As Dell and Reich (1981) note, the form-class constraint is close to being categorical, while sound similarities between exchanging words are better considered as probabilistic tendencies. The differences between sound and word exchanges in the distances they span also point to possible differences in the levels of processing at which they occur, although these levels may not be well represented by the distinction between deep and surface structure (as Garrett also notes, 1980, p. 217). Thus, there is evidence that *some* separation of processes is needed, even though there is at present little unambiguous empirical support for the claim that one of the representational vocabularies forms an abstract syntactic level of representation.

The Processes

The types of processes hypothesised to be involved in sentence generation are closely bound to the types of structures hypothesised to underlie it. Those theories that emphasise the role of surface phrase structure naturally rely on processing models that explain surface phrase structure generation, while those that assume two syntactic levels include processes designed to mediate between the underlying and surface representations.

Phrase Structure Generation. The most influential theory of phrase structure elaboration was proposed by Yngve (1960). According to the model, production processes generate a phrase structure tree from top to bottom and left to right, so the first part of the sentence to be elaborated is the left-most daughter. As the processor traverses this branch, it stores information about commitments to rightward branches that have yet to be elaborated. For example, to produce a simple sentence such as *The dog chased the rabbit*, shown in Fig. 9.1, the generator proceeds from the

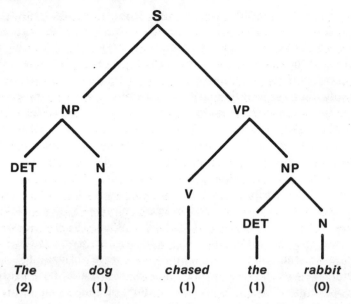

FIG. 9.1 A phrase structure tree for a simple sentence, with Yngve depth given in parentheses for each word. The mean depth of the sentence is 1.0.

sentence symbol, where a commitment must be made for one rightward elaboration (the verbal phrase), down past the noun phrase node, where it incurs a commitment to another rightward elaboration, and terminates with the article. The generator then returns to elaborate the noun phrase, generating the noun branch. Finally, it returns to the topmost symbol, the sentence symbol, and proceeds to elaborate the verb phrase.

Yngve's theory makes an interesting prediction about the effects of branching on the difficulty of producing a sentence. Since commitments to right branches are stored while the generator elaborates other branches to the left, the memory load may impair fluency in some way, perhaps slowing production or increasing the probability of error. The number of such commitments grows as a function of the depth in the tree of the left branches, with a corresponding increase in the memory load. This hypothesis has been tested in different ways, generally relying on a measure of the "mean depth" of the sentence to be produced. The mean depth is easily calculated by counting the number of *left* branches dominating each word of the sentence (which yields the number of right-branching commitments) and dividing by the total number of words. For the sentence in Fig. 9.1, the depth for each word is shown in parentheses. The mean depth for the whole sentence is 1.0.

This model has been examined by a number of investigators, including

Johnson (1966a, 1966b), Martin and Roberts (1966, 1967; Martin, Roberts, & Collins, 1968), and Perfetti (1969a, 1969b; Perfetti & Goodman, 1971). Little consistent support has been found for the detailed predictions of the depth hypothesis (see Fodor, Bever, & Garrett, 1974, ch. 5 and 6; and Frazier, 1985, for review and further discussion). Mean depth is probably not a sufficiently sensitive index of the syntactic processing that accompanies sentence formulation. There are at least two plausible reasons for this. One is that the measure is a global one, whereas many features of surface syntactic elaboration may create localised disruptions. A second is that detection of a speaker's processing problems may require on-line assessment of the formulation process. This has rarely been done; in fact, most tests of the depth hypothesis have employed recall measures.

Some support for a more general implication of Yngve's model comes from experiments by Forster (1966, 1967, 1968a, 1968b). Forster looked at the ease and speed of completing sentences with words deleted at the beginning or end, and found that it was more difficult to create the beginnings of sentences, as would be expected if the existence of rightward commitments burdens the generation of sentences. Evidence that this was not exclusively the result of practice in generating sentences from left to right came from comparisons of sentence completion performance across different languages. The languages differed in the degree to which their sentences characteristically branch to the left. The rationale was that speakers of left-branching languages should have more experience with rules that make substantial right context commitments before earlier portions of a sentence are elaborated, perhaps enabling them to cope better with the resulting increases in depth. Forster found the predicted difference: Speakers of left-branching languages were more successful and took less time completing left-deleted sentence fragments.

Of course, there is something decidedly odd about the task that Forster employed, although it is an oddity that it shares with Yngve's model. Speakers rarely know exactly how their sentences will end before they begin them (Lindsley, 1975), but depth calculations cannot be made precisely unless they do. Thus, Yngve's model would seem to require further specification in order to permit predictions about local sources of planning difficulty. While Forster's experiments generally supported the original theory, they involved a task that diverges from ordinary production in just the way that the theory does, making it unclear whether the results can be generalised to normal sentence formulation processes.

A different sort of support for Yngve's theory comes from the strong tendency for "heavier" or more complex constituents to appear later in sentences (Ross, 1967), which reduces their depth. Thus, the sentence *The boy offered the girl a magazine with a picture on its cover of Richard Nixon shaking hands with Ronald Reagan* sounds more natural than *The boy offered a magazine with a picture on its cover of Richard Nixon shaking hands with Ronald Reagan to the girl.* There is no comparable disparity between the formally similar sentences in the pair *The boy offered the girl a magazine* and *The boy offered a magazine to the girl.* A related phenomenon occurs in language acquisition, where subject-elaborated noun phrases appear later in the course of development than object-elaborated noun phrases (Nakayama & Crain, 1985; Pinker, 1984). However, these facts do not selectively support Yngve's model. As Frazier (1985) points out, they are compatible with any approach which assumes that complex constituents tend to appear at points of low complexity within a sentence.

In summary, there is scant support for the only theory of phrase structure generation that has received serious empirical attention. This is somewhat paradoxical, in view of the large body of evidence suggesting that phrase structure representations are in fact closely related to the utterances people produce. However, the difficulties of examining the time course of sentence generation processes in natural production tasks have impeded the development and elaboration of alternatives to Yngve's model. A specific, psychologically adequate processing model thus remains to be developed.

Transformations in Sentence Generation.   Yngve's model focused on the elaboration of surface phrase structure trees, and included no higher levels of processing that might be responsible for creating the representation that controls the selected form of the surface sentence. When such processes have been at issue, they have sometimes been equated with the syntactic transformations that relate deep and surface structures in transformational generative grammars.

An experiment that is sometimes cited in connection with the transformational hypothesis for production is Miller and McKean's (1964) matching study. Subjects in these experiments had to match pairs of sentences that were hypothesised to be related by differing numbers of transformations, and the amount of time required to make the match was assessed. The obtained relationship between number of transformations and time was very clear: The more transformations, the more time matching took. Now, it might be argued that the subjects actually used transformations to generate the target sentences in order to perform the matching task, and that such processing mirrors normal production, but Miller and McKean rejected these interpretations. They argued instead that, to the extent their subjects engaged in any syntactic operations at all, these probably involved ad hoc strategies rather than normal mechanisms of sentence production.

Most of the remaining arguments for transformational processes in production come from Fay's analyses of such syntactic errors in spontaneous speech as "Would you turn on the light on?" (Fay, 1980a, 1980b; Foss & Fay, 1975). Fay argued that such errors can be explained parsimoniously in terms of failures of transformations. For example, the particle movement transformation (which accounts for the difference between sentences such as "Turn on the light" and "Turn the light on") involves the movement of a particle (*on* in the example) from its immediate postverbal position in deep structure to a position after the noun phrase. Following Chomsky (1965), Fay's analysis assumed that this transformation consists of two elementary operations: copying to the new position, and deletion from the old position. When one of these elementary operations, deletion, fails to apply, the result is the error cited above.

Although Fay's analyses are ingenious, they are based on an unusually small sample of errors (fewer than 100; Fay, 1980a) spread across a relatively large number of categories. Furthermore, Fay (1982) and Stemberger (1982) have observed that many such errors can be explained in terms of different types of failures of phrase structure rules. Thus, "turn on the light on" might issue from a blending of two phrase structure rules: one that rewrites a verb phrase as verb + particle + noun phrase, and another that rewrites as verb + noun phrase + particle. Blending is a common source of word-level errors (as in "slickery," blending "slick" and "slippery"). Similar arguments can be made for other syntactic errors, including deletion, addition, shifting, and so on. The phrase structure account may therefore have the virtue of parsimony, since the converging evidence for phrase structure organisation in language production stands in significant contrast to the near-absence of such evidence for the transformational hypothesis.

To conclude this discussion of syntactic processing, it is worth repeating that little attention has been given to the details of the problem because of the difficulty of tapping critical features of production in ongoing time. This difficulty is highlighted by the frequency with which one encounters the claim that the structure of utterances is created automatically (Butterworth, 1980; Goldman-Eisler, 1968; Taylor, 1969): Goldman-Eisler, for example, was led to this conclusion by her failure to find systematic effects on pauses and hesitations that could be attributed to the syntactic features of sentences. Instead, she argued that such hesitations as she did observe were attributable to cognitive planning variables. Miller and McKean (1964) came to a similar conclusion, writing that:

> The general impression we have formed of how people perform syntactic operations in normal usage is that these operations are quite automatic and involuntary . . . Any deliberate and explicit control that a person can exercise over these linguistic operations is principally, and perhaps exclusively, at the semantic level (p. 308).

The apparent automaticity and opacity of these processes indicates that it will take considerable ingenuity to break into the system that creates structure in speech. Automaticity obviously does not imply that the system is simple. As with automatic transmissions, what is gained in external ease of operation may be purchased at the price of a substantial increase in the intricacy of the internal mechanism. The investigative burden is thus heavier, rather than lighter. We need to infer the structure of a device that is undeniably complex from output that is relatively error-free and, at the relevant levels of description, relatively invariant.

Integrating the Units of Expression with the Schema for Order

The two preceding sections reviewed evidence which suggests that the preparation of lexical units for utterances involves two interactive stages, a semantic stage and a phonological stage, and that the schema for ordering these units bears a rough similarity to the hierarchically organised constituent structures described in phrase structure grammars. What is still missing from the picture is an account of how the lexical units come to be integrated with or attached to the phrase structure representation. Serious theoretical controversies arise here, along with many of the unresolved questions about lexical and syntactic processes alluded to in the previous two sections. We will look first at Lashley's (1951) tentative suggestions about the nature of the co-ordination process and consider some of their weaknesses; then we will look at two more contemporary views.

Lashley's Proposal

In essence, Lashley's (1951) idea was that one set of elements may be primed, or partially activated, and then scanned by the mechanisms involved in serial ordering. He assumed that the set of primed elements are represented in parallel, linked to particular locations in an array (the nature of which Lashley left unspecified beyond the premise that it cannot code time or sequence). The sequence arises from the way these locations are scanned by the ordering schema, which transforms them into a temporal succession of elements. In terms of the evidence reviewed so far, the primed elements might be equated with phonologically specified words, and the ordering schema with phrasal representations.

Lashley did not speculate about the scanning process or the kinds of information it might use to pick elements out of the parallel array. This is where the central dilemma posed by the co-ordination process appears: If, as Lashley argued, the primed elements and the ordering schema are in important respects independent of one another, how or where do the obvious dependencies between words and syntax arise? Such dependencies are ubiquitous. Consider a few of the syntactic constraints imposed by different verbs. Some verbs permit direct objects (*The coach requested ten minutes*); others forbid them (**The day elapsed ten minutes*). Some verbs take *for-to* but not progressive complements (*I wanted the Spartans to beat the Jayhawks*; **I wanted the Spartans beating the Jayhawks*); others take progressive but not *for-to* complements (*I watched the Jayhawks beating the Spartans*; **I watched the Jayhawks to beat the Spartans*). Some verbs allow double objects (*The woman gave the Salvation Army an old bed*); others do not (**The woman donated the Salvation Army an old bed*). Some verbs take locative prepositional phrases optionally (*George drove the car into the garage*; *George drove the car*); others require them (*George put the car into the garage*; **George put the car*).

These examples suggest that lexical items have an impact on the syntactic frames in which they appear. However, in Lashley's framework, integration occurs only when the primed units are scanned by the ordering schema. The words should not influence the structure of the schema, but they appear to do so. In order to account for this, Lashley's outline of the processes needs to be expanded or modified. There are at least three ways in which this could be done.

One of these does not go very far beyond Lashley's proposals. It involves attributing lexical/syntactic dependencies to what Lashley called the determining tendency—in effect, the speaker's communicative intention. Perhaps the communicative intention selects a set of words adequate for its expression, and an appropriate syntactic schema. It could be that the constraints on the kinds of communicative intentions that can be expressed by particular sets of words and structures are sufficiently strong that the lexical set is usually compatible with the syntactic form.

There are two problems with this as it stands, both arising from the indirectness of the semantics-syntax connection. One of the examples above illustrates the first of them. Although the verbs *give* and *donate* are virtually identical in meaning in the sentences *The woman gave an old bed to the Salvation Army* and *The woman donated an old bed to the Salvation Army*, their syntactic privileges are not identical, as shown in the admissibility of *The woman gave the Salvation Army an old bed*, versus **The woman donated the Salvation Army an old bed*. It is hard to see how it would be possible to prevent the double-object construction from being created from the same communicative intention that would prime the word *donate* without some early interaction between lexical and syntactic processes.

The second problem is that this proposal flies in the face of one of the clearest intuitions speakers have about their use of language, which is that it is relatively easy to say "the same thing" in different ways. If there were rigid specification of the lexical and syntactic contents of sentences by communicative intentions, it would be difficult to explain the source of this intuition. In fact, this intuition constituted one of Lashley's original arguments for separating the ordering schema from the units of utterances.

Another possible modification to Lashley's co-ordination model would be to permit multiple ordering schemas or multiple lexical arrays, developed in parallel or successively. If multiple ordering schemas were developed, the first to incorporate all of the elements in the lexical array successfully would be the one to control the output process. Alternatively, if multiple lexical arrays were developed, the first to supply items appropriate for the ordering schema would be the one selected.

Such a system might work in principle, but it is hard to see how it could operate efficiently. Since there *are* dependencies between lexical forms and syntactic structures, it makes sense to consider a different sort of solution, one that involves the assumption that these dependencies are used early in the formulation process to select just the right set of words and structures. This could be accomplished by co-ordinating lexical representations with an abstract structural representation that guides the creation of the ordering schema.

Of course, this is exactly the function of the underlying syntactic representation that, as we have seen, receives equivocal support in research on sentence production. However, the rational necessity of something along these lines—something that captures lexical/syntactic dependencies, though not necessarily in the same way that it is done in the deep structure representations of transformational grammar—cannot be discounted. The most fully-developed account of the co-ordination process that incorporates such a level rests on arguments made first by Fromkin (1971) and elaborated by Garrett (1975, 1980). The model is outlined in the next section.

The Fromkin-Garrett Model

The major features of the Fromkin-Garrett model are schematised in Fig. 9.2. The production process begins with a nonlinguistic message. This is followed by a number of specifically linguistic processes that can be divided into those responsible for creating two representational levels, the functional level and the positional level. One critical distinction between these two levels has to do with the representation of serial order: Information at the functional level is not ordered, while that at the positional level is. A second distinction concerns the scope of the representation: The functional level spans a unit comparable to a clause, but the positional level spans a unit closer in size to a single phrase.

To form the functional level, semantically specified lexical items are

PROCESSING LEVEL	LEXICAL-SYNTACTIC COORDINATION	ROLE IN SENTENCE GENERATION
FUNCTIONAL	ASSIGN MEANING-BASED REPRESENTATIONS OF LEXICAL ITEMS TO FUNCTIONAL SYNTACTIC ROLES	CONTROL ELABORATION OF SYNTACTIC STRUCTURE
POSITIONAL	ASSIGN PHONOLOGICALLY-SPECIFIED REPRESENTATIONS OF LEXICAL ITEMS TO PLANNING FRAME	CONTROL ELABORATION OF PHONETIC FORM

FIG. 9.2   The levels of the sentence production process in the Fromkin-Garrett model (Fromkin, 1971; Garrett, 1975, 1980, 1982).

assigned to roles within an abstract syntactic structure. The types of roles assigned are not identified in Garrett's model, but could correspond to any of the several types of roles that have been proposed to serve as underlying structural relations in linguistic theories of syntax. These include logical relations (a predicate with its logical subject and object) or thematic roles (agent, patient, theme, etc.). Because the functional representation is completely responsible for the syntactic elaboration of the sentence at the positional level, it must encode all of the information necessary to construct the serially-ordered positional representation. Thus, all dependencies between lexical and syntactic features must be captured at this level.

At the positional level, the major syntactic process is the generation or selection of a positional structure or planning frame corresponding to a phrase structure description of the sentence. This frame specifies the order of words. Garrett (1980, 1982; Bradley, Garrett, & Zurif, 1980) has proposed that the frame includes closed-class words (function words), bound morphemes, and a representation of phrasal stress, so that the terminal elements of the planning frame for a sentence such as *The ambulance is hitting the policeman* might be something crudely along the lines of

The ____ is ____ ing the ____.

Other processes involved in forming the representation of a sentence at this level consist of the retrieval and assignment of phonologically specified words to positions in the planning frame. The positional level representation then guides the elaboration of the sentence's detailed phonetic form.

This model is motivated in part by differences in the distance and similarity constraints on word and sound errors in Garrett's corpus (1975, 1980). Word-exchange errors readily cross phrase boundaries, but rarely clause boundaries (only 20% of the word exchanges in Garrett's 1980 corpus occurred between clauses). Sound exchanges are most common within phrases. Further, word-exchange errors are governed by grammatical category, while sound exchanges occur more often between words of different form classes. The interacting elements in sound exchanges instead tend to be phonologically similar. These patterns led Garrett to a distinction between one level of representation that codes the proximity and phonological characteristics of lexical elements—the positional level—and one that codes the grammatical and semantic characteristics of lexical elements—the functional level.

In his separation of levels of processing, Garrett (1980) placed special emphasis on the characteristics of stem-morpheme exchanges. These exchanges create errors such as "She's already trunked two packs" (where "packed two trunks" was intended; Garrett, 1975) and "the flood was roaded" (where "the road was flooded" was intended; Stemberger, 1985). The stems of the open-class (content) words thus exchange, leaving their affixes behind.

Such errors are interesting on a number of grounds. First, they provide evidence for dissociations of lexical and syntactic processes, since inflectional affixes are syntactically governed. The stranding of inflectional affixes is a regular feature of such exchanges—it occurred in 89% of the errors in which it was possible in Stemberger's (1985) corpus. The inflections themselves rarely exchange: In Stemberger's corpus there were 135 cases of stem-morpheme exchanges, versus just one clear case of an inflectional affix exchange. It appears that these elements are specified prior to the open-class words, so the syntactic features of the planning frame seem to be set before other words are inserted.

A second interesting feature of stem-morpheme exchanges resides in their dual nature. On the one hand, the exchanging morphemes are independent lexical entries (and thus might be treated like other content words by lexical retrieval processes); on the other, they are only fragments of the full words planned for an utterance (and thus might be treated like sounds or syllables by phonetic elaboration processes). They therefore have considerable potential to illuminate further the stages of the sentence formulation process. Garrett's error data (1980) suggest that in two respects they behave much more like sound exchanges than independent word exchanges, being likely both to *violate* the form-class constraint and to *observe* the within-phrase distance constraint. These characteristics identify them with the positional level, providing additional support for distinctions among the processes involved in sentence formulation.

As a result of the division between the functional and positional levels, there are two separate points at which specific words are integrated with syntactic plans in the Fromkin-Garrett model. The first part of the integration process occurs at the functional level, where meaning-based representations of lexical items are assigned to the functional syntactic structure.

The second part of the process occurs at the positional level, where phonological representations of words are inserted into the planning frame that specifies their locations in the string. On this analysis, two separate lexical retrievals are necessary in the production of a sentence, one to recover a word's semantic and syntactic privileges at the functional level, and another to recover its phonological form at the positional level.

The double-retrieval hypothesis is generally consistent with the characteristics of word and sound exchanges, particularly their respective form-class and phonological constraints. Also consistent with double retrieval are the dissociations between word meaning and word form found in the investigations of lexical retrieval reviewed earlier, including tip-of-the-tongue phenomena, word-selection errors, and experiments on naming. All of these indicate that meaning and sound can be retrieved somewhat independently.

One problem for the double-retrieval hypothesis is that, whereas words are hypothesised to be specified in terms of their meanings at the level at which exchanges occur, strong meaning similarities between exchanging words seem to be uncharacteristic (Garrett, 1980). Garrett argues that such an effect may be absent simply because there is rarely an opportunity for it to occur, implying that words that are closely related in meaning may seldom occur in the same clauses. This claim has not been examined. However, a different implication of Garrett's hypothesis has been tested and supported experimentally.

Bock (in press) used an incidental priming task to contrast the effects of semantic and phonological priming on sentence production. The subjects received a mixed list of words and pictures of events in the context of a recognition memory experiment. As they took the recognition test, they pronounced each of the words aloud and described the event in each picture. On a subset of the trials, a picture would be preceded by a word that was either semantically or phonologically related to a particular target object in the depicted event. For example, a picture of lightning striking a church might be preceded by the word "worship" or "churn", and a picture of a horse kicking a cow by the word "pony" or "horn". The sets of semantic and phonological priming words were equated in their ability to elicit the target object names in a different task.

Garrett's model predicts that these semantic and phonological primes should have different effects on the syntactic forms of the picture descriptions. If the double-retrieval hypothesis is valid, semantic priming should influence functional-level processing and, thereby, the syntactic forms of sentences. Specifically, the priming manipulation should influence the use of active versus passive sentences by predisposing the primed words to occur as the subjects of the sentences more often than unprimed control words (by increasing their accessibility; see Bock, 1982). Phonological priming should have no effect on syntactic form, since its effect would be at the positional level, after the sentence's structure had been specified.

The predicted results were obtained in two separate experiments: Semantic priming had a reliable effect on syntactic form, and phonological priming did not. The two experiments differed in the types of phonological primes employed; rhyme primes in one case and "malaprop" primes (words with similar onsets, conclusions, and syllable structures, as in *hearse-horse*) in the other. Neither had a significant impact on syntactic form. This difference between semantic and phonological priming in their effects on syntax lends support to the division between processing levels and to the characteristics of the co-ordination process at each level.

The distinction between the functional and positional levels thus has some confirmation from both observational and experimental sources. However, it has also been disputed on several grounds. To understand these objections, it is necessary to clarify the processing relations between the functional and positional levels, particularly with regard to: (1) feedback from the lower (positional) to the higher (functional) level; and (2) the staging of the two levels—whether the functional level must be fully specified before the positional level is formed, creating a strictly serial system, or, alternatively, whether it can feed partial products to the positional level, yielding a more parallel or cascading system.

The theoretical stance taken on these processing questions is intimately related to the kinds of syntactic representations assumed to operate at each level (Bresnan & Kaplan, 1982). If representations similar to those of transformational grammar are assumed, with the functional level corresponding to the deep structure and the positional level to a transformationally derived surface structure, feedback would be blocked, and the amount of parallelism strictly limited. Feedback is blocked by the irreversibility of transformational operations, eliminating the possibility of relating elements of the surface representation to deep-structure elements. Parallelism is restricted by the fact that transformations operate over complete deep-structure representations, meaning that a full representation of the sentence would have to be developed at the functional level before the positional level representation could be generated. With representational assumptions derived from lexical-functional grammar (Bresnan & Kaplan, 1982) or generalised phrase-structure grammar (Gazdar, Klein, Pullum, & Sag, 1985), both feedback and parallelism appear to be permitted.

Garrett has not spelled out a specific set of representational assumptions for his model. Several of his arguments imply a transformational treatment (see, for example, Garrett, 1975, pp. 169–172), and he has acknowledged the connection without fully committing the model to this form of representation (Garrett, 1980, pp. 216–217). On the processing question, he has said (Garrett, 1982, p. 68) that the model permits no feedback from the positional to the functional level (consistent with the transformational assumption), but that the functional and positional levels may develop in parallel (Garrett, 1982, p. 69—which is inconsistent with the transformational assumption). Many criticisms of the model have assumed the transformational treatment (perhaps improperly), with its implied serial staging of levels. However, the claim that there is no feedback from the positional to the functional level is explicit, so evidence for such feedback constitutes a genuine challenge.

This does appear to be a vulnerable point. As noted earlier, there tend to be phonological relationships between exchanging words (Dell & Reich, 1981; Harley, 1984; Stemberger, 1985). If words are specified only in terms of their meaning and form class at the functional level, and if that level is the locus of word exchanges, phonological similarity should be unable to create such a predisposition toward reversals.

A further problem is that the phonological relationships between exchanging words are as strong for those exchanges that Garrett assigns to the functional level (exchanges between separated content words of the same grammatical category) as in those he would assign to the positional level (stem-morpheme exchanges) (Dell & Reich, 1981). Stemberger (1985) has also called into question the difference that Garrett noted between word and stem-morpheme exchanges in their observance of the grammatical category constraint. Like Garrett, Stemberger found that morpheme exchanges exhibit a relatively strong distance constraint, occurring predominantly within phrases (70% originated within the same phrase in Garrett's 1980 corpus). However, whereas Garrett reported that the elements in morpheme exchanges were less likely to observe the form-class constraint than word exchanges (only 43% did so in the 1980 corpus), Stemberger reported a different pattern. Restricting his attention to the morpheme exchanges that stranded inflectional affixes, Stemberger found no differences between word exchanges and morpheme exchanges in their observance of the form-class constraint (approximately 85% of both types observed the constraint, the same proportion reported by Garrett, 1980, for whole-word exchanges).

These kinds of problems with the Fromkin-Garrett model have led to a set of proposals that emphasise interactions between levels of processing. Some of those proposals are examined next.

Interactive Models of Production

Interactive approaches have often been endorsed as an alternative to a strictly top-down analysis (Bock, 1982; Dell, 1986; Harley, 1984; Stemberger, 1985). Dell's model (1985, 1986) gives an explicit and impressive account of phonological processes in production within an interactive

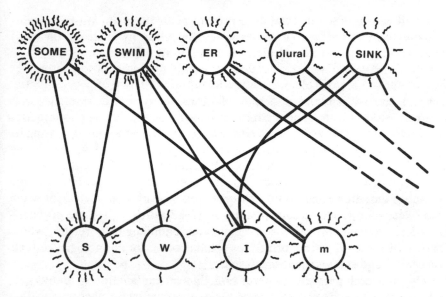

FIG. 9.3   An illustration of two levels of the lexical network in Dell's model of phonological processing in sentence production, showing a moment early in the production of the sentence *Some swimmers sink* (adapted and greatly simplified from Dell, 1986, p. 290). All links are bi-directional; many of them are not included in the figure. Highlights around nodes represent activation levels.

processing system, providing an example of this type of framework at its best.

The model takes phonological errors, both observed and experimentally elicited, as the primary data base. It assumes that the words required for an utterance retrieve or activate the phonological elements to which they are linked. The process is illustrated in Fig. 9.3, which shows a moment in the production of the sentence *Some swimmers sink*. Because retrieval or activation processes work in both directions, elements may begin feeding activation back to the units that initially activated them, and these in turn increase activation at the lower level. Although the phonological elements are linked to other words, which consequently receive some bottom-up activation, the beneficiaries of such casual activation will rarely achieve the activation levels that result from the resonating feedback relationships between the source word and its components. These relationships tend to enhance the activation of the strongest or most highly activated units, and reduce the activation of weaker units.

The ultimate effect is to ensure that the elements most tightly linked to the units that are activated at the highest level will in general be the ones produced. The only way to override this effect is through adventitious summation of the various sources of background activation, including residual activation from preceding utterances or intrusions from contemporaneous cognitive activity. These can momentarily increase the activation levels of a peripheral lower-level element, yielding an error.

Dell (1986; Dell & Reich, 1981) argues that similar interactions between the phonological and semantic representations of words in the lexicon may help to explain phonological effects on those errors that Garrett ascribes to the functional level. Activation of a word's phonological representation may feed back to the semantic representation, increasing its activation level. Changes in activation at the phonological level caused by phonological relationships among words could thus destabilise the patterns of activation at the semantic level. If this occurs as a representation of the sentence that draws on semantic information is being constructed (or when the rules that operate on semantically specified words apply), the probability of an exchange or other error involving phonologically related words should increase. The same principles could account for phonological effects on blends and semantic substitutions.

This approach provides an exceptionally neat explanation of many types of speech errors. However, there are certain syntactic phenomena that appear to depend on lexical processing in ways that require additional assumptions to be made. These phenomena are not errors, but simply normal variations in syntactic patterns that result from variations in lexical accessibility. One illustration of this comes from a further set of experiments (Bock, 1985) using the primed picture description paradigm described above. The experiments differed from the ones sketched earlier (Bock, in press) in two ways. First, they did not attempt to compare semantic with phonological priming, a comparison that required equating the strength of the semantic and phonological primes. The semantic priming conditions were therefore omitted. Second, the priming words were selected in a way that increased the strength of the phonological relationship between the primes and the names of target objects in pictures of various events. Thus, within limits imposed by the American English lexicon, the primes were maximally similar to the targets without being identical to them. The question was whether, with these increased phonological similarities, changes in the accessibility of the phonological representations of words would influence the syntactic structures of the sentences subjects produced.

The results revealed a clear effect of phonological priming: There was a significant tendency toward the production of sentences in which the phonologically accessible word served as the subject, rather than as the object, of active and passive sentences. Consistent with claims and findings that the effects of phonological relationships between words tend to be inhibitory (Colombo, 1986; MacKay, 1970; Meyer & Gordon, 1985; Slowiaczek & Pisoni, 1985; Stemberger, Elman, & Haden, 1985), the word that appeared as the head of the subject noun phrase was the *unprimed* rather than the primed word. The primed targets were therefore significantly more likely to appear later, rather than earlier, in the picture descriptions. Postexperimental debriefings revealed that the participants had not noticed the phonological relationships between the words and pictures, reducing the likelihood that the effects were due to conscious modifications of descriptions.

These results suggest that the deployment of the rules that create sentences is somehow influenced by the retrievability of lexical items, either directly or through changes in the structural representations to which the rules apply. Variations in activation patterns may thus have an impact not only on the lexical "data base" used in the formation of utterances, as Dell's approach emphasises, but also on the structures formed from the lexical representations. As a consequence, speakers say things differently from the way they would have, though these differences do not constitute errors. It may be that errors occur in part because rule application processes or the structures on which they operate fail to adapt to changes in lexical accessibility.

Such findings also pose problems for the Fromkin-Garrett model. Recall that Bock (in press) found that when sets of semantic and phonological primes were equated in their ability to elicit target words that appeared in sentences, semantic priming influenced sentence form, while phonological priming did not. This suggests that semantic factors have a much heavier impact at the level at which syntactic form is determined than do phonological factors. However, it appears that phonological processes *can* influence sentence structure if they are sufficiently perturbed or disrupted. There is no clear account of how this structural influence could occur in the Fromkin-Garrett approach, since the model permits no feedback from the positional to the functional level, and since the positional level plays no role in the determination of syntactic form.

To explain these and related findings (Bock & Irwin, 1980; Kelly, Bock, & Keil, 1985, 1986), it is necessary to develop an account of lexical-syntactic co-ordination that explains how variations in the form of the output from the lexical retrieval process could influence or interact with the application of rules or the development of "the schema for order." That problem is considered in the next section.

LEXICAL-SYNTACTIC INTEGRATION: ANOTHER LOOK

The approach I will sketch is a revised version of an earlier model (Bock, 1982) that bears resemblances to proposals made by Dell (1986), Harley (1984), Kempen and Hoenkamp (in press), MacKay (1982), MacWhinney (in press), Motley, Baars, and Camden (1983), and Stemberger (1985). Like the Fromkin-Garrett model, it requires the distinguishing of two points where lexical-syntactic integration processes occur. The first involves the assignment of semantically-specified lexical items to grammatical functions (functional integration), and the second involves the assignment of the phonological representations of words to constituent structures (constituent integration). Unlike the Fromkin-Garrett approach, it assumes that constituent integration processes can affect functional integration in ways that have consequences for the form in which utterances are produced.

The Two Levels of Integration

Functional Integration

Functional integration incorporates the processes that occur at Garrett's functional level, with the added assumptions that variations in what will be termed *conceptual accessibility* influence the assignment of words to grammatical functions, and that the grammatical functions correspond to surface- rather than deep-structure roles. The conceptual accessibility assumption has two parts. First, it makes the claim that the assignment of semantically specified words to grammatical functions such as subject and direct object will be affected by the ease of retrieving the words' semantic representations. Second, it assumes that, other things being equal, the subject is assigned first, with other functions following according to a hierarchy of grammatical relations (Keenan & Comrie, 1977).

The process can be argued to work roughly like this. Prior to functional integration there is a generalised priming of a set of lexical items that increases their levels of activation, along with tagging of the items by thematic role markers (agent, patient, and so on). Any lexical items that have relatively high levels of activation, from environmental sources or previous utterances, have the potential to gain additional activation from the priming process. (This aggregated priming may thus contribute to many of the word and morpheme intrusion and blending errors that occur in speech, where unintended words related to the message or to environmental events make their way into utterances.) Included in the primed set will be verbs marked for functional relations (mappings between thematic roles and grammatical relations), including different forms of the same verb (e.g. active and passive verbs, prepositional and double-object dative verbs).

Functional integration involves an attempt to link primed items together according to the functional relations specified by the verb, beginning by filling the subject role. Two important factors in this process are the accessibility or level of activation of alternative subjects (so a more accessible or more highly activated item capable of filling the subject role should be linked to a verb faster, other things being equal) and the strength of the verb form (since different verb forms will have different base strengths, the stronger form should be linked to a candidate subject more quickly, other things being equal). The first verb form that is linked to an appropriate subject head (i.e. one that matches the verb's functional relation specifications) should tend to govern the elaboration of the sentence.

During functional integration, then, lexical items are assigned to fill grammatical relations according to: (1) the thematic roles of the message elements they instantiate (agent, patient, beneficiary, etc.). (2) the ease of retrieving or activating their semantic specifications; (3) compatibility with the types of arguments allowed by the selected verb or predicate (i.e., the verb's specification of functional relations); and (4) the strength of alternative verb forms. The thematic role, in conjunction with the functional relations of predicates, determines a set of grammatical functions that a word could serve. For example, in describing an event such as one in which a bee (the agent) stings a man (the patient), *bee* may be either the subject of an active verb (*The bee stung the man*) or the object of a passive verb (*The man was stung by the bee*). If *bee* is more accessible, it should tend to be assigned to the subject role of the active form of the verb; if *man* is more accessible, it should tend to be assigned to the subject role of the passive form of the verb. However, because the active verb form has greater base strength than the passive, it has a higher probability of selection overall.

Some evidence for an integration process with these characteristics can be found in experiments by Bock and Warren (1985) and Bock (in press). Bock and Warren (1985) examined grammatical function assignments in sentences containing concepts that differed in imageability or concreteness. Greater concreteness of a concept increases the likelihood that any randomly selected predicate will accept that concept as an argument (Clark & Begun, 1971; Jarvella & Sinnott, 1972; Keil, 1979), meaning that it should be easier, on balance, for a verb to take a more concrete noun as its subject or direct object than a less concrete noun. Furthermore, the semantic specifications of concrete words may be more accessible than those of less concrete words. If functional integration proceeds by assigning the first available and appropriate noun to the subject role of one of the activated verb forms, as the accessibility hypothesis predicts, the subjects of sentences should tend to be more concrete than the direct objects. Likewise, concepts assigned as direct objects (defined as immediate postverbal objects, such as *university* in *The old hermit left the university the property*, or *property* in *The old hermit left the property to the university*) should tend to be more concrete than those assigned as indirect or oblique objects (defined as objects not in immediate postverbal position, such as *property* in *The old hermit left the university the property* and *university* in *The old hermit left the property to the university*).

This was the result that Bock and Warren obtained. There was a reliable tendency for more concrete concepts to appear as subjects rather than direct objects in active and passive sentences (see also James, Thompson, & Baldwin, 1973), and for direct objects to be more concrete than indirect objects in prepositional and double-object dative sentences. In addition, concreteness did *not* predict the order of words in conjunctive noun phrases (e.g. *time and winter*), suggesting that the effects were indeed attributable to the assignment of grammatical functions and not to simple serial ordering mechanisms.

According to the accessibility hypothesis, the integration process should also be influenced by semantic activation. Thus, a highly activated word should be integrated into a functional representation faster than a less activated word. As a result, highly activated words should tend to occur more often as the subjects of sentences than as the objects. These results were obtained in the experiment described above by Bock (in press): Nouns were more likely to be used as the heads of subject phrases when they were semantically primed than when they were not. Since this effect was significant for semantic but not phonological priming (when the sets of primes were matched in relatedness to the target words), it also supports the argument that the linking process occurs over semantically represented words.

These findings lend credence to the conceptual accessibility hypothesis. Functional integration proceeds by attempting to link concepts to the subject role, favouring more accessible or more activated concepts over others. The strength of the verb form itself seems to play a major role, however, as indicated by the overwhelming preference for active over passive verbs. It is clear that in the competition for a subject, the active wins more often than the passive. However, if the patient in an event (for example) is substantially more accessible than the agent, verb strength may be overridden by the ease or speed with which the word expressing the patient can be linked to the passive form, as its subject.

The functional representation created in this fashion initiates two further processes, the generation of constituent frames, and the activation of phonological representations. These are co-ordinated to form an ordered representation of lexical forms by constituent integration processes.

Constituent Integration

Just as in functional integration, the accessibility of lexical representations (though in this case phonological rather than semantic representations) influences the course of constituent integration. This is assumed to result from pressure to assign more accessible phonological representations to earlier phrases. The *phonological accessibility* hypothesis, then, is that the serial order of words is sensitive to the ease of activating or retrieving their phonological forms.

Much of the evidence for phonological accessibility comes from studies of conjoined phrases, including both conventional phrases (e.g. *salt and pepper, bread and butter, hale and hearty*) and spontaneous spoken phrases. Kelly (1986) has found that frequent words tend to precede infrequent words in conjoined phrases; since frequency affects phonological more than semantic retrieval processes (e.g. Huttenlocher & Kubicek, 1983), this may be attributable to the ease of retrieving or activating the phonological representations of words. Shorter words also tend to precede longer ones in phrasal conjuncts (Bock & Warren, 1985; Cooper & Ross, 1975; Kelly, 1986; Pinker & Birdsong, 1979), perhaps as a result of the greater accessibility of short words in memory (Baddeley, Thomson, & Buchanan, 1975; Brown & McNeill, 1966; Calhoon, 1935; see Bock, 1982 for discussion), although there is possibly a rhythmic component to the effect as well (Kelly & Bock, in preparation). Finally, Bock (1985) found that phonologically inhibited words tended to follow words that were not inhibited, both in phrasal conjuncts and in the major constituents (subject and object) of transitive sentences.

As long as two words that differ in phonological accessibility both occur as conjoined members of the same phrase, the tendency to order them according to their accessibility should create no problems for the constituent integration process. In many such cases, the syntactic roles of the words are identical, and there are no semantic or syntactic consequences of the order actually employed (the exceptions include such cases as *the old men and women*, which is ambiguous between *the [old men] and [women]* and *the old [men and women]*; in the former case *men* and *women* could not invert, while in the latter case they could, without affecting the intended meaning).

There are relatively few places in English where meaning-preserving inversions of this sort are possible: Generally, such inversions result from differences in grammatical function assignments, so a change in syntax accompanies the reversal even though the basic meaning is preserved (as in actives and passives, prepositional and double-object datives, and others like them). The problem is to explain those cases in which differences in phonological accessibility are correlated with word order in sentences in which such syntactic variations are a necessary correlate of the word-order variation. As noted above, Bock (1985) found such effects not only for phrasal conjuncts (where they are unproblematic for most theories) but also for active and passive sentences, providing evidence that the syntactic forms of sentences are likely to be adjusted to allow *phonologically* accessible words to appear early. This means that there must be some type of interaction between the processes that control the assignment of grammatical functions (functional integration) and those that control the assignment of phonological forms to serial positions (constituent integration).

Interactions Between Functional and Constituent Integration

Since grammatical functions are determined during functional integration, any systematic changes in functional relations that are attributable to events occurring during constituent integration imply that the lower level of processing can influence higher-level outcomes. There are two ways in which this might occur; through direct feedback from the lower to the higher level, or through parallel races among representations from the higher to the lower level coupled with lower-level selection among the competitors.

According to the feedback account, as proposed by Levelt and Maassen (1981), difficulties encountered during constituent integration could result in a signal being sent back to the functional representation. This signal instigates preparation of a different functional structure. The signal need not be an active or positive one: Failure to complete the constituent integration process might cause the decay or inhibition of the current functional representation. This could allow other verb forms activated during the initial priming phase to take over. The probability of any of these forms completing the constituent integration process may be heightened to the degree that they generate phrase structures that permit phonologically accessible words to appear early.

The alternative to the feedback account is a parallel race model. This assumes that more than one functional representation, perhaps created by different forms of the same verb, may start out the formulation process. The one that finishes the constituent integration process first (or integrates enough information to allow articulation to begin) should be the one to control the form of the output. A functional structure that generates constituent structures that permit phonologically accessible forms to be integrated into early parts of the utterance should, on the average, be more likely to win than one that does not.

There are arguments for both accounts. The feedback explanation is at least superficially more compatible with evidence that suggests a relationship between phonological accessibility and hesitations or utterance timing. Levelt and Maassen (1981, Experiments 2 and 3) found longer latencies to initiate utterances in which a less accessible word preceded a more accessible word, relative to utterances with the words in the opposite order. Furthermore, difficulties in lexicalising the second noun of an utterance appeared early in the preferred forms of utterances than when they that word to be postponed. Similarly, Streim and Chapman (in press) observed that in children's picture descriptions the use of low-frequency words early in sentences was accompanied by increased dysfluency. Finally, Bock (1985) found more dysfluency when phonologically inhibited words appeared early in the preferred forms of utterances than when they appeared later. Such findings suggest (though they clearly do not require) that the production system tries to fill in an active phrasal frame, rather than simply selecting among competing frames.

Other observations are more compatible with the parallel model. A variety of errors and infelicities of speech have the strong appearance of phrasal blends, mixing two alternative forms of expression. These include syntactic blends (e.g. "This is getting very difficult to cut this," a possible blend of "This is getting very difficult to cut" and "It is getting very difficult to cut this"; Stemberger, 1982) and blends of more distantly related linguistic expressions for the same idea (e.g. "we know the scope of how bad the problem is," "rain today, occasionally heavy at times," and "I miss being out of touch with academia"—spoken by a professor on leave in the computer industry). This kind of blending has received little attention except in work by Bolinger (1961), Butterworth (1982), Fay (1982), and Stemberger (1982). Butterworth discusses it under the heading of alternative plan errors, errors that result from interference between alternative linguistic formulations of the same thought (rather than interference from an unintended thought). Such errors suggest that different forms of expression can be activated at lower levels of processing.

Evidence for structural activation can also be found in syntactic perseveration, or the persistence of a particular form of expression across successive sentences in speech. Syntactic persistence has been observed in natural conversation (Schenkein, 1980), in sociolinguistic interviews (Weiner & Labov, 1983), and in controlled experimental contexts (Bock, 1986; Levelt & Kelter, 1982). For example, Bock (1986) found that subjects tended to repeat the syntactic form of a previously heard sentence when they were describing an unrelated event. A subject who had just heard the prepositional dative sentence *The governess made a pot of tea for the princess* was more likely to describe a subsequent picture as "A clerk showing a dress to a man" than as "A clerk showing a man a dress". The opposite pattern was found for subjects who heard the double-object dative, *The governess made the princess a pot of tea*. This occurred even though subjects were unaware of any relationships between the sentences and pictures.

This alternation between forms is compatible with the hypothesis that different structural realisations compete with one another. Resolution of the competition could be achieved in any of several ways. Recently used structures may tend to dominate less recently used structures (perhaps because of higher activation levels). The ease of constituent integration could also contribute to selection among alternative forms, with structures that permit earlier positioning of accessible lexical forms more likely to survive the competition than structures that place them late.

Clearly, none of the evidence for feedback or parallel activation is strong, let alone definitive. Indeed, *both* may occur. This would entail the activation of competing structural forms at every level, with feedback from lower to higher levels helping to select one of the candidates for further processing. In essence, this is the second of the three modifications proposed earlier for Lashley's (1951) co-ordination model, and the problem with it is the same. If there are a multitude of ways of expressing the same idea, and if all of these can be generated in parallel, the number of possible realisations and interactions among them is formidable. Without severe restrictions on the form or number of realisations for a given message, this approach could turn out to be intractable.

There are, then, at least two plausible ways in which events during constituent integration could influence events during functional integration. One involves feedback from the lower to the higher level, and the second involves parallel generation of competing lower-level structures by higher-level representations. Either or both of these may be operative in sentence formulation, serving to resolve conflicts between syntactic schemes and lexical forms.

A Summary and Some Predictions

The revised model combines the level features of the Fromkin-Garrett approach with an elaborated version of the accessibility hypothesis developed in Bock (1982). According to this hypothesis, the ease of retrieving, activating, or integrating lexical information during both functional and constituent integration influences the time course of formulation, the structure of the sentences produced, and the characteristics of the errors that occur. It makes a number of predictions that follow from differences in the lexical representations that are called on during functional and constituent integration, and from differences in the consequences of the integration processes for sentence form. Broadly, factors related to conceptual accessibility should affect functional integration, particularly assignments to grammatical functions. Factors related to phonological accessibility—the accessibility of phonologically-specified lexical forms—should affect constituent integration, particularly assignments to serially ordered positions in phrasal frames.

Some of the specific predictions of this model apply to normal, error-free speech, and others apply to errors. The remainder of this section summarises these in turn.

In normal speech, variables such as animacy, concreteness, and level of semantic activation should influence assignments to grammatical functions during functional integration. Functions high in the hierarchy of grammatical relations should take priority over those lower in the hierarchy, yielding a tendency to link conceptually accessible representations to verb forms that permit them to be subjects, other things being equal. (Obviously, other things are rarely equal. In particular, verb forms differ in strength, so that a strong form—e.g. an active—will generally dominate a weaker form— e.g. a passive. The prediction here is simply that the probability of a weaker form will increase over its baseline when that form allows the more accessible of two nominal arguments to be linked to a higher-level role.) Because grammatical function assignments affect serial order, there will often be an influence of conceptual accessibility on order, but an indirect one that occurs only as a result of the function assignment process. Support for these hypotheses has been found in experiments reported by Bock (in press), and Bock and Warren (1985).

Variations in phonological accessibility created by differences in frequency, phonological complexity, and level of phonological activation should influence the constituent integration process to a greater degree than functional integration. Furthermore, because the output of the constituent integration process directly determines serial order, phonological accessibility can have a more immediate impact on order than conceptual accessibility. Constructions in which order is not determined by differences in grammatical function assignment (as in conjunctive noun phrases) provide the clearest test cases, and strong support for the hypothesis (Cooper & Ross, 1975; Kelly, 1986; Kelly et al., 1985). For constructions in which order *is* determined by grammatical function assignments, variations in phonological accessibility may disrupt the constituent integration process, causing hesitations and dysfluencies, or prompting the development or use of a different structural frame with a different word order. Some support for these ideas has been found in experiments by Bock (1985), Levelt and Maassen (1981), and Streim and Chapman (in press).

Effects of accessibility should also show up in errors. During functional integration, semantic representations may be linked to the wrong grammatical functions, producing exchanges (e.g., *a wife for his job*; Fromkin, 1973b). The hypothesis predicts that such errors should reveal an accessibility effect, with more accessible words tending to show up in higher-level grammatical roles. Informal examination of a small set of word-exchange errors supported this prediction: In 10 out of 13 errors in which the words differed in concreteness and grammatical function assignments, the more concrete word appeared in a higher-level grammatical role than the less concrete ($P < .05$ by a sign test). In the single error in which the words were of equal concreteness but differed in animacy, the animate word appeared in the higher-level function. A different type of error, semantic substitution, ought to be more probable when a conceptually accessible word competes with a less accessible one for the same function, and this pattern seems to hold (Kelly, 1986).

The kinds of errors that occur during or after constituent integration should be more influenced by phonological accessibility than by conceptual accessibility. There is no principled reason why word exchanges cannot be initiated at this level, when phonological forms are inserted into constituent frames. Such exchanges would be expected to observe form-class constraints more often than not, since phonological forms are linked to terminal phrase structure positions according to form class. However, the form-class constraint may be weaker, since the same phonological form may represent words from several different form-class categories (e.g. /bæg/ may serve as a noun, adjective, or verb; cf. *paper bag*, *bag lady*, *bag a seat*). In addition, exchanges should occur less often during constituent integration than during functional integration, to the extent that they have to cross the boundaries of the primary units of constituent assembly or articulation. Thus, exchanges initiated during constituent integration may rarely be completed unless they are very close in the ordered string.

This predicts that the full exchanges most likely to show phonological accessibility effects are those that occur between phrasal units that are short enough to allow their elements to be assembled or articulated together, such as phrases containing bare nouns separated by a single preposition or conjunction (although exchanges are hard to diagnose in conjunctions, it is sometimes possible). Of the 5 exchanges meeting this criterion in Fromkin's published corpus (1973b), the more frequent word moves ahead of the less frequent in 4 (80%). In comparison, of the 14 exchanges separated by more than one word, the more frequent precedes the less frequent in only 8 (57%). If this hypothesis can be supported in a larger sample of errors, it may help to explain the high incidence of exchanges between words in prepositional phrases. There are effectively two points at which such errors can occur, versus just one for exchanges that span longer distances.

Another type of error that perhaps reflects a constituent integration problem is the shift. Shifts involve the apparent movement of a single word to a position earlier or later in an utterance (e.g. *You refuse me to let . . . to let me do it*; Stemberger, 1984). Words that move to earlier positions should tend to be phonologically more accessible, and Stemberger (1984) provides some evidence that they are. Closed-class words occasionally shift position in sentences, moving ahead of or behind open-class words. Since closed-class words are among the most frequent in the language, they should tend to move earlier rather than later if their accessibility is playing a role. Stemberger found that they were significantly more likely to move to an earlier position.

It appears that the model is consistent with an interesting range of data from errors and from normal, error-free speech. In addition, some of its principles may be extendable to levels lower in the formulation process. For example, accessibility seems to play a role even in errors involving individual sounds. Levitt and Healy (1985) used the error induction technique developed by Baars et al. (1975) to show that, in sound misorderings, frequent phonemes tend to occur earlier rather than later. Such data suggest that variations in accessibility influence processing at all levels of the speech production process.

CONCLUSION

The co-ordination of the lexical and structural components of sentences is strongly sensitive to dynamic features of information retrieval. The co-ordination appears to occur at two levels, one at which semantically specified lexical items are assigned to grammatical roles (functional integration), and a second at which phonologically specified lexical items are assigned to positions in a phrase structure representation (constituent integration). These levels differ in the kinds of information to which they are most sensitive, in what they do with that information, and in the effects of their operations on serial order. However, they are not fully independent. Constituent integration processes are influenced by factors that are beyond the control of the functional representation, such as the accessibility of phonological forms, and these can in turn affect the output from functional integration processes, either directly (through feedback) or indirectly (through selection among competing representations).

In the terms established by Lashley (1951) for the analysis of the co-ordination problem, the schema for order operates at the level of constituent integration. This schema, or frame, appears to take the form of a phrase structure representation of the sentence. It retrieves words, roughly in order, from a set of activated, phonologically specified lexical forms. In the ideal case, words should be more or less smoothly integrated into the frame, to be elaborated for articulation by phonetic processes. However, variations in the level of activation or accessibility of the phonological representations may produce errors, dysfluencies, or reformulations of the schema.

The ordering schema and the phonologically specified words are generated from or activated by an abstract representation of word meanings linked to grammatical functions, or the functional representation. This representation helps to ensure the compatibility of generated phrase structures with activated phonological representations, in some respects serving the function of Lashley's (1951) determining tendency—"[restricting] behavior within definite limits (p. 122)"—though Lashley had in mind a less language-bound, more ideational entity. It is formed by functional integration processes, which appear to respond to differences in the accessibility of conceptual arguments (the semantic representations of words) by varying grammatical function assignments. Sometimes this produces sentences with a changed structural form, and sometimes sentences with errors of functional assignment, as in word exchanges.

Lashley's analysis of the co-ordination problem is thus very much with us. Progress has been made in filling in the outlines he established, with the primary advances having come in describing the language structures and units that participate in the production process. We know considerably less about how information develops and flows through the system, how structural frames or ordering schemas are developed, and how the integrative links between structures and units are achieved. Because these processes of integration may hold the key to understanding much of the dysfluency, error, and structural variability observed in speech, they deserve serious attention.

Although co-ordination problems sometimes disrupt the flow of speech, there is also a positive side to the mechanisms of co-ordination. They seem to permit fluid modifications of speech, providing solutions for the kinds of information processing problems that speakers regularly confront, including problems in lexical retrieval and structural elaboration. Some of the more powerful ecological constraints on speech illustrate the importance of such capabilities. One of these is found in the relation of speech to time. Speech rates have both upper and lower bounds. The actual upper limit may be a matter of anatomy and physiology, but there is an effective upper limit imposed by the comprehension abilities of listeners. More important in the present context are the lower bounds created by the patience and politeness of audiences, or a speaker's willingness to impose on either. In speaking, people are rarely at liberty to take as much time as they might like to say what they have to say, or to find just the right word or turn of phrase. The maintenance of an acceptable rate of speech is therefore one of the goals of most speakers.

A second, closely related constraint arises in the effort after fluency: The linguistic events of speech should be distributed across time in a way that approximates not just an acceptable average rate, but also comes close to what Clark and Clark (1977) called the "ideal delivery." In the ideal delivery, "most types of clauses are executed in a single fluent speech train under one smooth intonation contour (p. 261)." as Clark and Clark note, some construct such as that of the ideal delivery is presupposed in all analyses of production, with deviations from that ideal pointing to a problem in formulation or execution.

Slobin (1977) has examined how such constraints may shape the form that language takes. Because speech must be producible (and understandable) in the time that is customarily available to its users, it must be reasonably efficient in its transmission of ideas, making accurate communication possible with minimal time and effort. Contraction (*I'm, they're, don't, wanna, lemme, gonna*) is one example of the many ways that speakers modify the language to achieve greater efficiency, changing a form to express an idea more rapidly.

Another way to achieve efficiency is through flexible use of the structural devices available for the expression of messages. Such flexibility provides a way of detouring around difficulties in lexical retrieval or problems in the creation of a syntactic plan. Speakers (at least neurologically intact speakers) are rarely stymied by formulation problems, suggesting that such detours help to sustain ordinary, day-to-day conversational interaction. The framework proposed above is compatible with the assumption that there are points at which formulation processes can make selections among alternative devices, drawing on those alternatives that are made available most rapidly. The places where these selections can be made help to define levels of processing in the creation of speech.

It would be a mistake, however, to regard these alternatives as existing in order to provide this flexibility. Instead, they may be available simply as a byproduct of the architecture of the language production system. This system permits the linguistic expression of ideas by linking a discrete vocabulary with generative procedures for the creation of sentences. The requirements of this linking process seem to create natural joints in the system, joints at which other forces in the communicative situation may have an effect.

What casts doubt on the claim that "the joints"—the points at which lexical-syntactic integration occurs—exist to facilitate communication is that they may just as often disrupt it. The problems are hypothesised to appear in the dysfluencies and errors that plague spontaneous speech. Errors and structural variation may thus be different sides of the same coin: If the processing system fails to detect or resolve a conflict, an error will result, but if the conflict is detected and negotiated, momentary speech disruptions or structural changes may occur. The trading relationship between speech rate and error rate lends support to this speculation, as does the complementarity in the contexts of hesitations and errors (Garrett, 1982).

In summary, language production requires the co-ordination, at several levels, of the units of language with the structures that order them in time. This co-ordination is made necessary by the processing system's solution to the central computational problem of production, the linearisation of thought in speech. The processes that effect the co-ordination must reconcile conflicts between systems (the conceptual system and the syntactic system, the syntactic system and the lexical system, the lexical system and the phonetic system) created by predispositions within each one. These conflicts sometimes produce errors, sometimes hesitations, and sometimes structural variability, exerting powerful control over the fluency and efficiency of speech.

ACKNOWLEDGEMENTS

Preparation of this chapter was aided by a Biomedical Research Support Grant from Michigan State University. Gary Dell, Michael Kelly, and Rose Zacks provided very helpful comments on an earlier version of the manuscript.

REFERENCES

Baars, B. J. (1980) The competing plans hypothesis; An heuristic viewpoint on the causes of errors in speech. In H. W. Dechert & M. Raupach (Eds.), *Temporal variables in speech: Studies in honor of Frieda Goldman-Eisler*. The Hague: Mouton, 39–49.

Baars, B. J., Motley, M. T., & MacKay, D. G. (1975) Output editing for lexical status in artificially elicited slips of the tongue. *Journal of Verbal Learning and Verbal Behaviour, 14*, 382–391.

Baddeley, A. D., Thomson, N., & Buchanan, M. (1975) Word length and the structure of short-term memory. *Journal of Verbal Learning and Verbal Behaviour, 14*, 575–589.

Balota, D. A. & Chumbley, J. I. (1985) The locus of word-frequency effects in the pronunciation task: Lexical access and/or production? *Journal of Memory and Language, 24*, 89–106.

Bawden, H. H. (1900) A study of lapses. *Psychological Monographs, 3*, 1–121.

Bever, T. G., Fodor, J. A., & Weksel, W. (1965) On the acquisition of syntax: A critique of "contextual generalisation." *Psychological Review, 72*, 467–482.

Bock, J. K. (1982) Toward a cognitive psychology of syntax: Information processing contributions to sentence formulation. *Psychological Review, 89*, 1–47.

Bock, J. K. (1985) *Lexical inhibition in sentence production*. Paper presented at the meeting of the Psychonomic Society, Boston, Massachusetts, November 1985.

Bock, J. K. (in press) Meaning, sound, and syntax: Lexical priming in sentence production. *Journal of Experimental Psychology: Learning, Memory, and Cognition*.

Bock, J. K. (1986) Syntactic persistence in language production. *Cognitive Psychology, 18*, 355–387.

Bock, J. K. & Irwin, D. E. (1980) Syntactic effects of information availability in sentence production. *Journal of Verbal Learning and Verbal Behaviour, 19*, 467–484.

Bock, J. K. & Warren, R. K. (1985) Conceptual accessibility and syntactic structure in sentence formulation. *Cognition, 21*, 47–67.

Bolinger, D. L. (1961) Verbal evocation. *Lingua, 10*, 113–127.

Boomer, D. S. (1965) Hesitation and grammatical encoding. *Language and Speech, 8*, 148–158.

Boomer, D. S. & Laver, J. D. M. (1968) Slips of the tongue. *British Journal of Disorders of Communication, 3*, 2–12.

Bower, G. H., Clark, M. C., Lesgold, A. M., & Winzenz, D. (1969) Hierarchical retrieval schemes in recall of categorised word lists. *Journal of Verbal Learning and Verbal Behaviour, 8*, 323–343.

Bradley, D. C., Garrett, M. F., & Zurif, E. B. (1980) Syntactic deficits in Broca's aphasia. In D. Caplan (Ed.), *Biological studies of mental processes*. Cambridge, Mass.: M.I.T. Press, 269–286.

Braine, M. D. S. (1963) On learning the grammatical order of words. *Psychological Review*, 70, 323–348.

Braine, M. D. S. (1965) On the basis of phrase structure: A reply to Bever, Fodor, and Weksel. *Psychological Review*, 72, 483–492.

Bresnan, J. (Ed.) (1982) *The mental representation of grammatical relations*. Cambridge, Mass.: M.I.T. Press.

Bresnan, J. & Kaplan, R. M. (1982) Introduction: Grammars as mental representations of language. In J. Bresnan (Ed.), *The mental representation of grammatical relations*. Cambridge, Mass.: M.I.T. Press, xvii–lii.

Brown, R. & McNeill, D. (1966) The "tip of the tongue" phenomenon. *Journal of Verbal Learning and Verbal Behaviour*, 5, 325–337.

Butterworth, B. (1980) Some constraints on models of language production. In B. Butterworth (Ed.), *Language production: Vol. 1. Speech and talk*. London: Academic Press, 423–459.

Butterworth, B. (1982) Speech errors: Old data in search of new theories. In A. Cutler (Ed.), *Slips of the tongue and language production*. Amsterdam: Mouton, 73–108.

Calhoon, S. W. (1935) Influence of syllabic length and rate of auditory presentation on ability to reproduce disconnected word lists. *Journal of Experimental Psychology*, 18, 612–620.

Chomsky, N. (1965) *Aspects of the theory of syntax*. Cambridge, Mass.: M.I.T. Press.

Chomsky, N. (1981) *Lectures on government and binding*. Dordrecht: Foris.

Clark, H. H. & Begun, J. S. (1971) The semantics of sentence subjects. *Language and Speech*, 14, 34–46.

Clark, H. H. & Clark, E. V. (1977) *Psychology and language*. New York: Harcourt Brace Jovanovich.

Colombo, L. (1986) Activation and inhibition with orthographically similar words. *Journal of Experimental Psychology: Human Perception and Performance*, 12, 226–234.

Cooper, W. E., Paccia, J. M., & Lapointe, S. G. (1978) Hierarchical coding in speech timing. *Cognitive Psychology*, 10, 154–177.

Cooper, W. E. & Ross, J. R. (1975) World order. In R. E. Grossman, L. J. San, & T. J. Vance (Eds.), *Papers from the parasession on functionalism*. Chicago: Chicago Linguistic Society, 63–111.

Cooper, W. E. & Sorenson, J. M. (1981) *Fundamental frequency in sentence production*. New York: Springer-Verlag.

Daneman, M. & Green, I. (1986) Individual differences in comprehending and producing words in context. *Journal of Memory and Language*, 25, 1–18.

Deese, J. (1984) *Thought into speech: The psychology of a language*. Englewood Cliffs, N.J.: Prentice-Hall.

Dell, G. S. (1984) Representation of serial order in speech: Evidence from the repeated phoneme effect in speech errors. *Journal of Experimental Psychology: Learning, Memory, and Cognition*, 10, 222–233.

Dell, G. S. (1985) Positive feedback in hierarchical connectionist models. *Cognitive Science*, 9, 3–23.

Dell, G. S. (1986) A spreading-activation theory of retrieval in sentence production. *Psychological Review*, 93, 283–321.

Dell, G. S. & Reich, P. A. (1981) Stages in sentence production: An analysis of speech error data. *Journal of Verbal Learning and Verbal Behaviour*, 20, 611–629.

Dommergues, J.-Y. & Grosjean, F. (1981) Performance structures in the recall of sentences. *Memory and Cognition*, 9, 478–486.

Ellis, A. W. (1980) On the Freudian theory of speech errors. In V. A. Fromkin (Ed.), *Errors in linguistic performance: Slips of the tongue, ear, pen, and hand.* New York: Academic Press, 123–131.

Ericsson, K. A., Chase, W. G., & Faloon, S. (1980) Acquisition of a memory skill. *Science, 208,* 1181–1182.

Fay, D. (1980a) Performing transformations. In R. A. Cole (Ed.), *Perception and production of fluent speech.* Hillsdale, N.J.: Lawrence Erlbaum Associates Inc., 441–468.

Fay, D. (1980b) Transformational errors. In V. A. Fromkin (Ed.) *Errors in linguistic performance: Slips of the tongue, ear, pen, and hand.* New York: Academic Press, 111–122.

Fay, D. (1982) Substitutions and splices: A study of sentence blends. In A. Cutler (Ed.), *Slips of the tongue and language production.* Amsterdam: Mouton, 163–195.

Fay, D. & Cutler, A. (1977) Malapropisms and the structure of the mental lexicon. *Linguistic Inquiry, 8,* 505–520.

Fodor, J. A., Bever, T. G., & Garrett, M. F. (1974) *The psychology of language.* New York: McGraw-Hill.

Ford, M. (1982) Sentence planning units: Implications for the speaker's representation of meaningful relations underlying sentences. In J. Bresnan (Ed.), *The mental representation of grammatical relations.* Cambridge, Mass.: M.I.T. Press, 797–827.

Ford, M. & Holmes, V. M. (1978) Planning units and syntax in sentence production. *Cognition, 6,* 35–53.

Forster, K. I. (1966) Left-to-right processes in the construction of sentences. *Journal of Verbal Learning and Verbal Behaviour, 5,* 285–291.

Forster, K. I. (1967) Sentence completion latencies as a function of constituent structure. *Journal of Verbal Learning and Verbal Behaviour, 6,* 878–883.

Forster, K. I. (1968a) Sentence completion in left- and right-branching languages. *Journal of Verbal Learning and Verbal Behaviour, 7,* 296–299.

Forster, K. I. (1968b) The effect of removal of length constraint on sentence completion times. *Journal of Verbal Learning and Verbal Behaviour, 7,* 253–254.

Foss, D. J. & Fay, D. (1975) Linguistic theory and performance models. In D. Cohen & J. R. Wirth (Eds.), *Testing linguistic hypotheses.* New York: Wiley, 65–91.

Frazier, L. (1985) Syntactic complexity. In D. R. Dowty, L. Karttunen, & A. M. Zwicky (Eds.), *Natural language parsing: Psychological, computational, and theoretical perspectives.* Cambridge: Cambridge University Press, 129–189.

Freud, S. (1920) *A general introduction to psychoanalysis.* New York: Washington Square Press.

Fromkin, V. A. (1971) The nonanomalous nature of anomalous utterances. *Language, 47,* 27–52.

Fromkin, V. A. (1973a) Slips of the tongue. *Scientific American, 229,* 110–116.

Fromkin, V. A. (Ed.) (1973b) *Speech errors as linguistic evidence.* The Hague: Mouton.

Garrett, M. F. (1975) The analysis of sentence production. In G. H. Bower (Ed.), *The psychology of learning and motivation,* Vol. 9. New York: Academic Press, 133–177.

Garrett, M. F. (1980) Levels of processing in sentence production. In B. Butterworth (Ed.), *Language production, Vol. 1, Speech and talk.* London: Academic Press, 177–220.

Garrett, M. F. (1982) Production of speech: Observations from normal and pathological language use. In A. Ellis (Ed.), *Normality and pathology in cognitive functions.* London: Academic Press, 19–76.

Gazdar, G., Klein, E., Pullum, G., & Sag, I. (1985) *Generalised phrase structure grammar.* Cambridge, Mass.: Harvard University Press.

Goldman-Eisler, F. (1958a) Speech production and the predictability of words in context. *Quarterly Journal of Experimental Psychology, 10,* 96–106.

Goldman-Eisler, F. (1958b) The predictability of words in context and the length of pauses in speech. *Language and Speech, 1*, 226–231.

Goldman-Eisler, F. (1968) *Psycholinguistics: Experiments in spontaneous speech*. London: Academic Press.

Green, T. R. G. (1979) The necessity of syntax markers: Two experiments with artificial languages. *Journal of Verbal Learning and Verbal Behaviour, 18*, 481–496.

Grosjean, F., Grosjean, L., & Lane, H. (1979) The patterns of silence: Performance structures in sentence production. *Cognitive Psychology, 11*, 58–81.

Grosjean, F., Lane, H., Battison, R., & Teuber, H. (1981) The invariance of sentence performance structures across language modality. *Journal of Experimental Psychology: Human Perception and Performance, 7*, 216–230.

Harley, T. A. (1984) A critique of top-down independent levels models of speech production: Evidence from non-plan-internal speech errors. *Cognitive Science, 8*, 191–219.

Humphrey, G. (1963) *Thinking: An introduction to its experimental psychology*. New York: Wiley.

Huttenlocher, J. & Kubicek, L. F. (1983) The source of relatedness effects on naming latency. *Journal of Experimental Psychology: Learning, Memory, and Cognition, 9*, 486–496.

James, C. T., Thompson, J. G., & Baldwin, J. M. (1973) The reconstructive process in sentence memory. *Journal of Verbal Learning and Verbal Behaviour, 12*, 51–63.

James, W. (1890) *The principles of psychology*, Vol. 1. New York: Dover.

Jarvella, R. J. & Sinnott, J. (1972) Contextual constraints on noun distributions to some English verbs by children and adults. *Journal of Verbal Learning and Verbal Behaviour, 11*, 47–53.

Johnson, N. F. (1965) The psychological reality of phrase-structure rules. *Journal of Verbal Learning and Verbal Behaviour, 4*, 469–475.

Johnson, N. F. (1966a) On the relationship between sentence structure and the latency in generating the sentence. *Journal of Verbal Learning and Verbal Behaviour, 5*, 375–380.

Johnson, N. F. (1966b) The influence of associations between elements of structured verbal responses. *Journal of Verbal Learning and Verbal Behaviour, 5*, 369–374.

Katz, J. J. (1977) A proper theory of names. *Philosophical Studies, 31*, 1–80.

Keenan, E. L. & Comrie, B. (1977) Noun phrase accessibility and universal grammar. *Linguistic Inquiry, 8*, 63–99.

Keil, F. C. (1979) *Semantic and conceptual development: An ontological perspective*. Cambridge, Mass.: Harvard University Press.

Kelly, M. H. (1986) *On the selection of linguistic options*. Unpublished doctoral dissertation, Cornell University.

Kelly, M. H. & Bock, J. K. (in preparation) *Rhythmic structure and lexical stress*.

Kelly, M. H., Bock, J. K., & Keil, F. C. (1985) *Sentence production and prototypicality: Conceptual versus lexical accessibility*. Paper presented at the meeting of the Psychonomic Society, Boston, Massachusetts, November 1985.

Kelly, M. H., Bock, J. K., & Keil, F. C. (1986) Prototypicality in a linguistic context: Effects on sentence structure. *Journal of Memory and Language, 25*, 59–74.

Kempen, G. & Hoenkamp, E. (in press) An incremental procedural grammar for sentence formulation. *Cognitive Science*.

Kempen, G. & Huijbers, P. (1983) The lexicalisation process in sentence production and naming: Indirect election of words. *Cognition, 14*, 185–209.

Klatt, D. H. (1975) Vowel lengthening is syntactically determined in a connected discourse. *Journal of Phonetics, 3*, 129–140.

Lachman, R. (1973) Uncertainty effects on time to access the internal lexicon. *Journal of Experimental Psychology, 99*, 199–208.

Lachman, R., Shaffer, J. P., & Hennrikus, D. (1974) Language and cognition: Effects of stimulus codability, name-word frequency, and age of acquisition on lexical reaction time. *Journal of Verbal Learning and Verbal Behaviour, 13*, 613–625.

Lashley, K. S. (1951) The problem of serial order in behaviour. In L. A. Jeffress (Ed.), *Cerebral mechanisms in behaviour*. New York: Wiley, 112–136.

Levelt, W. J. M. (1983) Monitoring and self-repair in speech. *Cognition, 14*, 41–104.

Levelt, W. J. M. & Kelter, S. (1982) Surface form and memory in question answering. *Cognitive Psychology, 14*, 78–106.

Levelt, W. & Maassen, B. (1981) Lexical search and order of mention in sentence production. In W. Klein & W. Levelt (Eds.), *Crossing the boundaries in linguistics*. Dordrecht: Reidel, 221–252.

Levitt, A. G. & Healy, A. F. (1985) The roles of phoneme frequency, similarity, and availability in the experimental elicitation of speech errors. *Journal of Memory and Language, 24*, 717–733.

Lindsay, P. H. & Norman, D. A. (1977) *Human information processing: An introduction to psychology*, 2nd ed. New York: Academic Press.

Lindsley, J. R. (1975) Producing simple utterances: How far ahead do we plan? *Cognitive Psychology, 7*, 1–19.

Lounsbury, F. G. (1954) Transitional probability, linguistic structure, and systems of habit-family hierarchies. In C. E. Osgood & T. A. Sebeok (Eds.), *Psycholinguistics: A survey of theory and research problems*. Bloomington: Indiana University Press, 93–125.

MacKay, D. G. (1970) Spoonerisms: The structure of errors in the serial order of speech. *Neuropsychologia, 8*, 323–350.

MacKay, D. G. (1973) Complexity in output systems: Evidence from behavioural hybrids. *American Journal of Psychology, 86*, 785–806.

MacKay, D. G. (1982) The problems of flexibility, fluency, and speed-accuracy trade-off in skilled behaviour. *Psychological Review, 89*, 483–506.

Maclay, H. & Osgood, C. E. (1959) Hesitation phenomena in spontaneous English speech. *Word, 15*, 19–44.

Martin, E. & Roberts, K. H. (1966) Grammatical factors in sentence retention. *Journal of Verbal Learning and Verbal Behaviour, 5*, 211–218.

Martin, E. & Roberts, K. H. (1967) Sentence length and sentence retention in the free learning situation. *Psychonomic Science, 8*, 535.

Martin, E., Roberts, K. H., & Collins, A. M. (1968) Short-term memory for sentences. *Journal of Verbal Learning and Verbal Behaviour, 7*, 560–566.

McCauley, C., Parmelee, C. M., Sperber, R. D., & Carr, T. H. (1980) Early extraction of meaning from pictures and its relation to conscious identification. *Journal of Experimental Psychology: Human Perception and Performance, 6*, 265–276.

Meringer, R. (1908) *Aus dem Leben der Sprache: Versprechen, Kindersprache, Nachahmungstrieb*. Berlin: V. Behr's Verlag.

Meringer, R. & Meyer, K. (1895) *Versprechen und Verlesen: Eine Psychologisch-Linguistische Studie*. Stuttgart: Göschensche Verlagsbuchhandlung.

Meyer, D. E. & Gordon, P. C. (1985) Speech production: Motor programming of phonetic features. *Journal of Memory and Language, 24*, 3–26.

Miller, G. A. & McKean, K. O. (1964) A chronometric study of some relations between sentences. *Quarterly Journal of Experimental Psychology, 16*, 297–308.

Morgan, J. L. & Newport, E. L. (1981) The role of constituent structure in the induction of an artificial language. *Journal of Verbal Learning and Verbal Behaviour, 20*, 67–85.

Motley, M. T. (1980) Verification of "Freudian slips" and semantic prearticulatory editing via laboratory-induced spoonerisms. In V. A. Fromkin (Ed.), *Errors in linguistic performance: Slips of the tongue, ear, pen, and hand*. New York: Academic Press, 133–147.

Motley, M. T., Baars, B. J., & Camden, C. T. (1983) Experimental verbal slip studies: A review and an editing model of language encoding. *Communication Monographs, 50,* 79–101.

Nakayama, M. & Crain, S. (1985) *Performance factors in children's sentence production.* Paper presented at the Boston University Conference on Language Development, Boston, Massachusetts, October 1985.

Nooteboom, S. G. (1973) The tongue slips into patterns. In V. A. Fromkin (Ed.), *Speech errors as linguistic evidence.* The Hague: Mouton, 144–156.

Nooteboom, S. G. (1980) Speaking and unspeaking: Detection and correction of phonological and lexical errors in spontaneous speech. In V. A. Fromkin (Ed.), *Errors in linguistic performance: Slips of the tongue, ear, pen, and hand.* New York: Academic Press, 87–95.

Oldfield, R. C. & Wingfield, A. (1964) The time it takes to name an object. *Nature, 202,* 1031–1032.

Oldfield, R. C. & Wingfield, A. (1965) Response latencies in naming objects. *Quarterly Journal of Experimental Psychology, 17,* 273–281.

Perfetti, C. A. (1969a) Lexical density and phrase structure depth as variables in sentence retention. *Journal of Verbal Learning and Verbal Behaviour, 8,* 719–724.

Perfetti, C. A. (1969b) Sentence retention and the depth hypothesis. *Journal of Verbal Learning and Verbal Behaviour, 8,* 101–104.

Perfetti, C. A. & Goodman, D. (1971) Memory for sentences and noun phrases of extreme depth. *Quarterly Journal of Experimental Psychology, 23,* 22–23.

Pick, A. (1913) *Die agrammatischen Sprachstörungen.* Berlin: Springer.

Pinker, S. (1984) *Language learnability and language development.* Cambridge, Mass.: Harvard University Press.

Pinker, S. & Birdsong, D. (1979) Speakers' sensitivity to rules of frozen word order. *Journal of Verbal Learning and Verbal Behaviour, 18,* 497–508.

Potter, J. M. (1980) What was the matter with Dr. Spooner? In V. A. Fromkin (Ed.), *Errors in linguistic performance: Slips of the tongue, ear, pen, and hand.* New York: Academic Press, 13–34.

Potter, M. C. (1985) *Lexical substitutions in immediate recall.* Paper presented at the meeting of the Psychonomic Society, Boston, Massachusetts, November 1985.

Rochester, S. R. & Gill, J. (1973) Production of complex sentences in monologues and dialogues. *Journal of Verbal Learning and Verbal Behaviour, 12,* 203–210.

Ross, J. R. (1967) *Constraints on variables in syntax.* Unpublished doctoral dissertation, Massachusetts Institute of Technology.

Rubin, D. C. (1975) Within word structure in the tip-of-the-tongue phenomenon. *Journal of Verbal Learning and Verbal Behaviour, 14,* 392–397.

Schenkein, J. (1980) A taxonomy for repeating action sequences in natural conversation. In B. Butterworth (Ed.), *Language production: Vol. 1. Speech and talk.* London: Academic Press, 21–47.

Seamon, J. G. & Chumbley, J. I. (1977) Retrieval processes for serial order information. *Memory & Cognition, 5,* 709–715.

Slobin, D. I. (1977) Language change in childhood and in history. In J. Macnamara (Ed.), *Language learning and thought.* New York: Academic Press, 185–214.

Slowiaczek, L. M. & Pisoni, D. B. (1985) *Phonological activation of lexical candidates in auditory word recognition.* Paper presented at the meeting of the Psychonomic Society, Boston, Massachusetts, November 1985.

Sorenson, J. M., Cooper, W. E., & Paccia, J. M. (1978) Speech timing of grammatical categories. *Cognition, 6,* 135–153.

Stemberger, J. P. (1982) Syntactic errors in speech. *Journal of Psycholinguistic Research, 11,* 313–345.

Stemberger, J. P. (1983) Inflectional malapropisms: Form-based errors in English morphology. *Linguistics, 21*, 573-602.

Stemberger, J. P. (1984) Structural errors in normal and agrammatic speech. *Cognitive Neuropsychology, 1*, 281-313.

Stemberger, J. P. (1985) An interactive activation model of language production. In A. Ellis (Ed.), *Progress in the psychology of language*, Vol. 1. London: Lawrence Erlbaum Associates Ltd., 143-186.

Stemberger, J. P., Elman, J. L., & Haden, P. (1985) Interference between phonemes during phoneme monitoring: Evidence for an interactive activation model of speech perception. *Journal of Experimental Psychology: Human Perception and Performance, 11*, 475-489.

Streim, N. & Chapman, R. S. (in press) The effects of discourse support on the organisation and production of children's utterances. *Applied Psycholinguistics*.

Tannenbaum, P. H., Williams, F., & Hillier, C. S. (1965) Word predictability in the environments of hesitations. *Journal of Verbal Learning and Verbal Behaviour, 4*, 134-140.

Taylor, I. (1969) Content and structure in sentence production. *Journal of Verbal Learning and Verbal Behaviour, 8*, 170-175.

Thumb, A. & Marbe, K. (1901) *Experimentelle Untersuchungen über die psychologischen Grundlagen der sprachlichen Analogiebildung*. Leipzig: W. Engelmann.

Weiner, E. J. & Labov, W. (1983) Constraints on the agentless passive. *Journal of Linguistics, 19*, 29-58.

Wingfield, A. (1968) Effects of frequency on identification and naming of objects. *American Journal of Psychology, 81*, 226-234.

Woodworth, R. S. (1938) *Experimental psychology*. New York: Henry Holt.

Yarmey, A. D. (1973) I recognise your face but I can't remember your name: Further evidence on the tip-of-the-tongue phenomenon. *Memory & Cognition, 1*, 287-290.

Yates, F. A. (1966) *The art of memory*. Chicago: University of Chicago Press.

Yngve, V. H. (1960) A model and an hypothesis for language structure. *Proceedings of the American Philosophical Society, 104*, 444-466.

Author Index

Abelson, R., 288, 300
Abramson, A. S., 126, 155
Ades, A. E., 213, 215, 227
Adlam, D., 329, 332
Aguiar, C. S., 78, 109
Aho, A. V., 184, 198, 227
Aibel, I. L., 129, 141, 142, 155
Aitken, P. G., 21, 22, 42
Akmajian, A., 183, 227
Alajouanine, T., 85, 88, 89, 108
Anderson, A., 281, 282, 296
Anderson, J. A., 14, 42
Anderson, J. R., 254, 298
Andrews, G., 62, 108
Antos, S. J., 100, 115
Arbib, M. A., 24, 42
Asam, U., 78, 108
Atkinson, M., 323, 332

Baars, B. J., 338, 371, 381, 384, 389
Bach, E., 263, 296
Baddeley, A. D., 375, 384
Badecker, W., 174, 227
Baer, T. 124, 125, 128, 155

Baker, E., 40, 42, 43
Baldwin, J. M., 374, 387
Balota, D. A., 348, 384
Bardwell, B., 78, 110
Barlow H. B., 14, 26, 42
Barney, H. L., 120, 156
Barratt, M., 321, 332
Bartlett, F. C., 288, 296, 312, 314
Bastian, H. C., 23, 42
Bates, E., 275, 296, 299, 319, 325, 332, 333
Battison, R., 354, 387
Bawden, H. H., 352, 384
Bay, E., 83, 86, 108
Beardsley, W., 283, 284, 298
Beaton, L. E., 75, 113
Becker, J. M. T., 21, 45
Beckers, W., 78, 108
Begun, J. S., 373, 385
Bellugi, U., 32, 42
Bengis, I., 93, 108
Benson, D. F., 72, 75, 78, 110, 111, 114
Benton, A., 64, 108
Berndt, R. S., 173, 228
Berry, T., 40, 42, 43

Bertram, B. L. R., 10, 47
Berwick, R. C., 206, 208, 209, 217, 227
Bever, T. G., 30, 31, 32, 37, 47, 53, 64, 65,
    66, 108, 176, 221, 229, 240, 251, 352,
    358, 384, 386
Birdsong, D., 375, 389
Blackman, H., 284, 300
Blumstein, S., 50, 64, 108, 117
Blumstein, S. E., 120, 124, 132, 153, 154,
    155, 156
Bock, J. K., 338, 339, 351, 366, 368, 370,
    371, 373, 375, 376, 377, 378, 379, 384,
    387
Bock, R. D., 86, 118
Bogen, J. E., 51, 53, 55, 58, 59, 61, 65, 71,
    92, 108, 117
Boggs, J. S., 62, 113
Bolinger, D., 52, 95, 97, 98, 102, 109, 263,
    296, 377, 384
Bond, Z. S., 138, 154
Boomer, D. S., 338, 347, 352, 353, 384
Borer, H., 324, 333
Borod, J., 69, 109
Bosch, P., 255, 259, 263, 265, 267, 297
Bouilland, J., B., 38, 42
Bower, G. H., 254, 296, 324, 341, 384
Bowerman, M., 328, 333
Bowers, K., 50, 54, 112
Boysen, S., 28, 29, 33, 46
Bradley, D., 174, 228
Bradley, D. C., 364, 385
Bradshaw, J. L., 53, 65, 109
Brain, A., 61, 86, 109
Brain, B. W. R., 23, 42
Braine, M., 323, 333
Braine, M. D. S., 167, 228, 325, 351, 385
Branch, C., 114
Bransford, J., 305, 312, 314
Brazier, M. A., 13, 42
Bresnan, J., 167, 181, 184, 192, 193, 210,
    228, 229, 333, 354, 367, 385, 386
Brill, G. A., 292, 298
Briones, A. V., 78, 109
Briscoe, E. J., 201, 210, 216, 228
Broca, P., 57, 109
Bronowski, J., 32, 42
Brown, G., 280, 297
Brown, J. V., 30, 31, 46
Brown, J. W., 75, 103, 109
Brown, K., 75, 109
Brown, R., 85, 109, 327, 333, 345, 375, 385
Brownell, H. H., 69, 73, 109, 111

Bruner, J. S., 318, 319, 325, 333
Bruun, A., 78, 109
Bruun, R. D., 77, 116
Bryden, M. P., 109
Buchanan, A., 60, 109
Buchanan, M., 375, 384
Buchwald, J., 75, 109
Burd, G. D., 10, 42
Butler, R., 63, 109
Butterworth, B., 356, 360, 377, 385

Caine, E. D., 78, 109
Calhoon, S. W., 375, 385
Camaioni, L., 319, 332
Camden, C. T., 371, 389
Canter, G. J., 50, 54, 55, 60, 65, 76, 92, 95,
    100, 109, 117
Caplan, D., 186, 228, 251
Caramazza, A., 173, 174, 227, 228, 234,
    251, 283, 284, 297, 298
Carling, C., 167, 230
Carlson, M., 247, 248, 249, 250, 251
Carmon, A., 64, 109
Carpenter, C. C., 10, 12, 42
Carpenter, P. A., 277, 278, 297
Carr, T. H., 348, 388
Carrell, T. D., 129, 145, 156
Carroll, J. M., 176, 226
Carter, A., 319, 333
Chafe, W., 97, 109
Chalkley, M., 326, 334
Chan, J. L., 50, 112
Chan, S. W.-C., 50, 114
Chang, F. R., 273, 285, 297
Chapman, R. S., 376, 379, 390
Chase, W. G., 345, 386
Cheek, W., 75, 109
Cheney, D. L., 10, 11, 16, 47
Chiarello, R. G., 64, 66, 108
Chomsky, N., 167, 171, 174, 178, 183, 184,
    203, 206, 228, 242, 251, 258, 262, 263,
    265, 297, 305, 307, 314, 322, 333, 354,
    360, 385
Chown, B., 30, 32, 43
Christiaansen, R. E., 275, 297
Chumbley, J. I., 341, 348, 384, 389
Church, K. W., 201, 228
Churchland, P. M., 160, 228
Cicone, M., 69, 111
Ciemins, V., 75, 109
Cirilo, R. K., 285, 297
Clark, E. V., 313, 314, 348, 349, 382, 385

Clark, H. H., 277, 287, 288, 290, 297, 298,
303, 313, 314, 348, 349, 373, 382, 385
Clark, M. C., 341, 384
Clark, R., 98, 109, 322, 333
Clarkin, J., 77, 116
Clifton, C., 248, 251
Cohen, D. J., 77, 78, 109
Cohen, J., 301, 314
Cohen, M. M., 143, 155
Cole, R. A., 124, 154
Collins, A. M., 358, 388
Colombo, L., 370, 385
Coltheart, M., 163, 228
Comrie, B., 27, 42, 372, 387
Connine, C. M., 147, 148, 155
Convis, C. L., 126, 154
Cooper, F. S., 120, 124, 132, 154, 155, 156
Cooper, W. E., 50, 61, 102, 108, 110, 124,
154, 350, 351, 375, 379, 385, 389
Copi, I., 312, 314
Corbett, A. T., 273, 297
Corbit, J. D., 148, 154
Coslett, H., 50, 112
Cotter, C. A., 290, 297
Coughlin, J., 92, 109
Cowey, A., 14, 26, 42
Craig, A., 62, 108
Crain, S., 196, 208, 220, 228, 234, 235, 238,
247, 248, 249, 358, 389
Creutzfeldt, O. D., 13, 42
Critchley, M., 69, 83, 86, 87, 88, 89, 91, 94,
102, 110
Crockett, H. G., 70, 110
Cullicover, H. G., 70, 110
Cullicover, P., 323, 324, 335
Cummings, J. L., 54, 65, 72, 78, 110, 111,
117
Cunningham, A., 29, 42
Curry, F., 63, 110
Curtiss, M., 279, 299
Cutler, A., 100, 117, 338, 345, 346, 353,
386
Czopf, J., 67, 110

Dalby, J., 136, 156
Dalston, R. M., 124, 154
Daneman, M., 277, 297, 348, 385
Danly, M., 60, 61, 110
Dardarananda, R., 50, 111
Darwin, C., 8, 41, 42
Davis, L., 40, 42
Dax, M., 57, 110

De Agostini, M., 109
Decker, L. R., 124, 156
De Divitis, H., 78, 110
Deese, J., 337, 385
De Groot, M. H., 78, 110
Delattre, P. C., 124, 132, 154, 155, 156
Dell, G. S., 286, 297, 338, 339, 346, 347,
352, 355, 356, 368, 369, 370, 371, 385
Denenberg, V. H., 24, 42
Dennett, D. C., 160, 228
De Roeck, A., 179, 228
De Saussure, F., 96, 110
Deschamps, A., 122, 154
Detlor, J., 77, 78, 109
Deutsch, G., 65, 117
Deutsch, W., 327, 333
De Villiers, J., 40, 42
De Villiers, J. G., 333
De Villiers, P. A., 333
Dewart, M. H., 235, 251
Dewson, J. H., 63, 110
Dexter, E. R., 133, 135, 155
Diamond, I., 63, 109
Diamond, I. T., 26, 42
Diehl, R. L., 126, 154
Dingwall, W. O., 29, 42
Dommergues, J.-Y., 354, 385
Dooling, D. J., 275, 297
Dore, J., 321, 333
Dowty, D., 211, 228
Dronkers, N. F., 73, 84, 110

Ebert, R. R., 124, 154
Efron, R., 64, 110
Ehrlich, K., 277, 278, 282, 284, 297
Eimas, P. D., 132, 148, 149, 151, 152, 154,
155
Eisenson, J., 69, 110
Ellis, A. W., 338, 386
Ellis, H. D., 64, 110
Elman, J. L., 370, 389
Erber, B. P., 143, 154
Ericsson, K. A., 341, 386
Ervin-Tripp, S., 55, 110
Erwin, I. J., 60, 118
Escalar, G., 78, 110
Espir, L., 67, 72, 82, 110
Estridge, N. M., 70, 110
Ettlinger, G., 31, 37, 45, 68, 110
Eyzaguirre, C., 74, 110

Faglioni, P., 64, 110

Falmagne, R., 314, 317
Faloon, S., 341, 386
Faltz, L. M., 263, 299
Fant, G., 124, 154
Fay, D., 338, 345, 346, 352, 360, 377, 386
Fedio, P., 76, 115
Ferguson, C., 320, 333
Ferguson, G. W., 10, 12, 42
Fernandes, A. C., 78, 109
Ferreira, F., 248, 251
Ferrier, D. 14, 43
Feyer, A. M., 62, 108
Feyereisen, P., 38, 43
Fillmore, C., 56, 96, 111, 319, 333
Fillmore, C. J., 168, 229
Finavera, L., 78, 110
Fischer-Jorgensen, E., 124, 154
Fisher, C. M., 75, 111
Fisher, J. M., 19, 43
Flagg, P. W., 303, 315
Flamm, L., 69, 111
Fletcher, C., 275, 296
Fodor, J. A., 13, 43, 130, 154, 160, 161,
  176, 205, 229, 240, 245, 251, 351, 358,
  384, 386
Fodor, J. D., 188, 190, 200, 205, 210, 220,
  221, 229
Foldi, N. S., 69, 111
Ford, M., 181, 192, 193, 210, 229, 354, 386
Forster, K. I., 119, 154, 234, 240, 242, 243,
  244, 251, 269, 297, 358, 386
Fortin, D., 64, 114
Foss, D. J., 360, 360, 386
Foster, R. E., 10, 43
Foucault, M., 330, 333
Fouts, R. S., 30, 31, 32, 43
Fowler, C. A., 140, 154
Fradis, A., 72, 93, 113
Francis, W. N., 303, 315
Frankel, M., 78, 111
Franklin, M., 319, 333
Franzen, E. A., 21, 22, 43
Fraser, B. 97, 111
Fraunfelder, U. 131, 155
Frazier, L., 181, 188, 190, 200, 210, 220,
  229, 245, 246, 250, 251, 252, 358, 359,
  386
Fredriksen, J. R., 270, 273, 264, 297
Frege, G., 254, 297, 298
Freiman, R., 39, 47
Freud, S., 338, 386
Fromkin, V. A., 50, 64, 117, 118, 338, 346,
  352, 353, 355, 363, 364, 379, 380, 386
Furness, W. H., 29, 43

Gaitenby, J., 60, 111
Gandour, J., 50, 111
Ganong, W. F. 111, 134, 154
Gans, S. J., 129, 145, 156
Gardner, B. T., 28, 30, 32, 43
Gardner, H., 40, 43, 69, 73, 109, 111, 118,
  306, 315
Gardner, R. A., 28, 30, 32, 43
Garner, A., 40, 42
Garnes, S., 138, 154
Garnham, A., 254, 256, 257, 276, 284, 287,
  291, 298
Garrett, M. F., 174, 176, 213, 221, 228,
  229, 234, 240, 251, 338, 339, 345, 346,
  352, 353, 355, 356, 358, 363, 364, 365,
  366, 367, 369, 383, 385, 386
Garrod, S. C., 280, 281, 282, 288, 290, 291,
  296, 298, 299, 300
Garvey, C., 284, 297, 298
Gay, T., 124, 154
Gazdar, G., 175, 184, 229, 324, 333, 367,
  386
Gazzaniga, M. S., 40, 48, 61, 65, 72, 111
Gelman, R., 303, 315
Gentner, D., 301, 303, 304, 305, 306, 308,
  311, 315, 325, 333
Gerstman, L. J., 124, 155, 156
Geschwind, N., 13, 43, 74, 79, 92, 111
Gibbs, R., 100, 111
Gill, J., 354, 389
Gill, T. V., 30, 31, 46
Gillan, D. J., 35, 36, 43
Giuliani, V, 275, 296
Givòn, T., 326, 333
Glaserfeld, E. C., 30, 31, 46
Gleitman, L., 324, 333
Gloning, I., 83, 111
Gloning, K., 83, 111
Goetz, C. J., 77, 111
Goldin-Meadow, S., 303, 315
Goldman-Eisler, F., 99, 111, 121, 122, 154,
  338, 347, 360, 387
Goldstein, K., 59, 68, 85, 86, 90, 111
Goodglass, H., 71, 83, 84, 85, 111, 114,
  174, 230
Goodin, L., 30, 32, 43
Goodman, D., 358, 389
Goodman, M., 7, 43
Gorden, H., 59, 92, 108

Gordon, H., 64, 71, 111
Gordon, P. C., 338, 370, 388
Gott, P. S., 66, 112
Green, H. D., 22, 43
Green, I., 348, 385
Green, K. P., 126, 129, 137, 140, 141, 142, 144, 145, 146, 154, 155
Green, T. R. G., 351, 387
Greenberg, J. H., 27, 43
Greenfield, P. M., 325, 333
Grober, E. H., 283, 284, 297, 298
Grodzinski, Y., 174, 231
Grosjean, F., 122, 123, 136, 154, 155, 156, 350, 351, 354, 385, 387
Grosjean, L., 350, 351, 354, 387
Grosz, B., 271, 298
Gruendal, J., 321, 334
Guiot, G., 76, 112
Gulick, W., 63, 112
Gupta, S., 284, 297

Haden, P., 370, 390
Hadler, B., 67, 69, 72, 84, 113
Hagen, A. C., 59, 63, 69, 112
Hall, W. C., 10, 43
Halliday, M., 319, 333
Halliday, M. A. K., 255, 298
Hankamer, J., 267, 268, 298, 299
Hanson, W. R., 75, 114
Hardy, J. A., 168, 228
Harley, T. A., 338, 356, 368, 371, 387
Harshaman, R., 64, 115
Hasan, R., 255, 298
Hassler, R., 76, 112
Hast, M. H., 19, 43
Hastie, R., 254, 296
Haviland, S. E., 288, 290, 298
Hayes, C. H., 29, 30, 43
Hayes, K. J., 29, 30, 43
Hayward, R. W., 21, 45
Head, A. J., 14, 46
Head, H., 5, 23, 24, 25, 30, 43, 83, 102, 112
Healy, A. F, 381, 388
Hecaen, H., 65, 109, 112
Heilman, K. M., 50, 69, 112
Hellige, J. B., 65, 112
Helson, H., 141, 154
Hempel, C., 52, 112
Hennrikus, D., 348, 388
Henriques, J., 329, 332
Henschen, S. E., 58, 88, 112
Heny, F., 183, 227

Hering, A., 78, 112
Herriot, P., 234, 241, 251
Hertzog, E., 76, 112
Herzog, M., 54, 55, 118
Hickman, A., 333
Hill, M. A., 78, 111
Hillier, C. S., 348, 390
Hillier, W. E., 70, 112
Hirst, W., 292, 298
Hobbs, J. R., 291, 298
Hockett, C., 52, 98, 112
Hoddinott, K. S., 62, 108
Hoenkamp, E., 371, 387
Hoff, H., 83, 111
Hoffman, R. R., 102, 112
Holmes, V. M., 354, 386
Honeck, R. P., 102, 112
Hoosain, R., 100, 115
Horowitz, L. M., 100, 112
Howe, C., 326, 333
Howie, P., 62, 108
Hubel, D. H., 14, 21, 43
Hughes, C. P., 50, 112
Hughes, E. C., 66, 112
Hughes, J., 39, 44
Huijbers, P., 351, 387
Humphrey, G., 343, 387
Hupfer, K., 22, 44
Hutchinson, J., 10, 47
Hutchinson, R. E., 10, 47
Huttenlicher, J., 303, 315, 348, 349, 375, 387

Irwin, D. E., 329, 371, 384
Isaacs, E., 120, 154
Isard, S. D., 178, 221, 222, 230
Itoh, K., 21, 45

Jackendoff, R., 168, 229
Jackson, J. H., 5, 6, 14, 15, 16, 18, 22, 23, 28, 44, 67, 80, 81, 87, 94, 102, 104, 112
Jaffe, J., 81, 112
James, C. T., 374, 387
James, W., 344, 387
Jarvella, R., 186, 229
Jarvella, R. J., 275, 298, 373, 387
Jasper, H., 14, 46
Jastrzembski, J., 304, 315
Jaynes, J., 103, 113
Jeeves, M. A., 14, 46
Jernigan, T. L., 21, 45
Jespersen, O., 52, 95, 113

Johnson, M., 102, 113
Johnson, M. K., 312, 314
Johnson, N. F., 351, 358, 387
Johnson, R., 179, 228
Johnson, T. L., 140, 154
Johnson-Laird, P. N., 211, 229, 234, 235,
240, 251, 252, 254, 256, 271, 275, 282,
287, 297, 298, 305, 315
Jolly, A., 11, 44
Jones, L. V., 86, 118
Jones, R. K., 62, 113
Jones, R. S., 14, 42
Juergens, U., 75, 113
Jung, R., 64, 113
Jurgens, U., 18, 19, 20, 21, 22, 44, 47
Jusczyk, P. W., 132, 149, 151, 154
Just, M. A., 278, 297

Kaas, J. H., 14, 25, 26, 44, 45
Kamp, J. A. W., 271, 298
Kaplan, D., 71, 181, 255, 299
Kaplan, R. M., 192, 193, 210, 229, 367, 385
Karmiloff-Smith, A., 328, 329, 334
Karten, H. J., 8, 44, 46
Karttunen, L., 267, 299
Katsuki, Y., 63, 113
Katz, J. J., 301, 315, 349, 387
Kean, M. L., 174, 229
Keenan, E. L., 263, 299, 324, 334, 372, 387
Keenan, J. N., 275, 299
Keil, F. C., 371, 373, 379, 387
Keller, N. J., 69, 118
Kellogg, W. N., 29, 44
Kelly, A. H., 75, 113
Kelly, M. H., 346, 348, 349, 371, 375, 379,
387
Kelter, S., 377, 388
Kempen, G., 350, 371, 387
Kempler, D., 67, 69, 72, 84, 113
Kennel, K., 37, 48
Kent, R. D., 113
Kidd, K. K., 78, 113
Kimball, J., 181, 183, 220, 225, 229
King, M., 7, 44, 179, 228
Kinsbourne, M., 57, 61, 67, 113
Kintsch, W., 167, 229, 275, 296, 299, 303,
315
Kirschner, A. S., 38, 44
Kirschner, H. S., 38, 46
Kirzinger, A., 21, 44
Klappholz, A. D., 273, 299
Klatt, D. H., 120, 155, 350, 387

Klawans, H. L., 77, 111
Klein, E., 175, 229, 367, 386
Kluender, K. R., 147, 148, 155
Koff, E., 68, 69, 109, 115
Kohler, W., 36, 44
Konorski, J., 14, 44
Koprowska-Milewska, E., 78, 113
Krashen, S., 64, 115
Kreiman, J., 54, 65, 117
Kreindler, A., 72, 93, 113
Kruger, L., 19, 44
Kubicek, L. F., 348, 349, 375, 387
Kucera, H., 303, 315
Kuczaj, S., 331, 334
Kudo, H., 21, 45
Kuhl, D. E., 75, 114
Kuhl, P. H., 21, 44
Kuypers, H. G. J. M., 21, 45

Laborwit, L. J., 62, 113
Labov, W., 54, 55, 113, 118, 377, 390
Lacan, J., 331, 334
Lachman, R., 348, 388
Lackner, J. R., 213, 229
Lakoff, G., 102, 113, 264, 299
Lamendella, J., 20, 45
Lane, H., 350, 351, 354, 387
Langacker, R., 261, 265, 299
Langendoen, D. T., 174, 229
Lapointe, S. G., 351, 385
Larson, C. R., 21, 22, 47
Lashley, K. S., 14, 45, 339, 342, 343, 361,
378, 381, 388
Lasnik, H., 264, 299
Laughlin, S. A., 21, 45
Laver, J. D. M., 338, 352, 353, 381
Leckman, J., 77, 78, 109
Lehiste, I., 120, 155
Lenneberg, E., 74, 93, 113
Lesgold, A., 279, 299
Lesgold, A. M., 341, 384
Leussenhop, A. J., 62, 113
Levelt, W. J. M., 353, 376, 377, 379, 388
Levin, J. A., 271, 299
Levine, D. N., 25, 45
Levine, H. L., 68, 72, 110, 115
Levita, E., 76, 116
Levitt, A. J., 381, 388
Levy, J., 71, 89, 113
Leyton, A. S. F., 19, 45
Liberman, A. M., 120, 124, 127, 128, 129,
130, 132, 139, 140, 141, 143, 149, 154,

155, 156
Lieberman, P., 11, 17, 45, 100, 113, 320, 334
Lieven, E. V. M., 320, 321, 326, 330, 334
Lindeman, R. C., 21, 22, 47
Lindsay, P. H., 341, 388
Lindsley, J. R., 358, 388
Linebarger, M., 174, 175, 229
Linebaugh, C. W., 69, 73, 114
Ling, P. K., 69, 111
Lisker, L., 126, 155
Lockman, A., 273, 299
Lomanto, C., 122, 123, 156
Lorch, M. P., 69, 109
Lounsbury, F. G., 95, 113, 347, 388
Luce, P. A., 120, 156
Luria, A. R., 15, 24, 45, 57, 58, 68, 84, 102, 113, 114
Lyons, J., 96, 102, 114, 166, 213, 229

Maassen, B., 376, 379, 388
McCauley, C., 348, 388
MacDonald, J., 143, 155
McFarland, H. R., 64, 114
McGurk, H., 143, 155
Mack, M., 124, 155
MacKay, D. G., 338, 339, 347, 352, 353, 370, 371, 381, 384, 388
McKean, K. O., 359, 360, 388
MacKinnon, J., 17, 45
McKoon, G., 285, 286, 297, 299
Maclay, H., 338, 347, 388
MacLean, P. D., 103, 114
McNeill, D., 345, 375, 385
McShane, J., 319, 321, 334
MacWhinney, B., 275, 299, 325, 333, 371
Magoun, H. W., 75, 113
Majeron, M. A., 78, 110
Malkiel, Y., 102, 114
Malt, B. C., 276, 299
Manelis, L., 100, 112
Mansfield, R. J. W., 26, 45
Maratsos, M., 326, 334
Marbe, K., 348, 390
Marcie, P., 68, 114
Marcus, M., 198, 208, 217, 229
Marie, P., 83, 86, 114
Marin, O. S. M., 173, 230
Marler, P., 10, 11, 17, 18, 45, 47
Marr, D., 162, 230
Marshall, C. R., 287, 297
Marshall, J. C., 163, 228

Marslen-Wilson, W. D., 119, 155, 176, 213, 221, 230, 234, 238, 239, 251, 252, 274, 280, 288, 300
Martin, E., 358, 388
Martin, M., 65, 114
Masling, M., 275, 296
Massaro, D. W., 143, 155
Mayer, J., 83, 84, 111
Mayhew, D., 275, 299
Mazziotta, J. C., 64, 66, 115
Mazzucchi, A., 174, 230
Mehler, J., 131, 155
Menn, L., 174, 230
Menzel, E. W., 36, 45
Meringer, R., 338, 352, 388
Mertus, J., 120, 154
Merzenich, M. M., 26, 45
Mesulam, M. M., 50, 69, 116
Metter, E. J., 75, 114
Meyer, D. E., 338, 370, 388
Meyer, K., 338, 352, 388
Miceli, G., 174, 230
Michel, D., 73, 109
Michelow, D., 69, 111
Miller, G., 178, 221, 222, 228, 230
Miller, G. A., 305, 315, 359, 360, 388
Miller, J. D., 21, 44
Miller, J. L., 122, 123, 124, 125, 126, 127, 128, 129, 130, 131, 132, 133, 135, 136, 137, 139, 140, 141, 142, 144, 145, 146, 147, 148, 149, 150, 151, 152, 154, 155, 156
Miller, R., 319, 333
Milne, R. W., 181, 230
Milner, A. D., 14, 46
Milner, B., 57, 63, 114, 116
Milner, P. M., 63, 114
Minsky, M., 287, 299
Mistlin, A. J., 14, 46
Mitani, A., 21, 45
Mitchell, T. F., 98, 102, 114
Mizuno, N., 21, 45
Molina, P., 76, 112
Montague, R., 216, 230
Moore, T., 167, 230
Morgan, J. L., 351, 388
Morrow, D. G., 283, 299
Morton, J., 119, 156, 163, 230
Moscowitz, A. B., 98, 114
Motley, M. T., 338, 371, 381, 384, 389
Mounoud, P., 324, 334
Mueller-Preuss, P., 75, 113

Mulroy, M. J., 10, 45
Muncer, S. J., 31, 37, 45
Mundinger, F., 76, 112
Murphy, G. L., 268, 269, 276, 299
Myers, P. S., 69, 73, 81, 114
Myers, R. E., 21, 22, 43, 45, 75, 103, 114
Myerson, R., 85, 114

Nachshon, I., 64, 109
Naeser, M. R., 50, 68, 114, 115
Naesser, M. A., 21, 45
Nakayama, M., 359, 389
Nass, R., 72, 111
Naughton, J. M., 40, 42
Nauta, W. J. H., 8, 46, 58, 114
Nebes, R. E., 65, 114
Neff, W., 63, 64, 109, 114, 115
Neilson, M., 62, 108
Nelson, K., 303, 315, 320, 321, 330, 334
Nettleton, N. C., 53, 65, 109
Newport, E. L., 351, 388
Nicholas, M., 69, 109
Nissen, C. H., 29, 43
Noll, J. D., 68, 115
Nomura, S., 21, 45
Norman, D. A., 341, 388
Nooteboom, S. G., 338, 352, 353, 355, 389
Nottebohm, F. N., 10, 42, 46
Nusbaum, H. C., 124, 156

Oakhill, J. V., 284, 298
Oblak, T. G., 10, 45
O'Connor, J. D., 124, 156
Ojemann, G. A., 58, 75, 76, 77, 115
Olbrei, I., 234, 240, 241, 251
Oldfield, R. C., 348, 389
Olsen, J., 94, 115
Ornstein, R., 65, 115
Ortony, A., 100, 115, 290, 299
Osgood, C., 100, 115
Osgood, C. E., 338, 347, 388

Paccia, J. M., 350, 351, 385, 389
Papcun, G., 64, 115
Paprotté, W., 325, 334
Parmelee, C. M., 348, 388
Partee, B. H., 263, 296
Pasnak, R., 37, 46
Passingham, R. E., 25, 28, 29, 46
Paton, J. A., 10, 46
Patterson, F. G., 31, 46
Patterson, K. E., 13, 46, 163, 228

Pauls, D. L., 78, 113
Pawley, A., 90, 96, 102, 115
Penfield, W., 14, 19, 46, 57, 58, 59, 61, 73, 77, 115
Perecman, E., 69, 115
Perera, H. V., 78, 115
Perfetti, C. A., 358, 389
Perrett, D., 14, 46
Peters, A., 320, 334
Peters, A. M., 98, 115
Peters, R. M., 115
Peters, S., 211, 228
Peterson, G. E., 120, 156
Peterson, L. N., 38, 46
Pettit, J. M., 68, 115
Pettito, L. A., 30, 31, 32, 37, 47
Phelps, M. E., 64, 66, 75, 114, 115
Piaget, J., 318, 321, 334
Pick, A., 83, 115, 343, 389
Pickard, K. A., 133, 135, 155
Pickens, J. D., 100, 102, 115
Pickett, J. M., 124, 156
Pieniadz, J M., 68, 115
Pinker. S., 361, 375, 389
Pisoni, D. B., 120, 129, 145, 156, 370, 389
Ploog, D., 16, 18, 19, 21, 22, 44, 46, 75, 113
Pollio, H. R., 99, 100, 102, 115
Pollio, M. R., 99, 115
Port, R. F., 124, 136, 156
Posner, M. I., 129, 156
Potter, D. D., 14, 46
Potter, J. M., 352, 389
Potter, M. C., 351, 389
Powelson, J., 73, 109
Premack, D., 28, 30, 31, 35, 36, 37, 39, 40, 43, 46, 48
Pribram, K. H., 74, 115
Pullum, G., 175, 229, 367, 386
Pulman, S. G., 205, 219, 230
Pylyshyn, A., 130, 156
Pynte, J., 213, 230

Quadfasel, F. A., 92, 111
Quinn, P. T., 62, 108

Radford, A., 201, 230
Radinsky, L. B., 7, 46
Raleigh, M. J., 16, 47
Ramer, A., 319, 333
Randall, J., 226, 334
Rasmussen, T., 14, 19, 46, 57, 114, 116
Ratcliff, R., 285, 286, 297, 299

Rayner, K., 246, 247, 248, 249, 250, 252, 278, 297
Reeves, A., 72, 111, 126
Reich, P. A., 338, 346, 347, 353, 355, 356, 368, 370, 385, 387
Reinhart, T., 262, 263, 264, 265, 266, 299
Remington, R., 64, 115
Repp, B. H., 120, 147, 156
Reyna, V. F., 301, 303, 304, 307, 308, 309, 310, 311, 312, 315
Reynolds, A. G., 303, 315
Reynolds, R. E., 100, 115
Richardson, E. P., 116
Riechert, T., 76, 112
Riege, W. H., 75, 114
Rieger, C., 167, 230
Riklan, M., 76, 116
Ritz, S. A., 14, 42
Roberts, D., 72, 111
Roberts, K. H., 358, 388
Roberts, L., 57, 58, 59, 61, 73, 77, 115
Robertson, M., 111
Robinson, B. W., 78, 103, 116
Rochester, S. R., 354, 389
Rondot, P., 76, 112
Rose, F. C., 67, 72, 82, 110
Rose, N., 331, 332
Rosenbeck, J. C, 113
Rosenblith, W. A., 63, 116
Rosenzweig, M. R., 62, 63, 116
Rosner, M., 179, 228
Ross, E. D., 50, 54, 61, 69, 116
Ross, J. R., 102, 110, 202, 230, 258, 261, 299, 358, 375, 379, 385, 389
Roth, S., 279, 299
Rubert, E., 29, 46
Rubin, D. C., 345, 389
Rumbaugh, D. M., 28, 29, 30, 31, 33, 46
Rumelhart, D. E., 271, 288, 299
Ryan, J., 318, 319, 334
Ryder, L. A., 234, 241, 251

Sachs, J. S., 254, 275, 299
Saffran, E. M., 173, 174, 175, 229, 230
Sag, I., 175, 229, 367, 386
Sag, I. A., 267, 268, 298, 299
Salfield, A., 329, 332
Sampson, G., 167, 179, 228, 230
Samson, H. H., 22, 47
Samuel, A. G., 147, 156
Sanders, R. J., 30, 31, 32, 37, 47
Sanford, A. J., 280, 281, 282, 288, 290, 291, 296, 298, 299, 300
Sapir, E., 102, 116
Satz, P., 69, 112
Savage-Rambuagh, E. S., 28, 29, 32, 33, 34, 46
Sawusch, J. R., 124, 156
Schaltenbrand, G., 76, 116
Schank, R. C., 167, 230, 288, 300
Schenkein, J., 377, 389
Schermer, T. M., 137, 140, 147, 148, 155
Schieffelin, B., 327, 334
Schlanger, P., 39, 47
Schlesinger, I., 323, 328, 334
Schlesinger, I. M., 182, 230
Schneider, W., 129, 156
Scholes, R., 50, 69, 112
Schuell, H, 71, 116
Schwab, E. C., 124, 156
Schwartz, M., 173, 175, 229
Schwartz, M. F., 174, 230
Seamon, J. G., 341, 389
Searle, J., 161, 230
Searle, J. R., 102, 116
Sebeok, T., 16, 47
Segalowitz, S. J., 53, 65, 116
Segarra, J. M., 92, 111
Segui, J., 131, 155
Seidenberg, M., 234, 239, 252
Seidenberg, M. S., 32, 47
Seligman, M., 303, 315
Semmes, J., 61, 116
Sengul, C. J., 277, 297
Seron, X., 38, 43
Sevcik, R. A., 29, 46
Seyfarth, R. M., 10, 11, 16, 47
Shaffer, J. P., 348, 388
Shallert, D. L., 100, 115
Shankweiler, D. P., 120, 155
Shapiro, A., 77, 78, 109, 116, 117
Shapiro, B., 60, 110
Shapiro, E., 77, 78, 116, 117
Shaywitz, B., 77, 78, 109
Sheer, P. E., 74, 116
Sheldon, A., 283, 284, 300
Sherlock, ??, 65, 109
Sherrington, C. S., 19, 45
Shifrin, R. M., 129, 156
Shillcock, R. C., 274, 300
Shimokouchi, H., 21, 45
Shinn, P., 124, 156
Sidner, C. L., 271, 300
Sidtis, J. J., 64, 116

Silverman, J., 69, 111
Silverstein, J. W., 14, 42
Simon, H. A., 90, 117
Simons, E. L., 7, 47
Sinha, C., 325, 334
Sinnott, J., 373, 387
Slobin, D. I., 234, 241, 252, 325, 327, 328, 334, 382, 389
Slowiaczek, L. M., 370, 389
Small, S., 167, 230
Smith, A. R., 58, 70, 74, 117
Smith, J. H., 325, 333
Smith, N., 166, 230
Smith, P. A. J., 14, 46
Smyth, G. E., 75, 117
Snyder, C. F., 129, 156
Soloman, G. E., 77, 117
Sorby, W. A., 62, 108
Sorenson, J. M., 350, 351, 385, 389
Souther, A. F., 126, 154
Sparck Jones, K., 165, 230
Speedie, D., 50, 112
Spellacy, F., 64, 117
Spencer, H., 5, 6, 13, 47
Sperber, R. D., 348, 388
Sperry, R. W., 14, 47, 64, 65, 117
Spinnler, H., 64, 110
Springer, S., 65, 117
Squire, L., 75, 114
Stamps, J. A., 10, 47
Steedman, M. J., 196, 208, 213, 215, 216, 220, 227, 228, 230, 234, 235, 238, 247, 248, 249, 252
Stein, B. E., 19, 44
Steklis, H. D., 16, 47
Stemberger, J. P., 338, 339, 345, 346, 347, 352, 356, 360, 365, 368, 370, 371, 377, 380, 389, 390
Stenning, K., 271, 300
Stern, K. K., 75, 117
Stevens, K. N., 120, 156
Stevenson, J., 10, 47
Stevenson, R., 254, 275, 298
Strange, W., 140, 154
Streim, N., 376, 379, 390
Studdert-Kennedy, M., 120, 155
Su, M. S., 50, 112
Sulloway, F. J., 14, 47
Summerfield, A. Q., 124, 126, 156
Summerfield, Q., 128, 133, 134, 136, 137, 139, 140, 143, 156
Sutton, D., 18, 21, 22, 47

Swadesh, M., 27, 47
Sweet, E., 25, 45
Sweet, K. D., 77, 116
Sweet, R., 77, 117
Swinney, D. A., 100, 117, 119, 156, 245, 250, 252, 274, 300
Syder, F. H., 90, 96, 102, 115

Tanji, J., 22, 47
Tannenbaum, P. H., 347, 390
Taveras, J., 75, 109
Taylor, I., 360, 390
Tembrock, G., 17, 47
Tenaza, R., 11, 17, 18, 45
Terbeek, D., 64, 95, 115, 117
Terrace, H. S., 29, 30, 31, 32, 37, 47, 48
Teuber, H., 354, 387
Thompson, J. G., 374, 387
Thompson, R., 62, 63, 73, 117
Thompson, V. E., 19, 43
Thomson, N., 375, 384
Thorpe, W. H., 10, 47, 48
Thumb, A., 348, 390
Trachy, R. E., 22, 47
Trimble, M. R., 78, 111
Tsvetkova, L. S., 84, 114
Tulving, E. 314, 315
Tunturi, A. R., 62, 117
Tyler, L. K., 119, 155, 176, 213, 221, 230, 234, 238, 239, 251, 252, 274, 280, 288, 300
Tyler, S. A., 102, 117

Ullman, J. D., 184, 198, 227
Urwin, C., 330, 331, 335

Van Buren, J. M., 76, 115
Van Hoof, J. A. R. A. M., 9, 48
Van Lancker, D., 50, 54, 55, 60, 64, 65, 67, 72, 76, 81, 84, 92, 95, 99, 100, 103, 109, 113, 117, 118
Van Pelt, D., 86, 118
Van Riper, C., 60, 118
Varga-Khadem, F., 26, 48
Varile, N., 179, 228
Velettri-Glass, A., 40, 48
Venn, C., 329, 332
Veroff, A., 40, 42
Vignolo, L., 64, 110
Vihman, M. M., 90, 99, 118
Volterra, V., 319, 332
Von Bonin, G., 57, 118

Waldron, T. P., 27, 48
Walker, A. E., 22, 43
Walker, C. H., 284, 289, 300
Walker, S. F., 24, 25, 28, 48
Walkerdine, V., 329, 330, 332, 335
Wall, R., 211, 228
Walle, E. L, 62, 113
Walsh, M. J., 72, 110
Wanner, E., 190, 230
Wapner, W., 69, 111
Ward, A., 75, 115
Warren, P., 210, 230
Warren, R. K., 373, 375, 379, 384
Wasow, T., 257, 260, 300
Wasterlein, C., 75, 114
Waters, R. S., 21, 48
Watson, R. T., 50, 54, 69, 112
Watters, G. V., 26, 48
Wayne, H., 77, 78, 116, 117
Wearing, A. J., 303, 315
Webb, W. G., 38, 44
Webber, B. L., 271, 272, 295, 300
Weinberg, A. S., 206, 208, 209, 217, 227
Weiner, E. J., 377, 390
Weinreich, V., 54, 55, 97, 118
Weinstein, E. R., 69, 118
Weir, R., 329, 331, 335
Weisel, T. N., 14, 21, 43
Weiskrantz, L, 13, 14, 48
Weizenbaum, J., 270, 300
Weksel, W., 351, 384
Wepman, J. M., 86, 118
Wetzel, A. B., 19, 43
Wexler, K., 323, 324, 333, 335
Whalan, D. H., 120, 157
Whipple, K., 66, 112
Whitaker, H. A., 92, 118
Whitehead, E. L., 279, 300
Whitfield, I. C., 63, 118

Wilks, Y., 165, 230
Williams, F., 347, 390
Wilson, A. C., 7, 44
Wilson, D., 166, 230
Wilson, W. A., 21, 48
Winer, J. A., 21, 48
Wingfield, A., 348, 389, 390
Winner, E., 69, 73, 118
Winograd, T., 270, 300
Winzenz, D., 341, 384
Witelson, S. F., 66, 118
Wong Fillmore, L., 90, 99, 118
Wood, C. C., 14, 48
Woodfield, A., 160, 230
Woodruff, G., 36, 37, 43, 48
Woods, W. A., 183, 231
Woodworth, R. S., 345, 390

Yakovliev, R. I., 103, 118
Yarmey, A. D., 345, 390
Yates, F. A., 341, 390
Yates, J., 284, 297, 298
Yekovich, F. R., 284, 289, 300
Yngve, V. H., 356, 390
Young, A. W., 69, 118
Yule, G., 280, 297
Yvonneau, M., 78, 118

Zaidel, E., 72, 118
Zamberietti, P., 78, 110
Zangwill, O. L., 57, 68, 118
Zatz, L. M., 21, 45
Zeki, S., 14, 48
Zemlin, W., 60, 118
Zollinger, W., 70, 118
Zuloaga, R. L., 78, 118
Zurif, E., 40, 42, 43, 173, 231
Zurif, E. B., 174, 228, 234, 251, 364, 385

Subject Index

A-chaining, brain maturation, 324
Absent object labelling, chimpanzees,
    32–4
Abstractness, relative, verbs/nouns, 302–3
Acoustic signal
    Intensity discrimination, 63–4
    Mapping, 120
        Phonetic categories &, 147–9
Acoustic-amnesic aphasia (Luria), 84
Adjectives, property as prototypic
    concept, 302
Agrammatism
    Broca's aphasia, 89–90, 172–5
    Sentence understanding, 173–5
    Syntactic & semantic information
        interaction, 234
Ambilaterality, cerebral, language, 68
American Sign Language (ASL), gesture
    system, chimpanzee training, 30–1
Amnesic (nominal) aphasia see Anomia
Analogical reasoning, chimpanzees, 35–6
Anaphora, 255–7
    Antecedent distance, 275–6
    Antecedent relations, 257, 260–6

Psychological aspects, 272
    Syntactic constraints, 265–6
Backwards, 255, 260–1, 263
Bound, 265
C-command condition (Reinhart),
    262–3
Contraints, non-syntactic approach,
    263–4
Deep/surface distinctions (Hankamer
    & Sag), 267–8
Discourse, 262
Examples, 256
Identity of reference, 267
Identity of sense, 267
Linguistic descriptions, 257–70
Meanings, 266–69
Precede & comand condition, 261–3
Semantic approach, 263
Syntactic aspects, 258
Syntactic form & distribution, 260
Transformational approach, 258–60
Anaphora resolution
    AI programs, 270–2
    Antecedent meaning &, 257

Backgrounding, 278–80
Experimental studies, 288–96
Knowledge-based, 287–9
Psychological aspects, 272–5
Referential continuity, 282
Structural factors, 276–85
Anomia, 79, 86
Left hemispherectomy, 71
Normal speakers, 93
Thamalic stimulation association, 76
Apes, relationship to man, 7
Aphasia, 6
Brain injury areas (Head), 24
Classification, 79, 84
Crossed, handedness, 68
Holistic speech use, 81–2
Idiosyncratic expressions, 88–9
Information-content-bearing language
defects, 83
Luria classification, 84
"Non-intellectectual" speech (Espir &
Rose), 82
Non-verbal communication, 38–40
Pantomime therapy, 39
Pantomimic actions, 6, 28
Prosody conservation, 81
Recurrent/occasional utterances
(Jackson), 87
Residual speech, 87–90
Unit size, 90–1
Stereotypic utterances, 87–90
Swearing, differences from coprolalia,
78
Wada test, 67
Articulation, motor pathway, 60
Articulation rate, 121
Changes, 122–3
Speech waveform acoustic fine
structure effects, 123–4, 125–7
Artificial languages, phrase construction,
351–2
Auditory pathways, Corti's organ/auditory
cortex, 62–4
Auditory perception, cortical control, 62–4
Autistic children, manipulable token
training, 40
Automatic speech see Propositional speech
Avian vocalisation, 10

Babytalk
Child speech segmentation, 320
Content word stress & intonation, 325

Backgrounding, anaphora resolution,
278–80
Backwards anaphora constraint, 255,
260–1, 263
Blending, 347–8, 360
Phrasal, 377
Bound anaphora, 265
Brain
Anatomy, 74
Damage, language evolution &
dissolution, 23
Dysfunction, reverse evolution
(Jackson), 6
Electrical stimulation, vocalisation,
18–20
Function, human/primate relationships,
13
Brain maturation
A-chaining, 324
Linguistic skill acquisition, 324
Broca's aphasia, 79
Agrammatism, 89–90, 172–5
Melody of speech, 60
Sentence understanding, 172–5
Broca's area homologues, primate
Electrical stimulation, 18–20
Lesions, vocalisation effects, 21–2
Broca's area lesions, speech output effects,
25

C-command condition (Reinhart),
anaphora, 262–3
Calculation, lateralisation, 64
Cataphora (Halliday & Hasan), 255,
260–1, 263
Categorical grammar, & parsing (Ades &
Steedman), 213–5
Category monitoring, syntactic/semantic
process interaction testing, 237–9
Category naming, chimpanzees, 34
Centre embedding, 176–9, 220–7
Memory limitation effects, 222–5
Paraphrasing effects, 178
Recursive nesting limitation, 222–5
Centrencephalic theory, brain function, 14,
74
Cerebral dominance, 57
Latent, post-trauma, 68
Cerebral hemispheres
Disconnected, language
comprehension, 72

Operating modes, 65–6
see also under terms Left & Right
Children
Language learning, 317–35
Language play, 329
Noun/verb meaning acquisition, 303
Referential, object-word based, 320
Social-expressive, language social use,
; 320–1
Word learning, 320–1
Chimpanzees
Intellectual skills, 30
Lip positioning control, 29–30
Symbolic communication training,
28–38
Throat, acoustic limitations, 29
Cingulate/supplementary motor area
In "readiness to vocalise", 22–3
Voluntary call initiation, 22–3
Click evoked responses, auditory pathway
studies, 62–3
Closure principle, parsing, 185, 187–8
Co-ordination problem
Components, 344–50
Lashley analysis, 342–3, 382
Cognitive development, children, 321
Cohesion degrees, idioms, 98
Collocations, 98
Colour naming errors, self-interruptions,
353
Communication
Auditory channels, 9–11
Non-verbal, 9
Aphasia, 38–40
Progression to speech, 318–20
Social interaction &, 8–9
visual channels, 11–12
Complex noun phrase constraint (CNPC)
(Ross), 202
Comprehension
Semantics/syntax interaction, 233–8
Serial Models, 238–42
Forster (1979), 242–4
Computational models
Interpretation, 159–60
Parsing, 159–231
Types, 159–60
Conceptual accessibility, word assignment
to grammatic function, 372–4, 378–81
Conceptual loss, left hemispherectomy, 71
Conceptual notation (Frege), 254
Configurational languages, hierarchical

arrangement, 340
Conjoined phrases, phonological
accessibility, 375
Consciousness, centrencephalic theory
(Penfield), 14
Consonantal contrasts, syllable-initial
position, articulation rate changes,
124–5
Context
Biasing, garden path sentences, 238
Dependence, 255
Conversation, right hemispherectomy
effects, 69–70
Coprolalia
Differences from swearing in aphasia,
78
Gilles de la Tourette's syndrome, 77–9
Klasomania, 78
Mental, 77
Normal speakers, 93–4
Cortical lesions, primate vocalisation
effects, 21–2
Corti's organ/auditory cortex, auditory
pathways, 62–4
Creativity, linguistic (Chomsky), 171–2

Deep anaphora, 267–9
Distance effects, 275, 276–83
Reactivated concepts, 285–6
Determinism, parsing (Marcus), 198–206
Diagram makers, localisation of function
theories, 23
Discourse anaphora, 262
Discourse model, anaphora AI
interpretation, 271
Disjunctive paraphrases, verbs, 313
Dissolution (Spencer), 6
Dualism, mental processes, 161
Dysarthrias, Parkinsonism, 76
Dyslexia, deep (Coltheart), 163

ELIZA AI program (Weizenbaum), 270
Emotional stress, Broca-like aphasia, 93
Epilepsy, 6
Ergative languages, 327
Exophora (Halliday & Hasan), 255, 265,
268
Explicit focus, memory, pronoun
antecedents, 280
Expressions
Character & content, 255
Context-dependent, 255

Different meanings assignment, 253–4
Focus sensitive structures (Bosch), 263–4
Sense [Sinn] & reference [Bedeutung] comparisons (Frege), 254
Units, syntactic ordering schema integration, 361–71
see also Utterances
Expressive aphasia (Luria), 84
Extra-striate cortex, visual analysis/synthesis locations, 26
Eye movements
Pronoun resolution, 277–9
Regressive, garden path sentence comprehension, 245–7

Feedback, lexical/syntactic integration, 376–8
Final arguments, parsing (Ford et al), 193–4
Fluent speech
ideal delivery, 382
Word predictability, 347–8
Focus sensitive structures, expressions (Bosch), 263–4
Focussing, anaphora AI interpretation, 271
Formulaic speech, 95–8
Aphasia, 85
Comprehension, brain damage effects, 72–3
See also Nonpropositional speech
Formulas, language acquisition, 98–9
Frame-system theory (Minsky), knowledge structure in long-term memory, 287–9
Free expressions, 95–8
Frontal lesions, bilateral, speech deficits, 26
Function word mastery, chimpanzees, 37–8
Functional and constituent interactions, lexical/syntactic integration, 376–8

Garden path effect
Context biasing, 238
Parsing, 181–3, 196–8
Syntax/semantics relationships, 244–53
General Problem Solver (Forster), 242–4
Gesticulation, pantomimic action differences (Jackson), 28
Gibbons, vocalisation evolution, 17–18
Gilles de la Tourette's syndrome, 77–9
Grammatical relations, sentence understanding, 167

Handedness
Crossed aphasia, 68
Language lateralisation relationships, 57
Hapax legomenon, nonfluent aphasia, 88
Heard speech reception, temporal lobe, 25
Hemispherectomy
Left, language impairment, 70–2
Right, postoperative language abilities, 69–70
Hemispheric specialisation see Lateralisation
Hesitations
Cognitive planning variables, 360
Word predictability, 347–9
Heterogeneity in language, 53–7
Propositional/nonpropositional dimension, 55–6
Hierarchical linking systems, 340–1
Hierarchical relationships
Configurational languages, 340–1
Sequential remembering, 341
Highly transitive events, child language expressions, 327
Holistic speech, aphasia, 81–2

Ideational speech, left hemispheric organisation, 61
Idiomatic stereotyping, gradient (Bolinger), 97
Idioms
Cohesion degrees, 98
Completion, aphasia, 92
Single lexicon meaning, 100
Transformationally defective, 97
Idiosyncratic expressions, recurrent, aphasia, 88–9
Implicit focus, memory, 281
Infants, pre-articulate, rate-dependent speech processing, 149–53
Inflectional linking systems, 340–1
Information-content-bearing language, defects, aphasia, 83
Interaction, syntactic/semantic
Comprehension, 235–40
Rhyme- and category monitoring task tests, 239–40
Intonation, phrase structure, 350–1
Invoked attachment, parsing (Ford et al), 194–5

Kaluli language, child learning, 327

Keyboard system, chimpanzee training, 31–2
Kimball, parsing principles, 183–8
Klasomania, von Economo's encephalitis, coprolalia, 78
Knowledge structure, AI approach, 287–9

Lambda abstraction, partial meanings, parsing, 219
Lanuage abilities, lateralisation, 50–1
Language acquisition, formulas, 98–9
Lanuage heterogeneity, 53–7
Language learning, early
  Continuity & change, 317–35
  Social & emotional factors, 330
  Subjectivity creation, 330–1
Language play, children, 329
Language specialisation, hemispheric, 57–8
Language understanding, theories 288
Lateralisation
  Handedness relationships, 57
  Language abilities, 50–1
    Functional interpretation, 66–7
    Nonpropositional speech, 56–7
    Singing, 58–9
  See also Localisation of function
Learnability theory, language development, 323–4
Left hemispherectomy, language impairment, 70–2
Lexical representation & retrieval, co-ordination problem, 344
Lexical retrieval
  Co-ordination problem, 344
  Object naming, 348
  Sentence production, experimental studies, 347–9
Lexical selection, errors, 345–7
Lexical units, primed, syntactic ordering schema integration, 361–71
Lexical/syntactic integration, 361–81
  Constituents, 374–5
  Determining tendency (Lashley) 362–3, 381–2
  Feedback (Levelt & Maasen), 376–8
  Fromkin-Garrett model, 363–8
  Functional 374–6
    Constituent interactions 376–8
  Parellel race model, 376–8
Lexigram categorisation, chimpanzees, 34
Limbic/supplementary motor area,

electrical stimulation, vocalisation, 19
Lip positioning control, chimpanzees 29–30
Local association, parsing, 189
Localisation of function, 6, 13–16
  Function components, 15–16
  Lower functions (Head), 25–6
  See also Lateralisation
Logical theory, cognitive ability, 163
Logogen theory (Morton), 163

Malapropisms, 345, 346
Materialism, mental processes, 161
Meaning, flexibility, nouns/verbs, 306–9
Melody of speech, Broca's aphasia, 60
Memory
  & comprehension, verbs, 305
  Explicit focus, pronoun antecedents, 280
  Implicit focus, 281
  Long-term, knowledge structure, Minsky's frame-system theory, 287–8
  Loss, left hemispherectomy, 71
Mental process, physical interactions, 161, 162
Metaphors, understanding, 306
Minimal attachment principle (Frazier & Fodor), 191–2
Mixed aphasia, 79
Mnemonic language systems, 341
Motor area, supplementary, electrical stimulation, 19
Movement, contralateral control, 59

Naming
  Categories, chimpanzees, 34
  Gesture-sign training, chimpanzees, 32–4
  Lexical retrieval, 348
Natural partitions hypothesis (Gentner), noun/verb acquisitions, 304–5
Nominal (amnesic) aphasia see Anomia
Nonfluent aphasia, hapax legomenon, 88
Nonpropositional language, right hemispheric representation, 67–73
Nonpropositional speech
  Clinical aspects, 79–83
  Fluent aphasia, 91–2
  Hemispheric specialisation, 56–7
  Neurolinguistics, 49–118
  Psycholinguistic studies, 99–100

Speakers' intuitions, 94–5
Subsets, 51–2, 55–6
Noun phrase anaphors, antecedent
    distance, 277
Nouns
    Conflicting verb modification, 307–9
    Extended meanings, 303–4
    Meaning components, 311
    Object as prototypic concept, 302
    Translatability, 303
    Understanding, verb understanding
        comparisons, 309–14
Number-consonant alphabet, 341
Numbers, reasoning, chimpanzees, 36–7

Object identity transmission, chimpanzees,
    33–4
Object naming, lexical retrieval, 348
Obsessive-compulsive disorders, Gilles de
    la Tourette's syndrome, 78
Occasional utterances, degrees in aphasia
    (Jackson), 87
Ordering problems, 342–3, 382
Ortholinguistics (Bogen), 51
Overt anaphora (Chomsky), 265

Palilalia, 86–7
Pantomimic actions
    Aphasia, 6, 28
    Gesticulation differences (Jackson), 28
Parallel function, pronoun anaphor
    comprehension, 283–5
Parallel race model, lexical/syntactic
    integration, 376–8
Paraphrasing, centre embedding &, 178
Parkinsonism, 76
    Dysarthrias, 76
    extrapyramidal disturbances, speech
        difficulties, 20
Parsing, 165–7
    Categorical grammer & (Ades and
        Steedman), 213–5
    Closure principle, 185, 187–8
    Computational models, 159–231
    Crain & Steedman, 196–8
    Deterministic (Marcus), 198–206
    Ford theory, 192–5
    Frazier & Fodor model, 188–91
    Garden path effect 181–3, 196–8
    Kimball's principles, 183–8
    Local association, 189

Preferences, sentence ambiguity,
    179–81, 182–3
Preliminary Phase Packager (PPP),
    188–91
Pulman theory, 217–20
Right association principle, 185, 186–8,
    189, 200
Sentence Structure Supervisor (SSS),
    188–91
Strategies, 183–98
Surface structure recovery, 183
Theory, objective, 175–83
Top-down (Kimball), 184
Two sentences principle, 185–6
Understanding &, 211–6
Part signified whole, child language
    development, 318
Pause rate, 121
    modification, speaking rate changes,
        122
Pausing, phrase structure, 350–1
Perception, linguistic category
    relationships, 325
Periaqueductal grey, language function
    association, 75
Peripheral speech mechanisms, cortical
    control, 58–64
Perseveration; syntactic, 377
Persistence, syntactic, 377
Personal geography, lateralisation, 64
Phonation
    Cortical control, 58–62
    Motor pathway, 60
Phonetic categories
    Boundary location changes, 147–9
    Syllabic rate change, 128–9
    Internal structure, auditory basis,
        147–9
Phonetic segment, mapping, 120
Phonological accessibility
    Conjoined phrases, 375
    Word serial ordering, 374–5
Phonological priming, sentence
    production, 366–7
Phonological substitutions, 345, 346
Phrase movement/displacement,
    transformational grammer 201–2
Phrase structure
    Artificial languages, 351–2
    Generation, Yngve theory, 356–59
    Pausing & intonation, 350–1
    Recall studies, 351

Speech errors, 352–4
Phrase-schemata (Lyons), 96
Phylogeny
    Communication & vocalisation, 7–12
    pre-adaptation &, 12
Pitch
    Control, left hemisphere damage &,
        60–1
    Discrimination, subcortical processing,
        63–4
Place, reasoning, chimpanzees, 36–7
Plastic token system
    Autistic child training, 40
    Chimpanzee training, 31
Plausibility, sentence comprehension,
    246–51
Pre-adaptation, & phylogeny, 12
Pre-articulate infants, rate-dependent
    speech processing, 149–53
Precede & command condition, anaphora,
    261–3
Preliminary phrase packager (PPP)
    (Frazier & Fodor), 188–91
Prepositions, correct gesture order,
    chimpanzees, 37
Preverbal communication, child language
    development, 318–20
Primates
    Brain function, language, 13–23
    vocalisation
        Cortical lesion effects, 21–2
        Hierarchical control, 16–18
Pronomials (Chomsky), 265
Pronoun anaphora, 258, 257–9
Pronouns
    Intrasentential syntactic constraints,
        266
    Referential (Bosch), 266
Propositional speech, 51
    Lateralisation, 67–8
    Left hemisphere damage effects, 67
    Left hemispherectomy effects, 71
    Voluntary speech differences, 80
Prosody conservation, aphasia, 81
Proto-declaratives, language development,
    319
Proto-imperatives, language development,
    319
Psychoanalytic theory, early language
    learning, 331–2
Pulvinar, electrical stimulation, anomia
    induction, 76

Readiness to vocalisé, cingulate/
    supplementary motor area, 22–3
Reading mechanisms
    Evolutionary aspects, 26
    Extra-striate cortex locations, 26
    Hereditary aspects, 27
Reasoning, chimpanzees, 34–8
Recurrent utterances, aphasia, 87
Recursion, in sentences, 176–9
Recursive nesting, centre embedding,
    222–5
Reference identity anaphora, 267
Referential continuity, anaphor resolution,
    282
Representational units, speech perception,
    119–20
Residual speech, aphasia, 87–90
    Unit size 90–1
Rhyme-monitoring, syntactic/semantic
    process interaction testing, 237–8
Right association principle, parsing, 185,
    186–8, 189, 200
Right hemisphere
    damage, language deficits, 68–9
    Speech formula comprehension, 72–3
Right hemispherectomy, postoperative
    language abilities, 69–70
Right recursion, 225–6

Schemata theory (Rumelhart and Ortony),
    language understanding, 288
Self-interruptions, colour naming errors,
    353
Semantic congruity effect, speech
    perception, 138–9
Semantic grammars, 167
Semantic inconsistency, sentence
    understanding, 307
Semantic plausibility, sentence processing,
    171, 172
Semantic priming, sentence production,
    366–7
Semantic processes, syntactic process
    autonomy, 240–4
Semantics
    "Bleaching out" 330
    Syntax relationship, 212–13, 233–40
Senario theory (Sanford & Garrod),
    language understanding, 288
Sense identity anaphora, 267
Sentence ambiguity
    Global, 181–3

Local, 181–3
    Parsing preferences, 179–81, 182–3
Sentence production
    Double retrieval hypothesis, 366
    Interactive models, 368–71
    Mean depth hypothesis, 357–9
    Phonological priming, 366–7
    Processes, 356–61
    Semantic priming, 366–7
    Transformations, 359–61
Sentence Structure Supervisor (SSS)
    (Frazier & Fodor), 188–91
Sentence understanding
    Agrammatism, 173–5
    Broca's aphasia, 172–5
    Grammatical relations, 167
    Semantic plausibility, 171, 172
    Syntactic information, 171
    Syntax involvement, 167
    Thematic (case) relations, 168–9
Sentence-schemata (Lyons), 96
Sentences
    Grammatical/acceptable, 178
    Semantically inconsistent, 307
    Shift-reduce algorithm, parsing, 216
    SHRDLU AI program (Winograd),
        anaphora understanding, 270–1
    Singing, lateralisation, 58–9
    Social interaction, & communication,
        8–9
    Sociolinguistic heterogeneity, 54–5
    Solipsism, methodological (Fodor), 161
    Sound discrimination, lateralisation, 64
    Sound exchanges, 352–3
        Within phrases, 365
        Word exchange contrasts, 355–6
    Speaking rate
    Acoustic properties characterisation,
        139–41
    Articulation rate, 121
    Changes, 121–7
        Speech fine structure effects, 125–7
    Pause rate, 121
    Physical versus subjective, 141–3
    Syllable acoustic-phonetic structure,
        139–40
    Visual information role 143–7
    Word identification, 137–9
    Word lexical status perception, 133–6
Speaking rate changes, obligatory
    processing adjustment, 129–39
Speech act theory (Ryan), 318

Speech, bilateral motor sources, 59
Speech errors, phrase structure, 352–4
Speech formulas, right hemisphere
    comprehension, 72–3
Speech perception
    rate-dependent processing 119–57
    Semantic congruity effect, 138–9
    Word lexical status, 133–6
Speech plans, word/syntax co-ordination
    337–90
Speech processing, rate-dependent, 119–57
    Basic phenomenon, 127–9
    Nature, 129–53
    Ontogenetic origins, 149–53
    Visual information, 143–7
Speech variations, information flow
    perturbation, 337–9
Spoonerisms, 352–4
Stem-morpheme exchanges, 365
Stereotypic utterances, aphasia, 87–90
Stereovision theory (Marr), 163
Stop consonant/semi-vowel acoustic
    contrasts, 124
Striatal (decorticated) cats, behaviours, 75
Stuttering, & lateralisation, 62
Subcortical structures
    Electrical stimulation 19–20, 76–7
    Injury, speech/language disturbances,
        74–5
    Speech & language processing, 73–9
Subjacency (Beswick and Weinberg), 206–8
Subject, linguistic role, adult speech, 323
Substitutions
    Phonological, 345, 346
    Word, 346–7
Sucking responses, high-amplitude,
    infant discrimination studies, 151–3
Surface anaphora, 267, 268–70
    Antecedent distance effects 275–6
Surface structure recovery, parsing, 183
Syllabic rate change, phonetic category
    boundary location change, 128–9
Syllables
    Acoustic-phonetic structure, rate
        specification, 139–40
    Length
        Identification time effects, 130–1,
            132
        VOT value relationships, 128, 133
    Speech processing unit 131–2
Syllogist reasoning theory (Johnson-
    Laird), 163

Symbolic communication training, chimpanzees, 28-38
Symbols, meaning, 161
Syntactic information, sentence processing, 171
Syntactic ordering schema, 350–61
  Expression unit integration, 361–71
Syntactic processing
  On-line semantic context effects, 238–40
  Semantic process autonomy, 240–4
Syntactic structures
  Abstract levels, 354–6
  Word and constituent order, 350–6
Syntax
  Mastery, chimpanzees, 37–8
  Semantics relationship, 212–13, 233–40

Taboo language, Gilles de la Tourette's syndrome, 77–9
Temporal integration problem (Lashley), 342–3
Temporal lobe, reception of heard speech, 25
Temporal order processing, lateralisation, 64
Tetrapods, vocalisation, 9–10
Thalamic animals, behaviours, 75
Thalamic damage, verbal memory dysfunction, 75
Thalamic haemorrhage, aphasia, 75
Thalamus
  electrical stimulation, speech rate effects, 76
  Lanuage function association, 75
  Language processing role, 73–4
Thematic (case) relations, sentence understanding, 168–9
Thematic selection hypothesis (Rayner) 249–51
Thought elements, unordered/cotemporal, 343
Throat, acoustic limitations, chimpanzees, 29
Time, reasoning, chimpanzees, 36–7
Tip-of-the-tongue states, 344–5
Tone frequency, spatial respresentation, auditory pathway, 63–4
Top-down parsing (Kimball), 184
Touch, in communication, 9
Transformational grammar
  Phrase movement/displacement, 201–2

Subjacency principle, 206–8
Transformations, sentence generation, 359–61
Transitive events, child language expression, 327
Transitive inference, language processes &, 35
Translatability, nouns/verbs, 303

Utterances
  Building, children, 322–8
  Word/constituent ordering schema, 350–61
  See also Expressions

Verb gapping, 206–7
Verb phrase ellipsis, 207–8
Verb understaing
  Memory &, 305
  Noun understanding comparisons, 309–14
  Verbal memory dysfunction, thalamic damage, 75
Verbs
  Conflicting noun modification, 307–9
  Disjunctive paraphrases, 313
  Extended meanings, 303–4
  Extensional processing, 313–4
  Intentional processing, 312–3
  Meaning components, 311
  Meaning extensions, 311
  Meaning generality, 311–2
  Relation as prototypic concept, 302
  Relational meaning, 301–2
  Translatability, 303
Visual comprehension, chimpanzees, 30
Visual information, speech processing, 143–7
Visual pattern recognition, lateralisation, 64
Vocal learning, 10–11
Vocalisation
  Anatomical pathways, 20–1
  Brain electrical stimulation, 18–20
  Evolution, gibbons, 17–18
  Hierarchical control, primates 16–18
  Subcortical structure stimulation, 76
Voice recognition, lateralisation, 65
Voice-onset time (VOT), voiced/voiceless consonants, 126–7
Voiced and voiceless consonants, voice-onset times, 126

Voluntary call initiation, cingulate/
  supplementary motor area, 22–3
Voluntary speech, propositional
  (automatic) speech differences, 80
von Economo's encephalitis, klasomania,
  coprolalia, 78

Wada test, aphasia, 67
Wants satisfaction, signs, chimpanzees, 32
Wernicke area homologues, lesions,
  vocalisation effects, 21–2
Wernicke's aphasia, 79

Word exchanges, 355–6, 365
  Sound exchange contrasts, 355–6
Word ordering
  Adult/child preverbal interaction,
    325–6
  Children, pragmatic aspects, 329
  Specific associations, 322
Word predictability, fluent/hesitant speech,
  347–9
Word substitutions, 345–7
Words, child learning, 320–1
Writing mechanisms, hereditary aspects, 27